BOLLINGEN SERIES L

*

The Notebooks of Samuel Taylor Coleridge

VOLUME 2

TEXT

Washington Allston: *Samuel Taylor Coleridge*
An unfinished portrait. Rome, 1806

THE 'NOTEBOOKS,

OF

Samuel Taylor Coleridge,

Edited by Kathleen Coburn

VOLUME 2, pt. 1

1804–1808

TEXT

BOLLINGEN SERIES L

PANTHEON BOOKS

THIS IS THE SECOND VOLUME OF
A COMPLETE EDITION OF THE NOTEBOOKS OF COLERIDGE
WHICH CONSTITUTES THE FIFTIETH WORK IN BOLLINGEN SERIES
SPONSORED BY BOLLINGEN FOUNDATION.
THE VOLUME IS IN TWO PARTS: TEXT AND NOTES

LIBRARY OF CONGRESS CATALOGUE CARD
NUMBER 56-13196
MANUFACTURED IN THE UNITED STATES
OF AMERICA
BY KINGSPORT PRESS, INC., KINGSPORT, TENN.
DESIGNED BY ANDOR BRAUN

IN THE PREPARATION OF THIS VOLUME THE EDITOR IS INDEBTED

FOR SPECIAL KNOWLEDGE AND CO-OPERATION

TO

Harold A. Bennett

Morchard Bishop

Beatrice M. Corrigan

George Whalley

Elizabeth Mary Wilkinson

CONTENTS

FOREWORD

THE second volume of *The Notebooks of Samuel Taylor Coleridge* comprises parts of sixteen notebooks, five of which have already been described in Volume I. Of the remainder, ten are among those in the British Museum, and one (Notebook K) is in the library of Victoria College in the University of Toronto.

Never in the late Lord Coleridge's collection, and hence not acquired by the British Museum in 1951, Notebook K is one of a small group of notebooks that until 1954 did not leave the possession of Coleridge's direct descendants. Most of these notebooks were first in the custody of Coleridge's son Derwent, then of his son, E. H. Coleridge, then of his son, the Reverend G. H. B. Coleridge, and recently of his son, A. H. B. Coleridge, from whom they were acquired by the Victoria College Library. They will be referred to by letter, an extension of Coleridge's own designation of one of them as "L".

Thanks are due here to the late Rt Hon Arthur Meighen, Q.C., and the J. S. MacLean Foundation of Toronto for preserving intact and making accessible the varied and useful Coleridge collection that included these notebooks.

To most of the institutions and individuals on whom levies were made in the first volume, I am again indebted. I must add two to the names on the half-title: those of Professor Harold A. Bennett, Principal Emeritus of Victoria College, who has gone over the Latin of both volumes, and whose sense of style and precision of thought may be relished in some of the translations here, and Professor Beatrice M. Corrigan, of the department of Italian in the University of Toronto, an Italianist whose wide special interests and unrelenting curiosity have all been brought to bear on the many problems raised by Coleridge's Italian studies. She has corroborated and corrected the text of the Italian entries, annotated them, and translated where printed

xi

translations were not available; Appendix A on Coleridge's knowledge of Italian is largely hers.

Without referring again by name to those scholars, friends, and colleagues who are referred to in the Foreword to Volume 1, many of whom have continued to help, I nevertheless renew my gratitude to them, and in addition accord it to the following: the Archivio Provinciale in Catania, the Clerk of Christ's Hospital School, and the County Archivist of Somerset, Ivor P. Collis, who obligingly searched records and solved problems; Mr John Beer, whose special knowledge of Coleridge's theological reading provided the source of a cluster of baffling entries; Mr Allan Cunningham, of Royal Holloway College, University of London, for researches in which his knowledge of both history and mountaineering was helpful; Professor Kenneth Curry, of the University of Tennessee, for information from and permission to use Southey material; Mr Bertram Davis, of Bristol, who lavishes on others his wealth of knowledge, especially about the Southey circle and Bristol, with a precision and a zest that are an education and a delight; Miss Helen Darbishire†, for information and insight that only she can give, and for the time- and energy-consuming kind of practical help represented by Appendix E to this volume; Professor Dorothy Emmet, of the University of Manchester, who took trouble to provide information not at all on her own beaten track; Mr Joseph Galea, of the Royal Archives, Malta, for unique and generous help and kindnesses; Colonel William F. Friedman, who applied his deciphering skill to a Coleridge passage; Professor Vittorio Frosini, of the Università Catania, for his spontaneous response to the inquiries of a stranger in Catania; Enzo Grima, Editor of the *Sunday Times of Malta*; Dr Walter Grossman, for help with the resources of the Widener Library; Mr W. S. Haugh, Librarian of Bristol, and Mr Peter Heaton, of the Bristol Central Library, for time and help and hospitality; Mrs. Beatrice Hogan†, for knowledgeable researches; Miss Hilda Lee, of London, for advice on Maltese problems; Mr Christopher Lloyd, of the Royal Naval College, Greenwich, and also the librarian of the Museum there; Professor Carmela Naselli, of the Università Catania, for help on the spot with Sicilian queries; Professor Erwin Panofsky, for comments on Coleridge's references to Michelangelo's *Last Judgment*; Miss Sybille Pantazzi, of the Art Gallery of Toronto, for persistence and success in a search for cherry-stone carvings, and Dr Gerd Betz, of the Zentralinstitut für Kunstgeschichte, Munich, for what in ice hockey would be called an "assist" therewith; Dr F. N. L. Poynter, librarian of the Wellcome Historical Library, London; the Reverend D. Rufus Price, Vicar of Ottery St Mary; Mrs Barbara Rossiter, for the useful and inspiriting gift of a collection of notes on Coleridge's notes made with all his characteristic energy by the late A. P. Rossiter; Sir Hannibal P. Scicluna, M.B.E., of Malta, the one and only guide for the Cathedral of St John, Valletta, for help and hospitality there; and Dr Donald Sultana, of Malta University, for practical co-operation by correspondence; W. T. Stearn, of the department of botany in the British Museum of Natural History, for skilled advice on botanical matters; Mr Ainslie Thin, of Oliver and Boyd, Edinburgh; W. A. Thorpe, of the Victoria and Albert Museum, Kensington; P. A. Tomory, of the Arts Council of Great Britain, who, as one-time Keeper of Art at the Leicester Museums and Art Gallery, gave detailed attention to Coleridge's notes on Sir George Beaumont's drawings; J. B. Trapp, of the Warburg Institute, London; Mr A. G. Wernham, for suggestions out of his special knowledge of Spinoza's theory of politics.

Toronto colleagues continue to be readily dragooned into service; in addition to those referred to in Volume I, I am indebted to Professor E. L. Fackenheim, of the department of philosophy; Dr Helen Hogg, of the department of astronomy; Reverend L. K. Shook, of St Michael's College; Professor E. M. Walker, of the department of zoology and the Royal Ontario Museum; and Dr H. G. Wiebe, of the department of German, and Dr R. S. Woof, of the department of English, both of University College.

I am particularly grateful for addenda and corrigenda, solicited and unsolicited, to the previous volume. Although various practical considerations have deferred the use of their information to the end of the work, I wish now to thank Mrs Elsie Duncan-Jones, of the University of Birmingham; the Reverend Richard Frothingham, of New York, and Mr J. C. Maxwell of King's College, Newcastle-on-Tyne, the last for especial generosity and unsparingness. Gratitude in this context was accurately defined in the seventeenth century as "a lively sense of favours to come".

Owners of paintings who kindly gave permission for reproduction here are noticed in the List of Plates; without their co-operation the volume would be not only less interesting but at some points less intelligible. Particular mention should be made of the generosity of the Bristol Public Libraries in allowing the publication here for the first time of a Constable wash drawing hitherto unknown.

KATHLEEN COBURN

Victoria College
in the
University of Toronto

INTRODUCTION

THERE is little to add here to the introductory statement of method in Volume 1. It may be pointed out that words or entries in cipher, that is to say, in Coleridge's cipher *systems* as distinct from his mere numerical substitutions or Greek characters for English words, have been traced line for line as in the manuscript, and transliterated line for line in the notes. These transliterations are in extract type, as are the translations of any length. The cipher is discussed in Appendix C.

It is tempting to speculate about the possibility of notebooks of this period having been lost. Looking back, we find, to make a rough calculation including many entries of imprecise date, and to take the first year for which entries run through the whole year:

in 1799:	251 entries	
in 1800:	269 entries	
in 1801:	199 entries	in Volume 1
in 1802:	248 entries	
in 1803:	459 entries	
in 1804:	600 entries	in Volumes 1 and 2
in 1805:	389 entries	
in 1806:	193 entries	in Volume 2
in 1807:	253 entries	

It will be seen that, except for 1801, the years show a crescendo of notes up to and including 1804, and then a sharp falling off in 1805, with an even more marked drop in 1806, and then again an increase (of about one third) in 1807.

The year 1801 was a bad one involving a good deal of restless moving about, considerable illness, and, probably more significant than either of these conditions, the most emotional period of Coleridge's love for Sara Hutchinson. But from 1799 to 1804 there are no inexplicably long intervals in memoranda-making. In April 1800, for

instance, we know that the translating of *Wallenstein* must have consumed the available time and energy. In 1801 the dating of many
entries is uncertain. Possibly a pocketbook did get lost on one of the
various journeys up and down the country. The year 1804 brought
illness in January (during which he filled two-thirds of N 16) and the
long journey to Malta. But it was a year when it was still possible for
STC to goad himself into activity, and to feel responsible for making
some return for the support of his friends. But what of 1805 and 1806?
From 1805 there are more obvious omissions. It is hardly conceivable
that Coleridge did not go to Palermo, for instance, either on the
Sicilian journey of 1804 or on his way home in 1805, or that if he went
he made no notes about it. And what of Messina and Catania?
Of other Sicilian historic sites and antiquities? Though Coleridge
disavowed any taste for antiquities as such, he was moved enough by
beauty and magnificence when he saw it in the Greek theatre at
Taormina to take some pains to describe it, and he must have seen
other glories in Sicily than the few he records. (We know he visited
Noto, for instance, though the visit is neither described nor confirmed in the extant notebooks.)

The same question arises about Rome and Italy generally, in 1806.
Surely there must have been descriptions of the Calabrian coast. And
of Rome and Florence? We know he took home prints of the Raphael
cartoons; is it not likely that he also, especially under Allston's
tutelage, made notes on them and other works of art? Or did the
great flow of talk, vividly described by Allston, preclude note-making?
And what of the journey home? Illness itself—and we know Coleridge
was miserable in body and mind on the return journey, and probably
for most of the first seven months of 1806—never prevented him
from writing his confidences to himself. Or were they too unbearable
in 1806? Perhaps we shall never know; but it is difficult to believe
that the only memorials of his weeks in Naples, Rome, and Florence
were those that have survived to us.

There is, moreover, more than one specific reference by Coleridge
at the time to his difficulties with his boxes and papers and to out-
right losses. In a letter of 18 Aug 1806, the first letter after landing in
England, he described to Daniel Stuart his problem in Naples in
Dec–Jan 1805–6: "By Mr Noble's advice I left every thing (but a

good suit of cloathes, & my shirts &c)—all my letters of credit, manu-
scripts, &c &c—with him.—I had not been ten days in Rome before
the French Torrent rolled down on Naples—all return was impossible,
all transmission of Papers not only insecure, but being English &
many of them political, highly dangerous both to the Sender and
Sendee—After two months sickening anxiety I received certain tidings that Mr N. had decamped (having admirably out-maneuvred the
French) with all my papers & effects; but whether to Malta, or
Sardinia was not known./But this is only a fragment of a Chapter of
Contents/—" (*CL* # 621). These boxes went first to Messina with
George Noble, and then probably to Malta to the custody of Stoddart,
from whom Coleridge extracted them, with unpleasant difficulties
about old debts and customs duties, in Dec 1807 (*CL* # 664); there is,
however, no absolute certainty whether the boxes in Stoddart's custody were the ones rescued by Noble or other boxes left by Coleridge
in Malta, or even whether the various boxes contained all the papers
he had left behind.

On the homeward journey there was clearly another misfortune; it
is referred to in a letter to Southey in Aug 1806: "My *MSS* are all—
excepting two pocket-books—either in the Sea, or (as is the case with
$\frac{9}{10}$ths) carried back to Malta—" (*CL* # 622). The story is told more
fully to Daniel Stuart: "Fortunately, I had perused with attention the
few political papers, which I had with me aboard ship, the very day
before the Spanish Privateer Ruffian boarded us—& which occasioned
& indeed necessitated the Captain to throw overboard his & my
papers promiscuously—so that the contents, tho' not the language,
are fresh in my memory—I likewise contrived to preserve two pocket-
books, full of memoranda, each as large as a large duodecimo Volume,
and a valuable paper on the present state of Egypt much fuller of
facts & more sober reasoning, than the one written for Sir A. B. to be
sent to the ministry—I collected every fact from respectable Eye-
witnesses, & not a few from Selim Effendi, the Mamaluke Minister at
Malta, with whom I was very intimate—For the rest of my papers I
must wait, till they come from Malta, & ought to be thankful, that
Noble made his escape with him [them?]" (*CL* # 623).

The gaps in correspondence and the occasional reference in contemporary memoirs to otherwise unrecorded episodes in the story of

Coleridge's Mediterranean journey remind us at any rate of how much of this period of Coleridge's life, especially of his literary activities in it, is unknown. Examples like the quotation preserved in 2741n and the following from the *Reminiscences of Michael Kelly* [by Theodore Hook] (2 vols London 1826) make the suspicion of memoranda lost the more tantalizing. Kelly describes the opening night of *Remorse*, concentrating on the music he had composed for it: "The chorus of boatmen chaunting . . . the distant peal of the organ, accompanying the monks while singing within the convent chapel, seemed to overcome and soothe the audience; a thrilling sensation appeared to pervade the great mass of congregated humanity . . ." He goes on to say, "I was fortunate enough to hear from the highly-talented author of the play, that my music was every thing he could have wished. I felt this as a high compliment from Mr. Coleridge; for I understood, when he was in Sicily, and other parts of Italy, he had this '*Miserere, Domine*' set to music by different Italian composers, none of whom satisfied him by giving his poetry the musical expression which he desired" (II 309–10). Even if something should be allowed for the exuberances of first-night conversation and its natural mutual acclaim (or for Hook's gift for improvisation), the question arises, with what musical composers in Sicily and Italy did Coleridge become acquainted? The circle connected with the opera house in Catania? In Palermo? Would some notebook have provided indications of an effort to write an opera in Italy, or a musical entertainment of some sort?

The numerous *contretemps* connected with Coleridge's books and papers, and luggage generally, in Malta, Sicily, and Italy in the war years 1804–6, the number of the custodians—Stoddart, Noble, Captain Derkheim, Mr Austwick, and what others we know not—the unsettled years between the return from Malta and the safe haven of Highgate, make one speculate, for all that has been preserved, on what may have been lost.

In later volumes there will be further evidence of missing notebooks, which, though perhaps belonging largely to a later period, may have contained Malta entries. Though Ernest Hartley Coleridge refers to "Malta notebooks", the phrase is a loose one and sometimes misleading. It would be incorrect to assume, for instance, that Italian entries, though naturally associated with this period, must be so dated. Coleridge resumed the reading of Italian, if he had dropped it, in *The Friend* period, perhaps an attempt at new bonds for old with the Wordsworths in the rather strained months of 1808–10. No more than the "German notebooks" are the "Italian" ones to be identified with one brief period.

Yet the notebooks of this little-known period of Coleridge's life have special characteristics and an atmosphere of their own—the mood more of despair than dejection, of work without hope yet not without vitality, curiosity, and struggle; they suggest the world of the child wandering with Cain in the desert, or of the self-examining not very old mariner alone on a sea much wider than the Mediterranean.

EXPLANATION OF EDITORIAL
SYMBOLS

⟨word⟩   A later insertion by Coleridge.

[?word]   An uncertain reading.

[?word/wood]   Possible alternative readings.

[word]   A reading editorially supplied.

⌐word⌐   A tentative reading, through crossings-out all but oblitera-
                   tive and usually post-Coleridge.

[. . .]   An illegible word. Each additional dot beyond three, up to
                   a maximum of ten, indicates another word. Longer
                   omissions are referred to in the notes.

⌐. . .⌐   An obliterated as distinct from an illegible word or pas-
                   sage, whether obliterated by ink, acid, or excision of
                   page or pages. A maximum of ten dots is used to sug-
                   gest the longer obliterations.

Other brackets, strokes, dashes, and devices are Coleridge's unless described
otherwise.

THE NOTEBOOKS

1804–1808

Entries 1843–3231

1843 16.226   Left Grasmere, Saturday noon, Jan. 14. 1804— *f70*
on foot/arrived at Kendal after a sweltring walk thro' heavy hot
air & the latter half of the Journey thro' Drizzle, at 5 °clock in the
evening—19 miles/in 5 hours, & I rested once to lunch.

1844 16.227   Images of Calmness on ~~Grasmere~~ Rydale Lake,
Jan. 14/~~new~~ fresh Delves in the Slate Quarry I *mistook* for smoke
in the reflection/An islet Stone, at the bottom of the Lake, the
reflection so bright as to be heaved up out of the water/the Stone
& its reflection looked so compleatly one, that Wordsworth remained for more than 5 minutes trying to explain why that Stone
had no Reflection/& at last found it out by me/the shore, &
green field, ~~with~~ a Hill bank below that Stone, & with Trees &
Rock forming one brilliant picture without was such, that look at
the Reflection & you annihilated the water/it is all one piece of
bright Land/just half wink your Eyes & look at the Land, it is
then *all* under water, or with that glossy Unreality which a Pros-
spect has, when seen thro' Smoke.

1845 16.228   Glasgow Horses, poor yet how heavily loaded—
2400 weight of coal Three miles—

1846 16.229   When a Vessel is seen off the Rock at Liverpool, *f70*ᵛ
the Bells of the nearest Churches begin pealing to welcome the
Mariners—a pretty Custom.

1847 16.230   The Subject is not new, and reflections will crowd
upon every Reader. The Notions in the meantime, which we en-
tertain, even in speculation upon a Subject so important, cannot be

entirely fruitless to mankind; & however little the Labours of the Speculative may influence the conduct of Men, one of the most pardonable Errors a writer can commit, is to believe that he is about to do a great deal of good, 350ᵗʰ page—of Adam Ferguson's Essay on the History of Civil Society.

1848 16.231   A School of Poetry has within a few years been set up by M̶ᵣ̶ Sir Lamb & some others whom it would be indecorous as their Works are not before us, where all harmony of Numbers is despised, all the regularities of Rhythm & Variety of Cadence are disregarded, and from which all the Graces of Language are contemptuously banished. This Harmony of Numbers, these regularities of Rhythm, and Varieties of Cadence, have, it is true, in many Instances been more attended to than chastity of Sentiment and vigour of Expression. Disgusted probably that these Ornaments should have been distributed with an ill-judged Profusion, this School, in order to reform the Taste, and enamour it *with* the charms of Simplicity, not content with stripping Poetry of her superfluous Embellishments and arranging tastefully those which would really adorn her Person, and set off her Beauties, has absolutely deprived her of the common decencies of Dress. The Nymph is now always pouting, always melancholy, always discontented & fretful/she may well be ashamed of her Nakedness, for she really is not fit to be seen. In this School too she has been taught an abominable Lesson of Affectation/instead of those high-bounding Spirits, that animated Eye, that healthy, generous and open Countenance, on which every Passion, as it arose, was faithfully pourtrayed, the affected little Minx is always sighing & crying, her Eye is always downcast, her Look demure, & her Countenance deceitful.—Her character is in every respect changed for the worse; & it is for the sole purpose of rescuing her from the further ill effects of such detestable Tuition, that we have been induced thus loudly to plead in her Behalf, & to express our Hopes that this School may be speedily broken up and forgotten.

M̲ʳˢ Barbauld Review of Lamb's John Woodvil Annual Review p.692. An affectation of plainness and simplicity, which is the flimsiest covering for Incapacity that was ever assumed/

f71

f71ᵛ

which is now-a-days offered to us as the very essence of Sim-   *f72*
plicity & Pathos.

1849 16.232
   Saturday from Grasmere to Kendal 14
   Sunday at King's Arm's Kendal, till 7 o'clock, evening 15
   Sunday Night Long Coach & Lancaster/
   Monday Night at Liverpool & from 7 °clock till 12
      at D' Currie's ⟨16⟩
   Tuesday D' Crompton's ~~18~~ 17
   Wednesday Ditto   18
   Thursday Ditto & M' Shepherd/19—

1850 16.233   O May we all avoid Hazletts on Jury!

1851 16.234   Friday Evening, Jan. 20, 1804. Observed in the
Garden of Eaton House the flight of the Brown Linnets, a large
flock of whom I had repeatedly disturbed by my foot-fall as I
walked by the thicket/1. Twinkling of wings. 2 Heavy & swanlike
rise & fall, yet so that while one was rising, another was falling—&
so 4. Their sweet straight onward motion/they swam on, not with   *f72ᵛ*
speed or haste, much less *hurry*, but with easy natural Swiftness—
& their graceful wheel round one half of a circle or more, & then
cut straight the diameter of it—4. Their change of position
amongst themselves/right to left, hindward to the front, vanguard
to the rear—these four motions all at once in one beautiful Whole,
like a Machine—

1852 16.235   A bright scarlet Pattern/I think that is a pretty,
modest Color/that I think will suit me/M' Pott's/to whom a
laurel Leaf & a scarlet pattern seem the same Color—

1853 16.239   Thursday Night—~~20~~ 19 or rather Friday M.   *f73*
1 °clock. Jan. ~~19~~ 20 1804—Seldom have I borne⌐. . . . .⌐

1854 9.5   Bought this pocket-book in Pall Mall, Thursday,   *f2ᵛ*
Jan. 26/having arrived in London, Tuesday Night, 7 °clock, Jan.

24. 1804—proceeded to T. Poole's, 16, Abingdon S[t], Westminster, & lodged at M[rs] Segurs, next door to the House of Lords—

1855 9.6   Called on Sir James Mackintosh who offered me a place in the E. Indies, & assured me on his Soul, on his Honor, that he was sincere. Called on Davy—more & more determined to f3   mould himself upon the age in order to make the age mould itself upon him.

1856 9.7   Met Tobin on the Stairs of Poole's Office on the Hunt for me/walked with him, called on Howell—on Sharp—on Lamb and Stuart/dine with S[t] on Saturday/with Tobin on Sunday—Interesting Story of Tobin's disappointment with Miss Savory—N.B. Nature of Property/she would have married him—loved him; but could not live for 600 £ a year!—

1857 9.8
f3[v]   Why rest thy Banners/lo the Eastern blush
                  Gilts thy ten thousand sails once more in Vain/
                  Or dost thou tremble at the stormy main
                  Or is thy dream of Blood & Conquest past

f4   3   Haste thou ~~Destroy~~ Usurper
                  Raise the battle storm
                  Tis Heavens decree thy Meteor fortunes fade
                  Inglorious Rout thy last sad Hour shall shade
f4[v]   No lingering hope thy dying Heart shall warm—

           2   Come thou Destroyer
                  With expecting eye
f5   A patriot Band awaits thy murderous host
                  The proud Avengers of thy ill timed boast
f5[v]   In awful power resolve on Victory

                              4

                  My Soul prophetic hears the dying groans
f6   Of those thy Victims, thy devoted slaves/

Their blood shall stain the bosom of the Waves
The Shore shall whiten with unhallowed Bones—

1858 9.9   The dread of mind that the possibility of my   *f6ᵛ*
feeling the Spirit of the Ludicrous while a great man is talking to
me with holy passion—Remember Jan. 26, 1804.—

1859 9.10   The silence of Newton's mind for 20 years—

1860 9.11   Sugar of Lead—

1861 9.12   Dirty Business.—Now—said I, with a great ef-   *f7*
fort to conquer my laziness, & a great wish to rest in the generality,
what do you mean under the words, dirty Business.—I note this
to remember the reluctance of the Mind in general to *analyse*—

1862 9.13   Too rash (PERHAPS) a generalization of Anger,
to assert that it is always the reaction of the living Power, offten
Fear/This is true of Anger—but are there not fits of passions not
explainable by this?—Poole's Jan. 27—Segur's Coffee House—   *f7ᵛ*

1863 9.14   Friday Night, Jan. 27 a wretched Night for the   *f3*
first part at least—yawning, & necessity of Sleep—& starts, dreadful dreams, & screaming, screaming, or preparation to scream/&   *f7ᵛ*
when I awoke—& to this hour, 10 °clock, Sat. Jan. 28, pain & tight-
ness at the chest, puffing & involuntary Yawning—I make this note
however to preserve the circumstance, that last night each time I
started from Sleep the one candle by my bedside were seen as two
distinct candles, for the first moment/. The least variation of the
organ, from its ordinary state ~~pre~~destroys single Vision.
    Jan. 28.—Rain—Rain! Rain!

1864 9.15   Sunday Morning, after the dreadful Dinner Ill-
ness of the Saturday, at dinner at Stuart's—I breakfasted at   *f8*
Greenough's & there & from him first heard & thought of Catania
& Mount Ætna from Greenough's recommendation/

G. B. Greenough.

Sunday Noon, Jan. 29. ⌐. . .⌐ lightly touched the [?Gown/ Gourd] out the Cupboard 16, Abingdon Sᵗ. O then my solemn, solemn Oath!—Merciful God! I pray thee to strengthen me/!!— Why not say your Prayers regularly at night!

f8ᵛ   1865 9.16   Lucky Escape/of the Irishman/~~my~~ his thighs & legs broken ⟨in falling from the Scaffold/⟩

1866 9.17   Monte Pelegrino—lumpy
                    Monte Catalfino—
                    Monte Giuliano—the Erix.

f1   1867 9.1   Chas Lamb
                                    Fitzroy Square
          Goodge St   Tottenham Chapel
          Howland St   N°/6 Northumberland Street [. . .]
          N°1 [. . . .]
                25 Upper Eaton St   Bull Inn
                    Pimlico   Whitehall
          6 Livres

f2   1868 9.2   ~~Tue~~hursday, ½ 4 °clock/—Mr [. . .]
                        1 Ease of Taxation fondly attributable to the Press, in its publication of Debates &c—

1869 9.3   Carbonate of Potash = Salt of Tartar large Tea Spoonful in a large Bason of Water   wash with a sponge—

1870 9.4   Friday, 5ᵗʰ dine with Ward.

f57ᵛ   1871 9.143   N° 4 Broad Sᵗ Buildings
                                        City

1872 9.144   Monday week, Mʳ Rickman with Davy

f58   1873 9.145   28, Geralrd Sᵗ

1874 9.146   8 Nightcaps + 2 Fl. Nightcaps
11 Shirts
10 Neck kerchiefs + [. . . .]
32 black Stockings—Pairs
3 Silk white striped
2 Cotton do.
3 Worsted or Yarn
10 Handkerchiefs
2 Flannel Waistcoats
3 Fl. und. Neckclothes
3 wash Waistcoats
6 nankeen Pantaloons

1875 9.18   Sunday Morning, Feb. 5. 1803—called on Lamb   ƒ8
fully expecting him to be from home, & intending all the way to
write a note to him, of apology—found him at note home, & while
sitting & talking to him, took the pen & note paper, & began to
write.

1876 9.19   Holcroft after Mʳˢ Wolstonecroft's Death took   ƒ8ᵛ
chaise & came with incredible speed to have Mʳˢ W *opened*—for   ƒ9
an extraordinary woman/

1877 9.20   Pat' de anno sexto Regii Johannis, 10. Salvus conduct' pro Lewelino Principe Northwall' et Madoc Fil' Griffin'
venient' ad Regem usque Wygorn' apud Wodestooke 29° July
Calendarium Rotulorum Patentium p.2—

1878 9.130 [. . . .]   ƒ55
Court Sticking Plaster
Ginger Powder
[. . .] Brandy
[. . .]
[. . .]
Concentrated Lemon
[. . .]   Parkinson's
[. . .]   1„1 8

Lamb, Inn, Postage   1„1—
L. B. & G. H.   3„0„0
                           1„1„0

Belum & Oddments   1„1„0
Lodg. Washg. Segur's   1„11„10
[. . . .] &c
          Inkhorn

1879 9.55

f16ᵛ

1066.	Will. 1.	1485.	Hen. 7
1087	W. 2	1509	Hen. 8
1100	Hen. 1.	1547	Edw. 6
1135.	Stephen	1553	Mary
1154.	Hen. 2.	1558.	Elizabeth
1189	Rich. 1	1603	James 1.
1199	John	1625	Charles 1.
1216	Hen. 3	1649	
1272	Edw. 1.	to	Republic
1307	Edw. 2.	1660	
1327.	Edw. 3	1660	Charles 2.
1377.	Rich. 2.	1685	James 2.
1399.	Hen. 4	1689	Will. & Mary.
1413	Hen. 5	1702	Anne
1422	Hen. 6	1714	George 1
1461	Edw. 4	1727	George 2
1483	Edw. 5	1760	George 3.
1483	Rich. 3	1788–9	Fr. Revolution

f14ᵛ 1880 9.48   "Honesty is a quiet passing over the days of a man's life without doing injury to another man. There is required in an honest man not so much to do every thing as he would be done unto; as to forbear any thing which he would not be content to suffer; for the essence of Honesty consists in forbearing to do ill. As Chastity is the Honesty of Women, so Honesty is the Chastity of Man. Either of them once impaired is irrecoverable. For Honesty doth not consist in the doing of one, or one thousand acts
f15 never so well; but in spinning on the delicate Threds of Life, tho'

not exceeding fine, yet free from bracks and stains. We do not call him an honest man, but a worthy man, that doth brave eminent acts; but we give him the title of an honest man, of whom no man can truly report any ill."

Sir Francis Walsingham's Anatomizing† of Honesty, p.335 of Cottoni Posthuma

† written, 1590.

Honesty gives a man a fair Report; *Justice* estimation and authority; *Prudence* respect and confidence; *Courtesie* & *Liberality*, *f15ᵛ* affection & a kind of dominion over other men. *Temperance* health; Fortitude, calmness of mind, & that full possession of all our moral & bodily faculties which justifies while it creates, self-reliance and a sense of dignity. Id.342.—The *Forti.* a little altered.

1881 9.49   It is neither right to praise bad Counsels because of their good success, nor to condemn good Counsels if the *Event* prove not Fortunate—lest many be animated to advise rashly, & *f16* others disheartned from counselling gravely.

1882 9.50   Remarks on Currency & Commerce by J. Wheatley Esqr. for Cadell & Davies

1883 9.51   The Latomies of the Capucins/at Syracuse—

1884 9.52   Dogs near Lentini could not hunt for Aromatic Flowers.

1885 9.53   Convent of Benedictines at Catania.

1886 9.54   Mazzalia, at Nicolosi, Guide, Granite, Porphyry, Basalt, Basaltic Hornblende, Chert, Schorle, and Feld Spar./

1887 9.56
A Jacket & Hood to fit on to my green Bag/to sleep in.   *f17*
Umbrella—
Pencils for presents—
Portable Soup. Mustard.

Get Jacket & Trousers at Malta/
A pair of *strong* Boots made *large:* High half-Boots—
Eau de Luce—

1888 9.57   Storia generale dell'Etna. Dall'Ab. Francesco
Ferrara. Catania, 1793.

f17ᵛ   1889 9.58   Catania three times destroyed by Earthquakes/
still they returned to the Houses of their Forefathers—Local attachment—Pleasures of Memory.

Oaks & Chestnuts in the woody region/
Smoke sole Cloud in Moonlight/now waterfallike
ocean seen below—sometimes [?but/oak] thro' the Trees—concealed—twinkling—bursting—

Views from Etna & such Heights are sublime/for they are a
true *Language*/crinkle crankle withered dried up lines—are these
beautiful/They are the description of a moonlight scenery by
Homer—

by slipping on the Crater you make yourself a footing

Sun's color varying thro' the smoke.

f9ᵛ   1890 9.21   Tuesday Night, 9 °clock, Feb. 7ᵗʰ, 1804, arrived
at Sir G. Beaumont's, Dunmow, Essex.—On Thursday, Feb. 2,
had the dreadful Rumpus with poor Godwin.

1891 9.22   erratum in our Last/For her Grace the Duke
read his Grace the Dutchess.—An Irish newspaper.

f72ᵛ   1892 16.236   Nicholl's History of Leicestershire—

1893 16.237   The water-lily = spurge—L. Beaumont

1894 16.238   Saffron Walden, Man on the Hay Stack sunk into
a nest of Adders &c.

1895 16.240   Sir G. B's Park Statue = Miss Gaites, the Cook *f73*

1896 16.241   We are not inert in the Grave—S' Paul's Corn in
the ground proves this scripturally: Infants growing in their Sleep
by natural analogy—What if our growth then be in proportion to
the length & depth of the Sleep—with what mysterious grandeur
does not this Thought invest the Grave! How poor compared with
this an immediate Paradise—

1897 16.242   I awake, & find my beloved asleep/gaze upon *f73ᵛ*
her/by the Taper that faintly illumines the Darkness—then fall
asleep by her side/& we both awake together for *good & all* ⌐in
the broad⌐ daylight of Heaven ⌐. . . . .⌐

1898 16.243   Men of Genius not believed clever because clev-
erness ⌐. . . .⌐ minded ⌐?capable⌐ of making rapid & sudden
⌐?Insight/Delight⌐—a man intoxicated with Genius makes large
Strides

1899 21.418   1. Foreground. Man on a drinking Horse, both *f90ᵛ*
beneath the Shadow of an ⟍⟍ ⟍ 2 ash, the 2 fork running out of
the Picture——Trees, a grove, in the other corner/a Town on the
slope of a Hill—A Church with a ruin of windows or arches just
beneath, and still higher a Castle—

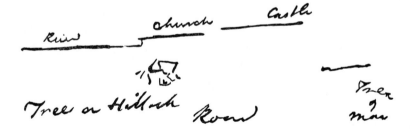

2. Uneven Ground, below which in the Front of the Picture,
A. a streamlet & low one-arched Bridge.—Above it & losing itself

in the A ~~edge~~ perpendicular Line of the Picture-frame the foot of
a Hill with Tufts of Trees.—On the B. perpendicular Line $\mathbf{I}$. a

noble old Stump of a Tree with its picture-ward
Horn not unantlered—: in the Center A ⟨solitary⟩ *Church* on a
Hillock, unenclosed, unrailed, wild—!! behind it you see *down*
~~into~~ *upon* a flat vale/: the whole back of the Picture filled by
Mountains in the Two Ridges—clouds upon them

N.B. A = the Right Hand of the Picture. B = the Left Hand.
$\mathbf{I}$ = the perpendicular Side-line of the Picture Frame. ⊢—⊣ = the
horizontal Line below. ⊢—⊢—⊣ horiz. line above.

f91　　　3. Flat, swampy, uneven Ground, with breasty Hillocks, trees
here & there in clumps & tufts:—⟨many of them pollard willows⟩—
a smoke from Lime kiln perhaps on the edge of the Channel—

Channel & Mountain line　　　　　　　　　　　　　　beyond
it, occupying $\frac{2^{rd}}{3}$ from B.—then open sea to A$\mathbf{I}$. a heavenly Picture—. N.B. River with swampy rushy Bank A ⊢—⊣ half extent
of ⊢—⊣

　　　3. B⊢—⊣. huge Stones, even almost to the Sea, which runs up
in a little Thumb here—above them a rough Hillside, a fine Tree,
Sheep on the Hill behind it.—The second Third of the View the

old Castle with three points　　　　　　　　　　　　last
Third to A$\mathbf{I}$. Boat with two men drawing in net, Sea, mountain
beyond—remarkably fine Clouds—

　　　4. Back of the Picture　　Cloud & Mountain *Fronton.*/Middle
from B$\mathbf{I}$ more than $\frac{2^{rds}}{3}$ ~~wood~~ Woods.—A$\mathbf{I}$ a serrated Ness with
two Trees on its Edge, one near the summit, one lower down—.
The front of the Picture—stones, a road, a man behind his loaded
Jack ass with stick on his shoulder, a bridge, & two men looking
over into the Stream which runs smooth & broad to A ⊢—⊣ .—A

road curving from the Bridge up to the Ness with a Man an inch
& a half from the bottom of the Ness. N.B. The Fronton of the
Mountain made by a Cloud which hides all but the Fronton.

5. A fine Rubens-like ~~Gentleman's~~ noble man's Seat with a Cottage ⟨or farm-house⟩ clustered close to AI.—all under a mountain
rising with two compleat curve lines

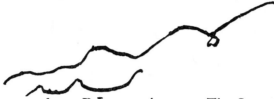

from B.I. to A ⊢—⊣. The Seat on a Hill, *f91°*
smooth I in the Front—another Hillock ~~B.I.~~ at BI. Trees on it,
and a man under their Shade—all the middle from BI to AI a
sweep-line of Trees, & the Mansion rising up above them, with
Trees climbing up the ~~Hill~~ Mountain behind it.
I Sheep & two figures on the smooth Hill in front.

6th. BI. A Group of Trees, amongst them a Pollard, on a
steep Bank. The Middle Third is a Road, winding & broad, with
a bank & Trees & Bushes Seaward; on the Bank two Figures, one,
with stick on his Shoulder, with his Back toward the Sea/; the
other, a Boy looking up in his face/; the remainder Sea & three
light Pinnaces—

~~8th~~ 7th./A Chamber ~~winding~~ of lofty Rocks, the floor a smooth
Pool of the River, over a waterfall—a Boat winding from out the
Turn of the Rock into this Chamber with two men—they now
hear the waterfall, & one with the Boat-pole *stays* the Boat.

8th. A Bridge (like Highbridge) over a lofty ⟨two-fold⟩ waterfall; ~~that~~ for making a deep pool half way (or somewhat more)
of the descent & then flowing over, ~~falls down~~ it makes a second

Fall, to the bed of the River ∫ —: Savage Banks; describe
Highbridge in short—a group upon it—Mountains & Nesses every
where—

f92   9ᵗʰ Two Inches square (of ten Inches' breadth, 5½ in length)
A (or Right-hand side) the Bank of a Hill stream, a Man half-
lying, half sitting, with his back to the Stream, close before him
(so as that the Toes of their Shoes must meet) a man standing, &
a dog with his Tail cocked up (whose Tail prolonged in the same
direction exactly ¼ᵗʰ of an Inch would touch the Breech of the upright man, the dogs' head smelling at the ground.—The next five
Inches square contains, 1. the waterslope from the overshot wheel,
one inch/then a smooth water, and then another steeper & shorter
slope;—and the remaining three Inches the 3ʳᵈ Turn of the again-
smooth water, having for its bank a rough Hillock 3½ Inches high,
and increasing in width from 1½ to 4½.—Over its Top the roof a

house, its gavel  —then a Tree overshadowing the
Chimney of the next House (note the Tree at Portinscale seared
by the smoke). This House with two chimney, and seen nearly to
the bottom/perhaps one third of the whole may be intercepted
aslant by the Ness Line of the Hillock.—Then the Trough, the
wheel of water—& within that Spout or wheel of foamy water the
wheel itself under the Trough, which Trough is supported by
three Posts—then another smaller House—and in the distance or
background a third House with 2 figures before it, to which third
House both the others refer as ∴ in a Triangle—The second
f92ᵛ   House ~~are~~ is higher up on the same Bank with the Men & dog.—
Trees & a Road to the right of the Houses, & straight above the
Figures.

10ᵗʰ a waterfall with three Streams, one bed of a river, ~~its~~ the
left Bank of the Waterfall a huge single detached rock, with little
detached Rocks resting *behind upon* it, the right bank a precipice
of Rock with a wild Tree just below its highest Jag-point. ‖ the
Background wood surmounted by

and from the bed of the River two figures, one above the other,
are scrambling up a Chasm of this Precipice.

11th. In the center of the utmost Distance a conical Hill—just under it a broad waterfall—below this ~~one~~ two falls one under the other, then a furious Slope—& lastly, two falls abreast, or rather rushing in to each other, so as to make a very rude inverted tri-

angle ⋁ —from the steep Precipice that forms the right *bank* of the furious Slope, & the *side* of the two Falls, a straight spout

from ~~a road,~~ ~~or~~ a water course on the top of ‡ the Bank all the rest wild Rocks. ⟨After Rain it would be all one Niagara.⟩

12. A river with well wooded banks thro' a plain with a mountain of the most beautiful outline,—filling the whole background. *f93*

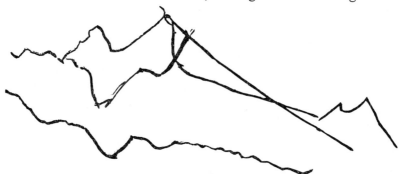

Miserable Scribble!
representing 3 ascending
Lines, the first with
two summits

the two others nearly the same line with the same inverted Triangle, 1 above the other.—

13th. A Church Yard ⟨with wall to two sides⟩—a noble Yew Tree overshadowing a beautiful Church Porch/with steps ⟨in the wall⟩ to its left.—a Hill behind in the distance to the left—In the centre of the Foreground a man ~~on~~ sitting on one Tomb Stone ~~and~~ who leaning on his Staff contemplates another.—

14. A Road winding between mountain Banks, like a River—. A. first Inch square two figures with their Backs to me—in the center of the Picture a man on Horseback watering *that* & a led

Horse at a Trough on the road Side—a natural Trough-Pool at the foot of a gentle Cascade/the mountain Banks well & wildly wooded.

15th. A. two inches *Sea,* a Bay & a Channel, for you see fire-lands, <u>A I</u> . *2 Inches* and A I . 1¼ from ⊢—⊣ , a boat with two men/ the remainder of the Picture a small Dwelling dimly coming out from BI. four inches and ½ from B ⊢—⊣; among Trees, that reach only not quite to the Top of the Picture/beneath them bushes & rough Stones, & steps, about 14, rudely winding up the Hill, up to the House—. The curve Lines of the Bay are divine.

f93°

16. Conway Castle, seaward—Sea—& on the steep Bank below the Castle wall Trees, under the Shadow of which a Bark is build-ing.—a beautiful Thought.

17. ⟨Three figures in the Lane.⟩ Inquire of Sir G. & annex it. ⟨It is only a view of a Back Lane, the town, & above that the Cas-tle of Conway.⟩

18. A gentleman's House with a curious Theatric Dome bulging out from it/a Lady on the Terrace above one smooth Slope & be-low another, moving slowly, as reading, to the House—she is now by the Poplar Trees.

19. A Bay of a simple semicircular curve—beyond the curve &

beyond the gentle ⟍ ness that forms it, a pinnace 2 Inches from A I —& (not quite) one Inch from A ⊢—⊣ a little Boy quite upright, & bending woman, with something in her Hands—& two somethings on the very brink of the Bay behind her—she & the Boy on the Brink.—~~Inquire~~—⟨She is washing her churn & Tubs.⟩

f94

20. A Waterfall, nay, a waterfury, a smoking Furnace of Fire! —~~five~~our Trees forming three Forks on its right more than per-pendicular jagged ~~ness~~ Bank,—with dripping Roots and lanky wet moss on the two highest Jags. In the Fork almost overhanging the furnace three figures, the first clinging to the second Tree-limb; (for this fork at least seems formed by two Trees growing from

the same Stump) the second figure is throwing, or pretending to throw, the third & innermost figure into the furnace—a bushy-like Tree (not bushy) on the other Bank must needs have one of its branches in endless motion; for it is over the summit of the furious Fall.

21. A Castle on the Sea Shore—on the very brink of the Bay—one of its walls running slope down into the Sea/

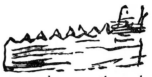

On B I & B ⊢─┤ —two Cypresses almost uprooted among the rocks on the Shore, and two figures are one sitting & pointing to the Castle, the other standing & listening.

22. High Bridge—

23. A Mad Yew-tree alone, ⟨with a grand S. Rosa-Eye more than half way up its rifted Trunk/⟩ a woodland tho' wide road between it, & the Skirt of a wood—an old Hag with a collection of sticks under her arm, a boy lying on the Ground, but looking up to her/the Yew Tree is old, its very Trunk split & shattered with age & lightning—its upright limbs finely intertwisted—

f94ᵛ

24. B I & ⊢─┤ —Trees, detached rocks, a Cottage with Chimney & *column* of smoke/but the rest of the whole Picture a river in a woodland Scene—with a very long bridge, railed on the inner side all the way along; not at all on the outer side/but the Half ⟨(not quite, 3¼)⟩ nearest the House is supported on two Arches/ the other half extending from A I. four Inches a thick Plank supported by two ⟨parallel⟩ Stakes in the middle/PA an old man with a stick & a boy before him are just stepping upon the first Arch from the Plank—. Two Pollards on the Bank by the House contrast prettily with two slender Pole-like Ashes, one bending over the Stream ❭❭❭ , the other quite straight ❭❭ .

25. A rude Plank bridge, railed off on each side, over a small waterpool, a man just got over & ascending to B I. front of the Picture the reedy rushy smooth Pool, the reeds & rushes on

⊢ , but its ~~other~~ side Banks rocky—the Back ground a Lock-up
of Mountains, Trees on each side the plank/—

f95   26. B**I**. Fine Trees—a man coming from between them—before him Cattle, just on the brink of the small Pond or Lake,
which with wood beyond it forms the center of the Picture, and
A**I** is occupied by woodiness, & a Church with

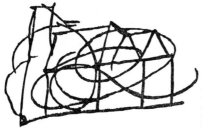

I cannot even mock it/only it
has a sort of Porch roof below
its Aisle Roof.

27. —Caystor Castle, the Tower remaining, & the lower window walls behind & below it thro' Trees—but the clear stream,
but the old Elm with its Roots, its Canopying Arms/the lovely
Cavern with the clear stream for a floor, & the Shadows/the eye
in the Trunk that is tall & upright behind the inclining Trunks of
the same root—the stone aside it, square & like a Seat/the rushes
on the brink

28. The remains of a Moat, the water as transparent as the
standing-places of a broad River. B**I** in the back almost of the
Picture, ~~nay~~ and only not in the centre, & intercepting the back
view,—at a good distance from ⊢ which is occupied by a turn of
the potamoeides Moat—a noble ruin of a Castle, one Tower and
*f95*ᵛ   its Turret entire,   this Tower & a part of wall ruined into rude
Steps (1/quite perpendicular from the rough ground, bushes
growing one third up this step and round the wall) 2. 3. 4. and
from the fourth you might perhaps climb into that window on the
right hand but a little above it)   this Castle & the ruined wall
abreast the clear water—then runs from the Turrett (across the
Picture) a wall with Window Holes, thro' which you see by
glimpses the blue distance. B**I** Trees, one single Tree on a hillock
over the water, but slanting & reclining *from* the water (N.B.
What would be its shadow?) The exact centre of the Picture is

the blue distance & a meadow seen thro' a gap & arch made by upright Trees, whose ~~arches~~ (branches *appear* to) meet—bushwork
between these *distant* Trunks & Roots.—/But O what a noble Balance to the B I does not the A I form!—from B I one fifth or a
little more of the ⊢—⊣ is the clear moat. then commences the point

of the ⌒⌒⌒ beautifully hillocked & serrated Bay, whose
other point reaches more than one third into the picture/near that
point comes out a ~~tongue~~ lingula of Land, one half as long as the
lingula which forms that inner point of the bay, & so forms a bay
within the bay, exactly a semi-oval, only that its inner line is
longer by the half than the line ⊢—⊣-ward. This ~~second Bay~~ Baylet   *f96*
is all overshadowed by one noble Branch from an elm, a very
large-trunked lofty Elm, which immediately above this Branch
~~splits~~ divides & rises up to its Top in two limbs, the limb A I-ward
the higher of the two/rich in autumnal hues.—On the other side,
toward the Back of the Picture, comes another Bay, not serrated—
a regular curve/and on the edge of this ~~one~~ Bay & on the Tongue
of Land beneath the great Branch, four ~~Boys~~ Maidens, one sitting
naked on the higher part of the Tongue which forms the steep
Bank of the second main-bay, his face to the water/his Back to
another figure—, ~~cloathed~~ shifted up to & around the middle/in
the second Bay, one ducking, and another swimming—A I a
Grove of Trees, of which two Trunks are seen, the one next the
great elm has a blighted branch touching the I ward limb of the
great elm, and above it the Tree slants of ⟋ into its
boughey Summit from an horse-shoe shaped Eye, from whence a
great branch must have been torn off—wild weeds on the Banks
of the moat ⊢—⊣ward.

29. Most picturesque wooden bridge, with gate-like railing on
each side, supported by stakes one strait down, one slanting ⋏
from that, into the clear smooth stream/thro' which the road dips
& goes & climbs up on the other side—a figure on horse back (with
one foot on each side of him) has just passed thro', has got on the

f96ᵛ Top of the ascent, & is going to descending—a very pleasing Country lies before, well-wooded. A I an old Tree, its stem only visible
(the other part lying out of the AI, the Bark of the stem all
ragged, & the lower third peeled off—by its side but farther in, in
the Picture, a delicate Ash in most exquisite curves. ∮ ~~B.A.~~

BI on the left of the Bridge, a grove of Trees, the stems of which
present all varieties of position & relation to each other/two by the
hither ⟨& inner part⟩ of the Bridge forming two parallel lines
slanting ~~from the~~ toward B I ∖∖ —on the other end of the
bridge two cross each other near the roots, then form an inverted
Triangle, ~~yet~~ nay, it is a complete Bow with the string —⊄ these
are magnificent Birches, the weeping Branches of which overhang
the road/I will get over on the other side of the Bridge, if only
to pass under that curious arch, a perfect Triangle, formed by two
Trees—and it is so solemn dark beyond, but the ∧ pointed passage arch & vault of Trees leads out into a glimmer of Light—
     On the woodwork on this side of the Bridge, part over water,
part over a rough Bank, three small stumps of a Tree, wild weeds
& grasses. B I Close to the slanting Trees an almost perpendicular
f97   *Scar*, a precipitous Bank of Clay, a tree which almost immediately
divides, and being aslanted by the slanting Tree forms a bow with
it, only that it is somewhat too like a ⟨ triangle//Light silvery
Clouds in the Sky/it is 4 or 5°clock in an autumnal Afternoon

     30. A I in the distance blue mountains or Hills

clouds/Sunny fields, bright yellow green, house on the edge
where they form the bank the river. A I ⊢⊣ one large rock-
stone half-hid in bushes & weeds aside a small hillock forming one
bank of the River—. Center of the Picture a one arched Bridge,

on the Castle—end of which 3 Figures looking over into the water, one in a scarlet cloak & hood—which lights up the whole Picture/. B I Conway Castle, with three ~~Towering~~ Turrets or Watch-towers in full view & entire—one in the distance is ruined, and the Castle wall with one watch Tower/Just under the wall a sweet modest nice white House among Trees/in autumnal variety of hues/ feathering & towering on to beyond the bridge/.—On the bank-edge of the sunny fields a nice white mansion, obscure in form of course.

31. The whole distance is a level & watered meadow with blue hills in the distance/but the beauty is that from the foreground (center) you look in upon it (as at Ulpha Bridge, where there is just such a sort of Table-meadow)—from this a stream descends, & coming full in sight makes a steep foamy rapid, then flows down smooth to the ⊢⊣ —beautiful B. bank of which at the foot of a Tree (and they could have been shadowed by a noble Arm of it, *f97ᵛ* but that is even now cut down, and the wound is still bare) a sweet woman, a child in her arms and lap, and ~~an~~ its older brother on the other side peeping over her knee/hitherward stretched along on his belly, in a red waistcoat coatless but with hat on a man look-ing up and either talking or listening to the woman/a little back-ward & between the man & woman, a tall elderly man standing up quite upright, & looking down on the group/quite in B I a man entering a wood, a boor rather stooping followed by a dog—enter-ing in between two Trees, of equal girth & heighth, & parallel, ~~a branch~~ an arm from one reaching the other forms a perfect gate-way—just one half of the height of the Trees.

1900 21.419   ⟨Lord Cadogan writes this to Lord Sᵗ Asaph⟩
    Lord Cadogan, 76 years of age, totally broken up, dropsical symptoms, & after any morsel of meat of any kind suffering all the Horrors of Indigestion—has recovered his Health perfectly by putting ⟨fine fatless⟩ Beef or mutton with as little water as would prevent the same from burning against the Vessel—into Papin's Digester & of this now jelly-fluid he took half a wine glass 10 or 12 times a day—or as often as the feelings directed
    Mr Mungay of Thetford recommended it/

f88   1901 22.150   Daniel's Poems, 2 Volumes, for Lady Beaumont—

f9ᵛ   1902 9.23   Friday Afternoon, Feb. 11, 1804, riding with Sir
G. B.—in Lord Maynard's was thrown off. &c &c—

f10   1903 9.24   Pure the Man that turnips cries &c

1904 9.25   When my Triplets you see
Think not of my Poesy
But of the holy Trinity.

1905 9.26   A blind man of my acquaintance exercising with
dumb Bells that having the Cover taken off were almost as shrill
as real Bells. "He liked the noise."

f10ᵛ   1906 9.27   When Lady Beaumont was a child, she told me,
that previously to her saying her Prayers she endeavored to think
of a mountain, or great River, or something *great,* in order to
raise up her Soul & kindle it—Sunday Morning, Feb. 13, 1804

1907 9.28   Painting & Engravings sends us back with new
f11 Eyes to Nature—as for instance the picture of the Cottagers by
Du Sart Engraved by Woollett/ the reciprocating influences of
Poetry, Painting &c—and Nature.

1908 9.29   Remember poor old King, & to do something for
him in the M. P. and Courier.

1909 9.30   Remember the Whisker bump.

1910 9.31   M Davenport
Mr G.   Swinton Street
Fricker.   Grays ⟨Lower⟩ Inn Lane
⟨N°/9.⟩

f11ᵛ   1911 9.32   Mʳ Welles, To enquire of the Law/

1912 9.33   Will you ask the maid to get me a Hackney
Coach? (Rickman's, Tuesday Night, Feb. 21. 1804, 11 °clock/the
day of the Receipt of that heart-wringing Letter from Sara, that
put Despair into my Heart, and not merely as a Lodger, I fear,
but as a Tenant for Life.)

1913 9.34   Poems in the Soother of Absence—
Ode on a Suicide for Love, whose punishment after his Death
consisted in the continuance of the same appetiteless heart-gnaw-
ing Passion which he could not reveal./The wanderings of this
Ghost thro' the world may be finely worked up—

1914 9.35   As if Judgment were overwhelmed like Belgic   *f12*
Towns, & shewed its Towers only at Dead-low water—

1915 9.36   Unmask the goblin Verse that frights the Page

1916 9.37
          Stuft, swoln, ungirt
          With grim, stiff iron verses jagg'd with Points

1917 9.38   Nothing but what a dying man might hear—
Berkenhead's Lines on Cartwright.

1918 9.39
          Clodds that can only sink a ship, whose Skull
          Can be at once exactly mad & dull.

1919 9.40   Gray's Orient Forms from Smallwood's Verses—

1920 9.41
                    And Snow, whose hanging weight   *f12*
          Archeth some still deep River, that for fear
          Steals underneath without a sound.

1921 9.42
                    These, Eumela! are not
          The Journies but Digressions of our Souls

That being once inform'd with Love, must work
And rather wander than stand still. I know
There is a Wisdom to be shewn in Passions,
And there are stay'd and settled Griefs! I'll be
Severe unto myself, and make my Soul
Seek out a regular motion/

ƒ13 1922 9.43   N.B. in my great Critical Work give a direct
close character of all the English Books of Criticism, of Note/

1923 9.44   The general Volunteer Spirit of the Nation illustrated in the protection of private Houses, not by the persons
or arms in the House, but by the confidence each man feels that
on any alarm every one of his Neighbors would rise up even in
his Shirt to assist—this quite National, & illustrated in every chase
ƒ13ᵛ of a Pickpocket & one noble instance of the influence of *national*
feeling, or public spirit, on the Hearts & Conducts of Individuals/
Contrast this with Lisbon, Rome, Naples/

This likewise illustrates the nature of selfishness or extremes
meet/an intensely selfish man does not care for even his distant
Self—every Coward instances this.

1924 9.45   Upper Seymour Sᵗ, 47.
                   W. Sotheby, Esqᵣᵉ.

ƒ14 1925 9.46   ⟨G.⟩ Dyer & the Hero Race/Mʳ Rickman's Aunt
—Your Aunt, Sir! is a very sensible Woman—. Why?—I read,
Sir! my Ode to her/& she said, it was a very pretty Thing. There
are very few women, Sir! that possess that fine discrimination, Sir!

1926 9.47   True Briton, purulent; but Cobbet, virulent.

ƒ98 1927 21.420   Dammee! they put me (says Wilson) between a
bottle of Port wine & of Lobster/& once ~~between~~ on one side of an
officer painted at full length which is worse than 10,000 Lobsters.

1928 21.421   The Law does not permit the identification of
Handwriting, the proving it to be the man's it was brought for-

ward as, by the examination of single Letters &c—for in this way
no man gains his knowlege of Hand-writings—but by the general
Effect—

1929 21.422   Tis with a large generous carelessness.

1930 21.423
　　　The Sun doth give
　　　Brightness to th'eye, and some say, That the Sun
　　　If not enlighten'd by th' Intelligence
　　　That doth inhabit it, would shine no more
　　　Than a dull Clod of Earth.　　　　　Cartwright

1931 21.424
　　　　　　　　　　　　　　Would you had
　　　Been there yourself! Would you had drank in all
　　　The Looks, Words, Graces, and Divinities
　　　That I have done! I am like the Priest, that's full
　　　Of his inspiring God! am fill'd, possessed,
　　　With such high Raptures, that *methinks I could*
　　　Bear myself up without a wing or chariot
　　　And hover o'er the Earth, still dropping something
　　　That should take root in Kingdoms & come up
　　　The Good of the People!　　　　　Ditto

1932 21.425
　　　　　those that come fresh from Visions:
　　　What saw you there?
　　　　　　　That which I still see, that
　　　Which will not away. I saw a Face that did
　　　Seem to participate of Flames & Flowers
　　　Eyes in which Light combined with Jet to make
　　　Whiteness be thought the Blot, & Black hereafter
　　　Purchase the name of Innocence & Glory.　　　*f98ᵛ*

1933 21.426
　　　　　　　　the appearance of a Star
　　　To one that's perishing in a Tempest.

1934 21.427   full of Instinct & Deity.

1935 21.428
My irritable Fears all sprang from Love—
Suffer that Fear to strengthen it/give way
And let it work—twill fix the Love, it springs from/

1936 21.429   Gin and Daisy Tea/dwarfs/a Mother used it
who wanted to breed up her Son for a Jockey/—⟨Those who
panegyrize a state of Society for a particular, because it has im-
proved/Xianity & Commerce, &c—without attempting to show
what Society by its natural growth might have been without it—a
good instance of the sophism of presuming cause from co-existence/
the child had *grown somewhat* from 3 to 14—& the mother attributes it to Gin/tho' the Boy is a Dwarf.⟩

1937 21.430
It is a pleasure to me to perceive the Buddings
Of Virtuous Loves
To know their minutes of Increase, their Stealth,
And silent Growings.—
A pretty idea, that of a good Soul watching the progress of an at-
tachment from the first glance to the Time when the Lover him-
self becomes conscious of it—A Poem for my Soother of Absence—

f55   1938 9.131   N° 29, Upper Gower S^t

1939 9.133
f55°   And this is your peculiar art, I know
Others may do like actions but not so:
The agents alter Things, and that which flows
Powerful from these, comes weaker far from those/

1940 9.134
There in some darksome Shade
Methinks, I'd weep
Myself asleep
And [?then/there] forgotten fade—

1941 9.135

There are two Births, the one when Light
First strikes the new awaken'd Sense/
The other when two Souls unite,
And we must count our Life from thence!
When you lov'd me and I lov'd you,
Then both of us were born anew—

1942 9.136

A Rotten Fellow   *f56*
I saw
In France a Monsieur only in the cutting
Of one cross Caper rise a man and come
Down, to the amazement of the standers by
A true extemporary Skeleton,
And was strait read on
⟨—ridicule this, with an "as if"—Sir F. D'Ivernois account of the
rottenness of Fr. Fin.⟩

1943 9.137

Love's Convert
by Cartwright
Fear never wanted arguments: you do
Reason yourselves into a careful bondage,
Circumspect only to your misery.
I could urge Freedom, Charters, Country, Laws,
Gods and Religion and such precious names;
Nay, what you value higher, Wealth; but that
You sue for Bondage, yielding to Demands
As impious as they are insolent and have
Only this sluggish name to perish full

1944 9.138   Liber 1. Epist. 17   *f57*
Est ergo mecum per diem totum eundem antequam scribam, eundem quum scripsi, eundem etiam quum remittor, non tamquam
eundem, lego. Quod te quoque ut facias et hortor et moneo. Neque
enim debet operibus ejus obesse quod vivit. An si inter eos, quos

f56ᵛ nunquam vidimus, floruisset, non solum Libros ejus sed etiam im-
agines conquireremus, ejusdem nunc honor præsentis et gratia,
quasi satietate languescet? At hoc pravum malignumque est, non
admirari hominem admiratione dignissimum, quia videre, alloqui,
audire, complecti, nec laudare tantum verum etiam amare con-
tingit.

1945 9.139

f57ᵛ   Sole Maid, associate sole, to me beyond
        Compare, above all living Creatures Dear—

1946 9.140
    Thoughts which how found they harbour in thy Breast,
    Sara, misthoughts of him to thee so dear.

1947 9.141
    I from the influence of thy Looks receive
    Access in every Virtue, in thy sight
    More wise, more watchful, stronger if need were
    Of outward Strength/

1948 9.142   I would as little wish Mʳ Wyndham in a Kingdom as a Monkey in a glass shop/

f58 1949 9.147   O that *endeavouring* face
When will your costiveness have done, good Orator!—

fₓ8 1950 9.59   Αγχωνην παιζειν—a barbarous custom mentioned by Athenæus, when men stood on a rolling globe, their
necks in a rope and a knife in their hands wherein if they failed
they lost their Lives to the Laughter of the Spectators—

1951 9.60   The ancients suck'd in the last Breath of their ex-
piring Friends. amavi—amatæ animulam—

1952 9.61   The nunnery situated on high Ground escaped

the Earthquake; but the Doors were thrown open/the nuns ran
about the Streets like mad/few returned/most became mothers,
many wives.   1783.

1953 9.62

Dialogue between a Mother & Child   *f18ᵛ*

Child (singing) "O Lady, lay your costly robes aside,
                   No longer may you glory in your pride/.
Mother/   Wherefore today art singing in my ear
                   Sad Songs were made so long ago, my dear?
                   This Day I am to be a Bride, you know/
                   Why sing sad Songs were made so long ago?
Child/   O Mother! lay your costly robes aside?
                   For you may never be another's Bride—
                   That Line I learnt not in the old sad Song./
M.   I pray thee, pretty one, now hold thy Tongue/
                   Play with the Bride maids & be glad, my Boy!
                   For thou shalt be a second father's Joy.   *f19*
C.   One Father fondled me upon his Knee—
                   One Father is enough alone for me.

1954 9.63   Oil of Turpentine, Oxyg.

1955 9.64   Ministers in arbitrary Governments insecure, not   *f19ᵛ*
to be relied on—BRIBED! Why not? They are Slaves/

1956 9.65   Ungrateful man is solstitial Heat under the
Shadow of a Tree/O! it only meant to shadow its own Roots &
Bark.

1957 9.66   Artificial Brow by the hand arched over the eye/   *f20*
                                                 quiet vision

1958 16.4   [. . .]   *f1*
                       [. . .]
                       Shirts

Cravats
pair of Stockings
14 Handkerchiefs
3 Waistcoats.
1 Flannel Drawers
1 Flannel Waistcoat
1 Nightcap
1 [. . .]
1 Neck [. . .]

1959 16.5   Pacchiaretti—

1960 16.6   Messrs. Alex Davison, Noel Templer, & Co,
                  34 Pall Mall,
                  London/

f21   1961 9.67   And these we invent and propose unto future en-
quirers, nauseating *crambe* verities and questions overqueried. Flat
and flexible Truths are beat out by every Hammer; but Vulcan
and his whole Forge sweat to work out Achilles' Armour. A large
Field is yet left unto sharper discerners, to enlarge upon this order
to search out the quarternion and figured Draughts of this nature,
and moderating the study of Names and mere Nomenclature of
Plants to erect generalities, disclose unobserved proprieties, not
only in the vegetable Shop but the whole Volume of Nature, af-
f21ᵛ fording delightful Truths confirmable by Sense and ocular information—which seems to me the surest Path to trace the Labyrinth
of Truth. For tho' discursive Enquiry & rational Conjecture may
leave handsome Gashes and Flesh wounds, yet without conjunction
of this expect no mortal or dispatching blows unto error.—
    Sir T. Brown, Quincunx mystically considered. 200.—O to write
a character of this man.—

1962 9.68   Virtue still Virtue; tho' you have met with a spe-
cious Rogue,—These rogues beget & seem to justify Selfishness—
be it my business to guard men against *them*, if possible, but still
f22 more against the *selfishness* to be generated, by shewing 1. its un-

reasonableness. 2. its folly 3. its meaning.—*For what were* you virtuous?—

1963 9.69   The generic how superior to the particular illustrated in Music, how infinitely more perfect in passion & its transitions than even Poetry—Poetry than Painting—& yet Genius how marvellous in all implements!!—March 10th/Lamb + John Lamb. Saturday Night—Knights Bronzes with eyes—Statues—

1964 9.70   A mattrass   f22ᵛ
                     Two single Blankets
                     Three single Sheets
                     Pillow & Pillow case
                     Counterpane + 3/10

1965 9.71   Fair mead Lodge; near Loughton, Essex/

1966 9.72   Mem. Nearchus for White

1967 9.73   Bentham by Dumont/translated—

1968 9.74   Sabbath promotes *public Spirit*/Men lay aside their peculiar Professions/One bond of feeling—hence the Sabbath breaking of Industry & its pernicious Consequences   f24

1969 9.75   I have shewed you my reasons and given you my Testimony, and yet you that have neither call this a *Notion.*

1970 9.76   The putrid Smell of the Stapelia—or carrion Flower tempts the ⟨large⟩ Flesh fly to deposit its young worms on its beautiful Petals, which perish there for want of nourishment, as applied to a really good hearted man who in youth swears, games &c/& yet the Scoundrels are all bit in him—to Henry 5th/.—

1971 9.77   Duellists such as Harvey Ashton, Best, Camel- f24ᵛ
ford, true *Assassins!*—Confute & indignantly ridicule Mackintosh's Defence of Duelling, as if it prevented Assassination/

1972 9.78   The huge Organ Pipe at Exeter larger than that at Haerlem—but *dumb!* Green determined to make it speak/tried all ways & means in vain/till at last he made a second Pipe pre-
f25 cisely alike, & placed it by it/—then it spoke.

1973 9.79   A complex Ship to Vandervelt as completely *one* Thing, one abstract, as an Egg or one of its ropes to an ordinary Artist. Sir G. Beaumont found great advantage in learning to draw from Nature thro' Gause Spectacles.

1974 9.80, 81   The Poles of Ice render the Torrid Zone Habit-
f25ᵛ able & the ~~la~~ very much later accumulation & Extent of Ice at the South Pole necessary to preserve the Ice at the North/?—How?
    The non-conducting Power of Fluids—else all ice/the high conducting power of the air/else all Scorch & Conflagration/—
    Davy's Hypothesis of the Aurora Borealis/—Sir Isaac Newton's of Light/each Particle every where in the course of Eternity.
    Contrast of colours—/two pillars/& wear green Spectacles/O what a lovely Purple when you pull them off//vice versa!

1975 9.82   Saturday, March 24, 1804—took my place,
f26 1,10„0 for the Portsmouth Mail for Tuesday Evening, March 27th

1976 9.83   Sunday, March 25th sate to Northcote for a Sketch, if possible, a Portrait of me for Sir G. Beaumont.

1977 9.84   N.B. Opium always in the day-time increases the puffing Asthma, eye closing, & startlings.

1978 9.85   West—yes, Sir!—& the Mad apothecary—long Story—frenzy—roll in his own Carpet—every Roll to his own advantage toward the Bell &c

f26ᵛ 1979 9.86   yawn—could not blast hiss

1980 9.87   Statuary easier than Painting—

1. James Northcote: *Samuel Taylor Coleridge*
From a sketch taken 24 March 1804. See 1976 and n

1981 9.88   Mr Farringdon's *conscientious* Views of North
Wales.—

1982 9.89   Ginger. Mustard. A knife & Fork. James's Powder. Bark.

1983 9.90   My spirit watched as constantly & as shily the
numberless kind attentions of Sir G. & Lady Beaumont, as an innocent young woman pleased & uncoy, the intelligible all of a
Lover's behaviour.

1984 9.91   Perpetual Church yard the Country to me—said
Northcote/melancholy—out of the reach of a city/especially the
Bleat of the Lambs at Sunset—

1985 9.132   Deficit only £ according to Stuart [. . . .] yet I   *f55*
still today had £20 independent of that [. . .] £ of small Gold
[?20/30] Capt. 20£

[?Harris]	25£
Dollars	5£
Expend.	8£/
Tot.	70£

1986 9.92   Davison, Noel, Templer, Middleton, Johnson, &   *f27*
Wedgwood, 34. Pall Mall.

1987 9.93   Left London, Tuesday Evening, on the Portsmouth Mail, March 27th, 1804: arrived safe at the Crown Inn (a
dirty doleful Inn) Portsmouth, ½ past 7, Wednesday Morning,
28th.

1988 9.94   The Star, Tues. Mar. 27. 1804—The Colonel expresses his conviction that they will live & die in defence of their
God. &c—

1989 9.95   Thomas Hope: every chair, designed each him-   *f27ᵛ*
self

1990 9.96   Maidlow,
Blendworth near Horndean,
Hants.

1991 9.97   A ~~parent~~ Mother dying of a contagious Disease
unable to give or receive the last Embrace to her Orphan Child.—

f28   1992 9.98   To the Memory of Henry Case of the Royal
Montgomery Militia, who serv'd as a Marine in the glorious Battle fought by Lord Howe on the 1ˢᵗ of June, 1794. This Stone was
erected by the voluntary Subscription of his Comrades, belonging
to Captⁿ Davies's Company. He died Nov. 5ᵗʰ 1798, aged 28.

Here lies a true Soldier whom all must applaud,
Much Hardship he suffer'd at home & abroad,
But the hardest Engagement he ever was in
Was the Battle of Self in the conquest of Sin.

f28ᵛ   Here lies I
Kill'd by a Sky-
Rocket in the Eye
In the year fortȳ

Here <u>I</u> lies all putrefaction
Waiting for the Resurrection = a fair statement of Priestley's intermediate State/

1993 9.99   Friday, April 6ᵗʰ, 1804—got on board the Speedwell, expecting to sail instantly/but the wind westerd again/
    Saturday April 7ᵗʰ/quite calm/beautiful sight/Isle of Wight,
& the Ships below it/and on the other side 9 men of war in
⌒⌒⌒ zigzag semicircle, & in the interspaces all sorts of smaller
f29   Ships, some with sails reefed, others all flying—the Sun on some,
some in shade/their different Shapes & sizes & distinctnesses, & the
Portsea Land &c a fine background, into which the sight dies away
& is satisfied. The different Signals, Drums, Guns, Bells, & the
sound of Voices weighing up & clearing Anchors. Wind all against

us/Saturday, went on shore/⟨but slept aboard⟩. Dined on board on Sunday.

Monday, April 9th, really set sail. In weighing anchor the men *f29ᵛ* grumbled aloud a sort of mutiny—not half our complement of men—Two pressed in the Downs/one ran away at Portsmouth, a rascal of a one-armed Cook better gone than stay'd/—now we are Captain, Mate, 2 boys, 4 men, 3 passengers, one Sheep, 3 pigs, several Ducks & Chicken, 1 Dog, a Cat & 2 Kittens.—Was sickish & feverish for a few Hours on Monday; but mended before dinner, eat a better dinner than my usual—and continued well. But by the Captain's persuasion lay on my bed/in consequence of which I dosed all night diseasedly, & all the morning—got upon deck, & formed different notions.—No Health or Happiness without *f30* Work/In consequence partly of the Build of the Brig, & partly of its being so heavily laden at its bottom, the Cabbin rocks like a Cradle, ~~as~~ when the cruel nurse~~r~~ rocks a screaming Baby.—/On Monday night we travelled like a ⟨Top⟩ Bough on a Larch Tree in a high wind/pitching & rocking at anchor in a Breeze that would have carried us 9 or 10 knots an hour/

This morning, Tuesday, April 10th, 1804, a fine sharp morning —the Sea rolls rough & high/but the Ships are before us & behind *f30ᵛ* us. I count 35, and the blue Land, the Start, to our right, & the lonely Gulls ~~fly~~ fish in among the Ships/& what a beautiful object even a single wave is! I shall employ this morning if only I can lay down a Plan for the rest of my Voyage.

1. Being broad awake, & it being day-light, get up, drink a dish of ginger Tea/& do all I can to clean myself, then ~~write something, either Letters Journal, or my Tours.~~ read Italian till breakfast Time/

1. Up—wash—ginger Tea hot. *f31*
2. Italian till Breakfast time.
3 Breakfast
4 Write or transcribe my Journal.
5th read the Theodicee & take notes for my Consolations.
6th Then write my Letters on literary Detraction/or a review of Wordsworth/in short, *something, beginning with this.*
7th between dinner & tea what I can/. Read some Italian if pos-

sible. After tea till bed time try to compose. God grant me fortitude & a perseverant Spirit of Industry!—

$f3I^v$ 1994 9.100   An exquisite purple upon part of the Sea/such as
I have often seen the glass of waterglasses.

1995 9.101   The wave itself—its crown of foam/its larger
Hollows—its puckers—its wrinkles, & 5th, its dimples & sunshine/

1996 9.102   Tuesday Night, April 10th, 1804/thought of a
Lullaby Song, to a Child on a Ship/great rocking Cradle with the
giant Rocker, Creak of Main top Irons, Rattle of Ropes, & Squeak
of the Rudder Rope running on the Block/And so play at bo peep
with the Rising Moon, and the Lizard Light/—There is thy native Country, Boy!—Whither art thou going to &c—

$f32$ The Ship at night moves like the crescent in a firmament of
Clouds & Stars in them, the Clouds now all bright with a moonlike
Light, now dim & watry-grey—now darting off—& often at such
distance that they lose all apparent connection with the Ship, &
seem each its own Lord, Spirits playing with each other//In my
tour to Germany I have described them most accurately, only that
now I observed close under the Ship side, a constant clear blue Sky
with coursing [?Star./Stars]

1997 9.103   Wednesday, April 11, 1804/Sea & Sky, & an ir-
$f32^v$ regular circle of Ships of which we seem the Center. Saw, a nice
black faced bright black-eyed white-toothed Boy running up to the
Main Top with a large Leg of Mutton swung, Albatross-fashion
about his neck/—"Rear'd" ~~like~~ for a Ship lad, taught every thing
by Curses—yet well-behav'd the while, & his Master shed a tear
when he died—for the Boy would sing on the Top Mast, a Song
neither of Love nor of Wine, & come down with Tears on his
Cheeks/

1998 9.104   Wednesday afternoon the Wind fell, & it was so
near a calm at one time that we went only a knot an Hour/Rain
$f33$ came—& with it my Drowsiness & Stupor/& tho' I eat nothing af-

ter dinner, & nothing but Soup & vegetables for dinner, I screamed in the night/. Mem. To examine whether Dreams of Terror & obscure Forms, ugly or not, be commonly preceded by Forms of Awe & Admiration with distant Love. Before three old Women, the dim Apparitions of three, attacked me in that dark passage I had seen a Lady, made up of Sir. C. Grandison's Lady & Sir P. Sidney's, talking with her Maid concerning Sir P. Sidney/—That Wednesday I opened out my Trunk, & examined the little Escritoire given me by Lady Beaumont. I had never connected any pleasure with neatness & convenience; now for the first time they *f33ᵛ* seized my Heart at once by a hundred Tentacula of Love & affection & pleasurable Remembrances. How could it be otherwise? Every thing had been so manifestly placed there by the Hand of affectionate Solicitude!

1999 9.105   April 12ᵗʰ/Thursday/the wind from N.E. has changed 5 points to S.E., but we go on pretty well, & with far less Rocking. "A neat handed Fellow who could shave himself in a storm without drawing blood." We are in the Bight of the Bay of Biscay, & tho' the Breeze blows fresh, yet I feel the Air more warm & genial and the Sky seems bluer.—

This day noon we are in 47 degrees 28 min. of Latitude.—

Delightful weather, motion, relation of the convoy to each other, all exquisite/—and I particularly watched the beautiful Surface of *f34* the Sea in this gentle Breeze! every form so transitory, so for the instant, & yet for that instant so substantial in all its sharp lines, steep surfaces, & hair-deep indentures, just as if it were cut glass, glass cut into ten thousand varieties/& then the network of the wavelets, & the rude circle hole network of the Foam/

And on the gliding Vessel Heaven & Ocean smil'd!

2000 9.106   Why an't you here? This for ever/I have no rooted thorough thro' feeling—& never exist wholly present to any *f34ᵛ* Sight, to any Sound, to any Emotion, to any series of Thoughts received or produced/always a feeling of yearning, that at times passes into Sickness of Heart.

2001 9.107   SICKLY Thoughts about M. mort. & W. ÷ Sā—
Hydrocarb./died looking at the stars above the top mast; & when
found dead, these Stars were sinking in the Horizon/—a large
Star? a road of dim Light?—Light of the Compass & rudderman's
Lamp reflected with forms on the Main Sail.

2002 9.108   Friday, April 13ᵗʰ, 1804.—A brisk Gale with high
Sea/between six & seven knots an hour/
 Morning, 9 °clock, about *46* Latitude, if we go on at this rate,
we shall stand opposite to, i.e. in the Line of Bourdeaux at 8 °clock
f35 this Evening, & perhaps see Cape Ortegal by this time tomorrow
morning. N.B. The great Sea-savannah acquires apparent extent by
the Ships' skirting its distance, & by its evident interminateness
conveys the feeling of Interminableness.

2003 9.109   After a certain force of wind you can go as fast,
& often faster, with less Canvass—πλεον ημισυ παντος.—
2. Throw nothing against the wind but ashes & scalding water.
3. The ship at the Forecastle always appears to move far faster
than it does.—4. Ship towed in a Convoy/Wyndham to tow Mʳ
Addington.

2004 9.110   The beautiful bright Slate, & the Soap stone colours by the Vessel's side, in a brisk gale, immediately under the
f35° mast in a froth-cream, that throws itself into network, with its *brisk*
sound, which the word brisk itself may be made to imitate by
hissing on the "isk," even better than the πολυφλοισβοιο
θαλασσης perhaps.

2005 9.111   To the Sheep/yesterday cropt its hay chearfully
—flashes of Lightning from the Tops & dimples of the gentle
waves, & the sweet murmur might have awakened the sensations of
dewy grass in sunshine, & the murmur of its Trees—but now/
kneeling its poor face to the Deck, its knees black, worn, & sore/—
up it starts, a great wave rushing over the ship—& staggers—&
f36 trembles under the Boat, with another on the Top of it, by the side
of the Pump, a Gun close before it/(the Boat a Pig Stye) alas! it
came from flat peaceable meadows—/Had it come from Black

Comb, or Muncaster Fell/—or even from Helvellin, or Fairfield, or Kirkstone/the dreadful Tempest of Sound, its Shelter behind the Rocks, the Snatching up of water, & of the waterfalls &c &c

2006 9.112   The Sea with its intermination & within the ken of the eye innumerable *multitude* of Sunshine—/Have I not seen   *f36ᵛ* masses of plumbago like the Sea/or rather Fire sides, Hobbs, &c, that in certain slant reflections resemble it?

2007 9.113   Friday Afternoon, 6 °clock/Commodore fired a Gun the smoke from which formed a cloud of a very picturesque Outline, which soon rose to the same apparent height with the other clouds, & only distinguished from them by its continuing Motion.

2008 9.114   Two beautiful Weather [?gales] this lovely after-noon/O for Sir G. B. to give permanence to these superlative Masses of Clouds over the Convoy, of which we are the foremost, even the Commodore lagging astern of us/to our Left—all under those Clouds.

2009 9.115   Half past 7 almost a calm/to the Left the arc of   *f37* Heaven which I have before me shipless, cloudless/I turn round, and lo! the arc which was behind me, & now to my right hand be-fore, the whole Convoy the Leviathan in the seeming centre & out-side of them (for our Ship is the foremost & the outermost by half a mile) exactly comprized under one magnificent twi-cleft white mountain of Cloud/beginning with & ending with the Ships/—/ or the other black clouds with stripes & streaks of darkening Gold/   *f37ᵛ* and mid way between our Top mast & the Right Horizon the cres-cent Moon with the old Moon in her Lap, and below it 20 times its own Diam. a bright Planet—⟨below it just $\frac{27}{190}$ of the Cope.⟩ While writing this we caught a young Bird a Lark as I believe.

2010 9.116   Moon 33,23ᵐ above the Horizon/the Star, 25,59. —8̶ 7 degrees from the Moon, the whole Cope of Heaven 190 de-grees.

2011 9.117   N.B. In my Consolations on narrowness of Heart

f38   —Lamb can't like the Brothers/ *Fox* does not like the Blank Verse
Poems/Misery! how is this possible without pleading guilty to
some defect of moral Being. If I do not like a poem, I can in my
own conceit at least shew a reason why *no* one ought to like/or
that they would be better off if they did not. Satur. April 14.

2012 9.118   Saturday Morning, Apr. 14/1804/fine, but we go
on slowly and we purchased the loveliness of last night by almost
~~by~~ a calm. The Lark alive and brisk.

The elements of this picturesque effect of a Ship/a man of war,
for instance.

f38°   1. Its height upon a flat surface/if a Steeple be so uniformly pleasing on a diversified meadow, how much more the Masts of a man
of war, referring as with a finger to the Sky, on this vast Level?
2. The proportion of the solid height to the Height above the
Hull, about as 40 to 160, made graceful & right by the strongly
felt Lightness & Airiness of the Sails/while yet
3. The elliptical figure of the Hull & its kindred motion prevent
all abrupt or harsh contrast between the wood & the Canvass—to
which the masts & in a [?brisk/fresh] gale the *stiff* Bellying of the
Sails are aidant.
4. The height of the naked mast above the sails, connected how-

f39   ever with them by Pennant & Vane, associated, I think, with the
human form on a watch-tower/a general feeling—ex.gr. the *Men*
on the tops of conical mountains & of others in Cumberland &
Westmor./
5. The harmony of the Lines—the ellipses & semicircles of the
bellying Sails & of the Hull, with the variety from the permanence
of the one & the contingency of the other/
6. The terminating Lines of the Sails forming ~~the~~ a similar curve
with the sail, yet by its determinateness producing a threefold ef-
fect/1. of a strongly felt variety in the Canvassage of the Vessel/
⟨2⟩ Secondly, I scarcely know how but its stiffness & determinateness always mingles a notion of natural Straightness which seems

f39°   to form a link of union with the masts, & so thro' the masts with
Hull making one whole of the whole Vessel/while the mast above

the Sails connects it with the beholder by obscure resemblance of the human form as seen at a distance or on a height/ 3. This determinateness of the stiff rope-hemm'd Edge Line of the Sails, not dying away into each other, weakening the *sensuous beauty* raises it to the picturesque, giving it the whole a greater facility of connecting itself & forming with other Ships as Forms, & of forming an interesting part of a common whole: which if it were a complete ƒ40 visual whole in itself, as a circle with its radii, &c it could not so ƒ40ᵛ easily do—

7ᵗʰˡʸ/Every one of these sails is *known* by the Intellect to have a ƒ41 strict & necessary action & reaction on all the rest, & that the whole is made up of parts, each part referring at once to each & to the whole/—and nothing more administers to the Picturesque than this phantom of complete visual wholeness in an object, which visually does not form a whole, by the influence ab intra of the sense of its perfect Intellectual Beauty or Wholeness.—To all these must be added the Lights & Shades, sometimes *sunshiny*, some- ƒ41ᵛ times *snowy:* sometimes shade-coloured, sometimes dingy—whatever effect distance, air tints, reflected Light, and the feeling connected with *the* Object (for all Passion unifies as it were by natural Fusion) have in bringing out, and in melting down, differences & contrast, accordingly as the mind finds it necessary to the completion of the idea of Beauty, to prevent sameness or discrepancy.— Of a Fleet of Ships more may be said: & probably more will sug- ƒ42 gest itself & of less obvious kind, on after quiet Looking: now that the Intellect has done its main business & rests.

They begin to cheat with the metallic pencils. I am forced to take a new one from another Book, having compleatly worn out the one belonging to it/instead of being about 2 inches it was scarcely one; & the metal far softer & more wasteful.

N°. 2. Proved by the ill look of a large Vessel with bare sails or the greater part of them reefed/unless it be made more than beautiful by becoming the Language of passion & peril/tho' it is most worthy of of Observation, that in such circumstance there is such a ƒ42ᵛ wonderful correspondency of the surrounding objects, clouds &

billow, & Ships, & their new relations to each other, & to the Stars, the Hull of One to the Masts of the other, &c &c—such a correspondency, I say, either by likeness or counteraction, that the whole Field of Vision becomes sensuallyously picturesque, & *the parts* become acquire as *parts* a charm which they have not as Things

f43 per se.—I mean to say, that divested of the passion that makes such a combination of Forms sublime, it would even sensuously *be grand*/if there be no other & better word.—Pursue this:—& add to the above the *outline* of the whole Ship, which especially in Merchant Ships, Brigs, &c is a beautiful Approach to the Oval/—the height of the whole Vessel taken in with the length of the whole/

f43° —& forget not to observe what a vast number of incidents the masts & sails of a Ship can represent, a sort of natural Telegraph, the distinctness of a Signal with the eloquence & absolute unarbitrary appropriateness of passion & reality.

2013 9.119   Saturday late Evening, about 8 °clock—I was gazing to the Starboard on the Clouds/& was musing that in this Bay of Biscay I had observed that the great masses on the Horizon split themselves into more Heads, & those more deeply cleft, chim-

f44 neys, obelisks, Turrets, & chiefly those larger loftier forms that have the Peak of the Mountain with the breadth & Proportions of the Tower. Yesterday I saw a strong resemblance of the most striking five Segments of Glencoe/the right hand side as you go *to* Ballachulish/& this Evening exactly over the Convoy, with it beginning & with it ending, I saw a delightful mockery of a Fleet,

f44° masts & Sails & Pennants/While I was thus musing, I turned to the Larboard side of the Vessel, & my Heart did indeed leap up/— Was it the Placefell Bank of Ulswater? Or the Benlomond side of Loch Lomond!?—Or Lochness?—or rather that which I saw in late eve at Letter Findlay? Or was it not a new Mountain with a new Lake/only so completely did the Sea between our Ship & it become a Lake, and that black substantial Squall Cloud the Moun-

f45 tain that formed & rose up from its banks, that it would be a positively falsehood to say, it was like. It was utterly indistinguishable/ I gazed & gazed again, & peered & scrutinized, & could find no distinction/a long level or nearly level ridge of low Mountain,

then gradually rising up into a ~~broad~~ Lambda with the top somewhat more rounded, & sinking down into a similar but not so far
stretching a mountain ridge/—exactly both in outline & in general   *f45ᵛ*
surface the same as to distinctness, as the opposite Shore of a Lake
a mile & a half or two miles broad has, in late evening, when the
air is now drizzly, & now cleared up by the uncertain winds—as
distinct if not more so/& the distinctness varying in the same way/
especially in the outline, which was now sharp, & defined, & O!
for a star to rest upon it, a bright large Star/& now light flying   *f46*
mantles of Clouds waving upon it, or snatched off from it/—Hoist
out the boat/I looked, till I half saw a Light on the Hill—In the
mean time the Captain paced up & down uneasy, & took in the
Sails/he feared that it had a Tempest within it/but the Squall-
cloud ⟨has⟩ dropt our wind, & ~~fell~~ falls in large rain/it is not past/   *f46ᵛ*
but our Stern is bethumpt with a rude Swell every 2 or 3 minutes/
& the Mate is whistling aloft for a wind.—What a sweet Image to
precede a Ship-wreck!—

2014 9.120   Sat. night, April 14ᵗʰ to Sunday April 15ᵗʰ, and
now Monday Morning, 9 °clock, April 16ᵗʰ, 1804.—
     All Saturday Night brisk Gales interrupted by Squalls with
heavy rains, during which variable or varying winds *shuttlecock'd*
our poor brig—then after a small Becalmment up springs the regu-   *f47*
lar Breeze again.—All Sunday it blew a brisk gale indeed, & we
went 9 knots an hour; & were going at that rate ~~last~~ yester evening
when the Commodore made us take in our Sails, to wait for Vessels
astern. But all day it rocked so deep, & the Sea so often gave the
Ship a smart & lusty Box o' the Ear, that there was neither sitting
or standing, without danger of Contusions—So tho' not at all un-   *f47ᵛ*
well by it, I kept to my Cot, which is the best possible sitting, eating, drinking, writing, even shaving, mantel, it fails only in its
original purpose, that of lying & sleeping; like a great Genius
apprenticed to a wrong Trade.—It is just 20 inches broad, & $\frac{F}{5}$, 1̇o
in length/with a Port-hole by leaving ⟨⟨D9, 32/3 in L.19. 4 deep
—23 broad. 19 L)⟩ Space & playroom to my right elbow, the lower
Half of which however I have so interlaced with cordage to & fro
& across thro' the iron rings, as to make me a nice cupboard, half a

f48　dozen Books or more, a Lemon or two, shaving Things—and on the flat of the Books (consisting of Sir T. Brown's works, sent down to me to P. by mistake, & Haüy's Mineralogy, packed up with Greenough's neatness—one parallelogram of brown paper) stand my Tea Cup, Soup plate, Glass of Lemonade—even my Ink Stand, by charm & talismannic Privilege/one of those Smooth Spaces in the Mediterranean, where the breakers foam in a circle around, yet send in no wrinkles upon, the mirror-bright, m-smooth Lacus in mare/Imperium in Imperio—

f48ᵛ　All night however it rocked so incessantly (for as aforesaid, as a sleeping & lying place it doth not *excel*) that I in my imperfect Dozings repeatedly lost all sense of support ab infra/I seemed to move to & fro, not because I was rocked, but because no spot being able to support me, each gave me on to another—or as if I moved to & fro, half by its Force, half by my own will/my own will giving a phantom transfer of a sort of will to this fancied *Surge* be-
f49　neath me/this somewhat that had force to displace & transfer, but not to support & sustain.—.This morning, a few minutes before 9, April 16, 1804,
I hurried on my great Coat, & shoeless &c went on Deck, & hailed the beautiful Coast of *Portugal*, & Oporto/—fishing boats on each side of us!—& I will write to Southey today.

2015 9.121　　Monday Noon.—Bear off from Land, but do not lose sight of it, nor of the Shadows of clouds, many and large and black on the broad Sides of the warm yellow green mountains/like
f49ᵛ　huge Phocæ sunning themselves on Sands. In the afternoon Cape Mondego stretched out, a bold Ness of deepest purple Blue. All day during the Sunshine watched with delight the two colors of the Ocean, richest Green—I had seen nothing like it hitherto, nothing so green, no green so bright & rich—and of violet purple, equal in light & richness: the V. P. now in large & small Islands among the Green, now almost halving the field of Vision, & their
f50　Colors forming two seas, each a Shore to the other—now the V. P. running up into the Green, & vice versâ in long Stripes, Coves, Spearheads, & Tongues. The Fishermen in their boat, 7—2 men, 3 Lads, and 2 boys. The two men had red Caps or nightcaps, the

Sails ocher brown, the Lads & Boys Caps olive less brown/—the
Colors remarkably soft & yet lively. I thought of Sir G. Beaumont
—At the side of the vessel the water itself, taken in separate wave-   *f50ᵛ*
lets astonishingly alive & brilliant—brilliant with Life, alive with
brilliance—In the afternoon slept t̶i̶l̶l̶ on the bare Deck/—Sun sets
in this Latitude 35ᵐ past 6, April 16ᵗʰ/I had so forgotten my
geography, so sedulously cuffed into my Ears/—that I was surprized at not finding the Length of Summer Days accompanying
their warmth!

2016 9.122   Sea Phrase μεταφορητικα
                Bear up and sail large—
                Half his Sails full, half aback = no progress—
often intentional in Mʳ Pitt.—&c.   *f51*

Every sail stretched, every rope in action; the sides of the Vessel
winged with Studding Sails, there he is, 2 leagues astern of the last
of the Convoy, the Commodore of which is moving on, with half
his masts bare   & he & the rest, what blessings they bestow on
this Lag Sheep of the Flock!—

Every night—& sometimes once a day beside—we lie aback for
2 or 3 hours, to wait for the Laggers.—

If a Vessel in the Convoy does not obey Signals, the Commodore   *f51ᵛ*
fires a *shot* at the Vessel/Commodore's strengthening *Pills* for the
Memory/—& charges the owner 5ˢ for the first, 10ˢ the next, & so
doubling each time.

2017 9.123   Blue *pierced* white.

2018 9.124   Tuesday Morning, ½ past 10, April 17ᵗʰ, 1804—
Last night Squalls, desperate Rocking, my Dreams full of Grief
& bitter weeping.
        Oft in his sleep he wept, & waking found
        His Pillow cold beneath his Cheek with Tears, And
        And found his Dreams
        (So faithful to the Past, or so prophetic)   *f52*
        That when he thought of what had made him weep,

He did not recollect it as a Dream,
And spite of open eyes & the broad Sunshine
The feverish Man perforce must weep again.
This in rhyme, & either greatly compressed or highly touched up.
And now for the Metaphysics/In cases of violent weeping is there
not always Pity mixed & predominant?—Do we not pity our past
Selves?—And Pity is has always pleasure as one of its component
Parts. Whence derived? Whence augmented? Sympathy will often
make a Sufferer weep/. Is not this always accompanied by Hope?
f52ᵛ "It makes the Images of the Past vivid, & so reproduces the first
effect."—So it may be said, I doubt—or if it does, is it not by decreasing the *feeling,* & making room for vivid Ideas. Are not vivid
Ideas themselves a sort of pleasure, as Music whether sad or lively,
is always Music.—This for *Consolations.* And now develope the
whole of that Phænomenon of Sleep, that I give (as I did last
night) the names, Characters, mine & their appropriate Language
& Feelings to 3 or 4 forms, having no one Likeness of the real
f53 Persons—as last night to Rickman. Poor Legrice, &c/No one of the
forms acting, as they, & so by me acted on, having one lineament
or even resemblance of Size?—Think of this.

I hear that the Rock of Lisbon has been in sight for some hours.
The rain is now over. I must be up.

How at sea to indulge yourself with breakfasting in bed—& how
in too great confidence of the Port Hole or carelessness, to scald
below the Hips.

2019 9.125   Long years of seriousness, of deep Passion, awful
Incident, seas traversed, & the famous Things of the world seen,
f53ᵛ and all connected with one abiding Hope, one Thought, one Love
—this will surely give a delicacy, an awe/a fear of saying ⟨or
doing⟩ *light* or *coarse* Things in her Presence/& lengthen out the
Passion by still combining it with a manly Feeling.

2020 9.126   Of your *good* men, who can conceive no object
of goodness not starving or dying. These men drive a *Trade:* &
every Thing smells of the Shop.

2021 9.127   The Rock of Lisbon, the yellow Sand-bank beyond it, but before you come to it, all that ridge which runs down   *f54*
into the Rock of Lisbon is as fine a Mountain, of the wild, striding

Edge, ⟨sketch⟩ kind, I ever saw/Especially the other ex-

⟨sketch⟩

tremity of the ridge, beginning with the Drunkards ⟨sketch⟩ —just
before that bold/village or villages, which I wished to be Cintra/
still farther back some very large building, 2 Towers visible to the
naked Eye/Palace or Convent?—very high, just ~~under~~ in a line
with 5 or 6 breast-shaped Peaks/After this Cape Espeichal, with a
grand *Dome*-shaped Mountain/&c.

2022 21.431   An account of the Signals made use of at Bam-   *f98ᵛ*
borough Castle, Northumberland. A Gun, a nine pounder, placed
at the bottom of the Tower to be fired as a Signal in case any Ship
or Vessel be observed in distress: namely *once*, if it be wrecked on
the Islands or any adjacent rock: *twice*, when any Ship or Vessel
is stranded or wrecked behind the Castle or to the N. of it, *thrice*
when any Ship &c is wrecked to the Southward of the Castle.
in order that the Customhouse officers and the Tenants with their
Servants may hasten—assist & prevent a plunder. *In every great
Storm two men are sent on horseback from the Castle to patrol
along the Shore* from Sunset to Sunrise, that, in case of an accident
one may remain by the Ship, & the other return to alarm the Cas-   *f99*
tle.—Whoever brings the first notice entitled to a premium in
proportion to the distance from the Castle; & if between 2 & 3 at
dark the premium to be double. A large Flag is hoisted, when any
V. is seen in distress on the Ferne Islands or Staples—that the
Sufferers may have the satisfaction of knowing that their Distress
is perceived from the Shore & that they will be relieved as soon as
possible. In case of bad weather the Flag will be kept up, a Gun
fired M. & evening, & a Rocket thrown up from the N. Turret,
till such time as Relief can be sent. These also are signals to the
Holy Island Fishermen, who by the advantage of their situation
can put off for the Islands at times when no boats from the main

land can get over the Breakers. Premiums are given to the first boats &c. A Bell on the S. Turret will be rung out every thick Fog, as a signal to the Fishing Boats; and a large Swivel, fixed on the East Turret, will be fired every 15 minutes as a signal to the Ships without the Islands.—

A large Weathercock is fixed on the Top of the Flag Staff for the use of Pilots: a large Speaking Trumpet is provided to be used when Ships are in distress near the Shore or run aground. An Observatory or Watch tower is made on the East Turret of the Castle, where a Person is to attend every morning at Day break, during the Winter Season, to look out if any Ships be in Distress.—M. & Com. of V. in Distress are to make such signals as are usually made by people in their melancholy situation.—April 17, 1804 off Cape Espeichel, below the Rock of Lisbon.

f54ᵛ 2023 9.128   Wednesday Morning, Ap. 18. Cape Sᵗ Vincent, low; but now at noon we are abreast of High land.—Tomorrow the Captain expects to be at Gibraltar. Wretchedly unwell the last day or two, that endless Rocking!—Like Hiccups or Itching—'Tis teazing, impertinent like the presence & tittle tattle of a shrill voiced Maiden Aunt in the company of the Beloved who loves—/ To day it is quit—Heaven!—And this is the 2ⁿᵈ of the whole voyage; & the 1ˢᵗ very inferior.

2024 9.129   Housekeeper—of eatables—I was determined to take enough of those—I always think them is comfortable/I don't know what I shall say to the Apricot Tarts at Malta—& so on— Every morsel eat for some reason, I must do so & so/that little Potatoe looks one smiling in the face/That little bit of &c &c [. . .]/for I always think &c—But [the man is the true] Sensualist

f55 —silent [. . . . . . .] so far a most interesting day [. . .] and the whole day—not at all sick or unwell.
plaintive
crying Yawns/

f3 2025 15.5   Memorabilia from Portsmouth, Monday, April 9ᵗʰ, 1804 to Gibraltar, and whithersoever else God will or suffer

me to go—Beginning Thursday, April 19—continued from the
Leaf but three of the red Pocket book with the word Chrono-
logical inked on its red Binding.

2026 15.7   Thursday Morning, April 19ᵗʰ, 1804.—Yester-   *f4*
night with a bright moon, the Light of which rolled, like an Island
of grey white Reeds on a tossing Lake—how hard to describe that
sort of Queen's metal plating, which the Moonlight forms on the
bottle-green Sea/the water bright, but the Green of the water not
bright—& therein Moonlight bright as if even it yet seemed to
partake ⟨of⟩ or rather to be modified by, the color in which it
floated—made a different color from its natural blue whiteness
without or only obscurely resembling that of the Sea water—*this*
as a Mem. that the moon silvering the Sea is not *lively* to Nature   *f4°*
—/However, under this moon we sailed at a large rate, and now
about 10 °'clock I sitting at the Rudder Case, my Desk, on the
Duck Coop, my Seat, have Spain, the Coast of Cadiz to wit, on
my left-hand, & Africa, the Barbary Coast, on my Right—perhaps
~~8~~ 6 miles distant from ~~each~~ ⟨the Spanish Coast, 13 from the Bar-
bary⟩ under mountain ridges both/but the Spanish Coast is of course
more distinct/I am right abreast of a high Bank, black brown
Heath with interspaces & large & small Scarifications of light red
clay—beyond this Mountain islands, alongside, & in file resembling Canoes & Boats with their Keels upward. We have a Breeze
that promises to let us laugh at Privateers & Corsairs that in a
calm will run out, & pick up a Merchant Vessel under the very   *f5*
stern of the Commodore, as a Fox will a Fowl when the Wolf dog
that guards the poultry yard, can only bark at him from his Chain/
This is Spain!—That is Africa! Now, then, I have seen Africa!
&c &c.—/Power of Names to give Interest!—When I first sate
down, with Europe on my left and Africa on my right, both distinctly visible, I felt a quickening of the movements in the Blood;
but still it felt as a pleasure of *amusement* than of Thought or
Elevation/and at the same time, and gradually winning on the
other, the nameless silent Forms of Nature were working on me,
like a tender Thought on a man, who is hailed merrily by some   *f5°*
acquaintance in his work, & answers it in the same Tone—. This is

Africa! That is Europe!—There is *division,* sharp boundary,
abrupt Change!—and what are they in Nature—two Mountain
Banks, that make a noble River of the interfluent Sea, ~~not~~ existing
& acting with distinctness and manifoldness indeed, but at once &
as one—no division, no Change, no Antithesis!—Of all men, I
ever knew, Wordsworth himself not excepted, I have the faintest
pleasure in things contingent & transitory. I never, except as a
forced Courtesy of Conversation, ask in a ~~Coach~~ Stage, whose
House is that—nor receive the least additional pleasure when I

f6   receive the answer. Nay, it goes to a disease in me—as I was gazing at a wall in Caernarvon Castle, I wished the Guide 50 miles
off that was telling me, in this Chamber the Black Prince was
born/or whoever it was—/I am not certain, whether I should have
seen with any Emotion the Mulberry Tree of Shakespere/. If
~~not~~ it were a Tree of no notice in itself, I am sure, that I should
feel by an effort with self-reproach at the dimness of the Feeling—
if a striking Tree, I fear, that the Pleasure would be diminished
rather than increased/that I should have no unity of Feeling, &
find in the constant association of Shakespere's having planted it
an intrusion that prevented me from wholly & as a whole man
losing myself in the flexures of its Branches & interweaving of its

f6ᵛ   Roots. No doubt, there are times & conceivable circumstances, in
which the contrary would be true, in which the Thought, under
this Rock by this Sea shore I know that Giordano Bruno hid himself from the Pursuit of the enraged Priesthood, & overcome with
the power & Sublimity of the Truths, for which they sought his
Life, thought his Life therefore given him that he might bear
witness to the Truth; & morti ultro occurrens, returned & surrendered himself—or here on this Bank Milton used to lie, in late
May, when a young man, & familiar with all its primroses made
them yet dearer than their dear selves by that sweetest line in the
Lycidas/And the rathe Primrose that forsaken dies/or from this
Spot, ~~Shakespere~~ the immortal Deer Stealer, on his Escape from

f7   Warwickshire, ~~fixed~~ had the first View of London, & asked himself—And what am I to do there? At certain times, uncalled and
sudden, subject to no bidding of my own or others, these Thoughts

would come upon me, like a Storm, & fill the Place with something more than Nature.—But these are not contingent or transi-
tory/they are Nature, even as the Elements are Nature/yea, more
to the human mind/for the mind has the power of abstracting all
agency from the former, & considering as mere effects & instruments, but a Shakespere, a Milton, a Bruno, exist in the mind as
pure Action, defecated of all that is material & passive/.—And the
great moments, that formed them—it is hard & an impiety against
a Voice within us, not to regard as predestined, & therefore things   *f7ᵛ*
of Now & For Ever and which were Always. But it degrades this
sacred Feeling; & is to it what stupid Superstition is to enthusiastic
Religion, when a man makes a Pilgrimage to see a great man's
Shin Bone found unmouldered in his Coffin, &c—Perhaps the matter stands thus: I ⟨could⟩ feel amused by these things, & should
be, if there had not been connected with the great Name, upon
which the amusement wholly depends, a higher & deeper Pleasure,
that will endure the Co-presence of so mean a Companion: while
the mass of mankind, whether from Nature or as I fervently hope
from Error of Rearing & the Wordliness of their after Pursuits,
are rarely susceptible of any other Pleasures than those of *amuse-*   *f8*
ment, gratifications of curiosity, Novelty, Surprize, Wonderment
from the Glaring, the harshly Contrasted, the Odd, the Accidental: and find the reading of the Paradise Lost † a task, somewhat
alleviated by a few entertaining Incidents, such as the Pandæ-
monium and Self-endwarfment of the Devils, the Fools' Paradise,
& the transformation of the infernal Court into Serpents, and of
their intended Applauses into Hisses.

† N.B.

To attack Johnson with all due severity on this phrase—Yes! and
the Bible too/& all good works, & the Fields, & Rivers, & Moun-
tains/they—& Dr. J. among the rest—die of Ennui in them—

This perhaps in the Consolations—on the virtues connected with   *f8ᵛ*
the Love of Nature, & vice versâ.

2027 15.8   Often even at noon under certain encloudments
of the Sun I observe a fine brassy Light on the sides of the waves.

2028 15.9   Thursday, One o'clock—A distinct View with my
glass of the Spanish Coast/Seaward a great Scar of Pink Clay or
Sand Stone; the Mountains above, drear & desolate, with bold
ascents & plunging Descents, the white Stone (granite or lime?)
staring & streaking thro' the black Heath & Brushwood—

2029 15.10   40^m p.2.—The Island & Town of Tariffa/The
surface of the Sp. Mountains (limestone) in fine sweeps, and horizontal Furrows & ridges. But the African Coast!—[?Moor/
Mount] behind Mount—& M. among M.—& three or four be-
f9 hind, like chimneys in the Clouds—and one old stooping Giant
looking in upon us 20 leagues inland. They most resemble Grasmere & the Maid of Glencoe.
     The famous Apes hill in front—a corruption of M. Abbila
     44^m p.2 The lowest Rock of Gibraltar called Europa point came
in view: along the Spanish Coast—we are now abreast of Tariffa,
which had the houses been slated instead of tiled, & would have
been so like Keswick—these are the green fields up Skiddaw, and
Skiddaw—& Carsleddam—rude resemblances indeed, but yet resemblances—& now the whole Rock of Gibraltar comes in view.
     The Shadows of the Ropes & Rope Ladders on the Convexcave
of the bellying Foresail & Top Sails.
     Between 4 & 5, Thurs afternoon, April 19—arrived at Gibraltar.

f9° 2030 15.11   *Cracker, Blazer,* and *Hasty,*
                          Spitfire, Sulphur, & *Strombolo.*

2031 15.12   Water by Halo Moonlight/grey yet very bright,
Fish Scales tossing about on it.

2032 21.432   To J. T. Esqre. April 19th, 1804. Men who ha-   ƒ99
bitually enjoy robust Health, have too generally the trick, and a
very cruel one it is, of imagining that they discover the secret of
all their Acquaintances Ill health in some Malpractice or other:
and sometimes by gravely asserting this here & there & every
where (as who likes his Penetration under a Bushel?) they not
only do all, they can, without intending it, to deprive the poor
Sufferer of that Sympathy which is always a Comfort, and in some
degree a Support to human Nature, but likewise too often implant
serious alarm & uneasiness in the minds of the person's Relatives
& his dearest and nearest connections. Indeed but that I have
known its inutility, that I should be ridiculously sinning against
my own law while I was propounding, and that those who are
most fond of advising are the least able to bear advice from others   ƒ99^v
(as the passion ~~for power~~ to command makes men disobedient),
I should often have been on the point of advising you against the
two fold rage of Advising, and of discussing characters, both the
one & the other of which infallibly generates Presumption, and
Blindness to our own Faults. Nay—more particularly where from
whatever cause there exists a slowness to understand or an aptitude
to mishear & consequently misunderstand what has been said—it
too often renders an otherwise truly ~~honest~~ good man a Mischief-
maker to an Extent, of which he is little aware. Our Friend's Reputation should be a Religion to us: & when it is lightly sacrificed to
what Self-adulation calls a Love of telling the Truth—in reality,
a Lust of talking (something seasoned with the Cayenne & Capsi-
cum of Personality) depend upon it, something in the Heart is
warped, or warping: more or less according to the greater or lesser
power of the counteracting Causes. I confess to you, that being
exceedingly low & heart-fallen, I should have almost sunk under
the Operation of Reproof and Admonition (—the whole too in
my own conviction grounded on utter mistake—) at the moment
I was quitting, perhaps for ever! my dear Country, and all that
makes it so dear—But the high Esteem, I cherish toward you, and
my Sense of your Integrity, and the Reality and Worth of your
Attachment and Concern, blows upon me refreshingly, as the Sea
Breeze ~~and~~ on the tropic Islander.—Shew me any one made bet-

ter by [?blunt/blank] Advice, and I may abate of my Dislike to
it. But I have experienced the good effects of the contrary in
Wordsworth's conduct to me; & in Poole & others have witnessed
enough of *its* ill-effects to be convinced that it does little else but
harm both to the Adviser & Advisee.—

2033 21.433   Ad hoc, dictu parva, sed magni eadem in re
gerendâ momenti res, congruens clamor a Romanis, eoque major
et terribilior; dissonæ illis, ut gentium multarum discrepantibus
linguis, voces.—Livii Lib. xxx. §§34.

f9ᵛ   2034 15.13   Muleteer with black velvet cap/. Boys with lean
asses paniered collecting the dirt, orange peels &c—12 Porters, 6
a breast—stop & rest, & ⟨the first six⟩ turning, face each other.—
Spaniards, Jews, Moors—a sweet English Lady/how straggled
that angel Face hither?

f10   2035 15.14   Soother of absence./O that I had the Language
of Music/the power of infinitely varying the expression, & individualizing it even as it is/—My heart plays an incessant music/
for which I need an outward Interpreter/—words halt over & over
again!—and each time—I feel differently, tho' children of one
family.

2036 15.15   What change of place, Country, climate, company, situation, health of Shrubs, Flowers, Trees/—moving Sea-
sons/& ever is that one Feeling at my Heart/felt like a faint
Pain, a spot which it seems I could lay my finger on/—I talk loud
or eager, or I read or meditate the abstrusest Researches, or I
laugh, jest, tell tales of mirth/& ever as it were, within & behind
I think, & image you/and while I am talking of Government or
War or Chemistry, there comes ever into my bodily eye some
Tree, beneath which we have rested, some Rock where we have
f10ᵛ   walked together or on the perilous road edging, *high above* the
Crummock Lake/where we sate beneath the rock, & those dear
Lips pressed my forehead/—or that Scale Force in its pride, as
we saw it—when they laughed at us for two lovers./

2037 15.16

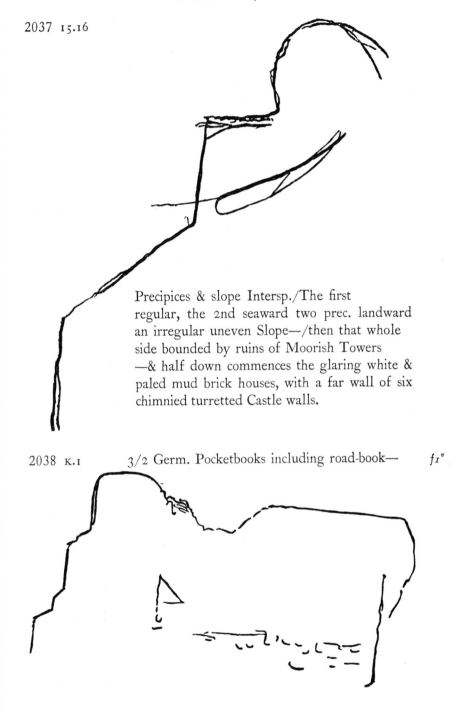

Precipices & slope Intersp./The first
regular, the 2nd seaward two prec. landward
an irregular uneven Slope—/then that whole
side bounded by ruins of Moorish Towers
—& half down commences the glaring white &
paled mud brick houses, with a far wall of six
chimnied turretted Castle walls.

2038 K.I   3/2 Germ. Pocketbooks including road-book—   ƒ1ᵛ

$f21^{v}$ 2039 K.51

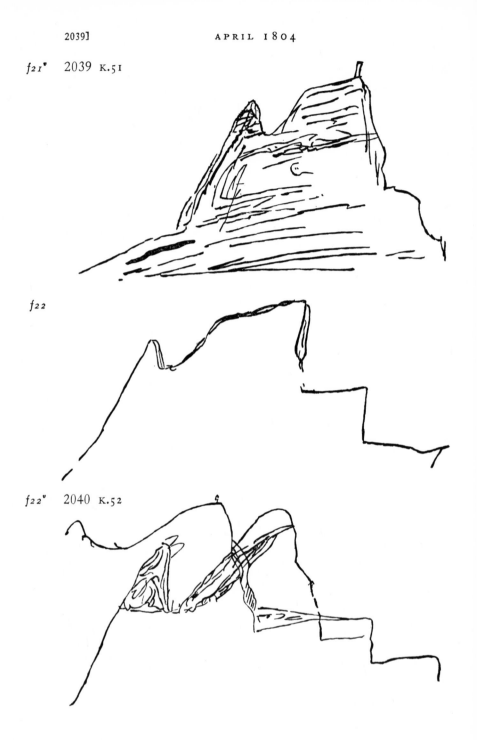

$f22$

$f22^{v}$ 2040 K.52

2041 k.53

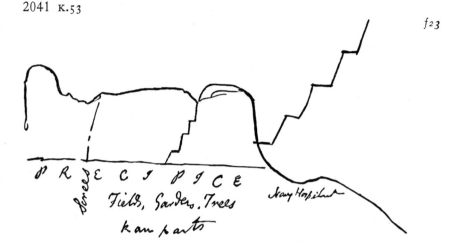

2042 k.2   That Brandy + water, especially + Ginger-sweet   ƒ1
poisons my Stomach. Mem. To take no more.—

2043 15.17   Facts—& I had it from a man on the Spot, who   ƒ11
saw it—&c and never have I been with 3, 4, or 5 *Men of the Spot*
who did not quarrel & dispute & contradict—

2044 15.18   Thursday, April 19th, arrived & anchored at Gibraltar, but did not get our Prattic till the next morning—next
morning, on shore, ⟨1⟩ Multier o the face & monkey teeth! with
stick thro' the strings of the waistband, traversing the Thighs behind— 2. Goat with his forefeet in the paniers of a Horse with
Grass in them stealing the Grass. 3. Porters, &c 4. Jews with ~~with~~
university Bumbazine Dresses, & fine family face. 5. Spaniards, dirty
dogs, with their cloaks, falling down very elegantly, & in groups
often *compose* excellently. 6. Greek Women, pretty Dowdies!
with ear rings ~~like~~ I have seen Chain rings on a landing place for
mooring Boats scarcely if at all larger— 7. English Officers &
Ladies, & Soldiers of all Regiments & Runaway Sailors. Friday
April 20th. I passed thro' the Town, my poor Nose paying dear   ƒ11[v]
for the amusement of my Eyes; walked by the Sea rampart, &
then wound up the Hill to Europa Point, pleased to see the

Geranium with pink flowers climbing down the walls, the top of which it completely cloathed & concealed, & here & there huge Plants of prickly ~~Aloes~~ Pear.—Higher yet I greeted my old favorite, the Broom, in full flower, of the size of a small Tree. I saw a young Ass, not much larger than a Mastiff, tethered under one of them. Rocks of dense grey marble, and many green plants, & many flowering weeds growing among and out of them, some of them old acquaintances, & new only from the time of their Flowering, others which I wished had had English Names. I walked

f12 calmly, slowly, happily, and regretted that I had delivered 2 Letters of Recommendation, & still more that I had promised my Captain and engaged with the Host to return to Dinner/My brain was active, my heart very full of Love, ~~and~~ tender Recollections, and if possible, yet more tender Hopes and Dreams of the Future. Reluctantly I returned to a noisy Dinner of 17 Sea Captains, indifferent Food, & burning Wines. Thence I called on Mr. Frome, a man of pleasant Countenance; engaged to dine with him the next day at 4°clock, and going back to the Inn forced home my now very tipsy Capt—whom I left still drinking in his own Cabin with 3 other Masters of Merchant Vessels, & went to bed, my

f12ᵛ whole Day resembling [?a Lover] divided up the middle, a scaly obscene Monster-fish all beside—

2045 15.19   Saturday, Ap. 21ˢᵗ went again on Shore; walked up to the furthermost Signal House, the Summit of that 3rd & last Segment of the Mountain Ridge, which looks over the blue Sea-lake to Africa—The Mountains around me did not any where arrange themselves strikingly, and few of their shapes were striking —one great pyramidal Summit far above the rest on the Coast of Spain, & an uncouth form, an ⟨old⟩ Giant's Head & Shoulders, looking in upon us from Africa far inland were the most impressive; but the Sea was so blue, calm, & sunny, so majestic a Lake

f13 where it is enshored by Mountains, & where it is not, having its indefiniteness the more felt from those huge Mountain Boundaries, which yet by their greatness prepared the mind for the sublimity of unbounded Ocean/altogether it reposed in the brightness & quietness of the noon, majestic, for it was great with an

inseparable character of Unity; and this the more touching to me
who had looked from far loftier mountains over ⟨a⟩ far far more
manifold Landscape, the fields & habitations of Englishmen, children of one family, one religion, & that my own, the same language, & manners, & every Hill & every River some sweet name
familiar to my ears, or if first heard remembered as soon as heard/
but here ~~below~~ on one side of me Spaniards, a degraded Race that   *f13ᵛ*
dishonour Christianity; on the other Moors of many Nations,
wretches that dishonor human Nature—if anyone were near now
& could tell me, that mountain yonder is called so & so, & at its
foot runs such & such a River, O with how blank an ear should
I listen to sounds, which probably my Tongue could not repeat, &
which I should be sure to forget, & take no pleasure in remember-
ing; & the rock itself, on which I stand, nearly the same in length
as our Carrock, but not so high, nor one tenth part as wide, what
a complex Thing!—At its feet ~~huge~~ mighty ramparts establishing
themselves in the Sea with their huge artillery—hollow Trunks
of Iron where Death and Thunder sleep; the gardens in deep   *f14*
Motes between lofty & massive walls;—a Town of All Nations &
all languages/close below me on my left fields & gardens & neat
small Mansions, Poplars & Cypresses & willowleaved Aspens, with
fences of the prickly aloe, strange Plant that does not seem to be
alive, but to have been a Thing fantastically carved in wood &
coloured, some Hieroglyph or temple Ornament of undiscovered
meaning—/on my right & immediately with and around me—
white Stone above stone, an irregular heap of Marble Rocks, with
flowers growing out of their Holes & Fissures, & Palmetoes every
where, uncouth thick Stem & leaves of 20 rushes growing together
in one fan, joining all a 4ᵗʰ from the bottom, & each having a
minor segment, a hand with long tapering fingers you cannot but   *f14ᵛ*
think of—& a 100 of these hands on each plant/—beyond these an
old Moorish Tower, & then Galleries & Halls cut out by human
Labor out of this dense hard, with enormous Cannon the apertures
for which no eye could distinguish from the Sea or the Sands below
them from the nesting Holes of Sea Fowl/—On the North side
aside these one absolutely perpendicular precipice the absolute
height of the Rock at its highest, a perp. precipice of 1450 feet/the

whole Eastern side an unmanageable Mass, of stones & weeds—
save in one place a perpend. Precipice of Stone slants suddenly off
ƒ15   in a swelling Slope of Sand, like the Screes of Wastwater—on the
other side of this rock 5000 men in arms, & not less than 10000
other inhabitants—on this sixty or 70 Apes!—What a multitude &
⟨almost⟩ discordant complexity of associations—the Pillars of Hercules, Calpe, Abbila, the Realms of Massinissa, Jugurtha, Syphax—
Spain, Gibraltar, the Dey of Algiers, dusky Moor & black African/
and O! how quiet it is to the Eye, & to the Heart when it will
entrance itself in the present vision, & know nothing, feel nothing,
but the Abiding Things of Nature, great, calm, majestic, and one.
From the Road I climbed up among the Rocks, crushing the
Tansy the strong smell of which the open air reconciled to me, &
reached the striding edge where as I sate I fell into the above musing.

ƒ15ᵛ   I descended with a good deal of Toil, regained the road, & by
mere accident/for I had passed it twice unnoticed/I blundered in
upon St. Michael's Cave. It is the very model of that which I had
described in my Tragedy/the most perfect I ever beheld.—First
descent forty striding Steps; about the 30th Step to your Left a
massy Pillar, a Stalactite 20 feet in Girth/a little beyond three
Stalactites depending, two inosculated, one distant an intercolum-
nation of its own size, each two feet perhaps in girth & hanging
down 5 or 6/ in the first Area there are at least 20 Pillars of the
Stalactite on the ground, some half way to the lofty roof, some
ƒ16   not 4 feet above the ground/but the substance & surface of the
Rock on my right!! the long grooves, & ribs—the crown upon
crown, a tower of crowns, the models of Trees in stone, here a
row of tall slender Pine Trees, or whatever else are thin & tall,
branching only at the top, with branching Stems/—here a full low
bushy-branched Oak/all forms of ornament, with nitches for
Images not there/excepting that there were no Saints or Angels,
it was perfect Gothic Extravaganza/close by this the first Side
Chamber, with a chasm & well & window precisely as I have described that in Osorio/but strait in are other chambers within
chambers, the bottom of which no one yet has reached, tho' many
have descended 300 & 400 feet, till the Smoke of their Torches

became intolerable—O if we do not sail till Thursday, surely, *f16ᵛ*
surely, I will try to go some way down it./—I returned having
spent the day *well*, & dined comfortably & drank temperately at
Frome's—& so on Shipboard.—But Sunday, April 22ⁿᵈ I stayed
aboard to write Letters: I was greatly intent on what I was reading in the Cabbin, but felt myself ill, a sense of suffocation & convulsive Snatches in my Stomach & Limbs/Mrs Ireland noticed
my laborious Breathing, & I looked up, & lo! it was raining hard/
& all the adjacent Country when I got on Deck, black & cloudy.—
The Rain, & Clouds & Easterly Wind went off; & so did my Illness, & I eat a tolerable dinner/but the E. returned all Night, I
passed a wretched Night—& tho' I had tasted no morsel since an *f17*
early dinner I could eat no Breakfast, & my Tongue was furred
white, my pulse quick & low, & my nostrils haunted with fever
smells—I went however on shore, called on Major Adye, having
heard that he had called for me &c, found him a kind pleasant
man, a quondam Pupil of my Brother George's/he sent a Corporal
with me, & I visited all the Batteries, the St. George's & Corn-
wallis's Hill &c/. But will these be as useful as they are wonderful?
—1. The Noise so deafening in these galleries on the discharge of
Guns, that the Soldiers' Ears have bled. 2. The Shower of Stones.
3. The Splinters &c—

Returned not very well but somewhat better/dined with the
Major/& if he be right, & we stay till Thursday instead of setting
sail tomorrow, we are to have a long Stroll together tomorrow,
and now for bed!—For it is Midnight, Monday, April 23ʳᵈ 1804. *f17ᵛ*
—And what will happen, & whether I shall awake, ⟨& be⟩ alive to
record what will happen, on Tuesday, April 24ᵗʰ, who on earth
can tell? Note the superstitious Trick of baffling & or appeasing
possible Evil by a feeling & expression of forced Fear, and encouraged Boding.

2046 15.20   Tuesday, April 24ᵗʰ, 1804.
⌈Darling⌉ could I tell in words or even embody in Ideas all that
has passed in my Heart since I wrote that last word. But so it is
ever/My poor Heart (& truly this seems to be something more
than a phrase or metaphor with me, so local is the feeling, so ap-

f18 parently co-present in the same [. . .] identical place with the gnawing, & palpitation—strange sense of Stopping) my Heart wishes & yearns, & stirs & bustles about you/& then stagnates upon you, ~~the~~ wishless from excess of wishing!—

f3ᵛ 2047 15.6   Monday Midnight—23 〈Ap.〉—or nearer—Tuesday Morning April 24/The Cloud *formed* by the Eastern Side of the Rock of Gibraltar & sending off detachments from it which float under the Moon over to the Spanish Mountains/one beautiful Dolphin-shaped Cloud is now floating, & what I have never seen in England, I here see, a Halo with bright stars just within, & a perfectly bright serene full moon in the center/. The planets larger/ the moon not/why?—

f18 2048 15.21   Edridge & his Warts cured by rubbing them with the hand of his Sister's dead Infant/knew a man who cured one on his Eye by rubbing it with the dead Hand of his Brother's— Comments on Ancient Mariner/—Our Captⁿ "Damn me! I have no superstition, I had as soon sail on Friday as on Saturday; but this I must say, that Sunday is really a lucky day to sail on/indeed to begin any sort of business upon/"

2049 15.22   Poem/dim not feeble is the waning 〈moon〉/the last curse of the waning moon/. The bright moon that follow'd suspended it, that when the moon waned again the Curse began

f18ᵛ to work, & was finished on the last day of the moon.

2050 15.23   Tuesday, April 24ᵗʰ, Noon/Had a long & instructive walk with Major Adye, round Europa Point, up the Mediterranean Stairs/to the Cavern again; & this I hoped to visit Wednesday—more & struck with it/the obelisks, the pillars, the rude statues of strange animals, episcopal Thrones, conical church yard monuments, reflected Lights in the interior that you must swear were windows/in short, such a very great populousness of forms so very various, yet combined by the sameness of the material, & yet such an unusual Spaciousness & grandeur when you look back

down upon the Arch & up the ascent to the dazzling Portal, & the
same with obscurity & indefiniteness when you look from the Portal.—From thence down to the Brewery &c/Converse of the *f19*
Capability of Gibraltar/Coup de main from the Spanish Coast

—Strength of Europa Point in its treble ⌇ and in that narrow
defile of rocks, with the strange *cellars* layed open on the left,
Europa Point to your Back.—D. of Kent—his Mishap/a good
Serjeant Major—Importance of Gibraltar decisive in my opinion
if we are to have a Mediterranean Commerce.—Struggle in the
minds of the Inhabitants between their Dislike of English Manners & their Dread of French Government/I find it a common
opinion that if the Peace had continued the French would have
monopolized the Commerce of the Levant, merely thro' the
partiality of the Inhabitants—is this possible?—

2051 15.24   Wednesday, April 25th, morning, ½ past X, we
were under weigh, the Vessel began its old trick of Rocking—I
was ill after dinner which I did not retain/the Mephitis of the *f19ᵛ*
Bilge burst forth, like a Fury/horrid Stench that turned the gold
red, & silver black, bemudded whatever part of the paint had been
before soiled, & covered the rest of it with ⟨quick-⟩silvery grease
drops. Hepatic Gas? Whence comes the Sulphur?—I dozed off the
Day & the Night, & Thursday Morning, about 10, found the
snowy mountains of Granada to the Larboard/
    A Vessell manned by Madmen, the Captain on Shore, fell foul
of 3 Vessels in getting under weigh, & having gotten under weigh
was so near running her forecastle on our beam, which (she was
twice our size) would have sunk us instantly, that when she
turned so as to pass close aside us, I could have knocked a shuttle
cock into her forecastle/& myself, the Capt. & the Mate all confessed, that our knees trembled under us. What a Death for an *f20*
old hardy skilful Mariner, to be run down while at anchor by a
set of Lubbers!
    We must have perished, if our Captain had not given them
directions.

2052 15.25　　　Friday, April 27th/At one time a dead calm ⟨the Ships how *thin!* Profiles/!—⟩ & for many hours nearly so—the Reflection of the Sun thro' the Sails & Ropes like a Vase or a circular Plume of flames in tortuous flakes of bright sulphur-blue; cherubic swords of Fire—now blowing all one way, now dividing, now

blossoming in a complete ⟨V⟩ crater-vase, ⟨a lily flower!⟩—Rudder tied (Ropes rotted, yet still the Tiller moved not/)—the ashes thrown over the Vessel's side remaining for Hours.

f20ᵛ　　Hints taken from real Facts by exaggeration—My Shadow the Head in the center of the crater which now forms a Glory about my Head; but my Shadow—⟨Shadow of me,⟩ from the waist upwards, of course, squares and masses itself into a mountain Shape,

& when I stretch out my arm, it is like a dim flake of blue cloud, a banner or streamer from the mountain-Cloud or cloudlike Mountain./We saw a bright golden Spot on the waters, which our Captn hailed for a Turtle; & tho' he had before talked to me prolixly of the utter worthlessness of the Turtles of these Seas of these Hawk's Bill Turtles, yet with all the whole Sailor's whole Bustle & Bellow, & Life & Death Impatience,^{xx} rapid, loud, eager, passionate Command, vehement reiteration, abrupt Transition,
f21　　every the lightest order conveyed in the form of Reproach & Abuse, with Oaths intermixed, like the Stars that start up, sparkle, dart flames & die away in the Snow of Foam by the Vessel's side, or flame-coloured Expletives, i.e. in image or idea, for they are Super-~im~completives in force—a large Beef Bone clean even to Polish of all Flesh without, but nathless full of marrow within/ as if his Mate^{xx} & some other prime Seaman with him had fallen overboard, & were screaming for Help, orders & himself maximafies as, the hoisting out of the Boat, and the Swede paddling

quietly on at length, the Captⁿ. leaning over the Fore /\ of the Boat with arms extended, some minutes & many yards before he came within reach it, catches the sleeper by the Tail, & holding him up in Triumph comes back with him. It was a small one & the Bill

exactly like that of a Parrot, but larger than that of the largest
Eagles; thick neck and with its two forepaws beats its breast, or   *f21ᵛ*
rather breast-plate, even as with two hands—& sighs so deeply!—
at the other end of its breast-plate its Tail, not distinguishable from
the fat rump of a plucked & picked Duck/—neither the Shell nor
the Flesh worth much.—The sluggishness of its motion on Deck,
or ~~the~~ its *movedness*, not motion, in sleep, on the almost Calm,
contrasted with the liveliness of its rapid Dip down on the instant
of its awaking. The Captn, Swede & I then went out for about a
mile or two in a circuit, among all the Calms; but without success
Cork + Orange + Bird on the Stick. Returned to Dinner, & while
at Dinner a Turtle alarm given, & Mr. Edridge went out, &
caught a much larger one.—Enormous Power of the animal's jaw.
—Plenty of Bonitos leaping up/likewise Porpoises, with a noise of
rushing, like that of a Vessel dashing on by steam or other power   *f22*
within itself, thro' the Calm, & making the Billows ⟨& the Breeze,
which⟩ it did not find/Ancient Mariner/—

In the afternoon I could not resist the Temptation of lying
down on my bed, my back ached so with sculling the water out of
the Boat in the hot Noon, nor being there of falling to sleep—a
bad bad practice, & which I feel to be so 9 times out of 10./During
my Sleep a Breeze started up; but "right wrong"—absolute East.
I watched the Sunset, & the Star rise/& Jupiter, first Star, like the
sonorous Savanna Crane of Bartram/—& at ½ past 9 the moon rise
/o the waning moon, there is certainly something in its look, a
melancholy something (that deserves to be explained). I walked
up & down in many and some sweet Thoughts, till Midnight/   *f22ᵛ*
having drank a small Cup of Rum Grog with the Captain which
instantly made me sick. Surely, I shall not be so contemptibly
weak as ever to do this again!—& went to bed.

ˣˣ writing in this manner may be compared to running downhill
after a man/if you run fast enough to overtake him, ten to one but
you overshoot/.

2053 15.26   Mem. A sense of the Height of high Mountains
independent of present comparison, a quadrant-like Measurement
of Sky-Altitude but seems no way connected with the feeling

sublimity, any more than a bright star gains in Sublimity by being 5 rather than 3 degrees above the Horizon.—This while looking on the Mountains of Granada.

2054 15.27   The Birds that never see land but live & sleep *f23* upon the [?waves]. Where do they breed? If on Shore or on some little Rock-island, that would make a beautiful illustration &c in my Soother of Absence.

2055 15.28   My Dreams *now* always connected in some way or other with Isulia, all their forms in a state of fusion with some Feeling or other, that is the distorted Reflection of my Day-Feelings respecting her/but the more distressful my Sleep, & alas! how seldom is it otherwise, the more distant, & Xst's Hospitalized the forms & incidents—& in one or two sweet Sleeps the Feeling has grown distinct & true, & at length has created its appropriate form, the very Isulia/or as I well described it in those Lines, "All Look" &c.

Jealousies the *Chills* of Fever.

2056 15.29   Saturday Morning, April 28th/All yesterday I could not beat off the feeling; no nor even the Idea of its being *f23ᵛ* Sunday—I forgot that it was not so half a dozen times, spite of as many Rectifications of my Error/—& this morning, X°clock, seems to me quite a Monday Morning after a July Sunday.— Breeze still point blank against us!—

2057 15.30   Afternoon could not but go to Bed/incessant Rocking, & this from Sea that crossed us, worse far worse than before—I passed a wretched time/retained not a morsel of my Saturday Dinner, & took no food whatsoever till Sunday afternoon when I swallowed & with some difficulty retained a little Rice. ⟨The Bilge-fury broke loose again⟩—all Saturday & all Sunday, April 29th, 1804, Rocked into unwholesome & painful Dozings; passed a better night on Sunday—and on Monday Morning, April 30th, find the wind still against us as before; but the rocking less *f24* violent. All Sunday Night it rained & lightened incessantly. N.B. Is it excess of Sympathy in *me* beyond others? or is it from a cause common to all men, namely, that we abstract the pleasant or the painful Sensations of others & so contemplate & sympathize with them as pure pain, or pure pleasure?—However this be, 20 times since my Departure from Portsmouth, I have felt as if it were impossible that I could sustain the *presence* of Sara, or Mary & Dorothy, on board a vessel for Malta—⟨suffering only what I suffer—⟩ much less endure the imagination of their being there & coming to *me*—yet all along feel that I could undergo it many times for them & for less ~~matter~~ ends/& that with such an end it would be greatly lightened. To [. . . . .]

Mem. To write to the Recluse that he may insert something *f24ᵛ* concerning *Ego*/its metaphysical Sublimity—& intimate Synthesis with the principle of Co-adunation—without *it* every where all things were a waste—nothing, &c—

2058 15.31   Being under the *Necessity* of being absent from you, Beloved! I could not will not to have the *Pain* of Absence. If it were in my power to have absence from you felt by me, as a Pleasure, would I, could I? O No!—And utterly do I protest against the absolute ~~Twin~~ Duumvirate, & twin Despotism of Pain & Pleasure! Great Springs of human conduct they are, main Springs perhaps; but not the sole Springs And I must hesitate with a perhaps whether unblamed to call them Main Springs, of which I doubt whether they are not derivative & secondary rather than primary movements. The Will = the Ego is the prime mover *f25* —& what is Reason?—And Love too—No! That too is no Creature of Pain & Pleasure—say rather the Parent *nursed* & sustained by its Children.

2059 15.2   abomination! The full moon came thundering *f1* down from Heaven, like a Cannon Ball; & seeing that nothing could be done went quietly back again! Dreamt these words before day light, May Morning, 1804. Put 'em into a Mrs. Jordan's mouth, ridiculing some pompous moral or political Declaimer.—

2060 15.32   Tuesday Morning, May Day, 1804!! In the *f25* Mediterranean plying wearily to the Windward off Carthagena— a wet foggy oppressive Weather, with the wind impotent or against

us!—And the Captn begins to look round for the Jonas in the
Fleet. Mem. One advantage of sailing in a *Convoy*. On a single
Vessel the Jonas must have been sought out amongst ourselves.
Hamburgh packet/did not like his giving up his Bed but thought
now that he was only a Fool/not the Devil. But he has muster
f25° enough. For ~~Royals & top gallant sails~~ Top Sails and top gallant
Sails, & Royals/—The Devil has help'd him to a Commodore's
Share/Aye! aye! the Devil knows his Relations &c &c/—Here
Vexation, which in a Sailor's mind is always linked on to Reproach
and Anger, makes the Superstitious seek out an Object of his
Superstition, that can feel his anger—Else the Star, that dogged
the Crescent or my "Cursed by the last Look of the waning moon,"
were the better—What an extensive subject would not superstition
form taken in its philos. and most comprehen. sense for that mood
of Thought & Feeling which arises out of the having placed our
summum bonum (what we think so, I mean) in an absolute Dependence on Powers & Events, over which we have no Controll.
While the Essayist treated of Sailors, Savages, Fishermen, rustic
Lovers, Farmers, Gamesters & the poor Gamblers at Lottery In-
f26 surances/in short, with all those who have no established Church,
or at least, a known Meeting-house of Superstition who Cloath it
in acknowleged & conventional Formulaes & Practices, attached
to the Traditional Part of Revealed Religion or dimly borrowed
of an old Idolatry, all would go on, the Essayist being a man of
right feeling, fleetly and fairly—in a current of interesting narration. The difficulty & the power of the work would begin with
the Superstition of those, who have no religion or only what is
called an entirely rational one, & who from infancy have been
taught to derive a self-importance from Contempt of & ⟨supposed⟩
Insight into all the common forms & conventional Outlets of
Superstition; & yet *are* superstitious, i.e. according to the definition. To trace out & detect its subtle Incarnations & Epiphanies &
to prove the sameness of the Genus. Hic Labor hic Opus est.

f26°   2061 15.33   Ships, & their Picturesqueness—/Have I noticed
the approximation to Round and Rondure, in the Square & triangular Forms—& that pleasure which depends on the subtle Sense

of Est quod non est?—Balance: Synthesis of Antithesis?—and secondly (& if I have not directly or by Implication anticipated it, of first-rate importance to me), that which in my last night's Dose I called the Polyolbiosis of each appearance from the recollections of so many others subtly combining with it/Sails bellying with Sails under reef—~~felt in modify appear~~ the Ideas of full Sail modifying the impression of the naked Masts, not on the eye but on the Mind, &c &c—. How much of the pleasure derived from the countenance of an old friend or woman long beloved—at least, continually gazed at, may we trace it to this in Dreams—so very *ʃ27* strangely do they instantly lead to Sara as the first waking Thought/no recollection giving a hint of the means, except only that in some incomprehensible manner the whole Dream seems to have been—about her? nay—perhaps, all wild—no form, no ~~image~~ place, no incident, any way connected with her!—What then? Shall I dare say, the whole Dream seems to have been *Her—She.*

Remember my repeated Memoranda—Dorothy, myself, &c in my Red Cottle Book. Does not this establish the existence of *a Feeling* of a Person quite distinct at all times, & at certain times *perfectly separable* from, the Image of the Person? And that this Feeling forms a most important Link of Associations—& may be combined with the whole Story of a long Dream just as well as with one particular Form no way resembling the true Image? I *ʃ27ᵛ* seem to see, tho' darkly, that the Inferences hence are many & important/Madness—Bulls—Self—God—Past Life + Present; or Conscience, &c—

2062 15.34   In my Soother of Absence to note my utter want of Sympathy with all the ordinary Love-poems, complaining of the Cruelty of my Mistress, of her attachment to another &c—in short, all that supposes that I could love with no knowlege of being loved in return—or even with the knowlege of the contrary.—In short, I shall have abundant matter for contemplation on the Subject in my Perusal of the Italian Love-poems.

2063 15.35   Tuesday Afternoon, one "clock, May Day—We are very nearly on the spot, where on Friday last about this same

ƒ28 Hour we caught the Turtles—And what are 5 days' toiling to
Windward just not to lose ground, to almost 5 *years!* Alas! alas!
what have I been doing on the Great Voyage of Life since my
Return from Germany but fretting upon the front of the Wind—
well for me if I have indeed kept my ground even!

2064 15.36   Wednesday, May 2nd/1804. To this hour six
° 'clock, afternoon, desperately sick, ill, abed, one deep dose after
another. Among other things beware of Rhubarb in the smallest
Quantities—it produces bilious sickness often & is always a pre-
carious medicine with me. Better in case of Costiveness to abstain/.
—This forenoon we were off Cape Pallas so that we have been
making about 8 or 10 miles a day, but still the Horizon is flannel-
petticoated all the way round—a cloud of the same height nearly
all round with a gausy white over it/—N.B. A great number of
small Birds about the Ship & Ship's rigging, all day to-day & all
ƒ28ᵛ   yesterday! Poet. interesting Thought of May 2nd & Thursday before May Night/Alas! how dear do these Thoughts cost you,
Coleridge?—

An Afterpiece called or at least the Scene layed at GIBRALTAR—
with Scenery, Cavern, &c, would be sure to answer—. 2. The present Royal Family, their character and influence on England, Europe, the World, at present—/one of the Noctes Politicæ, by a
Traveller, with his Heart at Home:— 3. D°/Faction, (Party lost
war: for *them* Principles were operant) the mean Elements of a
Faction, & how it yet acts on & finally transforms, the character
of the Leaders. *Remember* Courtney & Blair.— 4. Bonapart,
France, Sicily, Russia, &c &c &c—*one* Hecatomb of Gratitude to
Stuart.—

5. A Tragedy; scene Malta: & to try my Voyage in Verse—
this adesso. 6. Ship—all the ⟨3⟩ Topsails pulled down, & two or
three Reefs taken in/a whistle—and the men are on all the Ladders; & now they are up, & the yards are all manned, 10 or 12 on
each side of each yard—20 on the Main top sail/another whistle
—& in one minute they all three drop down, with a loud whistle
ƒ29   of their own thro' the Ropes & Rigging (o how far louder, & far
sweeter & altogether another whistle than that of the Boatswain's

which yet is not unpleasant) & in two minutes from the Boat's
swain's second Whistle the Reefs are taken in, the Sails a
top their masts again, and all the men now swarming the Ladders/
now *gone!*—This I saw Wednesday Evening; the Commodore
Frigate being almost within Stone throw of us.—There had been
Dancing & Music for an half hour on board the Frigate just before
—indeed broken by it. Music & Dancing & the yellow bellied Birds
on the Rigging; & that dreary Fog Bank all the *Semblance* of
Land!—I saw it was done in two minutes/140 pulses, in poetry,
which I might add, I counted partly to amuse Impatience, partly
to have some notion of the Time more exact than a Guess—twice
70.

7. *Fame* from Homer & Shakespere to K and X Y who *likewise*
answered the above Rebus in the Ladies' Diary—⟨Arithmetical⟩
Knowlege from the great Inventor of the Infinitesimal Calculus   *f29ᵛ*
to my poor old Grandam whose whole arithmetic consists & subsists in counting & muttering to herself the number of the Stitches
in her Knitting.

8. Stars—their natural Sublimity/whether indeed one or only a
Lanthorn on the mast.—And so of all the other objects of nature/
their sublimity to the man of nature, utterly ignorant of scientific
Ontology.—Seen by all at once: and drawing all at once to see—
&c—

9. A really important Hint suggested itself to me, as I was falling into my first Sleep—the effect of the posture of the Body, *open
mouth* for instance, on first Dreams—& perhaps on all. White
Teeth in behind a ~~dim~~ open mouth of a dim face—/My Mind is
not vigorous enough to pursue it—but I see, that it leads to a developement of the effects of continued Indistinctness of *Impressions* on the Imagination according to laws of Likeness & what ever
that may solve itself into.

2065 K.4   The apparent *divisibility* of *Life* in the Turtle &c/   *f1*
metaphysically what does it import?—⟨Mary Lamb's Friendship⟩

2066 K.5   Extremes meet. The Captains of a fastest-sailing
Vessel & the obstinately Laggardmost of a Convoy, equally vexed,
and restless.—

f_1^v 2067 K.6   A ⟜⟜⟜ polished Steel on the side of the
Wave.
Ebbolimento; a light Ebullition.
È meglio essere amici da lontano che nemici d'appresso.
1. Dark water-color, as that of Lakes in drizzly dark weather, but
rippling into the deepest indigo blue, & bright Foam, with the
Brightest, most delicate Sky-Blue—/
and how different from any of these the common far blue of the
Sea!—The blue Shades of Blue & Green, and the olive & yellow,
greens—Then the two bright Greens, the dark green of cut green
Glass, the other of a more Grassy Green—

2068 K.7   Shrouds = the higher Rigging—as the Futtock
Shrouds under the Main Top.

f_2 2069 K.8   Storm rolls over the Ship, she jerks her self with
a great plunge into the water windward/Lee-lurch—(taking a
Lurch)—when she does the same running from the wind, "brings
the wind on the other side, & lays the Sails all dead to the mast."
"Brace about the Head sails the other way, & keep the main top
sail shivering when she gathers way, and bring the wind aft again,
raise the fore-tack, & square the Head Sails, trim the Sails as they
were before & bring her to her course again."

f_3o   2070 15.37   Thursday, May 3rd—Wind as before, fag my Italian & get up I will and register an old observation or two from the
Black Book/
1. To enquire concerning Bilge Water of Davy—its hideous
Stench, its dropping quicksilver Drops on the clean paint, its red-
brown dirt color on the soiled part, its Red'ning of Gold, black'n-
ing of Silver not without a tinge of red-brown, and its turning the
red paint of the letters on the Sacks into lead or dove-colour./—
2. Image of moonlight at Gibraltar/The path from the Shore till
within a good Stone throw of the Vessel thickly swarming with
insect life, *all* busy-swarming in the path, their swarming makes—
but within the Shadow of the Ship it was—scattered at distances—
scattered O s, rapidly uncoiling into serpent spirals—O how slow a
word is rapidly to express the Life & time-mocking Motion of

that Change, always O s before, always Spirals, coiling, uncoiling, *being*.—But this afternoon I observed the Leopard ⊂⊃, and its *f30ᵛ* elongations and contractions, on the side of the Waves, in color & smooth brightness exactly ⊂⊃ into ⊂⊃ of polished Steel.—

During this heavy foggy flitting Eastern Wind the color of the Sea is the dark water-*dusk* of Lakes in drizzly overclouded weather/but rippling and breaking against the Sides of the Vessel into the very deepest brightest indigo Blue.—O what difference of Sea Colors!—From this now to the lightest delicate Starch Blue of Sunny Calms—& the common Blue of the Sea how different from either.—Then the Shades of Blue into Green—the olive Green, & lastly (in my present Recollection only) the two bright Greens, one as of cut Glass, the other Grass-green, tho' that is not so exact a Likeness as the cut Glass.—

N.B. Shrouds are the tight parts of the Rigging—What for in-

stance is the ╱ ╱ of the ≡ of the Ladder, that in Ship Ladders *f31* is the Shrouds. So too the Futtock Shrouds under the Main Top— This in memorial of my ignorance, who had identified them with the Sails.

A weather Roll, when the ship jerks herself with a great plunge into the water Windward. She takes a Lee-lurch, when she does the same away from the wind, brings the wind on the other side, & lays the Sails all dead to the Mast.—Thursday Night, Wind chopped about & about—once fairly to the *West*, for a minute or 2 —but now ½ past 9, the Captain comes down & promises a fair wind for Tomorrow.—We shall see.

2071 15.38   ~~Thurs~~Friday Morning, ½ past 8, May 4ᵗʰ, 1804. ~~Bravo Capt Findlay & Capt. ran Headlong when~~ the Squalls were flitting and fleering and the Vessel was tacking & veering.

Bravo, Captain Findlay *f31ᵛ*
Who foretold a fair Wind
Of a constant mind
For he knew which way the wind lay,—
Bravo! Captain Findlay!

A Health to Captain Findlay!
Bravo! Captain Findlay!
When we made but ill Speed with the Speedwell,
Neither Poet, nor Sheep could feed well
~~The Poet eat Muffin, the Sheep eat its Hay~~
And Poet & Pig! how [?grief] rotted Liver
And ⟨yet⟩ Malta, dear Malta as far off as ever
Bravo! Captain Findlay—
Foretold a fair wind
Of a constant mind,
For he knew which way the Wind lay.

————

Well/& we have got a wind the right way at last!—

2072 15.39   When young, come dancing in on the stage & O
then ~~we sing~~ we sing so pretty. The World for a Lass which we
exchange in age for that doleful Ditty, Alas for the World!—*for
a Song*, to be entitled—Transpositions! Wonders of Transpositions,

  ~~Where~~ By purpler Pimples ~~gem~~ gemm'd the Face one purple
ʃ32 Blotch/or Chin, Nose, Cheek, Brow one purple Blotch By purpler
Pimples gemm'd where two black shining Eyes forever shine and
shine/—And shine and shine, and as they shine for ever will shine
on, Till what with Brandy, what with Rum, The Liver's fairly
gone! Eyes that like watch *lights* shine, as if they were there not
for themselves to see with, but as a *sight* For others to avoid.

2073 15.40   Query as to the Posture of the Body we being
semi-demi-conscious of it in falling to sleep, does it not act sometimes by suggesting the postures of Objects, of inanimates so that
I could see them, of the animate partly so & partly so as they could
see me/& would look in on me:—On a subject so important no
Hint but deserves a Memorandum at least.

2074 15.41   I once talked of writing an Essay (& if I live, still
may) on the morals and manners of the makers of Dictionaries and
Grammars. In the "A new Method of Learning the Italian

Tongue &c by an Italian Master from the French of Messieurs de
Port Royal, p.159, in the Vocabulary under the title, or head, Ac-   *f32ᵛ*
cidenti e Infirmità, Accidents and Diseases, come these 4 together/
un buffetto, a fillip; un pugno, a Cuff; uno schiáffo, a box on the
ear; un cálcio, a kick—very comical. ~~But~~ I met with a run of a sad
accident to day!—What, my dear Sir!—Mʳ—— gave me first a
cuff, then pulled me by the nose, then gave me a box of the Ears &
lastly, kicked me.—!—

In the Imperfezzioni dell'Uomo, the Imperfections of man, the
last 8 or 9, un bazoso [*bavoso*], a slabber-chops, un ladro, a thief,
un guidone, a ~~thief~~ rascal, un boia, a hangman, un furfante, a
rogue, una ruffiana, a bawd, un mago, a magician, un stregóne, a
wizard, una strega, a witch, un cattivo, a wicked Fellow, un tristo,
a sad wretch./—

This to be mentioned first. I should *like* to dare look forward to
the Time, when Wordsworth & I with contributions from Lamb &
Southey—& from a few others   a few—should publish *a Specta-*
tor.—

2075 15.42   Lady B. bade me pray for her/that in my not   *f33*
merely versified Journal. T. for [?G/S]—whether we gain or lose
by that Dread of Prolixity which is the passion of highly polished
states of Society—from the diffusion of critical knowlege and of
the habit of criticism/from the multitude of Competitors—&c &c.
Still are those, who never did consider the Paradise Lost as a Task/
those who taking Spenser and reading him by small portions at a
time with his own "believing Mind" only wish & regret that lost
Half, in a more or less enviable State?—Does not this dread of
Prolixity in ourselves, & criticism of it in others, tend to make all
knowlege superficial as well as desultory—incompatible with the
pleasure derived from seeing things as they are, as far as the nature
of Language permits it to be exhibited.—Apply this to Wordsworth's Pedlar.—//

2076 15.43   English Constitution arising gradually & accord-   *f33ᵛ*
ing to no plan, out of the nature of things adapted itself to the
moral nature of Things, Struggles between the King una cum pop-

ulo, & the aristocracy between the People and the King &c &c/introduced checks and a spirit of suspicion suitable to the effects of Power on the human Character. The people had felt that external Conquests were made the mean & the pretext of domestic oppression/& that those whose names will *swell* with them (& whose situation leaves them no other *passion*) will see a national Interest that does not exist.—Hence *the Nation* does not impose upon us. In France all different & from this time it might have been foretold that it ended in Slavery.

2077 15.44   Saturday, ~~April~~ May 5ᵗʰ—after one day of Hope and Exultation lo! again a foul wind & hard rain. Yesterday after

f34 a hearty dinner I was seduced by curiosity & a sort of classical philanacreontic feeling, to drink a glass of wine from the Greek islands —and instantly my whole dinner was in the Sea/—and all the evening I continued writing till 12 "'clock, & the pressure on the chest with the motion from the Sea brought on at last the most painful ⟨& only⟩ genuine *sea*-sickness which I have had. Today I have kept to my bed, eat a small dinner slowly, & by silence & ⟨re⟩supine posture continued to keep it/nor am I worse or so bad as in such weather I should be on shore./But O! this weather! this weather!—Calms I had to expect—but heavy rains with heavy air —Small Birds of swallow flight skim about like [?slides/slivers]

f34ᵛ of darker shade above the ridges & sides of the waves. Marcus Antoninus Book 7—§54 the Sum & Essence of Quakerism/ *N.B.* Jeremy Collier's Translation!—L'Estrange out-heroded §67 of B.6 contains the sum of my Remark on the—not what he has done, but what is he?

2078 15.45   Sunday, May 6/From 3 "'clock a storm by the Captain's own emphatical declaration/the rough weather till then he laughed at me for calling a *little* stormy; would not allow it to be called even *rough*, but before 4 the Storm had carried away the foremost yard/it has increased & is increasing & the Captain does not like it.—I am perfectly calm tho' well for my body that there are the Doric Columns to my ~~Head~~ Bed!—I should be else broken, smashed, spilled 20 times an hour! fairly ejaculated, yet worse

than all this is the Bilge Water Fury—I am calm/& I trust with *f35*
all humility that I should remain so tho' all hope was over that I
should ever have it to tell how calm I had remained. Yet I can
scarcely imagine a less desirable mode of Death than to be drowned
at Sea in a Cabin, sea-sick, with that sick flatulence at the Stomach
which would make a sadder Sleep of every act of composure, and
resignation, & their natural bodily aids & accompaniments, the resting the Head & the closing of the Eyelids—& of these Sleeps, these
Horrors, these frightful Dreams of Despair when the sense of individual Existence is full & lively only ⟨for one⟩ to feel oneself
powerless, crushed *in* by every power—a stifled boding, one abject
miserable Wretch/yet hopeless, yet struggling, removed from all *f35ᵛ*
touch of Life, deprived of all notion of Death/strange mixture of
Fear and Despair—& that passio purissima, that mere Passiveness
with Pain (the essence of which is perhaps Passivity—& which our
word—mere Suffering—well comprizes—) in which the Devils are
the Antithesis of Deity, who is Actus Purissimus, and eternal Life,
as they are an ever-living Death./—and all this vanishes on the
casting off a puff of ill-tasted Gas from the Stomach/But O mercy!
what a Dream to *expect* Death with what a pillow-mate for a
Death-bed!

The Storm less violent about one o'clock. All the Crew but the *f36*
Captain had been sea-sick/but neither Mrs Ireland nor myself
were, which proves the wisdom of weak Passengers keeping *stiff* to
their Beds/—Doze & Doze & doze/One remarkably affecting
Dream in which I saw Sara, & the whole perfectly dramatic/how
comes it I so very rarely see those I love/I scarcely remember the
time when I *saw* Wordsworth or Dorothy or the Children & very
seldom Mrs. C. yet I often dream of them/—

2079 15.46   Monday Afternoon, May 7ᵗʰ—Swell heavy from
yesterday when the Storm dropped till this day, one o'clock.
[. . .] it ceased now—past 5 o'clock I have been very poorly &
sick. But the wind is veering [. . . . .] west wind.

The Chocolate which I had had made on Sunday afternoon I *f36ᵛ*
had heated up at 8 o'clock and past, that night/I have slept for 3
or four Hours and so sound that I was not awakened by the Tea's

being offered to me. The Chocolate stayed on my Stomach, & proved a Comfort/as it did.

2080 15.47   Tuesday Morning, May 8th. The wind this day about Noon, or one o'clock, turned to the first Course/. These last days in my frequent ⟨sudden⟩ awakings I have been much struck with the conversions of Forms ⟨& Lines⟩ into Human Faces, & Head Dresses, so as to startle, & that in a sort of contempt of Magnitude—a flower on the curtain expanded with the outlines of petals marked by brown Lines, & a polyandria Polygynia Tuft of yellow in the center with a bud beside turned into a very sweet Lady's Face & Head Dress, & arm extended & gently curved in a resting posture/This I could make into but one face, eyes, nose, & full face in the Port-hole, & this twice with open eyes of which I could not trace the external *occasionatives*.

f37

2081 15.48   Mr Hardy, Surgeon of the Maidstone.

2082 15.49   At one time awaking in the [. . .] pain & nervous agitation [. . .] flowers of the Curtain [. . . . .] became all at once [?several/yellow] faces, of various features and remained so for some seconds.

f37ᵛ   2083 15.50   Excellent story of Mr. Hastings' seaman concerning the Wager of Ingredients & utensils—he decided in favor of the utensils i.e. the Meat, Herbs, Pepper, & Salt the *Utensils* of a good Soup & the Pan the Ingredient

f1   2084 K.3   The Sails flapped unquietly, as if restless for the Breeze, with convulsive Snatches for air, like dying Fish.—May 8th.—

f38   2085 15.51   Tuesday Night, a dreadful Labor, & fruitless Throes, of costiveness—individuated fæces, and constricted Orifices. Went to bed & dozed & started in great distress—Wednesday Morning, May 9th—a day of Horror—tried the sitting over hot water in vain/after two long frightful, fruitless struggles, the face convulsed, & the sweat streaming from me like Rain, the Captn. proposed to send for the Commodore's Surgeon/& accordingly made sail for the Frigate but by Calm & one thing or other it was late evening before he could speak him. The Surgeon instantly came, went back for Pipe & Syringe & returned & with extreme difficulty & the exertion of his utmost strength injected the latter. Good God!—What a sensation when the obstruction suddenly *shot* up!—I remained still three-quarters of an hour with hot water *f38ᵛ* in a bottle to my belly (for I was desired to retain it as long as I could) with pains & sore uneasinesses, & indescribable desires—at length went/O what a time!—equal in pain to any before/Anguish took away all disgust, & I *picked out* the hardened matter & after awhile was completely relieved. The poor mate who stood by me all this while had the tears running down his face.—A Warning!

2086 15.52   Thurs. May 10ᵗʰ/—pretty well—a calm/and between 4 & 5 the Ships so near each other that the Cocks answered each other from 2 or 3 Coops—sweet Image for a Calm!

Calm continues—we catch large Turtles/beautiful, indeed heavenly Sunset, more than half the semi-circle of the Horizon on this side of the setting Sun about 5 diameters of the Sun high, of a de- *f39* licious Marone, a mulberry red—& this dying away into a rich smoky yellow-green/above it the new moon/—The double Path or double ⟨*deep*⟩ Column of white light from the Reflection of the Sails to each Ship in the daytime, a pleasant Image. Fish biting the Barnacles off the Turtle. At night the Ship rolled, tho' no breath of wind & so

Friday Morn. May 11ᵗʰ till a little before Sunset (S. sets at 7 °'clock here) a dead Calm with a heavy Swell from the Bay of Toulon which taking the Vessel on the broad-side kept her in one violent Roll.—Melancholy repetition of Whistles for Wind—but a light breeze 3 & 4 miles an hour started up—I have the disposition to Fever.

This Evening, or rather night, from ½ past 8 to 11 I had genial *f39ᵛ* feelings tho' not without an alloy of old Languor. But this is not the time—the barren sea, no related Mind, and a wearisome fickle Voyage/my limbs deprived of their natural motion, & my Stomach

& Bowels controlled by an unkind influence—this is not the Time
for me to begin my aweful Duty of considering & investigating the
real state of my Health—what I have to hope, what to fear. Yet
my Voyage in rough weather from Hamburgh forces itself upon
my recollections painfully! Whither have my Animal Spirits de-
parted? My Hopes—O me! that they which once I had to check

f40   [. . .] should now be an effort/Royals & Studding Sails & the
whole Canvas stretched to catch the feeble breeze!—I have many
thoughts, many images; large Stores of the unwrought materials;
scarcely a day passes but something new in fact or in illustration,
~~occur~~ rises up in me, like Herbs and Flowers in a Garden in early
Spring; but the combining Power, the power to do, the manly effective *Will*, that is dead or slumbers most diseasedly—Well, I
will pray for the Hour when I "may quit the tiresome Sea & dwell
on Shore; If not a Settler on the Soil, at least To drink wild wine
and to pluck green Herbs, And gather fruits fresh from their native Tree."—

Poetry a rationalized dream dealing [?about] to manifold
f40ᵛ   Forms our own Feelings, that never perhaps were attached by us
consciously to our own personal Selves.—What is the Lear, the
Othello, but a divine Dream/all Shakespere, & nothing Shakespere.—O there are Truths below the Surface in the subject of
Sympathy, & how we *become* that which we understandly behold
& hear, having, how much God perhaps only knows, created part
even of the Form.—[?and so] good night—

2087 15.53   Saturday, May 12ᵗʰ, 1804. Alas! the Wind fallen
again—not quite a calm indeed—but very light & lazy.—Seaward
—Evening a fine breeze & the right way but o! dear Friends did

f41   you see the crescent with its phantom moon, & the evening Star almost crowning its upper Tip!—They descended together Southward, while far away to the East the Signal Light on the Commodore's Top-Mast was undistinguishable from the planet Mars—
red, & sullen. But when the Moon & Evening Star approached the
Horizon, both became of a dusky sullen red/that the Signal light
shone bright by the comparison. Such is the force of Comparison.
The Moon set, till its upper Tip became a star of exactly the same

magnitude & appearance as the evening Star close above it/It set/
& in a few minutes its companion followed it/—I kept watch till
near 12, in a state of genial Feeling—but having taken some Rhu-   *f41ᵛ*
barb, of necessity, I was feverish when I went to bed, did not sleep
till 2 & in a few minutes was awakened half by good Mrs. I. half
by my own Screams/—& so three or four times/& the long Sleep
till Breakfast, tho' not sufficient to make me scream, was most
gloomy & distressful—even so as to leave a weight on my Spirits
the whole of
      Sunday, May 13ᵗʰ—till evening. On board Ship I cannot do with-
out aperients; & yet they act like poison on me. But God be
praised! the Breeze has continued, better & better/We came in
sight of Sardinia about 2 °'clock/like a Mountain Ridge with its   *f42*
round Rock Island/a fine outline/—Since 9 I have been in more
comfort & geniality/now ½ past 10, we are going at least six knots
an hour/& might go ten—& willingly forgive I the all-upsetting
Rolls of the reeler, that, tho' tipsy, knows well whither it is to go,
& makes good speed thither.

2088 **15.54**   To Cockermouth/& why I never went thither—
to remain a Dream.

2089 **15.55**   Brahman rescuing the Poison Snake sinks into one
mass of inorganized Slime!—this for my poem of strange
Thoughts & Sights/

2090 **15.56**   Hawk with ruffled Feathers resting on the Bow-
sprit—Now shot at & yet did not move—how fatigued—a third
time it made a gyre, a short circuit, & returned again/5 times it
was thus shot at/left the Vessel/flew to another/& I heard firing,
now here, now there/& nobody shot it/but probably it perished
from fatigue, & the attempt to rest upon the wave!—Poor Hawk!
O Strange Lust of Murder in Man!—It is not cruelty/it is mere
~~un~~ non-feeling from non-thinking.

2091 **15.57**   An Ode to Pleasure—not sought for herself, but   *f42ᵛ*
as the conditio sine qua non of virtuous activity—I not deprecating

f43 Pain, but Weight, Languor, & the soul-sickening Necessity of attending to barren bodily sensations, in bowels, in stomach, or organ
of Taste. Pain without gloom & anxious Horror, & from causes
communicable openly to all, rheumatism, &c O it is a sport!—but the
Obscure, or the disgustful—the dull quasi finger-pressure on
the Liver, the endless Flatulence, the frightful constipation when
the dead Filth *impales* the lower Gut—to weep & sweat & moan &
scream for the parturience of an excrement with such pangs & such
convulsions as a woman with an Infant heir of Immortality/for
Sleep a pandemonium of all the shames & miseries of the past Life
*f43*ᵛ from early childhood all huddled together, & bronzed with one
stormy Light of Terror & Self-torture/O this is hard, hard, hard!
—O dear God! give me strength of Soul to make one thorough
Trial—if I land at Malta/spite of all horrors to go through one
month of unstimulated Nature—yielding to nothing but manifest
Danger of Life!—O great God! Grant me grace truly to look into
myself, & to begin the serious work of Self-amendment—account-
ing to Conscience for the Hours of every Day. Let me live in
f44 *Truth*—manifesting that alone which *is*, even as it *is*, & striving to
be that which only Reason shews to be lovely—that which my
Imagination would delight to manifest!—I am loving & kind-
hearted & cannot do wrong with impunity, but o! I am very, very
weak—from my infancy have been so—& I exist for the moment!
—Have mercy on me, have mercy on me, Father & God! omnipresent, incomprehensible, who with undeviating Laws eternal yet
carest for the falling of the feather from the Sparrow's Wing.—
Sunday Midnight, May 13ᵗʰ, 1804.

2092 15.58   O dreary words!—the Captain comes off watch,
& I am in bed. Says Mʳˢ I. inquiring about the noise—They are
*f44*ᵛ setting the mainsail—it is almost Calm again!—I will go to bed,
tho' I have no sleep in my eyes—I have been trying to read
W. Wordsworth's Poem on the Formation of his mind, but I have
not been able to deliver myself up to it.—O bless you, all you
(Mary, William, the Babe, Dorothy, Sara) & my little ones!—and
Good Southey!—and thee, ~~thee!~~ the Mother of my Children, tho'
we have lived in Bitterness!

2093 15.59   Monday, May 14ᵗʰ/. Thank Heaven, "the almost calm again" was but for a few minutes. The Breeze did its duty broad awake all night, even to this Noon—Indeed not quite so much as there was, at this present time, but still a nice little Breeze.

Mem. I have marked down, I believe, in some one of my pocket *f45* books, an Idea from Darwin, meant to prove the entire dependence of all Sublimity on Association.—The sound of Thunder?—Sublime—No! it is a mistake—it is a cart over a hollow road, or going under an arch way.—Where is the Sublimity.—This fairly took me in, but now I see the fallacy. There is here no dependence—of Sublimity &c—but a true actual *Substitution* of the visual Image of a Cart and its low accompaniments and of the word *Cart* & its associations for the Sound first heard which was & always will be sublime if indeed it can be mistaken for Thunder. It is false that the Thunder clap depends for all its sublimity on our notion of the danger of Lightning & Thunder—with its height &c—These *aid* *f45ᵛ* but do not constitute/for how divinely grand in beauty is the great Aurora Borealis/yet no one will pretend that its crackling, tho' strange & impressive, is either sublime or grand or beautiful. But the fairest Proof a contra, & that which darted this Truth thro' my mind was the Commodore's Signal—which is truly sublime even as a Star is/so truly so, as long as I look at it or keep its Image before me, that even the word & visual Image Lanthorn & Candle only stands near it or under it, inert—Let that noise be produced by the Chariot Wheels of Salmoneus—So too recollect the Hawk's flying all that cloudy day falling like a shooting Star thro' a Jacob's *f46* Ladder or slanting Column of Sunshine—I am much pleased with this Suggestion, as with everything that overthrows & or illustrates the overthrow of that all-annihilating system of explaining every thing wholly by association/either *conjuring* millions *out* of o, o, o, o, o, o, o o—or into noughts.

2094 15.60   Wind dropt & ~~grew~~ became very light at eve/ most curious Sunset/

1. The Ball of Fire in the upper part of a square Pillar. 2. A granite Dome. 3. A square or four-square Rock with serrated outline. 4. an irregular-shaped rock. 5. a sugar loaf Rock of Fire, both

f46ᵛ exceedingly wildly jagged—& then as I sat it became green & vanished. I looked at it thro' the Glass, but it appeared the same to the
naked Eye, as I found by dropping the Glass every 2 or 3 seconds,
only it shewed more noble & magnificent thro' the Glass.—The
Green only I cannot answer for—whether or no it depended on the
Glass. The wind freshened—but Moon & Stars all dull & the corner
edge of the Crescent jagged—

2095 15.61   Tuesday Morn. May 15ᵗʰ/Wind continues; but
we see no Land, neither Maritimo nor Sicily, the horizon being
hazy.—The Wind continued quite fair till 4 °'clock, the morning
of Wednesday, May 16—& we were in full hope of seeing Malta
by eleven or 12, this day noon—But at 4 °'clock the Wind shifted
directly against us & continued between E. & S.E.—far more often
& longer the latter—all day—so that we have not made 10 miles
f47 the whole day. This is a true Sirocco; but it is cold or rather painfully chilly & penetrating: & affected my Health in a marked manner, with slight fever, slight pains all over me, and the menace of
a sore throat.—I will, please God that I arrive & live, keep a Journal of the Wind & weather at Malta or elsewhere, observe & note
down its influences on my Health, &c so as to be able on my return
to make a just comparison between the S.E. of the South, and our
English chill & rainy winds.—

2096 15.62   Thursday, May 17ᵗʰ, 1804—light winds, *for* now,
now against us, but a delicious day, & I uncommonly well. In the

evening a most noble view of Etna ⎓⎓⎓⎓⎓ blue on the

larboard & before us seen most dimly at eleven °'clock & only cer-
f47ᵛ tainly at evening/Divine Sunset/—on Wednesday Night I thought
how quietly I bore the disappointment of that day—as noted in the
dark on the Cover of this Book/Uncommonly well all day, &
neither slept nor felt an inclination to do so till past midnight—
sufficient proof of the nature of my Afternoon Sleeps!—

2097 15.63   Friday Morning, ½ past 6, May 18ᵗʰ, 1804, in full
clear sight of Malta/if no mischance drive athwart us, my Maltese
Journal will begin this Evening.—

2098 K.9   Sudden Bellow shot high up into the air with   *f2*
bomb-like Burst—Maltese Crier.

2099 15.64   We dropt anchor before even the Commodore,   *f47ᵛ*
about 4 °'clock. I went on Shore in the same Boat with Mrs. Ireland, with her Lover & Mr. Morrison, a rich Merchant, their pa-
tron. It was, however, six °'clock before I came to Stoddart's—
neither he nor Mrs. S. at home/the sister was, but not knowing it   *f48*
to be me, did not come down/—In above an hour she came down/
O ipsissima!—would not let the Servant, after 2 hours & a half go
to the next street to inform St. of my arrival/. *No! There was no
occasion!!—.—*
About 9 °'clock the Doctor came in & received me with an explosion of welcome—that *as it should be.*—I was much pleased with
Mʳˢ Stoddart's manners & countenance.
And here I will close this Book, leaving the blank paper for my
Sicilian Tour, if God permit *that,* when a Pencil will be more con-
venient than Ink.

2100 10.3   Friday Afternoon, 4 °clock, April[*]18ᵗʰ, 1804,   *f2*
the Speedwell dropt anchor in the Harbour of Malta—one of the
finest in the world/the Buildings surrounding it of all sides, of a
neat even new-looking Sand-free stone. Some unfinished, & in all
the windows placed backward looked like Carthage when Æneas
visited it/or a *burnt out* place—
Satur. April[*] 19ᵗʰ/—Found myself light as a blessed Ghost—
brought my Things from the Boat/in the after dinner hour walked
out with Stoddart & his wife—towards the Quarantine Harbour.
One's first feeling is that it is all strange, very strange; & when   *f2ᵛ*
you begin to understand a little of the meaning & uses of the massy
endless walls & defiles, then you feel & perceive that it is very
wonderful.—A city all of freestone, all the houses looking new,
like Bath; all with flat roofs, the Streets all strait & at right angles
to each other; but many of them exceedingly steep, a̶l̶l̶ none quite
level; of the steep Streets some *all* stepped with a smooth artificial

[* *April* for *May.* K. C.]

Stone, some having the footpath on each side in stone steps, the
f3   middle left for carriages; lines of fortification, fosses, Bastions,
Curtains, &c &c endless, endless—with gardens or bowling Grounds
below the high ones; for it is all height & depth—you can walk no
where without having whispers of Suicide, toys of desperation. Ex-
plosive Cries of the Maltese venders—shot up, broad & bulky
noises, sudden and violent. The inhabitants very dark, some almost
black, but straight clean limbed lively active/cannot speak in praise
f3ᵛ   of their cleanliness—Children very fair. Women from the use of
the Faldetto, or cloak hooding their Heads as Women in England
in a Shower throw over their aprons, & from the use of always
holding it down to one side of the face, all have a permanent lan-
guishing way of holding their heads one way—picturesque enough,
as expressive of a transient emotion; but shockingly insipid, *all* &
always.—The language Arabic corrupted with Italian & otherwise
perhaps.

f4   2101 10.4   Sunday. April[*] 20ᵗʰ, 1804. Still very well—
went to church, a plain Chapel with a picture behind the Pulpit
which I was not close enough to see, and at the other end in a nitch
a Cross painted! Was it there before? Or was it in complaisance to
Maltese Superstitions?—Called on Sir A. Ball & delivered my Letter—a very polite man; but no hopes, I see clearly, of any situa-
tion/there I met General Valette & delivered my Letter to him/a
f4ᵛ   striking room, very high, $\frac{3}{4}$ᵗʰˢ of its height from the ground hung
with rich crimson Silk or velvet; & the $\frac{1}{4}$ᵗʰ above a mass of colours,
pictures in compartments rudely & without perspective or art, but
yet very impressively & imagination stirringly representing all the
events & exploits of the Order—some fine pictures—one by Cor-
reggio—one of a Cain killing Abel, I do not know by whom/.
f5   Monday, April[*] 21ˢᵗ 1804. Hard Rain. Sir A. Ball called on me
& introduced Mʳ Lane & me to each other/his Chaplain & Son's
Tutor, &c. Invited me to dine with him on Thursday—& made a
plan for me to ride to Sᵗ Antonio on Tuesday morning, with Mʳ
Lane/& offered me a Horse—Soon after came on Thunder &

[* *April* for *May*. ᴋ. ᴄ.]

Storm, & my Breathing was affected a good deal; but still I was
in no discomfort—. April[*] 22nd—Tuesday Morning, 6 °clock was
on horse back & rode to St Antonio/ Fields with walls ▬▬▬ to
keep the Soil from the rains—mere desolation seemingly, & yet it   *f5^v*
is fertile. St Antonio a pleasant Country House, with a fine but un-
shaded Garden, save among the low Orange & Lemon Trees, still
thick with Fruit/on many of the Trees, Fruit ripe, blossoms, & the
next years Fruit/—Pepper Tree very beautiful/& the Locust Tree
not amiss.—Breakfasted with Sir A.—From Noon ~~very~~ unwellish—
& had a most wretched DEBILITATING night. [?Corporal] the next
morning told me it was a Sirocco the day—but could it be from   *f6*
that piece of green Oilskin at my Breast?—I went to bed early—&
it was a hateful Night. I took no *dose*—but let me try this the next
night that I feel myself well.—That day, visited St Johns—⟨o
magnificence!⟩—

2102 10.5   Wednesday, April[*] 23rd—General Valette I
called on at his Country House, just out of the Gates, near the end
of the Botanic Garden. Gen. V's the pleasantest place I have seen
here, the multitude of small Gardens & Orangeries among the huge
Masses of fortifications, many of them seeming almost as thick as   *f6^v*
the Gardens inclosed by them are broad.—Pomegranate in (beauti-
ful scarlet) Flower/under a Bridge over a dry Ditch saw the largest Prickly Pear/elk horns for Trunk, & then its leaves, but go &
look & look/. Hard rain/we sheltered in the Botanic Garden, yet
~~came~~ reached home not unwetted/As I was changing, G. Valette
called on me/—invited me & Stoddart for Sunday to dinner.—

2103 10.6   OF IDOLATRY philosophically investigated/Popery   *f7*
true Idolatry/& Moravianism—

2104 10.7   Dress their food out at their doors on pots of
Fire—
     Absurd to complain of the Maltese as semi-barbarous, & yet to
act towards them, servants for ~~English~~ instance, precisely as if they

[* Again, *April* for *May*. K. C.]

were English Servants, namely simply pay them their wages & expect them to do their Duty.

Every where I see the importance of treating human beings as good, by kindness, respect &c, Στοδδαρτ and the blind Woman—

ƒ7ᵛ   2105 10.8   I have found myself in a Bason always, sometimes on one side, sometimes in the Bottom.

2106 10.9   To enter a room, be loudly familiar with the Master & haughtily distant to a Stranger, a certain mark of a low mind.

ƒ13   2107 10.15   Desirous too neither to undertake or to be ~~thought~~ ~~to~~ suspected of having undertaken, a superfluous task, as I had taken some pains ~~to~~ ~~satisfy~~ ~~myself,~~ ~~I~~ for ~~my~~ ~~own~~ the satisfaction of my own mind, I could not but wish to satisfy yours, that nothing had appeared hitherto to supersede &c as I had diligently inquired for my own satisfaction, I wished to have it understood by others, that nothing had &c.—

ƒ73ᵛ   2108 16.244   Malta (Dʳ Stoddart's, his Majesty's Advocate, Strada de Forni, or N.º 4, Quarter 4, the House best known as the ci devant Casa de Sᵗ Poix—where I arrived ⟨Friday ~~after~~ late⟩ Afternoon, April[*] 18ᵗʰ, 1804.)

Thursday morning, 5 ºclock, April[*] 24ᵗʰ, awoke & found my Breast plate gone, as I thought but no! it had turned round, &

ƒ75   2109 16.245   20 minutes after 9, Tuesday morning, June 5ᵗʰ, 1804, Susan Stoddart died, born ½ after 11. Thursday Night, April 24, 1804.

2110 16.246   Forget not to impress as often and as manifoldly as possible the totus in omni parte of Truth, and its consequent non dependence on co-operation/& vice versâ the fragmentary character of Action, & its absolute dependence on Society, a majority &c/The blindness to this creates fanaticism on one side, alarm & persecution on the other—Jacobinism and Soul-*gougers*.—

[* Again, *April* for *May*. K. C.]

2111 16.247   Tiredness of the War and the Making of a Peace a direct subversion of the sole justifying end of the war in order just to take breath, compared to a poor waysore foot-traveller getting up behind a Coach that is going the contrary way to him/

2112 16.248   In the men of continuous and discontinuous minds explain & demonstrate the vast difference between the disjunction conjunctive of the sudden Images *seized* on from external Contingents by Passion & Imagination (which is Passion eagle-eyed)— The Breeze I see, is in the Tree—It comes to cool my Babe and me.—which is the property & prerogative of continuous minds of   *f75ᵛ* the highest order, & the conjunction disjunctive of Wit—

> And like a lobster boil'd the Morn
> From black to red began to turn,

which is the excellence of men of discontinuous minds— Arrange & classify the men of continuous minds—the pseudocontinuous, or *juxta-ponent* mind/metaphysician not a poet—poet not a metaphysician?—poet + metaphysician/—*the faithful* in Love &c—

2113 16.249   The very persons who deem you a strange Anachronism of Bigotry for connecting any horror with the Catholic Faith & its consequences, these so temperate, so smiling, so alltolerating, "there-are-good-&-bad-in-all-religions"—People, when Jacobinism came up, & some of its opinions appear to war against the rights of *Property* and for that all its other articles, with what horror! how dangerous! Gog & Magog—tho' common sense told aloud, that it was monster that would die of the convulsions it was born in/

2114 K.24   Godwin &c—O how little he reflected how much   *f4ᵛ* of the nature of Ital. [?city/cities] there was! even in Malta —jack asses—Cats—Cocks—Bells—Day cries—Night-bellowings— Guns.

2115 K.25   [?Justified in] Trifles of Enjoyment [. . . . . .   *f5* . . . .]

2116 K.28

f11ᵛ

ᴜ (or -) -,	ᴜ - ᴜ,	- ᴜ	figlio
ᴜ -,	ᴜ -,	ᴜ - ᴜ	raro
ᴜ -,	ᴜ -,	ᴜ - ᴜ	caro
ᴜ - ᴜ,	ᴜ - ᴜ,	ᴜ -	da te
ᴜ - ᴜ,	ᴜ - ᴜ,	ᴜ - ᴜ	esangue
- - ᴜ - ᴜ,	- ᴜ		ciglio
ᴜ - ᴜ,	ᴜ - ᴜ,	ᴜ - ᴜ	il sangue
ᴜ - ᴜ,	ᴜ - ᴜ,	ᴜ -.	diè

f57ᵛ 2117 21.329 There are Thoughts that seem to give me a power over my own Life—I could kill myself by persevering in the Thought—Mem: Describe as accurately as may be the approximating Symptoms &c—. I met something very like this Observation where I should least have expected such coincidence of sentiment, such sympathy with so wild a feeling of mine—on p.71. of Blount's Translation of the Spanish Rogue, 1623.

2118 21.330 Why are not you here? + O no! O no! I dare not wish you here.—A poem in 2 parts.

2119 21.331 Soldiers + Sailors, a drunken Squabble—Sailors swore, that the Soldiers said—Bring to, you ~~Buggers!~~—the Sold. that the Sail. said Damn your eyes! who stops the Line of March there.

2120 21.332   L.B. I——X. Yet this great Slasher, his ρασενδ μυθ against Bentley + Milton

f99ᵛ 2121 21.434 Why do we so very very often see men pass from one extreme to another? στοδκαρδια. Alas they sought not the Truth but praise, self-importance, & above all to see something f100 doing.—Disappointed they hate and persecute their former opinion, which no man will do who by meditation had adopted it, & in the course of unfeigned meditation gradually enlarged the circle & so got out of it/—for in the perception of its falshood he will form a perception of certain Truths which had made the falsehood plausible, & never can he cease to venerate his own sincerity of

Intention & Philalethie. For perhaps we never *hate* any opinion or can do so till we have *impersonated* it—we hate the persons because they oppose us, symbolize that opposition under the form & words of the opinion, & then hate the person for the opinion & the opinion for the person.

2122 21.435 *Facts!* never be weary of discussing & exposing the hollowness of these—every man an *accomplice* on one side or other/& then *human Testimony!*/"You were in fault, I hear—" said B to C and B had heard it from *A*. A had said, "& C, God bless her, was perhaps the innocent occasion." But what a Trifle this compared with the generality of Blunders!—

2123 21.436 English Hauteur—*horror carnis humanæ*—want of smiles—all seem to wither in the aspect of their Pride, Scorn, & true alienation—a me *alienum*.

2124 21.437 Blindness from putting out of your own eyes & *f100ᵛ* in mock humility refusing to form an opinion on the Right & the Wrong of the main Question "If we say so of the Sicilians, why may not Bonaparte say thus of the Swiss? &c &c. as if England and France, Swiss & Sicilians, were X, Y, Z, of Algebra/naked names of unknown Qualities?—To fix morals without morality, & general Rules to supersede all particular Thought/This never acted upon in reality, & yet the opinion pernicious—kills public spirit & deadens national Effort.

2125 21.438 Saw one side of his face & *instantly* not his Idea —but the Image of the *Place* in which they had been happiest, arose so vividly to her mind that well-nigh she fainted, & thoughts had she which seemed to give her power over her own Life.

2126 21.439 My whole body & heart panting & shivering like an ague fit of Love.

2127 21.440
Some innocent flowers, some sweet & virtuous Fruit
From the Tree of True Love.—

2128 21.441   And tho' they had all alike seen it, & that moment seen it, yet many related it over again to his ~~ges~~ eagerly
attentive neighbour, who listened as if that which indeed he had
that moment himself witnessed, was a new wild Story told to a
child/every where you saw men making strange gestures, no limb
—even of those alone, but was in some way or other acting over
the glorious Atchievement.

f101   2129 21.442   The little *point*, or sometimes minim *Globe* of
Flame, on the lighted Taper remaining unaltered 3 minutes or
more—given over then at once the flame darts or plunges down
into the wick, up again—& all is bright—a fair cone of Flame with
its black column in it, & minor cone shadow-colored-resting upon
the blue flame, the common base of the two cones, i.e. of the whole
flame.—A pretty detailed Simile in the manner of J. Taylor might
be made of this, applying it to slow Learners—to opportunities of
grace manifestly neglected, & seemingly lost & useless—&c &c.

2130 21.443   Die Liebe ist oft, ich möchte beynahe sagen, stets
das Werk eines Augenblickes. Ein Blick, mit dem man sich begegnet, ein Händedruck, ein Wort (a single *Tone*) ist nicht selten
der erste, der einzige *wahre* Bund, der zwey harmonirende Seelen
auf ewig verbindet. And I can explain this—& in that explanation
solve the immense difference between Love & *Habit* of attachment, between loving & *being in Love.*

2131 21.444
Nicht sterben? Und sie wollten mein Tröster seyn?
Gehen sie! Gehen sie!

2132 21.445   The Sun had set, a short half hour of tender
balmy darkness—& the moon rose, round & large, & scarcely confess'd its Waining—Stay Love! when the Sun had set, I said—
under the tender Darkness we sate, Under the Tree—the Nightin-
gale sings. the evening star is so large & beautiful. & the moon will
soon rise—/—/—O Evening,—when Loneliness is Dreariness—O
Love—inspirer. Love—demander, the lonely Heart aches—even

when it loves not, because it loves not—but Hope makes Dream/
but him who loves & is not beloved//but O! to him who loves &
is beloved, & never never must attain.—

2133 K.26   ~~Repet~~ Repeated Instances of the use of *ne*—   *f5*

1

Questo silenzio stesso e ⟨un⟩ mistero per li simplici, e la Censuria,
ne tirera un singolar' avantaggio—derive from it, or *hence*.—

2

Se non *ve ne* volete star' alla mia parola—if you are unwilling to
take my word *for it*—

3

La verità della quale è di tanta delicatezza che per poco che l'uom'
se ne retiri, cade nell'errore: e l'error del S. A. è di tanta sotti-
gliezza, che senza allontanar*sene* fa che un si trova nella verità.—

4

Mi voltai verso del mio Giansenista, e conobbi bene al suo gesto,
che non ne credeva niente.

5

Ma non rispondendo *egli* cosa veruna, io dissi: Io vorrei, che
quel che che voi dite fosse vero, e che voi *n'avessi di buone prove.*
Ne volete voi in questo punto, replicommi egli—*Io me ne vò a*
trovarvene—(I take me off from it = andarmene in the infinitive
—to find some for you—e anche delle megliori—& those too of the
best!—*lasciate far a me!* Detto questo, *se n'andò a* circar li suoi
libri.

acchiocciolarsi, *s'accroupir*, to sit squat on your Tail, e di più—and   *f4ᵛ*
moreover.—fate conto, che mai i Santi padri, i Papi, i Concili, ne la
Scrittura, ne alcun libro di pietà, *anche in questi ultimi tempi*
n'hanno parlato di questa sorte; ma per de' Casuisti, e de' nuovi
Scholastici *ve ne porterà in furia*/in vast abundance.—*E un danno*
(Pity!) mi disse *sotto* voce il mio &c. in an under voice—

2134 K.27
1 cosi—come = aussi—que   *f5ᵛ*
2 dove si son resolute cose tanto straordinarie, e si fuor d'essem-
pio, = *there* have taken place &c

3 Ne fanno concepire un Idea tanto grande, che non può credersi, non ci fosse un soggetto più che considerabile = *so great,* that one could not but believe they must have had &c/$^{che}_{that}$ as in English.

4 dove *vada a terminar'* un si gran fracasso = a quoy *se termine* un si grand Eclat.

5 Il che vi dirò

6 *dopo di essermene* perfettamente informato = after having _____ *myself of it*

f6   7 se il signor A. e temerario per haver detto nella sua seconda lettera/*whether*—for having said in—

8 Settant'uno Dottori = 71 Doctors

9 pigliar la sua difesa = undertake his defence—

10 non aver'egli potuto risponder'altro _____ se non che —— e che nondimeno ci ve le condanna, s'elle vi sono = could not _____ other, than that _____ and that nevertheless _____ if

11 che e quanto è = that & as much is = which is what has—

12 da quella banda = de ce costé-là: i quali = who

13. *senza di aver* voluto essaminare *se* quel ch'egli aveva detto era ver' o falso, avendo anche dichiarato che non trattavasi della verità, ma solamente della temerità della sua propos:—whether that which _____ the question here was not concerning—& Mem.

*f6*ᵛ   voluto e dichiarato &c/not voluti, &c.—

14 Poich'il Sign. A è tem: o no la mia coscienza non vi è interessata.   Whether or no—

15 E se mi venisse curiosità di sapere, se queste prop: sono in G., il suo libro non è tanto scarso, ne tanto grosso ch'io non _____ senza ricorrere alla S. _____ 16. per chiarirmene, = for to enlighten myself on the subject

17 Di manièra ch' io temo, che _____ non cagioni &c. So that I fear that this *will* &c Mind that seeming Expletive non, after temo etc. comparatives, &c—

18 Non _____ che quando __ not _____, unless

19 Ma com' i ho di già detto = but as I have just said

f7   20 —e come che la mia curiosità mi rendeva quasi tanto ardente che lui/almost as eager as he/

affinchè non si disputasse, in order that folks might not dispute—
più di tal = any longer of such a/

21 ⟨Tutto⟩ allegro di saper—and all in high Spirits *at know-ing,*—

22 ma che nondimeno e un uomo molto da bene; but who is nevertheless a very honest man.

23 per esser' meglio recevuto da lui io finsi d' esser' del suo partito/in order to be better received by him I pretended to be of his Party/—

24 Come, li diss'io, non è questa la vostra oppi⟨ni⟩one?—nò, replicommi egli—

25 Il mio uomo si riscaldò sopra di questo/my man grew warm on this/.

26 io davo parola di farlielo/sottoscriver col sangue loro—

27 bisogn'esser Teologo per penetrarne la finezza.—   *f7*ᵛ

28 *al quale* io dissi immediatamente *doppo* li primi complimenti —Ditemi, vi prego, *se voi* ammettete il poter &c/*to whom*— whether you—ditemi voi medesimo in che senso l'intendete, e allora vi dirò quel ch'io ne credo.—what I believe of it. Mem.— To be on my guard often to insert that *ne.*

29 —senza far moto, without disturbance—leviter—sans s'e-mouvoir/

30 Io l'intendo nel senso de Molinisti—*al che* replicò il mio uomo—a qual de M.? to which—to whom of the? to what part of the?

31 Essendo tutti uniti *nel disegno* di rovinar S. &c—accordarsi *di* questo tho' we should use "in" in ~~both~~ both cases—Practice &   *f8* the Della Crusca Dictionary can alone enable me to get over this Difficulty.

32 che gli uni e gli altri direbbono insieme, benche l'intendes-sero diversamente/

33 Ne sarete più sicuri sentendolo da lor medesimi. 34 Io non conosco ne l'uno ne l'altro/

35 se ne conoscerete qualcheduno di coloro/che io adesso vi nominerò/ne conobbi anche fra quei ch'ei mi nominò—I knew *some* too among those *whom*—

36 *E aver tutto* quel ch'e necessario in modo che niente manchi

per &c—per adempir*gli* = to fulfil *them*/in modo che non gli
manca cos'alcuna ne dalla banda d'Iddio./—/non e egli un giocarsi
delle parole? il dire che Is not this _____ the saying &c—

ƒ8ᵛ 37 Ma ho poi saputo che le lor visite non sono di rado, e che
continuamente si trovan gli uni con gli altri.

38 rizzandomi per lasciargli = rising to quit them.

e se bisognerà noi faremo venir tanti frati &c/and if it should be
necessary—

di modo che *non ci è, se non* la parola senz'alcun senso che corra
risico.—So that *it is only* the word &c that is in danger.

con *tal* pretesto/on such a pretext.

Se questo racconto non vi dispiace, io continuerò a darvi avviso
di quanto seguirà—Mentre sono &c—

ƒ9 Quanto tempo e che V. S. parlò Italiano?—How long have you
&c Non sono ancora due mesi/

Nel chiudere la lettera *which I was* closing up &c—
con la maggior' ventura del mondo per la mia curiosità—the most
luckily possible for my &c

Perche supposto che _____ non e piu naturale quant' il con-
cludere, che _____ nothing is more natural than to conclude
that—

Ell' è piu che sodisfatta/quite or very satisfied—

da pochi giorni in qua—since the last few days/Prima che—before that you have &c—Che portino la su le nostre ~~vale~~ valiggie—
Let them carry above stairs my portmanteaux/

ƒ9ᵛ Se voi credete di aver' scritto a me solo/ = *che voi avete.* Vedete *quel che* me ne scrive un Academico *de più* illustri *tra quelli*
uomini tutt' illustri, il quale *non* aveva veduto ancora *se* ³*non* la
prima = what *one of the most illustrious of*—³who as yet had
not seen any but the first—or—only the first.

la quale deve tanto alla memoria *del già* S. Card. R.   of the
late Cardinal R. &c

in quanto al = as for/in quanto al magnar e bere: as for your
eating & drinking

più alla distesa = more at length

senza altro =doubtless

già è tanto tempo—for so long a time past = Depuis si long-
temps.

In questo mentre   in the Interim/⟨bisognava che la Prop.⟩   *f10*
fosse &c.

per dover esser heretica.

di dove   from whence—

per esser egli stato freddo inverso di G. Christo—in consequence
of his being cold toward J. Christ. ⟨per cagione di sua freddezza—⟩

e prima di lui Santo Chr./and prior to him, (or before him)
S. C. had said/

è egli possibile, che in tutte le opere sue non habbino ⟨*abbiano*⟩
mai potuto trovar da opporli che solamente in tre righe, le quali
anche son prese *a parola per parola* (verbatim) *da i maggiori Dottori* della Chièsa G. e L.—from the two greatest Doctors

Scoperto, che ne averemo il veleno, noi la detesteremo; ma, fino a   *f10ᵛ*
che vi troveremo &c—(as *long as*)—non potremo tenerla che—we
cannot but hold them in, or we can not hold them otherwise than—

Questo è quello, di che ei si dolgono; ma ei son troppo penetrativi.
per noi, che non intendiamo le cose si al fondo, tenghiamoci in
riposo *senza intrigarcene.* without troubling ourselves of it = *ce ne.*

E in questo timore ho stimato necessario di consultar uno de più
dotti di coloro, che *per politica* furono neutrali nella prima disputa
—e l'ho *pregato di volermi dire* le circonstanze di questa discre-
panza, confessandoli francamente *di non vedervene pur una*

that I did see there any difference at all.—ne = our repetition of
the antecedent.—o che voi siete pur buono a creder, che ve ne sia!
That there exists *any there*   *f11*

che se ce ve ne avessero trovata qualcheduna/that if they could
have found any there/printed che s' c' ve n' avessero &c/che ei
hanno resoluti di—*a che prezzo si sia* at whatever price.—*senza dir
in che ne perche.*

alla meno parola che scappi alli Molinisti contro i principii
&c—at the least word that escaped from the Molinists—

Di maniera che doppo tante prove della loro debbolezza, hanno stimato *più a proposito,* e più util per loro il censurare ch'il replicare, essendogli assai più facile di trovare frati (monks) che ragioni

La lor censura per tutto censurabile *che la sia*—as it is.—la sarà conosciuta per quel ch'ell' e = known for what it really is.

f11ᵛ A loro questo basta. Vivono a giorno per giorno—

si son mantenuti *sino al presente*—thus &c.

da quel, che voi me ne dite—from what you tell me of this—cio ha fatto dire a un erudito Theologo.—it is this that made a learned man say—gave occasion to that saying of a learned man &c

i piu dotti tra di loro sono quei, che s'intrigano molto, che parlan poco, *e che non scrivono* nulla.
sin dal principio—since the &c.—

f12 Li essaminatori avendo voluto escir un poco di questo Metodo *non se ne* sono trovati bene; did not find themselves well off in it—

prima che la fosse conclusa/before it was ended
si parla poco per Tema di trascorrere troppo avanti   of running out too far—/

f12ᵛ 2135 K.31   Così è, lo confesso—A me toccáva di rispondere a V. S., e l'avréi fatto, *non meno per sodisfar al gusto, che al debito.* = as well to &c—as &c.

f12 2136 K.32   Io conobbi V. S. molto prima di fama, che di presenza.

Mettete dunque l'animo in riposo—set your mind at rest

e non temete *d'esser heretico* servendovi della propos: condannata/of being an Heretic in serving yourself of—*credete al* D. Le Moyne.—

Questa Prop. sarebbe Cattolica *in* un altra bocca: la Sorbona l'ha condannata solamente *nel* Signor Arnaldo/La grazia—non sara mai la vera fino a ch'ei la difenderà—as long as he shall defend it

f12ᵛ Lasciamo ⟨and so too mettiamo/⟩ dunque da una banda/lay aside/leave to themselves—

Noi, che non siamo Dottori, non abbiamo che far delle lor con-
tese = have nothing to do (i.e. no interest) in their Squabbles—
Li domandai non di meno *affin di sentire le sue ragioni*, per qual
causa &c—

2137 21.446   Wednesd. Morn. July 4ᵗʰ, 1804. At Breakfast at $f101^v$
Sir Alex. Ball's saw a Lady with Hair, Complexion, and a certain
cast of Countenance that on the first glance of her troubled me in-
conceivably—after a while I perceived the likeness to S. H. & was
near fainting—O what an inconceivable faintness with fondness—/
As I went away, I seemed to see clearly the possibility of loving
A. and B. A being dead, & B. strikingly like, as truly one soul in
two resembling Bodies.—⟨A 18 and A 35 years old.⟩

2138 21.447   Brave Tars—eager as Tygers for Battle. &c &c—
Sir *A. B.* assured me, that the men on board our most glorious
Warships *often run from their Quarters* tho' it was made a point
to hush it up/that it was the British *officers* & our Discipline/yet
believed their Men too braver & steadier than any other nation
except Danes & Swedes—
    Sir A. B. informed me on his own knowlege while he was on
the Coast of Africa, of the 75ᵗʰ   [*] Regiment consisting of
Welshmen being understood by the Negroes of that part, they
talking Welsh. What part of the Coast? Goree.
In what year?—
    Of the Colonel at Gibralter told me by Major Adye, who in
the conspiracy against the Duke in which he knew his own men
deeply engaged, interpreted their Shout of Welcome to the Regiment on whom they were about to be ordered to fire, as a shout of
Loyalty—& cried out/Thank you, my brave Lads! You are an
Honor to your ~~Country~~ King & Country! Fire!—and they fired!—
This to me appears far greater than Buonaparte's Strategem on his $f102$
return to Cairo from D'Acre.—Buonaparte at Malta called out the
2 Maltese Regiments raised by the order, amounting to 1500 of
the stoutest men of the Islands, harangued in them in a flaming
Speech on the Parade, that he had restored them to Liberty &

[* Coleridge's blank. K. C.]

would now giving them an opportunity of adding Glory to Freedom and asked who of them would march forward & be his Soldiers for Egypt—not one stirred/all refused—they were surrounded—marched to the Marino/forced on board Transports—
threatened with Death if one were seen on the Island, & at Alex-
andria always put in the front to save the rest, & only 50 survived/
who are now living.

2139 21.448   Monday Evening. July 9ᵗʰ, 1804, about 8 °clock,
the glorious evening coasted the moon, and at length absolutely
crested its upper Tip/true apparent Touch/Dʳ Sewell compared it
to the figure of a Cock. ✍—It was the most singular & at the
same time beautiful Sight, I ever beheld/O that it could have
appeared the same in England/at Grasmere.—

2140 21.449   On Wed. Morning July 11ᵗʰ, I took my bed & a
f102ᵛ few Cloathes and moved from the Palace in la Valette to the Palace at Sᵗ Antonio's/went that evening to Sᵗ Julian's, slept there,
rose a little after 4 next morn. & walked back/observed & tasted
the Locust Tree & Fruit/deepest verdure, most efficient shade of
any/but the Tree all made up of branches, like Ivy, these branches
oddly bossed or scabbed, ~~seems~~ looks as if meant to be a climber,
and to stand up per se only by compulsion/—The fruit looks exactly like the pods of the Scarlet Bean when grown to their full
size; and it is a pod, but full of an austere dulcacid Juice, that
reminds me of a harsh Pear. These Pods grow out of the Branches,
out of the very *wood* of the Tree, at the bottom of each of these
twisted upright branches, in a large Assemblage.—Pomegranate,
prickly pear, pepper Tree, Oleander, Date Tree (with its Wheel

of Plumage 〰 a complete circle including the enclosed part

of the Stem) Myrtle Bowers, Arbour of a scented Butterfly-flower,
but all conch-shaped, or cork-screw/the Standard beautiful spiral,
white stained with purple & the conformation of the Keel beautiful
& curious beyond my power to describe; it ends in a compressed

elastic cork-screw, which lies spire touching spire, but you can pull
it out into a compleat screw; and this is continued, as it were finely
spliced on to, & spun out into, the mast as we used to call it/t̶h̶e̶
which here seems rather to grow at the root of the Standard than
on the Keel, and which splits into exquisitely subtle Threads
I should like to see Linnæus on this Subject/Walnut, Mulberry,
Orange and Lemon

2141 21.450   The marks of carriage wheels on the extreme
edge of the sea coast opposite to Gozo/—

2142 K.33   E ciò basti per ora di me, e di cose private.   ƒ12ᵛ
Quanto alle publiche nostre d'Italia, veggo quel, che V. S. ne
scrive, e quel, che ne teme. Io nondimeno resto nelle mie speranze
di prima; e confido, che doppo un si buono aggiustamento nelle
cose di terre, *sia per cessare ancora* ogni novità *in* quelle di mare.
—*about to cease,* on the point of ceasing—&c.—In   The different
uses of *Nel* and *In?*—Il che piacia a Dio di far succedere quanto
prima: e che la nostra Italia *impari dalle miserie* di questa guerra
a goder tanto più *da qui inanzi* la felicità della pace.

2143 K.34   First, we exclude the French and deprive them   ƒ13
of a Port, which would furnish such facility to their Enterprizes
in the Levant, of whatever nature they might be and against whatever countries they might be directed as no maritime superiority
might be sufficient to counteract; while the presence of our troops
& Squadrons in that most commanding s̶i̶t̶u̶a̶t̶i̶o̶n̶ position not only
deprives them of that advantage, but opposes a positive obstacle,
wholly insurmountable to any considerable Expedition from the
French or Spanish Ports in that direction.   ƒ13ᵛ

2144 K.35, 37   Lizard half-erect stands still as I stop—I stop a
long while/he turns his head & looks sidelong at me/—Crawls
two or three paces by stealth—stops again/I walk off briskly, turning my head tho' & looking at him/he is too cunning—& has not
moved—at length I really move away—and off—he is gone!—
Glide across the sunny walk like shooting Stars, green, grey,
speckled/exquisite grace of motion/all the delicacy of the Serpent

and a certain dignity ~~from the~~ from even just the ~~semi~~ increasing
erectness of it to ~~the two low~~ its ~~forefeet~~ hind paws—/Dragon flies.

f14　1. purple. 2 & most common, a deep crimson—not so long in the
Sheath as our finest ones in England/Butterflies/glorious ones,
but their flight unwieldy—I could catch them with ease.—The
Lizard's motion, & the Dragon-fly's—both darting and angular, yet
how different/the Dr.'s always & naturally angular/the Lizard's
only by choice/—This is Friday, July 13th/at St Antonio's—Yesterday & to day I seem to *live*/O Sara!—yes, I could be happy
here with *you!*—Let me write to her to day.—Lizard green with
bright gold spots all over—firmness of its *stand-like* feet, where
the *Life* of the *threddy* Toes makes them both seem & be so firm,
so solid—yet so very, very, supple/one pretty fellow, whom I had
fascinated by stopping & gazing at him as he lay in a ⟨thick⟩ net-

f14ᵛ　work of Sun & Shade, after having turned his head from me so as
but for the greater length of its Tail to form a crescent with the
outline of its body—then turned his Head to me, depressed it, &
looked up half-watching; half-imploring, at length taking advantage of a brisk breeze that made all the Network dance & Toss, &
darted off as if an Angel of Nature had spoken in the Breeze—Off!
I'll take care, he shall not hurt you/—I should like if I could
know what they eat, or if they eat bread, to tame one/

　　Lizard driven headlong before a gust into the Harbour/
f15　turns his head & innocent eye sidelong toward me, his side above
his forepaw throbbing with a visible pulse—a minute & then a slow
timid creep off for an inch or so—then stops/

f14ᵛ　2145　K.36　　　A Banana, at least 20 feet high/the Leaves, 7
5eet in length & 2 feet in the broadest part of this green flag—
broken almost all at the Top into fillets more or less narrow according to the exposure, all however even where the whole Leaf

f15　flutters with a hundred fillets bound by the stem that runs up the
Leaf—as in a Lettuce/—a federal State out of a huge Empire =
Russia. The main Stems of the Banana green stained with black
as if by tarry Handling & Chains looks exactly like the painted
Mast of a royal Yacht/

2146 K.29   9ᵗʰ of May & 26ᵗʰ of June 1804 Earthquakes at   *f9*
Malta/Monday July 16ᵗʰ a few drops of the Rain from the [?dis-
turbance]

2147 K.30   Monday, July 16ᵗʰ, 1804 a few Drops of Rain at   *f10*
Malta/Tuesday ~~Noon~~ Midnight, & Wednesday ~~from~~ During 17ᵗʰ
& 18ᵗʰ of July, incessant Lightning, with little Thunder & rain
storm, with pleasant Showers thro' the Morning—and one fearful
Rain-storm in the afternoon before Dinner.

2148 K.38   Qu. in the inhabited Half of the Isle is it possible,   *f15*
in calm air, to be any where out of the Sound of Steeple Clock &
Church Bells

2149 K.39   Giorgona
                   Torre Gazza
                   Fontane
                   Bianche
                   Casibili F.
                   Cambli
                   Avola
                   Vittoria del

2150 21.451   In the Jacobinism of Anti-Jacobins note that   *f102ᵛ*
dreariest feature of Jacobinism, contempt of the Institutions of   *f103*
our Ancestors and of past wisdom which has generated Cobbets &
Juvernhas & contempt of Liberty of the Press, and of Liberty itself
—Men are not wholly unmodified by the opinions of their fellow-
men even when they happen to be enemies, or (still worse) of the
antagonist Faction.

2151 21.452   Saw in early youth as in a Dream the Birth of
the Planets; & my eyes beheld as *one* what the Understanding
afterwards divided into 1. the origin of the masses, 2. the origin
of their motions, and 3. the site or position of their Circles &
Ellipses—all the deviations too were *seen* as in one intuition of
one, the self-same, necessity—& this necessity was a Law of Spirit—

& all was Spirit—and in matter each all beheld the past activity of
others or their own—this Reflection, this Echo, is matter—its only
essence, if essence it be—and of this too I saw the necessity and
understood it—but I understood not, how infinite multitude and
manifoldness could be one. Only I saw & understood, that it was
yet more out of my power to comprehend how it could be otherwise—& thus in this unity I worshipped in the depth of knowlege
that passes all understanding the Being of all things—and in Being
their sole Goodness—and I saw that God is the one, *the* Good—
possesses it not, but is it.

⟨For my own Life—written as an inspired Prophet,—*throughout.*⟩

2152 21.453   Do not words excite feelings of Touch (tactual
Ideas) more than *distinct visual Ideas*—i.e. *of Memory?* If this
be the fact, it explains many of the popular notions concerning
Ghosts & apparitions, & their *vestiture* in *apparition* which is not
never attributed to them in genere.—But the Question is of great
Importance, as a general application—

2153 21.454   Motion at a great distance/its visibility increased
by all that increases the distinct visibility of the moving object—
f103ᵛ   This Saturday, August 3ʳᵈ, 1804, in the Room immediately under
the Tower in Sᵗ Antonio's, as I was musing on the difference,
whether ultimate or only of degree, between "auffassen" and
"anerkennen" (an idea received, and an idea *agnized*) I saw on
the Top of the distant Hill a Shadow ⟨on the sunny ground⟩ moving very fast & wavelike, yet always in the same place; which I
should have immediately attributed to the Windmill close by; but
the Windmill (which I saw distinctly too) appeared at rest. On
steady gazing however (& most plainly with my spy-glass) I found
that it was not at rest, but that this *was* its Shadow—The Windmill itself was sunny white in the sunshine & sunny white clouds
at its Back; the Shadow black on the white ground.—

2154 21.455   1. *con*scire. 2. scire quod est unum individuum
generis alicujus; (e.g. *a* sheep) 3. quod presens vel non presens,

i.e. *res;* sive *memoria* rei; sive *imaginatio*—Hæc tria Germani Metaphysici ~~ita~~ ~~operationem~~ Facultatis cognoscitivæ *inferioris* ~~dicunt~~ annumerant; superioris vero Facult. cognos. conscientiam congruentiæ sive contradictionis notionum duarum inter se, quædæ si immediata sit, *judicium* nuncupatur, si mediata, conclusio vel *deductio.* S.T.C.

2155 K.14   D' Stoddart   *f3*
                   H. M. *Advocate*
                   Admiralty
                   Malta
                   D' Stoddart
                   Strada de Forni.
                   o Casa di S' Poix.
                   Quarter 4, N.° 4. rear

2156 K.10   Duke di Gravino/Small Pox—inoculation of the   *f2ᵛ*
present king of Naples/England & Jamaica, & those cold Climates!

2157 K.11   Morea/June last—Depots of arms there.—

2158 K.12   Man that offered to stab the two English Gentlemen who would not pay 2 dollars & ½ instead of a Shilling/runa-
way—punished enough when taken said the King to Sir W. Hamilton—he would not have been taken if he had had any money
left—! I know it but I cannot help it—

2159 K.13   The young Prince—fowls & sheep cut open & applied hot to cure him of convulsions—

2160 K.15   Mezzo dì./   *f3*

2161 K.16   Story of Sir W. Hamilton who had a new king's
Head painted over George 2ⁿᵈ—This saved by Noble/Jacobin in
Naples shot at it/Sailor layed it down—punished the fellow—took
it up again & carried it off—

f3ᵛ   2162 K.17   Italians desire to be English, confirmed to me by
the most intelligent/—

2163 K.18   Specimen of a grievance in a Sicilian Village/—
Women & men with buckets & Pails, near a mile for water/the
Proprietor lived at Palermo, and was too poor & extravagant to
repair the Aqueduct, that a few years ago had brought the water
to the Village.
—20 per cent on Corn exported!—O wise S. Government!

f4   2164 K.19   The eye cannot behold the Sun   ἡλιοειδης ~~μη~~
~~γινομενος~~ μη γινομενος, nor the Soul God, θεοειδης μη γινομενη.
νοερᾳ επαφῇ—θειοτερον τι πασης αποδειξεως.
—The Light shines *about*, not *into* them.

2165 K.20   Ælian observes of the Stork that if the Night-owl
chance to sit upon her eggs, they become ~~up~~ υπηνεμια/and all
after-incubation rendered vain.

2166 K.21   Like the Gossamer Spider, we may float upon air
and seem to fly in mid heaven, but we have spun the slender
Thread out of our ~~fane~~ own fancies, & it is always fastened to something below.—

f4ᵛ   2167 K.22   κεντρον κεντρῳ συναψας—
an infant-christ formed in our Souls.

η δε δεισιδαιμονια τῃ αθεοτητι και γενεσθαι παρεσχεν
αρχην, και γενομενη διδωσιν απολογειαν, ουκ αληθῇ μεν ουδε
καλην, προφασεως δε τινος ουκ αμοιραν ουσαν.—Plutarch.

εις εαυτον επιστρεφων εις αρχην επιστρεφει.—

2168 K.23   ⟨Horses eat Barley, in Sicily not oats.⟩

f11ᵛ   2169 1.13   Childish minds alone, I am more than ever convinced, can attach themselves to (so called) antiquities.

2170 1.14   Aug. 19—Wed Thursday—Etna/
chiefly olives—then the Cactus vines—fig trees—about 3 miles
from Catania sweet view of woods & the Sea looked down on/
sweet gardens in little hollows on one side/high wild banks on
the other, rich odor filled the road from a file of asses browzing
on aromatics—a second still more lovely view 7 miles from Catania, before us the two breast shaped Mountains, M. Ross, bound-   f12
ing the view—within these a steeple in a direct line before us, &
woods & woody Hills behind us steps of woods, a steeple in the
distance in the line of the Road, in the same manner as the other/
& the Sea—we now came to the Smithery, a wearisome road indeed
but I took it leisurely, & came in to the Monastery cool/O what a
lovely place/Birches or Aspens; for it seemed Birch trunks with
Aspen Leaves—. & Pine trees before the white seeming large Farm-
house behind & around vineyards & woody hills & vine clad hills,   f12ᵛ
the vines growing in the powdered Lava, a marvel for it exactly
resembles the Dross-dust before a Forge Door/no particle of vegetable mould to be seen/I ascended the Hill, the ground scorching
my feet, & joyously entered the wood on the Top, composed chiefly
of Birches & Oaks.

2171 1.15   The objects seen from the wood are, 1. Vine Hill.
2. level fields of vines/. 3. the Monastery with its six pines & its
shivering Birches. 4. a small Vine Hill and on its summit a white
Chinese Summer House. 5. the desolate Lava from this distance
purple with a—smoke-white *Bloom* upon it. 6. green Hills & level
fields, all the cultivated green plain to the eye as far as the Sea/—
This the strait line/to my right 1. scattered Trees on the bare-
lava ascent of M. Ross—2. the Mont Ross, its cone & the inter-   f13
jacent Crater that formed them/of the color of the rich dark brown
Heath hills of the North/3. A strip of bare Lava as before/4.
Cult. plain with River, & one large Farm-house-looking Building
—& further to the right and the furthermost part of it under the
first Cone of M. Ross a green Hill with an elliptical Base; & a
crater at the Top of the same shape, with trees & verdure on it/
5. Cultivated plain bounded by yellow Hills/—To my left Hills
& Bottoms, of all Heights & Depths, all green & cultivated

bounded by a higher range of Hills which at my present Height cuts off the Sea, all but in the corner where are Temples & a Town, & the Sea./If there were a visible River or Lake, it would be a sweet Prospect like 1000 in England—

ƒ13ᵛ　2172 1.16　　　The golden Bracelets & Necklaces of the Chesnut Tree lying on its bare roots or interjacent connectives of trees growing round a Hollow Round—as if a huge Tree had been cut down/or on the green Fern, under which suspended by a single Thread of a Spider's web the dry yellow Leaf swings in the Breeze—

N.B.

The yellow high Hill was the low flat Sea beach lifted up by its color—& the clouds floating off like streamers. The Sand running into the Sea/& the Sea, that I could not see for the Hill was there & I thought it the Sky/and vice versa the Sun on Etna rose behind the Calabria out of the midst of the Sea, not the [. . . .] for the clouds lay [. . .] & were deep crimson, [. . . .], rather like skies ƒ14　colored with yellow a sort of Dandelion with [. . .] same seed tuft—in deep [. . .] the bare Lava, quite [. . .] in its stalk with light—2. *Prickly* pea green moss &c, & Pansy or little Celandine with Moss, its Socius

2173 1.17　　　What an image for the many forked spitefully-against-many-meaner-enemies-moving Tongue of a Dragon is not the first flame of a stick fire kindled in the excess of of wind—as against the Door of this Casina/August 20ᵗʰ/Etna/

2174 1.19　　　My good natured Guide came about ½ past 5 with wine, fruit &c—make a fire—With a stick *spitted* some pieces of ƒ14ᵛ　Heart or Liver—put two great stones, and on this unrevolving spit of natural wood set them to roast/Mem!—The Brother and 4 sisters—the eldest had been a *beautiful*, the youngest was—what a neck!—Voices shrill but melodious especially the *21 years* old wheedler & talker who could not reconcile to herself that I did not understand her/yet how short a time a man living so would understand a language/in 3 hours how much more I learnt here first hand, and they were women—

I ha~~d~~ve not eat flesh for a long time but I will try to eat of   *f15*
this/—After the Liver had been roasted some while he took up the
Spit, gashed the Liver, & then covered with a flap-skin/.

2175 1.20   *On Saturday, August 25*—re-ascended a Casina 4
full strides broad, & 11 long, with a door, but windowless, chim-
ney-less, a wooden pillar full of names & smoke-brown in the center
with a stone on the western side, & a huge heap of white wood
ashes, that seem to ever accumulate.

1 °clock Sunday
Yet the Sound of wind in the Trees pleasant to me & English/
moonshine   Trees, Moonshine & islands of Shadow//N.B.
Greenough

2176 1.24
            Quisquis hoc templum Hospes inquirat   *f18*
                Paulisper in limine consiste
            Locique sanctitatem venerare
            Temporis vicissitudine non extinctam.
                Nigris hic sub Arenis
            Piorum Ascetarum conduntur cineres.
                Ne mireris.
            Sterile Sabulum Sacrorum ossium [?Ætæte/Ac tactu]
                Gratos ubique contaminavit in fructus
                P~~a~~lomis Onustos palmites Dedit.
            Et qui viventes in carne
            Virtutum fuderunt Odores
                In Pulveres resoluti
            Adhuc vernant in floribus
                Adhuc olent in rosis.
            Ædem hanc ipsorum vita
            Ipsorum miraculis celeber
                Multipes inspice redivivam.   *f18ᵛ*
            Ætnei montis impetu jacuit
                Pulchrior e ruinâ surrexit
            Iterum terræ motu collis.

Nobiliorem induit venustatem
Eo adversæ Fortunæ Condumento
Ut varios tot inter casus
Pugnasse diceres et triumphasse Pietatem/
Fœlix ergo progredere
Divique tutelaris effigiem
Religioso cultu devoto prosequens
Prospera omnia ab ejus Patrociniis
[?Securus] tibi *polliceas.*

ƒ48 2177 15.65   12 ''clock Moonlight, 3 Horsemen loaded with
Bee Hives—Cava Secca [. . .] 24. Tombs of the [. . .] cut in the
Rock—view of Syracuse & the even slope of Etna—/wooded &
green the [?Slope] &c—[?Towns] on it [. . . .] [?right/night]
by its [?summit] [. . .] landing-place that [. . . . .] is of [?un-
known antiquity]

ƒ48ᵛ   Wine/Grapes/Heriots/
Village of Comi Gatania. *Every* door shaded with a Bower of
Vines on Casas/Fief of Alfeno/150 yards bridge/latter third one
Arch over a ravine 150 feet, with the Torrent at the Bottom/
wooded precipices—its banks, & some fassades wild Gate-Way with
two colossal Barbarous Images in nitches on each side/It is High-
Bridge to identity—

Rode on a ¼ of mile, wound down a road of huge pits, *dimples,*
& stairs of Limestone, and came to the view of the arch over the
Torrent. Wound down to the Torrent, the River leading our
ƒ49 Horses thro' such a steep narrow Gutter of solid Rock/O what a
place for Horses/on the Banks 2 High Stones on each side the
path, each ~~nearly~~ as large as Bowder Stone/in the Torrent Women
& Boys at least 50 washing, i.e. thumping & rubbing their cloathes
against the Stones in the Torrent. O this savage unforgettable
Scene! Huge Stones & huge Trees, & small & large Trees and
Stones & the HIGH HIGH great wall & all one long chamber!/& the
savage women of the Torrent, hairy *men*like legs—Oleander! Ivy!
Myrtle/and all the Pot herbs—lovely Lizards

The Paradise/the Gothic Arches. black with the [?Residue] of
that

The School of Archim. in Syr.—all for a sextant?—Is it any *f49ᵛ*
thing to eat?
Twisted Pillars from the old Olives—[. . .]
Meat sold—27ᵗʰ August Sunday, outside the Gates of Syracuse.
Wild Fig Tree a broad belt of spreading Branches round an ol-
ive, that grew out of the Top—
Brittleness of the Or. Trunks—in Half/

2178 15.66   Dr. Paolo Cesareo
Mon charmant, prenez garde—Mind what your Signior begs,
Ven you wash, don't scrub so harda/you may rub my shirt to rags.
While you make the water hotter, un solo I compose. Put in the
Pot the nice Sheep's Trotter, and de leetle Pettitoes. De Petty
Toes are leetle feet. The leetle feet not big great feet Belong to
this grunting Hog. The petty feet of the leetle Pig
    Come, Sara dear, carissima anima mia,   *f50*
    Go, boil the Kettle, make me some green Tea a.

2179 15.67   Black Faldetto = English Servant in mourning
caught in the Rain.—
    Every third ~~Door~~ Hour women lousing each other on ⟨on⟩ the
steps of the Shop-door.—viz—the Mistress &c of the Shop.
    In one street I met 5 or 6 Clergymen/and on no particular Day/
They are more numerous than even the Beggars./Immense influence of anticipation on language—MY difficulty in learning a
new language/I am not anticipated as well as &c—Just outside of
the Gates a bad-meat stall—10 yards from the Sea. 100 yards on
pass between 2 water troughs, that to the Right the engineers'!
Etna in the distance before me to my Right—white smoke over
white snow/turn, the harbor still to my left & [. . . . .] before *f50ᵛ*
me in one long line Hills, rampart-like, stony with white wrinkle
facing & grey-green with Olive Trees—to my left another straight
line of Hills lower almost nothing but white stone.

    Difficulty of learning Italian in Sicily—1. from the utter want of
distinct Ideas & of Judgment which makes a muddy *stream* of
sound, 2. bad It.—

Pass a bridge ¼ of a mile from the Gate with a seat and sort of Pillar on one side of it/a stream of clear water a yard wide runs under it, having run thro' that poisonous Marsh/O how easily it might be drained!

100 yards on & I began to see that I had passed the road so had about 300 yards to go back again.

2180 K.40

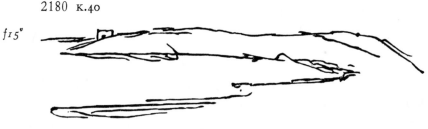

G. F. Leckie
Aug. 29 1804

2181 K.41

Br.
Harbour

2182 K.42   English & Italian word for word the same in the following sentence. Tutti questi eccessi mi facevano tener la salute loro per disperata. Ma voi m'insegnate ch'e' † la rendono sicura. † i.e. these very excesses.—

2183 K.43   in Aci./Consul. great House.—Sat some[?mom] with L.—Then both go to his [. . .]—spend half an hour/When L. arrived at Messina received a Letter, begging ⟨his⟩ Pistols, because he had *a violent passion* for them—

2184 K.44   ⟨Ne⟩ Sig' Lorenzo Albani
                   Tos. Antonio Manna
                   Cecilia Bertozzi
                   Tenor/Francesco Cariche
                   Carlotto Sommeri
                   ⟨Sig'⟩ Ignazio Moscuzzo

2185 K.45   Mi parea che sola sola f_{17}
                   del Guglielmi
                   Il mio destino ingrato
                   del Nasolini.
                   Questa' aura che spira
                       del Guglielmi
                   Parla, casella mia,
                   del Guglielmi.

2186 K.46   I gave 12 guineas to M' Noble.— f_{19}^v

2187 K.47   Linnæus forged Elegy on drowned Artedi "Thus
died by water this great Ichthyologist who had ever delighted in
that Element"/

2188 K.48   M' Dennison & the Pistol—2nd time it went off.
                   Leek

2189 K.49   The white poppy seed, sown in the months of f_{20}
October & November, the plants weeded to 8 inches distance, &
well watered till the plants are about ½ a foot high, when a com-
post of dung, without Earth, & Ashes is spread over the beds—a
little before the flowers appear, again watered profusely, till the
capsules are half grown, at which time the opium is collected/
     50£ tho' only one grain grew in one square foot of earth/; but
if we consider that one poppy produces from three or four to ten
heads, that from each head from six to 20 Incisions may be made
—& and that [from] many of Incisions I have taken away 2 or 3
grains.//

2190 K.50

f21

f103ᵛ　2191　21.456　　Syracuse, Sept. 1804—Tuesday Afternoon, 6°clock
long on my bed within the musquitoe curtain, which was not drawn
by its rings all round the iron rods of the bed, but was within half
a foot or a foot of my face/the curtain muslin with french grass-like
Streaks, a little less than ½ an inch broad/divided into three equal
parts, the middle red, the 2 outward green/—As I lay, if I directed
my eyes on these streaks, & *looked at* them, I saw them as they
were/but when I merely lay, & suffered myself to see them only
f104　because they were there, one streak straight before my eye appeared at first to be just by the iron ⟨perpend. rod⟩ at the foot of
the bed; but in a moment or so the iron rods were all within the
streaks—& by opening voluntarily the pupil of my eyes a little, &
rather thinking of them than looking at them, or to me still more
accurately, looking at the walls of the room, & merely letting the
streaks impress my eye, all these streaks fourfold or more as large
as they really were, and much, *very* much more vivid, lay on the
wall up to the very ceiling, bending ~~up to the very~~ with the wall
& ceiling (~~an~~ which formed an arch); and the iron rods all distinctly within these/—nay, by rapid glances I could produce a
momentary sensation of the real streaks in their natural size &
faintness, & real situation within the rods that were within these
long & vivid Streaks on the wall of the room—The wall was ~~about~~
just 10 feet from my eyes—a small window right opposite to my
eyes, the curtain about 9 feet or 9¼ from it/—

2192　21.457　　Thursday Night at the opera, Sept. 27, 1804 in
reflecting on the cause of the *"meeting* soul" in music, the seeming
recognizance, &c &c, the whole explication of *memory* as in the na-

ture of *accord* struck upon me/accord produces a phantom of memory, because memory is always an accord.

2193 21.8   Syracuse, Saturday, Oct. 5. 1804. ⟨A Serious mem-   *f2ᵛ*
orandum!⟩
     Mem. In company, indeed with all except a very chosen few,
never dissent from any one as to the *merits* of another/especially,
in your own supposed department/but content yourself with prais-
ing in your turn the really good. Praises of the unworthy are felt
by a good man & man of genius as detractions from the worthy, as
robberies/as so the *flashy* moderns seem to *rob* the ancients of the
honors due to them/& Bacon & Harrington are *not* read because
Hume & Condilliac *are*. This ~~may be~~ is an evil; but oppose it, if
at all, in books in which you can evolve the whole of your reasons
& feelings ⟨not in conversation, where it will be inevitably attributed to Envy⟩. Besides, they who praise the unworthy, must be the
injudicious; and the eulogies of ~~men~~ critics without taste or judgment are the natural pay of authors without feeling or genius—&
why rob *them*. ⟨Sint unicuique sua præmia.⟩ Coleridge! Coleridge!
will you never learn to appropriate your conversation to your company? Is it not desecration, indelicacy, a proof of great weakness &
even vanity to talk to &c &c, as if you [talk]ed [with Words]worth
& Sir G. Beau[mont?]

2194 21.458   Philosophy to a few, Religion with many, is the   *f104*
Friend of Poetry; as producing the 2 conditions of pleasure from
poetry, namely, tranquillity & the attachment of the affections to
generalizations. God, Soul, Heaven, the Gospel, miracles, &c are
themselves a sort of *poetry*, compared with Lombard Sᵗ & 'Change   *f104ᵛ*
Alley speculations. *Oct. 5. 1804.*

2195 15.68   Timoleon's, Oct. 10, 1804   Wednesday Noon.   *f51*
     The Gazæ a Tree at Tremiglia (Rocks with Cactus) pendulous
Branches, seed pods black at the same time with the orange yellow
flower, a little daisy-like tuft of silky hair/
     Above Tremillia Neapolis, & the ruins of its walls—Timoleon's
Villa supposed to be in the field *above* the present House/from

which you ascend = to 50 stairs.—Evident marks of Building on
the Spot. Grand View of the Harbour & the Sea over that Tongue
of Land which forms the anti-ortygian Embracing Arm of the
f51ᵛ   Harbour name/the Point of Plemmyrium where Alcibiades &
Nicias landed/([?tho some deny/the same day] that Neptune
died down there) & that round Bason. Came to the rushing of sub-
terraneous water/N.B. the Cipallaccid = a sort of poisonous Lily/
I left the aqueduct & crossed ascendingly to some ~~Hous~~ ruined
Cottages, beside a Delve with strait limestone *Walls* of Rock, on
which there played the shadows of the Fig-Tree, & the Olive/on
the Rocks surmounting this. I was in part of Epipolis, & a glorious
View indeed. Before me a track of stony common & fields, Acra-
dina, Ortygia, the open sea & the Ships, & the circular Harbour its
embracer, & the Sea over that/

f52   To my right that large extent of plain, green, rich, finely
wooded, the fields so divided & enclosed, that you as it were *knew*
at the first view that they are all hedged & inclosed, & yet no
Hedges or inclosures *obtrude* themselves, an effect of the vast number of Trees, all of the same sort/on my left stony fields, two Har-
bours, Manghisi, & its sand Isle, & *Augusta* and Etna whose smokes
mingle with the Clouds, even ~~while~~ as they rise from the Crater/
behind me that long range of green & stony Hills—where Cava
Sechia is—& another stony rampart, another—& more to the Left
—there are yet two other points, close to these on which the Castle
stands. A furlong off [. . . .] & thither I go—

f52ᵛ   On this point running along in ⋀ a continued Ass's back the
huge Stones that formed the Castle & its walls all oergrown with
bushes of a plant that is a sort of *spurge*, with corrosive milk/how
very *rich* the look-down on the Right is!—& on the left there is a
narrow long slip of fertility & cultivation, running like a River
thro' the Arabia Petræa on each side/Still on I walk the Lizard
gliding darts across the road & immerges himself under a stone/or
the grasshopper leaps & tumbles awkwardly strait before me/

f104ᵛ   2196 21.459   Oct. 11. 1804. Syracuse. Leckie's. Midnight—O
young man (*here the voice of Conscience whispered to me, con-*

cerning myself & my intent of visiting la P. D. tomorrow) O young man, who hast seen, felt, & known the Truth, to whom reality is a phantom, & virtue & mind the sole actual & permanent Being, do not degrade the Truth in thee by disputing—avoid it! do not by any persuasion be tempted to it—surely not, by vanity or the weakness of the pleasure of communicating thy Thoughts & awaking Sympathy, but do not even by the *always mixed* hope of producing *conviction*—This is not the mode—this is not the Time —not the Place—& by modestly and most truly saying, your arguments are all consequent, if the foundation be admitted—I do not admit the foundation/but this will be a business for moments of Thought, for the Sabbath days of your Existence, then perhaps a Voice from within will say to you better because more adapted to *you*, all I can say, but if I felt this to be that Day or that moment,   *f105* a sacred Sympathy would at once compel & inspire me to the Task of uttering the very Truth/Till then, I am right willing to bear the character of a mystic, a visionary, a self-important Juggler who nods his Head & says, *I could, if I would;* but I cannot, I *may* not bear the reproach of profaning the Truth, which is *my Life,* in moments when all passions heterogeneous to it are eclipsing ⟨it to the exclusion of⟩ its dimmest ray—I might lose my Tranquillity, & in acquiring the *passion* of proselytism lose the *sense* of conviction/ I might become *positive!* Now I am *certain!* I might have the *Heat* of Fermentation, now I have the warmth of Life!

2197 15.69   Oct. 12—the filth all along the Battlements & the   *f52ᵛ* Entrance to the Theatre/

2198 15.70   That beautiful green Lizard with scarlet Tail, yet   *f53* with a venomous Look—of which the E. Indians say—It never has bitten—it never does bite; but if it should bite, it would kill a village/—
They believe that a Cirra Manilla, if wounded it escape with life, will follow to his Death him who wounds, & league all other Snakes with him/so that the man must die by a snake. Thus a Moral or prudent allegory sinking into a reality of N. History/

2199 15.71   An assassin fetches water at Leckie's—

2200 15.72   15000 French; the Generals drew upon the King
of Naples for 18000 & pocketed the money.

2201 15.73   The opera of the Villane cantatrici—the Heroe
had fled from his Home for a Murder he had committed/no remorse is expressed by him, no Horror by others. It is a misfortune.

ƒ53ᵛ 2202 15.74   The Column in the middle of the Forum with the
Basis of ~~three others~~ 4 —The 3 first, the middle of which is the
standing Column, occupies from the ⟨beginning of the⟩ square of
the 1ˢᵗ part to the end of the Sq. of the Third 8 strides only—from
the end of the Square, in which the 3ʳᵈ Base stands, to the end of
the 5ᵗʰ is 12 Strides/the last glimmers thro' Brambles & the Lizard
suns itself on its sides—Two roads, I took that to the Right, walking beside a green Hedge of ⟨young⟩ Locust Trees/50 yards on
what a scene opens out upon me!—A Hill, an ascent from R, all
white, with many yawning caverns—black in the whiteness—the
perpend. Rocks steppy—it looked like a a huge place of Sepulchres,
ƒ54 the Sep. made of bones which the Sun & wind had bleached/Rooks
in flight were cawing over it/but behind me was the beautiful blue
Sea, seen on my right in a broad wedge, and as I turn my back a
little lake of it and a large boat with sails gliding across—it is now
gone!—forms the end of the vista made by the narrow well-
wooded Road—/pass by a Road with these cavern sepulchres on
each side of me—describe them—Women hanging out clothes to
dry upon them/the impurity of touching the Dead among the an-
cients/Pro & Con ~~to~~ between them & tis in this respect/Schiller's
Gotter. On the Top you have Etna before you and turning you see
ƒ54ᵛ beneath the Sea, then Harbour, Syracuse & the green Gardens
treed with high Trees here & there trimmed up to the Top like
our Elms in most parts of England—As I looked on Syracuse that
seemed rather like a monstrous Raft with Huts & Houses of
wooded painted to resemble Brick and Stone, which had just
touched the Shore & the Colony not yet disembarked than like a
part of the Land/That too will be swallowed up I said, & what
care I?—I now walked on by this—sweet Country Houses, & descended to the Bay of Manghisi—went into the largest of the Caverns which look toward the Sea above the road on the cape/—the

part admitting standing was 13 Strides by 8/a sort of window-like *f55*
opening above the entrance or mouth to its left a little as you enter.
 The Enchanter's Nightshade with white
blossom sent the light thro' its thin, green
leaves on the floor of the Cavern/I left the
Caverns, & turning a rock stood gazing at
the Sea/Etna and its floating mantle of
white smoke/in no respect distinguishable
from a white summer Cloud & ⟨seemed⟩ to
shut out the distance rather than to form it.
The fertility at its feet was dimly visible/
at the brink of the Bay the City of Augusta, then Bay, which is not
three stone throws from my feet/all that is distinctly visible is dreary
and stony—& to my right the blue cloud on the Horizon is Cala- *f55ᵛ*
bria/but stopping a few yards for wind I see the pretty village of
Belvedere in its olive Trees & thither I will go—but another Cavern larger than the former tempted me/it was that which seen
from my Lectiga in my journey from Cat delighted me/—it was
tressed by the long dependant Locks of the Caper, the Fig Tree,
one of which of considerable grew down almost from the center
stone of the Cavern Roof like a reflection in Water—& long dependant Tufts of the wild Time with ceaseless Hum of Bees—
From this Cavern you literally see only blank Ocean & mere Sky
—/This village of Targita & its olives & square/but this place of *f56*
Stones that I had been labouring over, without joke = to the Valley of Stones was a field, & a ploughed field too! and a Man with
2 oxen was ploughing it/it must have given a Somersetshire
Farmer strange feelings! Yet many say, that the Harvest is equally
great from a field thus strangely peppered as from a garden-clear
Field.—But the same idleness, which made the Forefather tell the
Lie to excuse itself, makes the Posterity believe it & act upon it/—
If they thought otherwise, they would not act otherwise.

Stone walls falling abroad into the roads—indeed every where a
subject well worthy of some remarks, of the hard labor & enormous
Prodigality of Lazy & penny-wise Barbarians— *f56ᵛ*

2203 15.75   The House-steads &c in the water at low tide in
the Porto minore—

2204 15.76   The Inquisition wanted to examine the Drugs in Sicily & Malta/INFAMOUS! Notice again & again the Error of supposing that a Government like an Individual can only do one thing at a time well.

2205 15.77   I do not believe that men ed. in the present system tell lies of self-interest more than our Calvinist Forefathers/ but Inaccuracies—careless observation followed by careless narration of Facts, recklessness with regard to Truth where the immediate Immorality or rather Dishonorableness does not stare them in the Face/this & utter want of Logic, produce that effect that "no thing I cannot, no person I can believe."

f57   2206 15.78   It was the village of Targea that I saw, with the olives, Tower, & *Stone* plough'd field—
Everything in R. Catholic Countries brought clearly, & hourly, & by efficient Faith to the calculation of mere Pain & Pleasure—so that thinking of a murder they think instantly of Hell—Purgatory and hope the poor man will *escape*/in short our Vices incline us to a bedimming of our future views; but in the vulgar they are made to ~~give~~ throw all their *glare* of passion upon it/& the Fiend of Hell is reconciled with the love of Vice/For of Heaven they *never* think/the best must go into *Purgatory*

f57ᵛ   2207 15.79   Saturday Morning—8 to 9 & a most tremendous Rain storm with Lightning & Thunder, one Clap of which burst directly over ~~our~~, Mr. L's House with the noise of an explosion of artillery—set the Dogs barking.
Vivid flashes in mid day, the terror without the beauty.—A ghost by day time/Geraldine.

f105   2208 21.460   Oct. 13. 1804. Saturday. Syracuse.—Each man having a spark (to use the old metaphor) of the Divinity, yet a whole fire-grate of Humanity (each therefore will legislate for the whole, spite of the De gustibus non est disputandum, even in trifles, till corrected by experiences—and at least in this endless struggle of presumption, really occasioned by the ever-working Spark of

the Universal, and the disappointments & baffled attempts of each, *f105ᵛ*
all are disposed to the jus extrinsecum fortioris ⟨(Spinoza)⟩ , &
recognize that reason as the highest, which may not be understood
as the best, but of which the Concrete Possession is felt to be the
strongest—Then comes Society, Habit, Education, Sleepiness, misery, intrigue, oppression—Then *Revolution*/& the circle begins
anew/:—Each man will universalize his notions, & yet each is variously finite. To *reconcile* therefore is truly the work of the Inspired! This is the true *Atonement*—/i.e. to reconcile the struggles
of the infinitely various Finite with the *Permanent*.

2209 21.461

⌐⟨The Soother of absence⟩⌐

⌐. . . . .⌐

⌐. . . . . in the Breeze,⌐
And let me float & think on ⌐?Asra/thee⌐
⌐And . . . . .⌐

⌐. . . . .⌐

⌐. . . . .⌐Body

⌐. . . . . myself in suffering⌐

⌐. . . . . . applied spiritually⌐

2210 21.462   Do not be too much discouraged if any virtue
should be mixed in your consciousness with affectation & imperfect
sincerity, & some vanity—*disapprove* of this—& continue the practice, & the good feeling even thus mixed—*it will gradually purify*   *f106*
itself. Probatum est. Disapprove! be *ashamed* of the Thought of
its always *continuing thus;* but do not too harshly quarrel with
your present Self: for all Virtue subsists in and by Pleasure. S.T.C.
Sunday ⟨Evening,⟩ Oct. 14. 1804.—///a great deal of this moreover is constitutional. That constitution which predisposes to certain Virtues, the Δωρον θεων has this Τεμενος Νημεσεως in it
—it is the *dregs* of Sympathy & while we are *weak* & *dependent* on
each other, & each is forced to think often for himself, Sympathy
will have its Dregs—& the Strongest, who have least of these, have
the Dregs of other Virtues to strain off.—~~to~~ 5/minutes of ten.

2211 21.463   To defend the *Opera* = all the objections against
equally applicable to Tragedy & Comedy without music, & all proceed on the false principle, that Theatrical representations are *Copies* of nature whereas they are imitations.

f57ᵛ 2212 15.80   Monday Morning, ½ 9, Oct. 15, 1804 set off in a
Boat with Dennison for the Pysma/The Shore to which we are approaching, before us, ⟨stretching⟩ & curving, the left & right, but
especially the left, green, woody, pastoral—the pillars of the Temple of Jupiter in the distance straight before us. The P. at its
mouth & for one furlong up ⟨to the 1 arched Bridge⟩ about 50
yards broad—discolored by the rain/otherwise it would have been
f58 translucent. The Stream narrowing between Mardges, we are now
obliquely bent over by the lofty Syrinx/The view up
the river—is wild, *Pan* like & water rushing into the River from a
small stream hidden in reeds, the reeds now meeting in sharp
arch, noise, shadows, and the King's fisher, most divine beauty.
Multitude of small black Dragon-flies—*libellulæ*.

   The Syrinxes leave the right side for a stone throw, but soon
recommence/obliged to desist from the stupidity & incompetency
of the Boat-boys—Went on shore to cross to Tremilla/observed
what I concluded to be the green bulb or tumour of a rush/Yet
why did I look again?—The understanding of the obscure feelings.
It was a green frog sticking to the Stalk like an old Bigot at his
prayers—His Hands up, & his under jaw membrane trembling
half bladder-motion, half life—What [?quantity]—how striking
yet [?bugbear]

f58ᵛ 2213 15.81   The monopolies of Syracuse/no market town in
Sicily. Mr Leckie killed an Ox last week, he was obliged to send
to a ~~particular~~ the public ⟨Shambles where, after the animal⟩ ~~is
called~~, there is the public Tagliator   [*] to cut it open/this
man had as his right the Heart, Liver ⟨Head, Tongue & all the⟩
Entrails &c & ~~20 Taris besides~~ ⟨and for this he is to give the⟩ Pro-

[* Coleridge's blank. K. C.]

prietor an Ounce/—who must however himself pay the Governor 35 Taris—But if Bread were to be made & sold at Tremiglia, the Officers of the Università would tear it out of the Hands of the Poor.

2214 15.82   The Lawsuit between the Marquis of Sortino & the Duke of Floridea & of the 18 *Perituri* [*paratori*], in which the water is carried off & supposed to be done by Quicksilver.

2215 15.83   48 Villages dependent on Messina all of whom   *f59* *must* go to Messina for bread proverbially execrable often a whole day without bread when the Floods are out, from the Poverty which prevents them laying in a [?store/stove] and the quality of the Bread which bad when new is scarcely eatable when kept.

2216 15.84   It may seem strange but it is fact, that the only big-bellied Men I have seen in Syracuse are Priests/Of them many most majestic Peripheries of Paunch.

2217 15.85(a)   Mem. Neptune buried at Tremiglia under a large Bay Tree, with vines wreathing about it/Sleep, Shade, & Quiet!— Oct. 16, 1804
     15.85(b)   Lucern choked by the Lupa that carpets the ground like ⟨horse-hair⟩ a beautiful yellow-yellow-green moss.

2218 21.464   Oct. 17. 1804. When you are harassed, disquieted,   *f106* & have little dreams of resentment & mock triumphs, in consequence of the clearest perceptions of unkind treatment, and strange misconceptions & illogicalities palpably from bad passions in any person connected with you, suspect a sympathy in yourself with some of these bad Passions—vanity for instance!—Tho' a sense of wounded justice is possible, nay, probably forms a part of your uneasy feelings, yet this of itself would yield at the first moment of reflection to Pity for the wretched state of a man, too untranquil & perpetually selfish to love any thing for itself, or without some end of vanity or ambition/—who detests all serious thought of   *f106ᵛ* permanent Things, abhors all poetry—tosses about in the impo-

tence of desires disproportionate to his powers—and whose whole
History of his whole Life is a tale of disappointment in circumstances where the Hope and ~~Expectation~~ Pretension was always
unwise, often presumptuous and insolent.—Surely an intuition of
this restless & no-end-having mood of mind would at once fill a
~~mind~~ heart having no sympathy with these passions with tender
melancholy, virtuously mixed with grateful unpharisaic Self-com-
placency. But a patient *almost,* but not quite recovered from madness, yet on its confines, finds in the notions of madness that which
irritates, & haunts & makes unhappy.

f59ᵛ   2219 15.86   Wolf remarks well in the Præfatio to his Theolo-
gia naturalis, that the a priori demonstration of Deity is in reality
a posteriori from the "rectius dici poterat exis. Dei hoc facto ex
contemplatione animæ demonstrari"/—Then after a bitter inquisi-
torque abuse & atheizing of Spinosa he says—ex notione igitur entis
perfectissimi existentiam veri numinis idem est ac eandem ex contemplatione animæ nostræ derivare, sic demonstratio non minus a
posteriori procedit, quam si ex contemplatione mundi hujus aspec-
tabilis derivatur. Vidit hoc pro acumine suo singulari, quod quo
quis acutior, eo magis suspicere tenetur, D. Thomas unde asseruit
f60   existentiam Dei a priori demonstrari non posse.

2220 15.87   Price's Annuities for Mr Leckie/

2221 15.88   Sicilian HORRIBLE Jangle of Bells contrasted
with their Love of & Taste for sweet Music.

2222 15.89   An excellent remark of Metastasio in his second
letter to M. de Chastellux/Ed in fatti non si può parlare ad un
pubblico e farsi chiaramente intendere, senza elevare, distendere,
e sostenere la voce notabilmente più di quello che suol farsi nel
parlare ordinario. Coteste nuove notabili alterazioni di voce esigono
un'arte, che ne regoli le nuove proporzioni; altrimenti produrreb-
bero suoni mal modulati, disaggradevoli, e spesse volte ridicoli.
Quest'arte appunto altro non è, che la musica, così a chi ragiona in
publico necessaria, che, quando manca agli attori quella degli

artisti destinati a comporla, sono obbligati a comporne una da se medesimi, sotto il nome di declamazione/—Apply this to London since the enormous size of *Th.*—observe how musical pieces were increased & became favorites—

2223 22.16   There is in Form (says Harrington) something *f17ᵛ* which is not elementary but divine. The contemplation of Form is astonishing to Man and has a kind of Trouble or Impulse accompanying it, which exalts his Soul to God. As the *Form* of a Man is the Image of God, so the Form of a Just Government is the Image of Man.—

And it may be added, the Image of those men *to* whom it is a *just* government.—By elementary Harrington means the sum of the component monads or ultimate particles—the very existence of which, except as entia rationis, I doubt.

Formation of Government is the Infusion of the Soul and Faculties of a Man into *a body of Men:* the formation of a good Government the infusion of the soul & faculties of a wise dispassionate Man—but it must be *infused*—not a mere *affusion/*which may produce a dewy lustre for a while, & still more perhaps refresh & prepare the people for a real assimilation—therefore Harrington adds wisely, that not the refin'd Spirit of a Man or of some, but only *f18* the refin'd Spirit of a nation can be a good form of Government—

A Parliament of Poets would never have written the Paradise lost—

Among the prophetic passages of Harrington's Works (Oceana, p.203. Toland's Addition) annumerate, Aph. 10. of Cap. vi. of a System of politics (p.506. Tol. Ed.)
If it be said that in France there is Liberty of Conscience in part, it is also plain that while the Hierarchy is standing this Liberty is falling, and that if, on the contrary, it comes to pull down the Hierarchy, it pulls down that Monarchy also: wherefore the Monarchy or Hierarchy, will be beforehand with it, if they see their true Interest.—N.B. Lewis the XIVᵗʰ took the Hint with a vengeance in the famous Edict of Nantz.

ƒ18ᵛ   A man may devote himself to Death or destruction to save a Nation; but no nation will devote itself to Death or Destruction to save mankind. Macchiavel is decried for saying, that "no Consideration is to be had of what is just or unjust, of what is merciful or cruel, of what is honorable or ignominious, in case it be to save a state or to preserve Liberty": which as to the manner of expression may perhaps be crudely spoken. But to imagine that a Nation will devote itself to Death or Destruction any more—upon Faith, given or an Engagement thereto tending, than if there had been no engagement made or faith given, were not Piety but Folly.—

The wisdom of late years seems rather to be cleverness—the cleverness of an embarrassed Spendthrift—tricks & shift off difficulties & danger, when close upon us—to keep them off at arms length, not in solid & grounded Causes to keep them truly *off*. We have expedient-mongers rather than Statesmen—fire-engines against Fires, boats against Inundations, no Houses built fire-proof, nor Dams to prevent Inundation. H. & S.T.C.

ƒ19   The deep waters wherein that Leviathan the minister of State, takes his Pastime. H.

Nemo unquam imperium flagitio acquis. bonis artibus exercuit, a wise rule to which even the reign of Augustus will be deemed a suspicious Exception, if only we recollect the deplorable & despicable state of minds, manners, & estates which were bared to view by the accession & reign of his immediate Successor.—S.T.C.

If the House stands awry, your Props do not stand upright. H. The People cannot see but they can feel.

Where the Spirit of the People is impatient of a Gov. by arms & desirous of a Gov. by Laws, there the Sp. of a Peop. is not unfit to be trusted with Liberty.

Man may rather be defined a religious than a rational Creature: in regard that in other Creatures there may be something of Reason, but there is nothing of Religion. On whom rests the onus probandi??

Caput Reipublicæ est nosse rempublicam. Cicero

Aut reges non abigendi fuerant, aut plebi re non verbo danda Libertas.—

2224　22.15　　　　New Metre—†.　　　　　　　　*f12*

> Und schweigend umarmt ihn der treue Freund,
> Und liefert sich aus dem Tyrannen,
> Der andere zieht [*ziehet*] von dannen.
> Und ehe das dritte Morgenroth scheint,
> Hat der [*er*] schnell mit dem Gatten die Schwester vereint,
> Eilt heim mit sorgender Seele
> Damit er die Frist nicht verfehle.

† (preceding leaf)　　　　　　　　　　　　　　　　*f13*

1. Amphibrach tetrameter
   hypercatalectic　　　　　∪ - ∪ / ∪ - ∪ / ∪ - ∪ / - †
2. Ditto trimeter acatalectic　∪ - ∪ / ∪ - ∪ / ∪ - ∪ / ※
3. Ionic a majore + Ditrochæus　- - ∪ ∪ / - ∪ - ∪ / ※
4. Two Amphib. + Epitritus　　∪ - ∪ / ∪ - ∪ / - ∪ - - †
   secundus
5. Anapæst tetramiacatalectic　∪ ∪ - / ∪ ∪ - / ∪ ∪ - / ∪ ∪ - †
6. Antibacchius + Dactyl +　　- - ∪ / - ∪ ∪ / - ∪ ††
   Trochee
7. Amphib. trimeter acatalectic　∪ - ∪ / ∪ - ∪ / ∪ - ∪ ††

An admirable metre.—For the Epitrit. secundus in the fourth line you may use a choriambus: i.e. either - ∪ - -, or - ∪ ∪ -, as may be more convenient.

> *Mute nature*—2.　　　　　　　*f12ᵛ*
> Und theilend meine Flammen Triebe
> Die Stumme eine Sprache fand, ⟨e⟩
> Mir wiedergab den Kuss der Liebe
> Und meines Herzens Klang verstand; ⟨e⟩
> Da lebte mir der Baum, die Rose,
> Mir sang der Quellen Silberfall;
> Es fühlte selbst das Seelenlose
> Von meines Lebens Wiederhall.—

⟨metre better 1 & 2nd Lines single, 3 & 4th double rhymes.⟩
the echo of my own Life—in inanimate Nature

3

- ᴗ ᴗ , - ᴗ ᴗ , - ᴗ ᴗ , - ᴗ
- ᴗ ᴗ , - ᴗ ᴗ , - ᴗ ᴗ , -
- ᴗ ᴗ , 　- ᴗ , - ᴗ ᴗ , - ᴗ
　- ᴗ , - ᴗ ᴗ , 　- ᴗ , - .
　- ᴗ , - ᴗ ᴗ , 　- ᴗ , - ᴗ ,
　- ᴗ , - ᴗ ᴗ , - ᴗ ᴗ , -
　　- ᴗ , - ᴗ ᴗ , 　- ᴗ , - ᴗ
- ᴗ ᴗ , 　- ᴗ , - ᴗ ᴗ , -

Windet zum kranze [*Kranze*] die goldenen Æhren
Flechtet auch blaue Cyanen hinein,
Freude soll jedes Auge verklären,
Denn die Königin ziehet ein—
Die Betsahmerin [*Bezähmerinn*] wilder Sitten,
Die den Menschen zum Menschen gesellt,
Und in friedliche feste Hütten
Wandelte das bewegliche Zelt.—

f13ᵛ　　　　　4　　　　　f15　　　　4
Dance, merrily, dance　　　　　　　-, - ᴗ ᴗ, -
Off, gloomy suspicion　　　　　　　-, - ᴗ ᴗ, - ᴗ,
Here be nothing but ~~happiness~~ amity　- ᴗ, - ᴗ ᴗ, - ᴗ ᴗ, -
Eyes looking askance　　　　　　　-, - ᴗ ᴗ, -
Tongues, courting contrition　　　　-, - ᴗ ᴗ, - ᴗ
Flee to, Ocean's extremity　　　　- ᴗ, - ᴗ ᴗ, - ᴗ ᴗ, -

⟨Where the subject admits a Stress on, and pause *after*, the first
monosyllable/but for other subjects for the first -, put an - ᴗ ./⟩

f14　　　　　　　[4a]
Reginam~~s~~ invitat gerendus nunc
Solenne parumper secundans
Eu! fletibus os inundans
Amatis innectunt languidum tunc
Vigilantem timore cruenta per hunc
Spirisque murmure rege
~~Formosus~~ Negatâ superbior lege.

In some part of the Soother of Absence introduce a passionate ad- *f15*
dress summo Poetæ, optimo maximo Amico, W.W.—to receive,
avow, support, sustain me, si quidem Asaharæ animum divine auda-
cem amor dedisset.—

5

Die Lerche sang, die Sonne schien,
Es färbte sich die Wiese grün,
Und braungeschwolle'ne Keime
Verschönten Büsch' und Bäume:
Da pfluct' [*pflückt'*] ich am bedornten See
Zum Strauss ihr, unter spätem Schnee,
Blau, roth, und weissen Güldenklee:
Das Magdlein [*Mägdlein*] nahm des Busens Zier,
Und nickte freundlich Dank dafür.

6

In diesem Wald, in diesen Gründen
Herrscht nichts, als Freyheit, Lust, und Ruh.
Hier sagen wir der Liebe zu,
Im dicksten Schatten uns zu finden:
Da find ich dich, ~~da findet~~ mich findest du.

7

Du Schmelz der bunten Wiesen,
Du neu begrünte Flur;
Sey stets von mir gepriesen,
Du Schmelz der bunten Wiesen!
Es schmückt dich und Cephisen
Der Lenz und die Natur!
Du Schmelz der bunten Wiesen!
Du neu begrünte Flur!—

8

f15ᵛ

Mein alter Freund, mein Schlaf, erscheine wieder!
  Wie wünsch' ich dich!
Du Sohn der Nacht, O breite dein Gefieder
  Auch über mich;
Verlass dafür den Wuchrer, ihn zu strafen,
  Den Trug ergetzt;

Hingegen lass den wachen Codrus schlafen,
Der immer reimt und immer ubersetzt [*übersetzt*].

9

Wilkommen [*Willkommen*], angenehme Nacht,
Verhüll in deine Schatten
Die Freuden, die sich gatten,
Und blende, blende den Verdacht;
Wann treue Liebe kussen [*küssen*] macht,
So wird der Kuss der Liebe,
So werden ihre Triebe
Beglückter durch die stille Nacht.

10

Ich sahe voll Gedanken
Durch junges Grün
In blauer Luft die blanken
Gewölkchen ziehn;
Da warf'st du mich, du Bübin,
Mit feuchtem Strauss,
Und flohst, wie eine Diebin,
Ins Gartenhaus.

ƒ16

11

Kommt, Gespielen, und springet   { single
Wie die Nachtigall singet,   { rhymes
Den[*n*] sie singet zum Tanz!
O geschwinder, geschwinder!
Rundherum, wie die Kinder:
Ringel, Ringelein, Rosenkranz!

A pretty metre might be made, by prefixing to each stanza two
Lines, each consisting of a Trochee with two Amphimacers, *one* of
the two, better perhaps the first always to be the same Line as the
last of the whole Stanza.—A Song of two Stanzas.

12

Kehre wieder, mein Bräutigam,
Kehre wieder in meinen Arm

Ach! wie zittr' ich, dich zu küssen!
Kehre wieder, Selino!

Hither, hither, Beloved one!
O return to my faithful arms!
Ah! to kiss thee, how I tremble!
Hither, hither, Selino!

13

1 Der Holdseligen
2 Sonder Wank
3 Sing' ich frölichen [*fröhlichen*]
4 Minnesang:
5 Denn die Reine
6 Die ich meine,
7 Winkt mir lieblichen Habedank.

Rhymes Three Syllable,
Tuneful Swan,
I tho' ill able
Murmur on:
For her maiden
Lips there play'd on
Smiles that solace the Woebegone.

14

Ich armes Mädchen
Mein Spinnerädchen
  Will gar nicht gehn,
Seitdem der Fremde
In weissem Hemde
Uns half beim Weizenmähn.

15

An meines Vaters Hügel
Da steht ein schöner Baum:
Gern singt das Waldgeflügel
An meines Vaters Hügel,
Und singt mir manchen Traum.

16

Scendi propizia
Col tuo splendore
O bella Venere
Madre d'amore

O bella Venere,
Che sola sei
Piacer degli huomini
E degli Dei—

&c &c &c

f17

17
Willkommen im Grünen!
Der Himmel ist blau
Und blumig die Au!
Der Lenz ist erschienen!
Er spiegelt sich hell
Am luftigen Quell
Im Grünen.

This last offends my ear: indeed the whole Stanza very closely resembles little Potatoes, inasmuch as it is *"no great Things"*— the following Song-metre is better.

18
Wenn kühl der Morgen athmet, gehn
Wir schon auf grüner Au,
Mit rothbeglänzter Sens; & und mähn
Die Wies' im blanken Thau.
Wir Mäher, dalderald*ei!*
Wir mähen Blumen und *Heu.*
Juch*hei!*

Drunk with I-dolatry—drunk with Wine.
a noble metre, if I can ~~form~~ find a metre to precede or follow
Sumptuous Dalila floating this way
Drunk with Idolatry drunk with Wine

f19ᵛ Siam passeggier erranti
Fra i vent' e le procelle
Ecco le nostre stelle

Queste dobbiam seguir
Con tal soccors'appresso
Chi perderà se stesso?
Con tanta luc'avanti
Chi si vorrà smarrir?

ᵕ ᵕ; I mean something between 2 long and two short syllables/ Two little words pronounced distinctly & with some emphasis; but yet quickly and not with much emphasis.

> Come il candore D'intatta nève
> E d'un bel core La Fedeltà.
> Un orma sola Che in sè riceve
> Tutta le invola La sua Beltà.

I observe in all the Italian Poets the frequent & seemingly un-limited liberty of using Trochees, one, & sometimes two together instead of Iambics,—I imagine that in reading they *spondaize* the two syllables and sometimes e contra an iambic in a place of the verse where a trochee seems to our ears almost necessary—

> Del gran padre Ocean lo speco angusto
> Nel piu riposto sen *l'onda* comprende;
> Lo speco, onde il Pastor del *marin* gregge
> Sulla fronte di Giove i fati legge.

ƒ20

Lònda as it cannot well be read l'on*da* must be spondaized *L'on da*—and so del marin must be read del ma rin gregge—& the same way with Sulla fronte. One trochee at the beginning gives a grace to any language—⟨⟨all this page is one blunder, but a blunder inevitable on the common rules of Italian Verse.—⟩⟩

Della piu calda Zon il cerch' accende and two, or more, together may be used to produce some particular effect, once or twice in a long Poem/of ~~many~~ some 1000 lines perhaps—

> Downward falling to the bottomless pit.

But to use it as the best Italian Poets almost in every stanza, &
often many times in the course of one stanza must be explained
from their more spondaic mode of speaking which it is the custom to *caricature*, as it were, when they read poetry. If you listen
to an Italian who speaks with propriety, you cannot but observe
this more equable *diffusion* of *accent*—words either spondees or
pyrrhics (- -, or ᴗ ᴗ), not as with us all Iambics or Trochees or
Anapæsts

ƒ20ᵛ   The airs &c of operas usually in the following metres./
   1. Sta zitta cospettoni   3 7 & sevens & one six—
   2. Voi contrastarm' ancora:
   3. Laric' in sulla prora
   4. Osservo ben di quà.
   5. Che dite non puol essere   you tell but not in verity
   6. Se Don Laric'e morto
   7. Or com' in questo porto
   8. Tornare mai potrà?
   9. Ma ch'ostinata cattiva!
   10. Lesbin' osserv'un poco
   11. Oi bo [*Oibò*] da questo loco
   12. Non vedo ben fin là.
   13. Un occhio molt'indegno
   14. Avet' in verità.
   15. Or ch' s'accost' il legno
   16. Sapremo chi sarà.
      The 1 & 5 often transposed, in short, I do not see but that if the
   Lines do not exceed 7 except here and there—a Vedetelo, toc-
   catelo/nor fall below six in the *fourth lines*, but that you may,
   retaining the same music make the rhymes where you like—

      Another metre of trochaic eights.
         Dropping balsams, show'ring blisses—
   with the 4th a seventh, an anacreontic
         Full of madness full of wine/
   The rhymes alternate; but this, I suppose no odds.

ƒ21   Vorrei che m'intendesse⎫
      Ma non m'intend'ancor ⎬following three times as a burthen to

S'amor'il cor v'accende
E mest'ognor vi rende
De più spitat'affanni
Sarete pred'ognor.
the intendesse metreizing to affanni, & rhyming or not as you
like.—

　　ᵕ　-　ᵕ　ᵕ̣　-　ᵕ
Per gust'e piacere　　　For rapture, for gladness
Per gioia e diletto
Il core nel petto
Balzando mi và.　　　　the ending of one/

N.B. with the finale of the Primo atto of the V. Cant. I have now
18 airs, Oct. 18, 1804.

Manfred, Precetti per la Musica.—
La systema del Tartini—

Fair is foul, and foul is fair　- ᵕ -/ ᵕ - ᵕ -/
Hover thro' the Fog and filthy Air　- ᵕ -/ ᵕ - ᵕ/- ᵕ -

19
6　　　10　　　10　　　10　　　7
1. old.　2. War.　3. abhor.　4. bold.　5. wooing.
10　　　9　　　10　　　11
6. Cold.　7. renewing.　8. shrouds.　9. ensuing.
12
10. clouds.

20.
4　　　5　　　6　　　8　　　9　　　10
1. good.　2. glory.　3. clear.　4. wood.　5. story.　6. Tear.
6　　　7　　　8　　　10　　　11　　　12　※

6 or 7　　　　　6 or 7　　　6 or 7 or else 7 or 9　f21ᵛ
1. singing or sing.　2. story or store.　3 ringing or ring.
6 or 7 or 7 or 9　　　10　　　10　　　10　　　10
4. gory or gore.　5. Jove.　6. mourn.　7. lorn.　8. grove.

      ~~8~~   8   8   10
9. grace. ~~10.~~ fur † 11. bent † 12. place. 13. her † 14. lent †
    10   12
15. Face.   16. Trace.   Not better than what
                                    accident may produce.
† If the first quatrain of the stanza should be single-rhymed,
then these may be double, thus, grace, furry, [?benty/beauty],
place, hurry, [?lenty/leuty]. Likewise the different Lengths of
the Lines may perhaps be altered—the second quatrain may be
all, or the former half of 8s instead of Tens.—

                    21.
1. an Hexameter. 2. a Pentameter. 3. Half a Pentam. 4. an
Hex. rhyming to 1. 5. a Pent. rh. to 2. 6. Half a Pent. rh. to 3.
1. glory. 2. care. 3. man. 4. story. 5. stare. 6. scan.—Any
thing of a light cast it ~~might~~ *would* suit/and from that one might
guess its other applicabilities, if any.

                    22
  ※ a variety of this—vide overleaf last line,
    4   5   6   7   8   9
1. good. 2. glory. 3. clear. 4. hoary. 5. wood. 6. story.
   10
7. tear.

                    23
    6   7   6   7   9
1. gone. 2. contracted. 3. one. 4. compacted. 5. exacted.
    8   7   7   10   7
6. woe. 7. Hamus. 8. lame us. 9. sow. 10. morals.
    9
11. laurels.—/6́ 7̀ 6́ 7̀ 9́/8̀ 7́ 7̀ 10́/7̀ 9́

f23ᵛ The Morlack Songs as given by Abbé Fortis are endecasyllables,
sometimes; ~~sometimes~~ but decasyll.—regularly, all trochaics.
            Kadlimuje ranam boglie bilo
            Ter poruça vjernoi Gliabi svojoi
            Ne çe kaime u dvoru bjelomu
            Ni u dvoru, ni u rodu momu.

Kad Kaduna rjeci razumjela
Josc-je jadna u toi misli stala.
I pobjexe Asan-Aghiniza
Da vrat lomi kule niz penxere.—
Rhymes consonant or assonant are intermixed as in Milton's Cho-
ruses in Samson Agonistes.

Da ne puza jadno ferze moje
Gledajuchi sirotize svoje—
A Kad bili Aghi mimo dvora

Dve-je chierze s'penxere gledaju
A dva sîna prid-gnu izhogiaju
Tere svojoi majçi govoriaju

24   ƒ24

Her Husband's to Aleppo/gone//Master o' the Tyger/
But in a sieve I'll thither sail
And like a rat without a Tail
I send him/to the Devils/Boys, South'ard o' the Nigre.

Amphibrachys, Pæon tertius, Ionicus a majore, Amphibrachys. It
is not however an Ionicus a majore, because there is not only a
pause between - , and - ∪ ∪ , but it evidently, tho' parted from it,
follows as its attrahant, the Pæon tertius.

25.

8 10 10 10 10 8. In Italian where all are double rhymes this is
a pretty measure: in English 3 double rhymes in one stanza if
there were more than two stanzas in the poem would never doe;
but the second line might be made rhymeless, tho' isometrical
with the 5 & 6ᵗʰ double-rhymed/

endless, gore, sor. .row, morrow, lore, sore/*or*
gore, endless, lore, sore, sorrow, morrow.

26.

6 6 6 6 6 6/6 7 7 6/7 7. a delightful fife-and-drum metre—for
poetry "of the animal Spirits./※ ※ on the opposite page—//

ƒ23ᵛ   ※ ※ In this brief notation (& most convenient one for all equable movements, whether Iambic, Trochaic, Dactylic, of amphibrachs, or amphimacers) ⌣ corresponds to ⌣ ; / to ´ ; but if ever a third rhyme is interposed, this is shown by a the circumflex: but when one set of rhymes is done with the / marks the notation to denote fresh rhymes.

ƒ24ᵛ   27

⌣ - / ⌣ - ⌣ / - ⌣ ⌣ / - ⌣ -
⌣ - / ⌣ - ⌣ / - ⌣ ⌣ / - ⌣ -
- - / ⌣ - - / - ⌣ - ⌣   {or - ⌣ / - ⌣ ⌣ / - ⌣ - ⌣
- ⌣ ⌣ / - ⌣ ⌣ / - ⌣ - ⌣   {or ⌣ - / ⌣ - ⌣ / - ⌣ - ⌣

then a second, ~~the first~~ so as to form one stanza of 8 lines, the 1 rhyming to 5, 2 to 6, 3 to 7, 4 to 8—or 4 to 5, 3 to 6, 2 to 7, 1 to 8.—Try both in semi-nonsense.

                                    28

ˋ ˜ ˋ ´ ´
7 10 7 9 11. Da Capo. Then an Epod of the metre of Milton's Christmas-day Hymn/9 & 11 of Sᵗ. and Antist: first an Amphib: followed by two Dactyls, the 11ᵗʰ a Trochee + amph: &c.

Dropping Balsams, dropping ~~nectar wine~~
    Descends the heavenly Herald, Maia's Son,
~~Comes the winged God, the Son of Maia~~
~~His feet are winged, the Caduceus~~
    Flying feet, and charmed Rod
The Sire of Quiet, wreath'd with Serpents
~~Comes wing'd Mercury, the Son of Maia~~
Mercurius winged Son of Maia.

He softly lighting on Sea,   ⌣ - ⌣ / - ⌣ ⌣ / -
                    wreathed with Serpent-twine
~~This~~ His mild Caduceus wreath'd with the sleepy snake,
- - / ⌣ - ⌣ / - ⌣ ⌣ / - ⌣ -
Yes! it is *He!* it is He!   - ⌣ ⌣ / - ⌣ ⌣ / -
The Valleys murmur not pleasureless,   ⌣ - ⌣ / - ⌣ ⌣ /
And the jubilating Ocean's (re)joicing is measureless.
- ⌣ - ⌣ - ⌣ - ⌣ (⌣) - ⌣ ⌣ / - ⌣ ⌣ /

Upon the mountain's Edge all lightly resting   *f25*
There a brief while
~~Now on its Edge~~ the Globe of splendor sits,
    seems a creature of this
And ~~a brief while belongs to~~ earth; but soon
    More changeful than the Moon
To Wane fantastic his great orb submits,
Or cone or mow
A distant Hill of Fire, ~~and~~ till sinking slowly
                he   s
Even to a Star at length ~~is~~ lessend wholly.

                    29
Abrupt, as Spirits vanish, ~~Earth~~ he is sunk/
A soul-like breeze ~~at once possess'd~~ possesses all the wood;
    The Boughs, the Sprays ~~all~~ have stood
As motionless, as stands the ancient Trunk,
But every leaf thro' all the forest flutters,
And deep the Cavern of the Fountain mutters

These lines I wrote as nonsense verses merely to try a metre; but
they are by no means contemptible—at least, on reading them
over I am surprised at finding them so good/16 Aug. 1805—
Malta.

Now will it be a more English Music if the first & fourth are
double rhymes; & the 5 & 6ᵗʰ single?—or all single; or the second
& 3ʳᵈ double? Try.

        Resembles Life, what once was held of Light,   *f25*ᵛ
        Too simple in itself for human Sight?

                    30
An absolute Self? an Element ungrounded?
All, that we see, all colors of all shade
    By incroach of Darkness made?
Is Life ~~pure act per se~~ (in its own nature)
        itself by consciousness unbounded,
And all the Thoughts, Pains, Joys of mortal Breath
A War-embrace of wrestling Life and Death?

Written in the same manner, and for the same purpose, but of
course with more conscious Effort than the two stanzas in the preceding Leaf—   16 Aug. 1805—the day of the Valetta
Horse-racing—Bells jangling, & stupefying music playing all Day—

f78ᵛ   The Elegiac Measure adapted to the English may be either,
with the preced: Hexam: in all cases, a common pentameter—or
else end with - ᴗ ᴗ / - ᴗ / - ᴗ : just ~~we~~ as we really *read* (tho' not
scan) the ancient Pentameter.

Jussit et invitos facta tegenda loqui.

the first half left open to all its original varieties as those may be
best expressed by English Emphasis—i.e. a syllable more or less—

Rideat assiduis—&c &c—or finally the last half of the Pentameter
may be

Treasures of Gold shall boast never to purchase faith.

f79   31
          Lieblich itzt wie über glatten Kieseln
            Silberhelle Fluthen rieseln,
            Majestätisch prächtig nun
            Wie des Donners Orgelton,
          Stürmend von hinnen itzt wie sic[*h*] von Felsen
          Rauschende schäumende Giessbäche wälzen/
            Holdes Gesäusel bald
            Schmeichlerisch linde,
            Wie durch den Aspenwald [*Espenwald*]
            Buhlende Winde—

                               32
          Excedit penitus corda latentia
          Et semper vigili spes stimulo furit.
          Spem de sollicitis tollite mentibus
            O quos implacidis juvat
            In fatis animi quies.

          Si non arboreis obvia fœtibus,
          Si non ora forent obvia fontibus

Quæ cursu refugo decipiunt sitim/
Pars de Tantaleis malis
O pars quanta recederet./

33   *f79ᵛ*

1 Latter Half of an Hexameter
2 Whole Hexameter.

34

Ten syllable Lines.—1. swift. 2. flaw. 3. drift. 4. law.
5. chime. 6. draw. 7. time. 8. clime. 8ᵗʰ. Alexandrine

35

No cold shall thee benumb   6
Nor darkness stain thy sight: 6
To thee new Heat, new Light 6
Shall from this object come: 6
Whose Praises if thou now wilt sound aright,
My Pen shall give thee leave hereafter to be dumb

10 8 10 8 10 12.—36

37

Den schwachen Flügel reizet der Æther nicht,
Im felsen neste [*Felsenneste*] fühlt sich der Adler schon
Voll seiner Urkraft, hebt den Fittig,
Hebt sich und senkt sich, und trinkt die Sonne.

38.

1. ᴗ - ᴗ. - - ᴗ. - - ᴗ. ᴗ - .   Two Antibacchiuses for Am-
                                  phibrachs
2. ᴗ - ᴗ. ᴗ - ᴗ. ᴗ - ᴗ. ᴗ - .   Amphibrachs catalectic
3. - ᴗ ᴗ. - ᴗ ᴗ. - ᴗ ᴗ. -   Dactyls hypercatalectic
4. - ᴗ ᴗ. - ᴗ ᴗ. - ᴗ - .   Two Dactyls with one Am-
                                  phimacer.
5. - ᴗ - . - ᴗ - . ᴗ
6. - ᴗ - . - ᴗ - . ᴗ   } Amphimacer with Ditrochæus
7. ᴗ ᴗ - . ᴗ ᴗ - . - ᴗ - . ᴗ ᴗ - Two Anapæsts. Amphimacer.
                                  Anapæst.

ƒ8o   I ~~heard a Bird~~ voice pealing in triumph ~~this to~~ Day,
O Freedom ~~divinest of Ardors~~ twas thine
Sumptuous Tyr~~anny floating~~ this way
Dr~~unk with~~ Idolatry, drunk ~~with~~ wine

  ~~Safe on the mountain rock, the storm and the eagle my guard-
  ians~~

                    38
I heard a voice pealing loud triumph today,
The Voice & the Triumph, O Freedom were thine,
Sumptuous Tyranny challenged the fray
Drunk with Idolatry, drunk with Wine/
Friend of ~~Humanity~~ Mankind! O Freedom, divinest of ardors
Whose could the Triumph! O Freedom but thine
  Stars of Heaven shine to feed thee;
  Hush'd are the Whirlbasts & heed thee,
By ~~the~~ her Depths, by her Heights Nature swears Thou art mine!

                            - - ᴜ / - - ᴜ /
1. Amphibrach tetrameter catalectic   ᴜ - ᴜ / ᴜ - ᴜ / ᴜ - ᴜ / ᴜ -
2. Ditto
3. Three psuedo ~~dactyls~~ amphimacers (& one long syllable—
4. Two Dactyls, and one perfect Amphimacer
5 = 1 & 2
6. - ᴜ - / - ᴜ - ᴜ
7. - ᴜ - / - ᴜ - ᴜ
8. - ᴜ - / - ᴜ - / - ᴜ - / - ᴜ -.

ƒ8oᵛ   39
  1̄0 1̄0 1̄0 1̄0 6́/1̄0 1̄0 1̄0 1̄0 6́/1́1 1́1 1̄0 1́1 6́ 6́ 1̄0 1̄2.—✳ †
✳ Variety of this metre, the 7th, 9th, and 10th lines///double
rhymes, instead of the 11th, 12th, and 14th.—
  † A second variety, the 13th, 15th, and 16th, only, double rhymes;
& the 17th & 18th to be omitted.

                    ~~40~~
  1́0 1̄0 1́0 1̄0/1́0 6́ 1̄0 1̄0 1̄0 1̄0 6́/1̄0 1̄0 1̄0 8́ 6́ 1̄0 1̄2.

41.

ĭō ĭō ĭō ĭō ĭō ĭō ĭō ĭ2.   or omit ĭ2.   34ᵗʰ.—a page back

Adaptation of Metre 23 to the English Language, which does not abound in hyperacatalectic endings.   6̆ 6́ 6̀ 6́ 6̀ 8 / 6̀ 8 8 1́0 7̆ 9̆./

Adaptation of M. 25—Trochaics.
 Thus she said; and all around
 Her diviner spirit 'gan to borrow;
 Earthly Hearings hear unearthly sound,
 Hearts heroic faint & sink aswound;   ƒ8ı
 Welcome, Welcome, spite of pain & sorrow,
 Love today, and Thought tomorrow.

Trautes Röschen, sieh wie hell
Unter Geissblatt dieser Quell
 Durch Vergissmeinnichten [*Vergissmeinnichtchen*] fliesset!
Reissender rauscht dort sein Fall,
Wo er mit des Donner's Schall
Und des Thales Wiederhall
 Über Felsen sich ergiesset.

Aber süsser ist er mir,
Mein herzliebstes Röschen, hier,
 Denn er gleichet meinem [*unserm*] Leben!
Seh' ich ihn so sanft and [*und*] rein
Gleiten in des Mondes Schein,
Röschen, dann gedenk' ich dein,
 Und der Freude Thränen beben.

42.
Within these circling Hollies Wood-bine-clad
Beneath this ~~holly~~ ~~peep~~ small blue Roof of vernal Sky
How warm, ~~it~~ ~~is~~ how still! tho' Tears should dim mine eye,
Yet will my Heart for days continue glad—
For here, my Love! thou art! and here am I!
       S.T.C.

ƒ81ᵛ   L. 6ᵗʰ in an English verse of my own, as is the above ~~without the~~
~~last line, without the last line it may be taken as a sample of the~~
~~work~~

[43]
How warm these woodland wild recesses!
LOVE surely hath been breathing here!
And ~~our~~ this sweet Bed of Heath, my Dear!
Swells up, then sinks with faint caresses
As if to have thee yet more near.

~~Eight Springs have flown since I~~

A variety of the same, & more melodious in our Language by substituting single for the two double rhymes. Thus:

I
How warm this woodland wild Recess!
Love surely hath been breathing here!
And this sweet Bed of Heath, my Dear!
Swells up, then sinks with faint caress
As if to have you yet more near.

2
Eight Springs have flown, since ~~I reclin'd~~ last I lay
On Southern Quantocks heathy Hills,
Where quiet sounds from hidden Rills
    here & there like things astray
Float ~~upward on the fav'ring wind,~~
And high o'er head the Sky-lark shrills!

On even such a bed as this
~~Alone~~ I lay, ~~and watch'd the Sky~~ a stranger to thine eye;
    Yet you
~~I knew thee not, yet whence that Sigh~~
Those yearnings ~~as~~ of approaching Bliss
Beloved! ~~was~~ flew thy Spirit by?

ƒ82ᵛ   3
On such a bed of heath as this
I lay, a stranger to ~~thine~~ your eye.

Yet whence that ~~sense of~~ aching Hope? that sign
Those yearnings ~~after~~ for an unknown bliss?
Beloved! flew thy Spirit by?

No voice as yet had made the air
Be music with thy name, yet why
That seeking [?Doze/Dream/Gaze]? that yearning sigh!
That promise without whence or where
Beloved! flew thy Spirit by?

As when a Mother doth explore
The sure mark on her long-lost Child,
~~I have seen First seen~~ I lov'd thee, maiden mild,
As whom ~~my Heart~~ I long had lov'd before;
So deeply ~~was the my Soul~~ had I been beguil'd—

44.—Nonsense Verses.   ƒ83

2 Ye fowls of ill presage,
1 Go, vanish into Night!
Let all things sweet and ~~all things~~ fair
Yield ~~willing~~ Homage to the Pair—
    From Infancy to Age.
Each Brow be smooth, ~~each eye be~~ and bright,
As ~~tranquil~~ Lake in evening Light
    Today be Joy! and Sorrow—
    Devoid of Blame
    The widow'd Dame
Shall welcome be tomorrow
Thou too, dull Night! may'st come unchid
This wall of Flame the Dark hath hid
With turrets, each a Pyramid!
For the Tears, that we shed, are Gladness
    A mockery of Sadness.

[44a] Nonsense Verses for the trial of the Metre/
Some sager Words two meanings tell
For instance, Love is such!
⌐. . . .⌐ cannot LOVE too *well*

And yet may *love too much*/
Would we make sense of this, we must
First construe Love as Love:/⌈. . . .⌉AΥ⟨ΣT⟩PIA

45. Nonsense

I wish on earth to sing
Of Jove the bounteous store
That all the Earth may ring
With Tale of Wrong no more,
I fear not Foe in field or tent,   5
Tho' weak our cause, yet strong his Grace—
As Polar Roamers clad in Fur
Unweeting, whither we were bent
We found as [?'twere] a native place,
    Where not a Blast could stir!   10
ƒ83ᵛ   For Jove had his Almighty presence lent,
Each ~~but~~ Eye beheld in each transfigur'd Face
The radiance bright of Joy, & Hope's forgotten Trace.   13.

46. Nonsense

I wish on earth to sing
Of Jove the bounteous store,
That all the Earth may ring
With Tales of Wrong no more.
I fear no Foe in Field or Tent   5
Tho weak our cause, yet strong his Grace,
As polar Roamers clad in Fur
Unweeting whither we were bent,
We found, as twere, a native place,
Where not a Blast could stir/
~~The Branches swing, the Woodwinds roar,~~
✗ Oh then I sing Jove's bounteous Store
On rushing wing ~~the~~ while Sea-mews soar,
And
The raking Tides rolls Thunder on the Shore.
✗ ⟨The 12ᵗʰ line had better be a repetition of the first & 2ⁿᵈ/
"~~I wish to~~ O then I sing Jove's bounteous store"⟩

47. Nonsense

Sing, impassionate Soul! of Mohammed the complicate story
  Sing, unfearful of Man, growing & ending in care,
Short the Command and the Toil, but endless & mighty the Glory
  Standing aloof, if it chance, vainly our Enemies scare/—
What tho' we wretchedly fare, wearily drawing the Breath,
  Malice in wonder may stare, merrily move we to Death.

48. Nonsense

O Sara! never rashly let me go
Beyond the precincts of this holy Place,
Where streams as pure as in Elysium flow
And flowrets view reflected Grace,
What tho in vain the melted Metals glow,
We die, and dying own a more than mortal love.

49th Metre/—Daniel's incomparable Epistle to the Lady Mar-   *ƒ85ᵛ*
garet, Countess of Cumberland, is written in Stanzas of eight lines,
Iambic Pentameter: the two last a couplet, the other six corresponding, the 1ˢᵗ to the 4ᵗʰ, 2ⁿᵈ to the 5ᵗʰ, the 3ʳᵈ to the 6ᵗʰ.—And
this metre certainly has a good effect in a poem of stately moral
sentences, and seems a serviceable medium between rhyme & blank
verse, attuned as it here is, by the rhymes of the last couplet. But
in the Epistle preceding, where this metre is adopted *without* the
couplet, it becomes a mere waste of rhymes, the poet having all
their restraint and trouble, while the reader has none of the effect,
unless indeed now and then an obscure sense of a *jingle* in the
monotonous blank verse.—Yet I rather am disposed to alter this
metre; whether I make the lines tetrameter or pentameter, in one
or other of the following ways—either by transposing the rhymes
from the 3ʳᵈ & 6ᵗʰ to the 3ʳᵈ & 5ᵗʰ, or from the first & 4ᵗʰ to the
first and 6ᵗʰ—breath, grave, men; death, when, gave: flew, renew.
or grave, breath, men; death, when, gave: flew, renew. or grave,
when, breath, death, men, gave, flew, renew. And I seem to antici-
pate, that for a moral poem all four modes may be adopted—In
short, I would always preserve the final couplet as the always an-   *ƒ87*
ticipable burthen of the metre, & which with the same number of
lines in all would make the whole poem sufficiently uniform/but

f86ᵛ the six first I would vary ad libitum, i.e. ring the changes—which would make ~~the~~ changes.

f95

∪ - ∪ / ∪ - ∪ / ∪ - ∪ / -
∪ - ∪ / ∪ - ∪ / ∪ - ∪ /
∪ - ∪ / ∪ - ∪ / - ∪
∪ - ∪ / ∪ - ∪ / - ∪ - / -
- ∪ - / ∪ ∪ - / ∪ ∪ - / ∪ ∪ -
- - ∪ / - ∪ ∪ / - - ∪ /
∪ - ∪ / ∪ - ∪ / ∪ - ∪

1	2	3	4
- -	∪ ∪	- ∪	∪ -
Spondee.	Pyrrichius.	Trochee.	Iambus.
5	6	7	8
∪ ∪ ∪	- - -	∪ - ∪	- ∪ -
Tribrach.	Molossus.	Amphibrach.	Amphimacer.
9	10	11	12
∪ ∪ -	- ∪ ∪	∪ - -	- - ∪
Anapæst.	Dactyl.	Bacchius.	Antibacchius.

1	2	3	4
∪ ∪ ∪ ∪	- - - -	- ∪ - ∪	∪ - ∪ -
Proceleusmatic.	Dispondæus.	Ditrochæus.	Dijambus.
5	6	7	8
- ∪ ∪ -	∪ - - ∪	- - ∪ ∪	∪ ∪ - -
Choriambus.	Antispastus.	Ionic. a mag.	Ion. a minori.
9	10	11	12
∪ - - -	- ∪ - -	- - ∪ -	- - - ∪
1. Epitrite.	2. Epit.	3. Epit.	4. Epitr.
13	14	15	16
- ∪ ∪ ∪	∪ - ∪ ∪	∪ ∪ - ∪	∪ ∪ ∪ -
1. Pæon.	2. Pæon.	3. Pæon.	4. Pæon.

16 + 12 = 28.

f22 2225 22.17   Id enim interfuit *Imperatorem* creare, non Regem, quod Imperator deducit, Rex vero abducit a populo susceptam sibi majestatem. Cum enim Rex creatur, (qualis creabatur apud Barbaros, quorum vile servitium Romani aversabantur) in eum omnis populi potestas publica recta confertur: est enim, uti Rex Persarum, αυτοκρατὴς καὶ ανυπευθυνος ut principem illum jus fasque quandoque perturbantem vitamque aliorum et bona rapientem si populus tollere conetur, cogatur civilem evertere statum, et publicam commutare voluntatem, novamque inde fundare republicam. Quo ne cives adigerentur, si Rex regni everteret reges publicas, jurare cogebant in leges; ut cujus potestas a populo coerceri amplius nequibat, sine regni eversione, auctoritate jusjurandi atque ultione divinâ contineretur. At Romanum Imperatorem sumentem sibi, minime vero absumentem S.P.Q.R. majestatem, si abuteretur Imperio, licebat, semperque licuit, nisi violentiâ militari muniretur, *f22ᵛ* nullâ variatione status civilis nullâque mutatione Reipublicæ, vel Imperio exuere vel vitâ. Ideo Imperatore creando eum ad jurandum in leges non adigebant, quia publicâ potestate in Populo et Senatu adhuc permanente, violentiam avertere licebat illius. Regnum nimirum Remp. totam exhaurit, et cum ea majestatem universam transfert in personam unius aut successorum—

Imperium contra est cumulus magistratuum—&c.—Non bene igitur Dion assequebatur sensum dominatoris Populi, quando mirabatur Populum Romanum, cum Regiam Potestatem per tot magistratus Imperatori contulisset, exultare tamen quod Regem non ferret. Nimirum quamvis Senator esset Dion, græcissabat tamen, neque tam serio ac Populus Romanus discrimen expendebat inter Regem et Regiâ Potestate præditum magistratum, sive civilem, *f23* quales erant consules, qui cum regiâ etiam potestate creabantur, quippe qui et in Regum loco successerant. Unde sicuti Consules, ita et Imperator, pars erant Reipublicæ universæ: cujus sub potestate simul cum ceteris magistratibus continebantur. *Gravina* Lib. Sing. de Romano Imperio. §§ 19.

The Placita or Imperatorial Edicts had not the force of Laws, except in the way that Precedents are, namely—postquam tempore invaluissent, atque inolevissent usu et consensu civitatis—/ The Emperor Macrinus had resolved to do all away all these mere Rescripts nefas esse, leges videri Commodi et Caracallæ et hominum Imperitorum *Voluntates.*

2226 15.90　　Boy saw 10 wolves at Cava Secchia, Oct. 18, *f60* 1804—

2227 15.91　　The Hospital Amer. near the Catacombs attacked by ruffians, windows broken, Doctor attacked/two men, sick, *ƒ60ᵛ* robbed—another who made resistance stabbed in 7 places/one taken/but the rest protected by the Convent Church of Sᵗ Lucia/ Friars have commonly a share of the Booty—Oct. 19. 1804

2228 15.92   This same morning Commodore Prebell told me a most interesting story of his own knowlege of an American Boy, not then quite 11 years old/Was following the men who were driving in the Cattle to the fold, & had a gun, powder balls, &c— the Gun had been given him by Commodore's Brother who always favored the Lad/his Dog barked, & the Boy thought a Squirrel was tree'd—and and then observed (it was evening) that the Dog barked at the foot of a vast pine hollow from top to bottom/and at the Bottom open (as the oak at the foot of Lattrig)—walked up —& saw the glare of the two Eyes of an immense Bear/he did not wait to put in a Ball into the gun, but went up & discharged the powder & small shot full in the animal's face/mad with pain & all bloody the Bear leapt out on the Boy, but leapt beside him & was shuffling on in pursuit of what was behind him, when his Dog attacked the Bear & turned him/ he then saw the Boy & made at him, but the Boy darted behind the Tree & his Dog again turned the *ƒ61*   Bear—& during this time the Boy had time to load & put a Bullet in the Gun/this done he followed the Bear, came up close to him, fired & broke his Thigh Bone/the Bear made at him, but was soon turned by the Dog—the Boy again behind a tree loaded again/but the Bear now made off, as fast as three legs would carry him/The Boy tracked him, till he came to a great fern & furze Brake/still went on, oftentimes, from the nature of the ground obliged to crawl on all fours, & it now being quite dusk/in three miles he came to the top of a very steep ascent at the Bottom of which was the Lake—now the Bear was half way down (for when wounded or hard pursued they take to the water—the Boy now made sure, & turning the Bear & irritating him as he faced shot him thro' the Heart/he twisted up & tumbled headlong down the Hill upon the Beach/the Boy went on, took a pole, & put his handerchief on it to be seen at a distance/ & went home to his alarmed family & told them his exploit/—They went by a different & round about road (for the Boy's road was not possible for a sledge) with two Oxen

& a sledge—& brought home the animal/that weighd 80 s^t·— *f61ᵛ*
larger than the largest cow the man had—This Boy Commodore
put to School for two years & wished the man to let him have the
Boy & make perhaps an Admiral of him/but the Father could not
& would not part with him/He is now 16—a handsome & very
clever Boy.—

Two Boys now on board Decatur's ship, 1 of 11, the other of
9—relations robbed &c &c &c waylayed surprized & one by one massacred by two Indians who saved the Boys for prisoners—found
wine—drank went to sleep—the eldest put up the musket to the
ear of one of the Indians, & placed his little Brother there, to fire
it off when he made the signal—himself took the Indian's Tomahawk, went, killed with it the Indian, making at the very stroke
the sign/the younger let off the musket & killed the other at the
same moment/they then went off, the eldest using the Tomahawk
to bark the Trees, & cut & scatter twigs to find the way back—

2229 15.93   Sicilians solicitously & from the earliest age taught
to fear Death by the Priests—informed me by a young Sicilian   *f62*
Nobleman, himself no small Bigot.

2230 15.94   Governor & the Commodore's Beef, which he
begged as a present & then sold at half its value to a Danish Captain.

2231 15.95   Tax on seed Corn.—

2232 15.96   All money-borrowers—this in my Journey to
Cava Secchia—one officer came & said—I shall want, 80 ounces—
Cavalierly said! and why?—he had robbed the military chest—&
trusted that one man of honor would assist another—

2233 15.97   A large Porcupine caught in the Cava Secchia Oct.
16. or 17, 1804.

2234 15.98   The Duke of Palermo's Son, in the Capuchins
(make a full story of this) without one single Book has a fine

Horse which he will not *shoe,* because he has been inform'd that English Gentlemen ~~never~~ ride their finest Horses always unshod—

ƒ62ᵛ 2235 15.99   The airs & songs generally audible in the court-yard of the Opera House, & even in the Street/and it is pleasant to hear the ragged boys & girls singing after the second or third representation of an opera, some ~~of the~~ one, some another, all the most pleasing airs of the opera with wonderful accuracy & agility of Voice—

ƒ106ᵛ 2236 21.465   Arrian. de Ven. in the κεφ.ε. (5ᵗʰ Chapter) occurs a passage which at once surprized & delighted me. How comes it that it has [not] been quoted & alluded to even to satiety. L. gave me the Book on account of the Epictetus included in it, & afterwards retracted the Gift—Αρριανου Τακτικα, περιπλοι κυνηγετικος και Επικτητου Στοικου εγχειριδιον—then a pictured Title page 4 in one page, then first, war & hunting, taking up the whole breadth of the octavo, the two last (ships in one, and the other a philosopher's Lecture-Table) compartite in one breadth—under this —Amstelodami, apud Ianssonio—Waesbergios 1683—Blancard's Edition, & a neater octavo I never saw—But now for the passage— I take up the last 4 lines of the 4ᵗʰ Chapter—Τριτα δε τα χαρωπα. ουδε γαρ, ουδε τα χαρωπα φαυλα εστιν, ουδε φαυλων κυνων συμβολα, ει και ταυτα τύχῃ καθαρα και γοργα ιδειν. (χαρωπα = light blue eyes? cæsius. Or grey?) /Κεφαλ; ε./Επει τοι ανεθ-ρεψα εγω κυνα χαρωπην οιαν χαραπωτατην. και αυτη ωκεια *ƒ107* τε ἦν, και φιλοπονος, και ευψυχος και ευπους· ωστε και τεταρσιν ηδε ποτε λαγωοις εφ' ηλικιας αντηρκησεν. και τα αλλα δε, πραοτατη τε εστιν (ετι γαρ μοι ην, οποτε ταυτα εγραφον) και φιλανθρωποτατη· και ουπω προσθεν αλλη κυων, ως αυτη, ουτε εμε εποθησεν, ουτε τον εταιρον τον εμον, και συνθηρον τον Μεγιλλον· επειδαν γαρ του δρομου απεπαυσατο, ουκ ετι ημωνγε, η θατερου απεαλλαττεται· αλλα ει μεν εγω ενδον ειην, αμα εμοι διατριβει, και προϊοντα ποι παραπεμπει, και επι γυμνασιον ιοντι εφομαρτει, και γυμναζομενῳ παρα-καθηται. και επανιοντος προεισιν, θαμινα επιστρεφομενη ως καταμανθανειν μη πῃ αρα εξετραπην της οδου. ιδουσα δε και επιμειδιασασα, αυθις αυ προεισιν. Ει δε επι τι εργον πολιτικον

ιοιμι, ηδε τῳ ἐ꜔ταιρῳ τῳ ἐμῷ ξυνεστιν, καὶ προς εκεινον τα αυτα
ταυτα δρᾷ· οποτερος δε ημων καμνοι το σωμα, εκεινου αὖ ουκ
απαλλαττεται. ει δε και ολιγου χρονου (χρονου = absence)
ιδοι, επιπηδᾷ ατρεμα, ωσπερ ασπαζομενη, και ασπασμῳ επι-
φθεγγεται, οια φιλοφρονουωενη· και δειπνουντι ξυνασα συν-
απτεται· αλλοτε αλλῳ τῶϊοῖν ποδοῖν, υπομιμνησκουσα, οτι και
ἀυτῇ αρα μεταδοτεον ειη των σιτίων. Και μην πολυφθογγος
εστιν, ως ουπω εγω ιδειν μοι δοκω αλλην κυνα· και οσων δει-
ται, τῃ φθωνῃ σημαινει· και οτι σκυλακευομενη μαγιστι εκολ-
αζετο, ει τις εις τουτο ετι μαγιστα ονομασειεν, προσεισι τῳ
ονομασοντι, υποπτηξασα λιπαρει, και το στομα εφαρμοζει τω
αστοματι, ως φιλουσα, και επιπηδησασα εκκρεμαται του αυχε-
νος, και ου προσθεν ανιῃσι, πρὶν τῆς απειλης αποπαυσαι τον   *f107ᵛ*
θυμουμενον. ωστε ουκ αν ~οκ꜔οκνησαι~ μοι δοκω και το ονομα
αναρραψαι της κονος, ως και ες υστερον απολελειφθαι αυτης,
οτι ἦν αρα Ξενοφωντι τῳ Αθηναιῳ κυων, Ορμη ονομα, ὠκυτάτη
καὶ σοφωτάτη, καὶ ἱερότατη.

2237 21.466   Oct. 21ˢᵗ. 1804—Monday night—Syracuse.—O
my God! or if I dare not continue in that awful feeling! yet oh
whatever is good in me, even tho' not in the *Depth*, tho' not in
that which is the Universal & Perfect in us yet oh! by ~the~ all the
ministering Imperfections of my nature that were capable of sub-
serving the Good—O why have I shunned & fled like a cowed
Dog from the Thought that yesterday was my Birth Day, & that
I was 32—So help me Heaven! as I looked back, & till I looked
back I had imagined I was only *31*—so completely has a whole
year passed, with scarcely the fruits of a *month*.—O Sorrow &
Shame! I am not worthy to live—Two & thirty years.—& this last
year above all others!—I have done nothing! No I have not even
layed up any material, any inward stores,—of after action!—O no!
still worse! still worse! body & mind, habit of bedrugging the
feelings, & bodily movements, & habit of dreaming without distinct or rememberable ⌈. . . . .⌉

2238 15.100   Dancing, when poor human Nature lets itself   *f62ᵛ*
loose from bondage & circumstance of anxious selfish care/it is
Madness—*Soother of Absence*

2239 15.101   Entered the corner ~~third~~ over a Break (downfall) in the wall—2 or 3 cavern openings & the huge detached Obelisk-ruin/and the great heaped wilderness of vast stones lying before & under this

D. ear   Rope

f63   Fine verbal echo just at the corner/then at the turn tear a bit of paper/the groove at the Top—/it is an angle formed by 2 curves joining at the Top at an acute angle but for the groove//undoubtedly the most interesting cavern I ever beheld—

The Rope walk a flat roof, but of 3 unequal heights/to the left supported by huge Structures of stone, with arches, & [?rises] toward the Air by three pillars, the first rather a huge side of the cavern than a Pillar, the two others perfect pillars, one square, one needle-like, smooth & thin, hiding its [?excrescences] & discontinuity by a necklace or neckerchief of weeds & bushes/

2240 15.102   The old Marquis of Casalia in order to prove his *memory* & knowlege of English, has learnt a very complex dance

f63ᵛ   & dances it without make one false step/more than 86 ! ! !

2241 15.103   Under Mellili in the estate of Bar. de fe (12 miles N. of Syracuse) a specimen of the Seed ~~sown there a specimen of the see~~ then sown there was Lolium among & a number of other ⟨among them blue flowers⟩ not corn seeds—some bad corn seeds—& certainly not above one *corn* in 10—one of them another intoxicating seed. Oct. 26, 18034.

2242 15.104   [?God/Aged] A catacomb, 4 or 5 feet high/

2243 15.105   Brudo, an old Capon-dog, goes & travels from Farm to Farm/a fortnight here, a month there, so long at one place, so long at another, & every where treated kindly, & welcomed/a rough shepherd's Dog, very fat, & at least 16 years old.

2244 15.122   The four fluted Doric Columns on the side of the   f66ᵛ
Temple of Minerva, now Sᵗ Paul's Church, contrasted with the tawdry modern Front and disproportion, stone flower wreaths, & little John Nobodies with chubby heads & wings looking up the Virgin's petticoats as roguishly as may be/

2245 15.123   Amid cruelly unlike Thoughts as I was passing up the green Lane with the garden on my left on my way to the Theatre, Nov—Monday, the aromatic Smell of the Poplars came upon me! What recollections, if I were worthy of indulging them.

2246 15.124   The flat roof of the Rope walk Cavern pink-colored, & continually dropping on the water below, now it is shallowly flooded, & in dimpling Circles from the Drops—

2247 15.106   In Sicily there is the Hawthorn:—but the Indian   f64
Fig—its advantages & disad.—Fodder—

2248 15.107   The Americans obliged to quit the Hospital—proof of bad air/all the Convalescents seized with agues.—And yet there is *no* damp marshy Land near it—it is high [⁇open and], dry.—The Pantinella is to be dried.

2249 15.108   At the Cava Secca they are gathering Saffron—/

2250 15.109   According to the Soil & the consuetudine, you give the *Massaro* (i.e. a Countryman with cattle—one without is Zapponaro) the Seed corn/if he provide Cattle himself, he pays simply 1. the seed Corn back again/then for each salm accor. to the goodness & custom of the Estate from two, the lowest, to 6 salms, the highest Terragio [*Terrazzo*]—in a good soil a salm of Land will produce from 12 to 16, nay, 22—nay, it *has been known*

32.—If the landlord find Cattle, the Mass. pays a Salm of Corn additional for each pair of Oxen—/i.e. about 8 per cent for your Money—/but then these Cattle feed in the Sallows & water land— if the Massaros own Cattle, they too feed. A Salm of Corn is at this present time (Nov. 6. 1804) worth 8 ounces = in common times 5 ounces. Cattle from 22 to 40 ounces.

f64ᵛ   2251 15.110   Of the culture of Hemp & its effects in Sicily.

2252 15.111   Captⁿ Arden who had his arm shot off, told L. that it was long before in running he could balance himself.

2253 15.112   Of the Lombardy Poplar that even undermines Houses in Pensylvania/Capt. Baron.

2254 15.113   Of the Palermo Ditches/enormous sluices of water [. . .] War./and [. . . .]

2255 15.114   Restuccia, the Stubble with green grass growing up amongst it ⟨for one year⟩ then Terriozza for another year, then the third year turned up and called Maggesi.

2256 15.115   Mrs. Leckie's opal surrounded with small brilliants/grey blue & the wandering fire that moves about it/& often usurps the whole/

f65   2257 15.116   Earthquake this autumn at Almeria, destroying all but the Church ded. to the Tributary Source with an unfathomable Gulph around it, *full of alligators*

2258 15.117   3 Instances mentioned by 3 credible witnesses of strange Thumps felt in the ~~Pharo O the Moditor~~ in perfect calm but nothing where Wind

2259 15.118   How can we explain the difference between India & Sicily? in India they even [?drain] the numerous Rice Grounds

[. . . .] a Rice Ground is the [. . .] of Fever, the Viper nest of
Pestilence. It is strange & strangely [. . .] Can the whole be explained by the mere want of Draining?—

2260 15.119   [?Perrit.] prevents adjoining farm grinding till
their 2000   suffer no body else/yet is never consumed [?Yet
Sicilian notions]—

2261 15.120   Syracuse, whose circumference in its splendor was   *f65ᵛ*
21 miles, and its Population 1200,000, is now zusammenge-
schrumpft into a corner of about 2 miles in circum/and about
12000 Inhabitants of whom at least 10,000 had better be out of
existence—this doctissima civitas of Cicero, I found no one native
with whom I could talk of any thing but the weather & the opera/
ignorant beyond belief—the churches take up the third part of the
whole city, & the Priests are numerous as an Egyptian Plague. I
have at times in half-dreaming moods looked at them, as a ~~man~~
~~who~~ being, not a man would look at them, who saw intuitively
the mischief & misery they caused,—our eyes the bites of Tygers
& Serpents!—! In the time of the Emperor Joseph—who had com-
municated his Tone of Thought in some measure to the Neapolitan
Court, attempts were made to free Syracuse from this enormous
burthen; but in vain! 2. next to Priests the necessity of carrying
all Law-suits to Palermo/the rage for Law among the Sicilians,
Marquis of Casalia—I have heard it stated that Syracuse sends
60,000 Scudi yearly to Palermo in Law business/Causes are—
1. the corruption of the Judges in general—2. the particular insti-
tution of the Tribunal of Patrimony and 3 & chiefly, the immorality, ignorance & *vacancy*, & utter absence of moral sense derived
from the Roman Catholic Religion/1361 Frederic the Simple gave
his Wife Constantia six cities for her revenue, Syracuse, Lentini,
Carlentini, Sanphilippo, Mineo & Vizini—these proved the Camera   *f66*
Reginale of which Syracuse was the Head—/hence the tent of
Justice for all these Territories was in Syracuse—but 1523 by an
act of Sic. Parliament they were re-united to the Royal Domain/
—want of Salary in the Capitano di Giustizia, necessitating a continual change and of course universal recklessness/for what can

be done in *one* year/scarcely knowlege enough acquired to form a wise plan of action.

Landholders are obliged to hold a third of their Corn at the Disposal of the Senate till March/if it be a scarce year, the Senate take it at a given price/if an abundant one, they say—dispose of it, but first we must dispose of ours.

f57ᵛ   2262 21.333   Man that made glass eyes—Emir expected to ~~read~~ see with it/man told him to wait—he could not expect that it would do so all at once.

2263 21.334   Phœnix lives a thousand years—& only one at a time yet Plutarch gravely says, that the Brain thereof is a pleasant Bit, but apt to occasion the Head ache.

2264 21.335

f58   Works of Bruno

1. De umbris idearum.	3 De progressu et lampade venatoria Logicorum
2 Acrotismus	4 Artic. 160. advers. Mathematicos
5 Candelajo, Comedia.	6 Della Bestia.
7. La Cena delli Ceneri	8 Dialoghi della ca—
9. Dell infinito &c	10 De triplici minimo &c.
11 Explic. triginta &c.	

2265 21.336   Coslovaz (in Dalmatia) è un povero luogo, come gli altri Casali di queste contrade; ma i boschi del suo Distretto abbondano di Frassini, che danno Manna in abbondanza, quando siáno opportunamente incisi. I Morlacchi non sanno farvi incisioni; e non conoscevano questo prodotto. Due anni sono andò a far colà delle sperienze Persona, che ne avea ottenuta la permessione dal Governo. Queste non corrisposero tosto alle speranze concepite, perche l'aria *erasi* rinfrescata *alcun poco*. Lo Sperimentatore perdette la pazienza, e abbandonò i Frassini tagliati. Al ritornare del caldo, eglino diedero esorbitante quantità di Manna, cui avidamente presero a mangiare i Morlacchi, trovandola dolce. Parecchi

di essi furono quasi ridotti a morte dall'uscite violente: la Manna
restò dopo pochi giorni abbandonata ai porci, e ai polli d' India.
Viaggio in Dalmazia dell' Abate Alberto Fortis.
volum: prim. p.36.

2266 21.337   Those crinkled ever varying circles, which the
moonlight makes on the not calm, yet not wavy, sea.—
Quarantine, Malta. Nov. 10. Saturday 1804.

2267 21.338   Beasts & Babies remember, man only recollects.
This distinction was made by Aristotle.—

2268 21.467   Nov. 22ⁿᵈ, 1804. Thursday Night, Garret, at the   *f108*
Treasury/4 windows in a room of 4 Strides by 4, but that the
seats & railed Covering (making a Toilet Table) of the Stairs take
up the greatest part & make this breadth only one Slip of a stride's
length, & this greatest Length only one stride in breadth—but
magnificently painted on the ceiling—Lord!—4 *winds* curly-pated
Face—heads spewing white smoke in a brush or wedge ⟨the broken
point at each mouth,⟩ and the mariners Compass in the middle/
but then such true & varied vomit-faces!!

2269 21.468   Nov. 22/1804. I have memorandum [. . . .]   *f108ᵛ*
my past Self—/In fine too, on a larger scale, take up the idea of a
Swedenborgian called on Sir Thomas Brown, & talking over Christianity with him/on Sir Thomas Moore—& on all odd fellows
whom I love & who ought to have thought less slavishly quod
Sanitatem &c. This Idea haunted me, as I was reading the Vulgar
Errors & Rel. Med. of Sir T. Brown.

2270 21.469   Of the French & Spanish Colonists why so much
better than the English & Dutch—& how they can venture to bap-

tize their Slaves—Gentleman from France explained it him in England/Xianity in England a sort of philosophy of *Rights;* but Catholicism a play thing.

f*109*   2271 21.470   Friday, Nov. 23, 1804
One of the heart-depraving Habits & Temptations of men in power, as Governors, &c &c is to make *instruments* of their fellow-creatures—& the moment, they find a man of Honor & Talents, instead of loving & esteeming him, they wish to *use him*/hence that self-betraying side & down look of cunning &c—and they justify & inveterate the habit by believing that every individual who approaches has selfish designs upon them.

f*58ᵛ*   2272 21.339   From the Courier, Monday, Aug. 13. 1804.
A case strictly the same in the only apparently miraculous part with the conversion of St. Paul.

STORM

The late tempest in Norfolk, Suffolk, Lincoln, Leicestershire, Warwickshire, &c. appears to have been more extensive in its course, and more violent in its effects, than was at first supposed; a number of horses were killed on different farms by the electric fluid. *Mr. R. Tower of Hempnall, Norfolk, was struck blind, as* } N.]
he was returning from Norwich, but has since received his sight.—
A large oak tree at Newton was split from top to bottom, and stripped of its bark twelve feet from the ground; some of the bark was carried 50 yards from the tree.—At Attleborough several large trees were split and shattered.—At Hundon, Suffolk, a double-barn, the property of J. Vernon, Esq. was consumed by lightning.—The fall of rain at Lynn was very great being nearly two inches in depth; and the thunder was the most tremendous ever remembered.—At Wolverhampton, the fluid descended the chimney of a house on Snow Hill, and consumed some linen which was hanging on a line. A fire-ball also fell upon a house at Monmore Green, to which it did much damage. At Stamford, the violence of the storm was dreadful.—At Holbeach, a fireball fell down the chimney of Mr. T. Peatfield, which it destroyed, and

forced its way into a room below, where it removed a particular wall, forced two opposite doors from their hinges, broke a looking-glass and other furniture, and carried away to the distance of 30 feet, the whole of the glass and lead of a large front window. Mr. P. who was coming down stairs, was knocked down by the shock, and remained a long time insensible. His wife had just quitted her bed, which the next moment was covered with the ruins of the chimney. At Sheffield, the lightning struck the house of Mr. E. Royle, at Shude-hill, and shattered to pieces a bed in which two children were asleep, but without doing them the least injury. Two sheep were struck dead in a field at Youlgrave, near Bakewell. At Wem, Shropshire, the lightning was uncommonly vivid, and the rain so heavy as to do great damage to the growing crops. An oak tree was shivered to pieces, and the fragments were scattered to the distance of 40 yards. The storm occurred at all the above-mentioned places between four and five o'clock on the morning of Friday se'nnight.

2273 21.340

 Look in mine eyeballs where thy beauty lies: *f59*
 Then, why not Lips on Lips, since Eyes on Eyes?

2274 21.341   Hard to express that sense of the analogy or like-ness of a Thing which enables a Symbol to represent it, so that we think of the Thing itself—& yet knowing that the Thing is not present to us.—Surely, on this universal fact of words & images depends by more or less mediations the *imitation* instead of *copy* which is illustrated in very nature *shakespearianized*/—that Proteus Essence that could assume the very form, but yet known & felt not to be the Thing by that difference of the Substance which made every atom of the Form another thing/—that likeness not identity—an exact web, every line of direction miraculously the same, but the one worsted, the other silk

2275 21.342   His pure mind met Vice and vicious Thoughts by accident only, as a Poet in running thro' terminations, in the heat of composing a rhyme-poem on the purest and best subjects, startles & half-vexedly turns away from a foul or impure word &c

2276 21.343   Commander's Balsam, from 10 to 15 D.

f109   2277 21.471   Pomp of confidence in a man in place of—In short, I should not wonder if it should please his M. M. to—have the usual contracts for beef for the navy—or some such stuff—a good scene even for a farce.

2278 21.472   Itaque id agitur, ut ignorantia etiam ab ignominia liberatur, by making it essential in those cases, to humanity & by ridiculing & maligning the attempts of more bold minds to lessen it—in metaphysics, origin of Evil.

2279 21.473   Soother of Absence. Days & weeks & months pass on/& now a year/and the Sun, the Sea, the Breeze has its influences on me, and good and sensible men—and I feel a pleasure upon me, & I am to the outward view of all cheerful, & have myself no distinct consciousness of the contrary/for I use my faculties, not indeed as once, but yet freely—but oh ⌈Sara⌉! I am never happy, never deeply gladdened—I know not, I have forgotten what the *Joy* is of ~~that~~ which the Heart is full as of a deep & quiet fountain overflowing insensibly, or the gladness of Joy, when the fountain overflows ebullient.—S.T.C.

f109ᵛ

2280 21.474   The beautifully *white* sails of the Mediterranean (so carefully when in port put up into clean bags) and the interesting circumstance of the Sparonara's sailing without compasses—by an obscure sense of time/

f66   2281 15.121   Casal Musta—the excellent Garden, and Vines planted on the outside of all the Walls & introduced thro' a = gutter-hole in the Wall/all these Bot. Gard/& the happy Luogo tenente! *Mem.*

f67   2282 15.125   The Bot. Gard. finished thence the expences applied to a great Farm in the *Uncul.*

2283 15.126   Of the bed of small stones on the Rock and under the Soil in all the Maltese Fields/Mem. Withering.

2284 15.127   Quietness, Security within & without in Malta/

2285 15.128   American Navy Officers & Clergy, numbers of
large fortunes & high Family/in favor of—Nobility, i.e. *No Nob.*/
—being *minus*.

2286 15.129   6 Richard 2. Scots ravaged Cumberland, West-
moreland, & the For. of Englewood—a great booty in which they
carried a horrible pestilence into their country/third part
died!—!—

2287 15.130   About a mile from the Pietà, on the elbow ⌣   *f67ᵛ*
fields as among rocks, Locust Trees more *tree-like* & well placed,
and loveliest green of the Almond Tree—*wings* pea green so very
lovely—

2288 15.131   Birca Cara, noble church, one Tower unfinished,
for want of money so common in Malta/rough columns &c—

2289 15.132   Cactus opuntia and Capers/this over and adown
the wall, the Tree rooted in the other side, the Caper growing out
of, & adown the walls, mark & characterize the Maltese Casals—
2. Splendid doorways and Stone Balconies, with wretched Door
and window shutters— + Stone—Wood.† & Pepper Tree & only
one! 3. † Pinks pendulous/4. Many children 5. Quietness
Maltese no Taste but for Stone & Fruit.

2290 15.133   Of my Dream of going into a Field with men on   *f68*
horseback all in blue which made me, then a Child of 7 years old,
burst into Tears in a corner of the Parlour at Ottery—the corresponding reality bursting on me near Reading in the 15th of Light
Dragoons.

2291 21.475   The το γελοιον of sensibility—refinement con-   *f109ᵛ*
sists not in the valuing or aiming at certain qualities, of purity,
unsensualized affection, &c, but in ~~insincerely~~ pretending to the
possession of them while ~~vanity~~ Self-conceit has hold of the Head,

Vanity of the Heart, & Concupiscence of the Tail. Friday, Dec. 7.
1804.

2292 21.476   640 acres in a square mile.

2293 21.477   Rings of Russet smoke from the evening Gun, at
Vallette.

2294 21.478   Beef fed on the cotton seed (& mutton too)—its
f110 fat congeals quickly & sticks worse than suet to the roof of the
mouth.

2295 21.479   *Tab.* For fear—for fear, for fear—now of Russia
—now of this—now that—but all for fear. The same day he said
—no moral feeling—the Cabinet would laugh ⟨aloud⟩ at such an
idea/we are none of us in these things actuated by any notion of
right or Justice, & we know it!!——

2296 21.480   So far from deeming it, ⟨in a⟩ religious ⟨point of
view,⟩ criminal to spread doubt of God, immort. & virtue (that
3 = 1!) in the *minds* of individuals, I seem to see in it a *duty*—
lest men by taking the *words* for granted never attain the feeling
or the true *faith*—that is, they only forbear even to suspect that
the Idea is erroneous or the communicators deceivers;—but do
not *believe* the idea itself—whereas to *doubt* has more of faith, nay
even to disbelieve—than that blank negation of all such thoughts
& feelings which is the lot of the Herd of Church and Meeting
Trotters.

2297 21.481   I have been obliged (Friday Dec. 7. 1804) to
read or look into Edwards' Hist. of W. Ind. for a foolish business
—it deserves a better reading—p.108. Vol. 2. those who recover
the Dead, having first administered a narcotic, why not supposed
sine qua non (over a X) to have adopted even those means of
f110ᵛ conveying truth/—more & more think of that habit of speculative
minds to turn all things into truth, as being all alike *falsehood*—/
—the *end* the sole.

2298 21.482   The smoke shot up, rocket or fountain like before the report is heard—the little moment before.

2299 21.483   The young man newly arrived in the W. Indies who observed (being seated next to him & by way of introducing a conversation), to Captain Reignier. It is a very fine day, Sir!— Yes, Sir! replied he abruptly—God and be damn'd to it! it is never otherwise in this damn'd rascally climate.

2300 21.484   Men taught at their Guns without powder who ran from their guns in action at the first explosion—

2301 21.485   The most common appearance in wintry weather is the appearance of the sun—under a sharp defined level line of a ⟨stormy⟩ cloud that stretches one third or half round the circle of the horizon, of thrice the height that intervenes between it & the horizon, which last is about a sun & a half—but the sun comes out a mass of brassy light, himself lost & diffused in his stormy splendor. Compare this with the beautiful summer set of color without cloud.

2302 21.486   In dreams one is much less, in the most tranquil dreams, a spectator only—one seems always about to do, or suffering or thinking, or talking—& I do not recollect that state of feel- *frri* ing so common when awake of thinking on one subject, & looking at another, or at a whole prospect/till at last perhaps, or by intervals, at least, you only look passively at the prospect.

2303 21.487   The monthly magazine a milleped Louse: & Mrs B. & D^r A two of the forelegs—or the whole Aikin family.

2304 21.488   How like Herrings, and onions our vices are the morning after we have committed them/& even lawful pleasures like the smell of a dinner room, when you have gone out & re-entered it, after dinner.

2305 21.489   85 Portraits sculpt on a cherry stone at Dresden/ X^t & the apostles, table & supper all drawn by the Letters of the text—at once portrait & language. This is a universal-particular language—Roman-catholic language with a vengeance.

2306 21.490   The holy ghost left all the Solecisms, hebraisms, & low, Judaic prejudices as evidences of the credibility of the apostles/so the Theopneusty left Cottle all his Bristolisms not to take away the credit from him & give it all to the Muses.

2307 21.491   Nothing & yet the very thing, like the white ⟨or blank⟩ in a wooden cut, that serves for hair &c.—

2308 21.492   Captain Rowley's Boat taking off by night the wounded men to prevent their falling into the hands of the Brigands—& such as died in the Boat, the Lieutenant by the Lanthorn read the funeral service over/—what a scene!

ƒ111° 2309 21.493   pigs in Naples tried for their lard-fat by running a hot wire into the nape of their neck, & instantly stopping when they pig squeaks—the wire shows the fat's depth.—Snow so injurious to the Roofs, cracks, & splits them/whenever it snows, Porters employed to throw it off, & often lives of the Passengers below are lost.—

2310 21.494   It is a remark that I have made many times & many times shall repeat, I guess—that Women are infinitely fonder of clinging to & beating about, hanging upon & keeping up & reluctantly letting fall, any doleful or painful or unpleasant subject, than men of the same class & rank. So to night (Tuesd. Dec. 11) M^{rs} Στοδσαγιττα & S. St. α ριγναρδο δι Νοβλε's χρυελτι το νεφυ.—Is it want of generalizing power & even instinct? I was thinking of Uncles (Petrus), Batchelors, Reason acting without Love, & therefore attracting Rages/for it must have some Leidenschaft—

2311 21.495   Of Caracciolo & his floating Corse that came to ask the King of Naples's Pardon

2312 21.496   Of the Ragusae All his men dead or dying of the yellow fever & forced out to sea from Malta.

2313 21.497   The Ship proudly with fair breeze sailing into harbour, then forced to turn about & beat round in the Quarantine *f112* Harbor.

2314 21.498   Poetry in its Grundkraft no less than the Vervollkommung'sgabe [*Vervollkommnungsgabe*] of man/the seraphic instinct.

2315 21.499   Final causes answer to *why?* not to *how?* & who ever supposed, they did—

2316 21.500   Mache ich mir vom GRUNDE aller Realität, ens realissimum, einen Begriff, so sage ich: Gott ist das Wesen, welches den Grund alles dessen in der Welt enthält, wozu wir Menschen einen VERSTAND anzunehmen nöthig haben, z.b. alles zweckmassigen [*Zweckmässigen*] in derselben. Er ist das Wesen, von welchem das Daseyn aller Weltwesen seinen Ursprung hat, nicht aus der NOTHWENDIGKEIT seiner NATUR (per emanationem) sondern nach einem Verhältnisse, wozu wir menschen [*Menschen*] einen FREIEN WILLEN annehmen müssen, um uns die Möglichkeit desselben verständlich zu machen.

2317 21.501   I addressed a Butterfly ⟨on a Pea-blossom⟩ thus —Beautiful Psyche, Soul of a Blossom that art visiting & hovering o'er thy former friends whom thou hadst left—. Had I forgot the Caterpillar or did I dream like a mad metaphysician the Caterpillars hunger for Plants was Self-love—recollection-feeling, & a lust that in its next state refined itself into Love?—12 Dec. 1804.

2318 21.502   Insects at the time of their rising into the powers *f112ᵛ* of propagation get wings = seeds of many plants plumes of down, for the same purpose—to spread & multiply.

2319 21.503   Different means to the same end seem to consti-
tute analogy. Seeing & Touching are analogous senses with respect
to magnitude, figure, &c—they would to a certain extent (& do)
supply each others place. The air-vessels of Fish & of Insects are
analogous to Lungs—the end the same, however however different
the means. No one would say, Lungs are analogous to Lungs—&
it seems to me either inaccurate or involving some true conception
obscurely, when we speak of Planets by analogy of ours—for here
knowing nothing, but likewise, we presume the difference from
the remoteness, & difficulty in the vulgar apprehension of considering these pin points as Worlds—So likewise instead of the phrase
"analogy of the past" applied to historical Reasoning, 9 times out
f113   of 10 I should say "by the example of the past." This may appear
verbal trifling, but "animadverte quam sit ab improprietate ver-
borum pronum hominibus prolabi in errores circa res." In short,
Analogy always implies a difference in kind & not merely in degree. There is an analogy between dimness, numbness, & a certain
state of the sense of Hearing correspondent to these (namely,
giving confusion with *magnification*) for which we have no name;
but between light green & dark green, between a mole & a Lynceus
there is a *gradation*, no analogy.   12 Dec. 1804

2320 21.504   Between Beasts & Men when the same actions are
performed by both, are the means analogous or different only in
degree? That is the question! The sameness of the end, & the
equal fitness of the means, proves no identity of means/I can only
read; but understand no arithmetic, yet by Napiers' Tables, or
the Housekeeper's Almanac I may even arrive at the conclusion
quicker than a tolerably expert arithmetician/Yet still reading &
reckoning are utterly different Things.—

f113ᵛ   2321 21.505   In Reimarus on the Instincts of Beasts Thom.
Wedgwood's ground principle of the influx of memory on perception is fully & beautifully detailed.

2322 21.506   It is often said, that Books are companions—they
are so, dear, very dear, Companions! But I often when I read a

book that delights me on the whole, feel a pang that the Author is not present—that I cannot *object* to him this & that—express my sympathy & gratitude for this part, & mention some fact that self-evidently oversets a second. Start a doubt about a ~~fourth~~ third—or confirm & carry a fourth thought. At times, ⟨I become restless: for my nature is very social.⟩

2323 21.507   What I have endeavored to say in a 100 forms is this, das[*s*] wir nicht einmal von einzelnen Dingen Begriffe haben, als vermittelst der eingesehenen Aenlichkeit [*Aehnlichkeit*] mit andern, und also vermittelst des algemeinen [*allgemeinen*] Erkentnisses.

——————————

From the above might not a corollary be deduced that Time is the effect of Memory, that is, of the collation of vivid impression with the phantasm thereof? ⟨Or thence too in part at least the notion of Reality or its perfect Likeness prevents the mind from thinking it two things, yet it is—how solve it/~~it~~ one is the effect of an abiding thing—or rather it is *Thought*, & this is *Thing*.⟩

2324 21.508   Well! (says Λαδι βαλλ) the Catholic Religion   *f114*
is better than none/Why, to be sure, it is called a Religion: but the ? is, is it, a Religion? Sugar of Lead/Well! better that than no Sugar. Put Oil of Vitriol into my Sallad—well, better that than no oil at all—or a fellow vends a poison under the name of James's Powders—well! we must get the best we can—better that than none!—So did not our noble ancestors reason, or feel—or we should now be Slaves, and even as the Sicilians are at this day— or worse: for even they have been made ~~wiser~~ less foolish in spite of themselves by others' wisdom.

2325 21.509   of the immense multitude of plants, & the curious regular *choice* of different herbivorous animals with respect to them/Reimar. Trieb. der Ins. 1. 184. & in the following pages of the pairing & equally wonderful young—& egg-laying insects—all in motion/the sea fish to the Shores or Rivers—the Land Crab to the Sea Shore—describe all the creation thus ~~agitationed~~ agitated by the *f114°* one or other of the three Instincts, self-preservation, childing & child-preservation—Darwin's Pain from Milk! O mercy! the blindness of the man!—& it is *Imagination,* forsooth, that misled him! too much *poetry* in his philosophy!—this abject deadness of all that sense of the Obscure & Indefinite, this superstitious Fetisch Worship of lazy or fascinated *Fancy!* O this indeed deserves to be dwelt on/

2326 21.510   Think of all this as an absolute Revelation, a real Presence of Deity—& compare it with historical traditionary religion. Two Revelations, the material & moral, & the former not to be seen but by the latter, as S⁺ Paul has so well observed—"By ~~philosophy~~ worldly wisdom no man ever arrived at God; but having seen him by the moral Sense then we *understand* the outward World, even as a Book/no Book of itself teaches a language in the first instance, but having by symp. of Soul learnt it we then understand the Book—i.e. the Deus minor in his work.

2327 21.511   The Hirschkafer in its worm state, makes its bed-chamber prior to its metamorphosis half as long as itself—Why? there was a stiff horn ~~under~~ turned under its belly, which in its fly state must project & harden, & this required exactly that length.

2328 21.512   The Sea Snail creeps out of its House, which thus *f115* hollowed lifts him aloft, & is his Boat & Cork Jacket/the Nautilus additionally spreads a thin Skin for a Sail.

2329 21.513   All creatures obey the great game-laws of Nature, & fish with nets of such meshes, as permit many to escape, & preclude the taking of many—So two races are saved, the one by taking part, & the other by part not being taken.

2330 21.514   Wonderful, perplexing divisibility of Life/it is related by D. Unzer, an authority wholly to be relied on, that an Ohrwurm (Earwig?) cut in half eat its own hinder half!—Will it be the reverse with G. Britain & America? The Head of the rattle-snake severed from the body bit at, & squirted out its poison/

Related by Beverley in his Hist. of Virginia. Lyonnet/ in his In-
sect-Theol./tore a wasp in half, & 3 days after the fore-half bit
whatever was presented to it of its former food, & the hind-half
darted out its sting on being touched. Boyle mentions a female
butterfly that when beheaded not only admitted the male but lay
eggs in consequence of the impregnation. But a Turtle has lived
six months with his Head off—& wandered about/yea, six hours
after its heart & bowels (all but the Lungs) were taken out—How
shall we think of this compatible with the *monad* Soul? If I say
what has Spirit to do with space—what odd dreams it would sug-   *f115ᵛ*
gest? Or is every animal a republic in se? Or is there one Breeze of
Life—at once the soul of each & God of all?—Is it not strictly analogous to generation, & no more contradictory to unity than *it?*—
But IT? Aye! there's the Twist in the Logic! Is not the reproduction of the Lizard a complete generation! O it is easy to dream, &
surely better of these things than of a 20,000 £ Prize in the Lottery, or of a Place at Court!—13 Dec. 1804. Malta.

2331 21.515   Darwin's story of the Bees in Barbadoes that finding Flowers all the year round left off making Honey confutes itself. It could not be the same species with ours—or else the young
ones would all perish, who absolutely require the Honey-broth for
their subsistence prior to their creeping out of their cells—

2332 21.516   To deduce instincts from obscure recollections of a
pre-existing State—I have often thought of it—Ey! have I said,
when I have seen certain tempers & actions in Hartley, that is *I* in
my future State/so I think oftentimes that my children are my
Soul./that multitude & division are not (o mystery) necessarily
subversive of unity. I am sure, that two very different meanings if
not more lurk in the word, *one.* S.T.C.

2333 21.517   The hot-blooded Paddy's *pruriency for Fight.*   *f116*
prurit in pugnam. Mart.

2334 21.518   Among my wild poem on strange things put into
an artificial Brooding-machine or Sand in the Sun three eggs, an
eagles, a Ducks, & a Serpent's/.

2335 21.519   The drollest explanation of Instinct is that of Mylius who attributes every act to Pain/and all the wonderful webs & envelopes of Spiders, Caterpillars, &c absolutely to fits of Colic, or paroxysms of Dry Bellyache!!

2336 21.520   This Tarantula Dance of repetitious & vertiginous argumentation in circulo, begun in imposture & ⟨self-⟩consummated in madness.

2337 21.521   While the whole planet (quoad its Lords or at least Lord-lieutenantry) is in stir & bustle, why should not I keep in tune with the time, & like old Diogenes roll my Tub about?

2338 21.522   A line like a river in a map, or rather like the wet track of a Fly on a Table, that has been rescued from drowning.

2339 21.523   I cannot too often remember that to be deeply interested & to be highly satisfied, are not always commensurates— apply this to the affecting and yet unnatural passages of the Stranger, or of John Bull—& to the finest passages of the Death of Cleopatra or Hamlet. But especially to the former, and such other operas where Music truly expresses Passion. Surely, surely, we are adapting all to the Vulgar, instead of raising up the Vulgar to the best.

f116

2340 21.524   15 Dec. 1804. Saw the limb of a rainbow footing itself on the Sea at a small apparent distance from the Shore, a thing of itself, no substrate cloud or even mist visible, but the distance glimmered thro' it as thro' a thin semitransparent hoop—

2341 21.525   ⟨Strada di S. Ursula in Malta all steps, from house door to house door 6 yards, the steps two feet in depth or breadth or length (I do not what to call it ⟍▬▬⟋ 6y *width*, I suppose, is the word—& they rise above each other in a tolerably steep ascent, 160 of them.⟩

2342 21.526   To be and to act, two in Intellect, (that mother of orderly multitude, & half Sister of Wisdom & Madness) but one in essence = to rest and to move = ▱ and a ◯ ! and out of the infinite combinations of these, from the more and the less now of one now of the other all pleasing figures & the source of all pleasure, arise. But the Pyramid △, that base of Stedfastness that rises yet never deserts itself—nor ever—approaches to the ◯ ? 16 Dec. 1804.   Sunday Midnight, Malta.

2343 21.527   The Pyramid in Art, I can make out no other   ƒ117 affinity to the circle but by taking its evanescence as the central point, & so having thus gained the radii *melt in* the circumference —look it into the Object; Extravagance! Why? Does not every one do this in looking at any three conspicuous stars together; does not every one *see*, by the inner vision & ⟨by⟩ its action upon our bodily eyes, a triangle. However, this is in art: but the Prototype in Nature is indeed loveliness—there there are no ⟨or all⟩ straight lines, ~~that comprehend~~ having the soul of curves ~~whose~~ from activity & positive rapid energy: ~~give the semblance of straightness~~— or ~~if it indeed appear~~ whether it seem curve or *straight*, here *is* motion, motion in its most significant form, it is motion in that form, which has been chosen to express motion in general, hieroglyphical from preeminence, & made to mean *all* by being there the most/therefore ⟨tho' it appear all straight, yet there's⟩ no need here of any curve, whose effect is that of embleming motion, & counteracting actual solidity by that emblem/here it is vice versa. Actual motion & therefore a balancing *Figurite* of Rest and Solidity.—But I will study the wood fire this evening at the Palace. Monday Morning, 17 Dec. 1804.

2344 21.528   O said I as I looked on the blue, yellow, green, & purple green Sea, with all its hollows & swells, & cut-glass surfaces —O what an Ocean of lovely forms!—and I was vexed, teazed, that the sentence sounded like a play of Words. But it was not, the mind within me was struggling to express the marvellous distinctness & unconfounded personality of each of the million millions of forms, & yet their undivided Unity in which they subsisted.

2345 21.529   A brisk Gale, and the spots of foam that peopled the *alive* Sea most interestingly combined with the numbers of *f118ᵛ* white Sea Gulls; so that repeatedly it seemed, as if the foam-spots had taken Life and Wing & flown up/the white precisely same-color Birds rose up so close by the ever perishing white wave head, that the eye was unable to detect the illusion which the mind delighted indulging—

2346 21.530   O that Sky, that soft blue mighty Arch, resting on the mountains or solid Sea-like plain/what an aweful adorable omneity in unity. I know no other perfect union of the sublime with the beautiful, that is, so that they should both be felt at the same moment tho' by different faculties yet each faculty predisposed by itself to receive the specific modification from the other. To the eye it is an inverted Goblet, the inside of a ~~gold~~ sapphire Bason; = perfect beauty ⟨in shape and color⟩ ; to the mind ⟨it is⟩ immensity, but even the eye ⟨feels as if it were to⟩ look *thro'* with dim sense of the non ~~differ~~resistence/it is not exactly the feeling ~~from a~~ given to the organ by solid & limited things/the eye itself feels that the limitation is in its own power not in the Object, but pursue this in the manner of the Old Hamburgh Poet—

2347 21.531   One travels along with the Lines of a mountain —/I wanted, years ago, to make Wordsworth sensible of this—/ how fine is Keswick Vale, would I repose? My Soul lies & is quiet, upon the broad level vale—would it act~~ed~~? it darts up into the mountain Tops like a Kite, & like a chamois goat runs along the Ridges—or like a Boy that makes a sport on the road of running along a wall, or narrow fence—

f117ᵛ 2348 21.532   (~~Tuesday~~ Monday Night, 11 °clock, 17 Dec.—I had turned over two leaves—this therefore is a long parenthesis): of the flame I see now that the eye refuses to decide whether it be surface or convexity—for the exquisite oneness of the flame makes even its angles so different from the angles of tangible substances.

Its exceeding oneness + its very subsistence in motion is the very *soul* of the loveliest *curve*/it does not need its *body*, as it were. Its sharpest point is, however somewhat rounded, & besides it is cased within its penumbra.

2349 21.533   Tuesday Morning, 18 Dec. 8 °clock.—Beautiful circumstance the improvement of the flower from the Root up to that crown of its Life & Labors †, that bridal chamber of its Beauty & its twofold Love, the nuptial & the parental—the womb, the cradle, the nursery of the future Garden—insect analogies. † Quisque sui faber—a pretty simile this would make to a young Lady producing Beauty by moral feeling.

2350 21.534   Of matter we may often say an unorganized mass; but I doubt, whether there exists a mass of unorganized matter.

2351 21.535   Nature, the πολυμηχανος Εγ⟨ρ⟩ανια, an ever industrious Penelope for ever unravelling what she had woven, for ever weaving what she had unravelled.

2352 21.536   To trace the if not absolute birth yet the growth & endurancy of Language from the Mother talking to the Child at her Breast—O What a subject for some happy moment of deep feeling, and strong imagination.—⌐Sara! Sara!⌐ O those dear ⌐children!⌐

2353 21.537   The adventures, rivalry, warfare, and final union f118 & partnership of Dr. Hocus, & Dr. Pocus.

2354 21.538   Country = contra/Gegend = gegen Geard, Guardian, Garden—Hat, Hüt, Hus, Haus, House, my Hat my Head's House. Word, *Werden*—that which is— ⟨Worth, worthy—Rede, Redlich⟩—Truth is implied in Words among the first men. *Tale* = tale. Word, wahr, wehr—truth, troweth, throweth i.e. hitteth = itteth =it is *it*. The aspirate expresses the exclamatia of action. Through, & Truth—Etymol. Spectre-colors pressed out of the eye closed under the Sunlight. Nos hæc novimus esse nihil.

2355 21.539   Idly talk they who speak of Poets as mere Indulg-
ers of Fancy, Imagination, Superstition, &c—They are the Bridlers
by Delight, the Purifiers, they that combine them with *reason* &
order, the true Protoplasts, Gods of Love who tame the Chaos.

2356 21.540   Of a Quintette in the Syracuse Opera/and the
pleasure of the Voices—one, and not one, they leave, seek, pursue,
oppose, fight with, strengthen, annihilate each other, awake, en-
liven, soothe, flatter, and embrace each other again, till at length
they die away in one Tone. There is no sweeter Image of wayward
yet fond Lovers, of Seeking and finding, of the love quarrel & the
making up, of the losing and the yearning Regret, of the doubtlet
then compleat Recognition, and ⟨of the total melting union. Words
not interpreters, but fellow-combatants.⟩

f119 2357 21.541   One of the most noticeable and fruitful facts in
Psychology is the modification of the same feeling by difference of
form/The Heavens lift up my soul, the sight of the Ocean seems
to widen it. We feel the same Force at work, but the difference
from Body & Mind both that we should feel in actual travelling
horizontally or in direct ascent, that we feel in fancy—for what
are our feelings of this kind but a motion imagined? with the feelings that would accompany that motion less distinguished more
blended, rapid, confused, & thereby coadunated—as white is the
very emblem of one in being the confusion of all.

                                                        S.T.C.

2358 21.542   Is it or is it not true, that whoever supermoralizes
unmoralizes? ⟨Instanced in the Catholic doctrine of marriage con-
cubitus cum pregn. &c &c.⟩

2359 21.543   Few phænomena of the Senses strike me with
greater wonder, lead me more to the twilight of matter and Spirit,
as a twofold motion, the Bowl of Ninepins for instance, or still
more beautiful, the rising up & whirling round of a hundred columns of sugar particles in [. . . . .] for you have

2360 21.544   Not to hastily to abandon & kick away the means   ƒ119ᵛ
after the end is or seems to be accomplished/so have I in blowing
out the Paper or Match with which I have lit a Candle, blown out
the Candle at the same instant.

2361 21.545   Of men (am not *I* included? O Heavens! What
name of Weakness, be it W. of Mind or W. of Heart, is there, ~~to~~
in which I am not included?) of men who cannot wait till their
works are finished, much less published, or even correct/who even
cannot stay till they are absolutely in any part written, but must
talk over, communicate, satiate and surfeit their impatient pert
vanity, ~~half~~ part busy-ness of mind, part incontinence of sympathy
with their Hints, Plans, chapters of Content, and first Fragments—
and so waste Life away, always *going to* do that & that, *never set
down at it;* affecting every thing (in the better sense of the word),
effecting nothing! What are these but Children with quills or stiff
Straws at the Cyder Press, drinking up the unmade, ⟨uncasked,⟩
unfermented, Liquor—& what is the consequence?—~~Ah~~ Aye! what
did *Thought do?*

2362 21.546   ⌈. . . . .⌉ Existence, S.T.C.   ƒ120

2363 22.12   with swimming hovering step—   ƒ11ᵛ
Are they bodiless Forms, colour but not substance? Are they moonlight Elfins? As ~~the~~ boats on the tossing sea, they toss as upon the
waves of the Melody—the melody hebt den atherischen Leib.

Jetzo, als wolt [*wollt*] es mit macht [*Macht*] durchreissen die
    Kette des Tanzes,
Schwingt sich ein holdes Paar dort in den dichtesten Reihn.
Schnell vor ihm her entsteht ihm die Bahn, die hinter ihm
    schwindet,
Wie durch magische Hand öfnet [*öffnet*] & schliesst sich der Weg.
Sieh! Jetzt schwand es dem Blick, in wildem Gewirr durch einan-
    der
Stürzt der zierliche Bau dieser beweglichen Welt—.
Nein, dort schwebt es frohlockend herauf, der Knoten entwirrt
    sich,

Nur mit verändertem Reiz stellet die Regel sich her.
Ewig zerstört, es erzeugt sich ewig die drehende Schöpfung,
Und ein stilles Gesetz lenk[t] der Verwandlungen Spiel.
Sprich wie gescheht's [*geschieht's,*] dass rastlos erneut die Bildun-
   gen schwanken,

f12   Und die Ruhe besteht in der bewegten Gestalt?
Jeder ein Herrscher, frei, nur dem eigenen Herzen gehorchet,
Und im eilenden Lauf findet die einzige Bahn?

It is harmony. Will you admire it in dance—& not in the Universe
—&c

f11   2364 22.11   Dec. 21. 1804. I cannot conceive any necessary
weakness of mind in the *then* belief of these supposed facts. It
seemed a discovery of powers in nature, like that of a magnet pro-
f11° ducing the effects of the Galvanic Electricity, which prove to be
false—as to the irrationality, it always seems to attach to new facts,
& one hopes that after discoveries will clear up the whole.

f12   2365 22.13   Jupiter & the Poet—cut your throat & come to
me? in Chabrerta—Jupiter divided the World—the Poet came in
after the division—he had been gazing on the Heaven—&c—

2366 22.14   In the Soother of Absence—introduce Domus
quadrata hortensis at Henley on Thames, the beautiful Girl—her
after fate—& my Struggle in London, 1804—Jan.—

f120 2367 21.547   Saturday, Dec. 22nd, 1804. The duty of stating the
power and in the very formation of the Letters, perceived during
the formation, the meaning of the injured mind. The Best remains! Good God! wretched as I may be bodily, what is there good
and excellent which I would not do—?—
   But this is written in *involuntary* Intoxication. God bless all!

2368 21.548   Sunday, Dec. 23rd/I do not understand the first
sentence of the above—I wrote ~~when nearly~~ them after that con-

vulsed or suffocated by a collection of wind in my stomach & alter-
nately tortured by its colic pangs in my bowels, I in despair drank
three glasses running of whisky & water/the violent medicine
answered—I ~~was~~ have been feeble in body ~~here this~~ during the   *f120ᵛ*
next day, & active in mind—& how strange that with so shaken a
nervous System I never have the Head ache!—I verily am a stout-
headed, weak-bowelled, and O! most pitiably weak-*hearted* Animal! But I leave it, ⟨as I wrote it⟩—& likewise have refused to
destroy the stupid drunken Letter to Southey, which I wrote in the
sprawling characters of Drunkenness/& If I should perish without
having the power of destroying these & my other pocket books, the
history of my own mind for my own improvement. O friend!
Truth! Truth! but yet Charity! Charity! I have never loved Evil
for its own sake; & ⟨no! nor⟩ ɪ ever sought pleasure for its own
sake, but only as the means of escaping from pains that coiled
round my mental powers, as a serpent around the body & wings of
an Eagle! ⟨My sole sensuality was *not* to be in pain!—⟩

2369 21.549   ⌐. . . . .⌐ should not be so!—S. T.   *f121*
                  Coleridge

2370 21.550   How opposite to nature & the fact to talk of the
one *moment* of Hume; of our whole being an aggregate of successive single sensations. Who ever *felt* a *single* sensation? Is not
every one at the same moment conscious that there co-exist a thousand others in a darker shade, or less light; even as when I fix my
attention on a white House on a grey bare Hill or rather long
ridge that runs out of sight each way (How often I want the german unübersehbar?) the pretended single sensation is it any thing
more than the *Light*-point in every picture either of nature or of a
good painter; & again subordinately in every component part of the
picture? And what is a moment? Succession with *interspace?* Absurdity! It is evidently only the Licht-punct [*punkt*], the *Sparkle*
~~of~~ in the indivisible undivided Duration. Christmas Day, 1804. In
the sky-chamber, with the four winds on the ceiling & the pencil of
Blast from each mouth of the curly-wigged No*bodies,* & the fine
Queen Elizabeth's ~~neck~~ Ruff of Cloud that serves them for neck/&

the mariners Compass, within them, ~~and~~ all within 5 or 6 Co-par-
allograms, only have ~~a~~ concave curves instead of corners,

those introcluded rims or borders various colored/& the green side-
board, with rails ~~all~~ round $\frac{3}{4}^{ths}$ of it, that is the ceiling at the same
of the winding stone Stair Case/& the four windows/& the whole
room in its extremes ~~by~~ 3 yards by 5/but with such deductions as
would leave its real capacity not more than 2 yds by 3 = six square
yards. Valletta, Malta:—Extremely unwell all last night.

f121   2371 21.551   A Rainbow strangely preserving its form on broken clouds, with here a bit out, here a bit in, & yet still a rainbow
even as you might place bits of colored ribbons at distances so as
still to preserve the form of a Bow to the mind. Dec. 25. 1804—

2372 21.552   There are two sorts of talkative fellows whom it
would be injurious to confound/& I, S. T. Coleridge, am the latter.
The first sort is of those who use five hundred words more than
needs to express an idea—that is not my case—few men, I will be
bold to say, put more meaning into their words than I or choose
them more deliberately & discriminatingly. The second sort is of
those who use five hundred more ideas, images, reasons &c than
there is any need of to arrive at their object/till the only object
arrived at is that the ~~readers~~' mind's eye of the bye-stander is daz-
zled with colors succeeding so rapidly as to leave one vague impression that there has been a great Blaze of colours all about
something. Now this is my case—& a grievous fault it is/my illustra-
f122   tions swallow up my thesis—I feel too intensely the omnipresence
of all in each, platonically speaking—or psychologically my brain-
fibres, or the spiritual Light which abides in ~~thate~~ brain marrow as
visible Light appears to do in sundry rotten mackerel & other *smashy*
matters, is of too general an affinity with all things/and tho' it perceives the *difference* of things, yet is eternally pursuing the like-
ness~~nesses~~, or rather that which is common/bring me two things

that seem the very same, & then I am quick enough to shew the difference, even to hair-splitting—but to go on from circle to circle till I break against the shore of my Hearer's patience, or have my Concentricals dashed to nothing by a Snore—that is my ordinary mishap. At Malta however, no one can charge me with one or the other. I have earned the general character of being a quiet well meaning man, rather dull indeed—& who would have thought, that he had been a ~~poet~~ Poet! "O very wretched Poetaster, Ma'am! As to the reviews, it is well known, he half ruined himself in paying cleverer fellows than himself to write them" &c—25   *f122ᵛ* Dec. 1804.

2373 21.553   How far one might imagine all the association System out of a system of growth/thinking of the Brain & Soul, what we know of an embryo—one tiny particle combines with another, its like. & so lengthens & thickens.—& this is at once Memory & increasing vividness of impression, one might make a very amusing Allegory of an embryo Soul up to Birth!—Try! it is promising!—You have not above 300 volumes to write before you come to it—& as you write perhaps a volume once in ten years, you have ample Time, my dear Fellow!—Never be ashamed of scheming—you can't think of living less than 4000 years, & that would nearly suffice for your present schemes—/To Be sure, if they go on in the same Ratio to the Performance, there is a small difficulty arises/but never mind! look at the bright side always—& die in a Dream! OH!

2374 21.554   The evil effect of a new hypothesis or even no-   *f123* menclature that many minds who had familiarized themselves to the old one, & were riding on accustomed to their ~~next~~ Horse on the road of discove~~red~~ry, put on a new animal lose time in learning how to *sit* him—while the others looking too stedfastly at a few facts which the Jeweller Hypothesis has *set* in a perfectly beautiful Whole, forget to dig for more, tho' Inhabitants of a Golconda. However, it has its advantages too—& these have been ably pointed out—it excites contradiction, is thence a stimulus to new experiments to *support*, & to a more severe repetition of those experiments and of other new ones to *confute*/& besides, a little Fancy, one must alloy severe Truth with it in order to mint it into current coin.

2375 21.555   In the Preface of my Metaphys. Works I should say—Once & all read Tetens, Kant, Fichte, &c—& there you will trace or if you are on the hunt, track me. Why then not acknowlege your obligations step by step? Because, I could not do in a *f123ᵛ* multitude of glaring resemblances without a lie/for they had been mine, formed, & full formed in my own mind, before I had ever heard of these Writers, because to have fixed on the partic. instances in which I have really been indebted to these Writers would have very hard, if possible, to me who read for truth & self-satisfaction, not to make a book, & who always rejoiced & was jubilant when I found my own ideas well expressed already by others, ⟨& would have looked like a *trick*, to skulk there not quoted,⟩ & lastly, let me say, because (I am proud perhaps but) I seem to know, that much of the matter remains my own, and that the Soul is *mine*. I fear not him for a Critic who can confound a Fellow-thinker with a Compiler.

2376 21.556   We notice a fact, and then generalize it—now in this generalization is it a fair comparison of a vast number of facts & an utter absence of all reason why it should ~~not~~ be otherwise in all included in the generalization, as in Euclid's demonstration of the equality of the Radii of a circle—This *is*—or is there an over-balance of apparent ⌐. . . . . ⌐

f124 2377 21.557   8000 men at Minorca useless & without quarters refused by General Fox at Lord Keith's earnest solicitation to garrison Genoa, that the 7 Austrians garrisoning it might have joined the army—& to have gone themselves.—!!

2378 21.558   Good Heaven! that there should be any thing at all—and not nothing—ask the bluntest faculty that pretends to reason & if indeed he have felt and reasoned, and he ~~may~~ must feel that something is which is to be sought after out of the vulgar track of Change-alley Speculation. If my researches are shadowy,

what in the name of Reason, are you—or do you resign all pretence
to reason, & consider yourself—nay, even that is a contradiction—
as a passive o among Nothings?

2379 21.559   How flat a commonplace! O that it were in my $f124^v$
Heart, Nerves, and Muscles—O that it were the *prudential* soul
of all, I love, of all who deserved to be loved, in every ~~thing~~ proposed action ask yourself—to what end is this? and how is this
the means?—and will it be the efficient means? and not the means
to something else foreign or abhorrent from my purpose?—Dis-
TINCT MEANS TO DISTINCT ENDS.—With Friends & Beloved ones
follow the Heart,/better be deceived 20 times, than suspect $\frac{1}{20}^{th}$
of once/but with strangers, or *acquaintances*, or enemies, or in a
quarrel, whether in the world's squabbles, as Dr Stoddart & D^r
Sewel in the Admirality Court, Malta, or in moral businesses, as
mine with Southey, or Lloyd (O pardon me, dear and honored
Southey that I put such a name by the side of yours—that stupe-
fied Self-luster for Self-love—does not express the whole)—in all
these cases, write your Letter, *vent, & ease yourself*, and when you $f125$
have done it—even as when you have pared, sliced, vinegared,
oiled, peppered & salted your plate of Cucumber you are directed
to smell to it—& then throw it out of the window—so, dear friend!
vinegar, pepper, & salt your Letter, cucumber argument—i.e. cool
reasoning—previously sauced with passion & sharpness—then read
it—eat it, drink it, smell it, with eyes & ears—(a small catachresis,
but never mind)—& then throw it into the fire—unless you can put
down in three or four sentences—I cannot allow more than one side
of a sheet of Paper—*the distinct End* for which you conceive this
Letter (or whatever it be) to be THE DISTINCT MEANS!—How
trivial! would to god, it were only *habitual!* O what is sadder
than that the crambe bis cocta of the Understanding should be and $f125^v$
remain a foreign dish to the efficient *will*—that the best and loftiest
precepts of Wisdom should be *trivial,* and the worst and lowest
modes of Folly *habitual.*

2380 21½.122   + means added to, × means multiplied with, $f75$
— means less by, deprived of = means the same as, equal to/
÷ means divided by.—

2381 21½.123   Luogot.° di Casal Safi il Sig.° Giuseppe Abdillo

ƒ74° 2382 21½.124   *Dec. 27. 1804*—1. We *feel.* 2. we perceive or imagine. 3. we *think.*

✕ These are the three distinct classes of psychological Facts, which all men are conscious of and which all languages express. Hartley, and his followers and the French Philosophers endeavor to resolve the latter two into the first//Leibnitz and Wolff the 1ˢᵗ & 3ʳᵈ into the second, "der Grundkraft (der einzige) ist der Vorstellungskraft"—and (as far as Thought may be considered as an self-activity of our Being), = the ⟨Will = the *Ich* or *I*⟩/Stahl & Fichte (and, as I believe, Plotinus, &c to Proclus) resolve the 1ˢᵗ & 2ⁿᵈ into the third. Still however the distinction must remain, alike in all—nor can any one be affirmed hitherto to have succeeded in *explaining* the three into one/. My *Faith* is with Fichte, but never let me lose my reverence for the *three distinctions,* which are as human & of our essence, as those of the 5 senses on which indeed a similar process has been tried.

So doing I may combine & harmonize Philosophy and Common Sense.

ƒ75   ✕ Shall we add a 4ᵗʰ, *Willing?* No. Because it is yet indefinite in the common ~~nonsense~~ *speculations* of ⟨speculative⟩ mankind whether ~~it~~ the Will be not a combination of all three as *wishing* evidently is whether wishing & willing are more than degrees of the same operation/And those who hold otherwise make it the Being itself, the absolute I or Self, not a modification or faculty— or if ever they ⟨may have⟩ identified ~~it~~ with the Third,/we still could not *add* it, we could only *substitute* it.—But to *act,* is not that a necessary 4ᵗʰ?

Answer. I would, that it were the grand comprising Term in Psiology for all the three; but a fourth it cannot make, inasmuch as "action," taken in the usual sense, implies *willing,* superadding *motion;*—and motion is either the first—i.e. feeling; or the 2ⁿᵈ— i.e. image (or τὸ perceptum definite) or both combined. And abstracted from outward contingency, action is the same as *"willing";* or at all events (for I perceive a distinction) it cannot be admitted,

BANDO

SUA Eccellenza il Sig. Commissionario Regio prendendo in consi-
derazione il vantaggio che dall'essere, e conservarsi in buono stato le
Strade ne ridonda al Pubblico, la sua premura per l'ottenimento di sì
importante scopo non gli permette di trascurare alcuno de'mezzi che
possan farvelo pervenire.

Considerando quindi che le ruote de'Calessi, e de'Carri, tali quali
si fanno attualmente, sono la cagion principale della deteriorazione e
guasto delle Strade ordina, e comanda, che in avvenire simili ruote
sien fatte sul modello da consegnarsi ai rispettivi Artefici, e senza che
i chiodi risultino sulle lamine di ferro, che contornan la loro circonfe-
renza, sotto pena agli Artefici controventori di pagare, tante quante volte
controvverranno, la pena d'oncie venti da applicarsi per metà al fisco,
e per l'altra metà al delatore.

Siccome poi spera Sua Eccellenza che la maggior parte dei Proprietarj de'Carri, e Calessi in vista del suo piacere, e del proprio lor
comodo vorran riformare le ruote de' Carri, e Calessi loro spettanti,
sebben già fatte, si ripromette fin da ora la soddisfazione di vedere
trapoco introdotto generalmente un sistema da far le ruote, che nell'atto
di risparmiare le Strade è pure di notabile vantaggio ai Proprietarj de'
Calessi, e Carri, essendo molto facile a comprendere, che le grosse, e
prominenti teste de' chiodi dando delle continue scosse ai Calessi, e Carri,
ed alle Persone, o cose condotte, distruggon più presto il Calesse, o Carro
istesso, ed in particolare le lamine di ferro, le quali ricevono immediatamente la scossa; scomodano chi è condotto; danneggiano le cose
condotte; ed affaticano vieppiù l'animale poichè quelle prominenti teste de'chiodi operano a guisa di tanti punti di resistenza, e di vetti op-
poste all'azione della forza movente.

Segreteria del Governo li 29 Gennajo 1805.

Samuel T. Coleridge Seg°.Pub.del Commis.Regio.

G. N. Zammit Prosegretario.

*Adi 31. Gennajo 1805. E' stato letto, publicato, ed affisso
nei luoghi soliti di q.te quattro Città e. gloriana a
suono di tromba in presa di moltissime persone.*

11. Possibly the first proclamation signed by Coleridge in his official
capacity as Public Secretary, Malta. 29 January 1805

See 2386n

till "the Will" either as a Thing per se, or ⟨else as⟩ = Ego, Anima, have been admitted.

Better 5. We 1. *feel:* 2. *perceive,* whether *things* or their represen-   *f74ᵛ*
tation in the Imagination. 3. *think* or *conc*eive: 4. *will:* 5. *move &*
impress motions.

2383 21½.2

1,	2,	3,	4,	5,	6,	7,	8,	9,	10,	11,	12,	13,	14,	15,	*f1*
a,	b,	c,	d,	e,	f,	g,	h,	i,	j,	k,	l,	m,	n,	o,

16,	17,	18,	19,	20,	21,	22,	23,	24,	25
p,	q,	r,	s,	t,	u,	w,	x,	y,	z,

Abbreviations.

$+ \times \ \sqsupset \ \mathrm{I} \ \mathrm{+} \ \text{⁂} \ \text{✳} \ - \ = \ \odot \ \psi \ \text{✳}$
and, to, they, of with from by, who, the, *I, me, you, ye, he, him, his*
&c

2384 21½.6   = the same as or equal to/ + added to × multi-   *f5*
plied by/ — less by/ ⋇ contrasted with.
—signifies who, or whom, or which, or whose, or what. ⊐,
they, them, these, those.

2385 21½.7   "E se quelli nobilissimi Scrittori furono ritenuti
per non offendere la memoria di coloro, di chi eglino avevano a
ragionare, se ne ingannarono, e mostrarono di cognoscere poco
l'ambizione degli uomini, e il desiderio che egli hanno di perpetuare
il nome di loro antichi e di loro. Nè si ricordarono che molti non
avendo avuti occasione di acquistarsi fama con qualche opera
lodevole, con cose vituperose si sono ingegnati acquistarla. Nè
considerarono, *come le azioni che hanno in se grandezza, come*
hanno quelle de' governi e degli Stati, communque elle si trattino,
qualunque fine abbino, pare sempre portino agli uomini più onore
che biasimo". Macchiav. Proemio delle Istorie Fiorentine.

2386 21½.8   And laurel Crown, the Enemy of Death,   *f5ᵛ*
                 If Life be action!

2387 21.599

f136 1/4, 1/5, 1/4, 9, 7, 8, 20, 22, 9, 20, 8, 15, ~~8~~, 21, 20, 9, 20, 19, 7, 21, ~~12~~, 9, 12, 20, 15, 6, 15, 16, 9, 21, 13, 1, 14, 4, 19, 16, 9, 18, 9, 20!—27 Dec. 1804.

2388 21.598   The survey of this pocket book—it might suggest and furnish matter for, a passionate address to my Lamp or Tapers, whose beautiful forms had been so often gazed at, & sometimes frightened of its perpendicular by my groans ⌐. . . . .⌐

2389 21.594 $\overline{W + D + MW} + SH + \overline{HDSC} = S\ T\ C.$
= Ego contemplans

2390 21.595   non s'e veduto

2391 21.596   do *think* of it; not merely dream—O by & by

2392 21.597   640 acres in a square mile.

f4ᵛ 2393 21.31   "It is not the place of any man's nativity, but his Domicil, not of his origination but of his habitation that subjects him to reprize: the Law doth not consider so much where a man was born as where he lives—not so much where he came into the World as where he improves it." Molloy de Jure maritimo.

f125ᵛ 2394 21.560   Wednes. Morning, 2 °clock, 9 Jan. 1805—Why am I not in bed?—Why have I occasion to notice that pressing the eyeballs close restores distinctness to the vision, when otherwise the words appear *fasericht*—hairy, ragged—with a rough irregular *nap* upon them/this last is the real feeling—& yet something resembling words written on blotting paper—not the mere sinking or running of the Letters, but that *fasericht* nappy essence of each Letter/. ⌐O Sara!⌐ I know not by what connection I then uttered your name/. I believe it was this, that thinking of my thus sitting up & of my intended Letter to poor *Stoddart* impress upon him the substance of this maxim of distinct means to distinct ends I

sighed—and instantly like a flashed of Lightning, I thought of
⌈. . . . .⌉

2395 21.561   Of the shameful resignation of Mathematics to   ƒ126
the French by the Countrymen of Barrow and Newton/the influence of our Engineer & artillery Corps so execrably educated,
compared with the French—What I once before observed, the
French Government, venal as Louis, in all matters of private Justice, will have no jobbing in public matters—and each man is found
out/the necessity of supporting *Science*, & perhaps every thing, by
Government & Patronage—and now combat stoutly the opinion of
a Public as a good thing/it is Perdition/trace it in every country
—while a Court is the great Judge, Poetry & Oratory becomes over-
decorous, over delicate, stupid stately/but when men of Learning
write to men of Learning, & the number of Readers is small, then
rise the Suns, Moons, and Stars out of the Chaos—but when the
Public are the Judge, O Heavens! Reynolds, Morton, Colman/
dullest parts of dull prose Tragedy with the grossest parts of
Farce, always a web of Jacobinism

2396 21.562   ⌈. . . . .⌉ learnt not always, *at all*, &   ƒ126ᵛ
seldom *harshly* to chide, those conceits of words which are analogous
to sudden fleeting affinities of mind/even as in a dance touch & join
& off again, & rejoin your partner that leads down with you the
whole dance spite of these occasional off-starts, all still not merely
conform to, but ⟨of, and⟩ in, & forming, the delicious harmony—
Shakespere is not a 1000ᵗʰ part so faulty as the ooo believe him/
"Thus him that over-rul'd I oversway'd" &c &c I noticed this to
that bubbling ice-spring of cold-hearted ~~violent~~ mad-headed Fanaticism, the late Dʳ Geddes—in the Heri vidi fragilem frangi;
hodie mortalem ~~mei~~ mori.

2397 21.563   11. Jan. 1805. Convoy has been off these four
days: and still cannot beat into the Harbour. But the Boat will go
off for the Letters.—O my poor anxious Soul! Lady Ball asked
me yesterday, if I was not excessively impatient—I surprized her
by saying—Not at all. Yet I felt that in telling the Truth I was

conveying falsehood—and endeavored afterwards to explain as far
I could with propriety that I was not impatient because I was anxious—that I had much Fear and little Hope/for the only things
that deeply interest me *being the Lives* & Health of Hartley,
Derwent, Sara—& W + D + MW + SH, whatever happens
anew, and implies change has either wherewith to frighten or not
wherewith to interest me. ⟨And Major Adye is dead! There died
a good man!—⟩

f127   2398 21.564   It is a most instructive part of my Life the fact,
that I have been always preyed on by some Dread, and perhaps all
my faulty actions have been the consequence of some Dread or
other on my mind/from fear of Pain, or Shame, not from prospect
of Pleasure/—So in my childhood & Boyhood the horror of being
detected with a sorehead; afterwards imaginary fears of the having the Itch in my Blood—/then a short-lived Fit of Fears from
sex—then horror of DUNS, & a state of struggling with madness
from an incapability of hoping that I should be able to marry Mary
Evans (and this strange passion of fervent tho' wholly imaginative
and imaginary Love uncombinable by my utmost efforts with ⟨any
regular⟩ Hope—/possibly from deficiency of bodily feeling, of tactual ideas connected with the image) had all the effects of direct
Fear, & I have lain for hours together awake at night, groaning
& praying—Then came that stormy time/and for a few months
America really inspired Hope, & I became an exalted Being—then
came Rob. Southey's alienation/my marriage—constant dread in
my mind respecting Mrs Coleridge's Temper, &c—and finally
stimulants in the fear & prevention of violent Bowel-attacks from
mental agitation/then ⟨almost epileptic⟩ night-horrors in my sleep/
& since then every error I have committed, has been the immediate
effect of the Dread of these bad most shocking Dreams—any thing
to prevent them/—all this interwoven with its minor consequences,
that fill up the interspaces—the cherry juice running in between
the cherries in a cherry pie/procrastination in dread of this—&
something else in consequence of that procrast. &c/—and from the
same cause the least languor expressed in a Letter from S.H.
drives me wild/& it is most unfortunate that I so fearfully de-

spondent should have concentered my soul thus on one almost as feeble in Hope as myself. 11 Jan. 1805.—

Important metaphysical Hint the influence of bodily vigor and strong Grasp of Touch in facilitating the passion of Hope: 5, 21, 14, 21, 3, 8, 19—in all degrees even to the full 5, 14, 19, 8, 5, 1, 20, 8 ment and the 2, 15, 20, 8 at once.   *f127ᵛ*

2399 21.565   The imperfection of the organs by which we seem to unite ourselves with external things—the tongue, the palate, the Hand—which latter becoming more *organic* is less passionate/ now take an organ as ~~in~~ the highest exponent of passion with the least possible machinery of power, that is, the most Feeling, ~~and~~ the least Touch, & no Grasp/it can only suit a universal idea/ ~~constantly~~sequently dim—& one by the dimness/~~of~~ ~~its~~ however complex it may or may not be. Observe that in certain excited states of feeling the knees, ancle, sides & soles of the feet, become organic/Query—the nipple in a woman's breast, does that ever become the seat of a particular feeling, as one would guess by its dormancy & sudden awakings—
Touch—double touch/¹Touch with the sense of immediate power ²with retentive power— ³retentive power extinguishing the sense of touch, or making it mere feeling—& the gradations preceding ~~these~~is extinction/⁴retentive power simply, as when I hold a thing with my Teeth/⁵with feeling not Touch in one part of the machinery, both in the other, as when I press a bit of sugar with my Tongue against my Palate/⁶with feeling & even touch but not ~~enjoyment~~ specific stim*ulari* (esse sub stimulo) as when I hold a quill or bit of fruit by my lips—1. mem. vi/Riley. inacts of E*ss*ex. 2. The Lips, or the thumb and forefinger in a slight pressure. 3. The Hand grasping firmly an inanimate Body—that is the one extreme of this third Class—the other would be a Lover's Hand grasping the soft white hand of his mistress/Here the retentive power and nisus modify but not extinguish the Touch—it tells the story still & the mind listens to it.—

2400 21.566   How often I have occasion to notice with pure delight the depth of the exceeding Blueness of the Mediter. Sea from my window/it is often indeed Purple; but I am speaking of its *Blueness*, perfect *Blue*, so very pure and one. The Sea is like a Night-sky; ⟨but for its Planicies, it were⟩ as if the Night sky were a Thing, that turned round & lay in the day time under the paler Heaven/& it is on this expanse that the Vessels have the fine white dazzling Cotton Sails/A Speronara with a fellow with a red Jacket, &

2401 21.567(a) ⌈. . . . .⌉

f128 then a positive boundary/while it acts at all, it is light/when the mind acts for itself, & feels the straining of ineffectual action, ineffectual for its ordinary purposes, it creates a darkness.

2402 21.567(b) This Evening (Tuesday, Jan. 15th, 1805) was the most perfect & the brightest Halo ~~around~~ circling the roundest and brightest moon I ever beheld—so bright was the Halo, so compact, so entire a circle, that it gave the whole of its area, the moon itself included, the appearance of a solid opake body—an enormous Planet/& as if ⟨this Planet had⟩ ~~there were~~ a ⟨circular belt-like⟩ Trough ~~over~~ of some light-reflecting Fluid for its rim, ⟨⟨that is the Halo⟩⟩ and its centre, i.e. the Moon a small circular bason of some fluid that still more copiously reflected, or that ever emitted light; ⟨and as if⟩ the interspatial area ~~being~~ were somewhat equally

substantial, but sullen/ —thence I have found occasion to meditate on the nature of the sense of magnitude; ~~and~~ its absolute dependence on the idea of *Substance;* the consequent difference between *magnitude* and *Spaciousness;* the dependence of the idea

f128ᵛ of substance on double-touch/& thence to evolve all our feelings & ideas of magnitude, magnitudinal sublimity, &c from a scale of our own bodies—so why if *form* constituted the sense, i.e. if it were pure vision, as a perceptive sense abstracted from *feeling* in the organ of vision, why do I seek for mountains when in the flattest countries the Clouds present so many so much more romantic & *spacious* forms, & the coal-fire so many so much more varied & lovely forms?—And whence arises the pleasure from musing on the latter/do I not more or less consciously fancy myself a Lilliputian, to whom these would be mountains—& so by this factitious scale make them mountains, my pleasure being consequently playful, a voluntary poem in *hieroglyphics* or picture-writing—*"phantoms* of Sublimity" which I continue to know to be *phantoms?* —And form itself, is it not its main agency exerted in individualizing the Thing, making it *this*, & *that*, & thereby facilitating this shadowy measurement of it by the scale of my own body? Yon long not unvaried ridge of Hills that runs out of sight each way, it is *spacious*, & the pleasure derivable from it is from its *running*, its *motion*, its assimilation to action/& here the scale is   *f129* taken from my *Life*, & *Soul*—not from my body. Space ⟨is one of⟩ the Hebrew names for God/& it is the most perfect image of *Soul*, *pure Soul*—being indeed to us nothing but unresisted action.— Wherever action is resisted, limitation begins—& limitation is the first constituent of body—the more omnipresent it is in a given space, the more it that is *body* or matter//but thus all body necessarily presupposes soul, inasmuch as all resistance presupposes action/Magnitude therefore is the intimate *union* blending, the most perfect union, thro' its whole sphere, in every minutest part of it, of action and resistance to action/it is spaciousness in which Space is *filled up; &* ~~feelingly stopped~~ ⟨as we well say—i.e. transmitted by incorporate accession, not destroyed⟩ ~~and~~ In all limited things, that is, in all *forms*, it is at least fantastically *stopped/*and thus from the positive *grasp* to the mountain, from the mountain to the Cloud, from the Cloud to the blue depth of Sky, ~~that~~ which, as on the top of Etna in a serene atmosphere, seems to go *behind* the Sun, all is *gradation*, that precludes division indeed, but not distinction/& he who endeavors to overturn a distinction by shewing that there is no chasm, by the old sophism of the Cumulus, or the   *f129*ᵛ horse's tail, is still diseased with the ✳ *Formication*, the (what is the nosological name of it?—the hairs or dancing infinites of black specks seeming always to be before the eye) the Araneosis of corpuscular materialism. S.T.C.

✳ When instead of the general feeling of the life-blood in its equable undivided motion, ~~we feel~~ & the consequent wholeness of the one feeling of the Skin, we feel as if a heap of Ants were running over us/*the one* corrupting into *ten thousand* &c So in the araneosis &c, instead of the one view of the air, or blue sky, a thousand webs, specks, &c dance before the eye. The metaphor is as just as of a metaphor any one has a right to claim, tho' it is clumsily expressed.

2403 21.568   Haslitt uttering something profound, & of course, paradoxical to Thelwall, who appealed to me with a triumphant grin/& H. is *right* here too, I suppose!—O no! I replied—very wrong—altogether mistaken/he has been talking excellent Greek to his ~~Aun~~ Grandmother.

2404 21.569   The least things how they evidence the superiority of English artisans—now the Maltese Wafers for instance/that stick to your mouth and fingers almost so as to make it impossible to get them off without squeezing them into a little pellet, and yet will not stick to the paper.

2405 21.570   In favor of Revelation, of the nature not logical *f130* but real—not what it ought to be but what it *is*—of historic faith/ and of the necessary aid, which this lends to the wavering convictions of the Reason, in matters concerning God and Immortality. Is it not the same aid as that which the Double-touch lends to to Sight and Hearing? Something may hereafter be found out to perform the same service, & yet to stand the severest test of Reason. Well! let that something be found out! Hitherto it has not been/and a Crutch may be an awkward Tool, but still the infirm want Crutches. Jan. 17. 1805. ⟨Historic faith is evidently evolvible from double-touch.⟩

2406 21.571   We have traced picture into hieroglyphic and hieroglyphic into arbitrary character—but go further! see the handwriting of men who write much yet not for others, as Scribes, but for themselves & for their own reading—see! how few diversities of character there are, so as often to make it impossible except by the sense to know whether a certain mark be an "e" or an "i" ⟨or an "a," or an "o" or an "u"⟩ or an "n" or an "r" or an "l," or even an "m" or "u" or "w"—~~as all legibl~~ ~~may~~ eleven letters have certainly been expressed by one mark—and see that "ly" at the end of "certainly" in the line above, who could distinguish it, by itself, from an ill-written GG?—So by increase & habit of increased Intellect may not any one thing come to mean all things?—S.T.C.

The foregoing observation seems a mere sophism a certain number of distinct marks preceding and awaking the idea it will no doubt turn any pothooks and hangers into the exponents of those ideas that necessarily connect the last distinct mark with the following ~~but~~ What if they all were

f130

—which characters perhaps may have been made by the scribble-scrabble-geniuses to mean every & each Letter—what if they were all to come together, much more if ~~each or~~ any *one* were to be uniformly repeated, what would the sublimest Intellect make of it?—No! all we can deduce is this, that the assimilating Intellect may reduce all forms into any one, and make any one in its place representative of all; but still Intellect demands Distinction, as its Essence, & Distinction implies diversity in the co-existent vision. That form which is now an "n" may elsewhere be an "a" or "w" or "i" or "r" or even a "d"—but no six similar characters could without foregoing & following diversity of distinct letters convey the word "inward." N.B. half a page wasted in Nonsense, and a whole page in the confutation of it. But such is the nature of exercise—I walk a mile for health—& then another to return home again.

f131

2407 21.572   Every one of tolerable education feels the *imitability* of Dr Johnson's & other such's, style, the inimitability of Shakespere &c/hence I believe arises the partiality of thousands to Johnson/they can ~~th~~ imagine *themselves* doing the same/Vanity is at the bottom of it. The number of Imitators proves this in some measure.

2408 21.573   Jan. 18. Morning 5 °clock—Thunder & lightning, during which Mr Macauley died like a sleeping Baby—without sigh or motion. I am appointed the Public Secretary pro tempore of Mr Chapman's Absence.

2409 21.574   On a heap of glowing wood embers throw a quantity of large and small Chips and Shavings—& they will all quietly and moulderingly change into the substance of fire—but apply even the smallest Match with the faintest blue *flame* and tho' with a thousandfold less Heat all it will set the whole instantly on flame. —A good Simile for sympathy of a predisposed multitude with the courage of some Massaniello—but physically, what is the reason of this phænomenon! that flame is ignited vapor says nothing till one knows what it is that ignites vapor. Can it be supposed that the tapering blue flame of a match or even of a bit of phosphorus is more intense † than that of a whole Hearth of glowing Embers?—Is not some business of affinity concerned here/the heat in the flame existing in a state of greater *repulsion* & therefore more eager to combine with bodies out of itself—† Yes! than equal space of embers.

f131^v

2410 21.575   Malta, 1805. Of the feelings of the English at the Sight of a Convoy from England—man cannot be selfish—that part of me (my beloved) wͨh is distant in space excites the same feeling as the "ich" † distant from me in time!—My Friends are indeed my Soul.—19. Jan. 1805.
† ⟨I have the same anxiety for my friends now in England as for myself that is to be, or may be—two months hence.⟩

2411 21.576   22 Jan. 1805.—I had sealed a Letter/I had not moved from my seat—& wanted the stick of sealing wax, nearly a whole one, for another Letter/I could not find it—it was not on the Table—had it dropt on the ground? I searched & searched—no!—I searched every where, my pockets, my fobs, impossible places/literally it had vanished and where was it?—It had stuck to my *Elbow*, I having leaned upon it ere yet it had grown cold.—A curious accident, & in no way similar to that of the Butcher with his Steel in his Mouth seeking for it/mine was true accident.—

f132 2412 21.577   23. Jan. 1805. Malta/. Of the principle of reciprocity, and its injurious consequences. Of the good effects of the

opposite, i.e. the Christian Principle in states/of those points, in which States may be exponented by Individuals, & those in which such analogies are absurd, as in national debts, doing only one thing at a time, &c &c, dependent apparently on this principle, that the absolutely moral is universal, & independent of number, and one of the $3 = 1$ of Use, Truth, Goodness—but Prudence is manifold.— N.B. Strictly to *define*, to *develope* ✕ Prudence/Apply this to French & Spanish Prisoners.
✕ Wherein is Prudence *distinguishable* from Goodness (or Virtue)—and how are they both nevertheless one and *indivisible*.

2413 21.578   Of the maxims that appear to govern the Courts of Admiralty—their *"betwixt & between"* of positive law & the dictates of right reason = inter Jus et æquitatem/of the advantages of this as far as it is a real *modification*. Its disadvantages as far as it appears *a jumble*.

2414 21.579   Seeing a nice bed of glowing Embers with one   *f132ᵛ*
Junk of firewood well placed, like the remains of an old Edifice, and another well nigh mouldered one, corresponding to it, I felt an impulse to put on three pieces of Wood, that exactly completed this perishable architecture, tho' it was 11 °clock, tho' I was that instant going to bed, & there could be in common ideas no possible use in it. Hence I seem (for I write, not having yet gone to bed) to suspect, that this desire of totalizing, of perfecting, may be the bottom-impulse of many, many actions, in which it never is brought forward as an avowed, or even agnized ⟨*anerkennt*⟩ as a conscious motive/—thence I proceed to think of restlessness in general, its *fragmentary* nature, and its connection if not identification, with the ⟨*pains correlative* to the⟩ pleasures derived from *Wholeness*— i.e. plurality in unity—& the yearning left behind by those pleasures ~~once~~ often experienced.
Mem. to collect facts for a comparison between a *wood* and a *coal*, fire, as to sights, sounds, & bodily Feeling.

2415 21.580   Sir A. Ball near Milford Haven + the French   *f133*
Ship, attempted to be put in tow which ran foul—

2416 21.581   the nephew of the Bishop of St David/& the vision that traversed his Eye.

2417 21.582   Of the Gentlemen, servant maid & gardener, the Dream.

2418 21.583   Of the man that arising from a dream repeatedly awoke his Brother to prepare for an engagement/at daylight a ship really discovered/procured himself to be tied to some post that he might not discover cowardice, as he had dreamt, he should— found dead without a wound, from Fear—
⟨Apply this incident to Miss Edgeworth's Tales and all similar attempts to cure faults by *detailed* Forewarnings—which leave on the similarly faulty an impression of *Fatality*, that extinguishes *Hope*. O Pain is = arsenic in medicine.⟩

2419 21.584   What precedes to the Voice, follows to the eye, as 000,1 and 100—/a b c were they men, you would say that "c" went first, being letters—things of voice & ear in their original, we say that 'a' goes first.
Many a man ~~who~~ & men who following made 1 = a thousand being placed at head become useless cyphers, mere finery for form's sake.

2420 21.585   Jan. 28th, 1805. Visited the Maltese Hospital, again & again to observe the indefatigable ubiquitarian intrusia of the Catholic Superstition, on every stair-case, by every bed side, in every chamber, along the roads, the traveller cannot help beholding it—the Sailor sees it the first thing—Contrast these hateful stone caricatures, these rascal-faces, especially that ghastly look of dead-drunkenness so common in the crucifix Jesuses, with the English Bible and Prayer Book seen in our Houses & Hospitals—and shew the absurdity of Pictures being the Books of the Poor/Christ by Titian, & one in the Roadside: a Parma Edition of with a ~~German~~ Bipont on the worst paper—in the latter you lose superfluous ornaments, at the utmost an increased facility of reading the letters, ~~in the~~ retaining the substance, in the former you lose both.

f133

In this Hospital among the Venereal Convalescents I saw ⟨in the same bed⟩ a child of 12 years old, and an old man at least 70!!—

2421 21.586   Of the pavement floors of the Quarantine apartments, like the pavement of a sepulchral Church/often draft boards cut out on it/often the same name Slovenly, then laboriously & pompously/the   curve dug round in the rocks at the walls, to waste the force of the undermining tide-billow.

2422 21.587   Prices of Articles.
Coffee at 4 or 5 Shillings a pound/not a berry in the Island. So in the Boston Gazette 3 Dec. 1804. Whale Bone 12 to 14 C.—None. Malaga Wine, 30 Dollars the quarter cask none.—

2423 21.588   1. Feb. 1805. Friday. Malta. Of the Millions that   *f134* use the Pen, how many (quere) understand the theory of this simple machine, the action of the Slit, etc?—I confess, ridiculous as it must appear to those who do understand it, that I have not been able to answer the question off-hand to myself, having only this moment thought of it.

2424 21.589
⌐My Love is . . . . . .⌐
⌐why have . . . . . .⌐
⌐. . . . .⌐
⌐. . . . .⌐
⌐What outward form and feature are
   guesseth but⌐
⌐He did but guess in part⌐
⌐. . . . . good and fair,⌐
⌐. . . . .⌐

2425 21.591   3 Feb. 1805. The gentlest form of Death, a   *f134ᵛ* Sylphid Death, passed by, beheld a sleeping Baby, became, narcissuslike, enamoured of its own self in the sweet Counterfeit, seized it/carried it off as a mirror close by the Green Paradise—the reviving airs awakening the Babe, & Death dying at the sudden loss.—

2426 21.592, 21.7 From Decembʳ 6ᵗʰ 1797 to Feb. 3, 1805, this Pocket-book has been filling—
       and now let it end/

f₁ᵛ
       ⌐. . .⌐! so begin! so end!
    Heart and Breathing no more life shall lend!
                                  S.T.C.

f₁ 2427 17.1 O that thou wert as my Sister, that sucked the Breasts of my Mother! Should I find thee without, I would kiss thee, yea, I should not be despised. I would lead thee and bring thee into my House!—
                                THE BIBLE.

2428 17.2
    Some glory in their Wealth, some in their Skill,
    Some in their Birth, some in their body's force,
    Some in their garments new yet changed still,
    Some in their Hawks and Hounds, some in their Horse:
    And every Humour hath its adjunct pleasure,
    Wherein it finds a Joy above the rest;
    But these particulars are not my Measure,
    All these I better in one general Best.
    Thy Love is better than high Birth to me,
    Richer than Wealth, prouder than garments' Cost,
    Of more delight than Hawks and Horses be,
    And having thee of all men's Pride I boast!
    Wretched in this alone, that thou may'st take
    All this away, & me most wretched make.
    But do thy worst to steal thyself away,
    For Term of Life thou art art assured *mine:*
    Since life no longer than thy Love will stay,
    For it depends upon that Love of Thine.
                            SHAKESPERE.

How like a Winter hath my Absence been   ƒ2ᵛ
From thee, the Pleasure of the fleeting Year!
What Freezings have I felt, what dark days seen,
What old December's Bareness every where!
                                        Shakes.

From you have I been absent in the Spring
When proud-pied April drest in all his trim
Hath put the Spirit of Youth in every thing
That heavy Saturn laugh'd and leap'd with him.
Yet nor the Lays of Birds nor the Sweet smell
Of different Flowers in Odour & in Hue
Could make me any Summer's story tell
Or from their proud Lap pluck them where they grew:
Nor did I wonder at the Lilies white,
Nor praise the deep vermilion in the Rose/
They were, tho' ~~fair~~ sweet, but ~~shadows~~ figures of Delight,
Drawn after you, you pattern of all those!
Yet seem'd it Winter still, and, you away,
As with your Shadow I with these did play.
                                        Shakespere.

Since I left you, mine Eye is in my mind
And that which governs me to go about
Doth part its function, and is partly blind,
Seems seeing but effectually is out:
For it no Form delicious to the Heart
Of Bird, or Flower, or Shape which it doth snatch/
Of its quick Objects hath the mind no part,   ƒ3
Nor its own Vision holds what it doth catch;
For if it see the rud'st or gentlest sight,
The most sweet Favour, or deformd'st creature,
The Mountain or the Sea, the Day or Night,
The Crow or Dove, it shapes them to your Feature/
Incapable of more, replete with you,
My most true mind doth make mine Eye untrue.
                                        Shakespere.

O never say that I was false of Heart,
~~That~~ Or that long Absence hath my love assess'd!
As easy might I from myself depart
As from my soul which houses in thy Breast.
That is my Home of Love! next Heaven, my best!
Never believe, tho' in my Nature reign'd
All Frailties that besiege all kinds of Blood,
That it could so prepost'rously be stain'd
To leave for nothing all thy Sum of Good!
For nothing this wide Universe I call
Save thou, my Soul! in it Thou art my All.
                                        Sh.

Let not my Love be call'd Idolatry
Nor my Beloved as an Idol shew,
Since all alike my Songs & praises be,
To one, of one, still such & ever so.
For as the Sun is daily new and old,
So is my Love still telling what is told.
                                    Shakes.

2429 17.3

My Sister and my Friend, and dearer yet
If in the Heart of Love one dearer name
Be found.
                            Wordsworth.

f2 2430 17.4   4 Feb. 1805, La Vallette, Malta, at the Treasury,
being the Public Secretary till the arrival of the Person who (if the
Appointment of the late Ministry be confirmed) is to succeed M^r
Macauley. ~~who died~~ Alex. Macauley, an intelligent honest, and
amiable old Man, died on the morning of the 18th of January,
1805, at 5 °clock, without moan or motion, calm as a sleeping Infant, during a tremendous Storm of Thunder and Lightning.—

f3° 2431 17.5   That one language may have advantages, which
another has not, that the English Language may excel all others

in the immense number of its practical words, ~~for~~ ⟨the trivial
names of⟩ the operations & component Parts of Ships, of manu-
factories, &c/that the French may bear the palm in the scientific
words of Trades, of military and diplomatic operations &c/that the
German exclusive of its world of mining, metallurgic, & miner-
alogical technical & scientific words has an incomparable army of
metaphysical & psychological Phrases, & both by its structure & greek-
rivalling facility of composition is of all others the best adapted to
logic & intellectual analysis, that the Italian is the sweetest, the
Spanish the most majestic in its sounds, (~~and~~ capable indeed of as
much sweetness as is desirable, ~~with~~ adding falernian strength, &
⟨thus⟩ calling forth all worthy powers of articulation) it may be   *f4*
considered as the perfection of Sound—at all events, very very
far more above the Latin, than it is below the Greek—that the
English by its ⟨monosyllabic, naturalizing, and⟩ marvellously
metaphorical Spirit (for the excellence wholly out of the Question
What language can exhibit a style that resembles that of Shakespere, Jeremy Taylor, or Burke?) can express more meaning,
image, and passion *tri-unely* in a given number of articulate sounds
than any other in the world, not excepting even the ancient Greek/
that on the other ⟨hand the⟩ French is at once the most perspicuous
& the most pointed language, & therefore the very own language
of conversation, & colloquial writing, of light passion, and the social
Vanity, which finds ~~the~~ its main pleasure in pleasing so as to be admired for pleasing, & attains its end by turns of phrase (that like
the painted dust-plumes on the Butterflies wing, or the colours of a
Bubble must not be examined by the grasp) by turns of phrase,   *f4*ᵛ
that, like flowery Turfs covering & wholly concealing ~~the~~ a Hollow,
~~beneath~~ seems to have, but ~~has no~~ have not, a Substratum & pre-
eminently too by a perpetual ~~Tickling of the appetites~~ Tampering
with the morals without offending the ‡ Decencies/all this I can

‡ "without offending the Decencies." The coadunated meaning of   *f7*ᵛ
mores so honorable to the Romans ~~is~~ was however a misfortune to
~~us/who~~ our language, we having altogether divided manners from
morals. We say "moral taste," "the moral sense"; but ~~the~~ neither
the Latin nor our own language seems to furnish a happy adjective

f4ᵛ ~~most~~ fully comprehend, & do most readily admit/consequently, I
can admit that in the narrative Epic and all the simpler modifications of Thought, and passion, and general Imagery the Italian
may yield only to the Spanish & the Spanish only to the Greek, and
that the It: and Span: really ~~excel~~ beyond the other living Languages ~~are~~ be adapted to the sorts of Poetry implied in this description, & that the English ~~is~~ not by accidental ~~of~~ Production of
Genius, but by its natural constitution stands unequalled for all
kinds of Poetry, in which the more complex and profounder Passions are united with deep Thought, for the Drama, whether Com-

f5 edy or Tragedy, so that it is *Poetry* ○ (for in modern Comedies
that professedly *copy* elegant conversation I am disposed to believe
that the French are our Superiors) for dramatic poetry, for impassioned and *particularized* ~~Imagery~~ Description, (see Burns'
description of a Brook, and Wordsworth's Poetry in a hundred
places) for rapid associations of sensuous Images and that species
of Delight ⟨from unexpected combinations of them⟩ which when
it excites a disposition to laughter or even to a smile is usually
called wit, ~~when~~ and fancy in other cases (this tho' the common
distinction, I perceive to be deficient/a better & perhaps the true &
only tenable distinction would be, (that where the manifest intention of the passage is to direct the attention chiefly to the combination for its own sake, for the sake of the pleasure derived from the
Surprize, it is properly called *wit*/but where the ~~intention is to~~
combination is introduced either for the sake of Some Reasoning or
Fact to be illustrated by it (even tho' the illustration should ~~out~~
bedazzle the res illustrate into obscurity by error of judgment in
the writer) or if introduced for its own sake, yet for the pleasure

f5ᵛ produced by the picture as gratifying the ~~eye~~ mental eye either by

---

expressive of "manners". A Frenchman's refined allusions to our
grosser gratifications do very grievously offend the moral taste,
but not that Taste which has manners for its object. It might have
been well if "ethic" instead of clinging to Titlepages and literary
Nomenclature a lame Semisynonime of "Moral" had been adopted
to express "mannery"; ⟨or if mannerly dared be thus used/e.g.
"the natural union and fatal disjunction of the moral and the
mannerly Taste."⟩

its colours, or its picturesque combination or both, and not chiefly
for the ~~pleasure~~ electric sensation derived from the surprize, then
it is properly called Fancy/the difference is indeed only in the
Tone of mind of the writer or speaker, & in the intention of the
sentence or sentences/but these two dispositions are ~~in~~ ⟨according
to⟩ the *predominance* of the one or the other characteristic of two
very very different sorts of intellectual power/the first belongs to
the men of Cleverness and Talent, the latter tho' by no means
essentially constitutive of Genius, has yet a close affinity to it, and
is most often an effect and attendent of it/) ⟨end.⟩

Now how to get back, having thus belabyrinthed myself in these
most parenthetical parentheses? Cut thro' at once, & now say in
half a dozen a Lines what a half a dozen Lines would have enabled
me to say at the very beginning/but my Thoughts, my Pocket-book
Thoughts at least, moved like a pregnant Polypus in sprouting
Time, clung all over with young Polypi each of which is to be a   *ʄ6*
thing of itself—and every motion out springs a new Twig of Jelly-
Life/—The Spanish ⟨including the Portugese.⟩ & Italian Languages from their sweetness and pomp of sound, & from many
political causes ~~from~~ having a less connection with the low and ludicrous in the words and consequent power of expressing common
things with dignity without deviating from nature and simplicity
(I am speaking, of the language not of the Thoughts) is better
suited than the other Eur. Tongues to certain sorts of poetry/the
English better to the *drama~~tic~~ poetry*, to distinct painting, rapid
association & combination both of images with images, & of images,
& combinations of images with the moral and intellectual world,
and vice versa words of passion and thought with natural images.

> Full many a glorious morning have I seen
> *Flatter* the mountain Tops with sov'ran eye/

and of the former take this as an illustration

> Was it the proud full Sail of his Great Verse &c

all this seems to me Just and true/

⊙ but I cannot admit that any language can be unfit for poetry, or
that there is any language in which a divinely inspired Architect   *ʄ6ᵛ*
may not sustain the lofty edifice of Verse on its two Pillars of Sub-

limity and Pathos. Yet I have ⟨heard⟩ Frenchmen, nay even Englishmen, assert this of the German/which contains perhaps an
hundred passages equal to the

"Ein Gott ist, ein heiliger Wille lebt
    Wie auch der menschliche wanke:
Hoch über der Zeit und dem Raume webt
    Lebendig der höchste Gedanke!
Und ob alles in ewigem Wechsel kreist,
Es beharret im Wechsel EIN ruhiger Geist.

and ⟨I have heard⟩ both Germans & Englishmen (and these ⟨too⟩
men of true feeling & genius, & so many of them that ~~the~~ ⟨such a⟩
company of my Betters makes me not ashamed to the having ⟨my-
self⟩ been guilty of this Injustice) assert that the French Language is unsusceptible of Poetry, in its higher and purer sense, ⟨of
Poetry⟩ which excites emotion not merely creates amusement,
f7   which demands continuous admiration, not regular recurrences of
conscious Surprize, and the effect of which is Love and Joy. Unfortunately, the Manners, religion, and government of France,
and the circumstances of its emergence from the polyarchy of
feudal Barony, have given a bad taste to the Parisians,—so bad a
one as doubtless to have mildewed many an opening Blossom. I
cannot say, that I know & can name any one French ~~name~~ writer,
that can be placed among the great Poets—but when I read the
Inscription over the Chartreux

C'est ici que la Mort et que la Verité
    Elevant leur flambeux [*flambeaux*] terribles;
C'est de cette demeure au monde inaccessible
    Que l'on passe à l'Eternité.

I seem to feel, that if France had been for ages a freer ~~or~~ and a
protestant Nation, and a Milton had been born in it, the French
Language would not have precluded the Production of a Paradise
f7ᵛ   Lost, tho' it might perhaps that of an Hamlet or Lear.

2432 17.6   Viscount and Sheriff only Lat. & Sax. for the

same County-Representative / Shire-reeve / So Share, Plough
share, & Shire, three perfect Synonimes so perfectly desynoni-
mized.—/—

2433 17.7   I   *f8*

The twentieth year is well nigh past,
Since first our sky was overcast:
Ah would that this might be the last,—
                         My Mary!

2

Thy Spirits have a fainter flow,
I see thee daily weaker grow/—
'Twas my Distress that brought thee low,
                         My Mary!

3

Thy needles, once a shining store,
For my sake restless heretofore,
Now rust disus'd and shine no more,
                         My Mary!

4

For though thou gladly would'st fulfil
The same kind office for me still,
Thy Sight now seconds not thy Will,
                         My Mary!

5   *f8ᵛ*

But well thou playd'st the Housewife's Part,
And all thy Threads with magic Art
Have wound themselves about this Heart,
                         My Mary!

6

Thy indistinct Expressions seem
Like Language utter'd in a dream:
Yet me they charm whate'er the Theme,
                         My Mary!

7

Thy Silver Locks once Auburn bright
Are still more lovely in my sight,
Than golden Beams of orient Light,
                My Mary!

8

For could I view nor them nor thee,
What sight worth seeing could I see?
The Sun would rise in vain ~~for~~ for me,
                My Mary!

9

Partakers of thy sad decline,
Thy Hands their little force resign;
Yet gently press'd press gently mine,
                My Mary!

10

Such feebleness of Limbs thou prov'st,
That now at every step thou mov'st
Upheld by Two/Yet still thou lov'st,
                My Mary!

11

And still to love thou prest with Ill,
In wintry Age to feel no chill,
With me is to be lovely still,
                My Mary!

12

But ah by constant Heed I know,
How oft the Sadness, that I shew,
Transforms thy smiles to looks of Woe,
                My Mary!

And should ~~m~~thy future Lot be cast   *f9^v*
With much resemblance of the Past,
Thy worn out Heart will break at last,
My Mary!
COWPER TO Mrs UNWIN
⟨※ See the second page of the next Leaf⟩

※ It is not without a certain sense of self-reproof as well as   *f10^v*
self-distrust, that I ask, or rather that my understanding suggests
to me the Quere, whether this divine poem (~~so~~ in so original a
strain of thought and feeling honorable to human nature) would
not have been more perfect, if the 3rd, 4th, and 5th Stanzas had been
omitted, and the 10th and 11th transposed so as to stand as the 3rd
and 4th. It is not—perhaps not at all, but certainly not principally—
that I feel any meanness in the "*needles*"; but not to mention that
the words "once a shining store" is a speck in the diamond, (in a
less dear poem I might perhaps have called it more harshly a
rhyme-botch) and that the word "restless" is rather too strong an   *f11*
impersonation for the serious tone, the *real*ness, of the Poem, &
seems to tread too closely ~~to~~ on the mock-heroic; but that it seems
not true to poetic feeling to introduce the affecting circumstance of
dimness of Sight from decay of nature on an occasion so remote
from the το καθολον, and that the 5th Stanza, graceful and even
affecting ~~even~~ as the ⟨*spirit* of the⟩ playfulness is, or would be at
least in a poem having less depth of feeling, breaks in painfully
here/the age and afflicting infirmities both of the Writer & his
Subject seem abhorrent from such trifling of—scarcely Fancy, for
I fear if it were analysed that the whole effect ⟨would be found to⟩
depend~~s~~ on phrases hackneyed, and taken from the Almshouse of
the Muses. The test would be this—read the poem to a well-edu-
cated but natural Woman, an unaffected gentle Being endued with
sense and sensibility, substituting the 10th & 11th Stanzas for these   *f11^v*
three/& some days after shew her the Poem as it now stands/I
seem to be sure, that she would be shocked/an Alien would have
intruded himself, & ⟨be⟩ found sitting in a circle of dear Friends
whom she expected to have found *all to themselves*. . . .
S.T.C.

f9ᵛ 2434 17.8   Thursday, 7 Feb. 1805
The ~~grandmother~~ Queen-bee in ~~the swarm~~ & hive of Popish Error, the great mother of the Swarm, seems to me their tenet
concerning Faith and Works, placing the former wholly in the rec-
titude ⟨nay, in the rightness,⟩ of intellectual conviction, and the
latter in the definite and most often the material action: ⟨conse-
quently, the assertion of the dividuous nature & self-subsistence
of Works.⟩ Hence the doctrine of damnation out of the Church
of Rome/of the one visible Church/of the absolute efficiency in
se of all the Sacraments, & the absolute merit of ceremonial ob-
servances &c &c—

f10 2435 17.9   Of the incalculable advantage of chiefly dwelling
on the virtues of the Heart, of Habits of Feeling, & harmonious
action, the music of the adjusted String at the impulse of the
Breeze—and on the other hand the evils of books concerning particular actions, minute case-of-conscience hair-splitting directions &
decision. O how illustrated by the detestable libidinous character
of most of the Roman Casuists of Diana de digito in maritali
fruitione!!—No actions should be distinctly described but ~~should~~
such as manifestly tend to awaken the Heart to ~~such~~ efficient Feelings, whether of Fear or of Love, ~~as tend to fill~~ actions that falling back on the Fountain, ⟨keep it full,⟩ or clear out the mud from
its pipes, ~~to~~ & make it play in its abundance, & shining in that purity, in which at once the Purity & the Light ~~or Defecation~~ is each
f10ᵛ the cause of the ~~Light~~ other, the Light purifying, and the purified
receiving and reflecting the Light, sending it off to others, not
like the polish'd mirror by rejection from itself, but by transmission thro' itself. S.T.C.

f11ᵛ 2436 17.10   8 Feb. 1805. Went to the Play performed by the
Officers of the Garrison; returned without waiting for the Entertainment. The longer I live, the more am I imprest with the
exceeding immorality of our modern Plays, and half-angry, half-
laughing, as either the impudence or the absurdity of the Assumption presents itself to my mind, I think of the pretences of the
moderns to superior morality compared with the Plays of Shake-

spere!!—In Shakespere the possible effect of inward operation, of *f12*
a righteous man's fervent prayer, on the world at large—but this
very assumption would of itself confute the supererogation-scheme.

2437 17.11   O me miserum!—Assuredly the doctrine of
Grace, atonement, and the Spirit of God interceding by groans to
the Spirit of God (Rom. VIII. 26) is founded on a constant experi-
ence/and even if it can be ever *explained away*, it must still remain
as the rising and setting of the Sun, yea, as the Sun itself, as the
Darkness and as the Light/it must needs have the most efficient
character of Reality, quod semper, quod ubique, quod ab omnibus!
—Deeply do I both know and feel my Weakness—God in his
wisdom grant, that my Day of Visitation may not have been past!
—S.T.C.—

2438 17.12   Sir A. B.'s reason against the Clergy having seats *f12ᵛ*
in the H. of C., that then men of large Fortune &c would enter
into the Church—& so swallow up those Funds for Literature &c
—that it would tend to take up the ⟨chief⟩ Ladder, by which the
lower Classes may climb up to the higher. Compare Latimer's
Sermon, on the Church owing its best members not to families of
Rank chiefly, but chiefly to the Yeomanry. Sir A. Ball is a great
man/I never knew an instance, in which *Prudence* was so like
Wisdom—he seems the binding *Link*, the Σοφοσωφρων—his
Intellect so clear and comprehensive, his Prudence on so large a
scale.

2439 17.13   9 Feb. Sat. Noon. Curious enough; but ⟨in con-
firmation of the preceding⟩ all this morning I have been walking
with Sophosophron, and enjoying a most interesting conversation
de se ipso et præterito et futuro; and the detail of his Voyage on *f13*
the uncertain Element of Promotion; the result being comprizable
in Hæc omnia fecimus nos ipsi, sapientia duce, fortunâ ~~adjuvante~~
~~vel saltem permittente~~ permittente vel ad summum adjuvante;
Luck gave him nothing, ~~worked~~ she in her most generous moods
worked with him, as ⟨with⟩ a Friend, not for him, as ⟨for⟩ a Fon-
dling: & still oftener, simply stood neutral, and suffered him to

work for himself. However, Fortune in this instance had ⟨certainly⟩ reconciled herself with Prudence, & gave the lie to the calumnious Proverbs, which confines her favors to fools. This proverb may be variously or rather perhaps multifoldly explained/~~by a number of co-operating causes~~.

Folly may often be only an abusive Term of Envy signifying Courage/Hardihood & Foolhardiness are as disparate as Green and Yellow; but Green and yellow will both appear yellow to the Jaundiced Eye. Courage multiplies ~~of~~ the chances of success, both by making, & by availing itself of, opportunities/and in this sense Fortune may be said to favor Fools by those who however wise *f13ᵛ* in their own eyes want valor and enterprize—Secondly, a superiorly good and wise man is pursuing other objects, and adapting the right means to the right end attains his object; but this not being what the world calls Fortune, neither money, nor artificial Rank, ~~this~~ his admitted Inferiors are said to be favored by fortune and he slighted, tho' the *Fool* did ~~no more than~~ the same in his line ~~that~~ as the Wise man in his/adapted means to ends and succeeded. In this sense, the proverb is current by a misuse or catachresis at least of both the Words, Fortune & Fools.—And thirdly and lastly, there is no doubt a true meaning attachable to Fortune, distinct from Prudence or Courage/*Luck* has a real existence in human affairs, from the infinity of co-existences and the co-existence of contingencies in an endless Flux with Necessities & general Laws/ex.gr. The moon is a necessity of nature in all her Phases, *f14* and so are the clouds, tho' the latter by the variety &c are not within human calculation like the former/The full moon on a clouded night/I am walking on in the dark aware of no particular danger/a strong wind rends the Cloud for a moment & the moon emerging discloses a pit or precipice a yard distant from me in the very track I was going. This is what is meant by Luck = the coexistence of infinite actions with each other, and the co-existence of those which from the multitude or the subtlety of the causes which produce ~~them~~ or determine them are *called* contingencies, ~~with~~ or of those which Virtue commands us to consider as *really* such, so far as they are the effects of the ⁂ *Arbitrement*

⁂ (Arbitrium = ego, et *agens*, not Voluntas = modificatio mei

per alterum, et passio—hoc *patior*, istud *ago;* et distinctio manet
sacra et immota etsi nulla sit nec esse possit, divisio, etsi etiam pa-
tiendo agam, necesse est, et agendo patiar)—of infinites ~~coe~~ the   *f14*^v
simple co-existence, and the co-existence of true or fancied contingencies with ~~some one or more~~ any regular and necessary Phænomenon (as the motions of the Planets in relation to the Sun and
to each other) produces coincidences, which when not calculable
or to be foreseen by human prudence form good or ill luck in
genere; & which will always appear as *Luck* to the mind, which
was not capable of such foresight/Some things are luck to all men,
others Luck only to the comparatively Ignorant/on a fine day
came on a sudden storm & spoilt ~~my~~ ⟨Hans Sachs's⟩ Hay, before
the invention of barometers—this is ill-luck/the same event took
place, I having an unfailing Barometer (we will *suppose* such an
instrument) but had neglected to look at it/this is no longer Ill-
luck, but Imprudence/. Now such coincidences taking place where
the causes that even without them have a tendency to produce the
same effect, as being ~~more~~ less *marvellous,* will draw ~~more~~ less   *f15*
attention, and the instances be ~~more~~ less remembered/that Wise
men should attain ~~For~~ certain objects seems natural, & we neglect
the circumstances that perhaps produced that attainment of themselves, without the intervention of the Wisdom/but dwell on the
fact, when the same happens to a † Fool, & so accumulating the
one sort of facts, and never collecting the other, we put a part for
the whole, as Poets ⟨do⟩ in language, and Quacks of all denomina-
tions in their reasoning.—/This is the third cause of the *Dogma,*
that Fortune favors fools/for in this sense it is a Dogma not a
Phænomenon/δοκει, ου φαινεται, or what the Germans express
by their Schein-phænomenon./
† Let a Lavoisier, or a Davy discover the ~~all~~ increase of specific
gravity in the combination of Mercury and Platina, tho' by an accident—it will excite no marvel, nor however admired will it be   *f15*^v
talked of as an instance of Luck; but let the very same accident
discover it to an illiterate Journeyman at Sheffield, & then what
Luck/but if the man ~~shall~~ should grow rich in consequence of it,
and half by the envy of his neighbours, & half truly be considered
as a man in general powers of mind much below Par—o what a

lucky Fellow! Well! Fortune favors Fools—it is always so.—and then come out half a dozen other instances.

2440 17.14   All gross and vulgar Spirits are inclined to Devil-worship equally with Savages. In G. Britain they cannot do it avowedly; but I have observed in all the late evangelical maga-zines, Christian Observer, the works of Wilberforce, Hannah Mooore, Porteus, and the whole of the Fanatics, Canters, or Sticklers for obsolete High-Church Orthodoxy for the sake of obsolete High Church Power a zealous advocacy for the existence ƒ16 & Agency of the Devil/who in this System is a sort of obnoxious Premier or Vizir of Providence, whose acts have no effect but in virtue of the Royal Signature, and yet his name & person take off the odium from the King—whom it is constitutional to abuse, in cases where without him Abuse would be Treason. All this has its uses; but nevertheless it is but a mask/and he who prays to God against the his Devil, like him those who petition his Majesty against his Ministers for measures which could not have taken place without the concurrence & authority of the Crown involve the Royal Person in the Blame actually, tho' in the least offensive manner. These glowing Diabolists have at the bottom the same state of religious feeling as their Cousins, the Theodiabolists of India or Africa/A. throws a sop to a savage Dog, B. offers a Bribe to his surly owner to keep him chained/—closely connected with ƒ16ᵛ this and using this as its means watch the love of Power; the pre-tence of *clerical conscience* attempted to be set up against the Laws of the Lands, in the Coroner's Verdict &c &c—in short, read with care the Christian Observer, & Works resembling it, & note down every instance/but priorly examine Warburton's Alliance of Church & State which contains the Germs of this Conspiracy. All these are mere, nay the merest *Hints:* the theme is, the Zeal for the existence and attributes of the Devil, and its conjunctions con-nective ⟨God and Reason require only virtue & reason; but the Devil needs an exorcist.⟩

2441 17.15   On Friday Night, 8ᵗʰ J̶a̶n̶ Feb/1805, my feeling, in sleep, of exceeding great Love for my Infant/seen by me in

the Dream/yet so as that it might be Sara, Derwent or Berkley/
and still *it was an individual Babe and mine.*

Of Love in Sleep, the seldomness of the Feeling, scarcely ever in   *f17*
short absences, or except after very long Absence/a certain indistinctness, a sort of *universal-in-particularness* of Form, seems necessary—vide the note preceding, and my Lines. "All Look or
Likeness caught from Earth, All accident of Kin or Birth, Had
pass'd Away: there seem'd no Trace of Aught upon her brighten'd
Face Uprais'd beneath the rifted Stone, Save of one Spirit, all her
own/She, she herself, and only she Shone in her body visibly."
This abstract Self is indeed in its nature a Universal personified—as
Life, Soul, Spirit, &c. Will not this prove it to be a *deeper* Feeling, & of such intimate affinity with ideas, so to modify them &
become one with them, whereas the appetites and the feelings of
Revenge and Anger co-exist with the Ideas, in not combine with
them; and alter the apparent effect of the Forms not the Forms
themselves./Certain modifications of Fear seem to approach nearest to this Love-sense, in its manner of acting.—

2442 17.16   Cornage (sergeantly when under the King, other-   *f17ᵛ*
wise Knights' Service) a personal Service of sounding the Horn in
warning of a *Raid.* or to find or pay for Scouts and Horners.

That Etymology is a Science/using this word in its laxest and
improper sense; but our Language has dropt the word "Lore" at
least except in poetry—the lehre of the Germans, the Logos of the
Greek—either we should have retained the word, and ventured
on *Root-lore,* Verse-lore, etc. or have adopted the Greek as a single
word, as well as a word in Combination/all novelties appear or
rather are felt as ridiculous, in language—but if it had been once
adopted, it would have been no stranger to have said that Ety-
mo*logy* is a *logy* which perishes from a Plethora of Probability,
than that the *Art* of War is an Art apparently for the destruction
& subjugation of particular States, but really for the Lessening of
Bloodshed, & the preservation of the Liberties of mankind/Art   *f18*
and Science are both too much appropriated—our language wants
terms of comprehensive generality, implying the kind not the degree or species—as in that good and necessary word "sensuous"

which we have likewise dropt, opposed to sensual, sensitive, sensible, &c &c—Chemistry has felt this difficulty, found the necessity of having one word for the supposed Cause, another for the effect, as in Caloric or Calorific, opposed to Heat/and Psychology has still more need of the Reformation/—

That Etymology is rendered uncertain as to any particular probability by the probality of all possible changes (e.g. amazement derived from the *Th* of the oriental Language, jour from dies;) or the more instructive Truth of the presence of all meanings in every meaning, as in Leibnitz felt & layed as the foundation of metaphysics in his representative Monads, or Vorstellungskraft; ƒ*18*° might be illustrated by asking a man whether he perceives any analogy between "Shyness" and "a Buckler." Yet I believe, that eschew and the German Scheu are both derived from Scutum; escuage or scutage being the sum paid in stead of the Shield, or personal appearance by our ancestors—and even this is perhaps only a secondary Stream flowing into the first, and that to shelter behind the *Shie*ld has an aboriginal brotherhood with shy, shame, &c.—Master and Mister = Wann, wenn, Property, Propr.

2443 17.17   Ucthred of Northumberland, Ranulph de Glanvil and Robert de Broy—Renfred de Deepdale/Ada de Morvil—*Idonea*. Evo de Johnby, and Philip Escrope. Ivo. Helwise = Heloise. Mary de Brus. Aeiparthen.

2444 17.18   "The inducement of a Form on a pre-existing material"—is this a true definition of Generation? Wherein then would Generation differ from Fabrication, or a child from a Statue ƒ*19* or Picture? It is surely the inducement of a Form on a pre-existing materials in consequence of the transmission of a *Life*, according to the kind of the living Transmitter, this principle of Life so transmitted being both the principalle of the ~~form induced and~~ induction of the Form, and of the adduction of the pre-existing materials—. The difference therefore between Fabrication and Generation becomes clearly indicable/the Form of the latter is ab intra, *evolved*, the other ab extra, *impressed*—the latter is representative always of something not ~~else~~ itself, and the more disparate that

something is, the more admirable is the Form, (as in Painting it
is more admirable than in solid Wax—in Iron or Bronze rather
than Wax/⟨supposing the forms to be⟩ forms of Flesh—&c)—but
the former is representative of its own cause within itself, i.e. its
causative self—and resembles, not represents, its any thing without Life and a Fluid are incompatible ideas; tho' it is easy to believe, that what we think fluid, may in truth be solid/i.e. have a ⟨*f19ᵛ*⟩
form of itself and from itself, permanent and organic, tho' its
visible *mass* may depend for its visible shapes wholly on outward
pressure or motion/as water in a bottle, or & blood in a bottle/
quoad form, both to the eye the same while at least the blood is
warm, in the one the microscope can, in the other cannot discover
organization. The text to this note is from Horsley's Charge, and
is not the only passage proving the laxity of the Bishop's Logic:
tho' I doubt not that on the whole he would have the Advantage
over Priestley/None but a thorough *Theologist* can combat suc-
cessfully with a *Christologist*—to shew the inanity of Jehovah,
Christ, and the Dove admit the adorable Tri-unity of Being, Intellect, and Spiritual Action, as the Father, Son, and co-eternal Proce-
dent, that these are God (and i.e. not mere general Terms, or
abstract ideas) and ⟨that they are⟩ one God (i.e. a real, eternal, ⟨*f20*⟩
and necessary Distinction in the divine nature, distinguishable Tri-
plicity in the indivisible Unity.)

2445　17.19　　The Platonic Fathers, instead of the Πατηρ, Υιος
and Αγιον Πνευμα, used Του Θεου, και του Λογου αυτου, και
της Σοφιας αυτου.—Θεος, Λογος, Σοφια, Ανθρωπος. Theophil.
as quoted by Horsley.—and this seems as precise and true as human words can be applied to so recondite a subject. 1. Being, the
eternal evermore I am = Deity, or eternal Life, or as we well say
the Supreme Being (which word Supreme is most often most grossly
apprehended, as synonimous to the Sublimest or Sovran, whereas
it is equivalent to *the Absolutest*)—2. Reason, Proportion, communicable Intelligibility intelligent and communicant, the Word— ⟨*f20ᵛ*⟩
which last expression strikes me as the profoundest and most comprehensive Energy of the human Mind, if indeed it be not in some
distinct sense ενεργημα θεοπαραδοτον. 3. But holy action, a

Spirit of holy Action, to which all holy actions being reducible as
to their Sine qua non, is verily the Holy Spirit proceeding fr at
once from Life and Reason, and effecting all good gifts, what more
appropriate Term is conceivable than *Wisdom:* which in its best &
only proper sense, involves action, application, habits and tendencies of realization the Good "A Bad man may be *intelligent;* but
the Good only are *wise.* He may be a clever fellow man, etc; but
I am sure, he is not a *wise* man." These common phrases shew the
f21   natural meaning of Wisdom; and in this way even now a true
Philosopher is something very different from a mere man of
Science—*he lived the Life of a Philosopher.*—But why the Son
should both create and redeem (for our Catechism seems to have
sacrificed Orthodoxy to a rhetorical division & appropriation of
offices in making the Father the Creator, not the Son. The Word
created all things, being with the Father, and redeemed all things
in like manner/& the Father both created and redeemed us by the
Son—) is of no very difficult solution, seeing that no ⟨*true*⟩ energies
can be attributed to an Ον αλογον; the moment we conceive the
divine energy, that moment we co-conceive the Λογος. But tho'
this may redeem, i.e. procure for us the *possibility* of salvation, it
is only the *Spirit* of *holy Action,* manifested in the *habits of Faith*
f21ᵛ   *and good works,* (the wings of the brooding Dove) that *sanctifies*
us, the Redeemer still co-operating in the completion of that work
of which himself is the Corner Stone—in truth, the A and the Ω,
seeing that the redeemed & sanctified become finally themselves
Words of the *Word*—even as lou articulate sounds are made by
the Reason to represent Forms, in the mind, and Forms are a
language of the notions—Verba significant phænomena, phænomena sunt quasi verba noematum (των νουμενων). As he in the
Father, even so we in him!
f20ᵛ   The practice in the Church ab initio of giving distinct offices to
the Father most pernicious.—

f21ᵛ   2446 17.20   Of my Mahometan Superstition—dread as to the
destruction of Paper. I am almost ashamed to confess to myself,
what pulling back of Heart I feel whenever I wish to light a can-
f22   dle or kindle a fire with a Hospital or Harbour Report/and what

a cumulus lie upon my Table, I am not able to conjecture what use
they can ever be, and yet trembling lest what I thus destroyed
might be of some use, in the way of knowlege. This seems the
excess of a good feeling; but it is ridiculous. Monday, Feb. 11,
1805.

2447 17.21   *Feb. Noon, 12.* Confining myself to the metaphysics and radical theology of the lower Platonists (not to the
magical and cabalistical ceremonies and operations which they
thought deducible from their philosophy) I dare affirm that their
doctrines are strictly conformable with the true meaning of Plato,
and harmonizable with the doctrines of the orthodox Xstian/yes,
even in the article of the eternity of the World, with which I
would begin the Proof.

2448 17.22   Tuesday, an hour ⟨and ½⟩ after Noon (½ after 1.)
Feb. 12, 1805—Thinking during my perusal of Horsley's Letters   *f22ᵛ*
in Rep. to Dʳ P. objections to the Trinity on the part of Jews,
Mahometans, and Infidels, it burst upon me at once as an awful
Truth what 7 or 8 years ago I thought of proving with a *hollow
Faith* and for an *ambiguous purpose,* my mind then wavering in
its necessary passage from Unitarianism (which as I have often
said is the Religion of a man, whose ~~Understanding~~ Reason would
make him an Atheist but whose Heart and Common sense will
not permit him to be so) thro' Spinosism into Plato and Sᵗ John/
No Christ, No God!—This I now feel with all its needful evidence, of the Understanding: would to God, my spirit were made
conform thereto—that No Trinity, no God.—That Unitarianism
in all its Forms is Idolatry, and that the remark of Horsley is most
accurate, that Dʳ Priestley's mode of converting the Jews & Turks
is in the great essential of religious Faith to give the name of
Christianity to their present Idolatry—truly the trick of Mahomet,
who finding that the Mountain would not come to *him* went to
the Mountain. O that this Conviction may work upon me and in
me/and that my mind may be made up as to the character of Jesus,   *f23*
and of historical Christianity, as clearly as it is of ~~Christ~~ the Logos
and intellectual or spiritual Christianity—that I may be made to

know either their especial and peculiar Union, or their absolute
disunion in any peculiar Sense.

2449 17.23   13 Feb. 1805. Wednesday afternoon walked with
Lieut. Pasley round the Works, &, on my return by water was wet
thro' by the rain-storm, the Boatman not a little terrified. The
view from the Cotenera Lines, just at Zeitun Gate, and another
a little further on, mounting a rude ascent, up to some Pauper
Houses, called the Ramp, are the most interesting, I have yet
seen in Malta./the first tho' without the fine lake-like Harbour
ƒ23ᵛ   view, which comes in the in the second, yet ple struck me the
most/—in both the scenery was various, the ground finely tossed up
and down, and instead of that Bason-view which I had every where
else noticed, the first Hills are backed by a second higher range,
and the buildings of Florean to the right—and in the 2ⁿᵈ view,
the whole of Valette & Florean, so silver-bright under the vast
black storm cloud, that cov *formed,* rather than *covered,* half the
cope of Heaven, was divine/—close by the ascent of savage, at
this season, most savage Pri: Pear Trees (Cactus opuntium) the
deep brilliant green fields, carpets among the bare white-bright
ƒ24   walls, the wild and yet harmonious complicacy & motion-counter-
feiting variety of the Heights, Slopes, and Bottoms, the variety
of light and shades so exactly suiting the populousness of the View
in all Modes of Buildings, Ships, &c &c/I have not seen any thing
that has pleased me so much since I left Sicily—shall I say, England? I mean to go with my Pocket-book, & minute its features.

2450 17.24   *A Hint.* Whether the Absence of Vowels in the
Hebrew is not a clue to the Alphabet, as according to my old old
theory consisting of symbols of whole Words/& whether the Aleph
does not add to the proof?

ƒ24ᵛ   2451 17.25   15 Feb. 1805. Mʳ England whose flowers of
Oratory I had noted down (a mixture of fine and learned words,
some used aright, others most ridiculously with the oddest & worst
Grammar-trample "He refused to pay the Duties: but I considered
this Tacitoonity as a Buggartel" What the manifesseses is that is

ralely repersentationed to the Custom House—ralely inclinated
to commerce with/what goods does come from England does pay
them there or such as them there Duties *there/inconsiderable* for
inconceivable—
this Gemman called on me this morning, and made a formal com-
plaint of Mr Chabots for impertinent and insolent Language used
to him in the performance of his Duty. O that I could but have
noted down every word of the large answer to my ? concerning
the particulars—The Vanity of the Man to tell all his own brilliant
Speeches caused him to represent *himself* as having used the
haughtiest and most insolent language, while the young man ac-   *f25*
cording to his account made only now and then a sheepish answer
of 4 or 5 words, meaning nothing. It was perfectly farcical!

2452 17.26   A chaise with four wheels turning freely on their
axles, and a man in it, all of ivory, drawn by a Flea, made by
Boverick in the Strand: The same, who made a Quadrille Table
with a Drawer in it, an Eating Table, a Side-board Table, a Looking-glass, twelve Chairs with Skeleton Backs, two dozen of Plates,
six dishes, a dozen knives and as many Forks, twelve spoons, two
Salts, a Frame and Castors together with a Gentleman, Lady, and
Footman, all contained in a cherry stone, and not filling much
more than half of it.—/Yet what *mass* is not this, compared with
the Parts and System of the Wheel-animalcule!—Oswald Ner-
inger made a Cup of a Pepper Corn which held 1200 other little
cups, all turned in ivory, each of them being gilt on the edges, and
standing upon a Foot/—& the Pepper-corn could have held 400
more!—

2453 17.27   Friday—Saturday 12–1 °clock/What a sky, the
not yet orbed moon, the spotted oval, blue at one edge from the   *f25°*
deep utter Blue of the Sky, a *mass* of *pearl*-white Cloud below,
distant, and travelling to the Horizon, but all the upper part of the
Ascent, and all the Height, such *profound* Blue, *deep* as a deep
river, and deep in color, & those two ⟨depths⟩ so entirely *one*, as
to give the meaning and explanation of the two different significa-
tions of the epithet (here so far from divided they were scarcely

distinct) scattered over with thin pearl-white Cloudlets, hands, & fingers, the largest not larger than a floating Veil/Unconsciously I stretched forth my arms as to embrace the Sky, and in a trance I
f26　had worshipped God in the Moon/the Spirit not the Form/I felt in how innocent a feeling Sabeism might have begun/O not only the Moon, but the depth of Sky!—the Moon was the *Idea;* but deep Sky is of all visual impressions the nearest akin to a Feeling/ it is more a Feeling than a Sight/or rather it is the melting away and entire union of Feeling & Sight/And did I not groan at my un-worthiness, & be miserable at my state of Health, its effects, and effect-trebling Causes? O yes!—Me miserable! O yes!—Have Mercy on me, O something *out* of me! For there is no *power,* (and if that *can* be, less *strength*) in aught *within* me! Mercy! Mercy!

Sat. Morn. 2 °Clock. S.T.C.

f26ᵛ　2454　17.28　　16 Feb. Saturday. Worse and worse! "Why will ye die?" The Soul is smitten with despair, and fears to form a resolution/Even to resolve is a Lie at the Heart, a Blasphemy! Those lines (composed in Ottery Church, or at Walthamstow?) of the *cold speck*—Prayer alone can save him. ΣΑΡΑ.

2455　17.29　　Of the Devil with a Memory, the first sinner/in order not to be baffled by the infinite ascent of the heavenly Angels he feigned that all, the T'Αγαθon, ⟨i.e. *God himself,*⟩ included, spring from nothing—& now he has a pretty task/to multiply with-out paper or slate the exact number of all the animalcules, & eggs, & embryos, of each Planet by those some other, and the ~~quotient~~ product by a third, that ~~quotient~~ product by a fourth and he is not
f27　to stop till he has gone thro' Half of the Universe, the number of which being infinite, it is considered by the Devils in general as a great Puzzle.—A dream in a Doze.

2456　17.30　　18 Feb. 1805.—Eight/①, 12/② 4/0.—

2457　17.31　　Misery of a bad stomach from intemperance caus-ing the Dream of a full highly ~~stored~~ set out Table, not as an object of Appetite, but of disgust and terror with remorse. a most *striking fact* this!

2458 17.32 Thursday, Feb. 21. 1805.—"Is it good or evil or indifferent, the writing or making intelligible marks, in places ~~that~~ where the eye must glance, memoranda of Caution against any habitual Infirmity, of Intemperance, Concupiscence, or Anger?—I fear, it is at least useless, and sometimes I even fear, that it is pernicious—as an acknowlegement and acquiescence in Weakness. What is to be done—o what a question! Is then regeneration a   *f27ᵛ* mechanical or chemical process that can be performed by a direction/or a medicine that can be made by a Recipe? Even Prayer, the only external means, requires half the conquest to have been attained/Quere? does not the Soul ~~cling to~~ repeat the *Vices* which it knows to be degrading & destructive, and really destests, in consequence of clinging to some *Passion,* which Reason—nay, of which it dreads to ~~enquire~~ question its reason?—This day now that dawned fair had I prayed and surrendered up my whole Heart to God and Reason, could this have been the Result?—"

> Thus ends the Day, so *hopingly* begun,
> Much Evil *perpetrated,* nothing *done!*

The Evil (occasionally) of Acknowlegement by its affinity with Acquiescence, an important Truth in the Theory of Self-Healing.—
To *flee* from Temptation/no excuses! better defer any thing than   *f28* the task of Self-amendment!—and even at the first impulse, say— What did Thought lead to? 21 Feb. 1805.
⟨Dramatic Hints these for Characters in my Comforts & Consolations.⟩

2459 17.33
> Insula parva situ sed rebus maxima gestis,
> Africæ et Europæ ac Asiæ contermina, Pauli
> Hospes, et alborum procerum gratissima mater.
>   Vincenzo Littara.—

2460 17.34   Circuit, 60 miles, breadth 12, length 20.—Transcribe Diod. Sicul. Lib. 5.—Quæ causa fuit (situs et commoditus portuum) ut loci ejus habitatatores Mercatorum beneficio statim et opibus augerentur et nomine inclarescerent.

2461 17.35   A world of Thoughts; (yet he was quiet as the Stars.)—the (   ) better by itself—too good for a conceit.

2462 17.36   The Egg of Light in the Palace 7 inches long, 4½ in diameter/

2463 17.37   No Bellows ~~in~~ among the Maltese/they *fan* the
f28ᵛ flame/a round piece of rush-matting with a stick/the shape of the Palm Tree as seen in the distance is the simple contrivance/it Answers very well ~~but~~ only that it blows out the smoke and ashes into the room & offends the Eyes of the Fanners.

2464 17.38   The small number of different names in proportion to the Population among the Maltese is a noticeable fact.

2465 17.39   "Lesto" in all its senses curiously synonimous to our "ready." Li Pomi di terra sono lesti   Io sono lesto.—un uomo lesto = astute, a *ready* fellow./*a ready Intellect.*

2466 17.40   The Effect of counting by *Dollars* on a Foreigner, to whom this is the *lowest familiar* coin/especially seen at auctions/ —4 or 5 Dollars sound to the feelings only like 4 or 5 Shillings at home—

f29 2467 17.41   Of the impurity and excitation of impure Thoughts, in certain *modest* women/who *accuse* every Look that falls on them/& by look and manner indict you of having lusted ~~of~~ after them. Λη χι.

2468 17.42   Monday Morning, which I ought not to have known not to be Sunday Night, 2 °clock, March 4—had been playing with Souter's pretty children/but went to bed with bad bowels —dreams interfused with struggle and fear, tho' till the very last not s̶t̶r̶ Victors—and the very last which awoke me, & which was a completed Night-mair, as it gave the *idea* and *sensation* of actual grasp or touch contrary to *my* will, & in apparent consequence of the malignant will of the external Form, actually appearing or (as sometimes happens) believed to exist/in which latter case tho' I have two or three times felt a horrid *touch* of Hatred, a *grasp*, or a *weight*, of Hate and Horror abstracted from all (Conscious) form or supposal of Form/an *abstract touch*/an *abstract* grasp—an *abstract* weight!—Quam nihil ad genium, Papiliane, tuum! i.e. This Mackintosh would prove to be Nonsense by a Scotch Smile.—/ The last that awoke me, I was saying, tho' a true Night-mair was however a mild one. I cried out early, like a scarcely-hurt Child who knows himself within hearing of his Mother. But anterior to this I had been playing with Children, especially with one most lovely Child, about 2 years old or 2½—and had repeated to her in my Dream, "The Dews were falling fast" &c—and I was sorely frightened by the sneering and fiendish malignity of the beautiful creature/from the beginning there had been a Terror about it, and proceeding from it/—I shall hereafter read the Visions in Macbeth with increased admiration.

f29ᵛ

f30

2469 17.43   The Remark, which escaped my memory, or rather my recollection while the importance of the same lay heavy upon my memory, was simply this—and is, I believe, a perfectly new observation/that the Devil and Devils among Christians form precisely the same System, with the same Feeling, of *one* and at the same time *many*, as among the Pagan Greeks and Romans the Ο Θεος, and οι θεοι/the more philosophic part used even the οι θεοι, as synonimous with Ο Θεος—something like the οι αμφι Αχιληα—or the Vos, and the Wie befinden sich die Hochdieselben, applied to a King or Sovereign Prince, at the first introduction/—but the Generality explained away this feeling as far as they could, by a Jupiter and his variously Subordinated Gods/—yet even with these an obscure feeling of unity remained/—and *God* or the divine Nature without particularizing an individual God was sufficiently common among them/—So with our Evil Spirit/ —*the Devil*/—and this again into Satan and his Subordinates.

f30ᵛ

Was not my bodily frame very nearly in the same state when I recollected this as when I first started it?—To think more and more of Memory.—

2470 17.44   Those Whispers just as you have fallen or are falling asleep—what are they and whence?

2471 17.45   In Illustration of what I have written in my Cottle-book on Envy suspected where only resentment is felt, & an uneasiness at a non-harmony, the wish not to see any thing admir-

f31 able where you find, especially in the moral character, any thing low or contemptible, and the consequent wish to avoid the struggle within, this anti monadic feeling, this (what shall I say?) *knowing, feeling,* a man to be *one,* yet not understanding how to think of him but as two—in illustration of this I confess that it has cost & still costs my philosophy some exertion not to be vexed that I must admire—aye, greatly, very greatly, admire *Richardson/* his mind is so very vile a mind—so oozy, hypocritical, praise-mad, canting, envious, concupiscent/—but to understand & draw *him*

f31ᵛ would be to produce almost equal to any of his own, but in order to do this, *"down proud Heart down!"* as we teach little Children to say to themselves—BLESS THEM!—(N.B. my fat Boy, Derwent! —)—all hatred down!—Charity, Calmness, an heart fixed on the good parts, tho' the *Understanding* is surveying all.—Richardson felt truly the defect of Fielding—or rather what was not his excellence, & made that his *Defect,* a trick of Uncharitableness often played chiefly, tho' not exclusively by Contemporaries. Fielding's Talent was *Observation* not *Meditation*—But Richardson was not

f32 Philosopher enough to know the difference—say rather, to understand & develope it/Strange! to bring two such names together, as Cottle's & Richardson's—Yet amid & in spite of the vast difference there are points of resemblance/& I must not be afraid to look steadily at them.—
N.B. That deep intuition of our *oneness*—is it not at the bottom of many of our faults as well as Virtues/the dislike that a bad man should have any virtues, a good man any faults/& yet something noble and incentive is in this/

2472 17.46   Of the rash Black Lead//&c of Stoddart in the L.B.—& reflections on the same as lessons & Cautions to myself/ that Judicial Pride.—Cave! cave!

2473 17.47   Dunnage = any thin thing interposed between *f32*ᵛ goods & the Ship to prevent the former from wet or injury—from *Dun*, thin?—
Hüt—or Hät-Money—compliment payed to the Captain for his Care of the Vessel—generally supposed to mean Money for the buying a ~~new~~ new Hat/this an instance of an unmeant *Pun*/

2474 17.48   The hypochondriac, or the intemperate man,— and his endless fruitless Memoranda/fruitless and perhaps perni-cious as familiarizing his mind to the Contemplation, the lazy Contemplation of his own Weakness.

2475 17.49   A Wood fire, full of moral illustrations. The first blowing—fanning—*puts out* apparently/—continue it—& the whole is a flame/and then the mass, so high &c, all *ashes!*

2476 17.50   The Bashaw of Tunis, Hamoudier, his Judgement *f33* on the 2ⁿᵈ of Decembʳ, 1804, with respect to the man who claimed his Wife—the Wife preferred her latter Keeper/the Dey said— "since this Woman seems to have caused the unhappiness, I'll settle it!—take her out and drown her." Which was done

2477 17.51   The Imperial Captain—the Jew—& supposed Jewess—all next day called Agar the Bey & cut off—

2478 17.52   The attempt by 3 to assassinate the Bey, who moves about and about from 10 Sleeping Rooms, & has always his *f33*ᵛ Prime Minister with him/—he has now the *Cut* on his Cheek—

2479 17.53   *America*
O. Bra/—/his answer—Do you know where the Sun sets?—Yes!— well it is there & only a great deal farther—

2480 17.54　　In my Room at the Treasury a Picture of the Crucifixion, the Top of which is Glory with a circle of Angels' Heads, and two full & bodied Angels, one playing a timbrel/. ~~Dow~~ Next, & stretching his arms so that each hand touches one

f34　end of the ⊤ tee-shaped Cross, & with the Head forming

a ◺ a triangle with a curve-base is a full figure of ~~the~~ God the Father/O Blasphemy! with an immense sweep of Petticoats, like those of a large fat old Woman/as far down as where the robe of decency runs across the right Thigh of the Saviour/but what is most remarkable is that the Holy Ghost in the shape of the Dove is so nested in the Father's flowing Beard as to be made to appear a part of the Beard/at a distance it is ~~Beard~~ Beard, look closer, it is a Dove!!—The Mother & the Beloved Disciple at the foot of the Cross, the latter clasping it in his arms, are drest as Friar

f34ᵛ　and Nun/Christ something better than usual for usually he looks like a man dead-drunk, with fallen jaws & loathsome aspect, beastly-drunk/What an answer to the Picturæ Pauperum Libri!

2481 17.55　　Canting Wretches! why not employ the time of your Laziness & Mock-offices of mock Religion in teaching your Poor to read?—As soon might an Enchanter order his ministring Fiends to destroy Hell & annihilate their own powers of Mischief!!!!!

2482 17.56

8 March 1805—
But yesternight I pray'd aloud
In Anguish and in Agony—
Help Lord! or I perish.

2483 17.57
9ᵗʰ/1 °clock Sunday Morning—, 1805.
O keep me from utter Despair! ah what Hope?　　S.T.C.

f35　2484 17.58　　March 16. 1805. Cause of the offence or disgust received by the *mean* in good poems when we are young, and its

diminution and occasional evanescence when we are older in true
taste/that at first we are from various causes delighted with *generalities* of Nature which can all be expressed in dignified words/
but afterwards becoming more intimately acquainted with Nature
in its her detail we are delighted with *distinct* vivid ideas, and with
vivid ideas most when made distinct/& can most often forgive
and sometimes be delighted with even a low image from art or low
life when it gives you the very thing by an illustration/as Cowper's
stream *"inlaying"* the level vale as with silver/& even Shakespere's   *f35ᵛ*
shrill-tongued Tapster, answering "shallow wits" applied to echoes
in an echo-full place/

2485 17.59   Mʳ Chapman not yet arrived! and I am to stay
another 2 months at least!/O God, guide me aright!

2486 17.60   Sunday Evening, March 17, 1805. A Day of
Evil/Wretch that Oμμααμ' S.ΣT./O a groan/deep & almost of
moral despair!
Of the not being able to know whether or no you are smoking in
the Dark or when your eyes are shut, item, of the ignorance in that
state of the difference of Beef, Veal, &c/it is all attention/your
eyes being shut, other images arise, which you must *attend to*/it   *f36*
being the habit of a *seeing* man to attend chiefly to *sight*—so close
your eyes, you attend to the ideal images—& attending to them
you abstract your *attention*/and it is the same as when deeply
Thinking in a reverie you no longer hear distinct sounds made to
you. But what a strange inference that there were no Sounds!

2487 17.61   The Drunken Man smoking a *Segar* and having
lay'd it down a moment put the wrong end in his mouth//Bra &
Snuff missing nose & in his right eye

2488 17.62   Of the contempt of Speculative men &c/Who
more so than Sir Walter Raleigh/& he, even *he* brought in the   *f36ᵛ*
Potatoe to Europe/Good Heavens! let me never eat a roasted
Potatoe without dwelling on it and detailing its train of consequences.—Likewise too, *dubious* to the Philosopher but to be

clapped chorally by the commercial World, he this mere wild Speculatist, introduced Tobacco.

2489 17.63   Of a Ship-wrecked Crusoe, who shot wild geese, swan, &c for his food, & who had preserved from the wreck two or three Score fine penknives—amused himself with carrying the art of penmaking to perfection—and layed up in his caves such vast stores of the best possible Pens that he at last freighted a large empty Vessel driven to that desart Island with them/A vessel forced to throw all her bales & stores overboard—& having by an active mind salted down & dried down a Vast quantity of Provision, he arrived in England worth—as it proved afterwards—9, or 10,000£/—⟨A dream this, in consequence of making 5 or 6 Pens just as I was going to Bed.⟩

f37

2490 17.64   Comparisons are odious/applied to the not wedding a widow/& this as an argument concerning the causes that would difficilitate Divorce even if the Laws permitted it.

*f37*ᵛ

2491 17.65   Leckie and the Marquis of Cannagattina, and the Cannagatarese/10 Dollars to the Campieri who shot him, & a promise of 20 for the next—

2492 17.66   Decater's grand Entertainment, & the Father in law of Cannagatina's Son, Baron Cannarella, stole two Silver Spoons, a curiously cut glass, & some Sugar/the Servant's address —When you have done looking at them Sir? &c

2493 17.67   Thomas de Sandford bequeathed to the Vicar of Warcop 20 Shillings for his *forgotten tythes*/as was the custom. A pretty use might be made of this, in morals.

f38   2494 17.68   I love Sᵗ Combe or Columbe, & he shall be my Saint/for he is not in the Cat. of Romish Saints, having never been canonized at Rome/and because this Ap. of the Picts lived and gave name to an Island in the Hebrides/& from him Switzerland. ⟨was Christianized.⟩

2495 17.69   Wednesday Night, 20ᵗʰ March, 1805, has past
into Thursday Morning, ½ past 2. I arose & as I past by the last
window of the Room made *a vow* aloud/O me! that I ever should
have had need to make such a Vow!—and *Mss* σε'τκο9/Can I
wonder that good men have joined in the cry of the Vileness of   *f38ᵛ*
Human Nature! There mistake was either logical or of nomen-
clature/they either said—H.N. was *evil* because there was *evil* in
H.N = false logic, since ~~you~~ they might equally say, H.N is good
for there is good in H.N.—& so either involve contradiction in
terms, or destroy the unity of H.N.—or else they *do* destroy the
Unity of H.N. & make the Association without *will* or *reason*, fan-
tasms and fantastic feelings, the concupiscent, vindictive, and *nar-*
cissine† part of our nature one separate, dividuous being, and the   *f39*
pure will and ever benevolent *Reason* they make another Thing, &
call it Grace, or the Holy Spirit, or God/Now this appears imprudent, as furnishing excuses for Despair and spiritual Sloth, and instead of that best prayer of putting our shoulders to the wheel with
upturned eyes, & heart, so that the co-operating muscles themselves
pray, we stand idle & gossip to ~~Jupiter~~ Hercules with our Tongues/
The Cart will never be out of the Slough or Rut. Merciful God!   *f39ᵛ*
grant that this Rising out of my Bed may be a Resurrection to my
better Spirit!—I rose for this cause/I felt myself in pleasurable
bodily feeling half-asleep and interruptively *conscious* of being
sweetly half-asleep/ and I felt strongly, how apart from all concupiscence (unless perhaps that dying away or ever-subsisting vi-
bration of it in the Heart & Chest & eyes (as it *seems* to us) which
is the symbolical language of purest Love in our present Embodi-   *f40*
ment/for if mind acts on body, the purest ~~feeling~~ Impulse can
introduce itself to our consciousness no otherwise than by *speaking*

† I mean, the not me becoming great and good by spreading thro'   *f38ᵛ*
and combining with all things, but all becoming me and to me by   *f39*
the phantom-feeling of their being concentrated *in me* & only valuable as associated in the symbolical sense (the eye in the seeing;
the ear in the blind/the taste in infants, the feeling in the adult   *f39ᵛ*
deaf, and blind, (& consequently dumb)—Stallmaster at Hanover)
with our own Symbol = to men in general, our visual Form.

to us in some bodily feeling)—(benevolificence, or rather ◡ - ◡, - ◡ - nĕvolificence)

I felt strongly how apart from all impurity if I were sleeping with the Beloved these kind and pleasurable feelings would become associated with a Being *out of me*, & thereby in an almost incalculable train of consequences increase my active benevolence ⟨= virtuous Volificence = benevolificence = *goodwilldoingness*⟩

O yes, Sara! I did feel how being with you I should be so very much a better man/—and why should it be a *Woman*, & a *beloved*

ƒ40ᵛ Woman? will the Sneerers ask. They have not the Heart to understand the answer; but I trust that if I have virtue enough to live, that I shall instruct the good to put the feelings of their own Souls into ~~their~~ a language, that shall kindle those feelings into tenfold heat and blaze—so that finally whatever is really & truly a part of our existing Nature, a universally existing part, may become an object of our love, & admiration—yea, that the Pressure of the Husband's Hand or swelling chest on the bosom of the beloved

ƒ41 Wife shall appear as strictly and truly virtuous, as *Actively* virtuous, as the turning away in the heat of passion from the Daughter of Lust or Harlotry. O best reward of Virtue! to feel pleasure made more pleasurable, in legs, knees, chests, arms, cheek—~~this~~ all in deep quiet, a fountain with unwrinkled surface yet still the living motion at the bottom, that "with soft and even pulse" keeps it full—& yet to know that this pleasure so impleasured is making us more *good*, is preparing virtue and pleasure for many known and many unknown to us. O had Milton been thus happy! Might

ƒ41ᵛ not—even in his own language—more than 20 million of Souls, & perhaps hereafter 20 times 20 million of human Souls have received new impulses to virtuous Love, till Vice was stared at as Voluntary Torment, slow gratuitous Self mangle-murder!—O and the thousand thoughts arising in this state, only connected with it, inasmuch as Happiness is a Fountain of intellectual activity, & connects the connected ~~with~~ a b with c, d—till Z.—yea, 1 and 2 with 3—& in a few moments with *595*, *876*, *341*. But I, Sara! But I am not worthy of you/I shall perish!—I have not good-

ƒ42 ness enough to hope enough/and tho' I neither game nor ever connect myself with Woman ⟨even by a Thought,⟩ yet my bod-

ily infirmities conquer me, and the cowardice of pain, or rather
of danger of Life, drives me to stimulants that cannot but finally
destroy me. O me/let me return!—Awake! awake!—

2496 17.70   Of the dissolving Sugar in the Tea, or the old   *f42*
Woman-plan of putting the lump in the mouth prest on the
Palate & let the Tea *wash* by it/—a lively illustration of something or other/my fancy does not say *what* at present.
3 °clock, 21 March. 1805.

2497 17.71   The noble Garden at Casal ⌜. . .⌝ Lucca, what a   *f42ᵛ*
picture/half or more finished, rich earth in level beds—this is
bounded by the yard or more smooth wall of Pebbles disclosing
the bed of the Garden, then quarries, rocks, men working, large
& small heaps of Soil, dug up from among the rocks—but the
surface most bare rock, and where else, it is only covered with
such vegetation as will grow in half an inch of Soil.—

2498 17.72   The deep Quiet of Malta & its security within &
without.

2499 17.73   Both here and in Sicily the Pinks &c are never
propped up; but are suffered to hang down, and are put in Pots
etc on balconies & walls, so as to give them play &-room. They
are large, & I think it far more beautiful way than ours/

2500 17.210

      But Love is there—   *f129ᵛ*
      The Clouds—but when they past,
      Did I not dance with all my waves
            hailed the Light renewed

2501 15.134   Of the Orange Trees loaded with Fruits, and   *f68*
Blossoms/24 March, 1805, Sᵗ Antonio, Malta.

2502 15.135   Negative Quantities/= opposed forces. Logical
by Contradiction ends in absolute nothing, nihil *negativum,* quod

f68ʳ est etiam irrepresentabile—a ball in motion & at the same time not in motion, motion in each sentence having been used in the same sense, is a contradiction in terms/in Nature it is *not*, or rather say, it *isn't*, so as not to give a moments reality by the use of the word per se, *is*—but there are oppositions without contradiction, & *real* —nihil privativum cogitabile—two tendencies to motion in the same body, one to the N. other to S., being equipollent, the Body remains *in rest*.—the second assumed Tendency is a real negative Quantity—better therefore called, a *privative* Quantity.

$- 4 - 5 = - 9$ is mere pedantry—there is no real *sub*traction/it is true *addition*. $-$ and $+$ have no meaning but as symbols of opposition.

2503 15.136   The Metapothecaries always kicking out at the
f69 *Mathe*maticians, the *Matter*maticians on the other hand aiming the same asinine Flings at the Metaphysicians. But real Metaphysicians and Mathematicians are Friends, and Lovers; always look at each other with respect and welcome, and often walk arm in arm.

2504 15.137   Blossoms on bare branches on Peach, Apricot, & Almond Trees= to what? Stench Blossom of the Spice Trees.

2505 15.274
f126   An uncut   11 of small
                                       3 of large
             10 times   13 Sticks of sealing Wax
                                       9 sticks
                     No anxious
             10   Impatience
             10
                 [. . . .] dotted off not for the use of Schools
                 love you—or is it [. . .]
                 Mercury—occultation of—
                         31 Bunches of Quills
                         25 March 1805

2506 15.138   To Casal Safi on Wednesday March 27—good   *f69*
Luogo tenente, his grandmother, Fratello, & two children/then
thro' Zerrid; no *blue* eyes, but round, like black cherries—when
black/but many not black/these from Hazel to Grey—no blue
ones. To Maccluba = Capuchin Gardens in Syracuse, only less than   *f69ᵛ*
nothing in beauty. Wonderful absorption of water/full, that immense bason with its gardens at the bottom (a true Topsy-turvy,
terra rovesciata) & gone in a few hours as it were—to Krendi/
sight just before Macluba of the fine Sea comb where Sir A.
landed. Thursday, 28—to the Conservatory hurry skurry, young
rabbit warren, escono cattivissimi/reflect on this deeply—to the
ospizio—the old man *bowing* cotton, and that other naked figure/
O for a Dante in Painting to go thro' the Hell of Trade, & Commerce!—

2507 15.139   The Caroubas when their Leaves glitter in the
Sun = Hollies.

2508 15.140   Gardens, say rather Garden Pots—beds at least
with Stone borders. The Maltese Fields.   *f70*

2509 17.74   Cause/Duty.—Now if I say to a Paleyan or   *f43*
Priestleyan my *mist,* my delving & difficulty, & he answers me in a
set of parrot words, ⟨quite satisfied, clear as a pike-staff,—nothing
before & *nothing behind*—a stupid piece of mock-knowlege, having no *root* for then it would have feelings of dimness from
growth, having no buds or twigs, for then it would have yearnings
& strivings of obscurity from *growing,* but a dry stick of Licorish,
sweet ~~and~~ tho' mawkish to the palate of self-adulation,⟩ acknowl-
eging no sympathy with this delving, this feeling of a wonder/
then I must needs set him down for a Priestleyan, Paleyan, Bar-
bouldian, &c &c &c &c &c—from Lock to Mackintosh.

2510 17.75   † To make this the beginning Stanza of the   *f43ᵛ*
Poem or Canto concerning to whom Virtue a path of Thorns and
Vice an *Impossibility*—to die! to die!—And this followed by the
consequences of Suicide O endless indefinite yearning thro' infinity.
March 28.

2511 17.76   To the Daisies in Malta/March 29.

2512 17.77   Of the Italian Language in Machiavelli & Boc-
cacio/wherein better, wherein worse, than the Latin. Of the present Gallicism and uniformity of construction throughout Europe,
& its effects.   29

2513 17.78   Our Polit. connect. with the Barbary States an
anomaly in Diplomatic, the whole a crazy old Fabric of Compro-
mise and Connivance, with no proportion, but/some/apartments
of/convenience/tho' there is no other way of getting to them but
by back stairs & thro' dark Passages.   29

                              my Letter to Oglander.

ƒ44   2514 17.79   ⌐ . . . . ⌐ & overcome by Love, by
very Love! that it has been quenched utterly in the memory, annihilated in the moral Being. That I may not lose and forget it,
let me remember to write that Poem on this subject at the end of
this Book.—

2515 17.80   Of country—Great Britain for me—none of your
romantics!—and what then do you mean? If my feelings are romantic, upon what are yours founded? Why should you love your
country at all? It is an axiom. Be it so! But still an Axiom implies
a definition, & is preceded by it. What do you mean by country?
The clod under your feet? or where you were born? What if I
had been born in a Sicilian Vessel, my mother an Englishwoman
being there brought to bed? No, where my Parents were born.—
What then if my Father had been so born, &c &c.

                              Saturday Night

ƒ44ᵛ   2516 17.81   Tis one source of mistakes concerning the merits of
Poems that to those read in youth men attribute all that praise
which is due to Poetry in general, merely considered as select language in metre (Little children should not be taught verses, in my
opinion/better not seen till ten or eleven years old—) two ~~sources~~
kinds of pleasure are procured, in the two master-movements &

impulses of man, the gratification of the Love of Variety with the grat. of the Love of Uniformity—and that by a recurrence, delightful as a painless and yet exciting act of memory, tiny breezelets of surprize, ~~the~~ each one destroying the ripplets which the former had made, yet all together keeping the surface of the mind in a bright dimple-smile—Hatred of Vacancy reconciled to with the love of Rest—These and other causes often make Poetry an overpowering Delight to a Lad of Feeling, as I have heard Poole relate of himself respecting Edwin and Angelina/—But so it would be with a man bred up in a Wilderness by unseen Beings, who should yet converse and rationalize—how beautiful would not *f45* the first other man appear, whom he saw, & knew to be a man by ~~its~~ the resemblance to his own image seen in the clear Stream/he would in like manner attribute to the man all the divine attributes of humanity, tho' haply it should be a very ordinary or even almost ugly man, compared with a hundred others. Many of us have felt this with respect to women, who have been bred up where few are to be seen/and I acknowlege that both in persons and in poems it is well *on the whole* that we should retain our first Loves, tho' alike in both cases evils have happened as the consequence—1 April, 1805.

2517 17.82   *31 ~~April~~ March, 1805.* Sunday Night, 11 oclock. —This day noon, a little after one o'clock Sir A. Ball sent for me— he not being in in his study I went into the Drawing Room, which *f45ᵛ* was full of Visitors—Lady Ball addressed me, asking me if I knew Captⁿ Wordsworth/I said, a little—Is he not a Brother of the Mʳ Wordsworth, you so often talk of?—No, I replied, still imagining she meant the Cousin/But you have heard his melancholy fate? What? said I/& the Ship? Here I turned pale & repeated the Question/Going from England, it sunk/& 300 men are lost—& only but one hundred saved. But the Captain/he is lost—said Lady Ball, her voice faltering, for she saw my Emotion/I could just say— Yes! it is His Brother/& retired from the Room/Sir Alexander followed me, upon Business—and Dʳ Sewel to invite me to dine *f47* with him/I was nearly strangled—and at last just got out—I have just heard of the Death of a dear Friend, Sir! excuse me/—& got home led by the Sergeant & followed to the Door by Sir A. B./O what an afternoon—O William, O Dorothy, Dorothy!—Mary—& you loved him so!—and o blessed Sara, you whom I in my imagination at one time I so often connected with him, by an effort of agonizing Virtue, willing it with cold sweat-drops on my Brow!—How shall I ever visit Langdale/O it will look like an hollow Vault—like a Cenotaph/his Tomb & a more heart-rending sight because ⌐ O Christ!⌐ Dear dear John! these Tears tho' from eyes

f47ᵛ that throb and smart are pleasure compared to what I have felt, to what I shall feel.—Methinks, it is impossible, to live/I shall hear next of Sara's Death/no, not of William's—no! no!—surely not—no surely, if there be intention in anything, or goodness in Providence/God forgive me!—I for myself despair of ever seeing my home. They are expecting me—did they not even so expect him!—O God have pity on us! O may Almighty God bless you, my Friends! and comfort you—dearest Dorothy, Mary, dear dear Mary—& Sara, deepest yet hopeless Hope! Ah venerated William/ how will you and Dorothy look at times ⌐. . . . .⌐

f70 2518 15.141   2 April, 1805   The first yellow green leaves. Of the figures scattered all over † the Tree, & yet thinly, & yet disclosing every branch & every grey twig resembled to a wonder a flight of large green Butterflies alighted on the leafless Tree/all shot through with Sunshine.

† no! only at the extremities of each twig.

2519 15.142   The beautiful Milk Thistle—with the milk-blue white veins or fibres up & athwart its dark green Leaves.

2520 15.143   All round the Fosses Civita Vecchia Garrison, the Gardens, where rocky trenches cut, & made Fruit gardens, Figs & Pomegranates/else Cotton—/& Culinary &c—noble.

f70ᵛ 2521 15.144   Sea & its Bays—
fields green with corn, interspersed with the dark crimson Sulla/ white with fields newly sowed—roughened here & there with fields in *building*—the many Casals/ the *tents* of *Stone* fields, i.e. stoocks as in Hopground/harbor running up as two lakes/barrenness every

where staring out, & every where conquered, or a-conquering—the
Sea like a blue wall around—so looked the scene from the Ramparts of Civita Vecchia looking down in the Bason towards S!
Paul's & S! Julian/Casals looking like burnt out Villages/the Har-   *f71*
bor like the grand Houses at Bristol left unfinished/a ruin of the
Purse/let me not forget how strongly and repeatedly this impressed me/It was travelling to Morrison's & again to St Antonio
on the high road that this first struck me and yesterday (Tuesday,
3 Apr.) on the same road I was impressed in the same manner.—

   Goats, Pigs—Calices—Faldettos—Streets all stairs, all across—
streets, stairs on each side/Bell-Jangling—Caricature Madonna
Looks of the (ugly!) Women in consequence of the Faldettos.—
Swarms of little Children/a Pig and a Goat eating off the same   *f71ᵛ*
piled Mound of Sulla, and a child astride of each, at a shop door/

the Swaddle of the Babes ⛾ —Multitude of Squinting People,

owing no doubt to the Swaddle/Maltese men & boys cast all in one
mould/their thighs & legs long in proportion to their stature, all
straight, clean-limbed ⟨fellows, limbs⟩ limber, straight, light, well-
rounded, the legs & thigh one limb/boys of six and 7 up to 25 or
more just one mould/—

   The prettiest Maltese women = pretty Jewesses.—Among the
men of advanced age, from 40 to 50, especially in the Casals, you
often meet with true Sancho Panzas.   *f72*

2522 15.145   I find by an accurate calculation that on each of
my fingers there is a yearly growth of nail amounting to 2½ Inches,
of course the whole growth of both hands is two feet and an inch/
On my feet about 18 Inches yearly, the sum total therefore of Nail
which my Body produces amounts to about 3 Feet, 7 inches in
length, or perpendicular measurement, but on an exact average ⟨of⟩
7 times that number in breadth, or horizontal measurement/

	Feet		Inches
Length	3	"	7
Breadth	25	"	1

                4 April, 1805.
⟨Cut a second time the two left finger nails Sat. morning 6 April.⟩

2523 17.226

f165ᵛ   Of the Judge that condemns to the tune of
"For 'keep all you take? [?turns/from] a Punt to a Brig
While your damn'd further Proofs to be made hugger-mugger
~~Turn~~ Change a Spanish Galleon to an empty Dutch Lugger

2524 17.227

f166   [. . . . .] the Gift is double
[. . . . .] once you give it
[. . . . .] double
He gives in [. . . . ?grievous] trouble

4 April 1805   S.T.C.

[. . .] that [?art] nor time nor trouble
So looks the hawk's wing double

or conceitfully
~~A single gift seem'd two so given~~
~~Without Delay or Trouble~~

Your Gift seem'd two, 'twas givn so fleetly
Warm Heart made cool Brain bubble
For Gratitude surprized so sweetly
Like Drunkenness, sees double.

f50   2525 17.83   ⌐ . . . . ⌐ mere *negative* evidence—"I
never felt that—never saw that—that is strange to me—" &c &c—
weigh with thee against the Honor & *Faith* due to that work.

2526 17.84   Midnight 5 April 1805. I will write as truly as I
can from *Experience* actual individual *Experience*—not from Book-
knowlege. But yet it is wonderful, how exactly the Knowlege from
good books coincides with the experience of men of the World, as
I have often noticed when much younger, in men of the World
f50ᵛ   who beginning to withdraw a little into themselves, commonly by
reading—I have noticed in them their deep delight in so many
passages, which had escaped me—so much in so many others which

I had never heard of *but from Booksellers*—/Experience necessary
no doubt, if only to give a *light* and *shade* in the mind, to give to
some ideas a greater vividness than others, & thereby to make it a
thing of Time and outward reality—practical—for all being
equally vivid = ⟨the whole becomes⟩ a dream. But notwithstanding
this & other reasons, I yet believe that the saws against Book-
knowlege are handed down to us from Times when Books conveyed only abstract Science or abstract Morality & Religion/
whereas in the present day what is there of real Life, in all its go-
ings on, Trades, Manufactures, high Life, low life, animate & in-   *f51*
animate that is not *in books*. Books are conversation at present. Evil
as well as Good in this, I well know/but Good too as well as Evil/

2527 17.85   O dear John! and so ended thy dreams of Tairns
& mountain Becks, & obscure vales in the breasts and necks of
Mountains! So thy dream of living with or among thy Brother &
his—O Heavens! Dying in all its Shapes; shrieks; and confusion;
and mad Hope; and Drowning more deliberate than Suicide;—
these, these were the Dorothy, the Mary, the Sara Hutchinson, to
kiss the cold Drops from thy Brow, & to close thy ~~his~~ Eyes!—
Never yet has any Loss gone so far into the Life of Hope, with
me. I now only fear.—6 Ap. 1805.

2528 17.86   6 April, 1805. Sat. Afternoon ½ past 4.—Tis   *f51ᵛ*
strange! it answers no purpose on earth/ ⌜. . . .⌝ do or deter
might do something, to be payed for in due time, but as to won, it
is lost, ~~neither~~ it does ⟨not⟩ Mʳ ∸ Macky! you chearful! or comfortable! even for the moment—? but tho' won, tis rather winn'd—
drowsy slips, painful struggling drums, leap up from within, start,
wake, chill/—and all for nothing. Tree, yon door.—

2529 17.87   Saturday Midnight. My Spirits exceedingly
low. I have much to write of my own feelings—but even to do
this, my solace when all else failed I have not now the
Heart. ⌜. . . . .⌝
          I couldn't die of the pain but in ⌜. . . . .⌝

f52   2530 17.88   Real + symbolical.—Motion + Rest at the Goal.
     Love—and the grandeur of loving the Supreme in her—the real
& symbolical united/—and the more because I love her as being
capable of being glorified by me & as the means & instrument of my
own glorification/In loving her thus I love two Souls as one, as
compleat, ⟨by anticipation, and yet in conseq. of anticipation⟩ as the
ever improving Symbol of Deity to us, still growing with the
growth of ~~my~~ our intellectual Faculties:—⟨and so uniting the moving impulse & the *stationary* desire.⟩ O that I may have heart &
soul to develope this Truth so important and so deeply felt. Well,
tomorrow I will take courage & write my *confession*—& try to
lighten my chest, my Brain/the something that weighs *upon* and
and *against* my Eyebrows! ⌜O Asra!⌝ Miserere mei, Domine!

f52ᵛ   2531 17.89   7 April, 1805. Sunday Morn: 4 ˚clock. How fee-
bly, how unlike an English Cock that Cock crows & the other answers!—Did I not particularly notice the unlikeness on my first
arrival at Malta?—Well! to day I will disburthen my mind. Yet
one thing strikes me—the difference, I find in myself now & for a
year or two past, *b* seemingly increasing in an increasing ratio, *d* decreasing in the same—by *d* I mean, my Enthusiasm for the Happiness of mankind in particular places and countries, & my eagerness
to promote it—by b, I mean, my sense of Duty, my hauntings of
conscience from any stain of Thought or Action! I remember the
having written a strong Letter to my most dear and honored
Wordsworth (Ah John Wordsworth—and Mary and Dorothy—
f53   perhaps they may have awaked, as I have done,—each or either—&
mourning for the one Brother ⟨. . . . .⟩ Mary will move herself
closer to William as if to let the ignorant *body* know, that *he* is
still here—he is not dead/& then, deep⟨-hearted⟩, & wide⟨-hearted⟩
Dorothy, my Sister! my Sister! so like to myself in the forms of
our Hearts/to thee 'tis *Shudder*, a phantom of—I cannot utter the
feeling!—O comfort us! comfort us!—but indeed I am very, very
hopeless & heartless! I was about to say that I ~~had written~~ once
wrote to W. in consequence of his Ode to Duty & in that letter explained this as the effect of ~~Selfinterest~~ *Selfness* in a mind incapable
of gross Self-interest—decrease of Hope and Joy, the Soul in its

round & round flight forming narrower circles, till at every Gyre its
wings beat against the *personal Self*. But let me examine this more   *f53ᵛ*
accurately. It may be, the phænomenon may come out more honorable to our Nature. The first is clear. Even in minute cleanliness it
~~is~~ holds good with me. I cannot endure the least atom or imagination of dirt on my person/but wash my body all over 20 times,
where 8 or 9 years I washed half of it once.

2532 17.90

> O! th' oppressive, irksome weight
> Felt in an uncertain State:
> Comfort, peace, and rest adieu,
> Should I prove at last untrue!
> Self-confiding Wretch I thought
> I could ~~serve~~ love thee as I ought,
> Win thee and deserve to feel
> All the love, thou can'st reveal.
> And still I chuse thee, follow still
> Every notice ⌐. . . . .⌐

2533 17.91   ⟨Is there not more than a mere diff. of graceful-   *f59*
ness between "that" and "which"—??⟩

2534 17.92   Mem.—to attempt to *understand* that craving
after indefinite sensations of comfort, the *Spera una delusione,*
Loda un inganno, and cerebelline Tint—the *manner* of its domina-
tion.

2535 17.93   It is as trite as it is mournful, but yet most instructive and by the genius that can produce the strongest impressions of novelty by rescuing the stalest and most admitted Truths
from the impotence caused by the very circumstance of their universal admission/(admitted so instantly as never to be reflected on,
never by that sole key of Reflection admitted into the ~~door~~ effective
legislative Council-chamber of the Heart) so true that they lose all
the privileges of Truth, and, as *extremes meet,* by being Truisms   *f59ᵛ*

correspond in utter inefficiency with universally acknowleged Errors—(~~Truisms~~ in Algebraic Symbols Truisms = Falshoodisms = 00) by that genius might good be worked in considering the old old Methusalen Law, that Evil produces Evil—One error almost compels another/tell one lie tell a hundred/O to shew this, a priori by bottoming it in all our faculties/& by experience of touching Examples.—Πανηγυριζε ~~Σιν~~ ειν ~~αγε~~ Ινγαννο + τιντσερεβελ υβερ νυκτα, σφεγλιατο ιν χονσ˙ δεσ μοργενς φρυ˙, ε ταλλορα περ μη ρεσταρε σφεγλιαντε ελπις εινα Δελυσιονε—Θεν ανξιετι, στιφλιν—αθμη

f61   2536 17.94   ⌜. . . . .⌝ explaining it—& by all sweet images conveying to *her* understanding, truth, and to *my own,* simplicity & the power of uttering abstrusest Truths as from the mouth of Childhood. But O me!—I am very mournful. Lord Nelson is pursuing the French Fleet & the Convoy is to be deferred/ I felt glad—how can I endure that it should depart without me? Yet if I go, whither am I to go?—Merciful Providence! what a cloud is spread before me/a cloud is my only guide by day and by night/I have no pillar of Fire, nothing definite to alternate with the Indefinite! ⌜. . . . .⌝

f61ᵛ   2537 17.95   8 Apr. 1805. Monday.—The favorite Object of all oriental Tales, & that which inspiring their Authors in the East inspires still their Readers ~~N.S. and West~~ every where, is the impossibility of baffling Destiny, & that what we considered as the means of one thing becomes in a strange manner the direct means of the Reverse. O dear John Wordsworth! what Joy at Grasmere that you were made Captⁿ of the Abergavenny/so young too! now it was next to certain that you would in a few years settle in your natives Hills, and be verily one of *the Concern.*—Then came your Share in the brilliant action with Linois—I was at Grasmere in spirit only. but in spirit I was one of the Rejoicers—As Joyful as any, & perhaps more Joyous!—This doubtless not only enabled you to lay in ~~more~~ a larger and more advantageous Cargo, but procured
f62   you a voyage to India instead of China/& in this a next to certainty

of Independence/—and all these were Decoys of Death!—Well!
—and but a nobler feeling than these vain regrets would become
the Friend of the man whose last words were—"I have done my
Duty! let her go!"—Let us do our *Duty:* all else is a Dream, Life
and Death alike a Dream/this short sentence would comprize, I
believe, the sum of all profound Philosophy, of ethics and metaphysics conjointly, from Plato to Fichte.—S.T.C.—

2538 17.96   I never had a more lovely twig of orange-blos-
soms with four old last year's Leaves with their steady green ⟨well-
placed among them,⟩ than to day—& with a rose-twig of three
Roses made a very striking Nosegay to an Englishman. The
Orange Twig was so very, very full of Blossom, that one fourth   *f62ᵛ*
of the number becoming fruit of the natural size would have broken the Twig off. Is there then disproportion here? Or waste?—O
no! no!—In the first place, here is a prodigality of beauty; and
what harm do they do by existing? & is not man a being capable of
beauty even as of Hunger or Thirst? and if the latter be fit Objects
of a final cause, why not the former?—But secondly, she hereby
multiplies manifold the chances of a proper number becoming
fruit/in this twig for a instance for one set of accidents that would
have been fatal to the year's growth if only as many blossoms had
been on it as it was designed to bear fruit, there may now be three
sets of equal accidents, and no harm done.—And thirdly, and lastly   *f63*
for *me* at least, or at least at present, for in nature doubtless there
are many additional Reasons, and possibly for me at some future
hour of reflection, after some new influx of information from Books
or observance—and thirdly, these Blossoms are Fruit, fruit to the
winged Insect, fruit to man/yea, and of more solid value perhaps
than the orange itself.—O how the Bees bethrong ⟨and bemurmur⟩
it, o how the Honey tells the Tale of its Birthplace to the sense of
Sight and Odours!—And to how many minute or uneyeable Insects beside!—So, I cannot but think, ought I to be talking to Hartley!—and sometime to detail all the insects that have arts or implements resembling human/the Sea snails with the nautilus at the
Head/the wheel Insect—the net—the Gun, the galvanic eel, &c &c
&c

f63ᵛ   2539 17.97   9 April. Wonderful Blending of Ideas in Dreams.
I have this very moment left my Bed—part of my Dream is too
strange & the feelings connected with the images in sleep too different from those which would have been connected with the same
awake to mention/I shall only therefore note these/There was a
Desk, like that of a Master's at the upper end of a School/for
School & Desk &c it always will be when I am ill; so deep has been
the impression of those days in which my ill-health no doubt origi-
nated!/and Middleton, who was my superior, my friend and Pa-
tron at School, my friend for the first year at College, who never
f64   quarrelled with me, but was quietly alienated, was there and received me kindly—with him was blended a series of images entirely
dependent, as I found on awaking, on the state in which Flatulence
had placed the different parts of my Body—he went away—& I
lay down at the bottom of the Desk, & heard a Clergyman quoting
aloud a Text from Sᵗ Paul, as from a Pulpit in the next Room/
without any feeling of surprize—the next instant it was Sᵗ Paul
himself, & no surprize did I feel!—Then Middleton returned &
reproved me severely for taking Liberties on the slightest encour-
agement, & sitting thus by *his Fire*/Till that moment it had been
the bottom of a Desk, & no Fire/but now there was a little obscure
Fire-place—all this without surprize—& I awoke—

f64ᵛ   2540 17.98   The best, the truly lovely, in each & all is God.
Therefore the truly Beloved is the symbol of God to whomever it
is truly beloved by!—but it may become perfect & maintained
lovely by the function of the two/The Lover worships in his Beloved that final consummation ⟨of itself which is⟩ produced in his
own soul by the action of the Soul of the Beloved upon it, and that
final perfection of the Soul of the Beloved, ⟨which is in part⟩ the
consequence of the reaction of his (so ammeliorated & regenerated) Soul upon the Soul of his Beloved/till each contemplates the
Soul of the other as involving his own, both in its givings and its
receivings, ~~in a mood that~~ and thus still keeping alive its *outness,*
f65   its *self-oblivion* united with *Self-warmth,* & still approximates to
God! Where shall I find an image for this sublime Symbol ⟨which
ever⟩ involving the presence of Deity, yet ~~tending~~ tends towards

it ever!—Shall it be in the attractive powers of the different surfaces of the earth?—Each attraction the *vice-gerent* & *representative* of the central attraction, and yet *being* ⟨no other than⟩ that
attraction itself.—By some such feeling as this I can easily believe
the mind of Fenelon & Madame Guyon to have coloured its faith in
the Worship of Saints—but that was most dangerous/it was not
idolatry in *them;* but it encouraged Idolatry ~~to~~ in others/—Now
⟨the⟩ pure Love of a good man to a good woman does not involve
this Evil, but multiplies, intensifies the Good.

2541 17.99   Of the Blows given by a person to himself, to his   *f65ᵛ*
hands, breast, or forehead, in the paroxysms of *Self-reproof*—sometimes do they not tend to force the bodily sensations into union
with that idea in the mind, which is the dictate of Reason & Duty—
so as to make the body itself feel the *condemnation* which the mind
feels so deeply?—(In using the words, *body* and *mind,* I always
pre-suppose such a definition of those 2 words to have preceded, as
removes all charge of unmeaning and sleight of hand management
of words—mysticism, &c &c—)—yet I at the same time reverence
that algebraic xyz of Reasoning, in which unknown quantities,   *f66*
known to be & to be different, but their difference not yet analysed,
are used—& right, deductions drawn. So the mere man's notions are
translated into Newtonianism, Newtonianism into Berkleianism,
Berkleianism into a finer—*ism*/yet all remain symbols of Truth,
~~true~~ actual tho' dim perceptions of it.—So—I standing on a mighty
Mass ⟨(as in the *Sun* for instance)⟩ or close beside it, perceived
that A there ⟨in the Planet, Jupiter, ex.gr.⟩ B. in an other distance,
⟨Venus,⟩ C in a third, D. in the same distance but quite different
relation, &c &c &c &c &c, all have seen this object, absolutely seen
it. I reconcile *all* their conceptions & justify them, ~~but~~ while they
dispute bitterly among themselves, each imagining a different Object. But I wish to explain fully that self-charged Insincerity, that   *f66ᵛ*
Histrionism (*Histrio* the Latin for an *Actor on a Stage*) ~~with~~ of
which the Soul half-accuses itself in many of its efforts at self-condemnation and self-reformation. I have before in my Hints and
Notes de Consolatione remarked, that this is a sad Strategem, as it
were, of Vice to detain the Prisoner, ⟨who is⟩ struggling to escape

from it, by inspiring Despondency—& in order to avert this from myself and others I would fain shew that this is the natural and necessary feeling, ⟨that must⟩ accompany~~ing~~ any ~~change~~ ⟨and every ⌘ spirit: Revol:⟩ any ⟨and every⟩ incipient change of Habit. It is, as I hope to shew fully, only the consciousness ⌐. . . . .⌐
⌘ spiritual Revolution

ƒ67   2542 17.100   Wednesday Night—Dreamt that I was saying, or reading, or that it was said to me, "Varrius thus prophecied Vinegar at his Door by damned frigid Tremblings"—just after which I awoke—I fell to sleep again, having in the previous Doze meditated on the possibility of making Dreams ⟨regular,⟩ and just as I ~~was~~ had passed on the other side of the confine of Dozing I afforded this specimen/"I should have thought it Vossius rather than Varrius—tho' Varrius being a great poet, the idea would have been more suitable to him/only that all his writings were *unfortunately lost in the Arrow*. Again I awoke. N.B. The Arrow Cap^{tn} Vincent's
ƒ67ᵛ   Frigate, taken by the French, ~~with~~ our Malta Letters and Dispatches having been previously thrown overboard, in Feb. 1805.— This illustrates the connections of Dreams—

2543 17.101   I humbly thank God, that I have for some time past been more attentive to the regulation of my Thoughts—& the attention has been blessed with a great measure of Success. There are few Day-dreams that I dare allow myself at any time; and ~~of these few~~ few & cautiously built as they are, it is very seldom that I can think myself entitled to make lazy Holiday with any one ⟨of them⟩. I must have worked hard, long, and well, to have earned that privilege/. So akin to Reason is Reality, that what I could *do* with exulting Innocence, I can not always *imagine* with
ƒ68   perfect innocence/for Reason and Reality can stop and stand still, ~~by~~ new Influxes from without counteracting the Impulses from within, and *poising* the Thought. But Fancy and Sleep *stream on;* and (instead of outward Forms and Sounds, the Sanctifiers, the Strengtheners!) they connect with them motions of the blood and nerves, and images forced into the mind by the feelings that arise out of the position & state of the Body and its different members. I

have ~~acted~~ done innocently what afterwards in absence I have ⟨likewise⟩ day-dreamed innocently, during the being awake; but ~~after~~ the Reality was followed in Sleep by no suspicious fancies, the ~~latter~~ Day-dream *has* been. Thank Heaven! however/Sleep has never yet desecrated the images, or supposed ‡ Presences, of those whom   *f68ᵛ* I love and revere.

    ‡ There is often a dim sense of the Presence of a Person in our dreams, whose form does not appear.

All the above-going throw lights on my mind with regard to the origin of Evil. ⟨υλη = confusio = passio = finiri—//Reason, Action, Forma efformans. (= means "the same as"://"opposed to".)⟩

2544 17.102   Saturday Morning—/A proof has struck me, say rather an illustration, or peep-cranny into the geometrical calculable nature of the merest contingencies in the plastic mind of the Universe—the Itch animalcule, those found only on tame Pigs, Flies that lay their eggs uniformly on the extruded anus of Horses, and become worms in the Horse's intestines—indeed the whole Entomology swarms with instances.

2545 17.103   A Treasure of Trash!   *f69*

2546 17.104   Saturday Night, April 14, 1805—In looking at objects of Nature while I am thinking, as at yonder moon dim-glimmering thro' the dewy window-pane, I seem rather to be seeking, as it were *asking,* a symbolical language for something within me that already and forever exists, than observing any thing new. Even when that latter is the case, yet still I have always an ~~obscure~~ cure feeling as if that new phænomenon were the dim Awaking of a forgotten or hidden Truth of my inner Nature/It is still interesting as a Word, a Symbol! It is Λογος, the Creator! ⟨and the Evolver!⟩

    What is the right, the virtuous Feeling, and consequent action,   *f69ᵛ* when a man having long meditated & perceived a certain Truth finds another, [? &/a] foreign Writer, who has handled the same with an approximation to the Truth, as he ⟨had previously⟩ conceived it?—Joy!—Let Truth make her Voice *audible!* While I was preparing the pen to write this remark, I lost the train of Thought which had led me to it. I meant to have asked something else, now forgotten: for the above answers itself—it needed no new answer, I trust, in my Heart. 14 April, 1805—

2547 17.105   The passion of the Maltese (of Catholics in general?) for Noise. Easter Sunday/This & the day preceding, what Bell jangling, what incessant firing of Guns, even the children ~~in~~ *f70* at every three yards letting off gunpowder-preparations—and where these cannot be had by them, clashing &c. Noise and Nothingness/this is the Sum of the *Indifferent* Parts of the Religion— the positive Good, ⟨nothing!—⟩ O—the positive Evil, immediate or in consequence, ah! what a gloomy Bulk of Catalogue, what a massy Doomsday Book!

2548 17.106   The English & North France, German &c Climates, ~~have~~ ⟨possess among many others this⟩ one little Beauty of † uniting the mysteries of positive, with those of natural, Religion —in celebrating the symbolical resurrection of the human Soul, in that of the Crucified, at the time of the actual resurrection of the "living Life" of Nature. Easter Sunday, 1805.
⟨† uniting⟩

2549 17.107   East. Sunday. That beautiful passage in dear and honoured W. Wordsworth's Michael respecting the forward-look- *f70ᵛ* ing Hope inspired pre-eminently by the birth of a child was brought to my mind most forcibly by my own ⟨independent, tho' in part anticipated,⟩ reflections respecting the ⌜immense⌝ importance of young Children to the keeping up the stock of *Hope* in the human Species/they seem as immediately the secreting-organ of Hope in the great organized Body of the whole Human Race, in all men considered as component Atoms of MAN, as young Leaves are the organs of supplying vital air to the atmosphere.

2550 17.108   Religion consists in Truth and Virtue, i.e. the permanent, the forma efformans, in the flux of Things without, of

feelings & images within/—well therefore the Scripture speaks of
the Spirit as praying to the Spirit—the Lord said to my Lord/&c—
God is the Essence as well as Object of Religion.

2551 17.109   April 17, Wed. 1805.—I would not willingly kill   *f71*
even a flower, but were I at the head of an army, or a revolutionary
Kingdom, I would do *my Duty*/and tho' it should be the ordering
of the military execution of a city, yet—supposing it my Duty—I
would give the order, & then in awe listen to the uproar, even as to
a Thunder-storm/the awe as tranquil, the submission to the inevitable, to the Unconnected with my own Self, as profound/It should
be as if the Lightning of Heaven passed along my Sword, & destroyed a man—

2552 17.110   There are times when my Thoughts flow, like
Music/O that they were more frequent!—How can they be? I
being so hopeless.†
    † ⟨and for months past so incessantly employed in official tasks,
subscribing, examining, administring Oaths, auditing, &c &c.⟩

2553 17.111   Does the sober Judgment previously meteeasure   *f71ᵛ*
out the banks between which the Stream of Enthusiasm shall rush
with its torrent sound/Far rather does the Stream itself plough up
its own Channel, & find its banks in the adamant Rocks of Nature?—
    A rude outline, like the wires placed on the black rosin-plate for
the electrical pictures of colored Powder.

2554 17.112   John Tobin dead—and just after the Success of
his Play!—
and Robert Allen dead suddenly!
    O when we are young we lament for Death only by sympathy or
as with the *general* ⟨feeling with which we grieve for⟩ Misfor-
tunes/⟨in general;⟩ but there comes a time, (and this year is the
time that has come to me) when we lament for Death, as *Death*,
when it is felt for itself, & as itself, aloof from all its consequences/   *f72*
—Then comes the grave-stone into the Heart—/with all its mourn-

ful names—then the Bell-man's or Clerk's Verses subjoined & the
Bills of Mortality are no longer common-place/

2555 17.113   The different gradations in which the Past or
Memory in the power of Imagination modifies the Present Impression, ~~would~~ appear to me a good ground-work for a Theory
concerning the Understanding & Souls of Brutes, and their relation
to that of man—The probability that there is in some other systems
or Planets Beings that form the intermediate links between man &
the most intellectual brute animals of this Planet/in some Planet
f72ᵛ it must be, in which the uppermost Creature is so greatly superior
to man, that the *softenings down* of man into the brute creation
of this Planet may be no softening down, no transition of his own/
may not do away that chasm, which Reason requires for self-es-
teem, & sense of distinct difference of kind. And here notice the bad
effects on the moral and intellectual character of the belief of mere
difference of degree. ⟨Such *may* be; but there is no reason to suppose it—because between Rational & Irrational there must be a
chasm, but all *chasm;*—between two Kinds is infinite.⟩

2556 17.114   Würde, Worthiness, Vɪʀᴛᴜᴇ consist in the mas-
tery over the sensuous & sensual Impulses—but Love requires Iɴ-
ɴᴏᴄᴇɴᴄᴇ/Let the Lover ask his Heart whether he can endure that
his Mistress should have *struggled* with a sensual impulse for an-
f73   other man, tho' she overcame it from a sense of Duty to him?—
Women are ʟᴇss offended with Men, from the vicious habits of
men in part, & in part from the Difference of bodily constitutions—
yet still to a pure and truly loving woman it must be a painful
thought/ That he should struggle with & overcome Ambition, Desire of Fortune, superior Beauty, &c ⟨or with objectless Desire⟩ is
~~not~~ pleasing; but *not* that he has struggled with positive appropriated Desire/i.e. Desire *with* an object.—
Love in short requires an absolute Peace & Harmony between all
parts of human Nature, such as it is; & it is offended by any War,
tho' the Battle should be decided in favor of the worthier. This is
f73ᵛ perhaps the final cause of the *rarity* of true Love, and the efficient
and immediate cause of its Difficulty. Ours is a life of Probation/

we are to contemplate and obey *Duty* for its own sake, and in order
to this we—in our present imperfect state of Being—must see it not
merely abstracted from, but in direct opposition to the *Wish*, the
Inclination/having perfected this the highest ~~part~~ possibility of human nature, he may then with safety harmonize *all* his Being with
this—he may love. To perform Duties absolutely from the sense
of Duty is the *Ideal*, which perhaps no human Being ever can ar-   *f74*
rive at, but which every human Being ought to try to draw near
unto—This is—in the only wise, & verily, in a most sublime sense
—to see God face to face/which alas! it seems too true that no man
can do and *live*, i.e. a *human* life. It would become incompatible
with his organization, or rather it would *transmute* it, & the process
of that Transmutation to the senses of other men would be called
Death—even as ~~the~~ to Caterpillars in all probability the Caterpillar
dies—& he either does not see, which is *most* probable, or at all
events he does not see the connection between the Caterpillar and   *f74ᵛ*
the Butterfly—the beautiful Psyche of the Greeks.—Those who in
this life *love* in perfection—if such there be—as in proportion as
their Love has no struggles, see God darkly and thro' a Veil. For
when Duty and Pleasure are absolutely coincident, the very nature
of our Organization necessitates that Duty will be contemplated as
the Symbol of Pleasure, instead of Pleasure being (as in a future Life we have faith it will be) the Symbol of Duty. This
other ⌜. . . . .⌝
this is the distinction between human and angelic *Happiness*. Hu-   *f75*
man Happiness—humanly happy I call him who in enjoyment
finds his Duty, angelically happy he, who seeks and finds his *Duty*
in Enjoyment—Happiness in general may be defined—not the aggregate of pleasurable sensations, for this is either a dangerous
error and the creed of sensualists, or else ⌜. . . . .⌝
wrong, and who in order to do right ~~has~~ is under no necessity of ab- *f75ᵛ*
staining from Enjoyment.

    O Sara! gladly if my miserable Destiny would relax, gladly
would I think of thee and of me, as of two Birds of Passage, recip-
rocaly resting on each other in order to support the long flight, the
awful Journey.—Not from self-flattery, for I have suffered exceedingly from the circumstances, ⌜. . . . .⌝

2557 17.115 ⌜. . . . .⌝

f76 that all the realities about me lose their natural *healing* powers, at least, diminish the same, & become not worthy of a Thought. Who that thus lives with a continually divided Being can remain healthy! ⟨And who can long remain body-crazed, & not at times use unworthy means of making his Body the fit instrument of his mind? Pain is easily subdued compared with continual uncomfort-ableness—and the sense of stifled Power!—O this is that which made poor Henderson, Collins, Boyce, &c &c &c—*Sots!*—awful Thought—O it is horrid!—Die, my Soul, die!—Suicide—rather than this, the worst state of Degradation! It is less a suicide! S.T.C.)—I work hard, I do the duties of common Life from morn to night/but verily—I raise my limbs, "like lifeless *Tools*"—The organs of motion & outward action perform their functions at the stimulus of a galvanic fluid applied by the *Will*, not by the Spirit of Life that makes Soul and Body one. Thought and Reality two distinct corresponding Sounds, of which no man can say positively

f76ᵛ which is the ~~Sound~~ Voice and which the Echo. O the beautiful Fountain or natural Well at Upper Stowey—⌜. . . . .⌝ The images of the weeds which hung down from its sides, appeared as plants growing up, straight and upright, among the water weeds that really grew from the Bottom/& so vivid was the Image, that for some moments & not till after I had disturbed the water, did I perceive that ~~they~~ their roots were not neighbours, & they side-by-

f77 side companions. So—even then I said—so are the happy man's *Thoughts* and *Things*—(in the language of the modern Philoso-phers, Ideas and Impressions.)—⌜. . . . .⌝

f77ᵛ by the face of him that lies down to drink at it, is worth 50 such/. Talent as opposed to Genius.

2558 17.116   ⌜. . . . . .⌝ in health than, ⌜. . . . . .⌝
                              April 21, 1805—

f78 2559 17.117   Of that wonderful connection between obscure feelings and Ideas—a speck of blood in the mouth, and immedi-ately a long dream of Blood, wounds flowing—torrents of Blood—

2560 17.118   So hard have I worked lately, & to so little effect
in consequence of my Health, so many calls and claims—& such
agitation & anxiety in consequence/that this morning ⟨awaking⟩
very early—a little after 2—mistaking the light of the Lamp which
~~was~~ had been placed in the second window-recess for the Dawn, my
Heart sunk within me/and when I detected the mistake, still I lay
dreading Daylight, wishing it a long Christmas Night—dark till
8!—O me!—It seems as if I should see no more the faces of those
whose blessed Countenances are the Light of Life to me. S.T.C.

2561 17.119   The two characteristics which *I* have most ob-   *f78ᵛ*
served in Roman Catholic Mummery, Processions, Baptisms, &c—
the immense *Noise* & Jingle Jingle, as if to frighten away the Dæmon, Common-sense; & 2. the unmoved stupid uninterested faces
of the Conjurers—I have noticed no exceptions.—Of Superstition
in general, is not its very nature, as being utterly *sensuous, cold,*
except where it is *sensual?*—Therefore the old form of the Idolatry, = the Greek Mythology, was so far even preferable to the
Popish/what Life did & could exist in Superstition, it brought forward & sanctified in its rites of Bacchus, Venus, &c/The Popish by
pretence of suppression warps & denaturalizes—in the Pagan it   *f79*
burnt with a bright flame, in the Popish it consumes the soul with
a smothered fire, that stinks in darkness/and smoulders—like gum,
that burns but is incapable of Light—

2562 17.120   To remember the Turkish Admiral, Captⁿ, Secretary (contrast of his Stupidity with the savage interruption-sup-
pressing Face of the Captⁿ, his hand always watchfully clasping his
dagger, in that *big-belly* of arms which he wore/Sir A. Ball, myself, Millar//&c

2563 15.146   From Sᵗ Julian to Sᵗ Antonio, one of the 6 or 7   *f72ᵛ*
grand Views of the Island/on top of the descent of the Hill, about
a mile from Sᵗ Julian's/to the left the grand curving Harbour that
incloses the Lazaretto & Fort of Manhoel, on the one side of which
Valletta &c, & the Casal churches beyond it, down to St Elmo
which is at the point of the one Tongue of Land, opposite to other
Tongue, making the mouth/Sᵗ Elmo of both Harbors—

Before you Birca Cara, the green Country/the Aqueduct in 3 or 4 different places/& Civita Vecchia on its hill cresting the whole—

f73 2564 15.147 Note among the wild flowers that *brightest-blue* dial-plate, the handsome Brother of my dear Flower in England with a golden eye/

The Lark-spur leafed Flower with bright ~~clo~~ crimson Petals/but above all the Stone-crop, with leaves full of juice very like indeed in color & shape to barberries, only rather more crimson that scar-

let/these starred all over with the most lovely star-like , exactly a star as there drawn, 6 petals equi-distant, most tender & delicate purple, with a white ground, as it were, attempting to gleam thro' it/and the little round of the o in the centre of the flower are of darkest crimson, very far darker than the barberry-shaped leaves/This plant covers the otherwise bare rock for stone throws/

f73ᵛ 2565 15.148 Having had showers (23 April) I smelt the orange blossoms long before I reached Sᵗ Antonio/when I entered, it was overpowering/the Trees were indeed oversnowed with Blossoms, and the ground snowed with the fallen leaves/the Bees ~~in~~ on them, & the ⟨golden ripe⟩ fruit on the inner branches glowing thro/Note/my reflection on the multitude of orange flowers.

2566 15.149 It would be a popular act of the Government, fully repaying the expence to finish the Tower of Birca Cara Church/

2567 15.150 Of the Maltese/my first impression, their ingratitude to the Order to whom they owe every thing, those splendid Towers of Balsan &c &c but after-recollection makes me feel that

f74 a People can only remember the past by the analogy of the Present and that it was the fault of the Order not to furnish any Link of historic memory.

2568 15.151 The Windmills—& seeming Terraces in the Views of Malta/on quitting Vallette it seems a great cumulus of *Gardens*/ walls + Trees &c

2569 15.152   On the stopping of the Calicé the noise of the
Wheels instantly substituted by the Hum of numberless Bees

2570 15.153   To a Fly drowneding in a glass of egged Brandy
& water/saved him/he flies from sugar to Flower to Grass, to Plate
—but the other miserable Drowning Man, the *Sot* the Drinker of
the egged Brandy???

2571 15.154   Cause of the silly mock-candour with respect to the   *f*74ᵛ
Papists, etc. is to be found in the inveterate habits of thinking always *personally*, thinking of the Roman Catholics, Priests or Lay-
men, entirely as *Causes and Agents*, which if they admitted the
evils of Popery, they are to detest—not as the *effects*, themselves
the objects of *Pity*. Thus mock-candour, in short, is most often
found accompanied with habits of personal Slander, called *Gossip-
ing*/Their whole thoughts, & conversation, of this *person*, and that
person, and another person/and as evil is more stimulating than
ordinary goodness, and detraction (alas! alas!) so much more sure
of Sympathy than honest Praise, these People are commonly ad-
dicted to base calumny, and by their *candour* to distant opinions,
and great *Bodies* of men, who are not the whit the better or happier   *f*75
for their candour, they compensate to their own conscience for their
want not of candour but of common charity to Individuals, who
may really be injured by it/who often are injured, and almost always disquieted.

2572 16.406

From Messina to Naples—	12 days	*f*130
Naples—	3 days	
Nap: to Rome—	2 days	
Rome—	3 days	
Rome to Ancona	3 days	
Ancona to Trieste or Venice		
including the Stay—	10 days	
at Ancona		
From Trieste to Vienna.	10 days	
	43 days	

2573 16.407   The Life & Reign of King Stephen, a good subject for an historic Play in the manner of Shakespere/especially the
legend of the Interview between him & the Empress Maud, ac-
quainting him that D. Henry was his own Son/—Milton—Death
& Sin & Satan/See the wild hist: of England, York & Pontefract
Castle, p.167.

_f130ᵛ_   2574 16.408   Gioseppe di [?Stefano Guardio]

_f75_   2575 15.155   Baron Dorello & his Hack before the Church of
C. Vecc. destroyed by the mob—good [?Loc/faith]
4ᵗʰ May

2576 15.156   An huge upright Stone, overgrown with Lichens,
supporting a fallen huge Olive Tree, both seemingly rivals in age,
of one colour, mossed and lichened alike/. the stone 4 feet high—

2577 15.157   The extreme rudeness & dryness of the white
rocks staring out & thro' the extreme formal regularity of the Orange Groves, fields & gardens of the Vale of the Boschetto/4 May,
1805.

_f75ᵛ_   2578 15.158   Liberty = Freedom?—No! No! No!—Not at
present, You _may_ use the latter without heinous offence, if you
take care to shew that it is necessary to the prosperity of Trade and
Commerce, a _necessary Evil_ in the process of moneygetting,—but
Liberty, O!—that Scoundrel will soon be in Newgate, I hope, is
the feeling of all who hear you use it.—This Remark I owe to Mʳ
Robert Dennison, at my room in the Treasury, 11ᵗʰ May, 1805.

_f76_   At the same time the feeling of Sorrow & national Degradation,
that 1000 such men as Sir A. B should _think_ COBBETT a national
Benefactor—!!—

In the autumn of 1798 Mʳ D. had fitted out a beautiful Ship,
noble Captain, fine Crew, well armed/some Friends admiring it
highly, said however, For God's sake alter the ✳ name/it is so obnoxious.

✳ The Liberty.

2579 15.159   ⌐Tuesday ⟨8⟩ night the . . . Lottery . . . . . .
. . . .⌐   •

2580 15.160   Pretended Originality/the Hydnora Africana on   *f76ᵛ*
the roots of the Euphorbia Mauritanica, & others, that seem to
grow out of the ground, having their roots below the surface yet
always fastened to the roots of some other Plant/these are the
Hypocrite-Parasite Plants.

2581 15.161   The Epidendrum *Flos Aeris* of Cochin china,
which taken from the woods & suspended in free air in multos an-
nos duret, crescat, floreat, et germinet.

2582 15.162
And as he gazed with his dull serpent eyes,
The Poison-duct behind the orbit of the eye   *f77*
Was working still; and ever as it work'd,
Created venom from the innocent Blood.—
a metaphor—

2583 17.175   Sunday Midnight, 12 May 1805, at the Treasury,   *f104*
La Vallette, Malta, in the Room, the windows of which directly
face the Piazzas, & vast Saloon built for the Archives & Library &
now used as the Garrison Ballroom/—sitting at one corner of a
large parallelogram Table well littered with Books, in a red arm

chair, at the other corner of which (diagonally)
Mʳ Dennison had been sitting, he and I having conversed for a
long time/he bade me good night, and retired—I meaning to retire
too however sunk for 5 minutes or so into a Doze, and on suddenly
waking up I saw him as distinctly sitting in the chair, as I had seen
him really some ten minutes before/I was startled, & thinking of   *f104ᵛ*
it sunk into a second Doze—out of which awaking as before I saw
again the same appearance, not more distinct indeed, but *more* of
his Form/for at the first time I had seen only his Face & Bust, but
now I saw as much as I could have seen if he had been really
there/the appearance was very nearly that of a person seen thro'

thin smoke, distinct indeed but yet a sort of distinct *Shape* & *Colour*
—with a diminished Sense of *Substantiality*—like a Face in a clear
Stream. My nerves had been violently agitated, yesterday morn-
f105   ing, by the attack of three Dogs as I was mounting the Steps to
Cap^{tn} Pasley's Door/two of them savage Bedouins, who wounded
me in the Calf of my left Leg.—I have noted this down, not three
minutes having intervened, since the Illusion took place.—Often
and often I have had similar Experiences/~~but~~ and therefore resolved to write down the Particulars whenever ~~they~~ any new
instance should occur/as a weapon against Superstition, and an explanation of *Ghosts—Banquo* in Macbeth—the very same Thing.—
I once told a Lady, the reason why I did not believe in the existence of Ghosts &c was that I had seen too many of them myself—
*f105*ᵛ   N.B. There were on the Table a common black Wine-bottle, a De-
canter of ~~Wh~~ Water; & between these one of the Half-Gallon Glass-
Flasks which Sir G. Beaumont had given me (4 of them full of

Port)   —the Cork in, covered with Leather, and having a
white   plated Ring on the Top/I mention this, because since

I wrote the former pages, on blinking a bit a third time, & opening
my eyes, I clearly *detected* that this high-shouldered hypochondri-
acal Bottle-man had a great share in producing the Effect/The
metamorphosis was clearly beginning, tho' I snapped the Spell
before it had assumed a recognizeable Form. The red-leather Arm-
chair was so placed at the Corner, as ~~to be~~ that this Flask was ex-
f106   actly between me and it/& the Lamp being close to my corner of
the large Table, & not giving much Light, the Chair was rather ob-
scure/& the brass nails where the Leather was fastened to the outward wooden room, reflecting the Light more copiously were seen
almost, for themselves. What if instead of immediately checking
the sight and then pleased with it as a philosophical *Case*, I had
been frightened, and encouraged it—& my Understanding had
joined its Vote to that of my Senses?
My own Shadow too on the wall not far from M^r D's Chair—
the White Paper, the Sheet of Harbour Reports lying spread

out on the Table, on the other side of the Bottles/—/Influence
of mere Color—influence of Shape—wonderful coalescence of scattered Colors, at distances, & then all going to some one Shape/&
the modification. Likewise I am now convinced by repeated Obser-   *f106ᵛ*
vation, that ~~if not~~ perhaps *always* in a very minute degree, ~~yet cer-~~
~~tainly~~ but assuredly in *certain* states ⟨& postures⟩ of the Eye, as in
Drowsiness, the state of the Brain & Nerves after Distress and Agitation, especially if it had been accompanied by weeping, & in many
others, we see our own faces, and project them, according to the
distance given them by the degree of indistinctness—that this may
occasion in the highest degree the Wraith, (vide a hundred Scotch
Stories, but better than all Wordsworth's most wonderful as well
as admirable Poem, Peter Bell, where he sees his own Figure—&
still oftener that it facilitates the formation of a human Face out of
some really present Object, and from the alteration of the distance,
among other causes, never suspected on the occasion, and *substra-*
tum.
        S.T.C.
N.B. This is a valuable note/re-read by me Tuesday morning, 14
May.

2584 17.176   Tuesday Morning, May 14ᵗʰ, 1805—With any   *f107*
distinct remembrance of a past life there could be no fear of Death,
as Death—no idea even of Death!—Now in the next State to meet
with the Luthers, Miltons, Leibnitzs, Bernouillis, Bonnets, Shake-
speres, etc/and to live a longer & better Life, the good & wise entirely among the good & wise, as a step to break the abruptness of
an immediate Heaven/—But it must be a human Life, and tho' the
Faith in a Hereafter would be most firm, most undoubting, yet still
it must not be a senuous remembrance of a Death passed over. No!
Something like a Dream/that you had not died, but had been taken
off, in short, the real events with the obscurity of a Dream, accompanied with the notion that you never had died; but that Death   *f107ᵛ*
was yet to come. As a man who having walked in his Sleep by rapid
openings of his eyes too rapid to be observable by others or rememberable by himself sees and remembers the whole of his Path, mix-
ing it with many fancies ab intra.—& awaking remembers, but yet as

a Dream.—Make out such a Dream/different Persons different—/
Man in a swoon, so buried/a person came to him in the night, there
had been a plot against him, his Beloved had given him a Potion/
he was to go on board Ship immediately, with a colony for some
new Islands—On Ship lands at the Green Islands of the Blest.—

ƒ76   2585   16.250   Power of the Eye/verily a window, thro' which
you not *look out* of the House, but can look into it too. A States-
man, and especially, a Diplomatist should for this reason always
wear Spectacles. 24 May, 1805

2586   16.251   Absurd Pedantry of transferring the Serpentine
Walks of cold bleak Countries to hot Climates : : to the pedantry
of transferring the straight ventilated Walks of Hot to cold Climates.

2587   16.252   Of the Soil found from ¼ of an inch to feet deep
under the free-stone, often like a plate or sheet dividing the Surfaces of Free-stone/always *red. Roots* + oxyd of Iron.

ƒ76ᵛ   2588   16.253   Creations emerging out of divine Ideas manifested by Jove to the Gods centuries before their mortal Incarnation—A report in Heaven of a unusually fair *Idea* of a Woman
emerging/Venus, fearful that her Son should become enamoured,
as of yore with Psyche, when he wandered alone, his bow unslung,
& using his sharp darts only to cut out her name on rocks or trees,
or at best to shoot humming Birds & Birds of Paradise to make
Feather-chaplets for her Hair, till the World grown loveless hardened into the Iron Age intreats of Jove to secrete this Form/but
ƒ77   Cupid, who had heard the Report, & fondly expected a re-manifes-
tation of Psyche hid himself in the hollow of the sacred Oak beneath which the Father of the Gods retired, the not to be
approached, beheld the Idea emerging in its first Glory, & was
struck blind by the *splendor* ere yet the Blaze had defined itself into
Form/Since then he strikes vaguely. This idea incarnate as Emme-
line &c

2589 16.254   A Poem on Andalusia, with the Traveller who had fought in strange Lands & preserved the Independence of a mountain Race against the Moors, &c but now weary of wickedness & enamoured of Peace in so peaceful a Form, &c for her Husband-lover/*a wish.*

2590 16.255   In the 11ᵗʰ Volume of the Carm: illust: Poet. Ital.   f77ᵛ
—p.177. Vida's most interesting Explanation & defence of the Worship of Saints/*Quote the whole*/& reply to it.

2591 16.256   A dazzling polished steel Extinguisher compared to the last Conflagration/the Light extinguishing all things—

2592 16.257   Negroes in America and W. Indies when flogged cruelly console themselves the wounds will turn white—

2593 16.258   Gravitation, all in all/nothing in any one part, as fluid, ether, or such like/—analogy of this to *Soul*, to Consciousness/that nothing-something, something-nothing/

2594 17.121   Latter end of May—&c—THE JEWS!   f79

2595 17.122   Of Uxoriousness & its extreme difference from conjugal Love/the latter is two eyes seeing one object ever/. The former, a horrible *Squint* in which the eyes *look* at each other.—

2596 17.123   Mem!—always to bear in mind that profound   f79ᵛ
sentence of Leibnitz/that men's errors (intellectual) consist chiefly in *denying*—what they *affirm* with feeling, is most often *right*/if it be *real affirmation*, & not affirmative in form, negative in reality/ as when a man praises the French Stage, meaning & implying his dislike of Shakespere &c/—

2597 17.124
O ~~Soul of~~ ⟨O⟩ Beauty, ~~beautifully~~ in a beauteous Body dight!
O ~~thou Fair~~ Body! that veiling ⟨Brightness⟩ becom'st bright/
Fair Cloud which less we see, than by thee see the Light!
in avvenenti spoglie
Bellissim' Alma!

ƒ8o   2598 17.125   Schiller disgusted with Kotzebueisms deserts
from Shakespere. What? cannot we condemn a counterfeit, & yet
remain admirers of the Original? This is a sufficient Proof, that
the first Admiration was not sound, or founded on sound distinct
perceptions/it was a sound feeling, but cloathed & manifested to
the consciousness by false Ideas. And now the French Stage, is to
be re-introduced/O Germany! Germany!—Why this endless Rage
of Novelty! Why, this endless Looking-out of thyself?—But stop!
let me not fall into the Pit, I was about to warn others of—let me
ƒ8oᵛ   not confound the discriminating character & genius of a nation with
the conflux of its individuals, in *Cities* & *Reviews*/Let England
be ⟨Sir P. Sidney,⟩ Shakespere, Spenser, Milton, Bacon, Harrington, ⟨Swift,⟩ Wordsworth, and never let the names of Darwin,
Johnson, Hume, *furr* it over!—If these too must be England, let
them be another England/—or rather let the first be old England,
the spiritual platonic old England/& the second with Locke at the
head of the Philosophers & Pope of the Poets, with the long list of
Priestleys, Paleys, Hayleys, Darwins, Mʳ Pitts, Dundasses, &c &c
be representative of commercial G. Britain/these have their merits,
but are as alien to me, as the Mandarin Philosophers & Poets of
ƒ81   China/even so Leibnitz, Lessing, Voss, Kant, shall be *Germany* to
me, let whatever Coxcombs rise up, & *shrill* it away in the Gras-
hopper-vale of Reviews/and so shall Dante, Ariosto, Giordano
Bruno be my Italy/Cervantes my Spain/and o! that I could find
a France for my Love/but ah! spite of Paschal, Madame Guyon,
and Moliere France is my Babylon, the Mother of Whoredoms in
Morality, Philosophy, Taste/the French themselves feel a for-
eigness in these Writers/How indeed it is possible at once to *love*
Paschal, & Voltaire?

ƒ89ᵛ   2599 17.159   Madrigals of Giovambatista Strozzi were published in Florence (nella Stamperia del Sermartelli) 1 May, 1593,
by his Sons Lorenzo and Filippo Strozzi, with a dedication to their
deceased Father's Brother or Cousin, Signor Leone Strozzi, Generale delle Battaglie di Santa Chiesa. My chief reason for extract-
ing the following specimens is to illustrate what appears to me a
striking point of difference between the Poetry of the 15 and 16 Cen-

turies, and that of the present Day—and I am inclined to extend
the remark to Painting likewise. In the present age the Poet pro-
poses to himself as his main Object & most characteristic of his art,
new and striking Images, incidents that interest the Affections or
excite the curiosity of the Reader; and both his characters and his
descriptions he individualizes and specifies as much as possible,
even to a degree of Portraiture/Meanwhile in his diction and
metre he is either careless (W. Scott) or adopts some mechanical
measure, of which one couplet or stanza is an adequate specimen,
with a language which ~~lae~~ claims to be poetical for no better reason, than that it would be intolerable in conversation or prose/—   *f90*
Just so, our Landscape Painters—their foreground and near distances are flat—but the great interest of the Landscape lies in the
background, Mountains, Torrents, &c, forbidding the eye to proceed, while nothing exists to repay it for going back again/Now
in the polished elder poets, especially of Italy, all is reversed—
Even as in their Landscapes, the front and middle are the most
interesting, and the interesting dies gradually away in the background, & the charm of the Picture consists not so much in the
specific Images which it conveys as a visual Language to the understanding, as to the exquisite beauty, and proportion of colors, lines,
and expression, with which the images are represented—and
novelty of subject was not so much sought for, as superior excellence in the manner of treating the same subjects—even so, in their
Poets—The imagery is almost always *general,* Sun, Moon, Flowers, Breezes, Murmuring Streams, warbling Songsters, delicious
Shades, &c—their thoughts seldom novel or very striking, while
in a faulty extreme they placed the essence of Poetry in the *art* of
Poetry, that is, in the exquisite polish of the Diction with perfect
simplicity, equally avoiding every word which a man of rank would
not use in common conversation, and every phrase, which none but a
bookish man would use—in the studied position of these words, so   *f90ᵛ*
as not only to be melodious, but that the melody of each should
refer to, assist, & be assisted by, all the foregoing & following
words of the same period, or Stanza, and in like labor, the greater
because unbetrayed, in the variety of harmony in the metres—not
as now by invention of new Metres, which have a specific over-

powering tune of their own (such as **Monk Lewis's** Alonzo &
Imogen, from the German, or **Campbell's** Hohenlinden, &c) but
by countless subtleties in the common metre of the class of Poetry
in which they are composing—.—Of this exquisite Polish, of this
perfection of *Art,* the following Madrigals are given as specimens,
and as mementos to myself, if ever I should once more be happy
enough to resume poetic composition, to attempt a union of these
—taking the whole of the latter, and as much of the former ~~and~~
as is compatible with a poem's being perused with greater pleasure
the second or the 20ᵗʰ time, than the first.

p.2.   MADRIGALI DELLO STROZZI.

> Nuova io non so, se stella,
> O' Sol dal Cielo in terra
> In forma di selvaggia Pastorella
> Scese per farmi guerra;
> E'l dardo, e la facella
> Fu'l dolce riso, e'l bel guardo soave:
> Altre costei non have
> Armi che queste; altr' io
> Scudo non ho che'l duolo, e'l pianger mio.

———

f91   p.7. Gelido suo ruscel chiaro, e tranquillo
> M'insegnò Amor, di state a mezzo'l giorno;
> Ardean le selve, ardean le piagge, e i colli.
> Ond'io, ch'al più gran gielo ardo e sfavillo,
> Subito corsi; ma si puro adorno
> Girsene il vidi, che turbar no'l volli:
> Sol mi specchiava, e'n dolce ombrosa sponda
> Mi stava intento al mormorar dell'onda.

———

p.8. Aure dell'angoscioso viver mio
> Rifrigerio soave,
> E dolce sì, che piu non mi par grave
> Ne l'arder, ne'l morir, anz'il desio;
> Deh voi'l ghiaccio, e le nubi, e'l tempo rio,

Discacciatene omai, che l'onda chiara,
E l'ombra non men cara
A scherzare, e cantar per suoi boschetti
E prati Festa ed Allegrezza alletti.

————

p.9 Schiera di lucid' AURE, amica schiera
Sempre compagna e scorta
Della purpurea e vaga Primavera,
Che'l bel tranquillo, e'l bel seren n'apporta,
Svegliati, apri la porta
Del bel cristallo orato;   *f91ᵛ*
E per questo e quel prato,
Questo e quel bosco ti trastulla e scherza,
Dolce volando, come Amor ti sferza.

————

p.10. AURE sempre di fiori,
Aure sempre di raggi inghirlandate,
E ben coi biondi Amori,
Scherzo, Gioco, e Piacer d'un parto nate,
(Tempo n'è ben) levate, uscite fuori
Co'l grazioso Aprile;
Che la Terra simile
Al Ciel si mostra, e'l Cielo
Se non al mio bel Sole, al suo bel velo.

————

p.11. Dive sù de'begli orti almi di rose
Oltra le serenissime contrade
Di luce, ove non cade
Il Sol, ne mai pur s'ombra; AURE pietose,
Deh girivi Pietade
A queste valli ombrose;
E vi accompagnin, quante   *f92*
V'ha Stelle, e Grazie, e Muse, e Ninfe sante!

————

p.12. Pacifiche, ma spesso in amorosa
Guerra co'fiori, e l'erba
Alla stagione acerba

Verdi Insegne del giglio e della rosa
Movete, AURE, pian pian; che tregua ò posa,
Se non pace io ritrove:
E so ben dove—. Oh vago, e mansueto
Sguardo, oh labbra d'ambrosia, oh rider lieto!

———

p.12. AURE, del bel seren lucido velo,
Della purpurea piuma
E della bionda chioma d'or, che'l Cielo
E tutto il Mondo alluma,
Regiratevi a noi, che l'aspra bruma
Dia luogo (e n'è ben tempo)
Al dolce tempo, e la viola e'l giglio
Con tutti i bei color tornin d'esiglio.

———

f92ᵛ   p.14 Torna AURETTA gentil col tuo bel Sole
A questi occhi miei, torna,
E'l cor fosco m'aggiorna
Rivestito di rose e di viole!
Amor lagrime e duol non sempre vuole,
Ma talor canto e riso
Avezzo in Paradiso
Suo dolce nido, avanti
Ch'egli albergasse ne'tuoi raggi santi.

———

p.15 Non perdonò quest'empia a'figli suoi;
E tu folle oggi in grembo le t'annidi?
E tu stolta le fidi
Quest' infelici tuoi?
Fuggi'l marmo spietato! e i dolci nidi
Appendi in qualche selva;
Non ha tale orca il Mar, la Terra belva!

———

This last Madrigal is imitated from a Greek Epigram on a Swallow, that had built its nest between the breasts of the Statue of Medea.—

p.17 Hor come un Scoglio stassi,
    Hor come un Rio se'n fugge,
    Ed hor crud' Orsa rugge,
    Hor canta Angelo pio; ma che non fassi?
    E che non fammi, O Sassi,
    O Rivi, O belve, o Dii, questa mia vaga
    Non so, se Ninfa, ò Maga,
    Non so, sè Donna, ò Dea,
    Non so, sè dolce, ò rea?

———

p.21 Tutte le notti Amor meco si stava
    Nel cor suo seggio antico;
    Del suo stato, e del mio mi ragionava
    Il mio fedele Amico!
    Hor non più nò: che suo mortal nimico,
    Sdegno sempre lo caccia;
    Ne lui solo minaccia, ma quant'ivi
    Son Pensier vaghi, e schivi,
    Ognun, come da strido
    Risvegliato Augellin, fugge di nido.

———

p.25 Dolce ritorna Amor cortese e pio
    Nell'angelico viso;
    Onde a gran torto Sdegno (o Sdegno rio)
    T'ha sì per me diviso;
    E deh teco, Signor, l'usato riso
    E'l bel guardo rimena;
    Che l'aspra pena, ch'io sostengo, a morte
    (Se pur vita quest'è) non mi trasporte.

———

p.25   Piangendo mi baciaste,
        E ridendo il negaste:
        In doglia hebbivi pia,
        In festa hebbivi ria:
        Nacque Gioia di pianti,
        Dolor di riso: O amanti
        Miseri, habbiate insieme
        Ognor Paura e Speme.

———

p.35 In bel sereno stella
       Non sì soave a mezza notte splende;
       Com'io vidi là'n quella
       Riva un bel FIOR; d'intorno a cui s'accende

       La fresca erba novella, e scherza, e ride
       Con l'aure, e l'onde a prova;
       E quanta il Ciel par, che dolcezza piova?
       Amor, ch'ivi s'asside,
       Giura, che mai non vide in seno ancora
       Un Fior sì vago alla vermiglia Aurora!

       ———

p.36 Bel FIOR, tu mi rimembri
       La rugiadosa guancia del bel viso;
       E sì vera l'assembri,
       Che'n te sovente, come in lei m'affiso:
       Et hor del vago riso,
       Hor del sereno sguardo
       Io pur cieco risguardo. Ma qual fugge,
       O ROSA, il mattin lieve?
       E chi te, come neve,
       E'l mio cor teco, e la mia vita strugge?

       ———

p.36 Hor lieve Ape foss'io
       Se non trepid'auretta fugitiva;
       Che via di riva in riva
       Io pur dietro volando al mio desio

       Nell'odorato mio candido FIORE
       Al fin mi chiuderei,
       Mille e mille fra mille sospir miei,
       E mille entro e di fuore
       Santi baci d'Amore
       Dandoli: oh qual soave il suggerei?
       Ivi ben sì, che volentier morrei.

       ———

p.37 Hor lieve ape foss'io, che tanto andrei
       Di bel fiore in bel fior per valli, e poggi,
       Ch'alla mia Fille anc'oggi

Così nascosa in sen mi troverrei;
Mille io ti pur darei
Caldi baci d'Amor, tenera Neve,
Ond'ella ha'l cor sì duro:
E suggerèti ancor soave e puro
Latte; ma lasso hor non le sia pur greve
Il solo mormorar pietoso e lieve.

————

p.45 Torna, Zefiro, torna, almo vitale ƒ95
Fiato del viver nostro,
Preda misera hor d'Ostro,
Hor d'Euro! ognun ne vince che n'assale.
Torna! E questo e quel mio languido e frale
Spirto reggendo aita;
Ne per me nò già vita
Cerco, ma sol per lei,
Che vita have pur tal da'sospir miei.

————

p.49 Filli mia, Filli dolce, oh sempre nuovo
E più chiaro concento,
Quanta dolcezza sento
In sol Filli dicendo? Io mi pur pruovo,
Ne quì tra noi ritruovo,
Ne tra cieli armonia,
Che del bel nome suo piu dolce sia:
Altro il Cielo, altro Amore,
Altro non suona L'Eco del mio Core.

————

p.57 Hor che'l prato, e la selva si scolora, ƒ95ᵛ
Al tuo sereno ombroso
Muovine, alto RIPOSO!
Deh ch'io riposi una sol notte, un hora!
Han le fere, e gli augelli, ognun talora
Ha qualche pace; io quando,
Lasso! non vonne errando,
E non piango, e non grido? e qual pur forte?
Ma poiche non sent'egli, odine, Morte.

————

p.59 Posa amica gentil, che'l mondo ignaro
  E folle chiama Morte,
  Apri di tuo sì caro
  E desiato Albergo, apri le porte!
  Ne piu tema ò speranza mi trasporte;
  Ma per quest'occhi lassi,
  Che piu vegghiar non ponno,
  Deh nel mio Cor tuo sonno eterno passi!

———

f96 p.60 Ecco l'Alba! Ohime che nuovo campo
  Di fatiche e di lagrime vegg'io?
  E chi schermo, chi scampo
  Ne'nsegna, altri che Morte al pianger mio?
  Deh Giorno, oh giorno rio,
  Vatten, fuggine a volo
  Col mio duolo! Tu, mia diletta vera,
  Torna, ma torna eterna, alma mia sera!

———

p.60 Riposata lunghissima, che mai
  Non ti risvegli, nostra ultima sera,
  Deh vienne, odine omai;
  Ch'una sol volta io pera,
  Non mille e mille, come a questa fera
  Piace, che'l Mondo chiama
  Vita; che sì'l mondo ama. Oh mondo cieco,
  Stanco io son, ne d'errar bramo piu teco!

———

f96ᵛ p.111 O benedetto mio gentil pensiero,
  Che mai non mi abbandoni;
  E c'hor pur sì leggiero
  Oltr'a quel'Alpi, hor sovra'l Ciel mi poni;
  Tu di lei, tu con lei sempre ragioni
  Che di Piacer mi sface;
  E tu rechimi pace
  A null'altra simile,
  O benedetto mio Pensier gentile!

———

p.89 All'apparir dell'odorato Maggio
    Fuggon le nubi e'l gielo;
    Ed ecco al nuovo raggio
    Tutto fiorito ogni arboscello e stelo:
    Ride la Terra, e'l Cielo intorno intorno,
    Ride la Notte, e'l Giorno;
    Quanto piu dolce ride il dolce Amore
    Entro'l mio Core, e nel bel seno adorno
    Suo sì caro diporto, e suo soggiorno!

———

p.152 Risi e piansi d'Amor; ne però mai   *f97*
    Se non in fiamma, ò'n onda, ò'n vento scrissi:
    Spesso mercè trovai
    Crudel; sempre in me morto, in altri vissi!
    Hor da'più scuri Abissi al Ciel m'alzai,
    Hor ne pur caddi giuso:
    Stanco alfin qui son chiuso.
                Il Fine

2600   17.211
                ⟨Malta⟩   *f139*
In a † Dream. "~~With~~ all the merely bodily Feelings subservient
to our Reason, coming only at its call, and obeying its Behests with
a gladness not without awe, like servants who work under the Eye
of their Lord, we have solemnized the long marriage of our Souls
by its outward Sign & natural Symbol. It is now registered in both
worlds, the world of Spirit and the world of the Senses. We therefore record our deep Thankfulness to Him, from whose absolute
Unity all Union derives its possibility, existence, and meaning,
subscribing our names with the blended Blood of this great Sacrament."
⌈so ended a . . . of Asra⌉

                        S. T. Coleridge

† a long Dream, of my Return, Welcome, &c. full of *Joy* & *Love*,
wholly without *desire,* or bodily Inquietude, tho' with a most curi-   *f139ᵛ*
ous detail of images, and imagined actions, that might be supposed
absolutely to *imply* awakened Appetite. A Proof this of the little

Power Images have over Feelings or Sensation, independent of the
Will—compared with the power of Feelings over Images:—a
proof too, one of a thousand, that by rigorous unremitting Purity
of ~~my~~ our Thought, when awake, joined with the unremitting
Feeling of intense *Love*, the imagination in Sleep may become
almost incapable of combining base or low Feelings with the Object of that Love.—In the Dream I supposed myself in a state of
Society, like that of those great Priests of Nature who formed the
Indian Worship in its purity, when all things, strictly of Nature,
were reverenced according to their importance, undebauched by
f140   associations of Shame ~~or~~ and Impudence, the ⟨twin-⟩children of
sensuality. The accursed effects of the extreme Contrary are to be
seen in every company, in every theatre, in almost every book of
the present Day—the sneers against women who study Botany,
the grave opinion that it cannot be studied, &c &c—O horrible!
⟨and the Jokes, in polite company, when tolerably intimate, O Mʳˢ
S. ah! what do you say to that?—Col. W.—Dʳ S.—&c &c⟩

2601 17.212   The ψευδο-poets, Campbell, Rogers, ⌐Cottle⌐
etc, both by their writings & moral characters tend to bring poetry
into disgrace/and but that men in general are the Slaves of the
same wretched infirmities, they would do it. And it would be well/
The true Poet could not smother the sacred fire/"His Heart
burnt within him, and he spake"—& Wisdom would be justified by
f140ᵛ   her Children/but the false Poet (i.e. the No poet) would be prevented from scribbling, finding poetry in contempt among the
Many, of whose Praise, whatever he may affirm, he is alone am-
bitious.

f92   2602 18.192   ⌐. . . . .⌐ the latter, only by looking at
my Lamp & there seeing the same/all the night before, deserved
misery, & sense of self-degradation in the long wretched Dose/—
Good God! and such a thing was possible/yes! tremble but write
it/—a Fenestra per Fenestra/molto miserabile—[?canestra]/
[?dixit]—ideotic/πλαν—ὁωρ—κeˣ/24 June/—this Sunday 23rd,
[?1805/1801]. O misery!—

2603 18.193   The *De crescent* still bright in heaven, very bright, & with its shadow moon, but giving no light, for the Dawn gave it/the unseen Sun an hour before his personal appearance ƒ92ᵛ gave it, yet suffered the Benefactress of the Darkness to retain awhile her full Dignity = the old System still formally established, & even honour-bright, yet still the power of the *coming* System diffused soberly over all/faint indeed, compared with its presence in the rising, not to think of it/as fully risen, yet even in its faintness being the true & by its superiority sole effective Light/

2604 18.194   Curious fact mentioned to me ⟨by Mr Dennison⟩ the Negroes often console themselves in their cruel punishments, ƒ93 that their wounds will become *white*/and looking on this as a grand Progression in their rank of Nature, spite of their abhorrence of the cruelty of white men. Their Love of *white*, their belief that superior Beings are white, even in the inmost parts of Africa where they have seen no White men/it is a color beloved by their good Deities & by the Supreme of all, the Immense, to whom they do not pray, but whose existence they confess. This among so many others in favor of permanent Principles of *Beauty* ƒ93ᵛ as distinguishable from Association or the Agreeable/

2605 17.213   From Baldwin's London Weekly Journal, May ƒ140ᵛ 2, 1805.—After an affrightful account of a little Chimney-sweeper, not six years old, having been placed nearly 6 hours, between a heated plate of Iron, and a mass of burning Soot, from which by a hole in the Chimney he was at last extricated, much scorched but still alive (this happened on the last day of April, 1805, on a Tuesday, at Mʳ Coutts' Banking-house in the Strand) follows—"The inhuman Father, apprehended some time since in Marybone Parish for cutting the back of his infant Daughter's Hand for at- ƒ141 tempting to take a piece of meat out of his Plate, was convicted at the Middlesex Sessions on Monday, April, 29ᵗʰ, and sentenced to two years' imprisonment in the House of Correction/

2606 17.214   27 June 1805. Malta.

To God.

Thou who the weak and bruised never breakest,
Nor ever triumph in the Yielding seekest/
Pity my weak estate, o now or never/
I ever yet was weak, and now more weak than ever.

S.T.C.—The Fish gasps on the glittering mud, the mud of this once full stream, now only moist enough to be glittering mud/the tide will flow back, time enough to lift me up with straws & withered sticks and bear me down into the ocean. O me! that being what I have been I should be what I am!—

f141ᵛ   2607 17.215   How shall I plead? I plead not/I dare mention no good quality, no palliation of the Bad—save only this, the ~~eager~~ earnest wish to be better/to be good for goodness' sake without a phantom of Vanity, "without a Daydream of Praise & Admiration"/But finally, it is Darkness, or a Mercy which I understand not. Yet still the Something within cries, Mercy!

2608 17.216

Gr.   20 = 1 ℥
℥ Scruple 3 = ℥
℥ Drachms 8 = ℈

f142   2609 17.217   Aconitum Neomontanum—Large blue Wolfsbane/from the mountain forests of Carinthia, Carniola, &c introduced by Stoerk—/half a grain of the inspissated Juice, or one to 2 grains of the dried Leaves in powder/on 10 grains of white sugar, twice or thrice a day—& gradually & *watchfully* increase the dose to 3, 4, 5 grains or the tincture of the dried Leaves in spirits of wine—~~2 drops~~ 1 part Ac. to Spir. W.—dose 5—up to 40 drops.

Sudorific, uretic—glandular swellings, ven. nodes, anchylosis, spina ventosa, itch, amaurosis, gouty & rheumatic pains/convulsions/

Allium—Garlic—Applied as a revulsive from the Head to the
Soles of the Feet—the expressed Juice dipped in cotton, and
changed 5 or 6 times a day, in the Ear for nervous Deafness—

Dropsy (Sydenham)—laxity of Solids/anthelmintic (Rosen-
stein) Oz in a pound of Milk, bruised/

Angustura—Diarrhœa, Acidity from weakness of the bowels—
Dyspeptic Flatulence—In powder, 5 to 20 gr. alone or with rhubarb, magnesia/in Infusion, one Drachm in 4 Oz. of water daily—   *f142ᵛ*

Arnica montana—German Leopard's Bane/One or two Scruples
infused in half a pound of water, & drank at proper intervals—
chronic Rheumatism—emmenagogue—internal pains, & conges-
tions from bruises—

2610 16.259   3 July, 1805—a few minutes before 4 °clock—the   *f78*
morning two shocks of an Earthquake very strong for Malta,
shook my bed like a strong arm/11 July, from near 10 to past 11
in the evening saw the moon full or very near it, considerably
above the Garrison Batt. & traversing its breadth, of the strangest
appearance/the Stars were bright in the Sky, the air even cold, the
milky way very full, yet the moon like a new-moon with the old
moon in her Lap, only that the silver Thread was not there, & its
color was reddish smoke-color/its continuance in the same shape—
What was it?—The whole Sky was crowded with Stars, & exactly   *f78ᵛ*
resembled a night of sharp Frost/in which many parts of the
Heavens are clear & the stars glittering, others red or hazy/it was
darker than by crescent Light, & the air felt raw & chill. When it
first struck my notice, the moon was *all* like a round of silver completely lost in egg-tarnish, or sulphuretted hydrogen gas—After
some time the Seaward Edge was brightened as by laborious Scour-
ing/till it became a crescent as before described/—nearer 12 than
11 it was a half moon, & the Stain lost its reddish tinge or discol-
oration, & became the whiter blue of starchy rain-clouds/—Yet to   *f79*
the very last the vapor never was seen out of the moon/to the last
all around the moon appeared blue sky, & at a very small distance
the milky way unusually rich/

I awoke at 2 °clock, Friday morning, 12 July, & then the full
moon was in all her Purity, bright, and the Stars were bold &

mighty that could abide her Presence.—What a picture this of a man commencing Life with a character utterly tarnished, & gradually scouring itself, & revealing by little & little till it became a Shakespere, or—

f79ᵛ Most ridiculous! it was a grand Eclipse; but I was led into the Blunder by Gioseppe (for I at first naturally took it for what it was) who assured me, it was a peculiar Vapor not uncommon in Malta. The Similie however holds good/I am not sorry/it is a good instance how a tolerably observing man would describe a total Eclipse of the moon, who had no idea of an Eclipse in his Mind.

2611 16.260   The Serjeant—his [?Papish/Papist] Recruit & Convert from the 7 to our 3 Sacraments. 3?—Yes, to be sure!— Bread & Wine & the Lord's Supper.

2612 16.261   Marriage made a Sacrament, to make the important & radicating *Temporal* a Spiritual—Points of difference only DOCTRINAL!!!—Elucidated by me: a Festuca then, & [?Relham/ Relhan]/the aromatic plants—/"*O! Included*, Sir! short grass & clover.—

f93ᵛ 2613 18.195   Saturday Morning-night, i.e. 3 °clock, with no glimpse of Dawn. 20 July 1805, Treasury—How often am I doomed to perceive & wonder at the generation of violent Anger, in dreams, in consequence of any pain or distressful sensation in the bowels or lower parts of the Stomach/When I have awoke in agony of pure Terror, my stomach I have found uniformly stretched with wind/but anger not excluding but taking the Lead of Fear, the bowels, and then most commonly it is "Le Grice"—
                                                        S. T. Coleridge

2614 18.196   Saturday Morning, ½ p. 9 °clock, and soon I shall
f94 have to brace up my Hearing, *in toto*/for I hear in my *Brain*/I hear (that is, have an immediate & *peculiar* feeling instantly co-adunated with the *sense* of external sound; ⟨ = means "correspond-ing"⟩ = [*] (exactly) to that which is experienced when one makes
f93ᵛ [*] " = " means "the same as," or "equal to"

a wry face & putting a one's right hand palm-wise to the right ear,   *f*94
& the left palm pressing hard on the forehead one says to a
Bawler (For mercy's sake, man! don't split the drum of one's
Ear.) Sensations analagous to this, of various degrees of pain even
to a strange sort of uneasy pleasure, I am obnoxious to from sound,
and therefore was saying (N.B. tho' I *ramble*, I always come back,
the life of the *sense* alive, tho' sometimes a Limb of Syntax
broken)—was saying that I hear in my Brain, & still more *hear* in
my stomach, and hear in my Bowels. For this ubiquity almost (For   *f*94°
I might with safety add the femur, my Toes, one or two at least, &
my knees) for this ubiquity of the Tympanum auditorium I am
now to wind up my courage/for in a few seconds that accursed
Reveillee, the horrible Crash, and persevering malignant Torture
of the Parade Drum, will attack me, like a party of yelling drinking N. A. Indians attacking a crazy Fort with a tired Garrison out
of an ambush/—The Noisiness of the Maltese every body must
notice; but I have observed uniformly among them the such utter
Impassiveness to the action of Sounds as that I am fearful that the
Verum will be scarcely verisimile. I h once seem heard screams of
the most frightful kind as of children run over by a Cart, & run to
my window, I have seen two Children in a parlour opposite to me   *f*95
(naked except a Kerchief tied round the middle) screaming in this
horrid fiendiness—for *fun!*—three Adults in the room, perfectly
unannoyed/& thus suffered to continue for 20 minutes—or as long
as their Lungs enabled them.—But it goes thro' every thing—
their Street-Cries, their Priests, their Advocates/their very Pigs
yell rather than squeek, or both together rather, as if they were
the true descendants of some half dozen of the Swine, into which
the Devils went, recovered by the Humane Society—the Dogs all
night long would draw curses on them, but that the Maltese Cats
in their amours—O it surpasses description/for he who has only   *f*95°
heard catterwauling on English Roofs can have no idea of a cat-
serenade in Malta. In England it has often a ⟨close and⟩ painful
resemblance to the distressful cries of young children, but in Malta
it is identical with the wide range of screams uttered by Imps while
they are dragging each other into hotter & still hotter pools of
Brimstone & Fire—it is the discord of Torment, and of Rage, and

of Hate, of paroxysms of Revenge, and every note grumbles away into Despair.

2615 18.197   His Massy Misery so prettily hidden with his Gold & Silver-leaf Happiness—Bracteata Felicitas! Seneca.

ʄ108   2616 17.177   Obituary, Month. Mag. May 1, 1804, p.394. At Blackburn, aged 26, Mʳ J. Towers, Iron-monger—
the above *endowments* (that is, *amiable manners* and *sincerity*) he possessed in so considerable a degree, as to entitle him to be denominated with peculiar propriety, in the opinion of his Friends, a fine model for any young man entering on business.—!—
March 1, 1804. Ditto p.199—In her 24ᵗʰ year, Miss Abigail Woolley, of Ratcliffe upon ~~Stoure~~ Soar/This Excellent and very engaging young woman was taken ill on the preceding Sunday, and in the short space of 48 hours this "fair Emblem of Nature's works" as she is aptly characterized by her Friends, was blasted for ever.—

ʄ108ᵛ   2617 17.178   To teach her (i.e. Andalusia D.) the existence of moral Evil, what man is, in general, as thro' a Veil, giving only one indistinct certainty that it exists/but how excellent man might be, how excellent some few *have* been, how excellent some few *are*, this to give in all its lines & colors of developement, an almost *Chinese* Painting, the Fore- & back-ground equally vivid & distinct, knowing no working of Distance.

2618 17.179   The two so very different senses in which I feel myself impelled to use the words Scotch & Scottish. Now the
ʄ109   Scotch simper, or grin castrate of managed malignity in a Mackintosh, *Scotch!*/The heroic Spartan sternness, & Plainness of *Paisley*/his *Wallace-like* mind & heart—it is not exactly English, i.e. S. Brittish/it is distinguishable from other equally noble characters whom (ah how few!) I have known in S. Britain/it is *Scottish!* N.B. Therefore among confidential company still to press in the distinction Scotch & Scottish/& in general company to avoid the former and its associated feelings from Awe of the Latter/ & wise Fear of being misunderstood.

2619 17.180 It never rains but it pours/First in comes poor *f109ᵛ* Reynell after 8 years' tossing/shipwrecks, Egypt, Aleppo, Smyrna, Africa, Spain &c &c &c—& he, my Disputer of Stowey, comes in on me—a most unaltered Being save in his Health (he will not live long) on me, Public Secretary at Malta/& to day, 22ᵈ July 1805 in comes a Gentleman/a face, whoмich I never saw before, & yet surely, there is in the face at least what I have seen before, but it was a Cloud that perhaps would *never* have dissipated, when he said No wonder, Sir! you do not know me/I should not have recollected your face—/my name is Merrick/that instant all was broad day- *f110* light/Jenny Edwards, the Sick Ward, 50 things, O power of words!—O the dignity of Language—! For this Merrick I was never intimate with—/I barely knew his person & name, except in those circumstances of a Joke played by Le Grice on poor Jenny by a Letter of Love in Merrick's name—/in one instant that Face, tho' it had a scar on it, from accident, & had been dissimilarizing itself for 15 years, or more, became as familiar as any face of my daily acquaintance, my acquaintance of the Day/This add to the Face in Sᵗ [? Mary's] church-yard—

2620 17.181 Caution in vain/the consul's Clerk of Tripoli, *f110ᵛ* stepping out of bed in the dark to go to the Dressing Table for Wa- ter & having made a few steps, bethought him of the Imprudence of it, & the probability of his treading on a Scorpion with bare foot, went back & slipped his feet into his Shoes, in one of which a scor- pion was & bit him mortally—. *Invention.*

2621 17.182 Miss, or Mʳˢ Viemanvill (wie man will) a good novel or play Name for a fair member of the Quicumque-vult Sis- terhood/or a "Lady of Lubricity," as Tom Coryat calls them.—

2622 17.183
Or as Lucina, giving *aid*. In birth to women—mild as any *maid* Full of sweet Hope her (or *his*) Brow seem'd; & her (*his*) Eyes
Like to the morning Skies
Seem'd more to shed than dart
Their comfortable Light upon the sick man's heart.

2623 18.1

f1ᵛ

William ⎫
Dorothy ⎬ Wordsworth
Mary ⎭

S. T. ⎫
Sara ⎬ Coleridge

⟨O blessed Flock! I the sole scabbed Sheep!   4½ ems
And even me they love, awake, asleep.⟩

$$W + D + M = \overline{W. + STC + SH} = \text{Ενοπεντας}$$

⟨Well—and if it be Illusion—yet surely an Illusion, which acts at
all times and in all moods and places, awake, asleep; sick, & in
health; alone, and in company; in sorrow and in Joy; present or
absent; in moments of self-condemnation and self-acquittal; o
surely that Illusion is hardly distinguishable, from Truth/*Reality*
it assuredly is—and such is the Illusion if Illusion it must be, that
I am persuaded, I love W.M.D.S. better than myself, & myself
chiefly in them.⟩

2624 18.2*

f1ᵛ,f2

ΣAPA Coleridge	W+M+D=W Coleridge
William Dorothy	William Mary

[* See General Note to N 18 for additions and variants. K. C.]

III. Notebook 18, $ff\,1^v$–2 (inside front cover and flyleaf)

See N 18 Gen Note

2625 18.200   <u>Marini.</u>   *f96ᵛ*

Sonnetto.

Non così bella mai per l'onda Egea
Con le Grazie e gli Amori in schiera accolta
Lungo il lido di Cipro uscìo talvolta
La sua conca rotando Citerea:
Come vid'io, non so se ninfa o dea
In ricca poppa assisa,—bionda e folta
La chioma a lievi Zefiri disciolta
Sul legno d'Argo il vello d'or parea.
Sospiravano i venti, e l'acque stesse
Al folgorar de la novella Aurora
D'amorose faville erano impresse;
E curvandosi il mar sotto la prora
Con rauco mormorio parea dicesse:
Ed io m'inchino a riverirla ancora.

This, & still more the following Sonnet, I have transcribed for the
sake of the Diction, and in order to catch its graces in English—as
the Style being its whole, my attention will be concentered and confined to this one Object while I am attempting to translate it.

Sonnetto.   *f97*

Sovra l'orlo d'un rio lucido e netto
Il canto soavissimo sciogliea
Musico rossignuol, ch'aver parea
E mille voci e mille augelli in petto.
Eco, che d'ascoltarlo avea diletto,
Le note intere al suo cantar rendea:
Ed ei vie piu garría, che lei credea
Vago, che l'emulasse, altro augelletto.
Ma mentre che tenor del bel concento
Raddoppiava più dolce, a caso scorse
L'imagin sua nel fuggitivo argento.
Riser le ninfe, ed ei ch'allor s'accorse
Schernito esser dal acque, anzi dal vento,
A celarsi tra rami in fretta corse.

I have transcribed this Sonnet for the sweetness and simple Flow of
the Style and of the Narration, regretting its *falseness* to Nature.
I cannot but think, that this mode of belying the lovely countenance of Things & *red-ochring* the rose, must be injurious to the
moral tact both of the authors & their admirers. S.T.C.

f97ᵛ   Sonnetto.

> Apre l'uomo infelice allor che nasce
> In questa vita di miserie piena,
> Pria ch'al Sol, gli occhi al pianto; e nato appena
> Va prigionier fra le tenaci fasce:
> Fanciullo poi, che non più latte il pasce,
> Sotto rigida sferza i giorni mena,
> Indi in età più ferma e più †† serena
> Tra fortuna ed amor more e rinasce.
> Quante poscia sostien tristo e mendico
> Fatiche e morti, in fin che curvo e lasso
> Appoggia a debil legno il fianco antico!
> Chiude al fin le sue spoglie angusto sasso
> Ratto così, che sospirando io dico:
> De la cuna a *la tomba* è un breve passo.

(†† In età più ferma, ~~ma non pero~~ ah! non pur più serena—??)

A Sonnet often imitated, but superior to all the imitations & copies
that I at least have seen. "*Serena*" seems to me rather an ill-chosen
word, if it mean—chiarezza del aria e del cielo liberi dalle nebbie e
nuvoli—still more if Franciosini is accurate in explaining it "chiara
senza sole, imperochè col sol si chiama splendore.—Splendente or
rather aprico ⟨is the true word, thus⟩ = *sunshiny*

f98   ⟨Mena i giorni sotto sferza nemica:
                      ~~In età più ferma~~
                      Indi in età più ferma e talor aprica.⟩

                          Sonnetto

            Sotto caliginose ombre profonde
            Di luce inaccessibile sepolti

Tra nembi di silenzio oscuri e folti
L'eterna mente i suoi secreti asconde.
E ⁜ s'altri spia per queste nebbie immonde
† I suoi giudizi in nero velo avvolti,
† Gli umani ingegni temerari e stolti
Col lampo abbaglia, e col suo tuon confonde.
O invisibile Sol, ch'a noi ti celi
Dentro abisso luminoso e fosco ††
E di tuoi proprj rai te stesso veli;
† Argo mi fai, dov'io son cieco e + losco,
†† Ne la mia notte il tuo splendor reveli;
Quanto t'intendo men, più ti conosco.

A noble poem; but with too many defects and botches for one of
14 lines only—

⁜ altri new-worded into † gli umani ingegni is *clumsy*—

†† luminous *and* dark (or dusky black) gives an apparent incompatibility without any notice of the author's ~~sense of~~ consciousness
of it or of its intentionality—⟨luminoso e bello—it should at least be
"yet" instead of "and"—& even thus how inferior to "dark with excess of light" in which the very wonder involves its own—but thus
it loses the sonnet metre⟩ involves its own explication, and while   ƒ98ᵛ
they excite that striving of thought and feeling of difficulty in the
reader, which ~~are~~ it is the Author's Object to do, yet reconcile it to
his understanding by the very same words; words at once expressing and explaining an approximation to Incompatibility.

†. *Argo*—grossly injudicious this pagan Fable used as a metaphor in an address to the metaphysical God of Reason and purest
Christianity.

+ cieco e losco, or lusco—*blind* and *short-sighted*—is either a
bull or something very like it.

††. This Line is a mere Make-weight, adding nothing to the line
preceding, wᶜʰ it merely *construes*, and neither leading to the line
following, nor having any bond of logical connection with it. Thus
then there are six grievous faults in 14 lines—and the first Line of
the Sonnet may without any hypercriticism be added & make a
seventh/for Da luce &c would be not only a sufficient but a far finer

ƒ99 beginning—And I at least should have hesitated long before I had admitted the third line—thick and obscure storm-clouds or rain-clouds of *Silence* (for that is the proper sense of *nimbus*)—oscuri is a beggarly Rag of Superfluity. Again after the line—"buried in Light inaccessible" the word "asconde" is flat with a vengeance—nay, it is not a flat—it is a *sink;* one steps into a hole when one was expecting to place the foot on a stair higher. Again, the eleventh Line, ~~an~~ excellent in itself, is but a repetition of the very same thought already expressed at least twice before—& that most ver-bosely—the 4 first Lines amounting to nothing more than is ex-pressed in this one line, the meaning of which is a second time crammed into the reader in the tenth, or preceding Line—& yet again a third time in line the sixth, or which the "in nero velo av-volti"—is bad all possible 1. It is a ~~wretched~~ ~~poor~~ anticlimax. 2. a metaphor at once harsh & mean. 3. It is a dull repetition, & 4. It is

ƒ99ᵛ almost a contradiction both to the preceding lines, & to the 10th & 11th which come after it; for tho' a luminous cloud may produce the effect of darkness by excess of splendor, yet assuredly a blinding Blaze of pure Light can never resemble a *black* Veil—for black or sable is a word of definite color, and perforce confined to the external appearance—& cannot like the word "dark" or "obscure" be used ad libitum either to characterize the outward Object & Cause ~~for~~ ~~the~~ ~~Cause~~ ~~Agent~~, (~~or~~ *modo* ~~of~~ ~~outward~~ ~~agency~~) or for the effect on the mind or senses of the spectator. Two more yet remain—the word "abbaglia" again repeats this endless *repeatable* of *over*-light—and both it and the col suo tuon confonde is a *tack'd* on thought miserable in its meanness & commonplace, but that is

ƒ100 not the worst—it is wholly out of the Texture—and not an inter-texture or even ornament of needle-work; but a bit of ⟨old⟩ Shoe-leather botched on upon the heel of a worsted Stocking, or a piece of Dowlas rather sewed in to the broken Stocking Calf in order to fill up a whole, & make it cover the Leg or Leg-last—Thus the Faults of this Poem are more in number than the Lines; and the faulty phrases, not much less than the number of Lines.—The last is the *atoning* Line—all the rest I read at first *well contented,* sav-ing the "Argo," and kindly took the will for the deed—I knew what the Author meant to say, & received it as actually said—This

being the ordinary State of mind in the mass of unmalignant
Readers, I have thought it worth the Trouble to analyse it thus
minutely. It may perhaps hereafter be serviceable in giving Hart-   *f100ᵛ*
ley or Derwent a gode and a guide to the close Hunt of Good
Sense, & fineness and steadiness to the right Scent—What then is
the Sonnet rendered without its faults?—This: Eternal Mind, that
in Light inaccessible buriest the mysteries of thy Essence & Providence, ~~hiding~~ veiling thy own Self from us by the abyss of thy own
Eradiance, out of my blindness thou makest Sight and Glory for
me—for how much less I understand, so much the more do I
know thee!—N.B. The invisible Sol, distinguished from the component Light & luminous Ocean, is verily Sun by name, & Sun by
nature—2 Souns out of one, i.e. a Sun beside itself—the proper
progeny of a poetical Son of a Gun (or Blunderbuss) who hap-   *f101*
pened to be a Man beside himself.

2626 17.184   The excellent Fable of the madning Rain I have   *f111*
found in Drayton's Moon Calf, most miserably marred in the telling!—inferior much to Benedict Fay's Latin Exposition of it, &
that is no great Thing/vide—his Lucretian Poem on the Newto-
nian System—/Never was a finer Tale for a satire, or rather to conclude a long satirical poem of 5 or 600 Lines.—

2627 17.185   Pasley remarked last night (2ⁿᵈ Aug. 1805) and
with great precision & originality/that *men* themselves in the present Age were not so much degraded, as their *sentiments*/This is
most true!—almost all men nowadays act and feel more nobly than
they think/yet still the vile cowardly selfish calculating Ethics of
Paley, Priestley, Lock, & other *Erastians*, do woefully influence &
determine our course of action/

2628 17.186   Yesterday (2 Aug. 1805) the Thermometer was
at 88 in the Shade, 134 to 140 in the Sun/& to day the Heat seems   *f111ᵛ*
equal or greater. The boards fly, with perpendicular Cracks, with
frequent and startling Sound/the Mahogany & stoutest woods from
England, in Tea chests, &c, literally explode & *burst* the Instru-

ment. Capt\ Lamb's Tea chest *went off*, as loud as a Pistol, fired at his Ear/& the Cooper's Shop (where there is at present a large quantity of Mahogany & English Oak) presents to the *Ear* a successive *Let-off* of Fire-works.—At St Antonio's, tho' we expected the sound every 4 or 5 minutes, yet still it was so loud that it startled us, each time (as we sat at dinner) not a board in the beautiful new dining Room but is split from top to bottom in two or three places—and this morning I was awaked out of a sound Sleep by one at the farther end of my long & spacious Bedroom/I have the prickly Heat on my Body, but without *prickling* or annoying me/& I am better than I have been for a long time/—In short, if my mind & heart were at ease, if my children, + SH + W.D.M.W. were with me, & they were well, I should be more than well/I should luxuriate, like a Negro, in the Oven of the Shade and the Blaze of the Sunshine.

f112

2629 17.187   3 Aug. 1805, Saturday—It is worthy notice, the instinctive passion in the mind for a *one word* to express a *one act* of feeling—i.e. in which, however complex in reality, the mind is *conscious* of no discursion, and Synthesis a posteriori. On this instinct rest all the improvements, and on the habits formed by this Instinct & knowlege of these Improvements, Vanity rears all the Apuleian, Apollonarian, &c &c Corruptions of Style—Even so with Dr Johnson/⟨shewn in the phrase, "I *envy* him such or such a thing —meaning only, I regret, I cannot share with him—have the same, as he, without depriving him of it or any part of it—⟩

f112" 2630 17.188   There are *Bulls* of action equally as of Thought/ not to allude to the Story of the Irish Mason's Laborer who layed his Comrade all his Wages that he would not carry him down in his hod from the top to the bottom of a high House down the Ladders/the feeling of vindictive Honor, in Duelling & the feudal Revenges enter in to Duelling, formed a true *Bull* for they were superstitious Christians, knew it was *wrong* & yet knew it was right/ they would be damned deservedly if they did it & if they did not, they thought themselves deserving of being damned/&c &c/—

2631 17.189   O! the complexities & the *Ravel* produced by Time struggling with Eternity!—a and b are different, and Eternity or Duration makes them one—this we call modification, the principle of all greatness in finite beings, the principle of all contradiction *and absurdity*.

2632 15.163   Sunday, 11ᵗʰ August, 1805, one o'clock—had ƒ77 taken Castor Oil in Gin & Water—when standing at the window and accidentally looking at my Seal, with many tender recollections I saw and (after noticing the circumstance) still continued to see it, like a fixed reality not dependent on my will, without dimness or swimmingness of Vision, *Two Seals*, of the same distance from each other as one eye from the other; but the Letters, ⅀ Ε⅀ΤΗ⅀Ε & the ƒ77ᵛ whole impression more large & distinct, *exactly* as if seen thro' a common Reading-glass.

2633 15.164   Frith, pompous ⟨mock-⟩learned Puppy/Sannazarii piscatory Eclogues opines the Port Ambassador/στραγγυρι

2634 15.165   Not men but sentiments degenerated

2635 15.166   Dogs *reviving* in the moonlight, & playing & gamboling in flocks at Malta/Aug. 12, 1805.

2636 15.167   Maltese Centry — Ha bibi! Himshi! nichts [?push/pish] la!

2637 18.189   About 5 °clock (can see by the Malta almanac) ƒ90ᵛ Wed. Morn.: 14 Aug. 1805—deeply depressed almost to despondence put on my Great Coat, and walked on the long Top of the House/—The Sea stretched out in a long width before me, a ~~wh~~ almost a whole turn of the Head/the Horizon dusky crimson, of the same height & degree of color along its whole extent—the half of the Sea nearest it was ~~calm~~ smooth, the hither half gently ruffled, ⟨& *inlayed*⟩ with curves and semicircles of smooth water— there were many boats at a small distance from the Shore, and so arranged that the Prow of the one appeared to touch the *wake* of the other/& this in 3 or four Lines of 4 or 5 boats each/so that each *File* seemed connected or *towed* by *ropes* lying stiff and tight on the surface of the water/—At length a particular Slice of the H. crimsoned deeper, & a large Ship was not far from it off to my right *f91* —when the Sun emerged, I felt as I always feel, as if it stepped in quick upon the Scene/occasioning a startlet ⟨it rose by the Ship, as by an ancient tower/⟩ (a breath of air on the surface of Tranquillity) & as if there were a contrast almost between the apparent motion of its first $\frac{1}{8}$th, & the slow solemn rising of the remainder/— When little more than a quarter risen, the Ship streaked it with a

transverse bar   —/but when almost full risen, & now standing on but not having yet left the surface of the water, it appeared like the short, strait, stiff Stalk of the beautiful Water Melon of Light/✳ ✳ ⟨turn back a Leaf⟩

f90   ⟨14 Aug. 1805—Sun rise. Conclusion of the Description. See the next page.⟩

✳ ✳ When risen & now with some interspace between it and the sea, the Ship seemed far *away* behind it, & the orb of Light seemed to have stepped forward out of the Horizon—, & to have left it behind it/but the road of light on the *calm*, a such a Roman Road, contrasted with the curved semicircular Roads of Calm in the Ruffle, & with its own continuation to the Ruffle, which faintly seemed but reflection/& when it rose higher, I caught it under a different aspect, no longer a road, but now a Column, beautifully proportioned/& now many high Towers, & the Continuation seemed indeed its Reflection.

f91   2638 18.190   5 °clock, Wed: Morn.: 14 Aug. 1805—⟨very unwell yester eve on my return from St Antonio—Boil on my arm fell back on my stomach, & gave me on the sopha an epileptic dream—alas! alas! the consequences—στιμυλος⟩ The dependence of ideas, ⟨consequently of Memory, &c⟩ on states of bodily or mental *Feeling* (a truth so important to my "*Consolations*") strongly exemplified in the first moments of awaking from a Dream/A

healthy man will often be utterly unable to do it within a few seconds of awaking—a nervous man, or one of perturbed or morbid
functions of the lower bowels, can often carry on the Dream in his
waking Thoughts/and often in its increasing faintness & irrecollecti-
bility has time to *watch* & compare—

2639 18.191   A flash of Lightning/struck terror into my Heart   *f91*
—yea—as if spiritual Things, *Beings of Thought* (Entia Rationis)
could cloath themselves & make a *space* of Light—the Shekinah of
the Conscience/—
   I seemed to see *my actions* in my mind/or my mind seemed to
have inclosed *that light* within its enlargened Circumference/—It
was real & spectral at the same moment/—These are the *Ideas*/a
cave, night, the Thunder & Lightning & the guilty man/had been
a Banditto, & drank & caroused but yet never killed his sensibility
—but drugged it &c &c &c—

2640 22.127   The Grotian Paleian Defences of X how injurious   *f74*
to X   develope/—never would the number of Infidels have been
so great, if to each attack it had been answered/Well, Brother! but
granting these miracles to have been false, or the growth of delusion at the time, and of exaggeration afterward from Reporter to
Reporter, yet still all the doctrines remain binding on thee? Still
must thou repent, & be regenerated, and be crucified to the flesh, &
this not by thy own mere being, but by a mysterious action of the
Moral world on thee, of the ordo ordinans. Still will the Trinity,
the Redemption, the assumption of Humanity by the Godhead remain Truth/& still will the Faith ~~of~~ in these Truths be the living
fountain of all true virtue, the seed like a mustard Seed, all the
leaves, sprays, flowers, & trunks of true good being only the developement of *that* form, & its combination with the ~~actual~~ real world,
it the vital form, that its materiale? Believe all these so as thy Faith   *f74*
be not merely *real* but *actual*/Then shalt thou know from God
whether or no Christ be of God—It is the importance and *essential-
ity* attributed to miracles that has tempted men to deny them!—
They are extra-essential, tho' not useless or superfluous.—

Answer to such as charge me with explaining away Christianity with an Allegory/—Allegory! what then is substance, if this be *allegory?*

2641 22.128   The revival & playfulness of the Dogs after Sunset till almost morning, in the open Space between the Treasury & Hall of Archives—& their continual noise, especially in their Combat with the Pigs.—The *Piggiad.*—16 Aug. 1805

2642 22.129   It is *me.* I doubt, whether this be necessarily bad grammar, psychologically analysed. Who was it, did that? It was I. Who were there? I and Thomas and William. And which of you was it they beat so?—O sir it was *me.*—Here comes the true Objective Case.

f75

2643 22.130   If you being afflicted with a particular Disease heard from a good and sensible man that he having had or having the like Disease had found great relief from a particular remedy, would you not wish it to be *true?* Would you not, if convinced it could do you no harm, examine it, give it a Trial?—Why, then do you proceed so differently with the averred remedies of human Sorrows, the Faith in God, Virtue, Immortality! Have not these been recommended to us *probata sunt* by many wise & good men/— Why, then this Scorn at the mention of them? This pleasure of Pride in your anticipation of proving them fallacies & impostures? —Have you in solitary moments disciplined your *Heart,* and seriously quieting the bustle of former Disputation questioned it as to the *Fact?*—Do I, or do I not, feel so? instead of, How shall I answer this?—What *words* shall I put together; &c &c—all in the *Head,* ⟨nothing in the *Heart*—⟩/your eyes glistening all the while and looking forward as if to an Audience, or with the look of one who is recollecting or anticipating an Audience?—Surely, there is something wrong at the Bottom of all this!—O that you had but once known, how sweet a Thing a deep Conviction is!—the blessedness of Certainty contrasted with the Bubble-bubble of *Positiveness!* —W. T. of Norwich/O I have wished to talk with him in some better moment by his Fire Side—

f75ᵛ

2644 22.131

Scarce half the Tale ‡
Impatiently he heard: then scour'd away
Swift as a famish'd Vulture scenting prey.
STC

‡ The ~~Tale was~~ Tidings were ecstacy to his ears; yet he listened   *f76*
to it, as if on the rack/scarce half the Tale, beating the earth with
his right foot, & his staff trembling in his hand, he heard, & even
that half ~~he~~ seemed rather to mould a dream than to convey the
simple Truth, then scourd away/—

2645 22.132

Of Infidels from Sir J. Davies—   *f75ᵛ*

"And tho' they would, they cannot quite be beasts."

Davies still more than even Daniel is a proof that our Language
has made no steps, endured no real alterations since the Time of   *f76*
Elizabeth, at least/Every 5 years, has its affectations; but he who
writes simply well, must write now, ~~as~~ both words & construction
as our ancestors, two or even three hundred years ago/

2646 22.133   /// Saturday 18 May 1805—Valetta—the persecution of the Jews commenced/

2647 22.18   It is a subject not unworthy of meditation to my-   *f25ᵛ*
self, what the reason is that these sounds & bustles of Holidays,
Fairs, Easter-mondays, & Tuesdays, & Christmas Days, even when   *f26*
I was a Child & when I was at Christ-Hospital, always made me
so heart–sinking, so melancholy? Is it, that from my Habits, or my
want of money all the first two or three and 20 years of my Life I
have been *alone* at such times?—That by poor Frank's dislike of
me when a little Child I was even from Infancy forced to be by
myself—or rather is it not, that from the distressful specific nature
of my ill-health, as well as from all these other causes, & from sundry accidents of my Life, I cannot be happy, but while awakening,
enjoying, and giving *sympathy* to one or a few eminently loved

Beings, and that when external Joyances call away my attention
from these Dreams, which are the poor substitute & wretched
Mock-indemnifications of that Sympathy & that Society I *feel*
my Hollowness? ⌐Surely, if ~~I were rich, & selfish and desired~~
ƒ26ᵛ   ~~Asra to come with me, I could~~⌐ (subtracting the force of former
Associations) be as ~~happy~~ joyous in watching men at a merry-make,
as I am *blessed* in worshipping the Loveliness of Fields, Lakes,
Streams, ancient Trees, mountains, & Skies—in the same Company?

2648 22.19   Man a creature only of some 6000 years: and how
much has he not had to do in that time?—Likewise, is it not a
ground of Hope if we can clearly see the causes of his wrecks and
mishaps (ex.gr. of the non-continuance of the Greek and Roman
Republics, of the irreligiousness of the present age) and see no
reason to deem either irremoveable or of necessary recurrence, having been removed!—For *my Comforts & Consolations*—

2649 22.20   Prelacy combined with Episcopacy the *better*/the
C. of E. Clergy are utterly removed from the Laity, the Laity
from Religion, by the want of *Elders*.

ƒ78   2650 15.168   One pleasant thing in Sicily/observed that the
men did not put their women to hard out of door work, but that
they were almost exclusively employed in spinning and management of the House/Holds good of the Maltese.

2651 15.169   20 Aug. 1805. Tuesday ⟨Morning⟩, Treasury
House, Malta, 9 °clock—I doubt, if it be not one of the "Signs of
the Times" that the Theses of the Universities of Oxford & Cambridge are so generally drawn from events of the Day/Stimuli of
passing Interests/Dʳ Dodds, Jane Gibbses, Hatfields, Bonapartes,
Pitts, &c &c &c &c, whereas the great end of that *ought to be* tranquil time should be to give a living Interest for the Permanent,
ƒ78ᵛ   the Generic, for that which is independent of Times, in short for
that which the Self-conceit of the Ephemerides has christened
Common-place. In this view, I confess, I would rather see "Mors
omnibus communis" as the theme, than *"Melita"* or Holkar Wel-
leslio devictus.

2652 17.222   24ᵗʰ August, 1805 = Saturday, 12 °clock, gave a   *f164ᵛ*
Doubloon.—Now note for one week all my expences/—

2653 17.223

Super ipsius ingens
Instat Fama viri, Virtusque haud læta tyranno.
Ergo anteire metus, juvenemque exstinguere pergit
                C. Val. Flacc. Argonaut.
                  Lib.1.30.

2654 17.224

Here I unclasp the book of my charg'd Soul,
Where I have cast the accounts of all my care;
Here have I summ'd my sighs; here I enrol
How they were spent for thee: look, what they are!
                  Daniel's Sonnets.

2655 17.225   "O Sir! I shall soon plug up that Shot-hole"—a   *f165*
Ship-carpenter arguing against a plausible objection/

2656 15.170   Saturday Afternoon Noon, ½ past 2, received the   *f78ᵛ*
blow & wound in my left Eye, by leaping out of the boat & meeting
in my full leap a rope stretched horizontally. 24 Aug. 1805.

2657 15.171   26ᵗʰ Aug. Eye very bad.—What an odd phrase/
But I did not like it *tho'*/—But I am sure of that *tho'*, as ⟨the last
words of the old Master of⟩ Trinity College, Cambridge, a famous   *f79*
Glutton, replied to one who told him "He was going to a better
place."

2658 15.172   The Modesty, the charming Modesty, of an Italian (& Latin) Dictionary "Connelino, dimin: di quella parte ver-
gognosa delle donne, il di cui nome non può scriversi." Accordingly, Conno is not inserted.

2659 16.262   How worldly men gain their purposes even with   *f79ᵛ*
worldly men by that instinctive Belief of Sincerity/hence (nothing

immediately and *passionately* contradicting it) the effect of the
ƒ80   "with unfeigned esteem," "devotion" & the other smooth speeches
of Letters/all in short, that Sea officers call *"Oil"*—and of which
they with all their bluntness well understand the use.

2660 16.263   The sick Warrior, starting with nervous pain at
the loud Night & Morning call of the collected *Drums,* to wc̄h of
yore his robust Heart had beat music & pleasure & high Hope &
Visions of Glorious Battle. Vallette.

2661 16.264   The more I reflect, the more exact & close appears to me the Similie of a Watch and Watches: the Sun & motion
ƒ80ᵛ   of the heavenly Bodies in general, to the conscience and consciences
∷ to the reason and goodness of the Supreme./Never goes quite
right, any one; no two go exactly the same, they derive their dignity and use as being Substitutes and Exponents of heavenly
motions/but still in a thousand instances they are & must be our
instructors, by which we must act, in practice presuming a co-inci-
dence, while theoretically we are aware of incalculable *Variations.*

2662 16.265   Pindaric Ode/mem. Coler. Dialogue between
Stroff. Antist, and Epode/
The March, the Counter march,

ƒ81   2663 16.266   ⌜. . . . .⌝ and Falsehood, and Torture
from ~~those~~is polypus growth of Contradictions!—These *Bulls*
(*Sbagli*) of Horror & Darkness!

2664 16.267   One cause of the continuance of ⟨two of⟩ the Sacraments even in the purest & most doctrinal Protestant Churches—
and which I have observed even in the society of "the *Disbelievers
only so far, at present*" (Arian and Unitarian Meeting-houses) the
Pride, the venial Self-consequence which is naturally felt in the
ƒ81ᵛ   performance of a *Ceremony*/at other times he is *talking*/in these
he is *doing* something, ~~and~~ something that must be done, and
which he alone can do. Hence Rome, the undoubted Anti-christ,

if there be any sense in the Word (i.e. if Christ mean the uncondi-
tional Obedience of the Free Will to the Law of pure Reason, and
Anti-christ a systematic actually-existing and most powerful Conspiracy to subvert the *Law*, to introduce in its stead all and every
Tampering of our sensuous *Nature, feelings*/pride, swellings up   *f82*
of Heart, melting fancies, (as Sᵗ Teresa) worldly Importance,
Terror, in all their minutiæ) Hence, I say, Rome has almost made
up her Church-discipline of *Ceremonies,* and hence too the only
Body of Christians who have wholly given up are the Quakers
who—and because they—gave up the sacerdotal Order. 6 Sept:
1805.

The Comparison between the aims and operation of the Mosaic
and Romish Ceremonies would make an interesting, & I believe,
new Theol. Tract.—To examine, in the early Fathers, what share   *f82ᵛ*
of the *Feeling* of Baptism belonged to the essence of *initiation* into
Christianity, indeed, most awful & *sacramental;* and how much to
the actual mode, the ceremony per se: & how far this latter was or
was not confounded with the former, as being the most general
mode of religious Proselytism. Give your repenting Enemy your
right-hand & press *his* in return. Make a Bow to your lawful Superiors.—

Might not a moral "Völkslehrer" [*Volkslehrer*] talk of these as   *f83*
absolutely necessary to Salvation, &c, they having been in his mind
Incarnations of the Truths involved?—all expressions belong to
the world of Sense—to phænomena/all are contingent, local, here
this, there another/but when ennobled into symbols of Noumena,
it is a common & venial error to forget the vileness in the worth, to
confound not to analyse—the contingent symbol with the divine
Necessity = Νουμενον

2665 16.268   6 Sept. 1805/Thursday Morning, Mʳ Chapman   *f83ᵛ*
                  arrived—at last!

2666 16.269   Friday Morning, 2 °clock/7 September 1805.—
Yes, a shocking recollection, that *years* have passed to a man in
the prime of manhood/on every night of which he has dreaded to
go to bed or fall asleep/& by that dread seduced to again & again

& again poison himself—/6ᵗʰ Sept. 5 °⟨clock morning⟩ Pain from having *cursed* a gnat that was singing about my Head.

ƒ84   2667 16.270   Not to deal in generals with the Rom: Cath: Rel: to fix on the Messerstich, the Knife-stabbing all over Neapolitan Dominions, how long it has lasted, and the means & the psychological Effects of such means, of the Priests to *prevent* ~~the~~ it. Prevent it?—no, to make men undergo a *Penance* all the effects of which are purely retrospective—& of the *act*—not of the disposition/nay, the very thought & anticipation of which Penance mingles with & increases the appetite of Revenge, & by a strange perversion renders it already *innocent,* because it *will have* been expiated,

ƒ84ᵛ   some time or other. But this is only a Hint—pursue it with as much psychological minuteness of inner Soul-Biography, as Richardson's visual consecutiveness.   9 Sept. 1805.—

ƒ79   2668 15.173   The Jew Minister of Algiers, Bushnak, who used often to boast that he held the Dey by the Beard, the plenipotent there, & the faithful agent of France, was shot by a Turkish Soldier on the 27ᵗʰ June, 1805. The Dey instantly sent him his Beads, the Stygian Oath in that country of irrevocable Pardon. The following Day the Jew's House was given up to Pillage/more than an hundred of that unhappy race massacred—their Bodies burnt/&

ƒ79ᵛ   Busnak whose funeral was followed by howls & shouts of curses & jubilation, was afterwards dug up & burnt. Sidi Ahkmet, of the old family of Oran, sent off to that Government, & likely to suppress the Rebellion/but the Jews all sent off except a few old people/two Ship-loads already gone.

2669 15.174   The Leach escaping out of his prison of the Bottle of Water—to die—a striking & new illustration of &c.

2670 15.175
                ⟨15 Sept. 1805. Sunday. MALTA/alas!⟩
Among the numerous examples of confusion of Heathen & Christian Mythology in the Poets of the 15ᵗʰ Century (pleasing inasmuch as they prove how intimately the works of Homer & Virgil &c were *worked* in & *scripturalized* in their *minds*—1. was

taught this hour, the other the next—or both together & by the
same man with the same countenance, with the same seriousness
and zeal, at the same early age—& in a time when Authority was
all in all—and what was publickly *taught* of Aristotle, was indi-
vidually & perhaps more generally, *felt* of *Homer*/in the various   *f80*
broken reflections of him throughout the Latin Poets & all men of
Education/& in the original & the echoing series of the other Greek
Poets to the Politians, &c &c,/—indeed, it requires a strong imagination as well as an accurate psycho-analytical understanding
in order to be able to conceive the *possibility*, & to picture out the reality, of the *passion* of those Times for Jupiter, Apollo &c/&
the nature of the *Faith* (for a Faith it was—it vanished indeed at
the Cock-crowing of a deliberate Question, in *most* men; but in the
ordinary unchecked stream of Thought it moved on, as naturally
as Contraband & Legal Goods in the same Vessel, when no Revenue Officers are on the Track.) Having as usual, thro' a Labyrinth
of Parentheses wandered out of the *Poss*ibility of connecting my
sentence grammatically tho' logically I have never *let go* of the
Thought, I aim to memorandum a striking instance of this gross   *f80ᵛ*
confusion of this Paganizing of Christianity, Jehovah : V. Mary : :
Jupiter to Leda, or Mars to the Mother of Romulus—in the *first*
Canzone of the darling Ariosto—5ᵗʰ Stanza or paragraph of it/

> Nè il dì, nè l'anno tacerò, nè il loco
> Dove io fui preso: e insieme
> Dirò gli altri trofei, ch'allora aveste,
> Tal che appo loro il vincer me fu poco.
> Dico, *da che il suo seme*
> *Mandò nel chiuso ventre il Re celeste,*
> *Avean le ruote preste*
> *Dell'Omicida lucido d'Achille*
> *Rifatto il Giorno mille*
> *E cinquecento tredici fiate*
> *Sacro al Battista, in mezo de la estate.*

2671 15.176   15 Sept. 1805. My tears & misery at the Thought
of not returning—my reflections on Captⁿ Pasley's feelings respect-   *f81*
ing the careless attack on the Scotch by Mackenzie.

ƒ84ᵛ   2672 16.271   26ᵗʰ Septʳ Syracuse *again*/& again the Prima
Donna/left Malta, Monday last/I was standing gazing at the
starry Heaven, and said, I will go to bed the next star that shoots/
Observe this in counting fixed numbers previous to doing any thing,
ƒ85   &c &c &c and deduce from man's own unconscious acknowlegement man's *dependence* on some thing *out of* him, on something
more *apparently* & believedly subject to regular & certain Laws
than his own Will & Reason/⌈. . . . .⌉ It is Saturday
morning, 27 Septʳ 1805/

2673 16.272   I quitted Malta on Monday 21 Sept/at 12 °clock
or past/and arrived on Tuesday morning/tho' but for the night
we might have been in the same day—

2674 16.273   If any man would be convinced of the [?obscen-
ity] of all [?from] *Climate* Malta—Syracuse—
ƒ85ᵛ   āāchch—Rōōah, the *every-minute* gentle Vitu-
peration of the Lettiga Driver/Septʳ/30ᵗʰ/

2675 21.348, 350
ƒ60   Wᵐ Denison
Syracuse 30 Septbʳ. 1805.
Lu suderi da a frunte mi grundâo.
Ciceri Ciceri.

2676 21.349   S. T. Coleridge left Malta, Monday 23 Sept.
1805—arrived at Syracuse, Tuesday Morning, 24ᵗʰ Sep/—left Syracuse,—alone! left Mr. & Mrs. Leckie. Monday 30 Sept. 1805.—

ƒ76   2677 22.134   Old Mariner ~~and his~~ on the little Lava Morta
at Catania reading the Italian "Carthaginisine"/[*Cartaginese*] of
the Death & Wreck of I. W.—

2678 22.135   Bēnabārazāārin/a good name for a moorish Bal-
lad/rhymes good-temperdly

2679 16.274   The Syracusans compared with the Maltese/the   *f85ᵛ*
uniformity of the Latter, the fearful Variety of the ~~Latter~~ former/
a few fair & beautiful, many such as seemed destined to have been
beautiful/& O how many seemed preserved by miracle from the
Tyger fangs & Talons, how many from the *withering* shrivelling
de-humanizing *Spell* & magical Blight of Death/Pilgrims from the
Upas Tree.

2680 16.275   Of the waste of Labor in Sicily & barbarous Countries /~~7~~ 6 mules to convey *me*, Mackenzie & Servant, with a very
small Luggage/& 3 men besides/9 to convey 3!!   *f86*

2681 16.276   7 miles ½ from Syracuse, 2½ from Prioli, 9 Salt-
hills, 40 Ton each at least—a farm-house between the first 2 and
the latter 7.

2682 16.277   Beyond Valverde, the next Village, 2 very beautiful young Ladies in ~~upon~~ chintz Trousers astride on very handsome ponies, man-fashion
Of the Fair Complexions, of the Women and children/very
fair, & very many so, from and in/Catania to Valverde, &c/
Never did I see out of England a place that more inchanted me
as a place of residence than Valverde/& the adjacent Hill.
The gray cloud-spotted cool in turn day, the Trees, the Fields, the   *f86ᵛ*
villages, all—had there been hedges instead of Stone-walls, might
have made us suppose ourselves in the most rich parts of Somerset
or S. Wales. 3 Oct. 1805/

2683 16.278   Glorious *Coroubas!*

2684 16.279   Oak, Pine, Walnut, Locust, Fig, orange, &
Lemon, Vine,

2685 16.280   Valverde,
St Antonio—
Gialli + Strada/!!!

ƒ87   2686 16.282

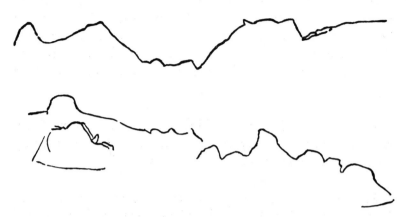

Leaf, of Prunus & Hop, & [?Vine/Pine]/

ƒ88   2687 16.283   ⟨Giardini below Taormina⟩/

Novo Albergo, the Lion/beware of the Landlord, & make a strict bargain with him.—The Wife, indeed the whole Household, are exceedingly civil and attentive but ⟨the man is⟩ *rapacious,* insatiable, even to unfeeling Impudence/Oct. 4. 1805. Friday morning.

N.B. One of your stout handsome hawk-nosed keen Rascals. I have often seen the Face in England

ƒ87ᵛ   2688 16.284   The view ~~from~~ on the Path from Taormina to the Theatre, & from the Theatre itself, surpasses perhaps all I have ever seen/the Sea with its lovely Twin Bays, the well-wooded cultivated Shore, the sudden fantastic savage Rise & Upland/—The high rock-hill that so fronted us with its proud Cone as we were entering Giardini/~~the~~Taormina, gray roofs & white fronts on its breast/Savage scenery, of various, leaping Outline, & *cut-glass* Surface/and the Clouds, & the Crater of Etna rising above/

On the Theatre you see on one side all Etna, & the Twin Bays,

                                  Sicily

Taormina, &c/and on your right the full Sea yet so

                                        Calabria

be-mountained as to form/a huge Harbour, in appearance—so com-   *f88*

pleatly is it land-locked except at the⌐⌐along the sea side, where all is so Montserratish!—Then passing immediately under Taormina a perpend. Precip. by the Church & Houses appearing to *rim* its edge/*rim*/

An immensely *steep* steep road with a precipice on my right   *f88ᵛ* Hand, as I ascended (out of the Lettiga) & took my Adieu of Giardini & Taormina on its Top. On the beginning of the Descent a new Scene tho' of the same character/to the Left a † precip. finely bushed ⟨with Cactus Opuntium⟩ († = perfectly perpendicular) & handsome Buildings peeping above/likewise to the Right the Sea with two Bays, but with one ruinous up-piled Island Rock-Hill created with a square Building, not above a stone-throw from the Shore—& about a stone-throw further a high savage Promontory of various outline with Buildings on it, running far into the Sea/The Island Rock has another naked Islet Rocklet at its Summit—a few yards—

2689 16.285   Syrinx—more beautiful than long/Cactus hanging   *f89* over blue Sea/

2690 16.286   Picturesque City or Town of Candelasia on the Top of the Mountain Rock/; but about 9 or 10 miles from Giardini, having dismounted for the execrable Road, were faced by a I

with a ruined Tower on its very Point/   /the wildest Precipice, the finest Pass I have seen/—a Hamlet/the Rock-mountains die off into green Hills, ~~with~~ interrupted by *cheosi*, O what a scene/ Four ⋀ 's/the first obtuse angled lying upon the 2nd larger,

higher, & still more obtuse-angled/the 3rd & 4th abreast, with a high   *f89ᵛ* Tower like a Minaret between/the 3rd more acute-angled than the 1 & 2, even had its line been prolonged to the Top, but its Top is a very sharp-angled Sugar loaf/the 4th a gibbous Shape, struggling

between a Triangle & semi circle/on these two the wild nest of
Houses & Churches/the whole of the Surface from Top to Bottom
grandly varied, & it forms so very distinct a feature. The Green

f90 Hills that follow it, *wavy!!*—After dinner & sleep, the bad road
with Tower ⟨where I got out⟩ & Gorge/then the ⟨thinly wooded⟩
Hills with circular steps or seat, & a Church Tower (*white*) most
romantically placed on ⋁ of one, just before the rise of an-

other/sometimes in the exact middle/the top often benested with
Towns, sometimes *crested* with a Tower/& the Mountain that often

peeps in from behind ♄ the Fork/above, or cloathed, or absolute rock, once or twice with a Tower like the Head of Cybele

2691 18.7

f2ᵛ   Friend, Lover, Husband, Sister, Brother!
Dear Names! close in upon each other!
Alas! poor Fancy's Bitter-sweet!
~~My name alone with her's can meet~~
Our names, and *but* our names, can meet!
                              Taurominum,
                                   Sicily.—

2692 18.8   Schinchimurra (a phrase of Boccace's to denote
astoundment) would be no bad name for the Fool in my Laugh
till you lose him/

2693 18.9   The admirable account of the Termites bellicosi,
arborum, viarum, by Smeathman/the aphides too, as virgin mothers

2694 18.10   The moon seen thro' a common Spy- or distance-
glass up closely, *exactly* resembles a ~~globe~~ flat circle of frozen
Snow, *thawing* here & there/and its first Start forward! But thro'
a real Telescope/

f90ᵛ 2695 16.287   6 Oct. 1805./arrived at Messina on Thursday
                    Night, 4 Oct. 1805—

2696 16.288   7 Oct. The view of Messina, rising up upon the
Mountain in almost the form of the *altar-screen* = like two or
three Churches in Messina, from the Terra Nuova ~~from~~ returning
from the Lazarette, the most impressive I ever beheld—not excepting Taormina/

2697 16.289   From 5 Rubles the Exchange popped up to 8, &
is now 10½, in Consequence of the sudden & imprudent Clamor for
Money at Constantinople & Odessa.

2698 16.290   — [?Gravitell's/Gravitelli], Sunday Morning
          Salvatore Campolo/

2699 16.291   Interesting Exper: of Mʳ Broadbent as to moist
air in discontinuing the practice of inundating the Flowers in Sum-   *f91*
mer which is done to cool and de-dustify. Sicily/

2700 16.292   Monday Midnight/or Tuesday Morning—Arose
from my Bed in a storm of Rain, Thunder, and Lightning/
⌜. . . . .⌝ almost: for the lamp blinds in its lowermost
Socket/and this morning I am to go off for Trieste/15 October,
1805./Albergo della Villa di Firenze, Messina.

2701 16.281   ~~First noticed that the abdomen growth~~   *f86ᵛ*
          Noticed the having an abdomen prominent, 15
Oct. 1805—or rather 16ᵗʰ/for it had passed one o'clock when I   *f87*
made the melancholy observation/

2702 16.293
          Sortibus coer⟨c⟩endis curandæ   *f91ᵛ*
          Quieti et Securitati publicæ pro Decori
          Augendi Viæ Ferdinandeæ

          ————

          Ferdinandi IV Regis
          Ut iusque Sicilia ab Hoc
          ⌜. . . .⌝ et Largitur
          ⌜. . . . .⌝

2703 16.294   20th October, 1805—My Birth Day!—O Thought of Agony! O Thought of Despair! drive me not to utter Madness!—

f92 2704 16.295   The pernicious effect of these terrifying Pamphlets &c from the Ministers

2705 16.296   20 Oct. 1805—And now I have again taken a solitary walk to Gravitelli, assuredly amongst the very loveliest Prospects, I have seen/soon after you have left the Suburbs of Messina, you are in the loneliness of a very narrow Valley, the Hill tolerably high and pleasantly wooded/but as the path narrowing, winds up the Hill, the richness of the woods before, above, & beneath increase/vines, & vineyards, and pleasant summer Houses, the Fig, the Olive, the Mulberry, Orange, Lemon, Peach, Plum,
f92 Apple, Pear/& here & there an Oak, & in two or three moist Places a grove of Poplars, now so deliciously aromatic/—Still as I rise, I am more & more enamoured of the marvellous playfulness of the Surface of the Hills/such swellings, *startings,* sinkings, and yet all so combined as to make it impossible to look at as many/no! it was a manifold *One!* but ere I had reached the summit of the first Hill, my friend Campolo's Summer House, the Sea came in on me over two Hills, the ships, [?isthmus] which appears to run in repeated

f93   Crescents, as   —one half filled

with massy buildings, the other half bare till it is terminated by the Light-House, bare & green/& the Mountains of Calabria, with their towns, & Villages across/—but above the House, O how shall I describe it/what I have already spoken of, is to my left and before me, as I look toward Messina/but now on my right I look down into a sister Vale, with a very even road winding thro' it, a vale so very *very rich* even up to the summits of its *very* high Hills—&
f93 those that would have been my Horizon, but that some bleak dark mountains of various outline outsoar, & as it were, *guard* them—/— Now too I see the whole town of Messina, its towers, & steeples/ now too I stand as in the middle with two mighty Castles cresting

two woody Hills to my right & left, about a mile distant right before me/Now too I see the Faro, that fair Tongue of Land, & the
Sea & the mountains beyond it—& the Vale on my right runs down
in one great winding Stream of of rich & varied greenness to the   *f94*
very edge of the Sea; & beyond it I see the open Sea, which by the
hither Shore & the Coast of Calabria appears shaped as a wedge
with an indefinite Base/the Ships, the beautiful sparonaras, the fishing Boats, the white Sails of the Mediterranean/O even but 3 years
ago how should I have *hoped & schemed amid all this, but now I
hope* no more. O this *is* a sore affliction to be so utterly estranged
from Hope/—O miserable on my Birth-day too/

2706 16.297   Castellaccio, Cast/di Gonzaga/   *f94ᵛ*

         Λ   Λ

2707 16.298   Braccio di Saraniero/

2708 16.299   Don Michaele Gaetani
                 alla Strada di Giudaica
                 vicino alle quatro Fontane/

2709 16.300
                 ⟨Proposed Rout—from Messina⟩
S. Gregorio, Bisso, Divieto, Bauso, *Spadafora,* on the Riv. Sapo-
nara, having passed two unnamed Rills at Divieto, and Bauso.—A
little on ~~leave~~ have *Tracuccia* to the left, with Valdina, *Venetico,*
Rocca, Monforte, running almost straight behind each other, thus
Pass the Larino, the Monforte River, & two nameless ones,
to *Pace,* having to the Right the Tongue of Land on which
Milazzo lies, tho' at too great a distance to turn out of the   *f95*
Road for it/*Pace* iself on the left of this Road, Archi nearer,
then cross the River S. Lucia, and the La Corda, and arrive at
Pozzo di Gotto and its stream/then by Pozzo di Gotto—to Barce-
lone then over four Streams, the Sᵗ Antonio, the Perilli, the Salice,
and the Grangotta, to *Furnari,* and its river of the same name/
From whence I am to try to make my way to Francavilla, by Maz-
zara to NOARA/but whether this is practicable on Mule or Foot I

do not know.—But suppose me at *Francavilla*—Maio, *Randazzo*, Maretto, *Bronte*, by the Simeto, *Aderno, Biancavilla*, Licodia, *Paternò*/From Paternò I may turn Northward some miles back but *f95*ᵛ by a different Road to *Centorbi, Regalbuto, S. Filippo d'Argiro*, Nissuria & Lionforte (with Asaro left on the left hand between them)—from Lionforte to make my way to *Castrogiovanni* (below Calatascibetta) to Piazza, & thro' or beside the *Bosco di Giummia* to *Calatagirone* (thence to make my way to *Mineo*, if that be Leckie's Lake-Hill, & from Mineo, if possible, to Gran Michele) N.B. from Cal. to Min.—there is a Road to Palma close by Mineo/ there are 3 ways—1. from Palma, to Palagonia, Castellana, Massaria di S. Nicola, *Lentini, Carlentini, Mililli*, SYRACUSE/2. G. Michele to Bucheri, thro' *Vizzini*, & thence straight to Syracuse/or 3. from Bucheri, Buscemi, Palazzolo, to *Noto*—and from Noto over the Casibile to Syracuse thro' Avola, and Blandini/—Or what *f96* if *Calatasibetta* I went to CALTANISETTA and thence followed the River Salso to Alicata, & went to Palma, *Naro* & GIRGENTI—& took a Sparonara from Girgenti to Syracuse/

2710 16.301   Of the ease with which Liars believe Lies, explained and applied to the French, the Sicilians, and Roman Catholics in general—

2711 16.302   The understanding of Metaphor for Reality (Loaves and Fishes = Apostles, Fisherman, Christ's Doctrine/&c &c) one of the Fountains of the many-headed River of Credulity which overflowing covers the world with miscreations & reptile *f96*ᵛ monsters, & then gives its huge supply thro' its many mouths into the Sea of Blood.

2712 16.303   To W.—in the progression of Spirit/once Simonides, or Empedocles or both in one?—O that my Spirit purged by Death of its Weaknesses, which are alas! my *identity* might flow into *thine*, & live and act in thee, & be Thou.

2713 16.304   The Story of Foscari, Son of the Doge F.—suspected of assassinating Almor Donato, one of the Council of 10, at

his own door, 5 Nov. 1450—Olivier, his footman, who had been
seen loit'ring near the House, & had fled the next day, occasioned
the suspicion/fled—but was tortured—confessed nothing/the same   *f*97
fate & result attended Foscari/who was condemned to banishment
for Life in Candia/gave a Letter to the Duke of Milan praying
his mediation/delivered by the agent to the Council of 10/Foscari
sent for—again tortured—avowed that he had given the Letter to a
known Traitor in order to be brought back in order to see his Father & Family/sent back to Candia, spite of the Doge/

Erizzo confesses on his Death bed the crime/Foscari sent for is
sent back a *Corse*/—his Father's & Mother's Darling.   *f*97ᵛ

2714 16.305   The plot of Marino Falliero, Doge of Venice, 80
years of age—to Murder the Grand Council merely to avenge an
affront offered to his *young* Wife by a young Ven. Noble/Beltrame
Bergamasco to save Nic Lioni, occasioned the Discovery—Doge
tried, & sentenced & executed/

2715 16.306   Bubalus Bison, Esqʳᵉ/ and Strenuous Inert,
                Ditto—

2716 16.307
        There ~~blooms~~ laves upon so white a Breast
        That well a Maiden's it might seem
        (I know not, if by Heaven's Behest
        Or by a longing Mother's Dream)
        A crimson Rose that shed no leaves
        ~~Yet~~ A man's large Heart beneath it heaves
        And He with the Rose on his Bosom bereaves &c/   *f*98

2717 16.308   One probable beginning of *Comedy* (in genere,
not as Greek but as of Man) I have this day (20 Novembʳ 1805)
seen just under my window at the Albergo del Sole Naples/A
Mountebank Fellow entertaining a mob—a forward Spectator, im-
pudent Boy, perhaps, interrupts him/mounts his Box/the dialogue
is found more stimulating of course than the monologue/&c &c &c
&c—/This took place & not by design/even this day—but it pro-

2718]

NOVEMBER–DECEMBER 1805

f98ᵛ duced so much more effect that tomorrow it will be by *design* & *provided*.—But o! how many other reflections did it not suggest to me—Horrible Indecency!—all of it *immorality!*—the Hor & Boy, placed often *a la Priapo*/& the Spectators, ⅔ from 12 to 17!!—Ever & ever think of that deep Epicureanism of the Papists, which now spreads as *Rationalism*, Unitarianism, &c, of fixing the whole attention on the *consequences*, not on the *nature*, & *symptomatic* charac-
f99 ter, of the action.—Inlet to Roman Catholicism in Protestant Countries/Methodists, Unitarians, Paleyans, &c &c!—And explain, & enforce this.

2718 16.309   The practical importance of religious (so called, the sustente) or philosophical i.e. truly religious *conviction* illustrated *in detail* by Λεχι. What has he to support him, animal Spirits being gone!—But they themselves are *nervous*—they always have fainting fits—they *will* die/what?—not the Stoic Pride of Virtue/that is lost in *common-sense* (i.e. pride of Ignorance)—not Xⁿ Hope/not Platonic Absorption of the Individual—or rather Individuous-matter.—

f99ᵛ 2719 16.310   Of Travellers, Sharpians, or Moorists—both bad, but the former as much better as the latter are more entertaining. Justify Sharp in parte/& REASON

2720 16.311
⟨Logic Friend of Perception!⟩
Vesuvius covered with smoke—cloud from the weight of the atmosphere/I saw on its sides two narrow streams or slips of Fire, rapidly undulating its flame-color in a fast-flowing Torrent of melted Gold or Copper/—but why begin there? why end there? I see no reason! I meditated & in that act cast my eye somewhat down/& again looking up, with an altered angle, perceived that it was two Pennants waving on this side the Bay, Logic the Friend of
f100 Perception. Q.E.D. There were 5 Masts, & two only had Pennants. These by splendor of reflection were thrown back upon the next intervening great object—Vesuvius—by the laws that regulate Distance.

2721 16.312   O how like Vesuvius to Skiddaw from the A. di Sole/& from the Bay on Ship-board & *close to it*, how like Rowling End to Grisedale Pike.

2722 16.313   Ready Command of a limited number of words = playing Cat-cradle dexterously with Language.

2723 16.314   A man's Imagination fitfully awaking & sleeping = the odd metaphors & no metaphors of modern poetry/Language in its first state without the *inventive* passion.

2724 16.315   Battle of Books/well! so a Battle of *Miracles* Catholic, Mahometan, Pagan. Metaphors mistaken for Reality one   *f*100ᵛ of the Springs of the many-headed Nile of Credulity, which in its Inundations having covered the Land with *miscreations* feeds by its many mouths the Sea of Blood.

2725 16.316   Plain contra-reasoning = fist-boxing/fierce Controversy is = boxing with cestuses i.e. lead-loaded Gloves—Virg. Æneid. But the Stiletto! but the envenomed Stiletto!—is there what worse (a *Germanism*) Yes! the poisoned Italian Glove of mock-friendship!

2726 16.317   God knows, that at times I derive a comfort even from my infirmities, my sins of omission & commission, in the joy of the deep feeling of the opposite Virtues in the two or three   *f*101 whom ⟨I love⟩ in my Heart of Hearts/Sharp therefore is the pain when I find faults in these Friends, opposite to my Virtues. I find no comfort in the notion of *average* for I wish to love even more than to be beloved & am so haunted by the conscience of my many Failings that I find an unmixed pleasure in esteeming & admiring, but in Esteem & Admiration I feel as a man whose good dispositions are still alive feels in the enjoyment of a *darling* Property on a doubtful Title. My instincts are so far dog-like/I love beings superior to me better than my Equals—but inferior is so painful to me, that I never in common Life, feel a man my Inferior except   *f*101ᵛ by after-reflection. What seems vanity in me is in great part attributable to this Feeling but of this hereafter I will cross examine myself.

2727 16.318   There are Actions which not done mark the greater man; but wͨh done do not imply a bad or mean man/Such as Martial's Compliments of Domitian/Dryden as opposed to Milton. By the bye we are too apt to forget, that Contemporaries have not the same *wholeness & fixedness* in their notions of persons characters that we their posterity have. They can *hope* & *fear* & *believe* & *disbelieve*/we make up an ideal, which like the Fox in the Fable or Lion, never changes. Ours is a Novel founded on Fact.

f102   2728 16.319   Modern Poetry characterized by the Poets ANXIETY to be always *striking*—The same march in the Greek & Latin Poets/Claudian, who had powers to have been any thing—observe in him the anxious craving Vanity! every Line, nay, every word *stops,* looks full in your face, & asks & *begs* for Praise. A Chinese Painting no distances no perspective/all in the fore-ground/and this is all *Vanity.* I am pleased that when a mere Stripling I had formed the opinion, that true Taste, was Virtue—& that bad writing was bad feeling.

f102ᵛ   2729 16.320   Instead of the Tale out of Burton/a wild story of Ceres's loss of Proserpine, and her final recovery of her by means of X̲ when he descended into Hell, at which time she met him & abjured all worship for the future/Conversion of a Heathen Goddess.—Mythol. that the Gods of Greece & Rome were some of the *Best* of the fallen Spirits—some were *converted* (Apollo & the Muses) & *Mars* became a favorite—How they became different Saints—Vide—Middleton's Letter from Rome.

2730 16.321   What a difficult Language the English (said an Italian to Capᵗ. Pasley)—4 words all pronounced the same/Ship, *f103*   Sheep, Chip, Cheap/adding to each the Italian Translation

2731 16.322   The Girl at Virgil's Tomb/E un pecccato [*peccato*]/Sono sfortunato assai nel avere un Confessore al quanto severo/The little darling Girl at Salerno—Non o Sento/what then? *Noi tutti/*!—Two wooden Images of Purgatory large as Life, with wooden Flames—the one with a *poor box* in its hand/—this over the Mantle piece of the Family Room.

2732 16.323   Thrasybulus, Demosthenes &c explain the conversational nature of the compound Epithets among the Greeks/—So we too if we had retained Praise-God-Barebones &c

2733 16.324   *Elliot!*—his Daughter (9 or 10 years old) her *f103ᵛ* sour looks, & choice of Delicacies. I think, that perhaps 20 dishes pass round the Table/this does, this does not please her palate.

2734 16.325   ⟨Minim Midge Esqʳᵉ married to Miss Thomasina Tit by the Reverend Leviathan Mammoth.⟩

2735 16.326   Of the sense of Light, the Eyeslids being shut, as when one fastens one's eye-lids, while puffing at a wood-fire to call out a flame/or when being half-a-sleep, we refuse to open them, on the entrance of the Candles/&c &c/—the effect on the images accidentally present to the mind at that instant, &c &c

2736 16.327   The Cross of the Mariners at Corfu, & to re-question C. Gregg as to the particulars.

2737 16.328   History of Heath: Gods wanting as a phil: *f104* School-book/how entertaining it would be, if it were only truly instructive. Boccacio *Genealogia*/Bacon &c &c—and Middleton's Letter from Rome/

2738 16.329   The system & coherency as well as the individual *meaning* of the Pagan Idols compared with the Catholic/indeed prefer the African Fetisches to them.

2739 16.330   Pan, Syrinx/Disappointment turning sensual into purer pleasures—disapp: Lust by regret, refining into Love & ending in Harmony.

f81   2740 15.177   What ~~is~~ was the Price of Corn in the first year of *Sir A. B.'s* Administ/the second? the third?—And what have been the prices in the Corresponding Years in Italy and Sicily?

2741 15.178   View of the ⟨Mountain⟩ cut or delved into projecting Hills bulging with deep intervenient Hills/on a kind of long ascending vale or semi-plain about midway the mountain a spacious Town/and below, up to the right on the summit of one of these bulging Hills, a Castle & Tower/seen from the black plain of Lava Sands on which the Troops were reviewed—at Torre d'Annunziata—Walls of the newest blackest Lava enclosing fields

f81ᵛ   of the same—on our journey to the place several Tombs.

2742 15.179   A *Jacket* of Stuff, of green commonly a stiff petticoat—a short apron and sandals = a *thick* wooden Sole, fastened over the instep by a strap of Leather so broad as just to permit the point of ⌂ the toes to appear uncovered save by the stocking. The Hair plaited and turned up ⟨often intertressed with silk Rope⟩ large & curious ear-rings. Little ~~children~~ girls as soon as they can walk drest exactly like their Mothers & elder Sisters—Women of Torre d'Annunziata

2743 15.180   Last day of Nov. 1805 from Naples to d'Annunziata & Castello del Mare/1 Dec. to Salerno.

f160ᵛ   2744 18.318   From Naples to Messina, along the Coast. Naples to Vietri/Road $\overset{+}{}$ good, Inn $\overset{=}{}$ tolerable. 28 Miles
(N.B. *R* signifies Road. *I* Inn. — , the Algebraic Symbol of negation signifies bad (Evil according to some of the Schoolmen, & to the Platonists, subsisting in negation: consequently the Devil himself may be painted too black, as the Proverb very profoundly observes, for Evil being Negation, if he were all evil, he would be nothing at all, which is a contradiction in terms—tho' perhaps the Priests were playing bo-peep with their Consciences, & by calling the Devil absolute Evil meant at once to *tell* the Truth & to convey

a Lie—holding up the Dæmon *Outis* in terrorem plebis—/—But
if we believe his Existence (as woe to him who does not, *adiabolism*
being co-ordinate in guilt of Heterodoxy ~~to~~ with *Atheism*, if indeed the latter be not subordinated to the former, as the common
phrase "He believes neither God, nor Devil" seems to imply)—:   *f161*
if, I say, the Devil exist, he must have some good Qualities; &
among these I should reckon meekness, patience, & long-suffering
—for no one denies him to be ~~both~~ bold *as a Lion* ("he goeth
about as a Lion, says Holy Writ")—and yet how quietly does he
suffer himself to be abused by the Hour together by Priests of all
Religions, except perhaps the Devil-worshippers in Africa & India/
—quietly & unresentingly/for to attribute the fiery and swoln
Noses of many of the dignified Clergy to their having been *pulled*
by the Devil is diving as low down as Hell for a reason which
might be found by ~~merely~~ diving ~~as low as~~ no lower than the
Cellar—/~~indeed he~~ To these may be added kind-heartedness—in
suffering himself to be the Scape-goat, ~~to every man~~ on which
~~he~~ each man lays all his follies & vices, and sends them off into
the unknown Wilderness—but this is a digression ex diverticulo   *f161ᵛ*
igitur in *viam*.
R signifies Road, I Inn. — signifies bad, —! very bad, + signifies
good, = middling or tolerable. ∧ signifies

		Miles
Naples to Vietri.	R +, I = :	28
Vietri to Supino	R +, I — :	30

(N.B. about half way between V and S. you pass outside Ebboli,
where there is a tolerable Inn.)

Supino to Auletta,	R ∧, I = :	8
Auletta to Sala	R ∧, I — :	46
Sala to Largo Negro	R ∧! I + :	24

The I is at the Post nicknamed *Mylords*.

Largo Negro to Rotonda. R —!! ∧ !!   27
This infamously bad & steep road is the worst between Naples &
Messina/it comprehends two posts. It is utterly impracticable for
a carriage/the Post-houses are at the miserable town of Castelluccio
and Auria—slept at the Cavʳ Girardo di Renaldis, who is kind   *f162*
without parade.

Rotonda to Castrovillari thro' the Campo Danese over a high mountain generally covered with Snow/the Road in some places =, in others —!

	Miles
No Inn in the Place but a bad public Stable—	16
Castrovillari to Cassano R =	8
Cassano to the Cassino of its Duke	4
Cassano to Cassino di Albenante :	26

N.B. Road +. Pass two Rivers in a Cart drawn by two Oxen/pass close to the Casino of the Duke of Corregliano, 16 miles, & within a mile of the towns of Corregliano (where there is a large Fair for Cattle on the 26 April, & 6 May) and Rossano, the latter 22 miles, a Priest, Bruinher, received us with hospitality. From Cassino di Albinante to the Cassino di Sign^r Michele Zito, passing the —! town of Carriati at 24 miles, Road = .   36 Miles

f104   2745 16.331   Naples, 2nd Lodging, 14 Dec. 1805.

2746 16.332   How affecting to read Ficinus's Prefaces to the Medici & compare them with the present Day.

f104^v 2747 16.333   Many a man's Secret Harm (to some favored Beings secret even to themselves) may be discovered by observing where they place their hand or hands when lost in thought, or vacant/& What is their commonest posture in Sleep.

2748 16.334   Sunday, 15 Dec. 1805—Naples/view of Vesuvius in the Hail mist/Torre Greca bright amid darkness, & the Mountains above it flashing here & there from their snows; but Vesuvius —it had not *thinned* as I have seen at Keswick (ah me!) but the air had so consolidated with the massy Cloud Curtain, that it appeared like a Mountain in basso relievo or an interminable wall of some Pantheon/

2749 16.335   Conceive an Eruption/two parts of the mountain visible, one a large circular space flashing sun-light from the Snows, f105   the other a straight Line from the Top to the Bottom, like a river, walled on each side with mist colored by the fire & ceiled by the Smoke.

2750 16.336

> Verecundia? imo, tyrannis hoc est!
> Quod cuivis adulor, negabis ipse;
> Nec non quod sapiam, haud negabis. Ergo
> Mores, et Sophiam, sacrasque Musas
> Uno nomine (dumque vivis ipse.)
> Dicturum, Gulielme—quæso, ~~quare~~ cur me, et
> ~~Quo me~~ Et quo Jure tuum "veto" coercet?
> Te vatem, atque Sophum, meumque ※ Regem
> Agn~~osceo~~ovi, ecce, ⟨usque⟩ lubens! at haud Tribunum.

※ Rex meus for the most honored Friend/Vide Martial, v.22. et passim.

2751 16.337   Lincoln! Aye—you may well call it Lincoln; for I was never so bit with Fleas in any place, in my whole Life.

2752 15.181   Antonio di Marco/Giustina Manilla/⟨Children⟩ ƒ82
—Giovanni, Josiello, Giacomo, Maria, Elisabetha, Felice, Anna/—
Uncle—Gaietano [*Gaetano*] de Faodis, Fortunata Manilla (& her Sister Giustina) Joanne, Matteo de Faodis—Deodata, Theresa, Grazia, Carmela/

2753 15.182   To notice with indignation the fortnightly Lotteries at Naples.

2754 15.183   Mem. The Pudels, who are genuine, have long [?depending/dependant] whiskers.

2755 15.184

~~Ἀλκαιον~~ Πίττακον, αγάσυρτον, ζοφοδορπιδαν ⟨blink-eye⟩
Χειροποδην ⟨split-foot⟩, σάραπον, σαραποδα ⟨drag-foot or broad foot/⟩
φύσκωνα ⟨πot-gut⟩, γάστρωνα, καὶ γαυρικα ⟨self-puffed⟩
      Blackguardisms of Alcæus.

2756 15.185

f82ᵛ Nouvelle Mappe Monde dédiée au progrès de nos connoissances. Hemisphere Maritime/Hem: Terrestre.

On presente cette Nouvelle Mappe Monde comme pouvant être utile per l'étude de la Geographie e pour la Theorie de la Terre, en plaçant sous un meme point de vue les quatre parties du monde, que l'on a désunies jusqu'a présent quoique la Nature les ait rassemblées sous un meme Hemisphere, en ne laissant dans l'autre qu'une pointe de l'Amerique singulierement brisée; et les mers continues semées de quelques isles, et de terrains Isolés peu considerables en comparaison des notres.

f83 La regularité ou meme l'espece d'affectation avec laquelle les grandes continens de l'Amerique et de l'Asie côtoyent le cercle qui les separe des mers de l'Hemisphere opposé est telle que l'on ne peut gueres la regarder comme un pur effet du Hazard. Mais plustôt comme une disposition consequente du quelque Loy Physique; et de quelques uns de ces faits de la Nature que nous ignorons. C'est ainsi un nouveau probleme dans la Theorie de la Terre que cette Mappemonde offre aux Physiciens de nos Jours dont le solution ne peut etre que fort interessant.

f83ᵛ C'est ancore une singularité fort grand que ce ne soit que sous le seul meridien de Paris et par un plan entre l'Equateur et l'Axe de la Terre que notre Globe puisse nous donner des spectacles aussi differens, &c &c. Cette proprieté est une sorte de preeminence qui doit a l'avenir le faire regarder comme le Premier meridien, sans l'Arc n'est point dans notre imagination, n'est pour ainsi dire dans la Nature—&c &c—

Mola di Gaeta/26 Dec. 1805. a map evidently in the first years of the Revolution/published at Venice/or republished.

2757 15.186   On descending the long winding Hill, into the vale like Sad. from Sᵗ John's—only you see it over the round back of a Hill below you/heard the first sweet Bird's Song, I plucking *f84* flowers. Passing the Battery Corn sown on the tops of ridges, entering the beautiful Vale of Fondi/—26 Dec. & Trees in their richest Autumnal Hues!—the Apennines round Hills—rising into sugar loaf Points/beautiful Orange Orchards on entering Fondi/trees so

large, and lofty & many full of fruits—[. . . .] Romantic round
Tower at projecting Battlements of Fondi/to the left in the very
distance the Appenines which end in the rock of Granite [. . .]
close to the Sea, of ~~one~~ [. . . .]

2758 15.187   From Naples Xmas Day, 1805—to 1 Aversa. 2.   ƒ84ᵛ
Capua/

2759 15.188   Dec. 31, 1805—Visited the Chiesa dellà [della]
Trinità de' Monti/vide Vasi; 1.227./—all completely ruined by the
Neapolitans when in Rome/most of the pictures annihilated, and
the famous Deposizione of Daniel da Volterra, left enough of to
excite one's deepest Horror of these Wretches.

2760 15.189   In the Cloisters all the French Kings & in the intervals blasphemous Pictures of the Miracles of Sᵗ Paolo Fr. de
Paola, out-Jesusing Jesus—among them close by the porch way "Sᵗ
Fr. de Paula Nativitas, celesti Splendore illustrata An. Ch. 1116"—
immediately under which is the oval opening of a Kitchen which   ƒ85
has so compleatly smoke-blacked the Splendor, that you can barely
perceive it to be a picture—
    Stopping ⟨falling⟩ Rocks, curing Lepers, opening Eyes with Spit-
tle, &c &c &c &c!!!!

2761 15.1   Pachiarretti   ƒ1

2762 15.3   Machines = Ballast tanks which by particular   ƒ2ᵛ
marks arising from the depth of the Barge determines the Quan-
tity/and on which a particular Duty/
    Ladzarette Duties, the In-equity of deriving from bulk

2763 15.4   To remember to send to Mʳ [?H] the seed of the   ƒ3
Nasturtium and—

2764 16.409   The Irishman who put his Burthen on his own   ƒ130ᵛ
Shoulders lest he should overload his Ass—
thro' the [?Shrouds]—from the North of Ireland, your Honour

2765 16.411

> 2 pr Stockings
> 3 Cravats
> 3 Shirts
> 1 pr of Drawers
> 1 und. waist
> 5 Handkerchiefs

f131   2766 16.412   When the moon waxes its $)$ has its back to the Right Hand/waning C to the Left.

2767 16.413   Brandy palpably affects my Breathing—

2768 16.414   *Bartel's* Reise durch Kalabrien &c

2769 22.136

f76ᵛ

Νωθον ὁ 'ἀλκστ βι μαν
Θατ ραππ ιν θις λεδμαν
῾Ατ ους ἀς ΑΔΙΕΜΑΝ
Λιες ἐρε νου α Δεαδμας
Θω ους Αλειφ, α βρᾶφ Μαγγτορ, γετ νου ις α με—
οφ ουρ ποορ Αλλ
Θε σουλ Βεινγ γον, 'Ε ις νου μηρλι Κορπορ.

2770 22.137   On a Gentleman's Grove was written Chastenut Grove/I justified the Spelling by the Latin Castanea, & it reminded me of the whimsical Latin Charade of Ariosto from the original Italian of Florio Angelo Monosinio/

> Arbos inest sylvis, quo scribitur octo figuris
> Fine tribus deruptis vix unam e mille videbis/

Which I imitated thus paraphrastically

Fair ~~Wood nymph~~ Nymph of the Forest, nor fairer than good
Sweet Wood Nymph, what art thou, I whisper'd & what is thy name,
And the ~~Wood~~ Wood Nymph made ~~answ reply~~ answer/Thro' the whole of this wood

Scarce one in a Thousand, that is not the same,   *f*77
Is there We're a Thousand to one all around you the same
Tis We've a name of 8 Letters, but ah! cut off the last three,
And alas in a Thousand scarce one will you see
It's but one in a Thousand—if e'en one you should see.

───────

Yet between us one Likeness remains, let the Name
Be eight Letters or five, still our fate's much the same
We are thrown to the Swine, save a few that are roasted
They
Yet not, O ye nine hundred, & ninety nine left
Between them and me some resemblance is left us & you is all
    Likeness bereft/
We are thrown to the Swine, save a few the best that are *roasted*
They You belong to horn'd Cattle, & the fairest being are *toasted*

2771   22.138
            On the De Epitaph on Major Dieman.

Know thou who walk'st by, Man! That enwrapp'd up in lead, man
What once was a Dieman, Now lies here a Dead man:
Alive, a proud MAJOR! but ah me! of oŭr poŏr ăll
The Soul being gone, he is now merely *Corporal.*

            ───────
            On the above.
    As long as e'er the Life-blood's running,
    Say, what can stop a Punster's Punning?
    He dares bepun even thee, O Death!
    To *pun*ish him stop thou his Breath.

2772   22.139
            On Fetid who died of a Catarrh.   *f*77°

Thee, Fetid! oft did armed Death attack,
As oft thou mad'st thy hungry King famin'd Foe draw back.
Thy Breath was dread, as Dragon's in Romance,
And carried farther than Death's missile Lance.
Ah! Whence then hear we then now at length thy Death-bell
    Knelling?

~~One March Night having had long time prowl'd without~~
~~Then enter'd suddenly a crowded Rout,~~
~~Has~~ Did Death ~~caught~~ too catch a Cold, & ~~los~~tose his sense of
Smelling!
His Wife ~~would not believe that~~ not crediting ~~that~~ he had died,
~~And let his Corse unburied still~~ Let ~~her~~ sweet FETID coffinless
remain,
Till when at length the ~~Carcase~~ putrified,
She haply wandering in a neighbouring Lane
Stops, ~~starts,~~ then shouts aloud—O Joy! he *breathes* again!

---

f78   "Sweet Fetid dead! No, No!" The Thought so shock'd her
His Widow would not in the House ~~remain abide~~
~~But still sought help with grief bewilder'd brain,~~ All grief-be-
wilder'd still she sought the Doctor
~~Ere she return But ere~~ she could return, he putrefied
And stepping o'er the Threshhold, ~~with the Doctor~~ wild of brain
~~She sniff'd~~ the air, then scream'd Joy! Joy! he *breathes* again!

"Sweet Fetid dead! No—No!" The Thought so shock'd her
His Widow would not in the House abide,
All grief-bewilder'd still she sought the Doctor—
Ere she return'd, her sweet Love putrefied—
And stepping o'er her Thresh-hold, wild of brain,
She sniff'd the air, then scream'd—Joy! Joy! he *breathes* again!

2773   22.140

f77ᵛ   On Gripe-all

One pitch-black Night there knock'd at Gripe-all's door
One who had sav'd his Life the year before,
Benighted now, way-wilder'd, tir'd, athirst.—
And Gripe-all let him in, not much unwilling,
f78   But from the window drove a bargain first,
And took the weary Pilgrim's only Shilling.
That night old Gripe-all dreamt, he had lost his Pelf—
~~Bare~~ Walk'd in his Sleep, & ~~dreaming~~ hung himself. ~~poor a~~
dream-distemper'd Elf,

And dreaming in good earnest hung himself.
His Soul and Corse are pent-up here below/
And this, they say, his Punishment & Fate is,
To lie awake, & ~~every hour~~ all day-long to know,
How many thousands read this *Tomb-stone gratis.*

2774 22.141   1. ~~Draw~~ an horizontal Line at ~~the~~ bottom of the   *f78*
Paper. 2. bisect it. 3. Alzate un ~~perpendicolare~~. 4. E Poi fate un
quadrato perfetto. 5. Poi ad ~~arbitrio~~ fissate il punto di vista. 6. Suppose you were drawing ~~a brick pavement~~, divide ~~it accurately into
equal parts or squares~~—digradano—fanno la sua digradazione/

2775 22.142   A poor chimney wretch fit to consort with Kitch-   *f82*
enists of all sorts, Salamanders to wit, Swallows, Bacon-flitches,
dried Pilchards, still drier Stock-fish, and red Herrings.—

2776 22.143   a poor good-man tell-clock

2777 22.144, 145 πολυφλοισβοιο θαλασσης = the *voiceful* Sea.

"As woo'd by May's delights I have been borne
    To take the kind air of a wistful morn
    Near Tavy's *voiceful* stream, to whom I owe
    More strains than from my pipe can ever flow."
        Brown's Britannia's Pastorals, *Song* iv.

2778 22.146
    The Daisy scatter'd on each mead and down,   *f84*
    A golden tuft within a silver crown—
    (Fair fall that dainty Flower! and may there be
    No Shepherd grac'd, that doth not honor thee!)
        Brown's Britannia's Pastorals, Song iii.

2779 22.149
                1 & 2   *f86*

    Of all the Tombs of Victims pack'd
    Close in the Church-yard, this (strange fact!)

Much grief must wake, much gladness win.
O ~~Joy! Jane was the last attack'd~~ For after
Jane were none attack'd
O ~~Grief!~~ But ah! Jane Burr is *not* within.

3

The yellow Fiend in Lust and Pride
Would clasp a Fury as his Bride,
And met his last Hour clasping HER
So of the Plague seven Thousand died,
And the Plague died of fierce Jane Burr—
S.T.C.

This Tombstone is sacred to the Relicts of Jane Burr—one time
or other/how soon Heaven knows/&c &c/the whole 1ˢᵗ Stanza re-
written, in two.

ƒ86ᵛ   ~~Amid this Waste of crowded Graves~~
                    ~~Where lie Contagion's Victim Slaves~~
                    ~~This Tomb with Grief & Joy must win~~/

On the Family ~~Tomb~~ Vault of the Burrs, a notorious Lady of
whose Household was the last person ~~attacked by the Pestilence~~
who caught the ~~Gibraltar~~ Fever at New York but recovered.

                    ~~Here near that From off yonder~~
                    For by that Town by Fever sack'd
                    Here of all
                    Where lie Contagions Victims pack'd
                    In all the Yard—This Tomb—strange Fact
                    This Tomb both Grief and Joy must win
                    Great Grief must wane, great Joy must win
                    ~~For Fien~~ O Joy! Jane Burr the last attacked
                    ~~That Fierce~~ But O Grief! Jane is *not* within
                    ~~Tis true grown vain with victor's pride~~
                    The yellow Fiend ~~dank clasp even he~~ in Lust & Pride
                    Would clasp a Fury as his Bride
ƒ87ᵛ   And the Plague died of fierce Jane Burr.
                                        S.T.C.

2780 22.162   The Child is born, the Child must die/Among the   *f89*
desert Sands/And we too all must die of Thirst/for not a Drop remains. But whither do we retire/to Heaven or possibility of
Heaven/But this to darkness, Cold, & tho' not positive Torment,
yet positive Evil—Eternal Absence from Communion with the
Creator. O how often have the [. . .] Sands at night roar'd &
whitened like a burst of of waters/O that indeed they were! Then
full of enthusiastic faith kneels & prays, & in holy frenzy covers the   *f88ᵛ*
child with sand. In the name of the Father &c &c/—Twas done/
the Infant died/the blessed Sand retired, each particle to itself,
conglomerating, & shrinking from the profane sand/the Sands
shrank away from it, & left a pit/still hardening & hardening, at
length shot up a fountain large & mighty/
How wide around its Spray, the rain-bow played upon the Stream   *f88*
& the Spray—but lo! another brighter, O far far more bright/it
hangs over the head of a glorious Child like a floating veil (vide
Raphael's God)—the Soul arises/they drink, & fill their Skins, &
depart rejoicing—O Blessed the day when that good man & all his
Company came to Heaven Gate & the Child—then an angel—
rushed out to receive them—

2781 18.4   The old gentleman at Edingburgh that wakes   *f2*
half an hour before Dinner to give a [. . . .] eat six whole ones
"It is a savour. I've eat six of them & I an't a bit hungrier than
when I begun—"

2782 18.5   She is "Fearfully & wonderfully made!"—

2783 18.6   3 is seven and twenty times more than 4!—
    Solution of this mystery. 111 is 27 times more than 4, for 27 ×
4 = 111.—and thrice two—six? No! but 222!!—How clever! Yet
I have seen logic very like it: for what matters it whether the pun
be between Letters & Cyphers, or Cyphers & Cyphers—or between
sounds and sounds/In both the same Symbol is used in two different Senses.

2784 16.338   Σωμα ψυχοπλαστον   Ψυχη σωμαπλαττουσα   *f105*
Reo = reor probably an obsolete Latin word, and res the second
person singular of the Present Indicative—If so, it is the Iliad of   *f105ᵛ*

Spinozo-Kantian, Kanto-Fichtian, Fichto-Schellingian Revival of Plato-Plotino-Proclian Idealism in a Nutshell *from* a Lilliput Hazel. Res = thou art thinking.—Even so our "Thing": id est, thinking or think'd. Think, Thank, Tank = Reservoir of what has been *thinged*—Denken, Danken—I forget the German for Tank/ The, Them, This, These, Thence, Thick, Thing, Thong, Thou, may be all Hocus-pocused by metaphysical Etymology into Brothers and Sisters—with many a Cousin-German/All little Miss Thetas, the ⊙ being a Circle, with the Kentron [*Kentrum*], or central Point, creating the circumference & both together the infinite Radii/ —the Central point is primary Consciousness = living Action; the circumference = secondary Consciousness ⟨or Consc: in the common sense of the word⟩ and the passing to and fro from the one to the other Thought, Things, necessary Possibilities, contingent Realities/ = Father, Son, Holy Ghost/the To Oν, Ο Λογος, η Σοφια/— The • is I which is the articulated Breath drawn inward, the O is the same sent outward, the ⊙ or Theta expresses the synthesis and coinstantaneous reciprocation of the two Acts, the Dualism of *Thought* by *Distinctions,* the Unity of *Thing* by Indivisibility/ and then the Radii, Ακτῖνες = Res in Theta (or perhaps Delta) = Αγω (acta) εν θητα (or Tau)—(O Lord! What thousands of Threads in how large a Web may not a Metaphysical Spider spin out of the Dirt of his own Guts/but alas! it is a net for his own super-ingenious Spidership alone! It is so thin that the most microscopical Minitude of ~~the minutest Midge~~ Midge or Sand-flea—so far from being detained in it—passes thro' without seeing it.—) These Words within the Crotchets—are Truth for the Worldlings, all without ⟨are⟩ Crotchets with a Vengeance ⟨to them⟩ but to me those Words are the Crotchets, the capapee Masquerade Domino of my own Convictions in the Opinions of the men of supposed gesunder Menschenverstand/the former are the naked Flesh & Blood, Bone and Muscle of my ⟨own⟩ individual Faith/

Rome—Jan. 1. 1806. Monday.

f106

f85   2785 15.190   1 Jan. 1806. Heard from Mr Jackson of the arrival of the French at Rome, to be expected on the 5th/To stay or not to stay—

2786 15.191   5 Jan. 1806—Santa Maria Maggiore/glorious
[. . .] in the right hand colonnade a picture of a Hermit ascetic
with his Hand resting on a book holding a Death's Head, & an
angel in the Clouds *fiddling* to him./

2787 15.192   Power misapplied = the Light of the Sun, which
falling on the eye would give the image of a human angel, or Or-   *f85ᵛ*
ange Tree full of green Leaves, and snow-white blossoms, and
Fruit both shagren and golden, falling on the nostrils makes—a
Sneeze!

2788 15.193   Log = promise of good in evil, (or + in −)/it is
slimy-wet at the ends (or outlets) because it is burning in the center.

2789 15.194   Mackenzie—Whirlwind in his Skirts

2790 15.195   ein Blitz der Seligkeit von Gottes Throne durch
mein Wesen, als ich sie wiedersah.

2791 15.196
2. Field inward flew a little Bird and poising herself in a column of
Sunshine/1. on a day when the Sky had but few lines & openings
of Blue/3. Sang with a sweet and marvellous voice. 4. Adieu!
adieu! I must away—5. Far far away! 6. I must set off to-day.

IInd

1. I listen'd to this sweet, strange song,
   Listen'd and gaz'd—Sight of a bird! Sound of a voice!
2. It went so well with me   mir war so wohl und doch so
   bang
   With gladsome Pain, with painful Gladsomeness.   *f86*
   Alternate rose and sank my Bosom/
5. Heart! Heart!
6. Breakst Thou for Joy or Smart?—

3

1. Yet, when I saw the Leaves fall, and all was cloudy,
2. Then said I, Ah! Autumn is here/

3. The Swallow, the Summer Bird, is gone/
4. And so will my Beauty fall, like the Leaves,
5. From my pining in Absence/
6. And so will his love fly away, like the Swallow—Away!
Away!
Swift as to day.

4

But lo! again came down the column of Sunshine,
And close by me pois'd in the column sang the sweet Bird
again—
And looking in my tearful face
Sang
        Love has no winter/
No! No! No!—It is ever true & is always Spring—

2792 15.197   Peter descendant of Lorenzo di Med. made Michaelagnolo make a *statue of Snow*, one snowy winter—good Sim. for men of Genius in Pamphlets and Newspapers.—

f86ᵛ 2793 15.198   The Sun when you gaze at it, dazzle-blinds you/ When you acknowlege its presence (know it by the absolute faith of habitual deduction, so rapid as to become identical with the stand-still of Intuition)—(= a wheel in its maximum of motion equal in the consciousness to Rest/there being no perceptible time between its being A (and) B)—all things become clear by it/—acknowlege the cause & avail yourself of its Effects.

f106ᵛ 2794 16.339   "He works too much with the Pipe in his mouth —looks too much at the particular Thing, instead of overlooking— ubersehen [*übersehen*]."—*Alston*/Thursday, Feb. 15. 1806.

2795 16.340   ⟨Trajano Wallis 10. anni⟩

2796 16.341   To conceive an idea of Olevano you must first imagine a round bason formed by a circle of mountains, the diameter of the Valley about 15 or 16 miles/These mountains all connected and one; but of very various heights, and the lines in which they sink and rise of various Sweep and Form, sometimes so high as to have no visible superior behind, sometimes letting in upon

the Plain one Step ~~behind~~ above them from behind, sometimes
two, and three; and in one place behind the third a bald bright   *f107*
Skull of a mountain (for the Snow that wholly covered it lay so
smooth & shone so bright in the Sun, that ~~it~~ the whole suggested
the idea of a polished Skull, and the Snow seeming rather a property or attribute than an accident or adjunct rendered the baldness
more intense rather than diminished it./

The other higher mountains that looked in from behind on the
bason with more or less command were lit up with snow-relicts,
scarcely distinguishable from Sunshine on bare and moist rock opposed to deep Shade, save when (as often happened) both the one
and the other were seen at the same time, when they formed one
of the gentlest diversities possible, and yet the distinction evident   *f107ᵛ*
and almost obvious—How exquisitely *picturesque* this effect is (in
the strictest sense of the word) Mʳ Alston has proved in his Swiss
Landskip, of which it is not too much to say—quam qui non amat,
illum omnes et Musæ et Veneres odere.—The vale itself is diversified with a multitude of Rises, from Hillocks to Hills, and the
~~northern~~ Eastern Side of the ⟨circular⟩ mountain Boundary ~~runs~~
vaults down into the vale in Leaps, forming Steps.—⟨The first⟩
Hills ~~that~~ sink to rise into ⟨a⟩ higher Hills that sinks to rise into a
yet higher and the mountain boundary itself is the fifth Step.—On
the third Step, which is broad and heaves in many Hillocks, some   *f108*
bare & like Cairns, some green, stands Olevano, its old ruinous
Castle with church-like Tower cresting the height of this third
Step/the town runs—down the Ridge in one narrow Line almost
like a Torrent of Houses; and where the last House ends, more
than half of the whole ridge, a narrow back of bare jagged grey
rock commences, looking like the ruins of a Town/a green field
finishes the ridge, which passes into the vale by a Copse of young
Oaks/one different heights on other Steps ~~and do~~ or other Hills
the towns of Civitella, Pagliano, Avita, Santo Spirito ~~all~~ stick like
Eagle-nests, or seem as if the rock had chrystallized into those
forms/but how shall I describe the beauty of the ~~rounds~~ roads,
winding up the different Hills, now lost & now re-appearing in
different arcs & segments of Circles—how call up before you those   *f108ᵛ*
different masses of Smoke over the vale—I count 10 from this one
point of view ⟨for they are burning weeds⟩ in different distances,

now faint now vivid, now in shade & now their exquisite blue glittering in Sunshine/~~but~~ Our House stands by itself, about a quarter of a mile from the Town and its steep Ridge, on a level Ridge a little lower than it.—This description I have written, standing or sitting on the ~~step~~ breast of the fourth Step, or that height ~~into~~ which ⟨immediately commands⟩ Olevano.—But from our House we look down into the Vale of Valleys—for so it may well be called, for the whole Vale heaves and swells like a Plate of cut

frog and knobby Glass, or a Spread of wood knotty and at the same time blistered/for the higher & larger Ranges of Hills include as in a plain a multitude of smaller elevations, swells, and ridges, which from a great Height appear as one expanse—even as a stormy Sea might appear from a Balloon; but lower down you see the Landbillows—& when in the Vale you are in a Labyrinth of sweet Walks, glens, green Lanes, with Hillsides for Hedges—some of the Hills & Hillocks wooded, some bare & pastured, several with white Cottages on their sides or summits, & one & sometimes two

frog" or three pines by the Cottage Garden Gate.

2797 16.342   What Tone to colors, chiaro-Oscuro to Light & Shade; viz. such a management of them that they form as beautiful whole, independent of the particular Images colored, lit up, or shaded.

2798 16.343
  The Winds on stern Blenkarthur's Height
    Are tyrannous and strong,
  And streaming forth unquiet Light
  From stern Blenkarthur's skiey Height
    As loud the Torrents throng!
  Beneath the Moon in silent weather
  They bind the Sky and Earth together—
  But ah! the Sky and all its Forms how quiet,
  ~~And ah~~! The Things ~~of~~ ⟨that love the⟩ Earth how full
    of Rage and Riot.

2799 16.344
  I know tis but a Dream, yet feel more anguish
  Than if 'twere Truth. It has been often so,

Must I die under it? Is no one near?
Will no one hear these stifled groans, & wake me?

2800 16.345   A sumptuous and magnificent revenge.

2801 15.199   Vino Rosso di Afile   *f86ᵛ*

2802 15.200   Torre nuovo/25 to 30 of the Peasantry weeding the new Corn, all in one file/Its brilliant variety of colors—March 6, 1806—

Monte Porcio & the fine town of Colonna cresting the bold woody Hill/18 miles from Rome   3 Capanne, Straw & Hound

2803 15.201   Il Vino Rosso di Afile   *f87*

2804 15.202   Cones

Palatana, good for the ℞—by the A's Studios

2805 15.203   "He's little, but he damn'd old"—Negro of his Pig, that he had sold.

2806 15.204

He died
In all the beauty and power of early Manhood—
Yet with such meek surrender of his Spirit
As quietly, as when the gliding Moon
Glides on into a black Cloud in mid Heaven—

2807 15.205   An History of Fools & Jesters/German Dict. a true *Sicklypaddy* of Jokes, Bulls, & funny Stories—with Notes, & a prefatory Essay on the Comic & Ludicrous, on Wit and on Humor.

A Panorama of Fables, chronologically, as before, &c.

Above all a true Pantheon of Heathen Mythology, with new Plates from the best Antiques—together with an Appendix containing a more compressed account of the Brahmen Idolatry, Tartar, Otaheitan, Northern, &c &c &c—with Plates, for the use of Schools, & young Artists—

f87ᵛ 2808 15.206 [*For drawing see plate facing next page*]

f88 2809 15.207	At Rome	6 . 29	15	6
	at Pallestrina	1	20	4
	Coach & men	12	21	6
	Genazzano to	5	24	2
	Olevano to the House	4		
	The Boy	3		

2810 15.208

f88ᵛ

Concave arch

—the Arch or recess of the Chapel/ chapel reflected with such depth in the pool with its pensile thread of ivy, with one leaf at the end/& when upright in the reflected!

f89

f89ᵛ 2811 15.209 In a figure from Life which Bonaparte ordered at Rome from an Italian Sculptor he bade him place the Lever of Archimedes in his Hand, Δος που στω.

2812 15.210   The Italian a most harmonious at least melodious
Language in the mouth of a sensible agreeably-voiced Englishman,
and the language of Love itself ~~from~~ set to the sweet tones of an
accomplished, *self-respecting,* and therefore of necessity *reflec-
tionate,* English Lady/but in the mouths of the Italians themselves
(at least 99 out of a hundred of all ranks, tho' of course more intensely in the lowest, and in the women worse than in the men) it
is beyond all comparison the most ear-insulting chaos of shrill and   *f90*
guttural, up and down, sounds that I have ever heard, tho' familiar
with the sounds of the corrupt Maltese Arabic, and the Platt-
Deutsch of the Hartz/. Rome is perhaps better than Naples, Florence &c, but bad is the best.—In the mouths of women of the Middle and lower ranks there are really no *words,* but a fusion of
sounds, the voice breaking off, *snapping* as it were, more often in
the middle, or after the first Syllable of a word, than at the end
of a word/there meaning bursting on into one virulent Variolæ
(quoad accents & tones) but quoad pauses & notes to express & fa-
cilitate the conception, the Variolæ are confluent/it is all one rough
ragged *Scab*-rough, ragged & uneven, yet still but *one.*—How in-   *f90ᵛ*
deed is it possible that persons so entirely unhabituated to reasoning, so wholly the creatures of habit and momentary passions &
impulses should talk harmoniously? Analyse the implied sense of
Harmony, & ~~it~~ the Supposition of its possibility will be found a
contradiction in Terms.—

Yet tho' ignorance, the yoke of Despotism & Priestcraft without
and of their own Passions within, and the consequent habitual un-
reasoningness, were the original cause of the Jargoning above-de-
scribed, there is no doubt that now this Jargoning re-acts, & ⟨heard
from Infancy⟩ tends to make the mind unreasoning & passionate.

I have often heard a long sentence & without its being repeated
found that I had understood it/yet for some sounds I have been   *f91*
so ear-poniarded with the physical sound, that it was like seeing
a fist that had just struck fire from your Eye.—Not so with the
French or German/

2813 15.211   Poem. Address on W. Alston's large Landscape
sent by sea to England/threnic on the perishability by accident as

well as time, & the narrow Sphere of action of Picture/Printing
yet even MSS, Homer, &c &c &c—but Apelles, Protogenes, ah
where?—Spenser's Faery Queen, vi last Books, & his Comedies/
but on what authority does this rest?—

f91   2814 15.212   Painter's Esel, in Italian Cavalletto (small
Horse) in French Chevallè, i.e. the same/is it not derived from
Esel, an Ass?

2815 15.213   To remember the fellow in the Market at Rome,
twisting the necks of near 200 Goldfinches, one after another, leaving them fluttering and gasping, he meantime chit-chatting with
a neighbour stallman, throwing his Head about, and sometimes
using the neck-twisting gesture in help of his Oratory—either
twisting them phlegmatically, his hands near his belly—sometimes
violently, both hands thrown out from him; but never intermit-
ting it.—

Oxen, Sheep &c killed in a most cruel manner in the open
Street—

Manner of milking on the Roman Farms, manus frictoria in
pudendis vaccæ.

f110   2816 16.346   March 8—1806—Olevano.
                "Non è per lui questa Arte"
                    Trajano Wallis.

2817 16.347   Sunday, March 9—Olevano—Am I at Keswick?
—The woods all peopled with Knots of Primroses, a plant which
is never seen at Rome or in the low Country/and now at 2 °clock
afternoon a thick Fall of Snow which see! how it falls on that or-
chard of Almond Trees already oversnowed with Blossoms—O
why is there no Lake? No River?—

2818 16.348   About a mile and a half from Olevano on a sand
rock beside the Road, on the as descent of the Hill, right before
you the ⟨end of the⟩ billowy vale rises all round into a circle of
Hills or Hillage, the South being low wooded Hills, the North

and North East high and indeed near Mountains—true Cumber-   *f110*
land Fells. Over the High bulging Hill on the North you see
three Ranges one behind the other still higher, on the lower of
which three stands ~~Civitella~~ Santa Vito/~~of~~ just peering over the
bulging Hill that walls the valley—close to the Right of this Hill,
divided from it by the softest descent, and ascent, the both forming a green & beautiful cultivated semicircular Sweep (like a broad
groove or flute in the Hill) and contrasted with the ragged woodiness or stoniness on ~~the~~ its either Side)—close to the right, with
only this interspace runs down that sharp Ridge, sharp as the
⟨bristling⟩ back of an enraged wild boar, the bottom jagged stones,   *f111*
running up into the Town, which occupying two thirds of the
steep strait Ridge, looks exactly ~~if~~ as the Rock had chrystallized
into that Form, & that the lower Third had been broken or im-
perfectly formed. Indeed, most of the Towns and Convents on
these bleak Heights, especially when seen thro' mists, or close beneath curtains of clouds, look like parts of the Rock, shot out in
chrystals, even as I have often seen real ~~chr~~ masses of chrystalliza-
tion look like Towns & Convents—⟨Exquisite effect of chiaro
Oscuro/⟩

2819 16.349   Sparklings countless on the Leaves of olive Trees
                 after Rain/

2820 16.350   Genoa/4 Olives/in the middle of them a round
Hole dug, in this Ropes & all sorts of woole~~ns~~, and woolen or   *f111*
greasy Rags, buried & covered over/the Rain ferments it, sets it on
a smothering heat or fire, & the ground & the Roots drink in ~~its~~
the Richness. This Mr Robert Sloane told me, whose Father had
sent *in one year* upwards of a million of pound weight of such Rags
to Emanuel Austin Mainero of Voltri, near Genoa/—and every
year ~~near~~ more than half that quantity

2821 16.351   About a quarter of a mile on, (near two miles
from Olevano, and on your left as you approach it) a ruined

House, from whose inner ~~wal~~ Ruins you have a very impressive
View of the deep deep Vale, with noise of unseen Waters (it has
been 3 days Rain) and its concave back sloping huge high wall,
f112   forming half an Ellipse 〰 with what bulges, inequali-
ties, Ridges, cultivation and varieties of cultivation, bareness &
variety of Bareness. But I notice it chiefly because from this Ruin,
in a direct Line above & behind the Ridge, crested by the Castle of
Olevano, rises the Town of Civitella, which in like manner crests
the bleak high grey Rock, which shuts out all further distance, and
seems to live with the Horizon. Tho' ⟨these Towns are⟩ three
miles distant, the interval ~~it~~ seems only like a great notch in the
Ridge/

2822 16.352   The *ribbed flame*/its snatches of impatience that
half seem & only seem that half, to baffle its upward rush/the in-
f112ᵛ   tense unity of individualities whose whole essence is in their dis-
tinguishableness/even as thoughts & fancies in the mind/the points
of so many cherubic swords, snatched back but never discouraged,
still fountaining upward/flames self-snatched up heavenward if
~~heaven~~ Earth supply the fuel, heaven the dry light air/themselves
shall make the current that will fan & spread them/Yet all their
force is vain if of itself, and light dry air, heaped Fuel, fanning
Breeze. As idle if no inward Spark lurks there, or lurks unkindled/
Such a Spark, O man! is thy Free-will the Star whose beams are
Virtues/

2823 16.353   This grove freely I dedicate all to thee, O
Priapus/Hunc lucum tibi dedico consecroque, Priape/

$$- \ - \left\{ \begin{array}{l} - \cup \cup, \ - \cup -, \ - \cup, \ - \cup \cup, \ - - \\ - \cup \end{array} \right.$$

f113   2824 16.354   Dʳ W. Hunter, & his designs on the pretty Servant maid who persuaded him to be carried by her to her Chamber,
cock-a-hoop/& she carried in to her mistress's Parlour full of Company—

2825 16.355 "Go call a coach &, let a coach be called &c"/Even so—"Call *Cràssamàtt*, and CrassaMATT/~~and~~ Both Crassamatt, Quinumquamavet, & Quashquamavet, and CRASSAMATT!—

2826 16.356 The desire of carrying things to a greater height of pleasure & admiration, than omnibus trutinatis they are susceptible of, one great cause of the corruption of poetry. Both to understand my own meaning, & to communicate it, ponder on Catullus's Hex. & Pent.—his numine abusum homines—his aut facere, hæc a te dictaque, factaque sunt/excrucies efficias, &c &c/—It is not whether or no the very same ideas expressed with the very same force & the very same naturalness & simplicity in the versification of Ovid & Tibullus, would not be still more delightful (tho' even that for any number of poems may well admit a doubt) but whether it is *possible* so to express them/& whether in every attempt the result has not been to substitute manner for matter, *point* that will not bear reflection (so fine that it breaks the moment you try it) for genuine sense & true feeling—& lastly, to confine both the subjects, thoughts, & even words of poetry within a most beggarly Cordon.—N.B. Metastasio—& in Pope the quaintness, perversion, unnatural metaphors & still more the cold-blooded use for artifice or connection of language justifiable only by enthusiasm & passion.

f113ᵛ

2827 15.214 Maunday Thursday Evening went with Sloane & Madame Amoreuse & the 4 years old Sloane to the Sistine Chapel; the mummery of putting out the Candles deprived of all possibility of effect by the rehearsal on the little ⌒ ⅄Chandelier/the divinity of the Miserere/the Pope in the Pauline Chapel, & the Ranelagh of the illumined Cross/my *after* adventure with the Child/

f91ᵛ
f92

2828 15.215 Ideal = the subtle hieroglyphical *felt*-by-all though not without abstruse and difficult analysis detected & understood, consonance of the *physiognomic* total & substance (Stoff) with the obvious *Path*ognomic/herein equi-distant from Opie-ism, *f92ᵛ* i.e. passions planted in a common face ⟨or portrait⟩ that might equally well have been the accidental Substrate of any other Passion, and the insipid personified passions of Lebrun, or the unmeaning abstractions of, mere Form of the Pseudo-Greeks. Take as an instance of the true Ideal Michel Angelo's despairing Woman at the bottom of the Last Judgment/

2829 15.216   All the senses in which "Beauty" is used/& which is the sole true sense, by the sole possible criterion, namely, that other words exist in the Language which would express those other senses without possibility of a misconception, but that ~~of~~ for the one sense there is no other word but Beauty.—Then of Truth. Now in *this* perhaps Language is more defective & tho' there may exist words for separate senses, yet their superior propriety will

f93 not strike the mind like a *sensation,* as in "delightful" for a rich cloud of one colour, or the smell of Attar of Roses, or "agreeable" of an irregular Face endeared to us by Habit & association of qualities suitable to our wants or dispositions—or "good" as applied to a bitter medicine or tooth drawing/in this case therefore I would make a numeration Table of all the senses in which the word ⟨"Truth"⟩ can be used without a palpable impropriety/shew, in what senses it is disparate, or contradictory to Beauty, and in what

f93ᵛ one sense it is perfectly, always, & necessarily identical with it/& then shew, that this is the only true *sense,* and that all others borrow their claim to it by some more or less distant participation in this Sense/ Good Friday, Rome, 1806.

2830 15.217   Yes! strange as I myself should have thought it a year or two ago, yet it is true, that a man makes fewer enemies, & creates inimical feelings of far less depth and permanence by talking boastfully of himself, than by enthusiastic eulogies—especially, if broad comparisons & sweeping Generalities form the woof and warf of his panegyric—on some other Individual.—And the Reasons are obvious/in the first, Envy is sopped by the ~~no~~ unamia-

f94 ble Light, in which the Egoist shews himself—2. Men feel it what

IV. Michelangelo: *Last Judgment*
Detail. Sistine Chapel, Vatican. See 2828n

v. Washington Allston: *Diana and Her Nymphs in the Chase*
Rome, 1805. See 2831 and n

they call, natural, i.e. they would do the same but for *prudence;* and the sense of their Superiority in this Prudence & Self-controll flatters them, & of course associates pleasure with the Object. 3. The Twist is mysterious to the cold blind-hearted οι πολλοι—& that of itself is painful & allied to Hatred, in all instances in which it is not capable of exciting superstitious Dread. 4. The sharp men of the world ⟨find *fancy* they escape⟩ at once from this mystery by— a poor *fool* (whom yet they hate because he is an unnatural fool: for their *Escape* is only a *fancy*) or a designing Knave.—And some more really penetrating men with worldly hearts will believe, and some of better nature will suspect, that the violence of praise is an effort of the mind to disguise its own envy from its own conscious-   *f94ᵛ* ness—& to bully it out of their Hearts by giving it the loud *Lie*, which is retorted from within by the whispered—you lie.—/What- ever be the interpretation, by the law of Association the Prais*ee* suffers as much as the *Praiser*/—if it were only the Evil of Antici- pation with extravagant Expectation, it would be an evil of itself— what then? when this Expectation is mingled with the hope & wish- ful look-out to be disappointed.—Never therefore speak of a con- temporary by Comparison or in generalities when you praise/but particularly & with as few epithets as possible. These are mere Hints/many feelings mingle in the play which have not been men- tioned in this note.

2831 15.218   Mʳ Allston's Landscape—   *f95* Lefthand of the Foreground/Side of a Rock, steep as a wall, of purplish hue, naked all but one patch of *Bushage,* breaking the Line of the Edge about a yard from the ground, and another much smaller and thinner a little above it/& here and there a moss- stain. Up the rock, a regular-shaped Pine, like its own Shadow, as I have observed in Nature/at the foot of the Pine & next the ⟨Side⟩ frame a bush with trodden Ferns at its feet, which almost hide a small Cleft or Fissure in the rock, beautiful purple-crimson mosses on the other side of the fissure and slopes down to the bottom, fissure with ferns & mosses & naked purple rock last/the small Cleft touches the junction of the side & bottom frame/& three

spans from thence commences the great chasm, & dark, bridged
over by the weedy tree, but slimy, the bark half-scathed & jagged/
oer a perilous bridge/take care, for heaven's sake/it begins smooth

*f95*ᵛ scathed & sattiny, mouldring, barkless, knotty/red Flowers growing up beside it/well, here rises the forked old Trunk, its left Fork
scathed and sattiny and seeming almost to correspond with the
bridge-tree.—Perilous ground between this Trunk and that noble
Tree which with its graceful Lines of motion exhales up into the
sky/for when I look at it, it *rises* indeed, even as smoke * in calm
weather, always the same height & shape, & yet you see it move/
who has cut down its twin bough, its brother?—Well—do not
blame it/for it has made such a sweet Stool at the bottom of the
Tree, ~~with~~ and the high top with its umbrella cloud of Foliage is
over your head—behind this and the Trunk is that red spot, scarlet
moss-cups or a lichen-stain.—from this Tree, bushes and a most
lovely pine tree, ⟨one of⟩ the boundaries of the left foreground
that, & a high brown bush behind, & the great Bowder Stone on its
left,   which at its bottom half touches the edge of the purple

f96 cloak   and I must climb over it to get the prospect of the far
valley, hidden by the Stone & the Rock, and a Tree all Foliage, growing behind the great stone & between it and the triangular Interspace of the Rock/and in this vale, dim seen, field & wood & sunshine shaft   is distanced by the snowy Mountain/

This is the left hand of the Picture/the middle the sunshiny
mountain all jagged and precipitous, in smooth plates of rock, yet
the whole all rough from their relative position to each other/its
scales of armour, behemoth/the Lake with filmy Light, the bushy
Island, the tree on its sloping bank, so steep! and shewing its steep-
ness by its own incumbency/*observe* its slim trunk seen through its
vapour-cloud of Foliage/and then the dog with its two hind feet

*f96*ᵛ on higher ground/But the right hand of the Picture, the tree with
its cavern-making roots stretching out to some faintly purplish

f96 Postscript * The divine semitransparent and grey-green Light on
the highest part of the Trunk of this Smoke Tree—

Stones that connect the right extremity with the purple rock on the   *f96ᵛ*
left extremity (—N.B. the color is really grey-paint, but in appearance & so call it, it is grey-blue faintly purplish)—& how by small
stones, scattered at irregular distances along the foreground even to
one in the very centre or bisection of the foreground, which seems
to balance & hold even all the tints of the whole picture, the key-
stone of its colors—so aided by the bare earth breaking in & making
an irregular road to the Lake on which that faery figure shoots along
as one does in certain Dreams, only that it touches the earth which
yet it seems to have no occasion to touch/but the delicate black & o   *f97*
how delicate grey-white Greyhound, whose two colors amalgam-
ated make exactly the grey-blue of the larger & the 12 small stones
behind & around them & even the halo ⟨still with a purplish grey⟩
of the crescent carries on the harmony, & with its *bright* white crescent forms a transition to the bright left-hand thick body-branch &
trunk of the largest tree/What a delicious trail of ivy-garlands the
old thin snaggy tree broken off one third from its summit, almost
a pole or huge stake/rotten & half hollow at the bottom/—but the
three Goddesses, for them I must trust to the moment of inspira-
tion/the Sky & Perspective of the Clouds—the many many newly
picturesque weeds.

2832 15.219   The quiet circle in which Change and Permanence   *f97ᵛ*
co-exist, not by combination or juxtaposition, but by an absolute annihilation of difference/column of smoke, the fountains before Sᵗ
Peter's, waterfalls/Gᴏᴅ!—Change without loss—change by a perpetual growth, that ⟨once constitutes & annihilates change⟩ the past,
& the future included in the Present//oh! it is aweful.

2833 15.220   Pretty Image of a deserted City/a large sign over
a door—"Magazzino di Acqua Vita, Rosoli, Spiriti, e Tabacchi, &c
&c &c &c." the lower half more than half veiled by tall nettles,
growing out of the Shed, in which the Sign Board was placed/
Rome, Borgo di Castello Sᵗ Angelo—

2834 15.221   [*For drawing see plate facing next page*]   *f98*

f98ᵛ   2835 15.222   Of the metres of the ancients/ Greeks

In reading Pindar, I was "struck on a heap" (to use a very vulgar but yet forcible & could it be divested of its associated meanness, highly *poetical* phrase) with the unpassable chasm between the ancient, and all the *possible* metres of *all* modern Languages of Europe. The Causes seem to be 1. That the common manner of talking was far far less caught from *spelling* & reading/consequently more streamy & tho' less intellectual in the colder ⟨might I not say meaner⟩ and contradistinctive sense of the word, and less facilitative of Intellect (as contra-distinguished from Passion, or Feeling) yet

f99   was necessarily more passionate and musical. ⟨⟨Mem!⟩⟩ The Italians even now compared with the English & Germans. Hence they not ~~run~~ only run lines into each other more easily & happily than we—at least, in all our lyric poetry—but with perfect ease fused words together, not only in the same Line, but even from one into another. This Latter had already become almost impracticable among the Romans, a less impassioned people. Hence the non-existence of any reputable Latin Poem in the Pindaric or Choric Metres. 2. And closely connected with the former, the Habit of always accompanying Poetry with Music, often instrumental, always vocal. They *sang* their verses literally. 3. From the great price of MSS it was an Art—the People knew it from the Theatres & public Reci-

f99ᵛ   tations. Consequently it remained artificial—till the downfall of all good things—tho' there is reason & facts to believe, that very early there existed Poetry Πολιτικη—i.e. read as the people naturally pronounced it/—Tertullian's Poems, & one supposed to have been written in Augustus' or Tiberius's Age.

f100ᵛ   2836 15.226   Received from Mʳ Russel on credit 4 Doppios and four Sequins—

2837 15.227   When by strong Blowing you have at length awakened the flame of Virtuous Resolution, then blow gently & with intermissions lest the Wind blows out what it kindled, but when there is a substratum of ignited materials then never heed

these transitory extinctions/Blow away, till all is one vigorous Flame.

2838 15.228   May/Wallis's—O *Still!!* This astonishing multiplication of Pain into itself, in dreams—I do not yet understand it. This Evening sleeping I—for the first time I recollect, had a most   *f101* intolerable sense of *Pain* as *Pain,* without affright or disgustful Ideas—a sense of an excruciating patience-mocking Rheumatism in my right arm/At length I awoke with it/& truly my right arm was in a painful state, partly from being pressed on, & partly I had felt it a little painful for a day or two/but the astonishing difference in the degrees of the Pain felt or supposed when asleep & when awaked—

2839 15.229   So much sorrow behind and before and around,   *f101ᵛ* no one Wish of the very Heart, which even the Reason, that keeps drowsy watch in a Day-dream, can suffer to pass into the Fancy, and to become the Material of a momentary Fabric of Pleasure— when every thing, that could give Happiness, presents its idea so closely interbodied with the immediate reflection of its impossibility, (& not a mere negative Impossibility but with the Reflection that it is made impossible by the actual presence of a positive, & sore heart-wasting Contrary) that the voluntary Mind shrinks   *f102* from all, it would endure all things to attain, as from a debt of Misery, as from a stern Creditor knocking at the door, who must be admitted, some time or other, but oh! not to-day—in this drear desolation of the happy Soul is Hope utterly exterminated?—Woe is me! No!—A Kettle is on a slow Fire/& I turn from my Book, & loiter from going to my bed, in order to see whether it will boil/— & on that my Hope hovers—on the Candle burning in the socket— or will this or that person come this evening—if he come at all, it   *f102ᵛ* must be within an hour—who when he comes neither gives me the least pleasure or does me the least good, as I well know, & have not the dimmest expectation that he will/or if I can by any wretched *usury* against myself, borrow half an hour's comfortable sensation ⟨to be repayed in pain⟩ at a 10,00 per cent interest. I make

a vision of the Liberation of Europe, & HOPE engarlands its brief
Halo around some ⌜. . . . .⌝

f105 2840 15.230   Monday, May   [*] saw Lord Bristol's
Collection/interesting from the strange mixture/2 Copies. 1. of the
Magdalen, 2ⁿᵈ of the 3 Graces of *Titian* by Mazzarese, admirable/
may be had for 100 £/they are even to connoisseurs *almost* equal to
the originals/to 98~~99~~—99 &c/

2841 15.231   Sorrowful yet true Speech of Artists/*burnt* or
gone to England which is the same as if the Picture were burnt—

f105ᵛ 2842 15.233   In the *S. of A.* to describe Sotting allegorically,
losing the way to the temple of Bacchus, come to the Cave of the
Gnome, &c &c.

2843 15.234   Gothic Building in whatever State of Ruin, is interesting but the Greek must have *some columns,* or else—⟨Mʳ
Baker⟩—

2844 15.235   To have Raphaels there must be a sale for such
things as even Raphaels in their *beginnings* must do/or else the
Horse starves while the grass is growing/[?Opulence/Hence] &
not the Churches the Cause of Painting flourishing in Roman
Catholic Countries/Madonna &c.

2845 15.236   On Sunday attended Sᵗ Peters' to see the Beatifi-
cation of Hieronymo de Francesco, a Jesuit//The Bronze image
in the embroidered Blanket & Tiara/

2846 15.237
f106   Amici, udite! Non fo piu credenza
                    Che son miei Libri pien di Debitori

[* Coleridge's blank. K. C.]

E per Altrui qualche convenienza
Ho perduto Denari ed Aventori/
Non trovo gia in me tal sofferenza
Che non fanno cosi miei creditori
Anzi con qualche loro impertinenza
Mi cavano da tasca [. . .]
Onde credenza non vo più [. . .]
E do dico di si non [. . . .]
Dico pero a chi non vuol Pagare
Desecrando spensar da [. . .] morte
Voler senza denar bere o mangiare
Gite lungi da me gite [. . .]

2847 15.238   Osteria at Porto 3 miles from Ostia/over the
ferry, with the blind ferryman,/he the only one

2848 15.232   Sunday, May 18, 1806/Left Rome with Mr Rus-   *f105*
sel/as far as Baccano not particularly interesting, bare Hills, with
slopes & bottoms/the broom by the roadside gay & cheering/tall
baron's Castle, like the Church Tower without the Church—impressive as a change from the magnificent remains in Rome, recall-
ing too such different æras—/—From Baccano the same, till we
came in sight of the Village of Monte rosso, with its red-tiled   *f106*
Houses mixed with Trees, beside a wood-patched Hill, & fields
more like English ones than any I had met with in Italy—from
thence in a short time we turned off into the Loreto road, & thro'
delightful wild broom—Hedges with rude woods on one side &
parkish fields & trees on the other—a *sweet* ride to Nepi, the most
romantic situation place I have seen, both when first its then round
ruined Tower & extinguisher-steeple peeped thro' the Trees—& it
continues improving to the very last/Its walls, ivy, double Gate,
picturesque & novel waterfalls between the 1st & second/the two   *f107*
Girls (with a little child) swinging under a great flowering Elder
growing out of the Wall, the swing suspended from it—indeed
from this place even to Terni thro' Borchetto,

[*] is a continued scene of beauty chiefly in the style of the River Wye—only the clefts are deeper, more romantic, & more wooded—but the river, is very inferior/The view of the bridge and side Arches, with the Acqueduct of two arches, not far from it, the mossiness & vestiture of the two side Arches (& the trout were very interesting) exquisite—especially as

f107ᵛ the road peeped above it—/the last 5 miles to Terni thro' an extensive Valley

2849   15.239

f108

The waterfall of Terni is composed of 1. a perpend. fall from the very summit of a flat-field—a-top a high Hill/on its left a *strip* thro' a mouth of its own, i.e.—a complete arbour of it/—and 2. of an elbow torrent, which at the elbow is bisected longitudinally by a mossy rock/& part of the first turn hidden by the edge of the hitherward Hill/After having winded up above a bushy Hill, all in

f108ᵛ shrubbery walks, we come out on an open bank, fronting the Fall/ to my left a lovely Valley, narrow, and of the character of Langdale, with the river Negra meandring thro' it not indeed with naked banks but always with visible Stream/to my right the rough lime-water torrent is forcing its ways among rocks, at the very toes of the opposite off-sloping Hills, its banks running up to the Rocky Hills in savage bush-works/this Stream is Negro + Villano/a peep of distant mountains, or else land-locked/

[* Coleridge left a line and a half blank. K. C.]

behind me as I write the off-sloping Hills & perfectly perpend.
bare Rocks—cypresses/N.B. the bisection commences about half   *f109*
way below the elbow, and the right Hand leaps down in a narrow
plaunge torrent-like, the left hand stream spreads out into a great
breadth and then falls [*over*] a convex semicircular brown & mossy
rock in fillets & broad aprons, then slides down shallow down a
smooth gentle slope, while its turbulent Brother is rushing down a
similar but much narrower declivity on an elevation ten yards
higher/all around bushy, mossy, rough with young fir-bushes &
bushes of Juniper/

Nothing can be conceived more lovely than the walk to & back to
take the objects backward/& then in transcribing I can reverse/
1. the wild shrubbery *climb* & N.B. the oranges & flowering shrubs/
2 Lime grove of great elegance/ 3./up thro' the L. G. to the right   *f109*
the jagged rocks fringed on the top with pines & cypresses, and one
rock of narrow, pointed & lofty cone as to resemble a Cypress without its naked Stem/4. Walk thro' the vineyard, small fields of
wheat, vines & olive Trees/Corn, Wine, Oil!—on the left hand
rocks, ivy & broom/pass under a pretty arch, half-man, half-nature
into the orange walk/having before me all this while the ~~Knoll &~~
~~town~~ Promontory arm of Papinio/⟨5⟩ on the summit of the Distance crested by Mirante the beautiful bridge of earth over the
joined river & view up and down most striking from bustle, greenness, & relief/6. The walk around & under Papinio & its wild ruins,
looking down into the bottoms that forms its trench, one of the   *f110*
richest scenes of woodland Shades & Sun-spots I ever beheld/7. &
the 3 Pines & 2 Cypresses, these on this, those on the other side of a
Cottage in the Bottom Terni-ward—/Mem. Not to forget our first
entrance in that lovely vale of Vineyards with the smoke rising up
behind a distant Hill as from burning weeds, & that was the Steam
of the Waterfalls of Terni—

On our return as I was looking out of the window of the Inn
(the Moro) saw two very large Carts built in the very form of our
heavy Coaches, a woman stretched at lazy length on the one, a boy
on the other/but all beneath Coops of Fowls—a huge Arc of   *f110*
Death's culinary Futura in rus—or at least in rure/Noticed at
Terni the dreadful prevalence of dram-drinking/Wine did them

all harm!—Coffee they did not care for/but Acqua Vita!—Aye, that indeed!—and on being supposed absent to my great amusement all coming to get a sup, one after the other/—O fearful!—

From Terni for 4 miles to Castanea the road leads along the breast of a Hill, the deserted Channel of a broad stream forming the whole vale/but the Hills on our right of such exquisite form & differences of Height, & some by natural steps & playful break- *f111* ups of Surface, green with young Corn, & rich with Shrubs & trees fascinate/so thro' a long valley, so narrow that the feet of the off-sloping Mountains were divided only by the bed of a stream, we winded on thro' winding galleries to Stretella/~~on~~ and again winded on till we came to the longest Ascent, I remembered to have known —drawn up by Oxen—I walked/on the ascent the bottom & scenery were on my left, as I descended on my right, the same sort of scenery however, namely, well wooded Mountains, with towns here and there surface, sometimes disclosing, more often hiding their *f111ᵛ* narrow valleys, seen only half way down, & in the distance their heads only seen, as billows—all together exquisitely green—& the lines playful and tossing—

f108 2850 15.240   At Perugia 12000 Inhabitants, 60 religious Instit. and 42 Churches/—and I suppose, that at Assisi the number is as great in proportion—

2851 15.241(a)
f111ᵛ   Where micant Conchs and micanter conchoids
           Do scintillate upon the Shores of Rhodes.

Dogana di Ossaia/
                              Ossaia
                    Una bella ragazza/

2852 15.241(b) Vincenzo Scoti/—

f125ᵛ 2853 15.271   No. 1504. Florence Gallery/Parmeggiano, Holy Family, the Christ evidently umarbeitet [*umgearbeitet*] into the Puck of Sir J. Reynolds & again into his Muscipula/

vi. Parmigianino: *The Holy Family*
Uffizi Gallery, Florence. See 2853 and n

VII A. Sir Joshua Reynolds:
Puck or *Robin Goodfellow*
See 2853 and n

VII B. Sir Joshua Reynolds: *Muscipula*
or *The Mouse-Trap Girl*
See 2853 and n

2854 15.272   The bad Effect of the Μενδικαντ Φριαρς not only in themselves, as sturdy Idlers & the true Dung of all the worst Ποισον-weeds of Superstition, but as by their Example spreading a spirit of mendicancy thro' all the lower Classes.

2855 15.273   In open tho' quiet street, & the perfectly suitable & most modest bed-dresses, with screens to place at the door side of any bed, when ⌐their⌐ delicacy required it/

2856 15.270   From Florence to Pisa/arrived at Pisa, Thursday   ƒ125
Afternoon 2 o'clock/thro' a heavenly country, especially the latter part of the Journey—a lovely plain, quite level, below you, so that you looked down upon it on your right and on your left, but not much below you, the road running thro' it like a Terrace Bank/of the hanging Tower, the Dome, the Cemetery, the Baptistery, I shall say nothing except that—being all together they form a grand & wild mass, especially by moonlight, when the hanging Tower has something of a supernatural Look/but what interested me with a deeper interest were the two Hospitals, 1 for men, 1 for women/ the breadth & the height ⟨of the rooms,⟩ the number largeness & good contrivance of the windows, the perfect cleanliness & good order—& what forms their strict peculiarity, the great door of open iron work, thro' which all who pass by/& it is in

2857 15.223   Benozzo Gozzoli   ƒ100
            Buffalmacco   1386
            Giotto
            Orcagna
            Laureati
            Ant. Veneziano
            Simon Memmi

2858 15.224   Hic Tumulus est Benotii Florentini qui proxime Has pinxit Historias, hunc sibi Pisanorum donavit Humanitas—1478—

2859 15.225   An Essay addressed to the Masters of Eton, Winchester, Westminster, St Paul's, Charterhouse, Christ's Hospital, Harrow, &c &c, respecting the pronunciation of Greek & Latin

f114   2860 16.357   June 7ᵗʰ 1806. O my Children!—Whether, and
which of you are dead, whether any, & which among you, are alive,
I know not/and were a Letter to arrive this moment from Keswick
(Saturday Night, June 7ᵗʰ, 1806, Leghorn/Gasparini's, or Arms of
England Hotel) I fear, that I should be unable to open it, so deep
and black is my Despair—O my Children, my Children! I gave
you life once, unconscious of the Life I was giving/and you as un-
consciously have given Life to me./Yes! it has been lost—many
f114ᵛ many months I past I should have essayed whether Death is what
I groan for, absorption and transfiguration of Consciousness—for of
annihilation I cannot by the nature of my Imagination have any
idea/Yet it may be true—O mercy, mercy!—Even this moment I
could commit Suicide but for you, my Darlings (of Wordsworths—
of Sara Hutchinson/that is *passed*—or of remembered thoughts to
f115   make a Hell of/) O me! now racked with pain, now fallen abroad
& suffocated with a sense of intolerable Despair/& no other Refuge
than Poisons that degrade the Being, while they suspend the torment, and which suspend only to make the Blow fall heavier/

2861 16.358   O dear John Wordsworth! Ah that I could but
have died for you/& you have gone home, married S. Hutchinson,
& protected my poor little ones. O how very, very gladly would I
have accepted the conditions. But thou art gone, who mightest have
f115ᵛ been so happy,—& I live—to be increasingly ⌜. . .⌝, body and
soul/*live*/to die minutely.

2862 16.359   After the being used to the sweet Roman Pronunciation, the Florentines appear to have lost the roof of the mouth &
so to *substitute* the throat, that the person who speaks most distinctly, quite *gargles*/and of those who speak least unpleasantly,
the words sounds to a foreigner's ear seem wandering about in the
roofless Hollow of the mouth seeking in vain for a something necessary to make them words/—So the Women!—Mercy/Ugly Ju-
f116   nos with Peacock Teat & Push of the Breast compared with lovely
Venuses, Graces, & Cupids &c of Rome/

2863 16.360   Baldwin's Lond: Week: Journ: March 22, 1806
—Saturday. At Lincoln Assizes on the 12ᵗʰ, T. Temporal found

guilty of the murder of a young woman in the Parish of South Hykeham, on the 3rd of November, in the morning, he married her/Temporal was a laboring *Banker* upon one of the Canals in the Neighbourhood of Lincoln, became criminally connected with the young Woman; she proved pregnant, the parish Officers *compelled* him to marry her. Within an hour he killed her, almost beating her Head from her body with the heavy club, he was known to walk with—
N.B. Robert Hanford

2864 16.361   Immense power of Language & [?active] Eloquence—Military men instead of giving injunction receiving it from [?Lowther] or Wyndham/a mere action by Language no confidence in fact   explain this fact of experience. ⟨a fact of repeated experience—by myself.⟩

2865 16.362   Alarming State of public morals in England & loss of lofty thinking, the perpetual Wyndham (*loud laugh*)/N.B. to call the public attention solemnly to this by an analysis of W's character, & that of his Joe Millerisms.   *f116ᵛ*

2866 15.242   Sunday, June 22nd 1806. Globe, Pisa. The conc*rete*   *f111ᵛ* in nature nearest to the *abstract* of Death is Death by a Flash of Lightning. Repeatedly during this night's storm have I desired that I might be taken off, not knowing when or where/but a few   *f112* moments past a vivid flash passed across me, my nerves thrilled, and I earnestly wished, so help me God! like a Love-longing, that it would pass through me!—Death without pain, without degrees, without the possibility of cowardly wishes, or recreant changes of resolve/Death without deformity, or assassin-like self-disorganization/Death, in which the mind by its *own* wish might seem to have caused its own purpose to be performed, as instantaneously   *f112ᵛ* and by an instrument almost as spiritual, as the Wish itself/!—

    Come, come, thou bleak December Wind,
    And blow the dry Leaves from the Tree!
    Flash, like a Love-thought, thro' me, Death
    And take a Life, that wearies me.

f114   2867   15.248   Fornacetti 9 or 10 miles from Pisa/all their drinking water brought from Pisa

2868   15.249   From For. to Castel di Bosco, 10 miles, number of begging children running with strange rattling shudder-whistle. Introduce Salisbury & the good coachman.

2869   11.1

f1

    1. *Uncomfortab*
    [2]. O + B.
    3. increased N E/.
    4. positive body pain
    5. Remorse + Despondency
    Let A—pleasurable feeling be assured—it is written by an immediate & ⟨by a⟩ four hours experience—that $A + O - B = A +$ pl. feeling + painful feeling + Αυτοτιμορευμενος [. . . .]—/at all events without the intolerable, & [. . .]
    Try little by little—

f2   2870   11.2   Bought Friday, Sept. 6th, 1806

2871   11.3

    Padre del Ciel, s'un tempo
    Si follemente ho pianto,
    Che'l fin del pianto non altro è, che pianto,
    Deh! dammi omai, ti prego
    Lagrime di te degne; amai, nol nego
    Beltà caduca e frale
    E lasciai l'immortale.

f2ᵛ
    Sana, Signor, con amoroso affetto
    L'amoroso difetto!
    Ascolta i prieghi miei;
    Non mi negar pietà, se Padre sei!
              S.T.C.
    25 Septr. 1806.

2872 11.4
Nel medesimo soggetto.

Signor, che del peccato,
E non del peccator, brami la morte,
Deh mira omai con che fallaci scorte
M'ha condotto a morire
Il mio cieco desire.
Ecco la pecorella tua smarrita,
Chiamala a tè sua vita;
Fà, che pianga il suo mal, pianga l'errore,   *f3*
Quanto pianse d'amore!

2873 11.5   Let me try—that I may have at least one good
thought to alleviate the pang of dying away—to pursue steadily
the plan of opening the eyes of the public to the real situation of
Needle-workers, and of women in general. Mary Lamb has prom-   *f3*ᵛ
ised me Facts in abundance.

2874 11.6   Captⁿ Burney's Story told him by Omai—of the
2 Stars near the Scorpion's *Head*—⟨by Antares⟩/or *Tail*, famine in
Otaheite/fish gained by man & his wife/Man would not suffer the
children to be awaked, tho' the Mother wished it/2 were awake,   *f4*
but feared to speake & pined & die/& were put up into Heaven &
then by their entreaty the Mother/

2875 11.7   If Miss James of Great Cumberland Place, a
friend of Mr Russel's, 5 Oct./1806.

2876 11.8   The Gentleman & his Servant at the assizes/
Prisoner, with Scar/all 3 after taken up for robbing the mails.

2877 11.9   Story of Odonase/

2878 11.10   Strong proof of the imaginary nature of Ghosts/   *f4*ᵛ
i.e. the sensation in the *ex toto* of Nature producing the Ghost,

not the Ghost the Terror, they (as from black dreams & reveries) no Ghost-seer *dies* or is the worst/whereas compare the frightful effects of tricks to frighten people, ideotcy, madness/Skeleton in the Girl's Bed/young man in the Cabin, who had suffered his Hat to float as if drowned/hid himself, & then appeared as his own Ghost/&c

ƒ5   2879 11.11   Sic perit Ingenium, Ingenii (*aliter. Genii*) ni pignora vitam Perpetuam statuant/

2880 11.12
    With never a whisper on the main
    Off shot the spectre ship:
    And stifled words & groans of pain
    Mix'd on each ~~trembling~~ murmuring lip/
    ⟨And⟩ We look'd round & we look'd up
    And Fear at our hearts as at a Cup
      The Life-blood seem'd to sip
    The Sky was dull & dark the Night,
    The Helmsman's Face by his lamp gleam'd bright,
      From the Sails the Dews did drip/
    Till ~~rose~~ clomb above the Eastern Bar
    The horned moon, with one bright Star
      Within its nether Tip.
    One after one, by the star-dogg'd moon,
        &c—

2881 11.13

ƒ5ᵛ

Antispast	∪ - - ∪	Pæon quartus	∪ ∪ ∪ -
Choriambus	- ∪ ∪ -	Pæon t̅r̅t̅s̅	∪ ∪ - ∪
Proceleusmatus	∪ ∪ ∪ ∪	Pæon scnd	∪ - ∪ ∪
Ionicus a m̅j̅r	- - ∪ ∪	Pæon p̅r̅m̅.	- ∪ ∪ ∪
Incs a minore	∪ ∪ - -	Epitritus 1.	∪ - - -
Dijambus	∪ - ∪ -	Epitritus 2	- ∪ - -
Ditrochæus	- ∪ - ∪	Epitritus 3	- - ∪ -
Dispondæus	- - - -	Epitritus	- - - ∪

Spondee - -	Dactyl - ᴗ ᴗ
Iambus ᴗ -	Trochee - ᴗ
Pyrrhychius ᴗ ᴗ	Anapest ᴗ ᴗ -
Molossus - - -	Amphibrach ᴗ - ᴗ
Bacchius ᴗ - -	Antibacchius - - ᴗ
Amphimacer - ᴗ -	

15 composite, 10 simple feet = 25.

Whole words not comprizable in any of the above feet: but by be- *f6*
ing in one word produce an effect, sometimes to be avoided, sometimes embraced, different from the same foot or feet made up of
two or more words—

ολυμπιονικαν.	ᴗ - ᴗ ᴗ - -
generosity.—	- ᴗ - ᴗ ᴗ
καταθυμοβορησει.	ᴗ ᴗ - ᴗ ᴗ - -
-ησε	ᴗ ᴗ - ᴗ ᴗ - ᴗ
Constantinopolitan.—	- - ᴗ ᴗ - ᴗ ᴗ
	- - ᴗ ᴗ - ᴗ -
Καλλιπλοκαμω.	- ᴗ ᴗ ᴗ -
ακαμαντοποδων.	ᴗ ᴗ - ᴗ ᴗ -
ποικιλογαρυν	- ᴗ ᴗ - -
Ὑπερβορεων	ᴗ - ᴗ ᴗ -
Ταλλαϊ*ω̈*νιδες	- ᴗ ᴗ - ᴗ ᴗ

2882 11.14   Picturesque Passages in Pindar.   *f6ᵛ*

ΟΛΥΜΠΙ:

Γ. 3ʳᵈ. Strophe β (2ⁿᵈ) & its Antistrophe, supposing Heracles to
have brought the Trees from Istria/—The Waggon with
young Olive-Trees, Horses, men—altars—Heracles—

"διχομηνις ολον χρυσαρματος

Εσπερας οφθαλμον αντεφλεξε"—the steep banks of
the Alpheus, & distant mountains.

Στ. 6ᵗʰ. Epod. β. κωλ. 6.—usque ad Strophen γ (3ʳᵈ) κωλ. 7.
Ἁ δὲ φοινικόκροκον—μελισσᾶν καδομενοι.—Evadne
with the new-born babe, the wild wood, on a bed of yel-

f7

low & purple violets—Lucina—the Parcæ—the two Serpents feeding it with honey—one holding the honey
comb in his folds & gyves, as in a vase/a slant ray thro'
a small opening in the Trees, falling full on the face &c
of the Infant/the Mother feeble, retiring, with reverted
face, full of mother's yearning.—Introduce the scenery
of Antist: γ. lines 6. 7. 8. & 9 to "σῶμα."

f11

2883 11.21

1 . 18	5 .3 Mʳˢ C. & Mʳ B.	2 wood boxlets
2 . 10		1 Escrutoire dark blue
. 10		1 long box
1 . 1		1 thick dᵒ
3 Turnpikes/		4 little
6 . 2/6		and 1 Naples Trunk
4 . 12 . 6		4 guin: 8. 6
1 . 10 . 0		1. 16. 3.
		2ⁿᵈ 18–
		18, 9. 6
		Chesterfield
		4 £, 1 × 18 × 11
		5 £.

2884 11.22   J Austwick
Bell Friday St.

2885 11.23   Mʳ Cruikshanks, Nᵒ 2, Great Sᵗ Helen's.

f50   **2886** 11.114   The Odes of Pindar (with few exceptions, & these
chiefly in the shorter ones) seem by intention to die away by soft
gradations into a languid Interest, like most of the Landskips of
the great elder Painters. Modern Ode-writers have commonly
preferred a continued Rising of Interest.

2887 11.115   Διθύραμβος = Liber pater, cujus nominis ra-
tiones reddiderunt diversas *Etymologistæ diversi,* ut solet genus
illud hominum ludere et ludi. Schmidt

2888 11.116   On what sufficient and decisive text or texts of *f52*
the New Testament is the 3rd of our 39 articles founded? If from
the Belief only, & the Tradition of the Church, how is this consistent with the 6th article/and even the enumeration of the canonical
Books, which cannot all be proved canonical out of Scripture, but
must rely on Tradition & critical deductions, lays open to the Roman Catholics an unarmed place. Strange! they will say, that Books
whose authority must rely on Tradition and the decision of Coun-
cils should be supposed to preclude & supersede the *necessity* of
Tradition & Church-sentence. I say, *necessity;* because our orthodox divines all admit their utility & *auxiliary* importance.

8th article—why not then adopt at once the very words of those
"most certain warrants of Holy Scripture"? The 20th & 21st art.
and wherein, as has been often asked & never answered, wherein *f51^v*
consists the difference between arbitrary ordination, & arbitrary
exposition, seeing that the effects are the same, and that the latter
equally as the former proceed from "an assembly of men, whereof
all be not governed with the Spirit and word of God"?—And do
not the R. Catholic divines justify all their Tenets out of Scripture,
expounded as they expound it, now literally & now mystically?—

The 18th article (& indeed the 13th) is it not in contradiction to
express words of St Paul, which clearly admit no second interpretation? and if we translate the word "ονομα" by the *power,* a sense
which in many passages it demands, why may we not conceive that
he who acts truly according to his ⟨uncorrupted⟩ Conscience—acts
by the power & is saved by the Spirit of Christ?

The 19th & 20th articles seem to be objectionable from the ex- *f51*
treme looseness & nugatoriness of the definition of the word,
Church. No ground is given to determine, who are *"faithful* men"
—or what is the requisite number. Are they to determine it by their
own vote? and what if an equal or greater number equally learned,
& to all human appearance, equally pious, & equally grounding
their faith on passages of Scripture according to their sense of
them, should differ—Who is to decide? And which of these are to
possess "authority in controversies of Faith"?—The C. of England's founders differed among themselves, and thus too of Art.
23rd.

f50ᵛ   23ʳᵈ/who chuses & who gives lawful authority in the congregation? The King?—One man?—And what if he be an Infidel, or
Heretic—& send such as himself. And who is to determine whether
he has or no?—It seems to me clear, that more power was intended by the Framer of the Article to rest on the Congregation or
Convocation than actually does exist in the Church/yet still, tho'
i̶n̶ with a less striking (& perhaps l̶e̶s̶s̶ a more mischievous) un-
foundedness the same difficulty returns:—On what or whom is the
practical authority finally built. This may be considered as one of
the two or three main vantage grounds of the R. Catholics, from
which their Fire commands the Eng. Church.

f47ᵛ   2889 11.109   S̶q̶u̶i̶r̶e̶ ̶D̶a̶v̶i̶d̶   T̶a̶l̶l̶b̶o̶y̶, a Welsh Esquire of
ancient Family—David Ap-Tall-boy,; the Etymology long taken
from the obvious circumstance of the tallness of the Family, one of
whom w̶a̶s̶ many 100 years ago is related to have been six foot/&
the Esquire himself, at present is 5, 9—a rare thing in Wales/but a
learned Chaplain has completely routed this, as one of the involuntary Puns of Ignorance, like Billy Ruffian for Bellerophon, &c/&
derives it most satisfactorily from the Race
       Ἀνδρῶν ἡρώων Ταφίων ἠδὲ Τηλεβοάων,
Virorum Heroum Taphiorum et Teleboarum/Hesiod. Ασπις
Ηρακλεους, v.19—one of whom had fled from the vengeance of
Amphitryon.

f48   2890 11.110   St⟨d⟩rt/passes over a poem as one of those tiniest
of tiny night-flies runs over a leaf, casting its shadow, 3 times as
long as itself, yet only just shading one or at most two letters at a
time. Minute Criticism.

2891 11.111   Ουθαρ = udder.

f48ᵛ   2892 11.112   A maid servant of Mʳˢ Clarkson's Parents had a
great desire to hear Dʳ Price, & accordˡʸ attended his Congregⁿ. On
her return being asked, well, what do you think &c—"A ī ī/replied
she/There was neither the Poor nor the Gospel." Excellent Hit
on the fine *respectable* attendants of Unitarian Chapels, and the
moonshine heartless Head-work of the Sermons.

2893 11.113   The mahogany Tables, *all* but especially the large
dining Table with the segments of circles, deep according the passion of the dice-box Plungers/chiefly half-circles/O the agony &   *f48*
spite with which many have been thrown/it is truly a written History of the fiendish Passions of Gambling—Oct. 12. 1806. New-
market

2894 11.108   Arrived in Cambridge, from Bury, on Thursday   *f47*
Noon, Oct. 16. 1806—after 12 years absence. Every thing the
same, thereby distinguished in its effect on the Feelings from the
Scenes of Childhood revisited in Manhood, which all seem ludicrously small/the young men seemed the very same young men,
I had left, the same faces, colored hair, complexions, &c/the only
alteration in myself, & the few old Handers of my own yellow/
they were altered indeed. I met with Brookses & Caldwells more   *f46ᵛ*
B. and C. than the men themselves.—Visited the Trin: Library
with Mʳ Jones—saw Porson & was introduced; but he took no
notice of me, not even by an act of common civility. His pitiable
State, quite *muddled.*—
                              S D   S D
    Payed a Bill of £ 1„1„0—4„6, paid of Mʳ Costobody, to Ann
Tiggin on behalf of her Husband deceased for a quarter's BELL-
RINGING.

2895 11.18   Never will alter a *Bill* on any account, after any   *f10ᵛ*
charge is once laid/the infallible & immaculate Landlord at Stamford.   Oct. 26. 1806.

2896 11.19   Abbe Bueè's Comparison of Romeau & de Lisle,
               & Haüy.

2897 11.24   (1) Suspension & (2) the Sense of Darkness, coin-   *f11ᵛ*
cident in the (1.) feeling, and the (2) visual spectrum *imitatively*
excited by it and accompanying it.—N.B. This seems important, =
i.e. mere feeling = darkness—but much remains to be explained,
namely, distinct image without Light, dᵒ with light, and 3ʳᵈˡʸ the   *f12*
Spectrum all Light/24 Oct, 1806. Ferry Bridge.

2898 11.25   M͟r͟ Dʳ Alexander
                 Preston

2899 11.20
ƒ10ᵛ   ⟨Oct. 25ᵗʰ, 1806⟩
There is "a good Few on the Road"—(of Cattle)—phrase for a
large number/hence possibly might "Few" come to mean "Many"
                  Ferry Bridge/

ƒ12ᵛ 2900 11.26   Supposing Christabel translated, or any similar
poem composed, in Greek, a good metre for it in the Prometh.
Vinct: thus 398ᵗʰ line/the Strophe A + St. β = Strophe A. Antistrophe α + Antist: β = Antistrophe B. Then the Epode from
the 286ᵗʰ to the 300ᵗʰ Line. Ηκω—βεβαιοτερος σοι.—

ƒ13   2901 11.27   Petch, Angel, Catterick.

2902 11.28   3. 1. 1. 2. 5—.

2903 11.29
1. ⁂ To ask about the Quicks, how much per thousand for
the best?—for Hedging/
2. To *send* to Mʳ Cookson one Magnum Bonum & one Peach
Tree—to nail against the wall—
⁂ 1. 1 per 1000. 3 years transplanted/

ƒ54   2904 11.124   To 38 past 10: my watch & W. 11. loses therefore
14ᵐ a̶n̶ h̶o̶u̶r̶ 11—52 in the [day] 38—8

ƒ13   2905 11.30   Arrived at Keswick on Thursday Evening, *Oct:*
30ᵗʰ 1806.

ƒ13ᵛ 2906 11.31   In malevolam animam non introibit Sapientia.

ƒ52ᵛ 2907 11.117   Shattering of long and deep-rooted associations
always places the mind in an angry state/& even when our own
understandings have effected the revolution, it still holds good/

only we apply the feeling to & against our former faith & those who still hold it/shewn in modern Infidels. Great good therefore of such revolution as alters not by exclusion but by an enlargement that includes the former, tho' it places it in a new point of view.

2908 11.118 Excellent cento in the "Instead of Venite exultemus" in the form of prayer for King Charles the Martyr. But is it consistent with the awe due to the incommunicable attributes of the Saviour GOD, especially the 18th verse/"the Son of man" &c not to mention its unfairness & *trick*?

2909 11.119 To Alston/After the formation of a new acquaint- *f53* ance found by some weeks or months unintermitted Communion worthy of all our esteem, affection & perhaps admiration, an intervening Absence—whether we meet again or only write—raises it into friendship, and encourages the modesty of our nature, impelling us to assume the language and express all the feelings, of an established attachment.

2910 11.120 To M[rs] W. & Sir G. B.—Much in us we can scarce endure ourselves to know, & one of the most fearful attributes of God his omniscience/yet often it would be desirable to have the real Wrong & its context known/Extremes meet, callous & anxious Affection.

2911 11.121 Φύονται δὲ καὶ νέοις *f53* ἐν ἀνδράσι πολιαὶ θαμὰ, καὶ παρὰ τὸν ἁλικίας ἐοικότα χρόνον.
Πινδ: Ολυμπ· δ. Επ. α.

2912 11.122 D[r] Hutton/ πολιᾶς εἶπε τιν' ἀυτὸς ὁρᾶν ἔνδον θαλάσσας αὐξομέναν πεδόθεν πολύβοσκον γαῖαν ἀνθρώ- ποισι καὶ ἔυφρονα μάλοις
Ολυμπ: Z. St. δ.

2913 11.123

Ἐλαφρὸν, ὅστις πημάτων ἔξω πόδα
Ἔχει, περαινεῖν νουθετεῖν τε τοὺς κακῶς
Πράσσοντας ἐγὼ δὲ ταῦθ' ἅπαντ' ἠπιστάμην.
Ἑκὼν, ἑκὼν ἥμαρτον, οὐκ ἀρνήσομαι.

Eschy. Prom. Vinct: L. 264.

f116ᵛ 2914 16.363   The Pine-tree top-blasted applied by Swift pro-
phetically to himself; the Chesnut a fine shewy tree and its wood
excellent but that, alas! it dies away at the *heart* first = poor me!

2915 16.364   Memory, a wan misery-Eyed Female, still gazing
with snatches of the eye at present forms to annihilate the one
thought into which her Being had been absorbed—& every form
recalled & refixed—In the effort it seemed to be fluttering off—the
moment the present form had been seen, it returned—She fed on
f117 bitter fruits from the Tree of Life—& often she attempted to tear
off from her forehead a seal, which Eternity had placed there;
and instantly she found in her Hand a hideous phantom of her own
visage, with that seal on its forehead; and as she stood horror-
struck beholding the phantom-head so wan & supernatural, which
she seemed to hold before her eyes with right hand too *numb* to
feel or be felt/itself belonging to the eye alone, & like a ⟨distant⟩
rock in a rain-mist, distinguishable by one shade only of substance/
(i.e. the vision enriched by subconsciousness of palpability by in-
fluent recollections of Touch)

2916 16.365   A Parson—Genuine old Port never hurt any
man/

f117ᵛ 2917 16.366   A moral painting/Glittering black eyes over ~~pur-~~
~~ple~~ dark crimson cheeks, & lips and the end of the nose with hues
of a bluish purple/in his right side under the false ribs a window,
& view of a swoln, schirrous, or half-eaten Liver.

2918 16.367   I scarcely know so pregnant a Thesis, as Fulke
Greville's Line 76ᵗʰ of his Alaham, Time ※ fashions ~~manners~~
minds, minds manners, manners Fate. Mem. my own note in the

waste Leaf of ~~the~~ his works. ⊗ In part, no doubt, this is a cycle; Time meaning the effect of the aggregate of minds and manners; but in part it may & does mean the effect of accidents, phys: mor: and polit:/as earthquakes, deluges/2. discoveries by individuals not rising out, as ~~a natural~~ the necessary growth of the then state of Society, as of the mariner's compass, printing, America, the Pox, f_{118} Potatoes, a Buonaparte, &c, tho' even these are, some more, some less, connected with & influenced by the state aggregate of men, but as a stimulant, or at the most a conditio sine qua non, not as an involving cause/3. Crusade, Stamp out, a numerous royal family, accidental presence or lack of great Talents in the Sovereigns of Europe, Philip 2nd, Henry 4th of France, Queen Elizabeth, Prince Maurice &c—Kings of—, Spain, Austria, Prussia, Russia, Naples, at present.

2919 16.368 Death first of all—eats of the Tree of Life/& becomes immortal describe the frightful metamorphosis/weds the Hamadryad of the Tree/their Progeny—in the manner of Dante/—

2920 16.369 A. In whom or what shall we find Help or Hope In these Extremities?—B. In whom or what? Passion by counter- f_{118}^v passion. ~~Extremes still propagating raise counter extremes~~ In the legitimate offspring of Extremity, Counter-extremes—which like some cruel popular & injured Prince Dethrone their Parent.

2921 16.370–1 A bodiless Substance, an unborrow'd Self, God in God immanent, the eternal Word, That goes forth yet remains, Crescent and Full, and Wanes. Yet ever ~~one~~ entire and one/—At the same time (it dawns & sets & crowns the Height of Heaven) the dawning, setting Son, at the same time the Tenant of each Sign Thro' all the zodiac/~~Yet~~ While each in its own Hour Boasts & beholds ~~the~~ exclusive Presence, ~~the~~ a Peculiar Orb. Each the great Traveller's Inn/Yet still the unmoving Sun—Great genial agent on all finite Souls, And by that action ~~cloathes itself with~~ puts on finiteness absolute Infinite whose dazzling robe Flows in rich folds & plays in shooting Hues of infinite Finiteness.

⟨Bright⟩ clouds of reverence sufferably bright
That intercept the dazzle not the Light
That veil the finite form, the boundless power reveal
Itself an earthly sun, of pure intensest White,
Adorn the sky—and what might be
disregard by ~~its~~ borrowed Beauty swells
To Honor without form/& what might be idolatry,
    makes spiritual worship—
Satisfies the mind's & eyes' necessity

f119   With form, a form that all informs against
itself, grateful proclaims its limited Honors whence
As silence too deep disturbs, tumultuates
distracts the mind that fain would feed itself
by awe, Some gentle Sound, Huge forests'
~~murmurs~~ whispers voyaging from far or musical
murmur of the distant ocean Preserves
the inner silence, makes it fruitful,
like prattling rill that trills down to
the roots, the dark & voiceless Parent
of the Tree, Its waving Branches, &
its fluttering Leaves, Sweet undersong
& hospitable Bower, and dear Repast
of hymning Birds—On ceremonies for Religion—
especially, the Cherubim &c of the Jewish Temple—

2922 16.372   To a former Friend who pleaded how near he
formerly had been, how near & close a friend—Yes! you were indeed near to my Heart, and native to my soul, ~~a~~ as Part of my
Being & its natural/Even as the Chaff to Corn,—but since that
time—~~By~~ thro' whose fault I'll be mute—I have been thrashed
out by the flail of ~~Flail~~ Experience—Because you have been, therefore nevermore Can you be part of the ~~winnow~~ grain.

2923 16.373   Too much & too little/This soar'd & burnt, the
other stoop'd & drown'd—

2924   16.374

   And sad experience saw your Treachery,
   Yet saw not half for the Tears that bedimmed her eyes//

2925   16.375

      For the true state of true Affection is Wonder $f119^v$
      at other's Worth; Faith without hire;
      Unwearied Toil; unrecompensed Desire.

                              F. Greville. Alaham.

      By fires of Hell which burn & have no light,
      By those foul Spirits which ill men only see
      For the true States &c

                              Ditto

an astrologer = *Star-divine.*

      Magnificence is princely Mystery: All great
      Estates by great expence are known. Prepare
      excess; let no cost be forgot/
      It makes men wonder tho' they honor not.—
      Music to fix the wandering Spirits voice,—
      and sweeten Envy's thoughts in unity—
      Lights of all kinds the light of Day put out:
      For Darkness so enamell'd is devout.

                              Ditto.

   When Fear propounds, Men ever choose with Loss,

                              Fulke Greville's (Lord
                              Brooke's) Alaham, Act
                              the 4th, Scene the 1st, line
                              47th.

   Zophi.
   Scorn'd, blind, I cannot harm. Ah! let me live!
   Let Power despise my needless, guiltless Blood.
   THE STRENGTH OF FEAR THE LOSS OF ALL THINGS,
   BUT OF LIFE CAN BEAR.

                              Act 4, Sc. 2/.

The whole Scene is excellent, even dramatically.

2926 15.243

f112ᵛ His own fair countenance, his kingly forehead
His tender smiles, Love's day-dawn on his Lips
~~Mild with smiles with~~ that put on such ~~an~~ heavenly spiritual light
At the same moment in his steadfast eyes/
Were virtue's native crest, the innocent Soul's
Unconscious meek Self-heraldry—to man
Genial, and pleasant to his guardian angel—
He suffered, nor complain'd: ~~yet~~ tho' oft, with tears,
He mourn'd the oppression of his helpless Brethren,
And ~~with a~~ sometimes with a deeper, ~~just~~ holier grief
Mourn'd for the oppressor:
                    S.T.C. ⟨but this in Sabbath Hours—⟩
                    a solemn Grief
     That like a Cloud at Sunset,
f113 Was but the veil of inward meditation,
Pierc'd thro'
And saturate with the intellectual rays, it soften'd.

2927 15.244   Self-respect, the Parent of Self-controll, by it supported, & sustain'd, as a dear Father by a duteous Child/

2928 15.245   Scene described between Albert & Maria after
some proud unfeeling Taunts from her respecting his College
unchastity. Chaste really, enraged at Osorio is supposed by Albert to be shocked concerning him/The extreme purity of his
Love for Maria one occasion negatively no connection with her—
no more than eating an unfit fruit—&c

2929 15.246   The ruins of Europe are as a shattered mirror,
that multiplies to his eye the images of his own countenance; & re-
f113ᵛ flect Shame and Despair on him (L. Grenv. or Wynd.) in each.

2930 15.247   Medea in banishment: the moral that extrava-
gancy from nature vitiates fatally the piety of the original Feeling,
& being Delusion must end in and be punished by Delusion—or
that means unauthorized by our natural feelings cannot be justified
by a good intention but rather prove that tho' the motives, of which

the mind is conscious, may be fair & of a saintly seeming, but that the mind itself is disordered and its *impulses* possessions of a familiar Spirit acting *upon* us, not inspirations of the representative *f114* of God within us, the general Spirit that acts in each for all; and in all for each.—The more I think, the more am I pleased with this Subject.

2931 15.250   Thierry & Theodoret give noble Hints; and Alaham nobler still. The characters are admirable/in both/not what they are, but what they suggest. Mem. to ⟨frame &⟩ write out a detailed Plot of each.

2932 15.251
  Bid winds tell whence they come, & turn them back—
  As vainly Strength speaks to a broken mind.

  better—Let Eagles bid the Tortoise sunward soar—

2933 15.252   To be sure, some good may be imagined in any *f114ᵛ* evil—as he whose house is on fire in a dark night, his Loss gives him Light to run away—

2934 11.32   The flame of a candle end, wrapped round with *f13ᵛ* thick paper. 1. The beautiful amber edges of the flame, including the yellow-white flame. 2. The unsteadiness of the outer flame; but which is most often the *head* of an Halbert, with about 1 and ½ of its length, of the spear-wood, to wch the head is fastened. But *f14* (3ʳᵈˡʸ, & to explain the words "outer flame":) the regular flame, amber-edged too, within the flame; and remaining of the same

form ⟋⟍ , horizontal circles decreasing to the keenest point, save

when this inner Soul forced the outer to combine with it for a moment, & the whole flame became, for a second of a second, one/ *f14ᵛ*

and of the form of the inner flame. Then again the halbert

Head.
                   Nov. 15. 1806.

ƒ54   2935 11.125   Keswick; finally resolved Wēsday, 15 Nov. 1806.

ƒ114ᵛ   2936 15.253   —like a lake beneath the Sun seemed to possess
in its own right & prodigally give the fiery Light, which by not
receiving it ~~sent~~ flashed forth/

2937 15.254   Æolian Harp motive for opening the Sash; & at
once lets in music & sweet air; purifies & delights, = moral Eloquence—Poetry—

2938 15.255   O Elpizomene! When shall I have to write a
letter to you, with no *other* Sorrow to communicate, than that absence from you, which writing itself implies?
                                    Friday, Nov. 28. 1806
ƒ115   I know, you love me!—My reason knows it, my heart feels it/
yet still let your eyes, your hands tell me/still say, o often & often
say, My beloved! I love you/indeed I love you/for why should not
my ears, and all my outward Being share in the Joy—the fuller
my inner Being is of the sense, the more my outward organs yearn
& crave for it/O bring my whole nature into balance and harmony.

2939 11.33
ƒ14ᵛ   Beneficium dando accepit, qui digno dedit—
                                                Laberius.

2940 11.34   Amabam Galliam (quatenus et quantum a vere
ƒ15   Anglo amari Gallia potest) vel eo nomine quod——nobis dedisset:
nunc odio eandem eo etiam ipso nomine prosequor.

2941 11.35   Stoicorum στοικώτατος.

2942 11.36   Vobis, bonis et multis scripsi ad *fructum;* non
paucis illis ac malis ad calumniam: vobis *cordatis,* qui ritus, mores,
historias recordamini; non oculatis istis, qui nihil, nisi quod ante
ƒ15ᵛ   oculos est, "vident, intelligunt, sapiunt," Animis denique scripsi,
non auribus—
          Farnabius ad Lectores in editione sua Juvenalis—

2943 11.37   Empires, States, &c may be beautifully illustrated
by a large clump of Coal placed on a fire—Russia for instance—
or of small coal moistened, & by the first action of the Heat of
any Government, not absolutely lawless, formed into a cake, as   *f16*
the Northern Nations under Charlemagne—then a slight impulse
from the ~~hand~~ fall of accident or the hand of patriotic foresight,
splits it into many, & makes each burn with its own flame, till at
length all burning equally, it becomes again one by universal similar action/& then burns low, cinerizes, & without accession of rude
materials goes out—

2944 11.38   To Fear—most men affected by belief of *reality*   *f16ᵛ*
attached to the wild-weed spectres of infantine nervousness—but I
affected by them simply, & of themselves—/but for the last years
I own & mourn a more deleterious Action of *Fear*—fear of horrors
in *Sleep,* driving me to dreadful remedies & stimuli, when awake,
not for the present Sensation, but to purchase daily a wretched
Reprieve from the torments of each night's Dæmons/selling my-   *f17*
self to the Devil to avoid the Devil's own Visitations, & thereby
becoming his *Subject.*

2945 11.39   Beauty of regular Government illustrated in the
nostrums of antiquity, under the Slavery even of republics, & still
more the decivism & total Slavery of the *Empire*/so the mirrors
of Archimedes & Proclus, the Steam Engines of Anthemius, the
Powder &c
        Of the different Monsters of the earth, the vivaparæous ~~Yellers~~   *f17ᵛ*
of the African Sands, the oviparæous [?~~Hessand~~] of Peru or Para-
guay, or the Deiparæ of Palestine and Indostan.

2946 11.98 $A + B = Z + G = Platinum/$ *f46*

2947 11.99   Playing a sad aftergame for his kingdom—

2948 11.100   Like the Cormorant or Sea Mew, careless what
course they veer, & only solicitous to float atop of ~~the~~ each Billow
as it rises whichever way it rolled—

2949 11.101   The Stag or Hart instantly on shedding his Horns, hides from his fellows in thickets never venturing out to pasture but by night.

New Horns are very painful: even the flies excite their sensibility.

ƒ45ᵛ   2950 11.102   The Rock of Names—indignant answer to Australis—/the view of the lake from Sunset—/the lines of Foam/"I have it down in my pocket-book"—/all the answer to be introduced in the Soother of Absence.

2951 11.103

~~Like the soft-eyed Hart (Hind)~~
Lur'd by her ~~Hunter with the Shepherd's Pipe~~ Flute,
~~Whose music~~ voyaging the twilight ~~wind breezes~~
~~Like~~ As the shy Hind, the soft-eyed gentle Brute,
Now moves, now stops, approaching by degrees
At length ~~emerginges~~ from the sheltring Trees,
Lur'd by her Hunter with the shepherd's Flute
Whose music travelling on the twilight Breeze
When all beside was mute,
ƒ45   She ~~lov'd to hear~~ oft had heard unharm'd & ever loves to hear,
She, fearful Beast! but that no Sound of Fear.

2952 11.104   Nimis augusta et divina res est nuspiam in errorem prolabi. Beveridge de Ling: orientalium Præstantiâ.
   Dies diem docet, et quod heri doctiorem latuit, hodie rudiori innotescat.   Idem.

2953 11.105   In any poem on Sleep the sleeps cum amatâ, familiar, confident/O! this felt with enthusiasm & so expressed
ƒ44ᵛ   enumerating all the other excellencies of Sleep/—Soother of Absence.

2954 11.106   Spite of Reason Anger & Resentment ~~called~~ carried on amid anguish & self-trouble by mere power of distinct Images and Thoughts.

2955 11.107   Of the profanation of the Sacred word, *the People*
— [?every/any] brutal Burdett-Mob, assembled on some drunken
St Monday of Faction, is *the People* forsooth—& ~~now~~ each leprous
ragamuffin, like a Circle in Geometry, is at once one, and all—&   *f44*
calls his own brutal Self, "us, the People!"—and who are the
Friends of the People? Not those who would wish to elevate each
of them, or at least, the Child who is to take his place in the flux
of Life & Death, into something worthy of Esteem & capable of
Freedom, but those who flutter & infuriate them, as they *are*.—A
contradiction in the very thought! For if really, they are good &
wise, virtuous and well-informed, how weak must be the motives   *f43ᵛ*
of discontent to a truly moral Being—but if the contrary, and the
motives for discontent proportionally strong, how without guilt
and absurdity appeal to them, as Judges & arbiters? He alone is
entitled to a share in the government of all, who has learnt to
govern himself—there is but one possible ground of a Right to
Freedom, viz. to understand & revere its Duties.

2956 11.40   A remarkably mild winter = to a Winter slum-   *f17ᵛ*
bring soft   seemed to smile at visions of Buds and Blooms, &
dreamt so livelily of Spring that his stern visage had relaxed, and
softened itself into a dim Likeness of his Dream. The Soul of the
Vision breathed thro' & lay, like light, upon his Face—   *f18*

2957 11.41   Saturday/Heavens! what an outrageous Day of
Winter this is & has been/Terrible weather for the last 2 months;
but this is horrible/Thunder, Lightning, floods of rain, & volleys
of Hail, with such frantic Winds.

Decemb. 1806—

2958 11.42
—To me the opening of thy bright blue eye
~~Seem'd to shed~~ Suffused with Light on every object nigh,
And shed a kind of Life.—

2959 11.43   Walton, in the Dale, on the Ribble/Church &   *f18ᵛ*
House on the Hill/House in a wooded *How*/
   Kendal; Cary Point, exquisite old man & Langdale/Sea & the
Islelike Headland Yews on the Precipice &c/

f121   2960 16.379   S.T. Coleridge
                             S.T. Coleridge
                             Dorothy Wordsworth
                             Sara Hutchinson

        2961 16.380   This *dwelling* Kiss—

        2962 16.381   Sick drooping children of a wretched Parent, =
yellowing leaflets on a broken twig, broke ere its June

        2963 16.382   A forced Marriage, a capital subject for a Trag-
                             edy.

        2964 16.383   Blest in the lovely marriage of pure words = the
                             Greek Language/

        2965 16.384
f121ᵛ
                             In a pamphlet Sheet, "LONDONS
                             FLAMES Discovered by
                             INFORMATIONS
                             Taken before the
                             COMMITTEE
                             Appointed to Enquire after the
                             Burning of the CITY of
                             LONDON
                             and after the Insolency
                             Of The (sm. Cap. *not Ital.*)
                             PAPISTS &c
                             London, printed in the year 1667.

f122   I find the following Lines containing the word avaunt//Taken
up at Leedes by Mʳ Thwaites Man a Recusant.

                             Cover the Fire, ye Hugonots,
                             That have so branded us with Plotts:
                             And henceforth no more Bonfires make
                             Till ye avaunt in the Stygian Lake, &c

        Dated the 5ᵗʰ of November, Anno Salutis 1666, & Anno primo
Restitutionis Romanæ Religionis in Anglia

2966 16.385   Stephen, King of Poland, said, Ego sum Rex Populorum, non Conscientiarum.—

2967 16.386   The Horrid Sin of Man-catching
The Second Part 1681.
p.1. In such a shamming Age as this wherein Shamming is become a Trade or Science, & the Workmen so ingenious, that no sooner is one *Sham* discovered but a new one is contrived to *sham* that, so   *f122ᵛ*
that for these last (3) years there hath been nothing but *Sham* upon Sham, or rather one continued *Sham* in several disguises—

2968 16.387   Many most ludicrously flat or insignificant lines quoted with a pompous epithet upon the Author/as the profound —says—or—as that galaxy of bright Imagination, Jer. Taylor—&c &c/remind me of Cicero de Oratore,

> sic a *summo Poeta* appellatus
> Egregie cordatus Homo Catus
> > Ælius Sextus.

2969 16.388
> Corrigere res est tanto magis ardua quanto,
> Magnus Aristarcho major Homerus erat
> > Ov. Pont. 1. 3. El. 11.

2970 15.256   Quartz, Felspar, Mica = Granite. Quartz, Fel-   *f115ᵛ*
spar, Mica, Hornblende = Sienite.—Various triple combinations of Q. F. M. & H. with shorl, serpentine, steatites, & garnets = Granitine. Quartz, Mica & Garnet = Norka of Murkstein. Quartz + Mica = Stell-stein.   Horn-blende + Mica = Grünstein.   Quartz + Steatites = Saxum Molare. Capillary Shoots of Shorl in Quartz = Hair-Stone—. Granilites = Granites of more than 3 Constituent Parts. Gneiss is = Granite, only fibrous instead of granular. The excess of mica over Quartz converts Gneiss to Schistose Mica. Porphyry = visible scatterlings of Felspar whether in a siliceous, or argillaceous, or magnesian, or calcareous Ground: though it should likewise contain Quartz, Hornblende, or Mica. Sandstone = small

_f116_ grains of flint, quartz, &c, either in calcareous, siliceous, argillaceous, or ferruginous ground. With mica = micaceus Sandstones.
Calcareous Stones: Calcar. Earth ⟨called Lime⟩ of a dry harsh
meagre feel:—Stones of which it forms a third part, never so hard
as to strike fire. Limestones, Marbles, Chalk, Tufa, Calc-Spars,
Stalactite, Stalagmite, Flos ferri, Pisolithus, Hammites or Roe-
stone, Alabaster, Sattin Spar, Swine-stone, in all their varieties are
Calc. Earth = Lime with Carbonic Acid. Lime supersaturated with
Carb. Acid makes an Elastic Marble, found in Switzerland & from
Dolomieu called Dolomite. With sulph. Acid = Selenite/the Gyp-
sums with Fl. Ac. = fluor Spar. Pure, i.e. unslacked, or quick Lime
+ water + sand = Mortar. Magnesia + silex and alumine =
Talcs. Mag. + oxide of Iron & carb. acid = the various Steatites.

_f116ᵛ_ 2971 15.257   The following Work I should suppose almost
secure of a considerable Sale; the four Gospels reduced into one
narration so that every thing in each not found in the other be
added to that which is common to all—(so far may probably be
found ready-done)—with a collection of all the striking parallel
Passages from the Ancient Moralists before Christ, and from those
of whom tho' after Christ there is no ⟨probable⟩ reason that they
had seen the Gospels: with an Essay, prefixed or annexed, concerning the nature and true point of the superiority of the Gospel
as a system of religion, Ethics, to that of the Ancient Philosophers,
of whatever Sect.

2972 15.258   A sort of experience like the effect of lightning
which striking on the eyes of sleeping men opens them to close no
more, and on those of waking men closes them to open no more.

2973 15.259   Aristotle in his reasonings concerning vision ad-
_f117_ duces an instance of one Antipho, who always saw his own perfect
image facing him the air, wherever he was or whithersoever he
moved. How many moral antiphos!
⟨Alas! a great moiety of the whole Race!⟩

2974 15.269   Mem. Mr Finch   *f124*
                 Travelling Tutorship &c &c &c

                 ———

                 Mr Warnford
                 [? Nab/Not/Box] Hill

2975 11.44   **The Epoch.**   *f18^v*
Saturday, 27th December, 1806—Queen's Head, Stringston, ½ a
mile from Coleorton Church, 50 minutes after 10/

2976 11.45   Fate-encircled Life: your days are tedious, & were   *f19*
it not for riotous Dancing at the hour when ~~all~~ matrons sleep,
dreaming of Babe or Husband—Husband or Babe or both by her
side, or in her arms there really being were it not for feasting,
dancing, wine, which drown and hang in you every honest Thought
And on your eyelids ~~hangs~~ so heavily, They have no power to
look so high as heaven, you'd muse yourself into a ~~present~~ Hell
of Thought By sense of the Hell that is already round you, upon
you, in you/an outcast from your nature, yea, only then being   *f19^v*
something that the Sun can shine on blameless when you pine in
anguish o'er that you were and are not.

2977 11.46   And the free Light may triumph in our faces—

2978 11.47   SUNDAY. Jan^ry 2

2979 11.48   The Coati-mundi and some of the long-tailed   *f20*
monkeys with a strange appetite delight in eating their Tails, "and
seem to feel no pain in wounding a part of the Body so remote
from the center of circulation." Buffon: = English ministers to
Ireland, E. Indies, America

2980 11.49   Of the Passion of Love in very young Children,
describe, paint, & explain, & deduce, for the Soother of Absence/

2981 11.50   Lurid in the fallen Snow the leafless Beeches   *f20^v*
                 Twigs—

2982 11.51   T. H. 25 July 1802.—
                         Aged 10 weeks—
                The Babe was sucking at the Breast,
                When God did call him to his Rest

                      83—and 87 years/
              Not more with silver Hairs than virtue crown'd
f2r   The good old Pair take up this Spot of Ground/
              Tread in their Steps & you will surely find
              Their Rest above, below their Peace of Mind—
                    Ashby Church Yard   6 Feb. 1807—

2983 11.52   Of the evil arising from all Revealed Religions,
in as much as by attempting to given motives to Reason & Goodness
f2r° beyond & alien to Reason and Goodness, it weakens and degrades
the Souls of men by an unnatural Stimulus; and at all events ~~the~~
so perverts the visual nerve of the mind that we still look at Virtue
asquint.

2984 11.53   Could I ~~fearel~~ for a moment the supremacy of
Love suspended in my nature, by accidents of temporary Desire;
were I conscious for a moment of an Interregnum in the Heart,
f22   were the ~~usurper~~ Rebel to sit on the *Throne* of my Being, even
tho' it were only that the rightful Lord of my Bosom were sleeping, soon to awake & expel the Usurper, I should feel myself as
much fallen & as unworthy of her Love in any ⟨such⟩ tumult of
Body indulged toward her, as if I had roamed, ⟨like a Hog⟩ in the
rankest ~~Stews~~ Lanes of a ~~prostitute~~ city, battening on the loathsome
f22° offals of Harlotry/yea, the guilt would seem greater to me/but
when Love, like a Volcano beneath a sea always burning, tho' in
silence, flames up in his strength at some new accession, o how can
the waters but heave & roll in billows!—driven by no wind on the
mere Surface, save that which their own tumult creates, but the
mass is agitated from the depths, & the waves tower up as if to
make room for the stormy Swelling.

f23   2985 11.54   A Cloud before the cleft of a high crag, like a
Sheep that stands alone, motionless, on the perilous ridge of a
mountain—

2986 11.55   τῷ καὶ ἐγὼ
καίπερ ἀχνύμενος
θυμον, αἰτέομαι
χρυσέαν καλέσαι
μοῖσαν. ἐκ μεγάλων
δὲ πενθέων λυθέντες,
μή τ᾽ ἐν ὀρφανία πέσωμεν
στεφάνων, μή τὲ κά-
-δεα θεραπευε. παυ-
-σάμενοι δ᾽ απρήκτων κάκων,
γλυκύ τι δαμωσώμεθα,
καὶ μετα πόνον·
      Πινδ. Ισθ: ειδ. Η.
       Διαιρ: α.

2987 11.56   Moonlight gleams, and massy glooms—   f23ᵛ

2988 11.57   In the forest the spots of moonlight of the wildest
outlines, not unfrequently approaching to so near to the shape of
man, & the domestic animals most attached to him, as to be easily
conjured into them by a fancyful, and mistaken by terror, moved
& started as the winds stirred the Branches; that it almost seemed,
like a flight of Faery lucent spirits, of Moonlight, Sylphs and
Sylphids dancing & capable of capering in a world of Shadows/
once where our path was completely overshadowedcanopied by by
the meeting Boughs for a stone-throw, as I halloo'd to those behind   f24
me, a sudden flash of Light darted down as it were, upon the path
close before me, with such rapid & indescribable effect, that my
life seemed snatched away from me—not by terror, but by the
whole attention being suddenly, & unexpectedly, seized hold of—
if one would could conceive a violent Blow given by an unseen
hand, yet without pain, or local sense of injury—of the weight
falling here, or there—it might not ill assist in conceiving the   f24ᵛ
feeling—This I found was occasioned by a some very large Bird,
who, scared by my noise, had suddenly flown upward, and by the
spring of his feet or body had driven down the branch on which he
was a-perch.

2989 11.58   I had a confused shadow, rather than an image, in my recollection, like that from a thin Cloud/as if the Idea were descending, tho' still in some measureless Height.

f25   2990 11.59   I languish away my Life in misery, unutterably wretched from the gnawings of the Disease, and almost equally miserable by the Fear of the Remedy.—or—harrassed by the Disease, and miserable from the Fear of the Remedy.—

While by the Delay not only the Remedy becomes more difficult, & the Fear consequently greater, in addition to the growing exacerbation of the Disease, but there is regularly annexed to it the pangs
f25ᵛ of Self-reproach & blackning Despair from the Delay.

And sapp'd Resolves, the rotten Banks of Fools against the swelling Tide of Habit. ⟨and my Heart *mantles* in its own delight.⟩

2991 11.60
The spruce and limber Yellow Hammer
In ~~early~~ the dawn of Spring, in the sultry Summer,
~~On the~~ In hedge, or tree his hours beguiling
With notes, as of one that Brass is filing.

2992 11.61   The Red-breast while singing opens and shuts the upper and lower mandible like a tiny pair of the finest scissors!

2993 11.62
With kindred earth-clods on a level
⟨No more in lusts to roll and revel⟩
Here lies the churl, call'd fat Tom Navel,
Who was a Beast and is a Devil.

2994 11.63   As when the Taper's white cone of Flame is seen double, till the eye moving brings them into one space; & there
f26   they become one—so did the Idea in my imagination coadunate with your present Form/soon after I first gazed on you with love.

2995 11.64

And in Life's noisiest hour,
There whispers still the ceaseless Love of Thee,
                    solace
The heart's *Self-commune*, & soliloquy.
                    the self-listning H⟨e⟩art

2996 11.65

You mould my Hopes, you fashion me within;
And to the leading Love-throb in the Heart
Thro' all my Being all my pulses beat.
You lie in ~~my~~ all my many Thoughts, like Light
Like the fair Light of Dawn, or summer-Eve
On rippling Stream, or cloud-reflecting Lake.

2997 11.66

And looking to the Heaven, that bends above you
How oft I bless the Lot, that made me love you.

2998 11.67   If I appear *little* (fretful and sullen concerning   *f26ᵛ*
Trifles) o! consider, Pασα that this is only, because my intense
Veol makes even Trifles that relate to W̲ = the Tree that fixes
its root even deeper than the grave, so great to me, that Wealth,
& Reputation, become trifles compared with it. And Fame, alas! I
am not *strong* enough to be *good* enough to look steadily at it, unless thro' the medium of the Delight, it would afford you.—And
even Virtue & the Hope of Heaven—O God! forgive me!—Can   *f27*
even the Eagle soar without Wings? And the wings given by thee
to my soul—what are they, but the Love & Society of that Beloved
⟨one⟩/I have, like the Exeter Cathedral Organ, a pipe of far-sound-
ing Music in its construction, yet is it dumb, a gilded Tube, till the
Sister ~~Tube~~ pipe be placed in correspondence/O *Beloved!*—Beloved!—ah! how ~~mightier~~ what are Words but air? & impulses of
air? O who has deeply felt, deeply, deeply! & not fretted & grown   *f27ᵛ*
impatient at the inadequacy ⟨of Words to Feeling,⟩ of the symbol
to the Being?—Words—what are they but a subtle *matter?* and
the meanness of Matter must they have, & the Soul must pine in

them, even as the Lover who can press kisses only ~~on his~~ this the
garment of one indeed beloved/O bear witness my Soul! bear witness the permanence of my Being!—even such a feeling must ac-
f28   company the strictest union, the nearest kiss, that can be—it is still
at once the Link & the Wall of Separation/O what then are Words,
but articulated Sighs of a Prisoner heard from his Dungeon!
powerful only as they express their utter impotence!—O then pity,
o pity me! but do not blame, if when I have been disappointed of
your society after having been permitted to hope for & expect it,
my heart-throbs have told the moment so loudly that Pain has
f28ᵛ   come on, and with Pain sad Thoughts, & sense of my own small
Worth & of others' superiority—my want of so much that must be
lovely in the Heart of Woman, Strength, Manliness, & Manly
Beauty—& thence Despondence, and a dream of painful fancies
overshining the taper-light of Reason—~~eyes~~ heart sunken, and eyes
incapable of looking at you! For whenever I seem to be slighted
~~for~~ by you, I think not what I am to you, but only what I have a
f29   *claim* to be—& then I sink—& but that it is a dream, & I still half-
consciously expect to awake from the night-mair—I could not but
die—die,/as an *act!*—O! SARA!

2999 11.68   I fall asleep night after night watching that perpetual feeling, to which Imagination or the real affection of that
organ or its appendages by that feeling beyond the other parts of
the body (tho' no atom but seems to share in it) has given a place
f29ᵛ   and seat of manifestation a shechinah in the heart.—Shall I ~~do~~ try
to image it to myself, as an animant self-conscious pendulum, continuing for ever its arc of motion by the for ever anticipation of
it?—or like some fairer Blossom-life in the centre of the Flower-
polypus, a life within Life, & constituting a part of the Life, the
includes it? A consciousness within a Consciousness, yet mutually
penetrated, each possessing both itself & the other—distinct tho' indivisible!—S.T.C.—

f30   3000 11.69   The 2. currents in the Straits of Gibraltar—one
flows in, the under current out—& what one adds, its opponent returns. = Passion and Awe/Body and Soul.

VIII. John Constable: *Coleorton Hall*

Wash drawing. C. R. Leslie, in his *Memoirs of the Life of John Constable* Chap VII, records from a letter to Mrs Constable for 18 Nov 1823: ". . . all that morning [a few days earlier] I had been engaged on a little sketch in Miss Southey's album, of this house, which pleased all parties here, very much." See 1938n and 3001

3001 11.70   Feb. 1807—Snow on the Hedge † on the Ashby-ward Road, ~~close by one of the~~ eagles claws & whipt-cream, the fungus, ⟨hat or tree—of vast size & divine,⟩ the elegant heart, ⟨or bladder-purse⟩ the icicles &c in the cavernlets of Snow/Lines of Motion, ⟨exquisite throughout; especially in the waving of the edges or brims.⟩

† extending about 20 yards, & beginning about 70 strides from the ~~third~~ second Gate below that which faces Coleorton New-farm

3002 11.71   The dawning Grey.—

3003 11.72

~~Not knowing Nor~~   you, ~~by you unknown,~~   *f30ᵛ*
~~No voice with fond regretful Tone~~
~~For me had made the mind-embodying~~ Air
Maid now ~~Thrill so deeply lov'd be music with your name.~~

I knew you not, I knew not that you were/
No Voice had made the mind-embodying air,
Be music with your name—

3004 11.73
Like some vast tropic Tree, itself a Wood,
That ~~crowns his Top~~ veils its head with clouds, beneath the flood
Feeds ~~his~~ its deep roots, & with ~~his~~ the jutting flank
Of ~~his~~ its huge Base controlls the fronting Bank
Scoop'd by the slanting current ~~from its way~~ to a Bay
Where lies the Boat for such as night or day
~~Pay~~ Bring here their gifts, & ~~tremble as they~~ bring in the
                                                                        distance kneel
~~Between his Fork the uncouth Idol sit~~
~~Beside the Fane below, the Dervise sits,~~
~~And his~~ To the ~~uncouth grim~~ dusk God, that makes them Woe
                                                                        or Weal–
Between ~~his~~ the Fork the uncouth Idol knits
His fluted Brows: low murmurs stir by fits,   *f31*
And by the Fane below the nail-boss'd Santon sits;
(Beside the Fane the Priest in steady Twilight sits)
And horror from ~~the~~ his broad Top's branchy wreath
Breathes on the rude Idolatry beneath.

As some vast tropic Tree, itself a Wood,
That crests its Head with clouds, beneath the flood
Feeds ~~his~~ its deep roots, and with the bulging flank
Of its wide Base controlls the fronting bank,
(By the slant currents pressure scoop'd away
The fronting Bank becomes a ~~froth~~ foam-pil'd Bay)
High in ~~the~~ its Fork the uncouth Idol knits
His channel'd Brows: low murmurs stir by fits:
And dark below the horrid Faquir sits;
An Horror from its broad Head's branchy Wreath
Broods o'er the rude Idolatry beneath.—

f31ᵛ   3005 11.74   The Pike of Teneriffe at the moment of Sunrise
not only covers the Isle of Teneriffe & Gomera &c but extends over
the visible Ile even to the visible Horizon, where it turns up &
appears to image its point on the air itself, & stoop of the Sky.

3006 11.75   The Golden Kingdoms of Africa between 15 & 17
N. Latitude & South of the Sanaga † & East of the great River or
Branch Falema, that runs ⟨due⟩ South out of it—the chief mines, or
rather impregnations of gold are † & north of the Gambra, are the
Mines of Segalla/~~namely~~ & of Ghinghi-faranna. (Item, to the
East of the Falema, 25 leagues from its confluence with the Sanaga,
& 5 leagues inland, between the Villages of Sambanura & Dallin-
f32   mûlet)—~~the~~ Segalla, 50 leagues from the mouth of the Falema,
and 500 paces to the Right, as you ascend the River/5 leagues
higher the Ghinghi-faranna, all full of Gold—/Then Nian-Sabana
on the River Sannon/at the very fountains of which are the rich,
RICH Mines of Tamba-awra/the Sannon ⟨Kolez⟩ is properly the
River of Gold—& from its fountains at Tamba-awra/thro' its whole
N. West course to its Fall into the Falema at the Gold Mines of
Naye washes earth of Gold & rolls on Golden Sands—

3007 11.76   A People of silent Traders near Jaye, on the
Gambra, far above Barrakonda, with Lips that would putrefy if
f32ᵛ   they did not continue put salt on them/Are Mʳ Windham's Lips
in the same necessity of the Sal atticum?

3008 11.77 A Snug of weather-fending Rocks [?butting/
buffing] stream

3009 24.1 Dr Crompton f_1
~~13~~ 13 Essex Street

3010 24.2 N.B. In preparation for my first important Work
—X^{tn} Rev^n. proved by X^{tn} Rel^n.—to try to procure an account of
the population of each separate Parish of Bristol—to subtract all
sectaries—& then to compare the remainder with the capacity of the
Parish Church. If I am not grossly misinformed, not one 5th of
those, who are professedly Church-people, could be crowded into
S^t. Paul's Church/This would be of eminent service/

3011 24.4 degne di sommo stilo sono le somme cose, ciòè la f_2
SALUTE, l'AMORE, e la VIRTÙ, e quelle altre cose, che per cagion di
esse sono nella mente nostra concepute, pur che per niun accidente
non siano fatte vili. Guardisi adunque ciascuno, e discerna quello
che dicemo: e quando vuole queste tre cose puramente cantare,
overo quelle, che ad esse dittamente, e puramente segueno, prima
bevendo nel fonte di Elicona (that is, *waiting for and seizing the
moment of deep feeling & of stirring imagination*) ponga sicura-
mente a *l'accordata liyra il* sommo plettro (tensis fidibis Lyræ), e
costumatamente cominci; ma a fare questa canzone e questa divi-
sione, come si dee, qui è la difficoltà, quì è la fatica/perciò che mai f_2
senza acume d'ingegno, ne senza assiduità d'arte, ne senza abito di
scienze non si potra fare.
E questi sono quelli che 'l Poeta nel vi. de la Eneide chiami di-
letti da Dio, e da la ardente virtù alzati al Cielo, e figliuoli di Dio,
avegna che figuratamente parli. E però si confessa la sciocchezza di
coloro, i quali senza arte, e senza scienza, confidandosi solamente
del loro ingegno, si pongono a cantar sommamente le ~~somme~~ cose
somme. Adunque cessino questi tali da tanta loro presunzione; e
se per la loro naturale desidia sono Oche, non vogliano l'Aquila,
che altamente vola, imitare.
Dante de la volgare Eloquenza, Lib: Secondo, Cap. IV.

f3   Quelli poi sillabe pari/per la sua rozezza non usiamo se non
rare volte; *perciò, che ritengono la natura de i loro numeri, i quali
sempre soggiaceno a i numeri caffi (uneven) sì come fa la materia
a la forma.*

                                                    Idem—Cap. v.

3012 24.5
                        Rime di Dante
        III

        Questa Donna, ch'andar mi fa pensoso,
        Porta nel viso la virtù d'Amore;
        La qual risveglia dentro nello cuore
        Lo spirito gentil che v'era ascoso:
        Ella m' ha fatto tanto pauroso,
        Posciach'io vidi il mio dolce signore
        Negli occhi suoi con tutto il suo valore,
        Ch'io le vo presso, e riguardar non l'oso,
        E quando avvene che questi occhi miri,
        Io veggio in quella parte la salute
        Che l'intelletto mio non vi può gire:
        Allor si strugge sì la mia virtute,
        Che l'anima, che muove li sospiri,
        S'acconcia per voler da lei partire.

f3ᵛ   XI. The last line is of the *Head,* not the Heart, and too much
resembles Wit. The rest is sweet and pathetic.

        Nelle man vostre, o dolce donna mia,
        Raccomando lo spirito che muore,
        E se ne va sì dolente, che Amore
        Lo mira con pietà, che 'l manda via:
        Voi lo legaste alla sua signoria,
        Sicchè non ebbe poi alcun valore
        Di poterlo chiamar, se non signore,—
        Qualunque vuoi di me, quel vo'che sia:
        Io so che voi ogni torto dispiace,

Però la morte, che non ho servita,
Molto più m'entra nello core amara:
Gentil Madonna, mentre ho della vita,
Per tal ch'io mora consolato in pace,
Vi piaccia agli occhi miei non esser cara.

3013 24.6   Conciòsia cosa chè la di vostra Excellenza Onori-
ficabilitudinitate m'ha tanto sovramagnificentissimamente ricevuto,
&c &c. Compared with this how *dwarfish* would be our—As the
honorable nature of your Excellency has received me with such   *f4*
surpassing magnificence, &c—

> Uomo da se vertù fatta ha lontana
> Uomo non già, ma bestia, ch'uom somiglia—

3014 24.7   Canzone xiv, fra le Rime di Dante is a poem of
wild & interesting Images, intended as an Enigma, and to me an
Enigma it remains, spite of all my efforts. Yet it deserves transcrip-
tion, and translation—P.195.—A.D. 1806

Tre donne intorno al cuor mi son venute
  E seggionsi di fore,
  Che dentro siede Amore,
  Lo quale è in signoria della mia vita.
  Tanto son belle, e di tanta vertute;
  Che 'l possente signore,
  Dico quel che è nel core,
  Appena di parlar di lor s'aita.
  Ciascuna par dolente e sbigottita,
  Come persona discaciata e stanca,
  Cui tutta gente manca,
  E cui vertute e nobiltà non vale.
  Tempo fu già, nel quale,
  Secondo il lor parlar, furon dilette;
  Or sono a tutti in ira ed in non cale.
  Queste così solette   *f4ᵛ*
  Venute son, come a casa d'amico;

Che sanno ben che dentro è quel ch'io dico.
Dolesi l'una con parole molto;
 E'n sulla man si posa,
 Come succisa/rosa:
Il nudo braccio di dolor colonna
Sente lo raggio che cade dal volto;
 L'altra mantiene ascosa
 La faccia lagrimosa,
Discinta e scalza, e sol di se par donna.
Come amor prima per la rotta gonna
La vide in parte, che'l tacere è bello;
 Di pietoso è felso,
 Di lei e del dolor fece dimanda.
 O di pochi vivanda
(Rispuose in voce con sospiri mista)
Nostra natura quì a te ci manda.
 Io che son la più trista,
 Son suora alla tua madre, e son drittura;
Povera (vedi) a'panni ed a cintura.
Poichè fatta si fu palese e conta;
 Doglia e vergogna prese
 Il mio signore, e chiese
Chi fosser l'altre due ch'eran con lei,
E questa ch'era sì di pianger pronta,
 Tosto che lui intese,
 Più nel dolor s'accese,
Dicendo: or non ti duol degli occhi miei?
Poi cominciò, Siccome saper dei,
Di fonte nasce Nilo picciol fiume
 Ivi, dove 'l gran lume
Toglie alla terra del vinco la fronda:
 Sovra la vergin onda,
Generai io costei, che m'è da lato,
E che s'asciuga con la treccia bionda:
 Questo mio bel portato,
 Mirando se nella chiara fontana,

f5

Generò questa che m'è più lontana.
Fenno i sospiri Amore un poco tardo:
   E poi con gli occhi molli,
   Che prima furon folli,
   Salutò le germane sconsolate.
Posciachè prese l'uno, e l'altro dardo,
   Disse: drizzate i colli;
   Ecco l'armi ch'io volli;
   Per non l usar [*l'usar*], le vedete turbate.
Larghezza, e temperanza, e l'altre nate
   Del nostro sangue mendicando vanno:
   Però se questo è danno,
   Piangalo gli occhi, e dolgasi la bocca
   Degli uomini a cui tocca,
   Che sono a'raggi di cotal ciel giunti:
   ~~Non noi siamo or punti~~
   Non noi, che semo dell'eterna rocca: *ƒ5ᵛ*
   Che se noi siamo or punti,
   Noi pur saremo, e pur troverem gente,
   Che questo dardo farà star lucente,
Ed io ch'ascolto nel parlar divino
   Consolarsi e dolersi
   Così alti dispersi,
   L'esilio, che m'è dato onor tegno:
   E se giudizio o forza di destino,
   Vuol pur che il mondo versi
   I bianchi fiori in persi;
   Cader tra' buoni è pur di lode degno:
   E se non che degli occhi miei'l bel segno
   Per lontananza m'è tolto dal viso,
   Che m'ave in foco miso,
   Lieve mi conterei ciò che m'è grave:
   Ma questo foco m'ave
   Già cosumate sì l'ossa e la polpa,
   Che morte al petto m'ha posto la chiave:
   Onde s'io ebbi colpa,

Più lune ha volto il sol, poichè fu spenta,
Se colpa muore, perchè 1 uom [*l'uom*] si penta.
Canzone; a'panni tuoi non ponga uom mano
Per veder quel che bella donna chiude
f6　　Bastin le parti ignude;
Lo dolce pomo a tutta gente niega,
Per cui ciascun man piega,
E s'egli avvien che tu mai alcun truovi
Amico di vertù, ed ei ti priega;
Fatti di color nuovi:
Poi gli ti mostra, e 'l fior ch'è bel di fuori
Fa desiar negli amorosi cuori.

f6ᵛ　　3015　24.9　　È cosa veramente molto naturale e ordinaria desiderare di acquistare; e sempre quando gli uomini lo fanno che possino, ne saranno laudati e non biasimati; ma quando non possono, e vogliono farlo in ogni modo, quì è il biasimo e l'errore.

Il Principe.

E se alcun dicesse, il re cedè—per fuggire una guerra; respondo con le ragioni dette di sopra, che non si debba mai lasciar seguire uno disordine per fuggire una guerra; perchè ella non si fugge, ma si differisce a tuo disadvantaggio.

Ditto

f7　　Let any man read the Capitolo Quinto of the Il Principe, then apply the whole to Buonaparte's Treatment of Holland—and then ask himself what would be the fate of England.

Facci adunque un Governo [*Faccia dunque un Principe*] conto di vincere e mantenere lo Stato, i mezzi saranno sempre giudicati onorevoli e da ciascuno lodati; perchè il Vulgo ne va sempre preso con quello che riusci, e con l'evento della cosa/e nel mondo non è se no [*non*] volgo.

Ditto

Sono di tre generazioni Cervelli—l'uno intende per se, l'altro intende quanto da altri gli è mostro, il terzo non intende nè per se stesso nè per dimostrazione d'altri.

Ditto

3016 24.10

    Drown'd in the Offender's penitence sincere
    The offence too dies—
    So gracious is a soul-sublimed Tear.

3017 24.11

[shorthand] ƒ7ᵛ

[shorthand] Dante:

Io miro i crispi [*crespi*] e gli biondi capelli [*capegli*]
De' quali ha fatto per me rete Amore,
D'un fil di perle, e quando d'un bel fiore
Per me pigliare, e trovo ch'egli adesca,
E pria riguardo dentro gli occhi begli,
Che passan per gli miei dentro dal cuore
Con tanto vivo e lucente splendore
Che propriamente par che dal solesca/.
Virtù mostra così che 'n lor più cresca,
Ond'io che sì leggiadri star gli veggio,
Così fra me sospirando ragiono:
    Oimè perchè non sono
A sol a sol con lei, ov'io la chieggio—
Sicch'io potessi quella treccia bionda
Disfarla ad onda ad onda,
E far di [*de'*] suoi begli occhi a miei due specchi
Che lucon sì che non trovan parecchi—&c   xv Canzone

[shorthand] ƒ8

3018 24.12

XVII.   202

Perchè nel tempo rio
Dimoro tutta via sperando peggio,
Non so come io mi deggio
Mai consolar, se non m'ajuta Iddio
Per la motte [*morte*], ch'io cheggio
A lui, che vegna nel soccorso mio:
Che miseri, com'io,
Sempre disdegna, come or provo e veggio.
Non mi vo' lamentar di chi ciò face;
Perch'io aspetto pace
Da lei sul ponto dello mio finire;
Ch'io credo servire
Lasso, così morendo,
Poi le diservo, e dispiaccio vivendo.
Deh or m'avesse Amore,
Prima che'l vidi, immantenente morto;
Che per biasmo del torto
Avrebbe a lei, ed a me fatto onore;
Tanta vergogna porto
Della mia vita, che testè non more:
E peggio ho, che'l dolore,
Nel qual d'amar la gente disconforto;
Che Amor è una cosa, e la ventura,
Che soverchian natura,
L'un per usanza, e l'altro per sua forza;
E mi ciascuno sforza,
Sicch'io vo' per men male,
Morir contra la voglia naturale.
Questa mia voglia fera
È tanto forte, che spesse fiate
Per l'altrui podestate
Daria al mio cor la morte più leggera:
Ma lasso per pietate
Dell'anima mia trista, che non pera;

f8ᵛ

E torni a Dio qual era;
Ella non muor; ma viene in gravitate:
Ancorch'io non mi creda già potere
Finalmente tenere,
Ch'a ciò per soverchianza non mi mova
Misericordia nova:
N'avrà forse mercede
Allor di me il Signor che questo vede.
Canzon mia, tu starai dunque quì meco,   *f9*
Acciocch'io pianga teco;
Ch'io non ho dove possa salvo andare
Che dopo il mio penare
A ciascun' altra gioja;
Non vo' che vada altrui faccendo noia,

3019 24.13

Di donne io vidi una gentile schiera
Quest'ognisanti prossimo passato;
Ed una ne venia quasi primiera
Seco menando amor dal destro lato.
Dagli occhi suoi gittava una lumiera
La qual pareva uno spirito infiammato;
Ed i'ebbi tanto ardir, che la sua cera
Guardando, vidi un angiol figurato.
A chi era degno poi dava salute
Con gli occhi, suoi quella benigna e piana.
Empiendo il core a ciascun di virtute.
Credo che in ciel nascesse esta soprana
E venne in terra per nostra salute:
Dunque beata chi l'è prossimana.

Un dì si venne a me Melanconia   *f9ᵛ*
E disse: voglio un poco stare teco.

E parve a me, che si menasse seco
Dolor ed ira per sua compagnia.
Ed io le dissi: partiti! va via!
Ed ella mi rispose, come un greco,
E ragionando a gran agio meco
Guardai e vidi Amore che venia;
Vestito di novo di un drappo nero
E nel suo capo portava un capello
E certo lacrimava pur da vero:
Ed io gli dissi: che hai, cattivello?
Ed ei rispose: io ho guai e pensero,
Che nostra donna muor, dolce fratello.

f32ᵛ   3020 11.78   Something shocking in the wanton anti-biblic opinion that there were many & various original Pairs of the human Being—one family—all Brethren & Sisters. Heavens! were it possible to make all men Kaimists, probably war over the earth ad internecionem would be the result. Difference = Hatred—Why?—

f33   3021 11.79   And Kisses, the mute Promises of Love.

3022 11.80   Miracles would effect a universal anthropomorphism if not infrequent & above all, unless confined to a small space and limited number. The first Jews anthropotheists and with a rancid Itch for Idolatry—the earlier Fathers to whom Miracles were familiar i.e. to whom miranda in miracula statim transeun[t] mira autem tot quot ignorata/Ignorantiæ regio extensæ labuit the
f33ᵛ   size of Terra incognita to Noah's grandchildren   they all anthropotheists, & therefore not Theanthropists.

3023 11.81   In all processes of the Understanding the shortest way will be discovered the last. and this perhaps while it constitutes the great advantage of having a Teacher to put us on the shortest road at the first, yet sometimes occasions a difficulty in the comprehension—/in as much as the longest way is more near to the existing state of the mind, nearer to what, if left to myself on starting the thought, I should have thought next.—The shortest *way* gives me *the knowlege* best; the longest way makes me more *knowing*.

3024 11.82   All the Linen at the Bridgewater Arms mark'd
"Stoln from the Bridgwater Arms."   *f34*

3025 11.83   The eyes quietly & stedfastly dwelling on an
object not as if looking at it or as seeing any thing in it, or as in any
way exerting an act of Sight upon it, but as if the whole attention
were listning to what the heart was feeling & saying about it/As
when A is talking to B. of C.—and B. deeply interested listens intensely to A, the eye passive yet stedfast fixed on C. as the *Subject*
of the communication—

3026 11.84   Deeply important that Incarnation & Transfiguration of Duty as Inclination, ? when it is that a sense of Duty lessens
inclination—from what imperfection in the sense this arises—&
how a perfect sense makes it impossible to will aught else. This
height of Love/—Reality in the external world an instance of a
Duty perfectly felt. How to make Duty add to Inclination. The   *f34ᵛ*
necessary tendency of true Love to generate a feeling of Duty by
increasing the sense of reality, & vice versâ feeling of Duty to generate true Love. All our Thoughts all that we abstract from our
consciousness & so form the Phænomenon Self is a Shadow, its
whole Substance is the dim yet powerful sense that it is but a
Shadow, & ought to belong to a Substance/but this Substance can
have no marks, no discriminating Characters, no hic est, ille non
est/it is simply Substance—& this deepliest felt during particular
phænomena with a consciousness that the phænomenon is in us but
it not in the phænomenon, for which alone we yet value the phænomenon, constitutes the craving of True Love. Love a sense of
Substance/Being seeking to be self-conscious, 1. of itself in a Symbol. 2. of the Symbol as not being itself. 3. of the Symbol as being
nothing but in relation to itself—& necessitating a return to the
first state, Scientia absoluta.—Discontent, when pain, when joy—
when is it quieted? In virtuous *action*—Sensuality itself a symbol   *f35*
of this or counterfeit action/

3027 11.85   I will use unimpassioned language because. 1. I
wish to relate, even as if I were a mere indifferent Historian con-

cerned only in the distinctness & accuracy of his representation, *what* I have felt. And because, the strongest words, the words most steeped in passion, would be poor and inadequate to express, *how* I have felt. When Nature has made the Heart ach, and beat, and swell, and sink, and sicken—the whole skull stiffen & feel rigid, and the eyes feel as if their business were to feel the horror & grief they expressed, & not to see or be seen/when the very limbs, the feet, the arms, seemed incapable of moving unless the mind recre-

f35ᵛ ated a new power by some sudden *flash* of resolve to let them indeed cease to be, as a fainting and overwearied man runs with violent speed to the place in which he is to rest/when such symbols as these have been employed by nature to express to my own mind *how* I have felt in ~~my~~ the ground of my Being, and yet still most inadequately hereby expressed it, what can modifications of air by the organs of articulation do?

> 3028 11.86   Hanrott, Burkitt,
>   & Winstanley,
>   7 Cheapside

f36 3029 11.87   Henry Pipers
>   Aldersgate Buildgˢ
>   N 10

3030 11.88

f36ᵛ Ὅπερ εἰμὶ, τοῦτο μένω, καὶ δυσφημούμενος καὶ θαυμαζόμενος.
>   Greg. Naz.

Omnia periclitabuntur aliter accipi quam sunt, si aliter quam sunt cognominantur.

>   Tertull: de Carne Christi, cap. 13.—

>   κωμωδία τοῖς εχθροῖς ἡ ἐμὴ τραγωδία.
>   Naz. Orat. 14.

3031 11.89   Sit tamen Domina Materque nostra Roma baculus in aqua fractus; et absit credere quae videmus.

Walter Mapes de nugis Curialium, distinct. 1.c.12.—on the gross Simony of the Pope in confirming the election of Reginald, bastard son of Joceline, Bishop of Sarum, into the See of Bath/

3032 11.90　　The primary powers of the Soul are in all men　*f37* the same & alike—these a principiis speciei—others, as Talent, Wit, Memory, &c—a principiis individui.

3033 11.91

Qui sibi nequam,
Cui bonus?

3034 11.92　　　　ᴜ -/ᴜ -/ᴜ - ᴜ/
　　　　　　　　　- ᴜ/- ᴜ/- ᴜ/-
　　　　　　　　　ᴜ -/ᴜ -/ᴜ - ᴜ/
　　　　　　　　　- ᴜ/- ᴜ/- ᴜ/-

3035 11.93
There is a Fate which flies with towering Spirit
Home to the Mark, & never checks at Conscience—

3036 11.94　　Think all is good *they* make so, who go on Secured by the Prosperity of their Crimes.

3037 11.95　　Man doth not nurse a deadlier piece of Folly To　*f37ᵛ* his high Temper and brave soul, than that of fancying Goodness and a Law to live by So differing from man's Life! As if with Lions,—Bears, Tygers, Wolves, and all those Beasts of Prey, He would affect to be a Sheep!—
(excellent speech for a Villain, like Buonaparte)—

3038 11.96　　When a man is once hated, his good deeds disserve him more than his evil—for the former provoke more malignant comments from more malignant feelings—because they will be interpreted as proceeding from an evil or base nature, & vice in the mask of Virtue excites more antipathy, than Vice in its own　*f38* Shape & avowed.　　　　—S.T.C.

3039 11.97   Many a party man talks as if he hated his Country, saddens at her prosperous events, exults in her Disasters, & yet
all the while is merely hating the opposite party, & would himself
feel & talk as a Patriot were he in a foreign Land. The true Monster is he (and such, alas! there are in these Monstrous days "vol-
lendeter Sündhaftigkeit") who abuses his Country when out of his
Country.

ƒiii   3040 19.1   ⌜Pacchiar⌝etti—

ƒɪ   3041 19.2   Friday afternoon, 22 May, 1807

3042 19.3

ƒɪᵛ

⟨An ounce and a half of the w⟩Weak Infusion of Colombo root
with a drachm of the Tincture of Colombo: and add 12 drops of
the muriated Tincture of Iron.—When going to bed, take from

half a grain to a grain of Aloes ~~mixed~~ joined to two grains † of
Calomel—or a grain of Aloes joined to a grain of Pill: Rusi.—/

† Grain & ½ may be taken at night, and the remaining Grain & ½
the next morn.

3043 19.4

3044 19.5

f2

3045 19.6

3046 19.7   A Or wren or linnet
In Bush and Bushet:
No tree, but in it
A cooing Cushit.

3047 19.8

3048 19.9

f2ᵛ

3049 19.10

3050 19.11   Die beste Staatsverfassung.
Diese nur kan[n] ich dafür erkennen, die jedem erleichtert
Gut zu denken, doch nie, dass er so denke, bedarf.

3051 19.12
What is fair, good & right Mankind wish in *general*
And this I have learnt from Confessions *auricular,*
(Said a shrewd Priest to me) but believe me, Sir! Men are all
Sad slippery Sinners in wishes *particular.*
A sly ~~learn~~nering

3052 19.13

f3

3053 19.14

3054 19.15

[shorthand/cipher text]

3055 19.16

[shorthand/cipher text]

3056 19.17

f3ᵛ   Who [shorthand] —:k [shorthand] cannot

Because he   [shorthand]

And ever frets and feeds his own   [shorthand]

[shorthand text]

f₁   3057 12.1   φιλοσοφια/philosophia

$$\begin{array}{r} 1815 \\ 726 \\ \hline 9075 \end{array}$$

3058 12.2   Susan Ashby.

3059 12.3

4840 square yards an English acre
$$4840 \times 3 = 14520.$$

3060 12.4   May 28th, 1807. Bristol. S. T. Coleridge/   f2
How villainously these metallic Pencils have Degenerated, not
only in the length & quantity but what is far worse, in the *Quality*
of the metal. This appears to have no superiority over the worst
sort of Black lead sold by the [?Maltese shopkeepers]

3061 12.5   Peperit olim Religio Divitias; at nunc matrem   f2^v
filia suffocavit.
                  Trithemius Abbas de viris illust. Ord. S. Bened.

3062 12.6

Mode of correcting Press Sheets.   f3

1. A wrong Letter in a word by drawing a short perpend. line
through it, with another oblique line in the Margin with the right
Letter round behind or before it. This   u\ or/u
2. But whole words by an horizontal rule, so   / line, thus
3. But where a space is wanting between two Words or letters
meant to be separated/the following mark should|be used   # /
4. Where the contrary error has place, the fol__lowing
5. Where there is a superfluous letter\ or or word: ∂/∂/
6. Where a Letter is upturned, as ə for e, thus   9/   f3^v
7. An unnecessary interspace between two\words, thus: |
8. If words misplaced should be with tr./ in the margin but if
          5   1   3   4   2
several misplaced words should be together, then add figures in
the Text to the same mark in the margin: tr./
9. Where you wish a new paragraph, put a | in the text, and in the
margin   [/
10. An improper Break thus [:] original instrument⌐   f4
              ⌐Whereby   no break. /
10. ── means that the word should be in Italics; ═══ in the
small Capitals, ═══ in Capitals, with   Ital / or S. Caps./
or Caps./ in the margin.

11. False punctuation marked by a | in the Text, and the stop in a circle in the margin: ⊙ ⊙ ⊙ ⊙

f4ᵛ   12. Where lines are to be added, write them at the bottom of the page⟩
But where more are to be added than can be so written, write them on another paper, attached to the page, & draw <u>a parallel</u> line to the paper, & place in the margin the words   *see separate copy* /
If 2 or more such additions are made, then number them, 1. 2. 3. &c.

(drawing an oblique line from the word where they are to be inserted down to words.

f5   13. Where a word has been struck out, & ~~afterwards~~ approved of,

then underdot the word, and write in the margin   *stet* /

14. The Hyphen is marked thus ∧ in the Text, and ~~by~~ in the Mar: by *H*   the apostrophe by **ꙮ** ; and the ellipsis Line *H*

3063 12.7

ϝορδσϝορθε.   ʽΟρδσόρθε.
Ούρδσέρθε.   Αξιολογος.
Επαξιος ϝιλιαμος.
ϝιλλελμος.

f5ᵛ   3064 12.8   Blue Sky through the glimmering interspaces of the dark Elms at Twilight rendered a lovely deep yellow green/ all the rest delicate Blue.

3065 12.9   Sed religionis Franciscanæ peculiare malum fuit, literarum Studium, quasi a vocatione ordinis alienum FRANCISCUS maluit nos orare quam legere. Ordinis periculum sensit, cum audivit

f6   literarum scholam Bononiæ institutam a JOANNE Ordinis Ministro Generali: *itaque ei maledixit, nec extremum spiranti maledictionem remittere rogatus voluit, asserens eam in cælo ratam esse, seque malle fratres suos orare quam legere.*
Asceticων Lib. Prim: Antonii Dadini Alteserræ, p.106.
Edit. Halensis a Glück.

3066 12.10   With struggles of Reform ut qui adverso flumine   *f6ᵛ*
lembum deicit, si vel minimum remigium remiserit, undis cedere
incessit—Sed vel minima remissionis damnum sentio heu! quantum!

3067 19.18   O how sweet *Hope* is!—that can no one feel who   *f3ᵛ*
is & has been full of Hope; but to have despaired/actively, or only
negatively to have been for months & seasons in a stupor ⟨& utter
lack of⟩ *personal* "This may yet *be* & ⟨be⟩ *mine*" and ~~yet~~ withal in
an activity of images desired/O to Him How sweet *Hope* is!
                                                31 May, 1807.

3068 19.19

3069 19.20   ⌐. . . . .⌐ put them one by one into   *f4*
large open glasses; and when the Glass is neatly filled, bind it over
with oiled Linen, well tied round the glass—& then let each glass
have two Inches of the Above Powders commixt below & above
and all round it.—Flowers may be kept the year thro' in the same
way.

3070 19.21   On the side of the Moderns relatively to the ancients, or in favor of the actuality of a progression on the whole, it
strikes me as adducible: that tho' the Ancient Greeks and Romans
held the *superstition* i.e. the *survivance* (supersto = supervivo) of
the soul exclusively/and tho' the Moderns (by which words, anc.
& mod., I always understand the Roman Empire and whatever
addition to its peculiar civilization Christendom includes, the
North of all Germany, Denmark, Sweden, & the Russian Empire)
hold the *resurrection* of the Body, and are vehemently acted upon
thereby—yet still anatomy & that of human Subjects has made incomparably greater progress, & won more decisive Victories over a   *f4ᵛ*
far more fierce and active Prejudice—a prejudice so strong as to
have converted the beautiful Genius with the inverted Torch into

a ghastly Skeleton, & the spicy funereal Pile, that in a moment restores to Nature her emancipated Elements, into the dark conservatories of suspended Animation, and Corses asleep.—Yet still Science presses forward against ferocious Mobs, & parliamentary Saints, conquering & still to conquer!

3071 19.22   Curious passage in Humphrey Wanley's Essay, Phil. Trans. Anno 1705—Abridgement Vol. 5. p.230. "other Books are post dated, that they might be accounted new."—

"The *reason* of these post dates *was, because, before* printing *came up* (*N.B. an exquisite specimen of the Slovenly Style*) a book was so much the more valuable, as it was newer. An old Book might be bought for an old song, as we say; but he that transcribed a fresh copy, must be paid for his pains. *And therefore* I have found in some Catalogues of the MSS. formerly extant in our Abbey Libraries, that when they said such a Book was Liber Vetus, ƒ5   they would often add, et inutilis; but liber novus was nitidus, eleganter scriptus lectu facilis, &c: which mean opinion of the ancient copies, by the bye, may have been the occasion of the loss of many a good Author."—Alter hand-writing into Style, & mode of thinking; & too well will this remark apply to modern Readers, & their opinions of new versus our elder writers.

bye the bye—? bye = vie, i.e. via?—

3072 19.23   An affecting remark of T. Poole's, how much the feelings of happy Childhood, when summer days appeared 20 times as long as now, may be re-produced by effective Industry— by monuments of Time well spent.—See the account of Abraham Sharp, Vol.5. Abridg: Phil. Trans. p.293.—Consolations.

3073 19.24   εσται και Σάμος Αμμος, ἐσεῖται Δῆλος αδηλος και Ρώμη ῥύμη.   Sib. Or:
        Erit Samus arena, erit Delos obscurus,
        Et Roma vicus.—
            So passes away even an Oracular *Pun.*

3074 19.25
    The strong and complex Cordage of its Roots
    Tying its almost self-supported Weighty
    To the firm earth in countless Intertwine
    Subtly embracing & soliciting,—

3075 19.26   My path becomes daily more rugged and mazy,   *f5ᵛ*
a cloud dwells upon my eyes, my heart is sick, and hope is dead
& ⟨yet⟩ the deep Yearning will not die, but lives & grows as in
a charnel house—and all my Vitals are possessed by an unremitting Poison.

3076 19.27   When the moist Vault alone shall weep for me,
Sole constant Mourner—

3077 19.28   We must fill our vessels promptly & in haste;
for we draw from a Rain Torrent—& soon the drops will not
fall from above, and the Channels below will be covered with
the Dust of Drouth—

3078 19.29   The weariness yet restlessness of the Bones, especially in the right thigh, knee, and leg—and more than all in
the Knee. Sometimes, in both legs; and sometimes, but seldomer,
in the left interchangeably. Soon follow on this a strangely dis-
quieting pain—shall I call it? or a painful unquiet—for the evil
seems rather in the exceeding Unquiet, than in the pain—a cruel   *f6*
sweat on the brow, & on the chest—windy sickness at the Stomach
—and in the mind a strong Temptation to, almost amounting if
not altogether to a sense of, a reprobate Despair, that snatches at
the known Poison, that suspends—alas! to aggravate the Evil, like
the pause in the balancing of the Javelin and the muscles, the
pause that defers the blow to make it the more forceful—and I
know it—and the knowlege, and the fear, and the remorse, and
the wilful turning away of the eye to dreams imperfect, that float
like broken foam on the sense of the reality, and only distract not
hide it, these are the wretched & sole Comforts, or rather these
are the hard prices, by which the Armistice is accompanied & paid

f6ᵛ   for. O who shall deliver me from the Body of this Death? Meanwhile the habit of inward Brooding daily makes it harder to confess the Thing, I am, to any one—least of all to those, whom I most love & who most love me—& thereby introduces and fosters a habit of negative falsehood, & multiplies the Temptations to positive, Insincerity. O God! let me bare my whole Heart to Dʳ B. or some other Medical Philosopher—if I could know, that there was no *Relief,* I might then *resolve* on something. But the one ineradicable Idea, and unquenchable Yearning!—and the Fear, that Death itself will but increase it! for it seems to have an affinity with Despair! O *Κψᴵ+.ᴵ Κψᴵ+.*

f7   3079 19.30   Dies, hora, momentum, evertendis dominationibus sufficit, quæ adamantinis credebantur radicibus esse fundatæ:— Casaubon.

What was said of Henry 3ʳᵈ of France and applied by Sir W. Raleigh to our Henry 6ᵗʰ, is at least as applicable to Lewis 16ᵗʰ— Qu'il estoit une fort gentile Prince, mais son reigne est advenu en une fort mauvois temps.

3080 19.31   For as Fortune's Favorite rides the Horse, so Fortune rides the favorite. Who when he is descended and on foot; the Man taken from his Beast, and Fortune taken from the Man; a base groom beats the one, and a bitter contempt spurns at the other, with equal Liberty.

3081 19.32   But let every man value his own wisdom, as he pleaseth. Let the rich man think all fools who cannot equal his abundance; the Revenger esteem all ~~buzzards~~ sheep, that have

f7ᵛ   not trodden down their opposites; let the Politician **deem** all **to be** gross **Buzzards** who have not merchandized their faith; yet when once we come in sight of the Port of Death, to which all winds drive us, and when by letting fall that fatal anchor, which can never be weighed again, the Navigation of this Life takes end —then it is, that our own cogitations (those sad and severe cogitations, formerly beaten **off** from us by Health and Felicity) return and **exact vengeance.** It is then, we cry to God for Mercy when ourselves can no longer exercise cruelty to others/it is only then when we ~~are~~ have no longer profit in deluding ~~even ourselves~~ our **Brethren,** that we are stricken through the soul with the terrible sentence, That God will not be mocked, **And yet still how oft do we attempt even then both to delude ourselves &** to mock our maker, ~~mockery inde~~ by regret and terror, instead of sincere remorse & repentances, and abhorrence of Sin even for its own exceeding Sinfulness. Mockery indeed! For if according to S⁺ Peter, The Righteous scarcely be saved, and that God spared not his Angels—where shall those appear, who having served their appetites all their lives, presume to think, that the severe Commandments of the All-powerful God were given but in sport—& that the short Breath, which we draw when Death presses upon us, if we can but fashion it to the sound of *Mercy* (without any kind of satisfaction or Amends) is sufficient? But what shall we call a mocking of God; if those men do not mock him, that think it enough for God to ask him forgiveness at leisure, with the last drawing **& beggarly relicts** of a malicious Breath? For what do they otherwise, that die this kind of well-dying, but say unto God;—I beseech thee, that thou wilt for my sake change thy nature, that thou wilt love oppressions, call ambition wisdom, and charity foolishness. For I shall prejudice my son (which I am resolved not to do) if I make restitution—and as to delivering the oppressed, how can I confess myself to have been unjust? Certainly, these Hopers have either found out a new God or made one/and in all likelihood such a leaden one as Lewis the 11ᵗʰ wore in his cap—(which he **used to kiss & make Promises to after his murders &c**) mockeries indeed fit to be used toward a leaden Image, but **of most horrible frenzy of folly and wickedness towards the everliving omniscient God.** But of this composition are all devotees of the World—that they fear all that is transient & ridiculous—They fear the plots and practices of their Rivals & their very whisperings, they fear the opinions of men which **like clouds sailing under clouds that impress shadows on shadows**—they flatter or forsake the prosperous and unprosperous—yet they dive under water, like Ducks

f8

f8ᵛ

f9

at every pebble thrown towards them—& on the contrary, they
shew an obstinate & blind valor against the Judgment of the Om-
nipotent—yea, they shew themselves Gods against God, & slaves
towards men—chiefly, towards **the worst & weakest** men whose
bodies **are rotting** and consciences are alike rotten!—

3082 19.33   and the amorous Spring.

3083 19.34   Veritas a quocunque dicatur, a Spiritu sancto est.
                                                        —Ambrose.
                 Quæ sacris saviunt, prophana non sunt.—

f9ᵛ 3084 19.35   Speaks with as great impudence & pomp of dicta-
tion as if Nature had shut up all light of Learning within the
Lanthorn of his hollow Jaws & ~~hollow~~ skull as hollow/

3085 19.36   Travels—whosoever in writing events of his own
times & witness, shall follow Truth too near the Heels, it may
haply strike his teeth out of his head—

3086 19.37   "Hoc ego non multis sed tibi—"

3087 19.38

         Upon Sir W. Raleigh's Execution & Death.

         Great Heart! who taught thee so to die;
         Death yielding thee the Victory?
         Where took'st thou leave of Life? if here,
         How could'st thou be so far from Fear?
         But sure thou died'st & quittedst the state
         Of Flesh & Blood before that Fate.
         I saw in every stander by
         Pale Death, Life only in thy eye.

3088 19.39   Universe—unfolded fragment of the Deity—
Fecisti mundum—de nihilo, pene nihil.—

f10 3089 19.40   To Memory—Great Guide of Things to come,
Sole Presence of Things Past.—

3090 19.41   Qui in factis Dei rationem non videt, ~~quia videt~~
suam infirmitatem videt—idque cur non videt, rationem videt—

3091 19.42   Dum furor in cursu est, currenti cede furori.
Ovid.

3092 19.43   Love will vent his inmost and veriest Griefs in
sweet and measured ~~sounds~~ ~~sweet~~ is it that—a divine Joy being its
end it will not utter even its woes and weaknesses, sorrows & sick-
nesses, except in some form of pleasure? pleasure the shadow &
sacramental Type of that Joy (which by union fit ~~and~~ et facit et
creat et creatur) or is it rather, that its essence being a divine synthesis of highest ~~order~~ reason—and ~~passion~~ vehementest Impulse,
it must needs the soul in its two faculties, or perhaps of the two
souls, vital power of Heat, & Light of Intellect—attract & com-   *f10ᵛ*
bine with poesy, whose essence is passionate order.

3093 19.44   "make themselves believe they love at the first
liking of a likely form, loving from the horror vacui, which is
still the law of Hearts preattuned to Love, not that they feel indeed the power of corresponding presence of that within and
without, which makes the heart find a reason in passion/

3094 19.45   Mʳ T. Poole of Nether Stowey in the C. of Somerset deems it an intolerable Tax on any person to find a Guest
Pen and Ink while in his House, and an unreasonable Expectation
on any Guest who should demand the same.

3095 19.46   Let a man once have felt Love indeed, & then   *f11*
he will *know* it—how shall he know that this is more Love than
his former Likings?—Even as the youth who carried away by
eloquent books had felt all the fermenting & busy heat of utmost
positiveness, the first time he has been made to demonstrate a
problem of geometry, feels the sense of *certainty*, & finds no difficulty save in words to distinguish it infallibly from the sensation
of positiveness.

3096 19.47
> The Wind that with Aurora hath abiding
> Among th'Arabian and the Persian Hills—

3097 19.48   an iron & injurious Age.

f11ᵛ 3098 19.49   Non relictus est hominum eloquiis de Dei rebus
alius quam Dei Sermo.

> > Hilarius de Trin. Lib. 7.

Etiam quæ pro religione dicimus, cum grandi metu et disciplinâ
dicere debemus.—Id.—

Etsi summis totius corporis doloribus oppressus, dubiâ spe vitæ,
spiritum miserè duco, fecit tamen summum meum et perpetuum
de te judicium, ut hos cruciatus, nescio quomodo frangerem, dum
supremo hoc literarum munere ad te perfungar.—ito igitur ubi
te per—

3099 19.50   As the Messenger was hastening off, he was discovered—& the Great Guns discharged at him/down he dropt, &
the Soldiers after him/had they found but his Message, all had
been ruined, but lo! Whiz, flew his right Arm close by me, with
a letter still grasped in his Hand/and at the same moment I saw
f12 his Left Thigh with about an inch or two of the leg—ran after it,
unsuspected, & found the Key of the Dungeon in his Breeches
Pocket—

3100 19.51
> > Sun-rise
> As all the Trees of Paradise reblossoming in the East.

3101 19.52
> > Wedg'd in and utterly crush'd
> > Between two dire Concurrences of Fate.

3102 19.53
> > Angels thy old Friends there shall meet thee
> > Glad at their own Home now to meet thee.
> > > > Crashaw.

3103 19.54
    What Soul soe'er in any language can
    Speak Heaven like her's, is my Soul's Countryman.
                                         Ditto

3104 19.55
    What can the Poor hope from us, when we be
    Uncharitable even to Charity?
                            applied to Malthus

3105 19.56   a supernumerary excellence—

3106 19.57   I fix this fair Indefinite—in spite of all the peev-
ish Strength of Weakness—/And soul-appeasing Melody—
           In such conspiracy of Charms

3107 19.58
    Fire, That slept in its Intensity, Life   *f12ᵛ*
    Wakeful over all knew no gradations,
    And Bliss in its excess became a Dream,
    And my visual powers involved such Sense,
    all Thought, Sense, Thought, & Feeling,
    and Time drew out his subtle
    Threads so quick, That the long
    Summer's Eve was ~~long~~ one whole web,
    A Space on which I lay commensurate—
    For Memory & all undoubting Hope
    Sang the same note & in the selfsame
    Voice, with each sweet *now* of
    My Felicity, and blended momently,
    Like Milk that coming comes ~~of its steady~~ & in its
    easy stream Flows ever in, upon the
    mingling milk, in the Babe's murmuring
    Mouth/or mirrors each reflecting each/—

                ———

    Life wakeful over all knew no gradation
    That Bliss in its excess became a Dream;

For every sense, each thought, & each sensation
Lived in my eye, transfigured ~~yet~~ not supprest.
And Time drew out his subtle threads so quick,
~~So softly too,~~ & And with such Spirit-speed & silentness,
That only in the web, of space like Time,
On the still spreading web I still diffused
Lay still commensurate—

What never is but only is to be
This is not Life—
O Hopeless Hope, and Death's Hypocrisy!
And with perpetual Promise, breaks its Promises.—

f13   Dark is the Sun, yet not a star ~~now in the Sky~~ peeps high,
〈Eclipse—〉
No constellations alphabet the Sky;
The Heaven ~~now one~~ large black Letter only shews
And ~~like~~ as a ~~wilful~~ Child beneath ~~the~~ its Master's blows
~~The groaning world~~ Utters at once its Task & its affright,
The groaning world now learns to read aright,
       ~~And~~ cries out, O!

The Stars that wont to start, as on a chase,
And twinkling insult on Heaven's darkened Face,
~~And~~ Like a ~~bold~~ conven'd Conspiracy of Spies
Wink at each other with confiding eyes,
Turn from the portent, all is blank on high,
No constellations alphabet the Sky—
The Heavens one large black Letter only shews,
And as a Child beneath its master's Blows
Shrills out at once its Task and its Affright,
The groaning world now learns to read aright,
And with its Voice of Voices cries out, O!

(I wrote these Lines, as an imitation of Du Bartas, as translated
by our Sylvester—)

f6ᵛ   3108 12.11   The Hayfield in the close hard by the Farm
House/babe, and totterer little more/old cat with her eyes blink-

ing in the Sun, & little kittens leaping & frisking over the Hay-
lines/

3109 12.12   8 miles from Taunton very good road/9 from   *f7*
Bridgewater, good from the Hill/

3110 12.13   What an admirable Subject for an Allston would   *f7ᵛ*
Tycho Brahe be listening with religious awe to the oracular
Gabble of the Ideot, whom he kept at his feet & used to feed with   *f8*
his own hands/

3111 12.14
                        On Planting Oaks.—
1. Any soil, but a Loam or Marl the best incomparably.
2. After cleaning the ground, it must be loosened & trenched
very deep, that the acorns may strike their Tap root well—on
this all depends. The lateral roots do little more than *steady* the
Tree. The Trenches 3 feet wide, and from 3 to 6 deep/as the   *f8ᵛ*
soil will permit—& 10 feet apart from each other.
3. Draw a drill in the center of each trench, two inches deep, if
in heavy loamy soil, three in light or sandy. In this place the
acorns, anxiously selected, two inches asunder, & cover them carefully with mould.   *f9*
4. When the plants appear, weed by hand in the Rows, & by Hoe
all around, once a month in the summer. In October pull up every other plant.
5. On the second year recommence thinning, &c, and prune any
remarkably strong Side-shoots.
6. On the third year thin as before; & then commence a general
Pruning, by cutting off smooth & close to the leading Stem all the *f9ᵛ*
side shoots of the first year. And this do yearly, *removing every*
year, very smooth & close to the main stem one year's growth of
side branches, leaving the branches of 2 years to form the head
of each third year/—In short, retain only the branches of the
first 2 years.
7. Continue this till the Tree arrives at a stem of from 40—to 60   *f10*
feet—then let it run to head, as it likes.

8. The removal of every alternate plant must be continued yearly, till the Trees are 30 feet apart.

By these means in 50 years you will have Oaks more worthy
f10ᵛ the name of British than the common ones of 100. The final emolument great, & much intermediate from young Poles/—advisable for a man of leisure, of small estate/The weeding &c a delightful exercise for himself & his Boys & Girls.—W.W. 37 years/John Tomlet 1 year/let 5 acres be planted, & Tom's Son at 23 will have a pretty Capital to set up in any Line/

f11ᵛ   I allow forty feet square for each Oak—363 Oaks in an Acre (Is not this some amabilis insania or rather damnabilis hallucinatio & cæcitas (seu cacitas) arithmetica of mine?) YES! Each Oak, timber & firing earns but 25£/363 × 25 = 9075£ per Acre. Huzza!
f12   Hurra! Give you joy, Master Tommy W.   9075   for 5 acres

$$\underset{45375£}{\underline{5}}$$

for T. Wordsworth's Son or Daughter at 23—Grandchild of W. Wordsworth Esqʳᵉ, the Poet. What an Event! But it would be fair, I think, to divide it too among all the Children, unless it is really advisable in order to render more secure (to securiorate) so noble a Breed, to found a family & therefore, thro' primogeniture to prevent final evanition by from [. . . . .]
f12ᵛ N.B. As I suspected/instead of 40 feet square each Tree will take up an 100 yards/and instead of 363 Oaks per acre read 43—and subtract from £45375 accordingly. Sic transit gloria Somnii.

f11   3112 12.15   Sunflower ought to be cultivated, the leaves being excellent fodder/the flowers eminently melliferous—& the seeds a capital food for poultry, none nourishing quicker or occasioning them to lay more eggs.

3113 12.16   ? Allapse of serpents/Serpentium allapsus timet.
                                              Horace—
What other word have we?
Pity that we dare not saxonize as boldly as our Forefathers by
f11ᵛ unfortunate preference latinized. Then we should have Onglide, angleiten, *Onlook*, Anschauung &c.

3114 12.17   Intersperse the layers of Hay not perfectly dried   *f12ᵛ*
with Salt/

3115 12.18   The *Crops,* or *Out-burst* of a Seam—in mines.

3116 12.19   Red, Green, & Violet the only colors.   *f13*
RED (from a to b.) = Red.
RED + *Green* (from b to c) = Orange
GREEN + *Red* (from c to d) = Yellow
GREEN (from d to e) = Green
GREEN + *Violet* (from e to f) = Blue
VIOLET + *Green* (from f to g) = Indigo
VIOLET (from g to h) = Violet

h   g   f   e   d   c   b   a

In the Dial of Colors any two colors from the opposite points of   *f13ᵛ*
each diameter = White. Thus a red ray + Green = White
orange + blue = White
Violet + yellow = White
which gives a presumption, that in each pair of colors the three
colors, Red, Green, & Violet are contained. *R. Gervy* or *G. Arvy.*
R.G.V. always combine into W.
I would that I were an expert and deep Algebraist, that I
might try my Luck in calculating all conceivable proportions of   *f14*
simple Light = + to Resistance, or Negation = − ; if so the different colors might be deduced from Light + No light, according to the notion of the first Thinkers among the Greeks. Thus:
if $\frac{2\frac{1}{2}}{5}$ W = Red, $\frac{1\frac{1}{2}}{5}$ = Green, and $\frac{1}{5}$ = Violet, of course the addition
would be 5 = W.—Still this would be mere *words,* if the differ-
ence in the paths of the Ray & in its comparative momentum must
be admitted as existing in outness, & not dependent on the form   *f14ᵛ*
of the Eye or subsequent act of the Imagination. For if *direction*
+ *momentum* α produce the sensation red, of course we must
call the unknown cause ab extra by the name of its sensuous effect.
Red: unless we can explain α by the circumstances of the reflect-

f15 ing body, or of the sense, either or both. Thus, if I could say that an homogene, Light, falling on a prism must necessarily strike the object at different angles, & that the difference of the refraction caused the colors, not the difference of the colors the refraction.

3117 12.20   Ὁν (Θεοπομπον) φασιν, ὑπο της ἑαυτου γυναικος ονειδιζομενον, ὡς ελαττω παραδυσαντα τοις παισι την βασιλειαν, η παρελαβε, μειζω μεν ουν (ειπειν) οσῳ χρονιωτερον.

Plut: in vitâ Lycurgi.

3118 12.21   Malice is blind, and Wickedness is Madness.

A. Sidney.

f3 3119 23.6   Given me by T. Poole, Esqre.

August 1807.

N. Stowey

f4 3120 23.7   Moral and Religious
Musings & Mournings

f54 3121 12.76   Pseudo-philosophus quidam, vel ut accuratius loquar, ψιλοσοφος—
Psilosophia Gallica
//philosophia Teutonica

3122 12.77   φίλτρον καὶ ἴϋγγα *of diction*

3123 12.78   And here my faithful Tears shall give a human Interest to the Flints on which I tread/

3124 12.79   Mild complaints tanquam gemitus Columbæ

f56 3125 12.80   Knapton
North Walsham
Norfolk

3126 12.81   + added to
                     — less by
                     = equal to, the same as
                     // contrary to

3127 12.82   Jiffling—restless motion/

3128 12.83   A Kitchen with smoke Jack &c/3½ Strides broad/   ƒ55ᵛ
5½ long.
     2. A good large pantry—
     3. The Hall 4½ broad, 6½ long—
     4. Parlour, 6 by 4 Strides.
     5. 2ⁿᵈ Parlor-Sitting Room. 5 Strides broad, 5 long, 2 windows
facing.
     Above Stairs 2 Servants rooms,   3 smaller room 4 one bed-
room 6 by four, another 5 by four—6 a third 5 by 4½.   ƒ55
     Two Stair Cases, all the 1 at each end of the House/the Bed-
rooms higher in proportion than rooms below/
     A Brew House with water cock & water in all possible conven-
ience—
     A Dairy
     A Cellar
     Pig Stie
     Palace of meditation
     G   Stables & one or other outhouses,   ƒ54ᵛ
     A pretty Garden & good Fruit round the House—
     [?Water/Walls], & the Prospect of Taunton Dean/ [. . .] &c

3129 12.84   Nicholson's Phil. Journal, Feb ~~178~~ 1804. For
Prognostics of the weather.—*Mem.*

3130 12.85   Trivédi Servoru Sarman to Sir W. Jones.
     To you there are many like me, yet to me there is none like

you, and you are always like yourself—there are groves of night flowers, yet the N.F. sees only the moon.

3131 12.46

*f33*ᵛ [1] Cumberland.
Wollt ihr zugleich den Kindern der Welt und den Frommen gefallen?
Mahlet die Wollust—nur mahlet den Teufel dazu.

[2] Der Prophet
Schade dass die Natur nur einen [*Einen*] Menschen aus dir schuf,
Denn zum würdigen Mann war und zum Schelmen der Stoff.

[3] Alles mischt die Natur so einzig und innig; doch hat sie
f34 Edel-und Schalksinn hier ach! nur zu innig vermischt.

[4] Zur abwechslung [*Abwechslung*]
Einige steigen als leuchtende Kugeln und andere zünden,
Manche auch werfen wir nur spielend das Aug zu erfreun.

————

[5] Eine grosse Epoche hat das Jahrhundert gebohren;
Aber der grosse Moment findet ein kleines Geschlecht.

————

[6] Hexen lassen sich wohl durch schlechte Sprüche citiren
Aber die Grazie kommt nur auf der Grazie ruf [*Ruf*].

————

[7] Das philosophische Gespräch.
Einer das höret man wohl, spricht *nach* dem andern, doch keiner
Mit dem andern: wer nennt zwey Monologen Gespräch?

————

[8] [?Poesie]
Reiner Bach, du entstellst nicht den Kiesel, du bringst ihn dem Auge
Näher, so seh ich die Welt, W—wenn du sie beschreibst.

[9]   Plain Sense, Measure, Clearness, Dignity, Grace   *f34*ᵛ
      over all, these made the genius of Greece.

[10] Nur an des Lebens Gipfel, der Blume, zündet sich neues
      In der organischen Welt, in der empfindenden an.

[11] Wirke Gutes, du nährst der Menschheit göttliche Pflanze,
      Bilde Schönes, du streust Keime der göttlichen aus.

[12] Auch in der sittlichen Welt ist ein Adel: gemeine Naturen
      Zahlen mit dem[,] was sie thun, Schöne mit dem[,] was
      sie sind.

[13] Ist das Auge gesund, so begegnet es aussen dem Schöpfer,
      Ist es das Herz, dann gewiss spiegelt es innen die Welt.

[14] "Welche Religion ich bekenne?" Keine von allen[,]
      Die du mir nennst. "Und warum keine?" Aus Religion.

[15] Diesen ist alles Genuss. Sie essen Ideen, und bringen
      In das Himmelreich selbst Messer und Gabel hinauf.

[16] Himmelan flögen sie gern, doch hat auch der Körper
      sein Gutes,
      Und man packt es geschick[t] hinter dem Seraph noch
      auf.

[17]   Licht und Farbe
      Wohne du ewiglich eines [*Eines*] dort bey dem ewiglich
      einen [*Einen*],
      Farbe, du wechselnde, komm freundlich zum Menschen
      herab.

[18] Allen gehört, was du denkst, dein eigen ist nur[,] was   *f35*
      du fühlest,
      Soll er dein Eigenthum sein, fühle den Gott, den du
      denkst.

[19] *Über* das Herz zu siegen ist gross, ich *verehre* den Tap-
      fern;
      Aber wer *durch* sein Herz sieget, er gilt mir doch mehr.

[20]　Selbst das Gebildete ist Stoff nur dem bildenden Geist.

[21]　Kannst du nicht *allen* gefallen durch deine That und
　　　dein Kunstwerk[,]
　　　Mach es *wenigen* recht, vielen gefallen ist schlimm.

[22]　　　　　　　Rogers
Weil ein Vers dir gelingt in einer gebildeten Sprache
Die für dich dichtet und denkt, glaubst du schon *Dichter*
zu seyn!

　　　　　Blumen moralische
1. Rosenknospe, du bist dem blühenden Mädchen ge-
　　widmet,
　　Die als die Herrlichste sich, als die bescheidenste zeigt.

2. Eine kannt' ich—sie war wie die Lilie schlank, und
　　ihr Stolz war
　　Unschuld—herrlicher hat Salomo keine gesehn.

3. Nachtviole, dich geht man am blendenden Tage vor-
　　über;
　　Doch bey der Nachtigall schlag [*Schlag*] hauchest du
　　köstlichen Geist.

ƒ35ᵛ　　　　　　Tuber rose
4. Unter der Menge strahlest du vor, du ergötzest im
　　Freyen;
　　Aber bleibe ~~from~~ vom Haupt, bleibe vom Herzen mir
　　fern.

5. Sagt! was füllet das Zimmer mit Wohlgerüchen?
　　Reseda,
　　Farbloss, ohne Gestalt, stilles und zierliches Kraut.

[23]　　　　Vergiss mein nicht.
Deine liebliche kleinheit [*Kleinheit*], dein holdes auge
　　[*Auge*], sie sagen
Immer, vergiss mein nicht! immer, vergiss nur nicht
mein!

———

[24] The seed beneath the snow—lives & shoots—but when
the Spring comes—o then it appears.

[25] Immer war mir das Feld und der Wald und der Fels
und die Garten [*Gärten*]
Nur ein Raum, und *du* machst sie, Geliebte[,] zum Ort.

[26] Alles wünscht' ich zu haben, um mit ihr alles zu theilen,
Alles gäb ich dahin, wär sie, die Einzige, mein.

––––

[27] Warum bin ich vergänglich, O Zeus? so fragte die Schön-   *f36*
heit,
Macht dich doch, sagte der Gott, nur das Vergängliche
schön.

[28] Und die Liebe, die Blumen, der Thau und die Jugend
vernamens [*vernahmens*],
Alle gingen sie weg weinend von Jupiters Thron.

––––

3132 12.47   Comparison between 1 the Anti-mysterii, or
Socinian, 2 the Lipo-mysterii/or common Latitudinarian C. of
England/3 the intellectual philo-mysterii (Methodist) 4 the
Catholic, & 5 the Quaker Systems of Christianity.

3133 12.48   August Serm. 57. de verb. Dom. Sic accipite, sic   *f36ᵛ*
credite, ut mereamini intelligere: fides enim debet præcedere in-
tellectum, ut sit intellectus fidei præmium.

3134 12.49   But should a friend think foully of that wherein
the pride of the Spirit's purity is in shrine—should he—&c—
O the agony! the agony!

Nor Time, nor varying Fate,   *f37*
Nor tender memory old or late,
Nor all his Virtues, great tho' they be,
Nor all his Genius can free
His friend's Soul from this agony!

f37ᵛ   3135 12.50   Those who embraced the Xn Religion in the
first instance from the perception of its conformity to the mysterious facts, and the plain or dim, yet alike inevitable revelations, of
their human nature fell into excess by forcing all, they could, into
the Scriptures—those of the latter days who have received Xtnity
by compulsion solely or at least principally on the historical evidence of its miracles have naturally per fas et nefas labored to
thrust out of it whatever the philosophy of Materialism would not
have taught them without it—receiving a contradiction to that
f38   system only in order to gratify a desire of continued Life/—&
resting this solely on a miracle & considering it in itself as an
absolute miracle, or violent interruption of the laws of nature,
thereby complement & confirm their philosophy. Thus Newcome
Cappe "It is essential to Gentile Christianity to believe that he
died and rose again, and was empowered to send from Heaven
the gifts of the holy spirit, and nothing else is essential. All the
rest is Verbiage—reference to natural religions, quotations from
the Old Testament, allusions to prefigurations or customs of the
Mosaic Economy; or terms & phrases of the language, people,
f38ᵛ   place, & time: in many respects exceedingly remote from the language of this Western World, & the accuracy of these modern
Times.

What is essential to the Jewish Christianity (which consists in
receiving Jesus for the Messiah promised to the Jews) is to receive him in that character, or to believe in him notwithstanding
that appearances are against it"—Cappe's Remarks on Scripture.

But—will the Deans, Vicars, & Rectors say—we, tho' we do
follow Paley & Grotius in our mode of receiving Christianity,
abhor these Heresies—Yes! but shew me any body of men not
payed, established, beneficed by the state, & tied down to a Liturgy
f39   & Articles, that beginning with Grotius have not gone on to
Socinianism, or near to it, or like Mʳ Cappe beyond it?—/

3136 12.51   ὁ τε ἐνθυσιασμὸς ἐπίνευσὶν τινα θεῖαν ἔχειν,
δόκει καὶ τῷ μαντικῷ γένει πλησιάζειν.
                                          Strab. Geogr. lib. 10.
Tho' Genius, like the fire on the Altar, can only be kindled from

Heaven, yet it will perish unless supplied with appropriate fuel to feed it — or if it meet not with the virtues, whose society alone can reconcile it to earth, it will return to whence it came, or at least lie hid as beneath embers, till some sudden & awakening Gust of regenerating Grace αναζωπυρει rekindles & reveals it anew. S.T.C.

3137 12.52   Prophetiæ veritas non confirmatur miraculis, is the maxim of Maimonides & all the Jews.—

3138 12.53   Earth = magna mater, Diana multimammia.   f39ᵛ

3139 12.54   Ridges shining with the Share like the Tops of crowded wavelets—the 6-furrowed ridge/

3140 12.55   Boiling the Thrush's Eggs.

3141 12.56   Dʳ Stock & his uxor Tyranna, & his scrape about W. in consequence of my reading.

3142 12.57   1. Discernible Size, 2. well differenced—3 akin to its appropriate faculty of sense or mind. 4—it stayed the needful while—5—and passed to me thro' proper unperturbed medium but distance due, 7. in the fit point of view. 8. My organ of sense entire & undepraved, and in full action.

3143 12.58   The Zahuris red of eye & dwarf in stature, have   f40 the power of seeing in the earth as if it were water, & all treasures, bodies, mines, springs, &c, appearing therein as substances in the bottom or middle of a transparent Fluid—see only on Tuesdays & Fridays, & are always born on Good Friday.—

3144 12.59   Αγνος rendered by the Botanists agnus castus, a pun covering a tautology. What is that? Ορος. Oh! it is Mons Oros, is it?

3145 12.60
         Tacitus, good Edit. & Gordon's Trans/for Poole/   f40ᵛ
         Locke's Works/

Selden's Works/
Berkley's Works
Barclay A. & Eup/
Stockdale's Shakespere/
Sh's poems.
Butler's An. & Serm/
Horæ Paulinæ & Nat/Theol/

3146 12.61   It is not the W's knowlege of my frailties that
prevents my *entire* Love of them/No! it is their Ignorance of the
ƒ41   Deep place of my Being—and o! the cruel cruel misconception of
that which is purest in me, which alone is indeed pure—My Love
of ασρα could not be, did I did not know that she knew it as if
she was it—herself & the Conscience of that self, beyond the
bounds of that form which her eyes behold when she looks ~~down~~
up on herself/O there is a form which seems irrelative to imprisonment of Space!

3147 12.62
ƒ41ᵛ   Templa pudicitiæ quid opus statuisse puellis
Si cuivis nuptæ quidlibet esse licet.

                                                              Tib. L.2.

3148 12.63   Every thing, that has been known or deemed fit
to win woman's Love, I have an impulse to make myself—even
tho' I should otherwise look down upon it—I cannot endure not
ƒ42   to be strong in arms, a daring Soldier—yet I know, I have no fear
of Life or dread of Pain, & that I am not that because I cannot respect it—again, I must be the high Intellect, that despises it—& both
at once. I must be a graceful & bold Horseman/I must sing & play
ƒ42ᵛ   on the Harp/I must be beautiful instead of what I am, and yet
she must love me for what I now am, even for myself & my exceeding Love/& what then mean these vain wishes? O I well
know! even to make her already loving me love me to that un-
utterableness, that impatience at the not enoughness of dependence, with which I love her! Oh and likewise because, if indeed she
ƒ43   do love me, I feel myself unworthy, not able to repay the debt—

I want, I yearn to make her Love of me delightful to her own
mind/I want to be every thing good & that good wearing every
attraction, wch even Evil has more often around it, & why? because she is all my Vanity & all my Virtue—Loving *her* I intensely   *f43ᵛ*
desire all that could make the greatest & (be it viceless) the weak,
if they be amiable, love *me*—I am so feeble that I cannot yearn
to be perfect, unrewarded by some distinct soul—yet still somewhat too noble to be satisfied or even pleased by the assent of the   *f44*
many—myself will not suffice—& a stranger is nothing/It must be
one who is & who is not myself—not myself, & yet so much more
my Sense of Being ⟨(The very Breath owes its power moral feeling)⟩ than myself that myself is therefore only not a feeling for
reckless Despair, because she is its object/Self in me derives its   *f44ᵛ*
sense of Being from having this one absolute Object, including all
others that but for it would be thoughts, notions, irrelevant fancies
—yea, my own Self would be—utterly deprived of all connection
with her—only more than a thought, because it would be a Burthen—a haunting of the dæmon, Suicide. O! what mad nonsense   *f45*
all this would sound to all but myself—and perhaps even She
would despise me for it—no! not despise—but be alarmed—and
learn from W̲—to pity & withdraw herself from my affections.
Whither?—O agony! O the vision of that Saturday Morning—
of the Bed/—O cruel! is he not beloved, adored by two—& two   *f45ᵛ*
such Beings—/and must I not be beloved *near* him except as a
Satellite?—But O mercy mercy! is he not better, greater, more
manly, & altogether more attractive to any the purest Woman?
And yet, and yet, methinks, love so intense might demand love—   *f46*
otherwise, who could be secure? Who could know, that his Beloved might not meet his Superior?—W. is greater, better, man-
lier, more dear, by nature, to Woman, than I—I—miserable I!—
but does he—O No! no! no! no! he does not—he does not pretend, he does not wish, to love you as I love you, Sara!—he does   *f46ᵛ*
not love, he *would* not love, it is not the voice, not the duty of *his*
nature, to love *any* being as I love you. No! he is to be beloved—
but yet, tho' you may feel that if he loved you, ⟨tho' only⟩ even
partly as I̲ love you, you should inevitably love him, love him to
a degree in which you *cannot* love *me*—yet still he does not *so*   *f47*

love you—⟨no!⟩ not in kind, much less degree—I alone love you
so devotedly, & therefore, therefore, love me, ⌐Sara!—   Sara!⌐
love me!

Awakened from a dream of Tears, & anguish of involuntary
Jealousy, ½ past 2/Sept: 13. 1807

N. Stowey.

f47ᵛ 3149 12.64   To lie in ease yet dull anxiety for hours, afraid
to think a thought, lest some thought of Anguish should shoot a
pain athwart my body, afraid even to turn my body, lest the very
bodily motion should introduce a train of painful Thoughts—

3150 12.65
> So herrlich stieg in seiner Blüthentracht
> Noch nie zu mir der *Engel Frühling* nieder!
> So rieselte mir nie durch Mark und Glieder—
> Wie? —— Nicht dass ——
> Du musstest erst in mir, Geliebte, du,
> Dem *Engel* eine Stätte zubereiten.

f48 3151 12.66   Our mortal existence a stoppage in the blood of
Life—a brief eddy in the everflowing Ocean of pure Activity,
from wind or concourse of currents—who beholds Pyramids, yea,
Alps and Andes, giant Pyramids the work of Fire, raising monuments like a generous Victor, o'er its own conquest, tombstones of
a world destroyed—yet, these too float adown the Sea of Time, &
melt away, Mountains of floating Ice/—

f48ᵛ 3152 12.67   Life knows only its Wirkung—therefore the To
Ἐν is the sole self-comprehender, because the Λογος of coeternal
Wirkung is ~~the~~ its perfect adequate Idea/therefore Trinity re-
jected, atheism, i.e. God = a blind unconscious Activity, the necessary consequence—

3153 12.68   Accords and Dissonances in their texture exquisite, a seeming Intertangle, yea, to the grosser eye a matted
mass, & witch-lock of confusion

3154 12.69   ? Every finite Being or only some that have the
temptation to become intensely & wholly conscious of its distinctness, thence tempted to division—thence wretched/—some so gross
by it as not even to acquire that sense of distinctness wholly swal-   ƒ49
lowed up in stupid instinct of Selfishness, not even = self-love—
to others Love the first step to re-union/A scoff, that Religious Enthusiasm borders on & leads to Lust—possibly because all our
powers work together/& it is the consequence of trying to stride
too vastly up the Ladder of existence, a great *round* of the Ladder
is omitted—namely, Love to some *verschiedene Eine* of our own
kind—then *let* Religion come/else Religion will not only partake
of, instead of being partaken by, & so co-adunated with, the summit of ~~real~~ Love, but necessary include the Nadir of Love, appetite/
thence, ~~the~~ dissensualize its nature into fantastic Passions, lewd
Idolatry of Paphian Priestesses.

3155 12.70   Auf einen Hieb fällt kein Baum: geschweig eine   ƒ49ᵛ
Zeder, die so viele Jahrhunderte, durch alle bekannte Zeitalter
steht, und mit ihrem immer grünendem [*grünenden*] Gipfel
jedem Sturm trotzt.
    —worin man von dem Erdgetümmel in die blauen heitern
Lüfte oben *wegverzückt,* und in dem unermesslichen Umfange
des Himmels athmet, befreyt von allen Banden.—I wish, I had
made a little collection of the most forcible combinations of the
German/Bürger, & Ardhingello, looked thro', would go far—and
additions would drop in at leisure.

3156 12.71   Time, Space, Duration, Action, Active, Passion,   ƒ50
Passive, Activeness, Passiveness, Reaction, Causation, Affinity—
here assemble all the Mysteries—known, all is known—unknown,
say rather, merely known, all is unintelligible/and yet Locke &
the stupid adorers of ~~this~~ that *Fetisch* Earth-clod, take all these
for granted—blinde Fenster der blossen Ordnung wegen an einem
Gebäude verträgt, wo gerade das beste Licht hereinbrechen und
die schönste Aussicht seyn sollte.—   By the bye, in Poetry
as well as Metaphysics, that which we first meet with in the Dawn
of our minds becomes our after Fetisch, to the Many at least—

blessed he, who first sees or the Morning Star, at least—if not the
$f50^v$ Sun—or purpling Clouds, his Harbingers. Thence is FAME desirable to a great man/& thence Subversion of vulgar *Fetisches* becomes a Duty.

⟨Rest = infinite Motion—either infinitely great or infinitely
small.⟩

Rest, Motion!—O ye strange Locks of intricate Simplicity,
who shall find the Key? He shall throw wide open the Portals
of the Palace of Sensuous or Symbolical Truth; and the Holy of
Holies will he find in the Adyta. Rest = Enjoyment, and Death!
Motion = Enjoyment and Life! O the depth of the Proverb, Extremes meet!

The Break of the Morning—& from Inaction a nation starts up
into Motion & wide fellow-consciousness!—The Trumpet of the
$f51$ Archangel, and a World with all its Troops & Companies of Gen-
erations starts up into an hundredfold Expansion, Power multiplied into itself, cubically, by the number of all its possible Acts—
all the Potential springing into Power!—Conceive a Bliss from
Self-conscience, combining with Bliss from increase of Action, the
first dreaming, the latter ~~not~~ dead-asleep, in a grain of Gunpowder
—conceive a huge Magazine of Gunpowder, & a Flash of Lightning awakes the Whole at once!—What an Image of the Resurrection, grand from its very Inadequacy. Yet again, conceive the
$f51^v$ living moving Ocean—its bed sinks away from under, and the
whole World of Waters falls in at once on a thousand times vaster
Mass of intensest Fire—& the whole prior Orbit of ~~its~~ the Planet's
successive Revolutions *is possessed by it at once* (Potentia fit
Actus) amid the Thunder of Rapture.—

3157 12.72   Bigness for Greatness—a Being so large, that accidentally passing by during the explosion of the Dr Darwin's
Chaos of the whole System of the Milky way, the Shot flew in
his face, & *pock-fretted him!*

3158 12.73   Form is factitious *Being*, and Thinking is the
$f52$ Process. Imagination the Laboratory, in which Thought elaborates
Essence into Existence. A Psilosopher, i.e. a nominal Ph. without

Imagination, is a *Coiner*—Vanity, the *Froth* of the molten Mass, is his *Stuff*—and Verbiage the Stamp & Impression. This is but a *deaf* Metaphor—better say, that he is guilty of Forgery—he presents the same ⟨sort of⟩ *Paper* as the honest Barterer, but when you carry it to the *Bank*, it is found to be drawn on—Outis, *Esqre*. His Words had deposited no Forms there, payable at Sight—or even at any imaginable Time from the Date of the Draft/

3159 12.74   The Sky, o rather say, the Æther, at Malta,   *f52ᵛ* with the Sun apparently suspended in it, the Eye seeming to pierce beyond, & as it were, behind it—and below the ætherial Sea, so blue, so ⟨a⟩ zerflossenes Eins, the substantial Image, and fixed real Reflection of the Sky—O I could annihilate in a deep moment all possibility of the needlepoint pinshead System of the *Atomists* by one submissive Gaze! Λογος ab *Ente*—at once the ~~essential~~ existent Reflexion, and the Reflex Act—at once actual and real & therefore, filiation not creation/Thought *formed not fixed*—the   *f53* molten *Being* never cooled into a *Thing*, tho' begotten into the vast adequate Thought. Est, Idea, Ideatio—*Id*—inde, hoc et *illud*. Idea—*atio*, seu *actio* = Id: iterum, ⟨Hoc + Id, & then⟩ Id + Ea (i.e. Coadunatio Individui cum Universo per Amorem) = Idea: Idea + actio = Ideatio, seu αγιον πνευμα, which being transelemented into we are mystically united with the *Am*— Ειμι —.

— minus, or deprived of. + added to. × multiplied into. = equal to, the same as.—

Hoc + Id: Id × Ea + Actio = αγιον πνευμα τῆς Ενωσεως—A   *f53ᵛ* Dew-drop, the Pearl of Aurora, is indeed a true *Unio:*—I would, that Unio were the word for the Dew-drop, and the Pearl be called Unio marinus.—

3160 12.75   Wer den reizbarsten, innigsten Sinn für die Schönheiten der Natur hat, ihre geheimsten Regungen fühlt, deren Mangel nicht leiden kann, und denselben *abhilft* nach seinen Kräften: der übt aller Religionen Wahrstes und Heiligstes aus.

O for the power to persuade all the writers of G. B. to adopt the ver, zer, and ab of the German—why not verboil, zerboil? versend, zersend? I should like the very words verflossen, zerflossen, to be naturalized—and as I look, now feels my Soul creative Throes, And now all Joy, all sense, Zerflows.

f54 I do not know, whether I am in earnest, or in sport, while I recommend this Ver & Zer: that is, I cannot be sure, whether I feel myself any thing ridiculous in the Idea, or whether the feeling that seems to imply this be not the effect of my anticipation of & sympathy with the ridicule of perhaps all my Readers.

f15ᵛ 3161 12.22 I guess that the gutta Asiatica or black Drop is = the Laudanum Helmontii Junioris.

 1. Of opium ¼ of a Pound
 2. Of the Juice of Quinces 5 pounds.
 3. Slice the O. thin & mince it small.
 4. Into the Quince Juice made luke-warm put in the Opium, & mix it well up—
 5. Then let it stay ten days to ferment in a moderate Heat.

f16 6. Then filter it.
 7. Then add of Cinnamon, Nutmeg, and of Cloves an Ounce, & let them infuse in this liquor in the same warmth three or four days—or better still, a week.
 8. Then filter it once more.
 9. Then let it evaporate till it become almost a semi-fluid—or

f16ᵛ if you choose, even to an extract from which pills may be made.
N.B. 10. After the spices have been put in (the Nutmegs powdered) the Liquor may be made to boil "a walme or two."
When in Malta, I might have easily tried it with Lemon Juice, instead of Quinces.

f17 11. Lastly, incorporate with it two Ounces of the best saffron reduced to powder; or still better as much extract as can be produced from two Ounces of Saffron.

3162 12.23 Arx, Tridens, rostris, sphinx, præster, torrida, seps, strix.

3163 12.24   We set Spies and Watches on the Sun—
We make Time give an account of itself & shall we not give an
account of Time?

3164 12.25   The Golden Rule for weak Stomachs, by S.T.C.   ƒ17ᵛ
Plain food rather than seasoned, ~~vege~~ animal than vegetable, solid
than fluid—and patience rather than medicine.

3165 12.26   Conception of a Planet without any general atmosphere; but in which each living Body has its peculiar atmosphere—to hear & understand one man joins his atmosphere to that
of another/according to the sympathies of their nature the aberra-
tions of Sound greater or less, & their Thoughts more or less intelligible, a pretty allegory might be made—

3166 12.27
       Two faces, each of a confused ~~con~~ countenance/   ƒ18
       And a confusion of countenance/as the last line/—

in the eyes of the one muddiness and lustre were blended, and
the eyes of the other were the same; but there was a red fever in
them, that made them more fierce/yet methought, the former
~~were~~ struck a greater trouble, a fear, and darkness of the mind/
and sometimes all the face looked meek & mild; but the eye was
ever the same.

3167 12.28   It is not repealing Scraps of Paper & Parchments,   ƒ18ᵛ
called Acts of Parliament, that will produce any advantage/Re-
peal the Ill-blood and Ill-will that subsists between this Country
and America—
                                        Lord Chatham

3168 12.29   Mʳ De Quincey
                     Dowry Parade
                     Hot Wells

3169 12.30   Tincture of Hops, 1 drachm/or Extract of Hops, 7 Grains.

f19   3170 12.31   That vegetable block of Rock-work, the short Oak in Enmore Park, 7 yards & a half, in circumference, and its shortness makes it monstrous. It is so gouty & double jointed/
The great lofty old Elm, in the Shrubbery 5¼ yards only.

3171 12.32   Shadow—its *being* subsists in shap'd and definite non-entity/

f19°   3172 12.33   I moisten the bread of Affliction with the water of Adversity.

3173 12.34
Enema domesticum/(Dr Hamilton)
Recipe—
Muriatis Sodæ unciam dimidiam.
Olei napi silvestris unciam
Aquæ tepidæ libram. misce.

Enema fœtidum,
Gummi resinæ ferulæ assæ fœtidæ drachmas duas
Aquæ tepidæ uncias decem (10)   Solve.

———

Enema purgans
Recipe
f20   Foliorum Cassiæ Sennæ drachmas tres,
Sulphatis Sodæ unciam,
Aquæ fervidæ libram.   Infunde et cola.

Haustus salinus effervescens.
Recipe—Carbonatis potassæ purificati scrupulos quatuor,
Aquæ fontanæ uncias quatuor.
Solve, et cum subsederint feces, cola.

Recipe—Succus Citri medicæ uncias duas,
Syrupi simplicis,
Aqua fontanæ, utriusque unciam   Misce.

Utriusque mixturæ uncia detur pro dosi; solutione carbonatis *f20ᵛ*
potassæ prius sumptâ, mistura e sueco citri medicæ illico porri-
genda est.

Infusum Cassiæ sennæ.

Recipe—Foliorum cassiæ sennæ unciam et dimidiam,
　　　Seminum coriandri sativi contusorum unciam et di-
　　　midiam,
　　　Supertartritis potassæ drachmas duas,
　　　Aquæ fontanæ libram.

Supertartritem potassæ in aquâ coquendo solve; deinde liquorem *f21*
adhuc ferventem sennæ et feminibus affunde; macera per horam
in vase aperto, et frigefactum cola.

———

Mistura diaphoretica antimonialis.

R—Aquæ fontanæ uncias quinque et dimidiam,
　　Sacchari purificati drachmam unam et dimidiam,
　　Vini tartritis antimonii drachmas duas,
　　Tincturæ opii guttas triginta. Misce.

Mistura diaphoretica salina *f21ᵛ*

R—Aquæ fontanæ uncias ɪv,
　　Sacchari purificati drachmas tres,
　　Carbonatis ammoniæ præparatæ grana decem.
　　Solve, et adde
　　Aquæ acetitis ammoniæ uncias tres,
　　Spiritus myrti pimentiæ drachmas duas. Misce.

Mistura mucilaginosa

R. Decocti Altheæ officinalis uncias quatuor,
　　Syrupi simplicis unciam dimidiam, Misce.

———

Potus acidus vegetabilis.

R. Decocti furfuris libras duas,
　　Supertartritis potassæ scrupulos quatuor, *f22*
　　Syrupi simplicis unciam.　　　Misce.

Solutio Gum: res: fer: ass. fœt.

R. Gummi resinæ ferulæ Assæ fœtidæ drachmas quatuor,
Aquæ fervidæ, uncias viginti-quatuor. Solve.

Aqua acetitis ammoniæ = (i.e. idem est, ac) = Spiritus Mindereri.
Aqua potassæ = Lixivium causticum.
Carbonas ammoniæ = Ammonia præparata.
Carbonas Magnesiæ = Magnesia alba.
Carbonas Potassæ = Lixivia purificata, seu Alkali fixum vegetabile
purificatum.

f22ᵛ Myrtus pimenta = Pimenta.
Submurias hydrargyri = Calomelas, seu Mercurius dulcis.
Sulphas Magnesiæ = Sal catharticus amarus.
Sulphas potassæ = Tartarum vitriolatum.
Sulphas sodæ = Sal Glauberi, seu Soda vitriolata.
Supertartritis Potassæ = Cremor Tartari, seu Crystalli Tartari.
Tartras Antimonii = Tartarus emeticus, seu antimonium tartaris-
atum.

1. Injicitur Enema domesticum. Then,
Recipe, Mercurii dulcis,
Pulveris Jalapæ,
Sacchari albi,
aa grana tria.
Tere in pulverem, quam primum sumendum.

f23 Toast & water for drink.

2nd day, *of Typhus*
Injiciantur Enematis domestici unciæ decem. Intra horam.
Recipe, Foliorum sennæ drachmam unam,
Extracti glycirrhizæ drachmam dimidiam
Aquae fervidæ uncias octo.
Sit Infusum duabus vicibus sumendum.

3rd day. Repetatur enema domest: vespere, et habeat haustum,
cum tincturæ opii guttis 15.

4th day. Magnesiæ drachmam unam
    Aquæ uncias quatuor
    Sacchari drachmam dimidiam.
Sit mistura cujus sumatur uncia dimidia, omni hora.   *f23ᵛ*
Repetatur haustus Anodynus vespere.
(Haustus Anodynus = Laudani guttæ 15 seu 25—Aquæ fontanæ
unciam, Syrupi simplicis drachmas duas)

Marasmus. 1 Day.
Recipe—Submuriatis hydrargyri grana decem,
    Sacchari drachmam dimidiam,
Tere intime, et divide in doses quatuor. Sumat unam
    quaque horâ.
Jusculi bovini librum unam, in dies.
2nd day.   *f24*
    Submuriatis hydrargyri grana tria, Sacchari, Jalapæ, singu-
    lorum grana sex. *mane* sumendus.
3 & 4th day. Ditto repeated, cum enemate domestico.
5th day—there was spontaneous vomiting/
    Recipe, Tincturæ Jalapæ,
        Syrupi Sacchari, utriusque drachmas duas.
Sit haustus mane et vespere sumendus: n.b. haustui vespertino in-
stillentur Laudani guttæ decem.
6th day. Repeated.   *f24ᵛ*
7th Repeated.
8th (no stool.)
    Recipe, Carbonatis magnesiæ, scrupulum unum,
        Supertartritis potassæ,
        Sacchari, utriusque grana decem.
    Sit pulvis, omni mane sumendus.
    Continuentur haustus cum tinctura Jalapæ.
9th Repeated.
10$^{th.}$ Ditto, sed intermisso haustu Jalapæ.
11. Submuriatis Hyd: grana duo,   *f25*
    Pulveris Jalapæ,
    Sacchari, utriusque grana sex. Sit pulvis vesperæ su-
    mendus.

Continuentur pulvis e carbonate magnesia.

12. Habeat pilulas aloeticas octo; sumat duas omni trihorio,
& take the Draught—Tincturæ Jalapæ drachmas tres,
Syrupi drachmam unam, Aquæ uncias duas, the first
thing in the morning.

ƒ25ᵛ   13. The Draught repeated.

14. After vomiting.

Recipe, Magnesiæ ustæ drachmam unam,
Mucilaginis Gummi Arabici unciam dimidiam,
Spiritus lavendulæ compositi drachmas duas,
Tincturæ Thebaicæ guttas viginti.
Aquæ uncias tres. Misce.

Sumat hujusce misturæ agitatæ unciam dimidiam, secunda
quaque horâ.

ƒ26   Oblinatur abdomen linimenti anodyni pauxillo, ter vel quater in
dies, et circumdetur panno laneo.

N.B. Throughout the whole 4 ounces of Port wine a day.

15. Solutionis Assæ fœtidæ unciam unam,
Aquæ, uncias quinque.
Sit mistura, ope fistulæ armatæ, per anum injicienda.
Continuentur alia, ut heri

16. Repetatur hoc enema, et continuentur alia.

17, 18. Continuentur et enema et alia.

19. Continuentur alia (i.e. vinum et mistura e magnesiâ).
ƒ26ᵛ   Omisse enemate.

20. Take only half doses.

After convalescence—

Habeat pulveris Jalapæ compositi unciam unam, in doses
sedecim dividendam. N.B. One to be taken once or twice
a day, so as to preserve a regular state of the Bowels.

———

Four Grains of Calomel, 3 or 4 of Aloes, & ten or 12 drachmas of
Rochelle Salt, will (either of them) generally *purge*—reduce the
ƒ27   dose, & they become laxative. J.D. complains of pain & sense of
weight at the epigastric region increased on pressure, vomiting of
Ingesta in an acid state with frequent eructations, headache &
vertigo, vague pains in her limbs—strength is impaired—loss of

Flesh—appetite bad—pulse 80—skin cool—tongue white & moist
—thirsty—habitually costive, catamenia suppressed—

Feb. 8ᵗʰ. No stool—

   Recipe—Extract colocynthidis composit. drachmam & di-
     midiam.

     Forma in pilulas viginti quatuor

     Sumat duas omni bihorio, usquedum responderit   *f27ᵛ*
     alvus.

9ᵗʰ. 3 copious stools of a dark greenish color & fetid—sense
   of weight at scrobiculus cordis—sixteen pills had been
   taken.

10ᵗʰ. 3 copious & more natural stools.

11ᵗʰ. Vomiting in the evening—Gastrodynia since morning.

   Recipe—Carbonatis magnesiæ scrupulos duos

     Pulveris rhei scrupulum,

     Sumantur ex aquæ menthæ piperitidis unciis dua-
     bus.

12. Gastrodynia gone—vomiting not recurred—no stool.

   Sumat statim infusi sennæ uncias tres, ex infusi lini unciis   *f28*
   sex.

   Serâ nocte enema purgans, si opus sit.

13. A copious, consistent, blackish, and fetid stool upon the
   exhibition of the Injection.

   general pain of Abdomen.

   pulse calm.

   Pilulas aloeticas sedecim.

   Tres omni trihorio.

14. Several stools, dark or greenish. 9 pills taken.

   Habeat salis polychresti drachmam dimidiam,

   Pulveris rhæi grana quindecim,   *f28ᵛ*

   Sit pulvis omni mane sumendus. Full diet.

18ᵗʰ. Has had regular stools, & continues convalescent.

   Recipe—Sulphatis Magnesiæ unciam.

       Supertartritis potassæ,

       Sulphatis potassæ cum sulphure, utriusque drach-
       mas duas.

   N.B. to be dissolved in a pint and a half of water, & a tea
   cupful taken each morning. Dismissed cured.

f29   3174 12.35   Αριστον μεν υδωρ—Lord Bacon = my Interpretation—

If Kings are Gods on Earth, they are likewise however Gods of Earth—

Ora tu, tu lege, tu protege, tuque labora.

Minos, Lycurgus, Solon, are grammar themes. For ancient Personages & Characters now-a-days use to wax Children again; *tho' that Parable of Pindarus be true, the best Thing is water: for common and trivial Things are many times the best, and rather despised upon pride, because they are* vulgar, than upon cause or use. Bacon—Of a Digest of Laws—Octavo Edition Vol.iv. p.377.

f29ᵛ   And in another place, which I cannot at place light on.—

Pope Urban the second in a brief to Godfrey, Bishop of Lucca, hath these very words which Cardinal Baronius reciteth in his Annals, Non illos homicidas arbitramur, qui adversus excommunicatos zelo catholicæ matris ardentes eorum quos libet trucidare contigerit.

Parisatis poisoned one side of the Knife with which she carved & eat of the same Joint, the next slice unhurt—happy illustration of affected self-inclusion in accusation—

f30   "I confess, I have somewhat of the cunctative"—Lord Bacon.

Heu! quam miserum ab illo lædi, de quo non possis queri—eheu, quam miserrimum est ab illo lædi, de quo propter amorem non possis queri—!—

Keeps his wounds green,
By moody day-dreams of Revenge.

Observation after reading Mʳ Sheridan's speech on Ireland, from Bacon—

Things will have their first or second Agitation: if they be not tossed in the arguments of Council they will be tossed on the waves of Fortune—

f30ᵛ   Death of an Immortal beautifully compared to the Indian Fig, which at its full height declines its branches to the Earth, & there takes root again.

I ought to do it; but my spirit mutinies against it.—

Read Lord Bacon Touching Non-residents & Pluralities, in his Tract on the Pacification of the Church—

Oct. Edit.—Vol.ii^{nd}, p.546.

For the ease of Chaplains——
I should think it were a juster reason why they should have no
Benefice, than why they should be qualified to have two.

3175 12.36   The Blast Rises & falls & trembles at its height—

3176 12.37   spitting flame, like a wet candle = a passionate   f31
woman. .

3177 12.38   Εις Ερωτα—duty & religion to that power, to
shew that tho' it make all things, wealth, pleasure, ambition,
worthless yea noisome for themselves—yet for *it* it can produce
all efforts, even if only to rescue its name from scoffs as the Child
& Parent of slothfulness/therefore works of general profit, works
abstruse/therefore activity, & above all virtue & chastity—

3178 12.39   Mess** Sealy's, Liverpool.   f31*

3179 12.40   Enumerate k, *ᵍyᵏ* qualities—First, perhaps I
ᴡ:μ; ι | ᶜ; ℓ / for them—at least I could not have without them;
but now I feel that I love them because they are hers.

3180 12.41   Samson Agonistes—Choruses of—
                ◡ - &c = a common blank verse line.

Samson.

I. ◡ - &c.
2. ◡ ◡ - ◡ ◡ ◡ / - / - ◡ / ◡ -
3. ◡ - / ◡ / - / ◡ / -
4, 5, 6. ◡ - &c.
7. ◡ - / ◡ - / ◡ -
8. ◡ - / ◡ - / ◡ -
9   ◡ - / ◡ - / ◡ -
10. - ◡ / ◡ - / ◡ - ◡ - ◡ -
11, 12. ◡ - &c
13   ◡ - / ◡ - / ◡ -.
From 13 to 28 ◡ - &c, except 25, = 3 Iambics
28, 29, 30 = 25.—Then concludes with 5 ◡ - &c.

f3²   Chorus

– – – – – ∪ ∪ –
– ∪ – ∪ – ∪ – ∪
∪ – ∪ – ∪ – / – ∪ ∪ –
– – – – ∪ – ∪ / – ∪ ∪ / ∪ –
∪ – ∪ – ∪ –
∪ – / – – / ∪ – ∪
∪ – / ∪ – / ∪ – ∪
∪ – ∪ / – ∪ / – – ∪ / –
∪ – ∪ –
∪ – / ∪ – / ∪ – / ∪ – / ∪ – / ∪ –. N.B. *Hex*ameter Iambic.
– ∪ – ∪ – ∪ –
– ∪ / – ∪ ∪ / – – / – / ∪ –
3 Hexameter Iambics.
∪ – ∪ – ∪ –
– – ∪ – ∪ – / – ∪ ∪ – ∪ ∪
Pentameter Iambic hyperacatalectic.
Pentam: Iamb: acatalectic
∪ ∪ – / – ∪ / –   ⎫
                      ⎬ rhymes
∪ – ∪ – ∪ – ∪ –   ⎭
Then 15 Pentam: & Hexameter Iambics mixt.

f3²ᵛ   3181 12.42   Vignette for my poems or other works—
A marjoram (from Gerard or later drawings) with—Abstine,
Sus! non tibi spiro—Swine having an antipathy to the fragrance of
this plant.

3182 12.43   The moulting Peacock with only two of his long
tail-feathers remaining, & those sadly in tatters, yet proudly as
ever spreading out his ruined fan in the Sun & Breeze—

3183 12.44   To speak to Lady Beaumont &c of Friendly Female Societies. Stowey/only 1½ pence a week/—1ˢ-9—after 70/but
chiefly for sickness.

f33   3184 12.45   Water wagtails, 7 or 8, following the feeding
Horse in the pasture/fluttering about & hopping close by his hoofs,

under his belly and even so as often to tickle his nostrils with their pert Tail/The H. shortens the grass—& they get the insects.

3185 19.59   ) β.υ;ノ ⌣ ,yλ:κ:ζλ;ι εω;+ ·   f13

3186 19.60   November 5, 1807—Miss Charlotte Brent's Birth Day/24
14 June, Mʳˢ Morgan's = Mary Brent—25—17 months differ-ence
C.B. The same Letters make the words *"Batchelor i'enter."*
~~B. C. A~~

3187 15.260   "A free confession of a Debt in a meaner man is   f117ᵛ
the amplest satisfaction to his Superiors: and I heartily wish that the world may take notice, and from myself that I had not to this time subsisted, but that I was supported by your frequent courtesies & favors"—
O me! I meant to have prefixed the preceding words too— Living as you have done inseparable in your friendship, I hold it as impertinent as absurd, in the presentment of my service ~~to you~~ in this kind, to divide you.
                                                    From Mass.
Massinger's Ded. of his Maid of Honor to Sir F. Foljambe, and   f118
Sir T. Bland—applied to Mʳ J. Wedgwood. 17 November

3188 15.261   Often it is only the not being permitted to ex-press affection in all those natural symbols, words, looks, και επαφαῖς αγναις that innocent & loving Brothers may to a twin Sister, that introduces aught more than the wish of these, yea, even the thought of aught beyond, into the mind. I may not—why? be-cause it may be understood—&c—

3189 15.262   When the cold Clod shall cover My clod-cold/   f118ᵛ
clay,   Body, and the moulder'd Earth on ~~my fast mouldring~~ this gay metamorphosis of Earth. Be rudely *should,* the mould upon the mould'ring

O tis a crazy tenement, this Body, a ruinous Hovel, which the ~~weary~~ striving Tenant, Tir'd out with the idle Toil of patching it, Deserts, and leaves it to the sap of the sure silent fire that masks itself In Air & Moisture, hides itself, Yet lords it, Like a disguised Monarch in the suit of ~~some~~ one ~~his~~ trusty servant—

Sap—Of early dews & late, of snow, rain, hail, the howling whirlwind, & the sigh-like Breeze, ~~and all and~~ whateer else makes *f119* up the Masquerade of Fire & Water/

My Fetters have eat in/the vital flesh Has grown up o'er them/ the unwilling Gaoler Leaves with a scornful Laugh the fruitless Task To the perplex'd Chirurgeon/

f171ᵛ 3190 18.329

       Amo te solo—G   ⎫ Dʳ Callcott

       Teneri miei sospiri F ⎬ Decʳ. 20. 1807

f13ᵛ 3191 19.61   Christmas Eve, 24 Dec. 1807. Bristol, Mʳ Morgan's

In proportion as a disposition, constitutionally as well as habitually susceptible of social & yet keener loving-kindness, has been by mishap banished from or stripped of, the Objects of these, does it become prone to quarrelsome & angry emotions, & the heart becomes a reservoir of predispositions to the same. Illustrate this by some simile—& introduce it into the Soother of Absence—/

f14 3192 19.62   I will suggest to Davy the propriety of confining archè, to that which causes a compound to *begin* to be; and to express the Base, by combining with which it begins that compound, by the affix "yl," from υλη, the Stuff, or material Substrate/at all events, the French Chemists were not justified in applying "gen" alike to Oxygen and Hydrogen/the former makes the thing acid, but the latter does make, but is made Water. The former is the true *Hydrogen,* or hydrarch, and if one wished to conjure up a triple Spirit from among the mighty Leaders that work under Lucifer, the Prince of the Air, Abracadabra, or Abraxas, would be tame on the Tongue compared with the ˣHydroxalkalarchic Gas! Nitrarchic. Hydryl, Sodyl, Potassyl, Strontianyl.

×Hydroxalkalarchico—Carbonic Gas! Hyperhydroxalkalchated
Muriatic Gas/for archated ⟨from αρχομαι⟩ offers no greater   *f14ᵛ*
violence to etymology than genated/from γινομαι.

3193 19.63   The abominable frequency of men, in ordinary
conversation after dinner, &c, who mistake opinions hazarded for
actions undertaken, and confound the monadic essence of Truth
with the necessarily social nature of Realization. So instead of
answering an argument, or correcting an Error, a man—especially
if a Clergyman or a Placeman—shakes his head, mumbles disap-
probation, & looks around the company's Eyes for Suffrages,
exactly as if a wrong Action had been proposed or commenced in
his Presence.—The dangerous Consequences of this almost always
selfish—Con-fettering of two things absolutely disparate, not so
much for the preclusion of Truth, tho' this be something, as for
the   hardening   ⌐ . . . .⌐   other.   If   A.   had   been   *f15*
⌐ . . . . .⌐ his Inferiors, a party for instance in an Alehouse, or a
crowd of Peasants, no wonder, if B. cried out against one, who
took such unfair advantages; and should thereafter be prejudiced
against the opinions themselves, right or wrong.

3194 19.64   My Love is built up far from accident.

3195 19.76   Mʳ Wickham has heard from some of his best   *f30ᵛ*
and most respected Friends, that Mʳ Champneys has propagated
Reports, which, if believed, would greatly injure Mʳ W's character. Mʳ W's Friends were at first so flattering as to assure him,
that they did not think it necessary for him to reply to these
Charges. But as Mʳ C. has continued to spread them beyond the
Circle of those, who have honored Mʳ W. with their particular
attention, he begs leave with the concurrence of his Friends to
distribute the following Statement hoping that the high Importance to himself of his Character will be accepted by those, to
whom this statement is sent—as an apology for this Intrusion on   *f30*
their attention.
    The Charges by Mʳ Champneys against Mʳ Wickham (as far as
the same have come to the knowlege of the Latter) are:

1ˢᵗ. That Mʳ Wickham induced Mʳ Champneys to execute to a Farmer, William Allard, of whom he had borrowed money, a warrant of Attorney to confess Judgement in a case where it was unusual and unnecessary to have this security, as Mʳ C. had also given a Bond, a Mortgage and an Assignment of a Policy of Insurance.

ƒ29ᵛ   2ⁿᵈˡʸ. That Mʳ W. induced Mʳ C. to execute a Warrant of Attorney to confess Judgement without informing him what the Instrument was.

3ʳᵈˡʸ. That the Mortgage and Judgement given to Allard was for £2100, whereas Allard's money was only £1200: and that the other £900 was a Debt due from Mʳ Champneys to Mʳ Wickham himself and not intended to be so secured: and that therefore Mʳ C. was imposed upon by the Insertion of the £900.

4ᵗʰˡʸ. That Mʳ Wickham joined with Allard in taking Mʳ Champneys by Surprize in levying an execution against him without giving him warning of such a Proceeding and that Mʳ Wickham even refused to take the Debt when tendered to him.

ƒ29   To answer the first Charge it is necessary to give the History of the Transaction: and it is necessary to Mʳ W's defence to state some Copies of Letters from Mʳ C., of which Mʳ W. is ready to shew the Originals. About the End of the Year 1801, Mʳ Champneys being very much distressed for Money discovered by means of his Butler, Mʳ Younge, that Farmer Allard had £1200 in his Possession, and Mʳ Champneys employed Mʳ Younge to try to get it for him. Allard (who had been a Client of Mʳ Wickham's (*but another Attorney had given Information of Allard's having this money*)) was resolved not to lend the money on any other

ƒ28ᵛ   security than a Mortgage; but was at last prevailed on by Mʳ Younge to lend 200£ on Mʳ C. giving him a Bond, *and a Promise* of a Mortgage. Mʳ Champneys gave the Bond accordingly, the 12ᵗʰ of January 1802. Mʳ C. knowing that Allard had still more Money pressed him to lend him a further Sum and again promised him a Mortgage. Allard at last consented, provided Mʳ Wickham would say, it was a safe Mortgage. Mʳ W. was by no means satisfied with Mʳ C's title to make a Mortgage and told him so repeatedly: and Mʳ W. knew too well Mʳ C's pecuniary Embarrass-

ments to advise a Client to take his *personal* security. Between the
12th January and 11th February 1802 many meetings and letters
passed, and Mr Champneys was very angry with Mr W., and
said, he threw Impediments in his Way, because he would not   ƒ28
assure Allard, that he knew the Mortgage was safe, when he believed the contrary. Mr Wickham told Allard, he might consult
some other Attorney, but he said he would not, that he was determined to rely on Mr W. and would employ no other. M^r W.
took every means to satisfy himself, that it was in M^r C's power to
make a safe Mortgage, but could not. Mr C. was pressing him at
the same time to assure Allard, that it was, and actually dictated
a Letter, 23rd Jany. 1802, and sent it to Mr W. to be copied by
him, & sent *as his own*, to assure Allard that a sufficient Mortgage
would be given at Lady Day, thereby to induce Allard to advance
the money immediately. Many *strong Efforts* were made by M^r   ƒ27^v
C. to prevail on Mr W. to satisfy Allard. Mr C. could produce no
Title Deeds, but said they were at his London Agents. Mr Wickham having particularly requested Mr C. to press his Solicitor in
London to send the necessary Deeds to perfect the Mortgage, M^r
Champneys sent him the following Letter—11 Feb. 1802.

"Dear Sir

Was I to send to Town, it would be Tuesday be-
fore the Coach could bring the Deed: which I can certainly get,
if it would satisfy this stupid Fellow. As I may by that Time
be called to Hampshire, I therefore send you *a Pacquet of
Parchments* which contains an assignment of £600 per annum,
I once raised and redeemed, and which *you may hold for him
as a security*, until one or the other is done. The Value of these   ƒ27
Deeds are *about Twopence*— †† That's nothing! He's a Fool,
and we ought to take this fair Advantage. I therefore think,
if you send him word, you have got *some Parchment for
him*, †† that might do—at all events pray try the Event.—Dear
Sir,

much yours
Thos. S. Champneys."

†† These ~~two~~ Words are so underlined in M^r C's Letter.

Mʳ W. as may be naturally expected felt indignant at this pro-
posal; & (it is needless to say) never executed it; but seeing very
clearly (to say nothing more disrespectful of Mʳ Champneys) that
he was determined, if possible, to get Allard's money without car-
f26ᵛ ing whether the security was or was not sufficient, Mʳ W. was more
and more determined, *that it should be sufficient* before he would
suffer Allard to advance the rest of the Money. However Mʳ C.
prevailed on a Tenant of his (Farmer West) who was thought to
have some property (about a thousand Pounds left him by his
Father) to agree to join with him, Mʳ C, in a Bond to Allard on
Mʳ C's promising him a Lease on his Farm, and Mʳ C. sent for
Allard to Orchardhigh, and (Mʳ Wickham not being present)
Mʳ C. prevailed on Allard to lend him 350£ more on West's
joining with Mʳ C. in a Bond for the whole 550£ (including the
former 200£). Mʳ Wickham had soon afterwards reasons for
f26 suspecting, that West had lent Mʳ C. some money without a sufficient Security, and of course West had lessened the Value of his
Bond to Allard. Allard had now advanced 550£ without sufficient
Security. Mʳ W. thought it better to advise him to advance 650£
more, which was the sum Mʳ C. wanted than run the risque of losing 550£ & advised him that if Mʳ C. gave a Warrant to confess
Judgment in addition to the other Security proposed, there would
be no great danger *while Mʳ C. paid the Interest.* Indeed Mʳ W.
in consequence of receiving this extraordinary Letter would have
broke with Mʳ Champneys at once, had he not thought it his Duty
f25ᵛ to have seen his Clients Allard & Middleton fully secured for their
Money.

Mʳ C's Solicitor never sent the Deed, nor has it yet appeared.
Indeed there was and is something suspicious in the way in which
Mʳ W's applications for Information to Mʳ C's Agents were answered. To some Letters Mʳ W. had no answer/sometimes Mʳ C.
himself has answered Mʳ W's Letters to the Solicitor, in some
Letters Mʳ C. violently abuses his Solicitors—and once Mʳ C. gave
them orders not to give any one Information about his Deeds—
but as Mʳ C—was very urgent and in fact much distressed for the
money, Allard by Mʳ W's advice advanced the 650£ more making
in all £1200/ and Mʳ W. made a Mortgage of Lands (which a

Mr Soane had held for his own Life only and whose Interest M^r   *f25*
C. had purchased—Mortgage dated 14th August & executed 28th
August 1802) from the best materials, he had—accompanied with
a Policy of Insurance for Mr Soane's Life. But this Mortgage was
certainly not a sufficient security for any Sum, it being accompanied
with no Title Deeds, to shew M^r C's power to mortgage further
than for the Life of Soane, and it being possible that a similar
Mortgage, or more than one, might have been previously given,
neither of which would be valid in case of M^r C's death further
than his *personal Security* and Mr W. well knew that in the event
of M^r C's omitting to pay the Premium on the Policy the latter
would be void—and he had very particular Reasons not to be con-   *f24ᵛ*
tent with M^r C's personal Security, *and was fearful, the Interest
would not be paid regularly*—Mr W. therefore advised a Warrant
of Attorney to confess Judgement to be given by Mr C—and which
the latter consented to—

&c &c

The remaining answers are of less interest—explaining the sum
of 900£ borrowed of Mr Middleton, Banker at Frome, but for
which Mr W. was answerable/finally, Mr C.—after having the
Sheriff's officers in his House & after various struggles & schemes,
ended in paying 2400£, costs &c included, instead of the 2000/&
paying Injury to boot—

3196 22.21
　　　　Dic mihi, Musa, sacri quæ tanta potentia Versus   *f27*
　　　Nam tibi scire datum, et versu memorare potenti,
　　　Cuncta vides, nec te poterit res tanta latere
　　　In regno Regina tuo/Vim, Diva, reclusam
　　　Carminis, et late penetralia ditia pande,
　　　Thesaurosque, et opes, et inenarrabile Sceptrum:
　　　Quæ sprevere homines, tandem ut mirentur amentque,
　　　Divisque accedat reverentia justa Poetis.
　　　　　　　　　　Cowleii Davideidos L.I.

Hinc in nos nata est Numerorum sancta potestas.
　　　　　　　　　　　　　　Idem.

3197 22.22　　　Not only ~~not~~ Chaucer ~~nor~~ and Spenser; but even Shakespere and Milton have as yet received only the earnest, and scanty first gatherings of their Fame—This indeed it is, which gives its full dignity and more than mental grandeur to Fame, this which at once distinguishes it from Reputation, and makes its attainment a fit object of pursuit to the good, and an absolute duty to the Great; that it grows with the growth of Virtue & Intellect, and co-operates in that growth; it becomes wider and deeper, as their country and all mankind are the countrymen of the man of true and adequately exerted Genius/becomes better and wiser.

*f*27ᵛ　3198 22.23　　　The Inscription on the Statue of Senacherib in the Temple of Vulcan in Egypt would make a striking Inscription on the Tomb of any one who had died under memorable circumstances—

　　　　　Ἐις ἐμὲ τὶς ὁράων εὐσεβὴς ἔστω.

3199 22.24　　　Bellarmin makes sweating & crowding one of the great Torments of Hell; which Lessius no doubt after an actual & careful Survey affirms to be exactly a Dutch mile (5 English?) in Diameter. But Ribera (he however only deduces it out of the Apocalypse) makes it 200 Italian Miles—which differ from ours only by a trifle—. I suppose, Lessius was a Protestant, for whom a smaller Hell would suffice/—.

3200 22.25

　　　Ite hinc Camœnæ!—
　　　Dulces Camœnæ (nam fatebimur verum,
　　　Dulces fuistis) Et tamen meas chartas
　　　Revisitote: sed pudenter et raro.
　　　　　　　　　　　Virgilii Catalectus

　　　Posterius graviore sono tibi Musa loquetur
　　　Nostra: dabunt cum securos mihi tempora fructus.
　　　　　　　　　　　Virgil: Culex

3201 22.26   Nella beltà si fà uno di più—Pitagora:—   *f28*
    Here is (an unusual thing) a *force* as well as elegance of the
Italian, which painfully exemplifies the great poverty of our Language in philosophical Language—every word with us expresses
degree, defect, excess, not kind/In Beauty the Many is made one./
But to the word *many* is attached the idea of ⌜. . . . .⌝
La connessione d'Amore e di beltà—nella beltà si fa uno di più—   *f29ᵛ*
nell'amistà si fa uno di piu. Amore è che giugne e unisce l'amante
colla persona amata—E perocchè le cose congiunte communicano
naturalmente intra sè le loro qualità, intantoche talvolta è, che
l'una torna del tutto nella natura dell'altra: incontra, che le pas-
sioni della persona amata entrano nella persona amante, sicchè
l'amor dell'una si communica nell'altra e così l'odio, e 'l desiderio,
e ogn'altra passione—perchè gli amici dell'uno sono dall'altro
amati, e li nemici odiati—S.T.C.

3202 22.27   *f29*

3203 22.28   When I can, & if I can, to trace the origin, his-   *f28ᵛ*
torical & metaphysical, of Allegory—its slight traces in the ancients,
& the causes of that slightness from the nature of a philosophical
Idolatry, which conjoined with *actual worship* too much realized
their personification, so that even *in Ovid* the most allegorical they   *f29*
only verge towards or partake of allegory, Cebes &c/As the belief
of reality, & as the *action* of corporeal forms to which a reality by
faith had been attached, weakened, allegory *grew*—the causes that
prepared the world for a mundane, as opposed to a national religion, a religion of *man*, as opposed to the religion of Greece with
its Olympus, Delos, Delphi, &c, likewise encreased the feeling for
allegory—with the full establishment of the mundane or Christian   *f30*

Religion it became *Compleat—Prudentius—*&c/Platonism favor-
able to it, therefore Apuleius &c—Then thro' the dark Ages—& at
the dawn of modern Literature read Dante's prose intermixed with
Poetry, Il convito, Vita nuova, &c, & all the works of the old Ital-
ians prior to, contemporary with, or the immediate successors of
Dante/then go to Bellay, &c in France/then to Chaucer &c &c—to
Spencer, in English—& then trace the decline of Allegory & its
Causes.

f30ᵛ   3204 22.29   The bequest of Lewis XI to the Virgin Mary of
the whole & entire of his Country of Boulogne, saving & excepting
the *Revenues.*

3205 22.30   Heber, Heremon, and Eth (or Ith)—

the title of Dalkaïs

to go to law with the Devil, in a court held in Hell, with Satan's Lord Chief Justice on the Bench/~~and~~ before a packed Jury ~~of~~
half of caudacornute ⋇ Courtiers & the other half of Brimstone-
Contractors. "meet men and apt in the profession of the Law."—

⋇ or cercoceractic/a $\kappa\epsilon\rho\kappa\circ\varsigma$, cauda ut bestiarum, et $\kappa\epsilon\rho\alpha\varsigma$, cornu/
$\kappa\epsilon\rho\kappa\circ\varsigma$, a beast's Tail, and $\kappa\epsilon\rho\alpha\varsigma$, a Horn.

$\kappa\epsilon\rho\kappa\circ\kappa\epsilon\rho\omega\nu\upsilon\chi\alpha$ $\Sigma\hat{\alpha}\tau\alpha\nu$

N.B. to examine the ? respecting the practical superiority or in-
feriority of a love of freedom derived from national established
hereditary privileges, & that which is derived from cosmopolitical
philosophy—the cruel Tyranny of all free nations over their col-
f31   onies & slaves—England, Switzerland, Holland, contrasted with
France, & with Spain too, after their first enormities of conquest.

"brayed as in a mortar with
Sword, pestilence, & famine/"

In the wars of Elizabeth they thus forced the Irish literally to eat
each other/and then the English Commander tried & executed the
Survivors for the crime of Cannibalism/actually hung a party of
old women on this pretence/Sir Arthur Chichester found 3 little
children eating the body of their dead Mother/

3206 22.31   Lydia Chard, in Finsbury Square, a young Lady of 22—while attending her Mother who had fainted away, caught fire—the servants one screamed, the other fainted/she in vain wrapt herself up in the Carpet Rug—in the confusion a woman came in, & pretending to assist suffered her for near 10 minutes to be burning in her stays &c & then got off having cut away & taken off bothe her pockets/19 Novem: [?1804/1807].—

3207 22.32   And under his brow, that moved not at all, ~~in~~ his head & body motionless, his eye he turned round, as it was an imp that could move of itself—or as if twere of glass & went on a pivot, or was plucked by a string, like the ~~eyes~~ head, arms, and legs of a little child's Mommock.   f31ᵛ

3208 22.33
Thinking many a merry thought
All by himself alone.—

3209 22.34   Told to no one any what the passion of his Heart/ A Hope he had within his Heart, but kept it to himself—he ~~thought~~ talked of many other things, he talked & tried to think, but always thought of this sweet Hope, a thought still going on/ Sometimes he seemed to see it, sometimes he seemed to hear it, according as the feeling or blended with the stirring power of eye or ear, whichever from whatever cause then happ'd to be most ac- tive/Just as if this Hope at heart were itself a formal spirit/—

3210 22.35   Changes of the Metre of the Epistle to the Count. of Cumberland/mark'd 49ᵗʰ.
a,b,c; a,b,c.
b,a,c; a,b,c
c,a,b, a,b,c.
c,b,a; a,b,c
b,c,a; a,b,c.
————
~~a,b,c; b,a,c.~~
~~a,b,c, c,b,a~~

f69

3211 22.113

> Nor do the Ocean Tides more ceaselessly
> Entring each Bay & voicing on each shore
> Still wake and watch ~~our~~ around our British Isle,
> Than did the Flux and Reflux of his Thoughts/

3212 22.114

> For Milton (from Chapman's Sonnet to The
> Earl of Suffolk among the Sonnets
> prefixed to his Odyssey—

> Who can be worthier men in public weales
> Than those (at all parts) who prescrib'd the best?
> Who stirr'd up noblest Virtues, holiest zeals,
> And evermore did live as they profest?

3213 22.115   Το τα μικρα, μεγαλως και τα κοινα, καινως.
Now is ~~this~~ it or not the Business and Duty of the genuine Poet?
Or is it not a principle falsely abstracted from Homer, without
adverting to the novelty in his age of Arts & Implements now
most common/so that with him it was τα μεγαλα μεγαλως, και
τα καινα μετα δεινοτητος—i.e. with the natural excitement & passion from sense of novelty & admiration/instead of being justly
drawn from Grounds of universal Reason.—

3214 22.116   The question fairly stated how far a man can be an
adequate, or even a good, as far as he goes, tho' inadequate Critic,
of Poetry who is not a Poet at least in *posse?*—Here are the questions—adequate, & good tho' not commensurate/but another distinction—supposing he is not only not a Poet, but is a *bad* Poet?—
Irene.—

f69ᵛ   **3215** 22.117   I trust, you are very happy in your domestic
being; very—because, alas! I know that to a man of sensibility, &
more emphatically, if he be a literary man,—there is ⟨no⟩ medium
between that and—The secret pang that eats away the Heart.
    The sole Hope being an Idea,/wᶜʰ in all our general associa-
tions (which must needs either overpower, or perplex and over-

gloom any partial or accidental association) is a form of Despair, relatively to others—& if contradictorily, unnaturally, made the substance of Hope, the tertium quid of the combination frightens the Heart with Guilt in its approach—Hence even in dreams of Sleep the Soul never *is*, because it either cannot or dare not be, any ⟨ONE⟩ THING; but lives in *approaches*—touched by the outgoing pre-existent Ghosts of many feelings—It feels for ever as a blind man with his protended Staff dimly thro' the medium of the act instrument by which it pushes off, & in the act of repulsion, O for the eloquence of Shakspeare, who alone could feel & yet know how to embody these conceptions, with as curious a felicity as the thoughts are subtle. As if the finger which I saw with eyes Had, *f70* as it were, another finger invisible—Touching me with a ghostly touch, even while I feared the real Touch from it. What if in certain cases Touch acted by itself, co-present with vision, yet not coalescing—then I should see the finger as at a distance, and yet feel a finger touching which was nothing but it & yet was not it/ the two senses cannot co-exist without a sense of causation/the *touch* must be the effect of that Finger, I see, yet it's not yet near to me, ⟨and therefore it is not it; & yet it is it. Why,⟩ it is it in an imaginary preduplication. N.B. there is a passage in the second Part of Wallenstein, expressing not explaining the same feeling— The Spirits of great Events Stride on before the events—it is in one of the last two or 3 Scenes.

How few would read this Note—nay, *any one?*/and not think the writer mad or drunk!

3216 22.118   Two kinds of Madness—the Insania pseudo- *f70ᵛ* poetica, i.e. nonsense conveyed in strange and unusual Language, the malice prepense of vanity, or an inflammation from debility— and this is *de*generate/the other the Furor divinus, in which the mind in a by infusion of a celestial Health supra hominis naturam erigitur et in Deum transit—and this is Surgeneration, which only the Regenerate can properly appreciate.

3217 22.119   It is worth noting & endeavoring the to detect the *f70* Law of Mind, by which in writing earnestly while we are thinking, we omit words necessary to the sense. It will be found, I guess,

that we seldom omit the material word; but generally the word by
which the mind expresses its modification of the verbum materiale.
Thus in the preceding page, 5ᵗʰ line, medium is the *materiale;*
that was its own brute inert sense/but the *no* is the mind's action,
its *use* of the word.

f70ᵛ   I think this a hint of some value. Thus *the* is a word in constant combination with the passive or material words; but *to* is
an act of the mind, a modification/and I had written *the* detect,
instead of *to* detect. Again, when my sense demanded "the" to express a distinct modification of some *verb. mater.* I remember to
have often omitted it in writing. The principle is evident—the
mind borrows the materia from without, & is passive with regard
to it as the mere subject *"Stoff"*; a simple event of memory takes
place; *but* having the other in itself, the inward Having with its
f71   sense of security passes for the outward Having—or is all memory
an anxious act, & thereby suspended by vivid security—or are both
reasons the same—or if not are they consistent, & capable of being
co- or sub-ordinated.—. It will be lucky, if some day after having
written on for two or three Sheets rapidly and as a first Copy,
without correcting, I should by Chance glance on this Note, not
having thought at all about during or before the time, of writing
—/& then to examine every word omitted—/

The mind's actions is 1. the Copula, is, was, &c. 2. decision
whether the *Stuff* is represented as belonging or not belonging to
the particular Thought, i.e. whether it is privative ~~or not~~/such as
no—not—none—for the mere absence ⟨of the privative—⟩ or negative symbol marks its appurtenance. I have houses. The positive is
expressed by the absence of any visual symbol (for emptiness ~~or~~ &
absence, silence, darkness as Spinoza observed ~~for whom~~ whose
pocket Mr Locke picked of it without after confession, are as positive Vorstellungen as Light, Sound, Image)—but this not being
existent cannot be outwardly omitted, & the mind can never arrive
at any consciousness of any hallucination/but no—&c—

f73   3218 22.125   ~~DʳCallott~~
                Dʳ Callcott, Kensington Gravel Pits, near the Ux-
bridge Road.

3219 22.126

    Canzon, i' credo, che saranno radi   *f73ᵛ*

    Color, che tua ragione intendan bene,

    Tanto lor parli faticosa e forte/

                    Convito di Dante

    Voi che 'ntendendo, il terzo ciel movete &c

3220 24.14

Whom should I choose for my Judge? the earnest *impersonal*   *f9ᵛ*
    Reader

Who in the work forgets me and the world and himself.

———

Ye who have eyes to detect and Gall to chastise the Imperfect,

Have you the Heart too that loves, feels and rewards the com-   *f10*
    pleat.

Whenceat is the meed of thy Song? ~~From~~ 'Tis the ceaseless, the
    thousandfold Echo

Which from the welcoming Hearts of the Pure repeats and pro-
    longs it,

Each with a different Tone, compleat or in musical fragments.

                or

This be the meed, that thy Song ~~awakens~~ to a thousandfold echo

~~The~~ ~~other~~ * Welcoming Hearts: ~~of~~ ~~the~~ ~~Pure~~ ~~Hearts~~ ~~that~~ ~~re-~~
    ~~ceive~~ ~~and~~ ~~retained~~ ~~it~~ ~~and~~ ~~prolonged~~ ~~it~~ is it their voice, or is
    it thy own voice?

~~Yea~~ List! the Hearts of the ~~Good~~ Pure, like Caves in the ancient
    Mountains

Deep, ⟨deep⟩ *in* ~~their~~ bosom, and ~~deep~~ *from* the Bosom resound it;

Each with a different tone, compleat or in musical fragments

~~Meets~~ ~~thy~~ ~~strain~~ ~~and~~ ~~prolongs~~ ~~and~~ ~~for~~ ~~ever~~ ~~&~~ ~~ever~~ ~~repeats~~ ~~it~~,

Meet the Song, they *receive*, and retain, and resound, & prolong it!

* Welcoming Souls! is it their Voice, sweet Poet! or is it thy own
Voice?

3221 24.15   Was uns hierinn eine stärkere Zuversicht zu   *f10ᵛ*
geben vermag ist die Harmonie, in der wir mit mehreren stehen,

ist die Erfahrung dass wir nicht allein—wenn wir uns in mehreren wieder finden.

So wenig er auch bestimmt seyn mag, andere zu belehren, so wünscht er doch sich denen mitzutheilen, die er sich gleichgesinnt weiss oder hofft, deren Anzahl aber in der Breite der Welt zerstreut ist, er wünscht sein Verhältniss zu den ältesten freunden [*Freunden*] dadurch wieder anzuknüpfen, mit neuen es fortzusetzen, und in der letzten Generation, sich wieder andere für seine übrige Lebenszeit zu gewinnen. Er wünscht der Jugend die Umwege zu ersparen, auf denen er sich selbst verirrte—

Das Publicum—ein Werk verlangt das ihm gefalle—und meistens wird sich der Künstler gern darnach bequemen, denn er ist ja auch ein Theil des Publicums, auch er ist in gleichen Jahren und Tagen gebildet—. thence acting & acted on whole whole nations, while ages have been warped.

f11   Das schlechteste werk [*Werk*] kann zur empfindung [*Empfindung*] und zu einbildungsgefühl [*Einbildungsgefühl*] (nicht kraft) sprechen, indem es sie in bewegung [*Bewegung*] setzt, los und frey macht, und sich selbst uberlässt; das beste Kunstwerk spricht auch zur Empfindung, aber eine höhere Sprache, die man freilich verstehen muss; es fesselt die Gefühle, und die Einbildungsκραft, es nimmt uns unsre Willkühr—wir können mit dem Vollkommenen nicht schalten und walten, wie wir wollen; wir sind genöthigt uns ihm hinzugeben, um uns selbst von ihm, erhöht und verbessert, wieder zu erhalten.—

3222 24.16   Rais'd by her love the Earthly of my nature rose, like an exhalation that springs aloft, a pillared form, at the first full face of the rising Sun, & intercepting full his slant rays ~~storm~~ burns like a self-fed fire, & wide around on the open Plain spreads

f11ᵛ   its own splendor & now I sink at once into the depths as of a Sea of life intense—pure, perfect, as an element unmixt, a sky beneath the sky—yet with the sense of weight of water, pressing me all around, and with its pressure keeps ~~my being~~ compact my being &

my sense of being, presses & supports—what else diffusing seemed—

[shorthand/Greek manuscript notation]

3223 24.17   Common minds—component drops of the stream of Life; men of genius, the large & small Bubbles. What if they break, they are still as good as the rest—drops of water—

3224 24.18   *For* and because: the latter now used *exclusively* *f12* to signify a causative connection between the ideas themselves; the former both this and likewise to explain the reason of mentioning it to the Auditor or reader.—Dampier, using because instead of for (they no doubt being originally perfect Synonymes, the latter a translation of the former) will exemplify this/Vol.11 Part 11. p.77.—"But poor Daniel, not finding any assistance waited till the beast opened his Jaws to take better Hold, *because* it is usual for the alligator to do so"—we should now say *for*, or "it being usual." Instance of desynonimization—

3225 24.19
                                   Hints.   *f12ᵛ*

Great minds can and do create the taste of the age—/and men of genius yielding to it, in part, & in part ~~actinged~~ ~~on~~ on by it, is one of the contingent causes, warping the taste of nations & ages.— one cause of the popularity of vicious poems—see p.19
   Das schlecteste [*schlechteste*] werk

3226 24.20   an unsuspicious Testimony in favor of Education in its best sense in Dampier—V.2. P.2. p.89. I have particularly observed there & in other places that such as had been well bred, were generally most careful to improve their Time, & would be very industrious & frugal where there was any probability of con-

siderable gain. But on the contrary such as had been inured to hard
Labor & got their Living by the Sweat ⌐. . . . .⌐

3227 23.1   Pacchimaretti

ƒ1 3228 23.2   καὶ ἐξ ἐκείνου θανατᾶ μου ἡ ψυχὴ—"and from
that moment my Soul yearns to die."—

ƒ2 3229 23.3   SυνThνηCκω.
CHE SARA SARA   *fosse stato.* ⟨"Che" in Italian, both
"that" & "what"—and *"that"* both as a conjunctive, and as a pro-
noun Relative.⟩ Thus "che sarà, sarà" is what will be, will be—
but "che Sara Sara, i.e. fosse stato: = "O that S. were S."

3230 23.4   I see it—I see it—the Spirit of the Nation is gone
—for we all want to be made believe, that our Pleasure is our
Duty, not to make our Duty our Pleasure.—What then is the
secret of the French Power? of the vicious French? Consistency,
unanimity in vice & energy. That is the secret.—and great men,
as to action, the product of the Revolution—

3231 24.21

ƒ13   Ad Vilmum Axiologum

⟨See p. 30⟩

Me n' Asræ perferre jubes oblivia? leni
Aversos oculos fronte videre meæ?
Scire et fœdifragam, crudelem, quæ mihi semper
Grata fuit, semper grata futura mihi?
~~Hancque pati jubes~~
  ~~Me lucem noctemque pati~~
Meque pati lucem, cui falsam perdite amanti
  Quicquid Naturæ est, omne mihi titubat?
Cur non ut patiarque fodi mea viscera ferro,
  Dissimulato etiam, Vilme! dolore jubes?
Quin cor, quin oculosque meos, quin erue vel quod
  Carius est, si quid carius esse potest!
Deficientem animam, quod vis, tolerare jubebis?

Dum Asræ dum superet me moriente fides.
At fidis inferias vidi, et morior! Ratione
　Victum iri facili?—me *ratione* putas?
Ah pereat qui in amore potest rationibus uti!
　Ah pereat qui, ni perdite, amare potest!
Quid deceat, quid non, videant quibus integra mens est:
Vixi! et vivit adhuc immemor ⌐Asræ mei.⌐

Ad Vilmum Axiologum.

f13ᵛ

a fragment

This be the meed, that thy Song creates a thousandfold Echo!
ˣSweet as the warble of woods that awake in at the gale of the
　Morning!
List! the Hearts of the Pure, like Caves in the ancient Mountains
Deep, deep *in* the Bosom, and *from* the Bosom resound it,
Each with a different Tone, complete or in musical fragments,
Meet and All have welcom'd thy Song Voice, and receive and re-
　tain and prolong it!
This is the word of the Lord!—it is spoken, and things Beings
　Eternal
Live and are born, as an Infant—the Eternal begets the Immortal!
Love is the Spirit of Life, and Music the Life of the Spirit.—

———

　　　What is Music?—*Poetry* in its grand sense?
　　Answer.
Passion and order aton'd! Imperative Power in Obedience!
　　　What is the first and divinest Strain of Music?
　　In the Intellect—"Be able to *will*, that thy maxims (rules of
individual conduct) should be the Law of all intelligent Being."
　　In the Heart—or practical Reason—Do unto others, ands
thou would'st be done by.
　　This in its widest extent involves the Text—Love thy Neigh-　*f14*
bour as thyself and God above all things.—For conceive thy Being
to be all-including, i.e. God, thou knowest, that *thou* wouldest
command thyself to be beloved above all things.—
From what reasons do I believe a *continuous* (& ever continua-

ble) *Consciousness?* From *Conscience!* Not for myself but for my
conscience—i.e. my affections & duties toward others, I should
have no Self—for Self is Definition; but all Boundary implies
Neighbourhood—& is knowable only by Neighbourhood, or Relations.—Does the *Understanding* say nothing in favor of Immortality!—It says nothing for or against; but its Silence gives
consent, and is better than a thousand arguments such as mere
Understanding could afford?—But miracles!—Do you speak of
them as Proofs or as natural consequences of Revelation, whose
Presence is proof only by precluding the Disproof that would arise
from their absence?—Nay, I spoke of them as of positive funda-
mental Proofs.—

*f14*ᵛ　　Then I dare answer you—"Miracles in that sense are Blasphe-
mies in Morality, Contradictions in Reason. God, the Truth—the
Actuality of Logic—the very *Logos*—he deceive his Creatures,
& demonstrate the properties of a Triangle by the confusion of all
Properties!—If a Miracle merely mean an event before unexperi-
enced, it proves only itself, and the inexperience of mankind/
whatever other definition be given of it, & rather attempted (for
no other not involving direct contradiction can be given)—it is
Blasphemy—It calls Darkness Light, & makes Ignorance, the
Mother of Malignity, the appointed Nurse of Religion—which
is Knowlege as opposed to mere calculating, & conjectural Understanding.

f15　　Seven years ago, but oh! in what happier times—then only deluding, not deluded & believing the echo of my own voice in an
empty vault to be the substantial voice of its indwelling Spirit—I
wrote thus—

> O ye Hopes! that stir within me!
> Health comes with you from above!
> God is *with* me! God is *in* me!
> I *cannot* die: for Life is Love!

And now, that I am alone, & utterly hopeless for myself—yet still
I love—& more strongly than ever feel that Conscience, or the
Duty of of Love, is the Proof of continuing, as it is the Cause &
Condition of existing, Consciousness. How beautiful the Har-

mony! Whence could the Proof come, so appropriately—so con-
formly with all nature, in which the cause & condition of each
Thing is its revealing & infallible Prophecy!—And *for* what reason, say rather for what cause, do you believe Immortality?—Because I *ought*—& therefore *must!*

Ad Vilmum Axiologum ƒ15ᵛ

Me n' Asræ perferre jubes oblivia? et Asræ
Me aversos oculos posse videre meæ?
Scire et eam falsam, crudelem, quæ mihi semper
    Cara fuit, semper cara futura mihi?
Meque pati lucem, cui vanam perdite amanti,
    Quicquid Naturæ est, omne tremit, titubat!
Cur non ut patiarque fodi mea viscera ferro,
    Dissimulato etiam, Vilme, dolore jubes?
Quin Cor, quin Oculosque meos, quin erue vel quod
    Carius est, si quid carius esse potest!
Deficientem animam, quod vis, tolerare jubebo,
    Asræ dum superet, me moriente, fides,
At Fidis Inferias vidi! et morior!—Me Ratione
    Victum iri facili, me *Ratione*, putas?
Ah pereat, qui in Amore potest rationibus uti!
    Ah pereat, qui, ni perdite, amare potest!
Quid deceat, quid non, videant quibus integra mens est:
Vixi! vivit adhuc immemor Asra mei.

A CHRONOLOGICAL TABLE

A CHRONOLOGICAL TABLE

Dates in square brackets are not supplied in Coleridge's text. Dates in pointed brackets are later insertions in the entry in question.

Series	N Entry	Date	Series	N Entry	Date
			1878	9.130	[c 6 Feb 1804]
			1879	9.55	[26 Jan–7 Feb 1804]
		1804	1880	9.48	[26 Jan–7 Feb 1804]
			1881	9.49	[26 Jan–7 Feb 1804]
			1882	9.50	[26 Jan–7 Feb 1804]
1843	16.226	14 Jan 1804	1883	9.51	[29 Jan–7 Feb 1804]
1844	16.227	14 Jan [1804]	1884	9.52	[29 Jan–7 Feb 1804]
1845	16.228	[15–16 Jan 1804]	1885	9.53	[29 Jan–7 Feb 1804]
1846	16.229	[16 Jan 1804]	1886	9.54	[29 Jan–7 Feb 1804]
1847	16.230	[16–18 Jan 1804]	1887	9.56	[29 Jan–7 Feb 1804]
1848	16.231	[16–18 Jan 1804]	1888	9.57	[29 Jan–7 Feb 1804]
1849	16.232	[19 Jan 1804]	1889	9.58	[29 Jan–7 Feb 1804]
1850	16.233	[19 Jan 1804]	1890	9.21	7 Feb 1804
1851	16.234	20 Jan 1804	1891	9.22	[7–10 Feb 1804]
1852	16.235	[20 Jan–6 Feb 1804]	1892	16.236	[7–16 Feb 1804]
1853	16.239	20 Jan 1804	1893	16.237	[7–16 Feb 1804]
1854	9.5	26 Jan 1804	1894	16.238	[7–16 Feb 1804]
1855	9.6	[26 Jan 1804]	1895	16.240	[7–16 Feb 1804]
1856	9.7	[26 Jan 1804]	1896	16.241	[7–16 Feb 1804]
1857	9.8	[26–27 Jan 1804]	1897	16.242	[7–16 Feb 1804]
1858	9.9	[26–27 Jan 1804]	1898	16.243	[7–16 Feb 1804]
1859	9.10	[26–27 Jan 1804]	1899	21.418	[7–16 Feb 1804]
1860	9.11	[26–27 Jan 1804]	1900	21.419	[7–16 Feb 1804]
1861	9.12	[26–27 Jan 1804]	1901	22.150	[c 7–16 Feb 1804]
1862	9.13	27 Jan [1804]	1902	9.23	[10] Feb 1804
1863	9.14	28 Jan [1804]	1903	9.24	[10–12 Feb 1804]
1864	9.15	29 Jan [1804]	1904	9.25	[10–12 Feb 1804]
1865	9.16	[29 Jan–5 Feb 1804]	1905	9.26	[10–12 Feb 1804]
1866	9.17	[29 Jan–5 Feb 1804]	1906	9.27	[12] Feb 1804
1867	9.1	[26 Jan–27 Mar 1804]	1907	9.28	[13–16 Feb 1804]
1868	9.2	[26 Jan–27 Mar 1804]	1908	9.29	[13–16 Feb 1804]
1869	9.3	[26 Jan–27 Mar 1804]	1909	9.30	[13–16 Feb 1804]
1870	9.4	[26 Jan–27 Mar 1804]	1910	9.31	[17–18 Feb 1804]
1871	9.143	[Jan–Feb 1804]	1911	9.32	[17–18 Feb 1804]
1872	9.144	[Jan–Feb 1804]	1912	9.33	21 Feb + [Mar] 1804
1873	9.145	[Jan–Feb 1804]	1913	9.34	[c 21 Feb–c 8 Mar 1804]
1874	9.146	[Jan–Feb 1804]	1914	9.35	[c 21 Feb–c 8 Mar 1804]
1875	9.18	5 Feb [1804]	1915	9.36	[c 21 Feb–c 8 Mar 1804]
1876	9.19	[5 Feb 1804]	1916	9.37	[c 21 Feb–c 8 Mar 1804]
1877	9.20	[5 Feb 1804]	1917	9.38	[c 21 Feb–c 8 Mar 1804]

Series	N Entry	Date	Series	N Entry	Date
1918	9.39	[c 21 Feb–c 8 Mar 1804]	1970	9.76	[8–24 Mar 1804]
1919	9.40	[c 21 Feb–c 8 Mar 1804]	1971	9.77	[10–24 Mar 1804]
1920	9.41	[c 21 Feb–c 8 Mar 1804]	1972	9.78	[10–24 Mar 1804]
1921	9.42	[c 21 Feb–c 8 Mar 1804]	1973	9.79	[19–24 Mar 1804]
1922	9.43	[c 21 Feb–c 8 Mar 1804]	1974	{9.80	[19–24 Mar 1804]
1923	9.44	[c 21 Feb–c 8 Mar 1804]		{9.81	
1924	9.45	[c 21 Feb–c 8 Mar 1804]	1975	9.82	24 Mar 1804
1925	9.46	[c 21 Feb–c 8 Mar 1804]	1976	9.83	25 Mar [1804]
1926	9.47	[c 21 Feb–c 8 Mar 1804]	1977	9.84	[25–26 Mar 1804]
1927	21.420	[Feb–Mar 1804]	1978	9.85	[25–26 Mar 1804]
1928	21.421	[Feb–Mar 1804]	1979	9.86	[25–26 Mar 1804]
1929	21.422	[Feb–Mar 1804]	1980	9.87	[25–26 Mar 1804]
1930	21.423	[Feb–Mar 1804]	1981	9.88	[25–26 Mar 1804]
1931	21.424	[Feb–Mar 1804]	1982	9.89	[25–26 Mar 1804]
1932	21.425	[Feb–Mar 1804]	1983	9.90	[25–26 Mar 1804]
1933	21.426	[Feb–Mar 1804]	1984	9.91	[25–26 Mar 1804]
1934	21.427	[Feb–Mar 1804]	1985	9.132	[26–27 Mar 1804]
1935	21.428	[Feb–Mar 1804]	1986	9.92	[26–27 Mar 1804]
1936	21.429	[Feb–Mar 1804]	1987	9.93	28 Mar 1804
1937	21.430	[Feb–Mar 1804]	1988	9.94	[28 Mar–8 Apr 1804]
1938	9.131	[Feb–Mar 1804]	1989	9.95	[28 Mar–8 Apr 1804]
1939	9.133	[23 Feb–8 Mar 1804]	1990	9.96	[28 Mar–8 Apr 1804]
1940	9.134	[23 Feb–8 Mar 1804]	1991	9.97	[28 Mar–8 Apr 1804]
1941	9.135	[23 Feb–8 Mar 1804]	1992	9.98	[28 Mar–8 Apr 1804]
1942	9.136	[23 Feb–8 Mar 1804]	1993	9.99	10 Apr 1804
1943	9.137	[23 Feb–8 Mar 1804]	1994	9.100	[10 Apr 1804]
1944	9.138	[23 Feb–8 Mar 1804]	1995	9.101	[10 Apr 1804]
1945	9.139	[23 Feb–8 Mar 1804]	1996	9.102	10 Apr 1804
1946	9.140	[23 Feb–8 Mar 1804]	1997	9.103	11 Apr 1804
1947	9.141	[23 Feb–8 Mar 1804]	1998	9.104	[11 Apr 1804]
1948	9.142	[23 Feb–8 Mar 1804]	1999	9.105	12 Apr [1804]
1949	9.147	[23 Feb–8 Mar 1804]	2000	9.106	[12 Apr 1804]
1950	9.59	[Feb–10 Mar 1804]	2001	9.107	[12 Apr 1804]
1951	9.60	[Feb–10 Mar 1804]	2002	9.108	13 Apr 1804
1952	9.61	[Feb–Mar 1804]	2003	9.109	[13 Apr 1804]
1953	9.62	[Feb–Mar 1804]	2004	9.110	[13 Apr 1804]
1954	9.63	[Feb–Mar 1804]	2005	9.111	[13 Apr 1804]
1955	9.64	[Feb–Mar 1804]	2006	9.112	[13 Apr 1804]
1956	9.65	[Feb–Mar 1804]	2007	9.113	[13 Apr 1804]
1957	9.66	[Feb–Mar 1804]	2008	9.114	[13 Apr 1804]
1958	16.4	[Feb–27 Mar 1804]	2009	9.115	[13 Apr 1804]
1959	16.5	[Feb–27 Mar 1804]	2010	9.116	[13 Apr 1804]
1960	16.6	[Feb–27 Mar 1804]	2011	9.117	14 Apr [1804]
1961	9.67	[9–10 Mar 1804]	2012	9.118	14 Apr 1804
1962	9.68	[10–12 Mar 1804]	2013	9.119	[14 Apr 1804]
1963	9.69	10–[12] Mar [1804]	2014	9.120	16 Apr 1804
1964	9.70	[12 Mar 1804]	2015	9.121	16 Apr [1804]
1965	9.71	[12–13 Mar 1804]	2016	9.122	[16 Apr 1804]
1966	9.72	[13–26 Mar 1804]	2017	9.123	[16 Apr 1804]
1967	9.73	[8–24 Mar 1804]	2018	9.124	17 Apr 1804
1968	9.74	[8–24 Mar 1804]	2019	9.125	[17 Apr 1804]
1969	9.75	[8–24 Mar 1804]	2020	9.126	[17 Apr 1804]

Series	N Entry	Date	Series	N Entry	Date
2021	9.127	[17 Apr 1804]	2073	15.40	[4 May 1804]
2022	21.431	17 Apr 1804	2074	15.41	[4 May 1804]
2023	9.128	18 Apr [1804]	2075	15.42	[4 May 1804]
2024	9.129	[18 Apr 1804]	2076	15.43	[4 May 1804]
2025	15.5	19 Apr 1804	2077	15.44	5 May [1804]
2026	15.7	19 Apr 1804	2078	15.45	6 May [1804]
2027	15.8	[19 Apr 1804]	2079	15.46	7 May [1804]
2028	15.9	[19 Apr 1804]	2080	15.47	8 May [1804]
2029	15.10	19 Apr [1804]	2081	15.48	[8 May 1804]
2030	15.11	[19 Apr 1804]	2082	15.49	[8 May 1804]
2031	15.12	[19 Apr 1804]	2083	15.50	[8 May 1804]
2032	21.432	19 Apr 1804	2084	K.3	8 May [1804]
2033	21.433	[19 Apr 1804]	2085	15.51	[10 May 1804]
2034	15.13	[20 Apr 1804]	2086	15.52	10 May [1804]
2035	15.14	[20 Apr 1804]	2087	15.53	13 May 1804
2036	15.15	[20 Apr 1804]	2088	15.54	[13 May 1804]
2037	15.16	[20 Apr 1804]	2089	15.55	[13 May 1804]
2038	K.1	[c 20 Apr 1804]	2090	15.56	[13 May 1804]
2039	K.51	[c 20 Apr 1804]	2091	15.57	13 May 1804
2040	K.52	[c 20 Apr 1804]	2092	15.58	[14 May 1804]
2041	K.53	[c 20 Apr 1804]	2093	15.59	14 May [1804]
2042	K.2	[20–23 Apr 1804]	2094	15.60	[14 May 1804]
2043	15.17	[20–23 Apr 1804]	2095	15.61	16 May [1804]
2044	15.18	[20–23 Apr 1804]	2096	15.62	17 May 1804
2045	15.19	23 Apr 1804	2097	15.63	18 May 1804
2046	15.20	24 Apr 1804	2098	K.9	[18 May 1804]
2047	15.6	24 Apr [1804]	2099	15.64	[18 May 1804]
2048	15.21	[24 Apr 1804]	2100	10.3	[c 23 May] 1804
2049	15.22	[24 Apr 1804]	2101	10.4	[c 23 May] 1804
2050	15.23	24 Apr [1804]	2102	10.5	[c 23 May 1804]
2051	15.24	26 Apr [1804]	2103	10.6	[c 23 May 1804]
2052	15.25	27 Apr [1804]	2104	10.7	[c 23 May 1804]
2053	15.26	[27 Apr 1804]	2105	10.8	[c 23 May 1804]
2054	15.27	[27 Apr 1804]	2106	10.9	[c 23 May 1804]
2055	15.28	[27 Apr 1804]	2107	10.15	[c 23 May 1804]
2056	15.29	29 Apr [1804]	2108	16.244	[24–25 May 1804]
2057	15.30	30 Apr [1804]	2109	16.245	5 June 1804
2058	15.31	[30 Apr 1804]	2110	16.246	[5 June 1804]
2059	15.2	1 May 1804	2111	16.247	[5 June 1804]
2060	15.32	1 May 1804	2112	16.248	[5 June 1804]
2061	15.33	[1 May 1804]	2113	16.249	[5 June 1804]
2062	15.34	[1 May 1804]	2114	K.24	[May–June 1804]
2063	15.35	1 May [1804]	2115	K.25	[May–June 1804]
2064	15.36	2 May 1804	2116	K.28	[May–June 1804]
2065	K.4	[2–3 May 1804]	2117	21.329	[July 1804]
2066	K.5	[2–3 May 1804]	2118	21.330	[July 1804]
2067	K.6	[2–3 May 1804]	2119	21.331	[July 1804]
2068	K.7	[2–3 May 1804]	2120	21.332	[July 1804]
2069	K.8	[2–3 May 1804]	2121	21.434	[July 1804]
2070	15.37	3 May [1804]	2122	21.435	[July 1804]
2071	15.38	4 May 1804	2123	21.436	[July 1804]
2072	15.39	[4 May 1804]	2124	21.437	[July 1804]

Series	N Entry	Date	Series	N Entry	Date
2125	21.438	[July 1804]	2176	1.24	[19–26 Aug 1804]
2126	21.439	[July 1804]	2177	15.65	27 Aug [1804]
2127	21.440	[July 1804]	2178	15.66	[27 Aug 1804]
2128	21.441	[July 1804]	2179	15.67	[27 Aug 1804]
2129	21.442	[July 1804]	2180	K.40	29 Aug 1804
2130	21.443	[4 July 1804]	2181	K.41	[29 Aug 1804]
2131	21.444	[4 July 1804]	2182	K.42	[Aug–Sept 1804]
2132	21.445	[4 July 1804]	2183	K.43	[Aug–Sept 1804]
2133	K.26	[1–6 July 1804]	2184	K.44	[Aug–Sept 1804]
2134	K.27	[1–6 July 1804]	2185	K.45	[Aug–Sept 1804]
2135	K.31	[1–6 July 1804]	2186	K.46	[Aug–Sept 1804]
2136	K.32	[1–6 July 1804]	2187	K.47	[Aug–Sept 1804]
2137	21.446	4 July 1804	2188	K.48	[Aug–Sept 1804]
2138	21.447	[4 July 1804]	2189	K.49	[Aug–Sept 1804]
2139	21.448	9 July 1804	2190	K.50	[Aug–Sept 1804]
2140	21.449	[12] July [1804]	2191	21.456	[25] Sept 1804
2141	21.450	[12 July 1804]	2192	21.457	27 Sept 1804
2142	K.33	[1–13 July 1804]	2193	21.8	5 Oct 1804
2143	K.34	[13 July 1804]	2194	21.458	[5–11] Oct 1804
2144	{ K.35	[13 July 1804]	2195	15.68	10 Oct 1804
	{ K.37		2196	21.459	11 Oct 1804
2145	K.36	[13 July 1804]	2197	15.69	12 Oct [1804]
2146	K.29	[c 16 July 1804]	2198	15.70	[12 Oct 1804]
2147	K.30	[c 18 July 1804]	2199	15.71	[12 Oct 1804]
2148	K.38	[July 1804]	2200	15.72	[12 Oct 1804]
2149	K.39	[July 1804]	2201	15.73	[12 Oct 1804]
2150	21.451	[12 July–3 Aug 1804]	2202	15.74	[12 Oct 1804]
2151	21.452	[12 July–3 Aug 1804]	2203	15.75	[12 Oct 1804]
2152	21.453	[12 July–3 Aug 1804]	2204	15.76	[12 Oct 1804]
2153	21.454	3 Aug 1804	2205	15.77	[12 Oct 1804]
2154	21.455	[3 Aug 1804]	2206	15.78	[12 Oct 1804]
2155	K.14	[19 Apr–10 Aug 1804]	2207	15.79	[13 Oct 1804]
2156	K.10	[Aug–Nov 1804]	2208	21.460	13 Oct 1804
2157	K.11	[Aug–Nov 1804]	2209	21.461	[13 Oct 1804]
2158	K.12	[Aug–Nov 1804]	2210	21.462	14 Oct 1804
2159	K.13	[Aug–Nov 1804]	2211	21.463	[14 Oct 1804]
2160	K.15	[Aug–Nov 1804]	2212	15.80	15 Oct 1804
2161	K.16	[Aug–Nov 1804]	2213	15.81	[15 Oct 1804]
2162	K.17	[Aug–Nov 1804]	2214	15.82	[15 Oct 1804]
2163	K.18	[Aug–Nov 1804]	2215	15.83	[15 Oct 1804]
2164	K.19	[Aug–Nov 1804]	2216	15.84	[15 Oct 1804]
2165	K.20	[Aug–Nov 1804]	2217	15.85	16 Oct 1804
2166	K.21	[Aug–Nov 1804]	2218	21.464	17 Oct 1804
2167	K.22	[Aug–Nov 1804]	2219	15.86	[16–18 Oct 1804]
2168	K.23	[10 Aug–7 Nov 1804]	2220	15.87	[16–18 Oct 1804]
2169	1.13	[19 Aug 1804]	2221	15.88	[16–18 Oct 1804]
2170	1.14	19 Aug [1804]	2222	15.89	[16–18 Oct 1804]
2171	1.15	[20 Aug 1804]	2223	22.16	[before 18 Oct 1804]
2172	1.16	[20 Aug 1804]	2224	22.15 [?1801]–18 Oct 1804–[?1807]	
2173	1.17	20–Aug [1804]	2225	22.17	[?Oct–Dec 1804]
2174	1.19	[20–26 Aug 1804]	2226	15.90	18 Oct 1804
2175	1.20	26 Aug [1804]	2227	15.91	19 Oct 1804

468

Series	N Entry	Date	Series	N Entry	Date
2228	15.92	19 Oct 1804	2280	21.474	[23 Nov 1804]
2229	15.93	[19 Oct 1804]	2281	15.121	[Nov 1804–1805]
2230	15.94	[19 Oct 1804]	2282	15.125	[Nov 1804–1805]
2231	15.95	[19 Oct 1804]	2283	15.126	[Nov 1804–1805]
2232	15.96	[19 Oct 1804]	2284	15.127	[Nov 1804–1805]
2233	15.97	[19 Oct 1804]	2285	15.128	[Nov 1804–1805]
2234	15.98	[19 Oct 1804]	2286	15.129	[Nov 1804–1805]
2235	15.99	[19 Oct 1804]	2287	15.130	[Nov 1804–1805]
2236	21.465	[17–21 Oct 1804]	2288	15.131	[Nov 1804–1805]
2237	21.466	21 Oct 1804	2289	15.132	[Nov 1804–1805]
2238	15.100	[19–26 Oct 1804]	2290	15.133	[Nov 1804–1805]
2239	15.101	[19–26 Oct 1804]	2291	21.475	7 Dec 1804
2240	15.102	[19–26 Oct 1804]	2292	21.476	[7 Dec 1804]
2241	15.103	26 Oct 1804	2293	21.477	[7 Dec 1804]
2242	15.104	[26 Oct 1804]	2294	21.478	[7 Dec 1804]
2243	15.105	[26 Oct 1804]	2295	21.479	[7 Dec 1804]
2244	15.122	[5 Nov 1804]	2296	21.480	[7 Dec 1804]
2245	15.123	[5] Nov [1804]	2297	21.481	7 Dec 1804
2246	15.124	[5 Nov 1804]	2298	21.482	[7 Dec 1804]
2247	15.106	[6 Nov 1804]	2299	21.483	[7–11 Dec 1804]
2248	15.107	[6 Nov 1804]	2300	21.484	[7–11 Dec 1804]
2249	15.108	[6 Nov 1804]	2301	21.485	[7–11 Dec 1804]
2250	15.109	6 Nov 1804	2302	21.486	[7–11 Dec 1804]
2251	15.110	[6 Nov 1804]	2303	21.487	[7–11 Dec 1804]
2252	15.111	[6–7 Nov 1804]	2304	21.488	[7–11 Dec 1804]
2253	15.112	[6–7 Nov 1804]	2305	21.489	[7–11 Dec 1804]
2254	15.113	[6–7 Nov 1804]	2306	21.490	[7–11 Dec 1804]
2255	15.114	[6–7 Nov 1804]	2307	21.491	[7–11 Dec 1804]
2256	15.115	[6–7 Nov 1804]	2308	21.492	[7–11 Dec 1804]
2257	15.116	[6–7 Nov 1804]	2309	21.493	[7–11 Dec 1804]
2258	15.117	[6–7 Nov 1804]	2310	21.494	11 Dec [1804]
2259	15.118	[6–7 Nov 1804]	2311	21.495	[12 Dec 1804]
2260	15.119	[6–7 Nov 1804]	2312	21.496	[12 Dec 1804]
2261	15.120	[6–7 Nov 1804]	2313	21.497	[12 Dec 1804]
2262	21.333	[July–Nov 1804]	2314	21.498	[12 Dec 1804]
2263	21.334	[July–Nov 1804]	2315	21.499	[12 Dec 1804]
2264	21.335	[July–Nov 1804]	2316	21.500	[12 Dec 1804]
2265	21.336	[July–Nov 1804]	2317	21.501	12 Dec 1804
2266	21.337	10 Nov 1804	2318	21.502	[12 Dec 1804]
2267	21.338	[10 Nov 1804]	2319	21.503	12 Dec 1804
2268	21.467	22 Nov 1804	2320	21.504	[12–13 Dec 1804]
2269	21.468	22 Nov 1804	2321	21.505	[12–13 Dec 1804]
2270	21.469	[23 Nov 1804]	2322	21.506	[12–13 Dec 1804]
2271	21.470	23 Nov 1804	2323	21.507	[12–13 Dec 1804]
2272	21.339	[Nov 1804]	2324	21.508	[12–13 Dec 1804]
2273	21.340	[Nov 1804]	2325	21.509	[12–13 Dec 1804]
2274	21.341	[Nov 1804]	2326	21.510	[12–13 Dec 1804]
2275	21.342	[Nov 1804–?1808]	2327	21.511	[12–13 Dec 1804]
2276	21.343	[Nov 1804–?1808]	2328	21.512	[12–13 Dec 1804]
2277	21.471	[23 Nov 1804]	2329	21.513	[12–13 Dec 1804]
2278	21.472	[23 Nov 1804]	2330	21.514	13 Dec 1804
2279	21.473	[23 Nov 1804]	2331	21.515	[13 Dec 1804]

Series	N Entry	Date	Series	N Entry	Date
2332	21.516	[13 Dec 1804]	2384	21½.6	[c 27 Dec 1804]
2333	21.517	[13 Dec 1804]	2385	21½.7	[c 27 Dec 1804]
2334	21.518	[13 Dec 1804]	2386	21½.8	[c 27 Dec 1804]
2335	21.519	[13 Dec 1804]	2387	21.599	27 Dec 1804
2336	21.520	[13 Dec 1804]	2388	21.598	[27 Dec 1804]
2337	21.521	[13 Dec 1804]	2389	21.594	[c Dec 1804]
2338	21.522	[13 Dec 1804]	2390	21.595	[c Dec 1804]
2339	21.523	[13 Dec 1804]	2391	21.596	[c Dec 1804]
2340	21.524	15 Dec 1804	2392	21.597	[c Dec 1804]
2341	21.525	[15 Dec 1804]	2393	21.31	[1804–1805]
2342	21.526	16 Dec 1804			
2343	21.527	17 Dec 1804			
2344	21.528	[17 Dec 1804]		**1805**	
2345	21.529	[17 Dec 1804]			
2346	21.530	[17 Dec 1804]			
2347	21.531	[17 Dec 1804]	2394	21.560	9 Jan 1805
2348	21.532	17 Dec [1804]	2395	21.561	[9–11 Jan 1805]
2349	21.533	18 Dec [1804]	2396	21.562	[9–11 Jan 1805]
2350	21.534	[18 Dec 1804]	2397	21.563	11 Jan 1805
2351	21.535	[18 Dec 1804]	2398	21.564	11 Jan 1805
2352	21.536	[18–22 Dec 1804]	2399	21.565	[11 Jan 1805]
2353	21.537	[18–22 Dec 1804]	2400	21.566	[11 Jan 1805]
2354	21.538	[18–22 Dec 1804]	2401	21.567(a)	[15 Jan 1805]
2355	21.539	[18–22 Dec 1804]	2402	21.567(b)	15 Jan 1805
2356	21.540	[18–22 Dec 1804]	2403	21.568	[15–17 Jan 1805]
2357	21.541	[18–22 Dec 1804]	2404	21.569	[15–17 Jan 1805]
2358	21.542	[18–22 Dec 1804]	2405	21.570	17 Jan 1805
2359	21.543	[18–22 Dec 1804]	2406	21.571	[17 Jan 1805]
2360	21.544	[18–22 Dec 1804]	2407	21.572	[17 Jan 1805]
2361	21.545	[18–22 Dec 1804]	2408	21.573	18 Jan [1805]
2362	21.546	[18–22 Dec 1804]	2409	21.574	[18–19 Jan 1805]
2363	22.12	[21 Dec 1804]	2410	21.575	19 Jan 1805
2364	22.11	21 Dec 1804	2411	21.576	22 Jan 1805
2365	22.13	[21 Dec 1804]	2412	21.577	23 Jan 1805
2366	22.14	[21 Dec 1804]	2413	21.578	[23 Jan 1805]
2367	21.547	22 Dec 1804	2414	21.579	[23 Jan 1805]
2368	21.548	23 Dec [1804]	2415	21.580	[23–28 Jan 1805]
2369	21.549	[23–24 Dec 1804]	2416	21.581	[23–28 Jan 1805]
2370	21.550	25 Dec 1804	2417	21.582	[23–28 Jan 1805]
2371	21.551	25 Dec 1804	2418	21.583	[23–28 Jan 1805]
2372	21.552	25 Dec 1804	2419	21.584	[23–28 Jan 1805]
2373	21.553	[25 Dec 1804]	2420	21.585	28 Jan 1805
2374	21.554	[25 Dec 1804]	2421	21.586	[28 Jan–1 Feb 1805]
2375	21.555	[25 Dec 1804]	2422	21.587	[28 Jan–1 Feb 1805]
2376	21.556	[25 Dec 1804]	2423	21.588	1 Feb 1805
2377	21.557	[25 Dec 1804]	2424	21.589	[1 Feb 1805]
2378	21.558	[25 Dec 1804]	2425	21.591	3 Feb 1805
2379	21.559	[25 Dec 1804]	2426	21.592 / 21.7	3 Feb 1805
2380	21½.122	[c 27 Dec 1804]			
2381	21½.123	[c 27 Dec 1804]	2427	17.1	[c 4 Feb 1805]
2382	21½.124	27 Dec 1804	2428	17.2	[c 4 Feb 1805]
2383	21½.2	[c 27 Dec 1804]	2429	17.3	[c 4 Feb 1805]

Series	N Entry	Date	Series	N Entry	Date
2430	17.4	4 Feb 1805	2482	17.56	8 Mar 1805
2431	17.5	[4–7 Feb 1805]	2483	17.57	[10 Mar] 1805
2432	17.6	[4–7 Feb 1805]	2484	17.58	16 Mar 1805
2433	17.7	[4–7 Feb 1805]	2485	17.59	[16 Mar 1805]
2434	17.8	7 Feb 1805	2486	17.60	17 Mar 1805
2435	17.9	[7 Feb 1805]	2487	17.61	[17–20 Mar 1805]
2436	17.10	8 Feb 1805	2488	17.62	[17–20 Mar 1805]
2437	17.11	[8–9 Feb 1805]	2489	17.63	[17–20 Mar 1805]
2438	17.12	[8–9 Feb 1805]	2490	17.64	[17–20 Mar 1805]
2439	17.13	9 Feb [1805]	2491	17.65	[17–20 Mar 1805]
2440	17.14	[9 Feb 1805]	2492	17.66	[17–20 Mar 1805]
2441	17.15	[9–10 Feb 1805]	2493	17.67	[17–20 Mar 1805]
2442	17.16	[9–10 Feb 1805]	2494	17.68	[17–20 Mar 1805]
2443	17.17	[9–10 Feb 1805]	2495	17.69	21 Mar 1805
2444	17.18	[9–10 Feb 1805]	2496	17.70	21 Mar 1805
2445	17.19	[9–10 Feb 1805]	2497	17.71	[c 21 Mar 1805]
2446	17.20	11 Feb 1805	2498	17.72	[c 21 Mar 1805]
2447	17.21	12 Feb [1805]	2499	17.73	[c 21 Mar 1805]
2448	17.22	12 Feb 1805	2500	17.210	[?c Mar 1805]
2449	17.23	13 Feb 1805	2501	15.134	24 Mar 1805
2450	17.24	[13 Feb 1805]	2502	15.135	[24–27 Mar 1805]
2451	17.25	15 Feb 1805	2503	15.136	[24–27 Mar 1805]
2452	17.26	[15 Feb 1805]	2504	15.137	[24–27 Mar 1805]
2453	17.27	[16 Feb 1805]	2505	15.274	[25 Mar 1805]
2454	17.28	16 Feb [1805]	2506	15.138	27 Mar [1805]
2455	17.29	[18 Feb 1805]	2507	15.139	[27 Mar 1805]
2456	17.30	18 Feb 1805	2508	15.140	[27 Mar 1805]
2457	17.31	[18 Feb 1805]	2509	17.74	[c 28 Mar 1805]
2458	17.32	21 Feb 1805	2510	17.75	28 Mar [1805]
2459	17.33	[21 Feb–3 Mar 1805]	2511	17.76	29 Mar [1805]
2460	17.34	[21 Feb–3 Mar 1805]	2512	17.77	29 [Mar 1805]
2461	17.35	[21 Feb–3 Mar 1805]	2513	17.78	29 [Mar 1805]
2462	17.36	[21 Feb–3 Mar 1805]	2514	17.79	[29–30 Mar 1805]
2463	17.37	[21 Feb–3 Mar 1805]	2515	17.80	[30 Mar 1805]
2464	17.38	[21 Feb–3 Mar 1805]	2516	17.81	1 Apr 1805
2465	17.39	[21 Feb–3 Mar 1805]	2517	17.82	[1 Apr 1805]
2466	17.40	[21 Feb–3 Mar 1805]	2518	15.141	2 Apr 1805
2467	17.41	[21 Feb–3 Mar 1805]	2519	15.142	[2 Apr 1805]
2468	17.42	4 Mar [1805]	2520	15.143	[2 Apr 1805]
2469	17.43	[5 Mar 1805]	2521	15.144	4 Apr [1805]
2470	17.44	[5–8 Mar 1805]	2522	15.145	4 + ⟨6⟩ Apr 1805
2471	17.45	[5–8 Mar 1805]	2523	17.226	[4 Apr 1805]
2472	17.46	[5–8 Mar 1805]	2524	17.227	4 Apr 1805
2473	17.47	[5–8 Mar 1805]	2525	17.83	[1–4 Apr 1805]
2474	17.48	[5–8 Mar 1805]	2526	17.84	5 Apr 1805
2475	17.49	[5–8 Mar 1805]	2527	17.85	6 Apr 1805
2476	17.50	[5–8 Mar 1805]	2528	17.86	6 Apr 1805
2477	17.51	[5–8 Mar 1805]	2529	17.87	[6 Apr 1805]
2478	17.52	[5–8 Mar 1805]	2530	17.88	[6 Apr 1805]
2479	17.53	[5–8 Mar 1805]	2531	17.89	7 Apr 1805
2480	17.54	[5–8 Mar 1805]	2532	17.90	[7 Apr 1805]
2481	17.55	[5–8 Mar 1805]	2533	17.91	[7 Apr 1805]

Series	N Entry	Date	Series	N Entry	Date
2534	17.92	[7 Apr 1805]	2586	16.251	[May 1805]
2535	17.93	[7 Apr 1805]	2587	16.252	[May 1805]
2536	17.94	[7 Apr 1805]	2588	16.253	[May 1805]
2537	17.95	8 Apr 1805	2589	16.254	[May 1805]
2538	17.96	[8 Apr 1805]	2590	16.255	[May 1805]
2539	17.97	9 Apr [1805]	2591	16.256	[May–July 1805]
2540	17.98	[9 Apr 1805]	2592	16.257	[May–July 1805]
2541	17.99	[9 Apr 1805]	2593	16.258	[May–July 1805]
2542	17.100	[10 Apr 1805]	2594	17.121	[May–June 1805]
2543	17.101	[10 Apr 1805]	2595	17.122	[May–June 1805]
2544	17.102	[13 Apr 1805]	2596	17.123	[May–June 1805]
2545	17.103	[13 Apr 1805]	2597	17.124	[May–June 1805]
2546	17.104	[13]–14 Apr 1805	2598	17.125	[May–June 1805]
2547	17.105	15 Apr [1805]	2599	17.159	[May–Aug 1805]
2548	17.106	15 Apr 1805	2600	17.211	[c June 1805]
2549	17.107	15 Apr [1805]	2601	17.212	[c June 1805]
2550	17.108	[17 Apr 1805]	2602	18.192	24 June [1805]
2551	17.109	17 Apr 1805	2603	18.193	[24 June 1805]
2552	17.110	[17–21 Apr 1805]	2604	18.194	[24 June 1805]
2553	17.111	[17–21 Apr 1805]	2605	17.213	[c 27 June 1805]
2554	17.112	[17–21 Apr 1805]	2606	17.214	27 June 1805
2555	17.113	[17–21 Apr 1805]	2607	17.215	[c 27 June 1805]
2556	17.114	[17–21 Apr 1805]	2608	17.216	[c 27 June 1805]
2557	17.115	[17–21 Apr 1805]	2609	17.217	[June–Aug 1805]
2558	17.116	21 Apr 1805	2610	16.259	12 July 1805
2559	17.117	[c Apr 1805]	2611	16.260	[12 July 1805]
2560	17.118	[c Apr 1805]	2612	16.261	[12 July 1805]
2561	17.119	[c Apr 1805]	2613	18.195	20 July 1805
2562	17.120	[c Apr 1805]	2614	18.196	[20 July 1805]
2563	15.146	[23 Apr 1805]	2615	18.197	[July 1805]
2564	15.147	[23 Apr 1805]	2616	17.177	[July 1805]
2565	15.148	23 Apr [1805]	2617	17.178	[July 1805]
2566	15.149	[c 23 Apr 1805]	2618	17.179	[July 1805]
2567	15.150	[c 23 Apr 1805]	2619	17.180	22 July 1805
2568	15.151	[c 23 Apr 1805]	2620	17.181	[July 1805]
2569	15.152	[c 23 Apr 1805]	2621	17.182	[July 1805]
2570	15.153	[c 23 Apr 1805]	2622	17.183	[July 1805]
2571	15.154	[c 23 Apr 1805]	2623	18.1	[July–Oct 1805]
2572	16.406	[Apr 1805]	2624	18.2	[July–Oct 1805]
2573	16.407	[Apr 1805]	2625	18.200	[?July–Oct 1805]
2574	16.408	[Apr 1805]	2626	17.184	[3 Aug 1805]
2575	15.155	4 May [1805]	2627	17.185	3 Aug 1805
2576	15.156	[4 May 1805]	2628	17.186	3 Aug 1805
2577	15.157	4 May 1805	2629	17.187	3 Aug 1805
2578	15.158	11 May 1805	2630	17.188	[Aug 1805]
2579	15.159	[May 1805]	2631	17.189	[Aug 1805]
2580	15.160	[May 1805]	2632	15.163	11 Aug 1805
2581	15.161	[May 1805]	2633	15.164	[12 Aug 1805]
2582	15.162	[May 1805]	2634	15.165	[12 Aug 1805]
2583	17.175	12–14 May 1805	2635	15.166	12 Aug 1805
2584	17.176	14 May 1805	2636	15.167	[12 Aug 1805]
2585	16.250	24 May 1805	2637	18.189	14 Aug 1805

Series	N Entry	Date	Series	N Entry	Date
2638	18.190	14 Aug 1805	2689	16.285	[4 Oct 1805]
2639	18.191	[14 Aug 1805]	2690	16.286	[4 Oct 1805]
2640	22.127	[c Aug 1805]	2691	18.7	[4 Oct 1805]
2641	22.128	16 Aug 1805	2692	18.8	[4 Oct 1805]
2642	22.129	[Aug 1805]	2693	18.9	[4 Oct 1805]
2643	22.130	[Aug 1805]	2694	18.10	[4 Oct 1805]
2644	22.131	[Aug 1805]	2695	16.287	6 Oct 1805
2645	22.132	[Aug 1805]	2696	16.288	7 Oct [1805]
2646	22.133	[Aug–Nov] 1805	2697	16.289	[7–14 Oct 1805]
2647	22.18	[c Aug 1805]	2698	16.290	[7–14 Oct 1805]
2648	22.19	[c Aug 1805]	2699	16.291	[15–20 Oct 1805]
2649	22.20	[c Aug 1805]	2700	16.292	15 Oct 1805
2650	15.168	[c 20 Aug 1805]	2701	16.281	16 Oct 1805
2651	15.169	20 Aug 1805	2702	16.293	[15–20 Oct 1805]
2652	17.222	24 Aug 1805	2703	16.294	20 Oct 1805
2653	17.223	[24 Aug 1805]	2704	16.295	[20 Oct 1805]
2654	17.224	[24 Aug 1805]	2705	16.296	20 Oct 1805
2655	17.225	[Aug 1805]	2706	16.297	[20 Oct–20 Nov 1805]
2656	15.170	24 Aug 1805	2707	16.298	[20 Oct–20 Nov 1805]
2657	15.171	26 Aug [1805]	2708	16.299	[20 Oct–20 Nov 1805]
2658	15.172	[26 Aug 1805]	2709	16.300	[20 Oct–20 Nov 1805]
2659	16.262	[July–Sept 1805]	2710	16.301	[20 Oct–20 Nov 1805]
2660	16.263	[July–Sept 1805]	2711	16.302	[20 Oct–20 Nov 1805]
2661	16.264	[July–Sept 1805]	2712	16.303	[20 Oct–20 Nov 1805]
2662	16.265	[July–Sept 1805]	2713	16.304	[20 Oct–20 Nov 1805]
2663	16.266	[July–Sept 1805]	2714	16.305	[20 Oct–20 Nov 1805]
2664	16.267	6 Sept 1805	2715	16.306	[20 Oct–20 Nov 1805]
2665	16.268	6 Sept 1805	2716	16.307	[20 Oct–20 Nov 1805]
2666	16.269	7 Sept 1805	2717	16.308	20 Nov 1805
2667	16.270	9 Sept 1805	2718	16.309	[20 Nov–14 Dec 1805]
2668	15.173	[c 15 Sept 1805]	2719	16.310	[20 Nov–14 Dec 1805]
2669	15.174	[c 15 Sept 1805]	2720	16.311	[20 Nov–14 Dec 1805]
2670	15.175	15 Sept 1805	2721	16.312	[20 Nov–14 Dec 1805]
2671	15.176	15 Sept 1805	2722	16.313	[20 Nov–14 Dec 1805]
2672	16.271	27 Sept 1805	2723	16.314	[20 Nov–14 Dec 1805]
2673	16.272	[27 Sept 1805]	2724	16.315	[20 Nov–14 Dec 1805]
2674	16.273	30 Sept [1805]	2725	16.316	[20 Nov–14 Dec 1805]
2675	21.348 / 21.350	30 Sept 1805	2726	16.317	[20 Nov–14 Dec 1805]
			2727	16.318	[20 Nov–14 Dec 1805]
2676	21.349	[c 30 Sept 1805]	2728	16.319	[20 Nov–14 Dec 1805]
2677	22.134	[Sept–Nov 1805]	2729	16.320	[20 Nov–14 Dec 1805]
2678	22.135	[Sept–Nov 1805]	2730	16.321	[20 Nov–14 Dec 1805]
2679	16.274	[30 Sept–3 Oct 1805]	2731	16.322	[20 Nov–14 Dec 1805]
2680	16.275	[30 Sept–3 Oct 1805]	2732	16.323	[20 Nov–14 Dec 1805]
2681	16.276	[30 Sept–3 Oct 1805]	2733	16.324	[20 Nov–14 Dec 1805]
2682	16.277	3 Oct 1805	2734	16.325	[20 Nov–14 Dec 1805]
2683	16.278	[3 Oct 1805]	2735	16.326	[20 Nov–14 Dec 1805]
2684	16.279	[3 Oct 1805]	2736	16.327	[20 Nov–14 Dec 1805]
2685	16.280	[3 Oct 1805]	2737	16.328	[20 Nov–14 Dec 1805]
2686	16.282	[4 Oct 1805]	2738	16.329	[20 Nov–14 Dec 1805]
2687	16.283	4 Oct 1805	2739	16.330	[20 Nov–14 Dec 1805]
2688	16.284	[4 Oct 1805]	2740	15.177	[Sept–Nov 1805]

473

Series	N Entry	Date		Series	N Entry	Date
2741	15.178	[30 Nov 1805]				
2742	15.179	[30 Nov 1805]				
2743	15.180	[1 Dec 1805]			1806	
2744	18.318	[Nov–Dec 1805]				
2745	16.331	14 Dec 1805				
2746	16.332	[14 Dec 1805]		2784	16.338	1 Jan 1806
2747	16.333	[14 Dec 1805]		2785	15.190	1 Jan 1806
2748	16.334	15 Dec 1805		2786	15.191	5 Jan 1806
2749	16.335	[15 Dec 1805]		2787	15.192	[5 Jan–6 Mar 1806]
2750	16.336	[15 Dec 1805]		2788	15.193	[5 Jan–6 Mar 1806]
2751	16.337	[15 Dec 1805]		2789	15.194	[5 Jan–6 Mar 1806]
2752	15.181	[1–26 Dec 1805]		2790	15.195	[5 Jan–6 Mar 1806]
2753	15.182	[1–26 Dec 1805]		2791	15.196	[5 Jan–6 Mar 1806]
2754	15.183	[1–26 Dec 1805]		2792	15.197	[5 Jan–6 Mar 1806]
2755	15.184	[1–26 Dec 1805]		2793	15.198	[5 Jan–6 Mar 1806]
2756	15.185	26 Dec 1805		2794	16.339	15 Feb 1806
2757	15.186	26 Dec [1805]		2795	16.340	[15 Feb–8 Mar 1806]
2758	15.187	[26 Dec 1805]		2796	16.341	[15 Feb–8 Mar 1806]
2759	15.188	31 Dec 1805		2797	16.342	[15 Feb–8 Mar 1806]
2760	15.189	[31 Dec 1805]		2798	16.343	[15 Feb–8 Mar 1806]
				2799	16.344	[15 Feb–8 Mar 1806]
				2800	16.345	[15 Feb–8 Mar 1806]
				2801	15.199	[6 Mar 1806]
				2802	15.200	6 Mar 1806
		UNDETERMINED DATES		2803	15.201	[6 Mar 1806]
				2804	15.202	[6 Mar 1806]
				2805	15.203	[6 Mar 1806]
				2806	15.204	[6 Mar–3 Apr 1806]
2761	15.1	[c 1805]		2807	15.205	[6 Mar–3 Apr 1806]
2762	15.3	[c 1805]		2808	15.206	[6 Mar–3 Apr 1806]
2763	15.4	[c 1805]		2809	15.207	[6 Mar–3 Apr 1806]
2764	16.409	[?1805]		2810	15.208	[6 Mar–3 Apr 1806]
2765	16.411	[?1805]		2811	15.209	[6 Mar–3 Apr 1806]
2766	16.412	[?1805]		2812	15.210	[6 Mar–3 Apr 1806]
2767	16.413	[?1805]		2813	15.211	[6 Mar–3 Apr 1806]
2768	16.414	[?1805]		2814	15.212	[6 Mar–3 Apr 1806]
2769	22.136	[c 1805]		2815	15.213	[6 Mar–3 Apr 1806]
2770	22.137	[c 1805]		2816	16.346	8 Mar 1806
2771	22.138	[c 1805]		2817	16.347	9 Mar [1806]
2772	22.139	[c 1805]		2818	16.348	[9 Mar 1806]
2773	22.140	[c 1805]		2819	16.349	[9 Mar 1806]
2774	22.141	[c 1805]		2820	16.350	[9 Mar 1806]
2775	22.142	[1805–1807]		2821	16.351	[9 Mar 1806]
2776	22.143	[1805–1807]		2822	16.352	[c Mar 1806]
2777	22.144 / 22.145	[1805–1807]		2823	16.353	[c Mar 1806]
				2824	16.354	[c Mar 1806]
2778	22.146	[1805–1807]		2825	16.355	[c Mar 1806]
2779	22.149	[c 1805]		2826	16.356	[c Mar 1806]
2780	22.162	[1805–1816]		2827	15.214	3 Apr [1806]
2781	18.4	[1805–1819]		2828	15.215	[3 Apr 1806]
2782	18.5	[1805–1819]		2829	15.216	4 Apr 1806
2783	18.6	[1805–1819]		2830	15.217	[4 Apr–11 May 1806]

Series	N Entry	Date	Series	N Entry	Date
2831	15.218	[4 Apr–11 May 1806]	2883	11.21	[c 9 Oct 1806]
2832	15.219	[4 Apr–11 May 1806]	2884	11.22	[c 9 Oct 1806]
2833	15.220	[4 Apr–11 May 1806]	2885	11.23	[c 9 Oct 1806]
2834	15.221	[4 Apr–11 May 1806]	2886	11.114	[5–12 Oct 1806]
2835	15.222	[4 Apr–11 May 1806]	2887	11.115	[5–12 Oct 1806]
2836	15.226	[4 Apr–11 May 1806]	2888	11.116	[5–12 Oct 1806]
2837	15.227	[4 Apr–11 May 1806]	2889	11.109	[12 Oct 1806]
2838	15.228	[1–11] May [1806]	2890	11.110	[12–16 Oct 1806]
2839	15.229	[1–11 May 1806]	2891	11.111	[12–16 Oct 1806]
2840	15.230	[12–18] May [1806]	2892	11.112	[12–16 Oct 1806]
2841	15.231	[12–18 May 1806]	2893	11.113	[12–16 Oct 1806]
2842	15.233	[4–18 May 1806]	2894	11.108	16 Oct 1806
2843	15.234	[4–18 May 1806]	2895	11.18	23 Oct 1806
2844	15.235	[4–18 May 1806]	2896	11.19	[23–25 Oct 1806]
2845	15.236	[4–18 May 1806]	2897	11.24	24 Oct 1806
2846	15.237	[4–18 May 1806]	2898	11.25	[24 Oct 1806]
2847	15.238	[4–18 May 1806]	2899	11.20	25 Oct 1806
2848	15.232	18 May 1806	2900	11.26	[Oct 1806]
2849	15.239	[20–21 May 1806]	2901	11.27	[Oct 1806]
2850	15.240	[20–21 May 1806]	2902	11.28	[Oct 1806]
2851	15.241(a)	[20–21 May 1806]	2903	11.29	[Oct 1806]
2852	15.241(b)	[20–21 May 1806]	2904	11.124	[Oct 1806]
2853	15.271	[May–June 1806]	2905	11.30	30 Oct 1806
2854	15.272	[May–June 1806]	2906	11.31	[30 Oct 1806]
2855	15.273	[May–June 1806]	2907	11.117	[Oct 1806]
2856	15.270	[May–June 1806]	2908	11.118	[Oct 1806]
2857	15.223	[May–June 1806]	2909	11.119	[Oct 1806]
2858	15.224	[May–June 1806]	2910	11.120	[Oct–Nov 1806]
2859	15.225	[May–June 1806]	2911	11.121	[Oct–Nov 1806]
2860	16.357	7 June 1806	2912	11.122	[Oct–Nov 1806]
2861	16.358	[7 June 1806]	2913	11.123	[Oct 1806]
2862	16.359	[8–17 June 1806]	2914	16.363	[Oct–Nov 1806]
2863	16.360	[8–17 June 1806]	2915	16.364	[Oct–Nov 1806]
2864	16.361	[8–17 June 1806]	2916	16.365	[Oct–Nov 1806]
2865	16.362	[8–17 June 1806]	2917	16.366	[Oct–Nov 1806]
2866	15.242	22 June 1806	2918	16.367	[Oct–Nov 1806]
2867	15.248	[June 1806]	2919	16.368	[Oct–Nov 1806]
2868	15.249	[June 1806]	2920	16.369	[Oct–Nov 1806]
2869	11.1	[6 Sept 1806]	2921	{ 16.370 / 16.371	[Oct–Nov 1806]
2870	11.2	6 Sept 1806			
2871	11.3	25 Sept 1806	2922	16.372	[Oct–Nov 1806]
2872	11.4	[25 Sept–5 Oct 1806]	2923	16.373	[Oct–Nov 1806]
2873	11.5	[25 Sept–5 Oct 1806]	2924	16.374	[Oct–Nov 1806]
2874	11.6	[25 Sept–5 Oct 1806]	2925	16.375	[Oct–Nov 1806]
2875	11.7	5 Oct 1806	2926	15.243	[Oct–Nov 1806]
2876	11.8	[5 Oct 1806]	2927	15.244	[Oct–Nov 1806]
2877	11.9	[5 Oct 1806]	2928	15.245	[Oct–Nov 1806]
2878	11.10	[5 Oct 1806]	2929	15.246	[Oct–Nov 1806]
2879	11.11	[5 Oct 1806]	2930	15.247	[Oct–Nov 1806]
2880	11.12	[c 5–12 Oct 1806]	2931	15.250	[Oct–Nov 1806]
2881	11.13	[c 5–12 Oct 1806]	2932	15.251	[Oct–Nov 1806]
2882	11.14	[c 5–12 Oct 1806]	2933	15.252	[Oct–Nov 1806]

Series	N Entry	Date	Series	N Entry	Date
2934	11.32	15 Nov 1806			
2935	11.125	15 Nov 1806			
2936	15.253	[28 Nov 1806]			
2937	15.254	[28 Nov 1806]		1807	
2938	15.255	28 Nov 1806			
2939	11.33	[Nov–Dec 1806]	2978	11.47	[4] Jan [1807]
2940	11.34	[Nov–Dec 1806]	2979	11.48	[4 Jan–6 Feb 1807]
2941	11.35	[Nov–Dec 1806]	2980	11.49	[4 Jan–6 Feb 1807]
2942	11.36	[Nov–Dec 1806]	2981	11.50	[4 Jan–6 Feb 1807]
2943	11.37	[Nov–Dec 1806]	2982	11.51	6 Feb 1807
2944	11.38	[Nov–Dec 1806]	2983	11.52	[Feb 1807]
2945	11.39	[Nov–Dec 1806]	2984	11.53	[Feb 1807]
2946	11.98	[Nov–Dec 1806]	2985	11.54	[Feb 1807]
2947	11.99	[Nov–Dec 1806]	2986	11.55	[Feb 1807]
2948	11.100	[Nov–Dec 1806]	2987	11.56	[Feb 1807]
2949	11.101	[Nov–Dec 1806]	2988	11.57	[Feb 1807]
2950	11.102	[Nov–Dec 1806]	2989	11.58	[Feb 1807]
2951	11.103	[Nov–Dec 1806]	2990	11.59	[Feb 1807]
2952	11.104	[Nov–Dec 1806]	2991	11.60	[Feb 1807]
2953	11.105	[Nov–Dec 1806]	2992	11.61	[Feb 1807]
2954	11.106	[Nov–Dec 1806]	2993	11.62	[Feb 1807]
2955	11.107	[Nov–Dec 1806]	2994	11.63	[Feb 1807]
2956	11.40	[6–13 Dec 1806]	2995	11.64	[Feb 1807]
2957	11.41	[6–13] Dec 1806	2996	11.65	[Feb 1807]
2958	11.42	[20–21 Dec 1806]	2997	11.66	[Feb 1807]
2959	11.43	[20–21 Dec 1806]	2998	11.67	[Feb 1807]
2960	16.379	[?1806]	2999	11.68	[Feb 1807]
2961	16.380	[?1806]	3000	11.69	[Feb 1807]
2962	16.381	[?1806]	3001	11.70	Feb 1807
2963	16.382	[?1806]	3002	11.71	[Feb 1807]
2964	16.383	[?1806]	3003	11.72	[Feb 1807]
2965	16.384	[?1806]	3004	11.73	[Feb 1807]
2966	16.385	[?1806]	3005	11.74	[Feb 1807]
2967	16.386	[?1806]	3006	11.75	[Feb 1807]
2968	16.387	[?1806]	3007	11.76	[Feb 1807]
2969	16.388	[?1806]	3008	11.77	[Feb 1807]
2970	15.256	[?1806]	3009	24.1	[1806–1808]
2971	15.257	[?1806]	3010	24.2	[c May 1807]
2972	15.258	[?1806]	3011	24.4	[c May 1807]
2973	15.259	[?1806]	3012	24.5	[c May 1807]
2974	15.269	[?1806]	3013	24.6	[c May 1807]
2975	11.44	27 Dec 1806	3014	24.7	[c May 1807]
			3015	24.9	[c May 1807]
			3016	24.10	[c May 1807]
			3017	24.11	[c May 1807]
			3018	24.12	[c May 1807]
	UNDETERMINED DATES		3019	24.13	[c May 1807]
			3020	11.78	[Feb–May 1807]
			3021	11.79	[Feb–May 1807]
			3022	11.80	[Feb–May 1807]
2976	11.45	[1806–1807]	3023	11.81	[Feb–May 1807]
2977	11.46	[1806–1807]	3024	11.82	[Feb–May 1807]

Series	N Entry	Date	Series	N Entry	Date
3025	11.83	[Feb–May 1807]	3077	19.28	[1807]
3026	11.84	[Feb–May 1807]	3078	19.29	[1807]
3027	11.85	[Feb–May 1807]	3079	19.30	[1807]
3028	11.86	[Feb–May 1807]	3080	19.31	[1807]
3029	11.87	[Feb–May 1807]	3081	19.32	[1807]
3030	11.88	[Feb–May 1807]	3082	19.33	[1807]
3031	11.89	[Feb–May 1807]	3083	19.34	[1807]
3032	11.90	[Feb–May 1807]	3084	19.35	[1807]
3033	11.91	[Feb–May 1807]	3085	19.36	[1807]
3034	11.92	[Feb–May 1807]	3086	19.37	[1807]
3035	11.93	[Feb–May 1807]	3087	19.38	[1807]
3036	11.94	[Feb–May 1807]	3088	19.39	[1807]
3037	11.95	[Feb–May 1807]	3089	19.40	[1807]
3038	11.96	[Feb–May 1807]	3090	19.41	[1807]
3039	11.97	[Feb–May 1807]	3091	19.42	[1807]
3040	19.1	[c 22 May 1807]	3092	19.43	[1807]
3041	19.2	22 May 1807	3093	19.44	[1807]
3042	19.3	[May 1807]	3094	19.45	[1807]
3043	19.4	[May 1807]	3095	19.46	[1807]
3044	19.5	[May 1807]	3096	19.47	[1807]
3045	19.6	[May 1807]	3097	19.48	[1807]
3046	19.7	[May 1807]	3098	19.49	[1807]
3047	19.8	[May 1807]	3099	19.50	[1807]
3048	19.9	[May 1807]	3100	19.51	[1807]
3049	19.10	[May 1807]	3101	19.52	[1807]
3050	19.11	[May 1807]	3102	19.53	[1807]
3051	19.12	[May 1807]	3103	19.54	[1807]
3052	19.13	[May 1807]	3104	19.55	[1807]
3053	19.14	[May 1807]	3105	19.56	[1807]
3054	19.15	[May 1807]	3106	19.57	[1807]
3055	19.16	[May 1807]	3107	19.58	[1807]
3056	19.17	[May 1807]	3108	12.11	[July 1807]
3057	12.1	[May 1807]	3109	12.12	[July–Oct 1807]
3058	12.2	[May 1807]	3110	12.13	[July–Oct 1807]
3059	12.3	[May 1807]	3111	12.14	[July–Oct 1807]
3060	12.4	28 May 1807	3112	12.15	[July–Oct 1807]
3061	12.5	[28 May 1807]	3113	12.16	[July–Oct 1807]
3062	12.6	[28 May 1807]	3114	12.17	[July–Oct 1807]
3063	12.7	[28 May 1807]	3115	12.18	[July–Oct 1807]
3064	12.8	[28 May 1807]	3116	12.19	[July–Oct 1807]
3065	12.9	[28 May 1807]	3117	12.20	[July–Oct 1807]
3066	12.10	[28 May 1807]	3118	12.21	[July–Oct 1807]
3067	19.18	31 May 1807	3119	23.6	Aug 1807
3068	19.19	[31 May 1807]	3120	23.7	[Aug 1807]
3069	19.20	[1807]	3121	12.76	[May–Sept 1807]
3070	19.21	[1807]	3122	12.77	[May–Sept 1807]
3071	19.22	[1807]	3123	12.78	[May–Sept 1807]
3072	19.23	[1807]	3124	12.79	[May–Sept 1807]
3073	19.24	[1807]	3125	12.80	[May–Sept 1807]
3074	19.25	[1807]	3126	12.81	[May–Sept 1807]
3075	19.26	[1807]	3127	12.82	[May–Sept 1807]
3076	19.27	[1807]	3128	12.83	[May–Sept 1807]

Series	N Entry	Date	Series	N Entry	Date
3129	12.84	[May–Sept 1807]	3182	12.43	[c Oct 1807]
3130	12.85	[May–Sept 1807]	3183	12.44	[c Oct 1807]
3131	12.46	[c Sept 1807]	3184	12.45	[c Oct 1807]
3132	12.47	[c Sept 1807]	3185	19.59	[Nov 1807]
3133	12.48	[c Sept 1807]	3186	19.60	5 Nov 1807
3134	12.49	[c Sept 1807]	3187	15.260	17 Nov [1807]
3135	12.50	[c Sept 1807]	3188	15.261	[Nov 1807]
3136	12.51	[c Sept 1807]	3189	15.262	[Nov 1807]
3137	12.52	[c Sept 1807]	3190	18.329	20 Dec 1807
3138	12.53	[c Sept 1807]	3191	19.61	24 Dec 1807
3139	12.54	[c Sept 1807]	3192	19.62	[Dec 1807]
3140	12.55	[c Sept 1807]	3193	19.63	[Dec 1807]
3141	12.56	[c Sept 1807]	3194	19.64	[Dec 1807]
3142	12.57	[c Sept 1807]	3195	19.76	[1807]
3143	12.58	[c Sept 1807]			
3144	12.59	[c Sept 1807]			
3145	12.60	[Sept 1807]		UNDETERMINED DATES	
3146	12.61	[Sept 1807]			
3147	12.62	[Sept 1807]	3196	22.21	[1807–1808]
3148	12.63	13 Sept 1807	3197	22.22	[1807–1808]
3149	12.64	[Sept 1807]	3198	22.23	[1807–1808]
3150	12.65	[Sept 1807]	3199	22.24	[1807–1808]
3151	12.66	[Sept 1807]	3200	22.25	[1807–1808]
3152	12.67	[Sept 1807]	3201	22.26	[1807–1808]
3153	12.68	[Sept 1807]	3202	22.27	[1807–1808]
3154	12.69	[Sept 1807]	3203	22.28	[1807–1808]
3155	12.70	[Sept 1807]	3204	22.29	[1807–1808]
3156	12.71	[Sept 1807]	3205	22.30	[1807–1808]
3157	12.72	[Sept 1807]	3206	22.31	[1807–1808]
3158	12.73	[Sept 1807]	3207	22.32	[1807–1808]
3159	12.74	[Sept 1807]	3208	22.33	[1807–1808]
3160	12.75	[Sept 1807]	3209	22.34	[1807–1808]
3161	12.22	[c Oct 1807]	3210	22.35	[1807–1808]
3162	12.23	[c Oct 1807]	3211	22.113	[1807–1808]
3163	12.24	[c Oct 1807]	3212	22.114	[1807–1808]
3164	12.25	[c Oct 1807]	3213	22.115	[1807–1808]
3165	12.26	[c Oct 1807]	3214	22.116	[1807–1808]
3166	12.27	[c Oct 1807]	3215	22.117	[1807–1808]
3167	12.28	[c Oct 1807]	3216	22.118	[1807–1808]
3168	12.29	[c Oct 1807]	3217	22.119	[1807–1808]
3169	12.30	[c Oct 1807]	3218	22.125	[1807–1808]
3170	12.31	[c Oct 1807]	3219	22.126	[1807–1808]
3171	12.32	[c Oct 1807]	3220	24.14	[1807–1808]
3172	12.33	[c Oct 1807]	3221	24.15	[1807–1808]
3173	12.34	[c Oct 1807]	3222	24.16	[1807–1808]
3174	12.35	[c Oct 1807]	3223	24.17	[1807–1808]
3175	12.36	[c Oct 1807]	3224	24.18	[1807–1808]
3176	12.37	[c Oct 1807]	3225	24.19	[1807–1808]
3177	12.38	[c Oct 1807]	3226	24.20	[1807–1808]
3178	12.39	[c Oct 1807]	3227	23.1	[1807–1808]
3179	12.40	[c Oct 1807]	3228	23.2	[1807–1808]
3180	12.41	[c Oct 1807]	3229	23.3	[1807–1808]
3181	12.42	[c Oct 1807]	3230	23.4	[1807–1808]
			3231	24.21	[1807–1810]